EXCEPTIONAL CHILDREN

Introduction to Special Education

FOURTH EDITION

Daniel P. Hallahan
James M. Kauffman

University of Virginia

Prentice Hall, Englewood Cliffs, New Jersey 07632

Library of Congress Cataloging-in-Publication Data

Hallahan, Daniel P.
    Exceptional children.

    Includes bibliographies and index.
        1. Exceptional children—Education—United States.
I. Kauffman, James M.   II. Title.
LC3981.H34   1988   371.9   87-14467
ISBN 0-13-295585-7

Editorial/production supervision: Serena Hoffman
Interior design: Levavi and Levavi
Design supervision: Judith A. Matz-Coniglio
Cover design: Judith A. Matz-Coniglio
Cover art: *Two Sisters*
    © 1980 C. Crist Delmonico.
Manufacturing buyer: Carol Bystrom and Margaret Rizzi
Photo research: Teri Stratford
Photo editor: Lorinda Morris-Nantz

CHAPTER OPENING QUOTES: (1) and (2) Richard H. Hungerford, "On Locusts," *American Journal of Mental Deficiency,* 1950, *54,* 415–418.   (3) Neil Diamond, "Brooklyn Roads." Copyright © 1968 Stonebridge Music. All rights reserved. Used by permission. International copyright secured.   (4) Neil Diamond, "Shilo." Copyright © 1967 Tallyrand Music, Inc. All rights reserved. Used by permission. International copyright secured.   (5) Gerald Jonas, *Stuttering: The Disorder of Many Theories.* Copyright © 1976, 1977 by Gerald Jonas. By arrangement with Farrar, Straus & Giroux, Inc. and International Creative Management. This selection originally appeared in *The New Yorker.*   (6) Helen Keller, *The Story of My Life.* New York: Doubleday, 1954.   (7) Leonard Gershe, "Butterflies Are Free." Copyright © 1969 by Leonard Gershe.   (8) Words by Chuck Mangione. Copyright © 1971 Gates Music, Inc. All Right Reserved.   (9) *Autobiography of Mark Twain,* edited by Charles Neider. New York: Harper & Row, 1959.   (10) Bob Dylan, "The Times They Are A-Changin'." Copyright © 1963 Warner Bros., Inc. All Rights Reserved. Used by permission.

Prentice-Hall International (UK) Limited, *London*
Prentice-Hall of Australia Pty. Limited, *Sydney*
Prentice-Hall Canada Inc., *Toronto*
Prentice-Hall Hispanoamericana, S.A., *Mexico*
Prentice-Hall of India Private Limited, *New Delhi*
Prentice-Hall of Japan, Inc., *Tokyo*
Simon & Schuster Asia Pte. Ltd., *Singapore*
Editora Prentice-Hall do Brasil, Ltda., *Rio de Janeiro*

Contents

3

Learning Disabilities 99

4

Emotional Disturbance/ Behavioral Disorder 159

5

Speech and Language Disorders 207

6

Hearing Impairment 259

7

Visual Impairment 307

8

Physical Disabilities 357

9

Giftedness 411

10

Normalization and Attitudes toward Disabled People 461

Glossary 512

Index 521

Preface

This book is a general introduction to the characteristics of exceptional individuals and their education. While we have placed the major emphasis on the classroom practices that make up the discipline of special education, we have also covered the special psychological, medical, and sociological aspects of the various handicapping conditions. We think much of this material will be meaningful to general educators as well as to special educators. This recognition of the significant role of the general educator in dealing with students with a variety of learning and behavioral problems is in response to the continuing trend to educate exceptional youngsters as close as possible to the general education mainstream. In addition, much of the information we present should be of interest to parents of exceptional children.

We begin with a chapter on introductory and historical concepts underlying the education of handicapped individuals; we end with a chapter on the philosophical principle of normalization and societal attitudes toward handicapped people. Between these two chapters are eight others, each devoted to a traditional category of special education: mental retardation, learning disabilities, emotional disturbance/ behavioral disorder, speech and language disorders, hearing impairment, visual impairment, physical disabilities, and giftedness.

We are aware of the noncategorical position in special education—the position that the educational needs of exceptional children, especially those who are mildly handicapped, are generally similar regardless of categorical designation. However, we have continued to organize this book categorically through its four editions because we believe that an introductory book should reflect the general viewpoint of the special education profession, and the prevailing approach to educating exceptional students remains categorical. We also believe that our primary task as authors of an introductory book is to inform readers of things as they are, not as any particular advocacy group thinks they should be. In addition, some information is more logically presented by category. For example, the nature of the individual's condition (e.g., with visually impaired children, defects of the eye) and the educational methods used (e.g., with visually impaired children, Braille, large print books, compressed speech devices, canes) are sometimes so specialized that a clear presentation of them necessitates categorical organization. And finally, many instructors who have continued to use the three previous editions have told us they appreciate our well-organized, categorical format. Because the noncategorical orientation is an important position within special education, however, we do discuss it at relevant points in the text.

Believing the reader is not merely interested in the facts and figures of exceptional students, we continue to approach exceptionality in as informal a manner as possible without falling prey to folksiness. We want our readers to come away knowing basic facts about handicapping conditions: definitions, causes, psychological and behavioral characteristics, and educational approaches. But we also think it important that they have an appreciation of what it's like to have a handicap. To encourage sensitivity to the very personal impact a handicap can have on an individual, as well as on those around him or her, we have chosen quotes from literature or songs to begin each chapter. Each quote introduces the reader to the realities of being exceptional.

Based on positive comments from users, we've continued to include other special features designed to provide a better understanding of exceptional individuals and those who work with them. Perhaps the most popular new feature in the previous edition was "One Professional's Perspective." These interviews of practitioners with excellent reputations, we are gratified to learn, have helped readers realize what it's like to be a professional faced with the day-to-day realities of working with exceptional students. The honesty of the response to the questions we posed to these professionals has also contributed to readers' appreciation of exceptional students. And it is refreshing that, without being Pollyanish, each of these professionals exudes a high degree of enthusiasm for his or her professional role—an attitude that reflects the recent national concern for excellence in all of education.

We start each chapter with boxed material listing common misconceptions. We are still amazed at the considerable number of myths surrounding exceptional people. A few (far too few) have been deleted since our first edition in 1978, only to be replaced by others. Each of these myths is discussed within the chapter, but we highlight them by placing them at the beginning of the chapter so students can preview some of the salient topics to be presented.

We also provide boxed material throughout the book. These boxes are primarily of three types: first, some highlight particularly interesting research findings and their applicability to educational practice: second, some discuss particularly interesting and important issues facing the field; and third, some present the human side of being exceptional. In the latter case, they stress the inherent paradox of being exceptional—that the exceptional individual is, at once, both different from and the same as the rest of humanity. But because a person is different in *some* ways does not mean that he or she is different in *all* ways.

Each categorical chapter ends with a section called "Managing the Child in School." Although this section was originally conceptualized primarily as an aid for readers having a general education background, feedback from users indicates that special educators find it useful too. We don't intend these suggestions to be exhaustive (we've restrained the urge to expand them in revised editions); they are meant to serve as guiding principles for working with exceptional students.

And we again include a glossary for readers' convenience. Words appearing in boldface within the text are listed in the glossary at the end of the book.

Mostly out of loyalty to the many instructors who used our previous editions so faithfully, we have made modifications in this fourth edition cautiously. We have thoroughly updated information on all aspects of the field of special education—a task that becomes more challenging with each new edition because of the ever-expanding nature of our field. It is, however, a pleasure for us to be chroniclers of the many new and exciting developments in the field, technological and otherwise.

In addition, we have made four other changes worth noting. First, we have expanded the chapter summaries to help the reader glean the most salient points in each chapter. Second, in keeping with trends in the field, we have increased the coverage of early childhood as well as secondary and postsecondary programming. Third, after careful analysis, we have added and deleted boxes. Finally, we have reorganized and expanded the last chapter, "Normalization and Attitudes Toward Disabled People." Although the focus of the chapter is still on society's attitudes toward handicapped people, we have added coverage of several timely issues. We discuss the disability rights movement, led by disability activists who liken their cause to that of the civil rights movement of the 1950s and 1960s. We cover the media's treatment of disabilities, noting that many authorities believe TV, movies, literature, newspapers, and magazines tend to depict disabilities in an inaccurate and stereotypical fashion. And we discuss the current debate concerning the regular-education initiative—the position that general, rather than special, education should be primarily responsible for educating handicapped students, especially those with mild handicaps.

Prentice Hall has done its share of seeing that our book will be of utmost utility to instructors and students. First, they have produced an extraordinary attractive book. The eye-appealing nature of the book, we believe, befits the status of the special education field. Second, they have produced an excellent package of instructor aids:

Student Study Guide. The author is Amy P. Dietrich, Memphis State University.

Interactive Study Guide: Software for the IBM or Apple that allows students to review the text material and test their mastery of it.

Instructor's Manual. The authors are Michael S. Rosenberg and Cay Holbrooke, Johns Hopkins University.

Test Item File: 1100 questions in multiple choice, true/false, and essay format. The author is James Van Tassel, Ball State University.

Floppy Disk Testing: Test Item File on a disk, available for the IBM or Apple.

Gradebook Software: Program for the IBM that allows instructors to keep class records, assign grades, average grades, compute class statistics, print graphs of individual test grades and final grades, and sort by student name or grade.

Telephone Test Preparation Service: Instructor selects up to 200 questions from the Test Item File and phones them in to a toll-free 800 number; Prentice Hall prepares the test (and an alternate version if requested) and mails it within 24 hours, together with an answer key.

Videos/Films: Free film rental or video to adopters of 100 copies or more in a given semester.

Special Education on a Disk: Software for the IBM or Apple consisting of activities that allow students to apply textbook theory to classroom experience. The authors are Jack Barnette, Gary Morrison, and Steve Ross, Memphis State University.

By way of appreciation, we are thankful to reviewers of our previous edition and drafts of some of our revised chapters: Katherine G. Butler, Syracuse University; Kathryn P. Meadow-Orlans, Gallaudet University; Richard L. Thurman, University of Missouri-St. Louis; June H. Elliott, Lyndon State College; Richard F. Rodriguez, Western New Mexico University; Dr. Helen W. McRae, Trenton State College; and Carolyn Callahan, University of Virginia.

We want to express our appreciation to Joe Perry Sutton and especially to E. Paula Crowley, students who put in countless hours assisting us on various phases of the revision process. We also thank Ms. Karen Dwier for her extraordinarily accurate and rapid typing of some of our references and for her many trips to the post office for us. At Prentice Hall, we are grateful to Shirley Chlopak, Jeannine Ciliotta, Serena Hoffman, and Susan Willig for their help during the project.

We also want to thank those instructors and students who have given us feedback on our previous editions. Your comments are always welcome because they help us in our quest to write a scholarly, informative, interesting, and readable introduction to special education.

Daniel P. Hallahan
James M. Kauffman

About the Artists

The art work on the cover of this book was drawn by C. Crist Delmonico. Mr. Delmonico was visually limited from infancy until his teen years, when he became blind. He began to express himself in the visual arts at that time, using pencil, chalk, and other media to manipulate line, shape, and color into illusory abstract patterns. Mr. Delmonico's works, entitled "Dreamscapes," are created by visualizing images and designs, aided by memory. The resulting statement evokes illusions through which the viewer finds personal interpretations, along with the artist's intended perceptions. These "Dreamscapes" are included in a nationally touring exhibition, "Art of the Eye," which explores the nature of perception by visually impaired artists. A recipient of numerous awards and international recognition, Mr. Delmonico resides in Morristown, New Jersey.

The art work that opens each chapter of the book was done in classes taught by Erin Wells in Charlottesville, Virginia, and by Marcia Matthews at the Norman Bleshman School in the Special Services District of Bergen County, New Jersey. We are extremely proud of these talented young people:

Chapter 1: Ellen Goldstein, 6th grade
Chapter 2: Chrissy Isbister, 2nd grade
Chapter 3: Jamar Johnson, 8 years old
Chapter 4: Tina Johnson, 14 years old
Chapter 5: Meredith Wells, 8th grade
Chapter 6: Owen Wells, 8th grade
Chapter 7: Bari Kim Goldrosen, 16 years old
Chapter 8: John Edmonson, 6th grade
Chapter 9: Ellen Goldstein, 6th grade
Chapter 10: Lane Kneedler, 4th grade

1

Introduction

Only the brave dare look upon the gray—
upon the things which cannot be explained easily,
upon the things which often engender mistakes,
upon the things whose cause cannot be understood,
upon the things we must accept and live with.
And therefore only the brave dare look upon difference without
flinching.

(*Richard H. Hungerford, "On Locusts"*)

The study of exceptional children is the study of *differences*. The exceptional child is different in some way from the "average" youngster. In very simple terms, such a child may have problems or special talents in thinking, seeing, hearing, speaking, socializing, or moving. More often than not, such a child has a combination of special abilities or disabilities. Today over 4 million such "different" children have been identified in public schools throughout the United States. The statistic that about one out of every ten children in American schools is an exceptional child, coupled with the fact that even many so-called normal children have school-related problems, makes the study of exceptionality a colossal task.

The study of exceptional children is also the study of *similarities*. Exceptional children are not different from the "average" in every way. In fact, most exceptional children are average in more ways than they are different. Until recently, professionals, and laypeople as well, tended to focus on the differences between exceptional and nonexceptional children, almost to the exclusion of the ways in which all children are alike. Today more attention is being given to what exceptional and nonexceptional children have in common—to similarities in their characteristics, needs, and ways of learning. As a result, the study of exceptional children has become more complex, and many so-called facts about handicapped and gifted children have been challenged.

The student of one of the hard sciences may boast of the difficulty of the subject matter because of the many facts that must be pieced together and remembered. The plight of the student of special education is quite different. To be sure, there are facts, but they are relatively few in number. Any study of human beings must take into account inherent ambiguities, inconsistencies, and unknowns. In the case of the child who deviates from the norm, we must multiply all the mysteries of normal human behavior and development by those pertaining to the child's exceptionalities. Because there is no single accepted theory of normal child development, it is not at all surprising that relatively few definite statements can be made about exceptional children.

There are, however, patches of sunshine in the bleak gray painted by Hungerford (see page 1). It is true that in the vast majority of cases we are unable to identify the exact reason why a child is exceptional. But progress is being made in determining the causes of some disabilities. In a later chapter, for example, we discuss the rather recent detection of causal factors in Down syndrome—a condition resulting in the largest number of children classified as moderately retarded. Likewise, retrolental fibroplasia—at one time a leading cause of blindness—has been greatly reduced since the discovery of its cause. The cause of mental retardation associated with a metabolic disorder—PKU (phenylketonuria)—has been discovered. Soon after birth, infants are now routinely tested for PKU so that any mental retardation can be prevented if they should have the disorder. Besides these and other medical breakthroughs, research is bringing us a more complete understanding of the ways in which the handicapped child's psychological, social, and educational environments are related to learning problems. For example, special educators, psychologists, and pediatricians are increasingly able to identify environmental conditions which increase the likelihood that a child will have learning or behavior problems (Werner, 1986).

Educational methodology has also made strides. In fact, in comparison to what is known about causes, we know a lot about how exceptional children can be taught and managed effectively in the classroom. Although special educators constantly

MISCONCEPTIONS
ABOUT EXCEPTIONAL CHILDREN

Myth	*Fact*
Special education originated in America.	The origins of special education are found in the work of nineteenth-century European physicians.
Public schools may choose not to provide education for some children.	Federal legislation specifies that in order to receive federal funds, every school system must provide a free, appropriate education for every child regardless of any handicapping condition.
By law, the handicapped child must be placed in the least restrictive environment (LRE). The LRE is always the regular classroom.	Law does require that the handicapped child be placed in the LRE. However, LRE is *not* always the regular classroom. What LRE does mean is that the handicapped child shall be segregated as little as possible from home, family, community, and the regular class setting. In many, but not all, instances this will mean placement in the regular classroom.
It is a relatively easy matter to determine the prevalence of exceptional children.	A host of variables—vague and changing definitions, overlapping diagnoses, sampling errors, school-defined nature of exceptionality, and the deliberate avoidance by some of having their children labeled exceptional—make it exceedingly difficult to arrive at accurate prevalence figures.
The causes of most disabilities are known, but little is known about how to help children overcome or compensate for their disabilities.	In most cases, the causes of children's disabilities are not known, although progress is being made in pinpointing why many disabilities occur. More is known about the treatment of most disabilities than about their causes.

lament that all the questions are not answered, we do know considerably more today about how to educate exceptional children than we did ten or fifteen years ago. In particular, once reasonable people realized that behaviorists did not really want to create George Orwell's nightmare world of *1984,* the methods of behavior modification were adopted by many special educators. Behavior modification is not a total solution, but it is often a highly effective, humane educational tool.

Before moving to the specific subject matter of exceptional children, we must point out that we vehemently disagree with Hungerford on an important point: We must certainly learn to "live with" handicapping exceptionalities, but we must never "accept" them. We prefer to think there is hope for the eventual eradication of many of the disabling forms of exceptionality. In addition, we believe it is of paramount importance to realize that even children whose exceptionalities are exotic or extreme can be helped to lead a fuller life.

Jim Abbott was born with a disability, but he's about to realize a lifelong dream

I
T IS THREE-quarters of a mile from Room 111, Rumsey Hall at the University of Michigan, to the baseball field at Ray Fisher Stadium, and as Jim Abbott walks across the sprawling campus, he has plenty of time to think and fret, as any freshman pitcher would. He thinks freshman thoughts. He has freshman doubts. He wonders if a high school fastball is good enough for college hitters.

"I feel the pressure," he says. "After all that's happened to me in my life, I don't want to get lost in the shuffle now. I don't want to be just another high school pitcher who got lost in college."

Jim Abbott, 18, is not just another lefthanded high school phenom, no matter what happens when the varsity baseball season begins for real this month in Ann Arbor. Jim Abbott was born without a right hand.

As he heads across campus each day, he smiles nervously as he readies himself for practice. He has come too far to fail. He smiles because he is eager.

"I'm battling against the odds again," Abbott says. "I've got to prove myself all over again, because I'm different. I'm back at the bottom, working my way up. But I'm going to make it."

In the 10 years of my job as a newspaper columnist, I have never been as touched by an athlete as I have by Jim Abbott, the one-handed kid from Flint, Mich., who has been different, at least so far in his young life, because he has been better, not because he is crippled.

"I'm just at another crossroads," he says, "with people staring at me."

His right arm ends at a narrow stub—a wrist that quit—with one small finger protruding. The right arm is about 10 inches shorter than the left. On the mound, Abbott starts with the stub stuck in the pocket of his glove, which has the pocket turned around, facing home plate. At the end of his follow-through, as a fastball already is being Federal Expressed to the plate, the good hand slides into the glove as easily as a knife going into soft butter.

When he must catch the ball, he takes it in the glove. Then, with deftness and economy, the glove is being turned around as it is tucked under his right arm, the ball comes out, and Abbott has it in his left hand, ready to throw again.

Ted Mahan, Abbott's Connie Mack League coach in Flint, says, "He used to drop the glove once in a while. I can't remember the last time he did *that*."

If Abbott could not make the switch, he could not pitch. He was outfitted with a hooklike prosthesis when he was 4. He threw out the hook when he was 5. He would play the hand he was dealt.

"I *hated* that [artificial] hand," Jim Abbott says now. "That's why I gave it up before I got to the second grade. It limited the things I could do. It didn't *help* me do anything. It was ugly, it drew attention to me, and I threw it out."

I say to him: "But you had to know having one hand was going to draw attention to you your whole life."

He says: "I planned to be different because I was a great baseball pitcher."

His boyhood seems artificial because it is out of some improbable storybook. Jim Abbott knew hurts. There were, briefly, nicknames like "Stub."

"He heard all the predictable mean things that 5- and 6-year-olds say," says his father, Mike Abbott. But the jokes and nicknames did not last long. Jim Abbott became the best in the

Ken Regan/Camera 5

Freshman Jim Abbott holds baseball in University of Michigan locker room. He's battling the odds again, but it's an old familiar battle, and the outcome is always the same.

The Kid Who Wins One-Handed

BY MIKE LUPICA

SOURCE: *Parade Magazine,* March 2, 1986, pp. 4–5. Reprinted by permission of International Creative Management.

Some exceptional individuals learn to live with and overcome their handicaps in ways that surprise most of us. Their differences do not keep them from leading full and normal lives as children or as adults. Sometimes special education plays no role in their lives because their own personal strength and support from their families neighborhood, in all the games. But mostly baseball. "He was going to show everybody," his father says.

The father, a 37-year-old account executive for Anheuser-Busch, watched the son over hundreds of boyhood hours throwing a ball against a brick wall. He would throw. Switch the glove. Catch. Put the glove under the arm. Take the ball out. Throw again. And again.

Jim started in a Flint Midget League when he was 12. There was a story about him in *The Flint Journal*. The road to deciding between a University of Michigan baseball scholarship and a Toronto Blue Jays bonus contract as a high school senior had begun.

"The only thing that would have been a handicap for me," Jim Abbott said one day last summer, sitting on his stoop, pounding his fist into a new Rawlings glove, "is if anyone had ever been negative around me. If anyone at any point had said, 'You can't do this' or, 'How do you expect to do *that* with one hand?' I probably wouldn't be playing ball of any kind right now. But my mom and dad and my coaches and my teammates have always said, 'Just go do it.' So I've played. I love playing basketball. I love football. I'm going to miss playing football now that I'm out of high school. But I just kept getting better and better at baseball. And I've been successful at every level I've pitched."

"We told him a long time ago," says his mom, Kathy Abbott, 37, a Flint attorney, "that if he wanted to play, he had to be able to do what the other kids do."

"I'm not going to tell you there weren't nights when he came home crying," says Mike Abbott. "But there really weren't a lot. He has been blessed with a great heart."

Jim Abbott is 6 feet 4 and 200 pounds. With his shock of sandy hair and open, ingenuous face, he looks like he ought to be starring in one of those summer movies for teens. He shot up to his present size between his sophomore and junior years at Flint Central High. No more brick walls by then, of any kind. Most times when the ball came back to him, it came from his catcher, because the batters were swinging and missing so often. Abbott was throwing baseballs past high school teams in the spring. Connie Mack teams in the summer. The scouts, college and pro, began to hear about this one-handed kid ("Huh? One-handed pitcher? *Come on!*") who was lighting up the radar guns with a 90 mph fastball. The scouts came to watch. When they saw the left arm, they forgot about the missing right hand.

In his senior year at Flint Central, Abbott had a 10-3 record with a 0.76 earned run average. He struck out 148 batters in 73 innings. He gave up just 16 hits. That works out to two strikeouts an inning, a hit every four or five innings. When batting, he stuck the stub at the end of the bat, near the handle, and closed his big left hand around it.

Using this system, Jim Abbott only managed to hit .427 for Flint Central, with seven homers. He also played quarterback on the football team. Flint Central went 10-2. Against Midlands High, Abbott threw four touchdown passes in the first half. There isn't a rule anywhere that says The Natural has to have two hands.

Jim Abbott, bottom, at age 4 with prosthesis he later discarded; right, warming up for college photo session (note glove cradled on right hand); and in football uniform.

Asked if there's anything he can't do, he replies: "I can't button the darn buttons on my left cuff."

When I first heard about Jim Abbott, one-handed pitcher, I remembered Monty Stratton, the one-legged pitcher for the White Sox, and how hard it was for him to field bunts. I asked Jim about bunts, first thing.

Jim: "One game when I was pitching in the ninth grade, they bunted on me eight times in a row. I threw out the last seven. That was enough of that."

Mike and Kathy Abbott married young. They were each 18 when their first son was born without a right hand. Like him, they have learned as they've gone. They have helped him turn the abnormal into the normal, a potential negative into an inspiring and uplifting positive. Jim Abbott would be a more complete baseball player with two hands. I find it impossible to believe he could be a more complete person.

"We think," says Mike Abbott, "that if the baseball thing went up in smoke tomorrow, Jimmy would be adjusted enough to go live his life without baseball."

Once, quite seriously, I asked Jim Abbott what he *can't* do.

Quite seriously, he replied: "I can't button the darn buttons on my left cuff."

"Who does it?"

"My mom, usually. My roommate in college."

"After watching him pitch, I didn't think of the right hand at all—*at all*," says Don Welke, one of the scouts who has helped make the Toronto Blue Jays' farm system into one of the best in baseball. "For me, he was just another outstanding prospect."

The Blue Jays felt that Abbott's impairment might discourage other teams, so they waited until the 36th round of last year's amateur draft before taking him. Some saw it as a publicity stunt—as a backhanded compliment, if you will. The Blue Jays were, and are, serious about Jim Abbott's future.

"His drafting wasn't for publicity," says Don Welke, who urged the team to take Abbott. "We look down the road and see him as a major leaguer. He has a major league arm, a major league heart."

Jim Abbott, however, had that major league heart set on Michigan.

"A couple of years ago," he says, "to play college ball at any level was a dream I never thought could come true. I remember on my first visit to Ann Arbor, I looked at the campus and thought how pretty things were and how neat it would be for someone to go there. Then I stopped short and said to myself, '*You* can have this. It's you they want. You can play college baseball here.' I think I can have both my dreams. I can play college ball and have pro ball still waiting for me down the road."

A week before he left for college, I asked Jim if he was afraid about the future. "I am," he said. "But I really think they're just normal fears for a guy going off to college. You're talking about my hand, right? I had to stop being afraid a long time ago. What fear there's been, I've used to get better."

We were sitting in front of the Abbott house. He was showing me his new glove. "You know," he said, "I hear a lot about how inspirational I am. But I don't see myself as being inspirational. Whether you're rich or poor or one-handed or whatever, your own childhood just seems natural, because it's the only one you know. I've met kids with one hand lately, or one arm—8-year-olds, in that range— and they tell me I've helped them by example, and I do feel great about that. But I don't think *I'm* that great. If I can inspire kids in any way, I'd just hope they could get the same enjoyment out of sports I've had."

And now, on this afternoon, it was time for a game of catch. Jim Abbott walked about 30 yards away and began tossing the ball to me. It began to make bigger and bigger popping noises in my glove as the kid got loose. After about five minutes, I promise I did not notice the shortened right arm, or the glove switch, any of it. I just made sure to watch the ball. I wanted to be sure I was quick enough with *my* glove so that a baseball thrown by Jim Abbott did not hit me between the eyes.

I thought: I'm like the hitters. I feel overmatched. But I wanted to remember this game of catch, because I began to feel strongly that it would be important someday that I knew Jim Abbott when.

I have used the word hero a lot in writing about sports, carried away by the moment. Jim Abbott is a hero. He is like most true heroes. He doesn't make a big deal out of what he does. He just gets on with things. He plays the hand dealt him, at the University of Michigan now. Without bitterness and without complaint, he has become a champion, no matter what happens in Ann Arbor this spring.

and communities are sufficient to allow them to overcome obstacles. A case in point is Jim Abbott, a student at the University of Michigan. But many others, some with differences less obvious or extreme than Jim's, need special education programs and related professional services to help them live full and happy lives.

DEFINITIONS

Exceptional Children

Exceptional children are those who require special education and related services if they are to realize their full human potential. They require special education because they are markedly different from most children in one or more of the following ways: they may have mental retardation, learning disabilities, emotional disturbance, physical disabilities, disordered speech or language, impaired hearing, impaired sight or special gifts or talents. In the chapters that follow we will define as exactly as possible what it means to be a member of a group of exceptional individuals.

Special Education

Special education means specially designed instruction that meets the unique needs of an exceptional child. Special materials, teaching techniques, equipment and/or facilities may be required. For example, children with visual impairment may require reading materials in large print or Braille; children with hearing impairment may require hearing aids and/or instructions in manual communication; children with physical disabilities may need wheelchairs, ramps, and a variety of equipment available only in a special medical facility; and children with special gifts or talents may require access to working professionals. Related services—special transportation, psychological assessment, physical and occupational therapy, medical treatment, and counseling—may be necessary if special education is to be effective.

Special Education Services

Special education may be provided according to several types of administrative plans, from a few special provisions made by the child's regular teacher to twenty-four-hour institutional care. The type required depends on the extent to which the child differs from the average; children with greater differences usually need more continuous, prolonged, and intensive intervention.

Beginning at the least intensive level of intervention, the *regular classroom teacher* who is aware of the individual needs of children and skilled at meeting them may be able to acquire materials, equipment, and/or instructional methods that are appropriate. At this level the direct services of "experts" may not be required—the expertise of the regular teacher may meet the child's needs.

At the next level the regular classroom teacher may need consultation with a *special educator* or other professional (e.g., school psychologist) in addition to the special materials, equipment, or methods. The special educator may instruct the regular teacher, refer the teacher to other resources, or demonstrate the use of materials, equipment, or methods.

Going a step further, a special educator may provide *itinerant services* to the exceptional child and/or the regular classroom teacher. The itinerant teacher establishes a consistent schedule, moving from school to school and visiting the classroom to instruct exceptional children individually or in small groups, provide materials and teaching suggestions for the regular teacher to carry out, and consult with the regular teacher about special problems.

At the next level, a *resource teacher* provides services for the children and teachers in only one school. The children being served are enrolled in the regular class-

The emphasis today is on providing special education services that are tailored to individual students' unique needs. Here one student who has difficulty controlling a pencil for written work is using a manual typewriter in the conventional way, while another who hasn't the use of his arms and fingers is learning to use a headstick to type his written work. Meanwhile, other students in the class are completing their assignments with paper and pencil. (Ann Chwatsky/Leo de Wys Inc.)

room and are seen by the specially trained teacher for a length of time and at a frequency determined by the severity of their particular problems. The resource teacher continually assesses the needs of the children and their teachers and usually teaches children individually or in small groups in a special classroom where special materials and equipment are available. Typically, the resource teacher serves as a consultant to the regular classroom teacher, advising on the instruction and management of the child in the classroom and perhaps demonstrating instructional techniques. The flexibility of the resource teacher plan and the fact that the child remains with peers most of the time make this a particularly attractive and popular alternative.

Diagnostic-prescriptive centers go beyond the level of intervention represented by resource rooms. In this plan children are placed for a short period of time in a special class in a school or other facility so their needs can be assessed and a plan of action can be determined on the basis of diagnostic findings. After an educational prescription is written for the child, the recommendations for placement may include anything from institutional care to placement in a regular classroom with a particularly competent teacher who can carry out the plan.

Hospital and homebound instruction involves teaching the child in the hospital or at home because of a physical and/or psychological condition. This type of service is most often required by children who have physical handicaps, although it is sometimes employed for emotionally disturbed or other handicapped children when no alternative is readily available. Typically, the child is confined to the hospital or the home for a relatively short period of time, and the hospital or homebound teacher maintains contact with the child's regular teacher.

One of the most visible—and, in recent years, controversial—service alternatives is the *special self-contained class*. Such a class typically enrolls fifteen or fewer exceptional children with a particular diagnostic label (e.g., mental retardation). The teacher ordinarily has been trained as a special educator and provides all or most of the children's instruction. The youngsters assigned to such classes usually spend the whole school day segregated from their normal peers, although sometimes they are integrated with nonhandicapped children during part of the day (perhaps for physical education, music, or some other activity in which they can participate well).

Special day schools provide an all-day, segregated experience for exceptional children. The day school usually is organized for a specific category of exceptional children and may contain special equipment necessary for their care and education. These children return to their homes during nonschool hours.

The final level of intervention is the *residential school*. Here exceptional children receive twenty-four-hour care away from home, often at a distance from their home communities. These children may make periodic visits home or return each weekend, but during the week they are residents of the institution, where they receive academic instruction in addition to management of their daily living environment.

The major features of each type of placement or service alternative, examples of the types of students most likely to be served in each, and the primary roles of the special educators who work in each type of placement setting are shown in Table 1.1. Note that while these are the major administrative plans for delivery of special education, variations are possible. Many school systems, in the process of trying to find more effective and economical ways of serving exceptional students, combine or alter these alternatives and the roles special educators and other professionals play in service delivery. Furthermore, the types of students listed under each service alternative are *examples only;* there are wide variations among school systems in the kinds of placements made for particular kinds of students. Note also that what any special education teacher may be expected to do includes a variety of items not specified in Table 1.1. We discuss these expectations for teachers in the following section.

Special education law requires placement of the child in the **least restrictive environment (LRE).** What is usually meant by this is that the child should be segregated from normal classmates and separated from home, family, and community as little as possible. That is, his or her life should be as "normal" as possible, and the intervention should be consistent with individual needs and not interfere with individual freedom any more than is absolutely necessary. For example, children should not be placed in a special class if they can be served adequately by a resource teacher, and they should not be placed in an institution if a special class will serve their needs just as well. While this movement toward placement of exceptional children in the least restrictive environment is laudable, the definition of "least restrictive" is not as simple as it seems. Cruickshank (1977) has pointed out that greater restriction of the physical environment does not necessarily mean greater restriction of the child's psychological freedom or human potential. In fact, it is conceivable that these children could be more restricted in the long run in a regular class where they are rejected by others and fail to learn necessary skills than in a special class or day school where they learn happily and well. It is important to keep the ultimate goals for the child in mind and to avoid letting "least restrictive" become a hollow slogan that results in shortchanging children in terms of their education. As Morse has noted: "The goal should be to find the most productive setting to provide the maximum assistance for the child" (1984, p. 120).

Although considerable variation in the placement of handicapped students is found from state to state and among school systems within a given state, most exceptional children are educated in regular classes. Figure 1.1 shows that, nationwide, over two-thirds of handicapped children and youths are served primarily in regular classes. Most of these students receive special instruction for part of the school day from special education resource teachers. About one-fourth of all handicapped children and youths in the United States are placed in separate special

Figure 1.1 *Percent of all handicapped children served by age range in four educational environments, school year 1983–84*
SOURCE: *To Assure the Free Appropriate Public Education of All Handicapped Children. Eighth Annual Report to Congress on the Implementation of the Education of the Handicapped Act,* Vol. 1 (Washington, D.C.: U.S. Department of Education, 1986), p. 56.

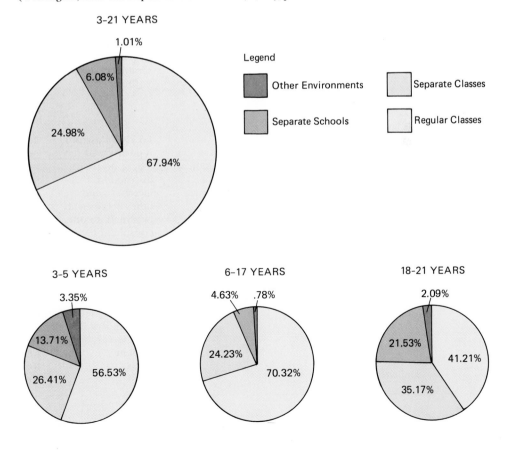

Table 1.1   Examples of Service Alternatives for Special Education

	LEST INTENSIVE AND MOST INTEGRATED			
Type of Placement	**Regular Class Only**	**Regular Class with Consultation**	**Itinerant Teacher**	**Resource Teacher**
Major features of placement alternative	Regular teacher meets all needs of student; student may not be officially identified or labeled; student totally integrated	Regular teacher meets all needs of student with only occasional help from consultant(s); student may not be officially identified or labeled; student totally integrated	Regular teacher provides most or all instruction; special teacher provides intermittent instruction of student and/or consultation with regular teacher; student integrated except for brief instructional sessions	Regular teacher provides most instruction; special teacher provides instruction part of school day and advises regular teacher; student integrated most of school day
Examples of types of students served	Student with mild learning disability, emotional disturbance, or mild mental retardation	Student with mild learning disability, emotional disturbance, or mild mental retardation	Student with visual impairment or physical disability; student with speech impairment	Student with mild to moderate emotional, learning, or language impairment
Primary role of special education teacher	None	To offer demonstration and instruction and to assist regular class teacher as requested	To visit classroom regularly and see that appropriate instruction, materials, and other services are provided; to offer consultation, demonstration, and referral for regular teacher and assessment and instruction of student as needed; to work toward total integration of student	To assess student's needs for instruction and management; to provide individual or small-group instruction on set schedule in regular class or resource room; to offer advice and demonstration for regular teacher; to handle referral to other agencies for additional services; to work toward total integration of student

			MOST INTENSIVE AND LEAST INTEGRATED	
Diagnostic Prescriptive Center	Hospital or Homebound Instruction	Self-Contained Class	Special Day School	Residential School
Special teacher provides most or all instruction for several days or weeks and develops plan or prescription for receiving teacher; student totally segregated while in center, but may be partially or totally integrated following diagnosis and prescription	Special teacher provides all instruction in hospital or home until student is able to return to usual school classes (regular or special) from which he or she has been temporarily withdrawn; student totally segregated for short period	Special teacher provides most or all instruction in special class of students with given categorical label; regular teacher may provide instruction in regular class for part of school day; student mostly or totally segregated	Special teacher provides instruction in separate school; also may work with teachers in regular or special classes of regular school; student totally or mostly segregated	Same as special day school; special teacher also works with other staff to provide a total therapeutic environment or milieu; student totally or mostly segregated
Student with mild handicap who has been receiving no services or inadequate services	Student with physical disability; student undergoing treatment or medical tests; pregnant student	Student with moderate to severe mental retardation or emotional disturbance	Student with severe or profound physical or mental handicap	Student with severe or profound mental retardation or emotional disturbance
To make comprehensive assessment of student's educational strengths and weaknesses; to develop written prescription for instruction and behavior management for receiving teacher; to interpret prescription for receiving teacher and assess and revise prescription as needed	To obtain records from student's school of attendance; to maintain contact with teachers (regular or special) and offer instruction consistent with student's school program; to prepare student for return to school setting (special or regular)	To manage and teach special class; to offer instruction in most areas of curriculum; to work toward integration of students in regular classes	To manage and teach individuals and/or small groups of handicapped students; to work toward integration of students in regular school	Same as special day school; also to work with residential staff to make certain school program is integrated appropriately with nonschool activities

classes, and only about 7 percent are segregated in separate schools or other environments (e.g., institutions, hospital schools, and homebound instruction).

Note that Figure 1.1 indicates differences in educational placement by age. Children under the age of 6 are less often educated in regular classes and more often placed in separate schools than are children who have reached the usual school age. Special classes, separate schools, and other environments such as homebound instruction are used more often for older teenagers and young adults than for students of elementary and high school age. These differences can probably be explained by two facts. First, preschoolers and young adults who are identified for special education tend to have more severe disabilities than youngsters of school age. Second, regular public school classes for preschoolers and young adults are not found in every public school system in the United States. Thus, placements in other than regular classes are typically more available and more appropriate for many preschoolers and young adults.

The environment that is least restrictive depends in part on the child's handicapping condition. Figure 1.2 illustrates the differences in educational placement of children with different disabilities. There is almost never a need to segregate a child whose primary disability is a speech/language impairment in a separate class or

Figure 1.2 *Percent of handicapped children (ages 3–21) served in four educational environments by handicapping condition, school year 1983–84**
SOURCE: *To Assure the Free Appropriate Public Education of All Handicapped Children. Eighth Annual Report to Congress on the Implementation of the Education of the Handicapped Act,* Vol. 1 (Washington, D.C.: U.S. Department of Education, 1986), p. 60.

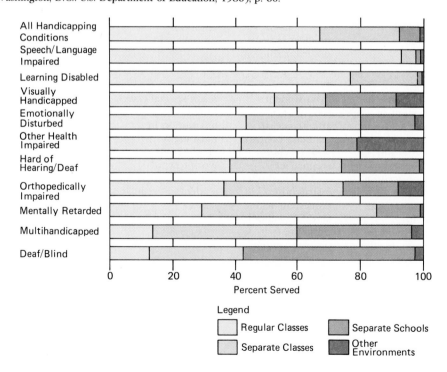

separate school. Most children with learning disabilities can be appropriately educated in regular classes. On the other hand, the resources needed to teach deaf/blind children require that most of them attend separate schools or classes.

WHAT SPECIAL EDUCATION TEACHERS ARE EXPECTED TO DO

We have noted that most students in public schools who have been identified as handicapped are placed in regular classrooms. Furthermore, there is good reason to believe that a large number of public school students not identified as handicapped share many of the characteristics of exceptional children. Thus regular teachers must obviously be prepared to deal with exceptional children.

We stress here that a student should not be referred for special education unless extensive and unsuccessful efforts have been made to accommodate his or her needs in regular classes. Before referral, school personnel must document the strategies that have been used to teach and manage the student in general education. Only if these strategies have failed is referral justified.

The student preparing to become a teacher should understand that the roles of general and special education teachers are not always clear in a given case. Sometimes, uncertainty about the division of responsibility can be extremely stressful; for example, teachers may feel very uneasy because it is not clear whose job it is to make special adaptations for a child or just what they are expected to do in cooperating with other teachers (Crane and Iwanicki, 1986; Morrison, Lieber, and Morrison, 1986).

Whether specifically trained in special education or not, a teacher may be expected to participate in educating handicapped students in any one of the following ways:

1. *Refer for evaluation.* By law, all public school systems must make extensive efforts to screen and identify all handicapped children and youths of school age. Teachers must observe students' behavior and refer those they suspect of having handicaps for evaluation by a multidisciplinary team.
2. *Evaluate academic abilities and disabilities.* Although psychologists or other special school personnel may give a referred student formal standardized tests in academic areas, adequate evaluation for special education requires the teacher's assessment of the student's performance in the classroom. Teachers must be able to report specifically and precisely how the student can and cannot perform in all academic areas for which they are responsible.
3. *Participate in eligibility conferences.* Before students are placed in special education, their eligibility must be determined by an interdisciplinary team. Therefore teachers must be ready to work with professionals from other disciplines (psychology, medicine, or social work, for example) in determining a student's eligibility for special education.
4. *Participate in writing individual education plans.* A written individualized plan for his or her education must be on file in the records of every handicapped student. Teachers must be ready to participate in a conference (possibly including the student and/or parent, as well as other professionals) in which the plan is formulated.
5. *Communicate with parents or guardians.* Parents (sometimes surrogate par-

ents) or guardians must be consulted during the evaluation of their child's eligibility for special education, formulation of the individual education plan, and reassessment of any special program that may be designed for their child. Teachers must contribute to the schools' communication with parents about their child's problems, placement, and progress.

6. *Participate in due process hearings and negotiations.* When parents, guardians, or handicapped students themselves are dissatisfied with the school's response to the child's needs, they may request a "due process" hearing or negotiations regarding appropriate services. Teachers may be called upon to offer observations, opinions, or suggestions in such hearings or negotiations.

A high level of professional competence and ethical judgment is required to conform to these expectations. Teaching demands a thorough knowledge of child development and expertise in instruction. Furthermore, teachers are sometimes faced with serious professional and ethical dilemmas in trying to serve the needs of students and their parents on the one hand, and in attempting to conform to legal or administrative pressures on the other (Bateman, 1982). For example, when there are indications that the child may have a handicap, should a teacher refer that child for evaluation and possible placement in special education, knowing that only inadequate or inappropriate services will be provided? Should a teacher who believes strongly that teenage students with mild retardation need sex education refrain from giving students any information because sex education is not part of the prescribed curriculum and is frowned upon by the school board?

In addition to being competent enough to meet the six expectations we listed above, special education teachers must attain special expertise in the following areas:

1. *Academic instruction of children with learning problems.* The majority of students with handicaps have more difficulty learning academic skills than do the nonhandicapped. This is true for all categories of handicapping conditions because sensory impairments, physical disabilities, and mental or emotional handicaps all tend to make academic learning more difficult. Sometimes the difficulty is slight; often it is extreme. Special education teachers must have more than patience and hope, though they do need these qualities; they must have the technical skill to present academic tasks so that students with handicaps will understand and respond appropriately (see Algozzine and Maheady, 1986; Engelmann and Carnine, 1982; Lloyd and Carnine, 1981).

2. *Management of serious behavior problems.* Many students with handicaps have behavior problems in addition to their other disabilities. Some, in fact, require special education primarily because of their inappropriate or disruptive behavior. Special education teachers must have the ability to deal effectively with more than the usual troublesome behavior of students. Besides understanding and empathy, they must possess the mastery of techniques that will allow them to draw out particularly withdrawn students and control those who are hyperaggressive and persistently disruptive (see Kerr and Nelson, 1983; Morris, 1985; Nelson, 1981; Polsgrove, 1983; Strain, 1981).

3. *Use of technological advances.* Technology is increasingly being applied to the problems of teaching handicapped students and improving their daily lives. New devices and methods are rapidly being developed, particularly for students with sensory and physical disabilities. Special education teachers

need more than mere awareness of the technology that is available; they must be able to evaluate its advantages and disadvantages for teaching the exceptional children with whom they work (see Stowitschek, 1984).

4. *Knowledge of special education law.* For good or ill, special education today involves many details of law. Handicapped students' rights are spelled out in considerable detail in federal and state legislation. The laws, and the rules and regulations that accompany them, are constantly being interpreted by new court decisions, some of which have widespread implications for the practice of special education. Special education teachers do not need to be lawyers, but they do need to be aware of the law's requirements and prohibitions if they are to be adequate advocates for students with handicaps (see Ballard-Campbell, 1981; Bateman and Herr, 1981; Blackhurst, 1982).

We caution here that the specific day-to-day expectations for special education teachers vary from school system to school system and from state to state. What we have listed here are the general expectations and areas of competence with which every special educator will necessarily be concerned.

PREVALENCE OF EXCEPTIONAL CHILDREN

Government figures show that about 11 children and youth out of every 100 attending public schools have been identified as handicapped for special education purposes (U.S. Department of Education, 1986). The total number of children served by special education is over 4 million. Most of these children and youth are between the ages of 6 and 17. Although preschoolers and youths 18 to 21 are being identified as handicapped with increasing frequency, school-age children and youths in their early teens comprise the bulk of the identified population.

Before considering the difficulties of determining the prevalence of handicapping conditions, we need to clarify the statistical terminology used in most reports on the numbers of handicapped children.

The terms *incidence* and *prevalence* are often used interchangeably in speaking of the number of exceptional children. Technically, *incidence* refers to the number of new cases of children with an exceptionality in a given period of time (usually a year). *Prevalence* applies to the total number of existing cases (new and old) in the population at a given point in time. For instance, we might find that the incidence of blindness among children in Chicago was 200 for 1984, meaning that in 1984 there were 200 new cases of blindness in children. We might find too that the *prevalence* of blindness in the child population of Chicago in 1984 was 3,000, meaning that in 1984 there were 3,000 blind children in Chicago. *Prevalence* is also used to refer to the percent or proportion of the population that falls into a given category. Thus we might state that the prevalence of blindness in Chicago in 1984 was 0.03 percent, indicating that 3 of every 10,000 children in Chicago were blind in 1984. Obviously, establishing accurate figures depends on obtaining accurate counts of the number of handicapped and nonhandicapped children in the population in question.

It would seem that the task of determining the number of children who need special education should be a simple, straightforward matter. Why would it be any more difficult to count handicapped children than to count nonhandicapped children? Several factors make it hard to determine the number of handicapped children in a given area with accuracy. These include problems involving definition, diagnosis, sampling errors, the role of the school, and stigma.

The Effect of Vague and Changing Definitions

An accurate accounting of the number of individuals falling into any category of exceptionality depends ultimately on a clear, unambiguous definition. The way we have defined exceptional children in this book, and the way they have been defined by others as well, leaves room for error. There may be honest disagreement among professionals regarding whether or not a given child has a handicap. And when one considers the definitions of specific handicapping conditions, the problem of counting instances becomes more obvious.

There is a continuing debate over the definition of some of the most common handicapping conditions, as you will see throughout this book. For example, who should be counted among those with mental retardation, and who should not? Should someone who scores below 85 on an IQ test be considered to have mental retardation, or should the cutoff score be lower, say 70 (see Edgerton, 1984)? We do not want to mislead you here. Mental retardation is not defined simply in terms of IQ. But IQ is one of the criteria mentioned in almost all definitions. The crux of the problem is this: Depending on just how mental retardation is defined, there will be many more or many fewer individuals who have that disability. Especially in those categories of special education having the highest incidence and prevalence—mental retardation, emotional disturbances, learning disabilities, and speech and language disorders—definitions are subjective and subject to change (Forness, 1985).

When people do not have a precise and unvarying definition of what it is they are counting, it is no wonder they have difficulty agreeing about the number of instances they have observed.

The Effect of Overlapping and Changing Diagnoses

Even if it is granted that a clear definition of a handicapping condition has been agreed upon, there may be confusion about how a particular child should be classified for the purposes of incidence or prevalence estimates. The child may have more than one pertinent set of characteristics. For example, he or she may have both mental retardation *and* emotional disturbance, blindness *and* retardation, speech-handicaps *and* blindness, or cerebral palsy, blindness, *and* emotional disturbance. If the child is counted only once, then in which category? Furthermore, a diagnosis that fits a child today may be inappropriate next year, or even next month. Frequently, children who are handicapped by speech defects, behavior disorders, or learning disabilities improve to such an extent that they should be considered nonhandicapped. Occasionally, a blind child gains sight or a hearing-impaired child becomes able to hear normally. And of course children can acquire handicapping conditions through disease, accidents, and other factors. Incidence and prevalence estimates must take into account the fact that children's intellectual, emotional, and physical characteristics may change.

Sampling Errors

Incidence and prevalence figures typically are estimates based on the number of children counted in a sample. The sample is a subgroup or subset of the total population for which the estimates are made. That is, if incidence and prevalence data are desired for the United States, it is not necessary to count each and every child. Rather, samples are drawn from various parts of the country, and the counts obtained in these samples are then used as the basis for estimating what the count is in the entire country. It is possible to obtain a biased sample that does not accurately reflect the frequency with which a handicapping condition occurs in the general population.

The School-Defined Nature of Exceptionality

Still another factor that makes it difficult to determine the prevalence of exceptional children has to do with the role of the schools. Some exceptionalities are defined almost totally by the child's response to the demands of school. In the case of learning disabilities, school performance is very nearly the essence of the problem. It is failure to achieve at school that *defines* the child as having a learning disability in nearly all instances. Much the same can be said of mild mental retardation—that is, a child may be considered retarded in school but may function quite adequately elsewhere (see Edgerton, 1984). The point to consider here is that when an exceptionality is defined by the school, there is no accurate way of estimating the incidence or prevalence of that exceptionality in preschool children or in individuals beyond school age. Moreover, many exceptional children and youth do not attend public schools, from which federal prevalence and data are drawn. They may attend private schools or be incarcerated as juvenile delinquents, for example (Murphy, 1986). And the prevalence of the disability may vary considerably from school to school simply because the demands on children differ from school to school.

The Stigma of Identification

Finally, as we have already noted, many parents are reluctant to have their child identified as exceptional. Roos (1975) has described the reactions of parents to having a handicapped child: loss of self-esteem, shame, ambivalence, depression, self-sacrifice, and defensiveness. "Parents may anticipate social rejection, pity, or ridicule and related loss of prestige. Social withdrawal may be a common consequence" (p. 343). The cartoon illustrates with a bit of humor how facing up to the fact of a child's handicap can be a painful and unpleasant experience—one that many parents try in every way possible to avoid. It is not surprising that incidence and prevalence data can be distorted as a result.

SOURCE: Reprinted by permission of the National Education Association.

THE HISTORY OF SPECIAL EDUCATION

There have always been exceptional children, but there have not always been special educational services to answer their needs. During the closing years of the eighteenth century, following the American and French revolutions, effective procedures were devised for teaching children with sensory impairments—those who were blind or deaf (Winzer, 1986). Early in the nineteenth century the first systematic attempts were made to educate "idiotic" and "insane" children—those who today are said to have mental retardation and emotional disturbance. In the prerevolutionary era the most society had offered exceptional children was protection—asylum from a cruel world into which they did not fit and in which they could not survive with dignity, if they could survive at all. But as the ideas of democracy, individual freedom, and egalitarianism swept America and France, there was a change in attitude. Political reformers and leaders in medicine and education began to champion the cause of handicapped children and adults, urging that these "imperfect" or "incomplete" individuals be taught skills that would allow them to become independent, productive citizens. These humanitarian sentiments went beyond a desire to protect and defend handicapped people. The early leaders sought to normalize exceptional children to the greatest extent possible and confer on them the human dignity they lacked.

The historical roots of special education are found primarily in the early 1800s. Contemporary educational methods for exceptional children can be traced directly to techniques pioneered during that era. And many (perhaps most) of today's vital, controversial issues have been issues ever since the dawn of special education (see Ball, 1971; Kauffman, 1976, 1981, 1985; Lane, 1976). In our discussion of some of the major historical events and trends since 1800, we will comment briefly on the history of people and ideas, the fall and rise of special education, the history of professional and parent organizations, and the history of and perspectives on legislation and litigation.

People and Ideas

Most of the originators of special education were European physicians. They were primarily young, ambitious people who challenged the wisdom of the established authorities, including their own friends and mentors (Kanner, 1964).

Jean Marc Gaspard Itard (1775–1838), a French physician who was an authority on diseases of the ear and on the education of deaf students, is the person to whom most historians trace the beginning of special education as we know it today. In the early years of the nineteenth century, this young doctor began to educate a boy of about 12 who had been found roaming naked and wild in the forests of France. Itard's mentor, Philippe Pinel (1745–1826), a prominent French physician who was an early advocate of humane treatment of insane persons, advised him that his efforts would be unsuccessful because the boy, Victor, was a "hopeless idiot." But Itard persevered. He did not make Victor nonhandicapped, but he did dramatically improve the wild child's behavior through patient, systematic educative procedures (see Itard, 1962; Lane, 1976).

Itard's student, Edouard Seguin (1812–1880), emigrated to the United States in 1848. Before that, Seguin had become famous as an educator of retarded children, even though most thinkers of the day were convinced that such children could not be taught anything of significance. Seguin received his M.D. degree from the City University of New York in 1861. His book *Idiocy and Its Treatment by the Physio-*

logical Method (published in the United States in 1866) described in detail his interpretation and elaboration of Itard's methods. It also provided much of the foundation for the work of Maria Montessori (1870–1952).

Montessori, the first woman in Italy to receive a medical degree, became known not only as an educator of mentally retarded children, but also as an advocate of early education for children (Montessori, 1912, 1917). The extent of Seguin's influence on Montessori is reflected by the fact that she laboriously copied by hand all 600 pages of his book (see Lane, 1976).

Jean Marc Gaspard Itard.
(Harvard University Press)

Maria Montessori.
(American Montessori Society)

Rev. Thomas Hopkins Gallaudet.
(New York Public Library)

Samuel Gridley Howe.
(Perkins School for the Blind)

Are All Handicapped Students Receiving Special Education?

PL 94-142 requires that all handicapped students be identified and given appropriate special education. Some government officials claim that all or nearly all handicapped pupils are being served, but some educators question this. These differences of opinion are partly a result of discrepancies between prevalence estimates and reports of the percentage of schoolchildren identified. From the 1950s until the early 1980s the federal government's Department of Education published estimates of the prevalence of exceptional children in various categories. These estimates, which remained remarkably stable for many years, were approximately as follows:

Exceptionality	Percent of School Population
Speech impaired	3.5
Mentally retarded	2.3
Emotionally disturbed	2.0
Learning disabled	2.0
Hearing impaired	0.6
Deaf/blind and other multihandicapped	0.6
Crippled and other health impaired	0.5
Visually handicapped	0.1

Starting in the early 1980s the Department of Education began to publish estimated prevalence *ranges* (e.g., 1.2–2.0 percent for emotionally disturbed), partly in recognition of the difficulties of obtaining accurate estimates. Since the mid 1980s, *Annual Reports to Congress on the Implementation of Public Law 94-142* have contained no estimates of the prevalence of handicapped children, only statistics regarding the number of handicapped children served by special education. Recent reports indicate that about 40 million children and youth are enrolled in American public schools (preschool through grade 12). Of these 40 million, the following were served by special education in 1985 (according to the U.S. Department of Education):

Exceptionality	Percent Enrolled in Special Education
Learning disabled	4.73
Speech impaired	2.86
Mentally retarded	1.68
Emotionally disturbed	0.95
Other health impaired	0.14
Multihandicapped	0.22
Hard of hearing and deaf	0.17
Orthopedically impaired	0.14
Visually handicapped	0.07
Deaf-blind	0.01
Total	**10.97**

The federal government's prevalence estimates and statistics regarding the percent of the school population served have been matters of controversy since PL 94-142 went into effect in 1978 (see Hallahan, Kauffman, and Lloyd, 1985; Kauffman, 1980, 1981, 1984, 1985, 1986a, 1986b; Magliocca and Stephens, 1980). Far fewer handicapped students are being identified than was anticipated, particularly in the categories of emotional disturbance and mental retardation. However, the percentage of the school population served under the category of learning disabled is far higher than anticipated.

Moreover, statistics indicate that only about 60 percent of the nation's population between 3 and 21 years of age is enrolled in public schools (U.S. Department of Education, 1984). Some educators suspect that many of the nearly 30 million individuals in the 3 through 21 years age range who are not enrolled in public schools are handicapped and require special education. Many handicapped children in some categories may not have been identified because: (1) the definitions of some categories are vague and subjective, allowing school systems to avoid identifying children who are not obviously handicapped; and (2) school systems do not have the money required to serve many more handicapped children if they were identified.

Lane summarized the links between Itard and Montessori as follows:

Itard had set out to train an *enfant sauvage;* by his journey's end he had become the originator of instructional devices, the inventor of behavior modification, the first speech and hearing specialist, founder of otolaryngology, creator of oral education of the deaf, and father of special education for the mentally and physically handicapped. Sensory education was gaining breadth and momentum as his student Seguin took the helm. Seguin went on to establish the education of the retarded world-wide and to discern the vast panorama beyond, where the training of the handicapped opened out to the training of all mankind. Montessori, coming later, saw the course she must follow more clearly; extending Itard's program first to the early stages of child development, before formal education, then to revising our conception of education itself, whatever the age of the learner. Montessori died just two decades ago. But our society has so thoroughly absorbed what this evolving system offered that we barely recognize its features, understand why they were sensational discoveries at the time, or appreciate the struggle and vision of those who rode the stream of history and also changed its course, from Itard to Montessori. (1976, pp. 285–286)

What were those sensational discoveries of the last century? These are a few of the revolutionary ideas of Itard, Seguin, and their successors:

- *Individualized instruction,* in which the child's characteristics rather than prescribed academic content provide the basis for teaching techniques.
- *A carefully sequenced series of educational tasks,* beginning with tasks the child can perform and gradually leading to more complex learning.
- *Emphasis on stimulation* and awakening of the child's senses, the aim being to make the child more aware of and responsive to educational stimuli.
- *Meticulous arrangement of the child's environment,* so that the structure of the environment and the child's experience of it lead naturally to learning.
- *Immediate reward for correct performance,* providing reinforcement for desirable behavior.
- *Tutoring in functional skills,* the desire being to make the child as self-sufficient and productive as possible in everyday life.
- *Belief that every child should be educated to the greatest extent possible,* the assumption being that every child can improve to some degree.

As will become obvious in this book, these ideas form the foundation for present-day special education.

So far we have mentioned only European physicians who figured prominently in the rise of special education. While it is true that much of the initial work took place in Europe, many Americans contributed greatly during those early years. The Americans stayed informed of European developments as best they could, some of them traveling to Europe for the specific purpose of obtaining first-hand information about the education of handicapped children (Kanner, 1964; see also Rosen, Clark, and Kivitz, 1975).

Among the young Americans concerned with the education of handicapped students was Samuel Gridley Howe (1801–1876), an 1824 graduate of Harvard Medical School. Besides being a physician and an educator, Howe was a political and social reformer, a champion of humanitarian causes and emancipation. He was instrumental in the founding of the Perkins School for the Blind in Watertown, Massachusetts, and was also a teacher of deaf/blind students. His success in teaching Laura Bridgman, who was deaf and blind, greatly influenced the education of Helen Keller. Howe was also a force behind the organization of an experimental school for retarded children in Massachusetts in the 1840s and was personally acquainted with Seguin.

Thomas Hopkins Gallaudet (1787–1851) was a minister who had met and tried to teach a deaf girl when he was a student at Andover Theological Seminary. He traveled to Europe to learn about education of deaf students, and upon his return to the United States in 1817 established the first American residential school for deaf students in Hartford, Connecticut (now known as the American School of the Deaf). Gallaudet University in Washington, D.C., the only liberal arts college for deaf students in the world, was named in his honor.

We could name many others, European and American, whose fascinating and brilliant careers helped to shape special education. But at this point it might be more helpful to sketch the historical trends that will enable us to understand current issues in the field.

The Fall and Rise of Special Education

The early years of special education were vibrant with the pulse of new ideas. It is not possible to read the words of Itard, Seguin, Howe, and their contemporaries without being captivated by the romance, idealism, and excitement of their exploits. The results they achieved were truly remarkable. But despite the energy, optimism, and accomplishments of these early leaders, special education lost its momentum in America during the last part of the nineteenth century. Humane and effective treatment turned to ineffective institutionalization and human warehousing; hope turned to despair. Not long after they were first opened in the late 1800s, special public school classes for exceptional children became dumping grounds for all kinds of misfits (Hoffman, 1975; Sarason and Doris, 1979).

The reasons are not simple. Many factors contributed to the decline, including at least the following: overzealous claims, which led the public to expect miraculous cures; bickering among professionals; unwillingness of the public to foot the bill (especially during periods of inflation and recession) when it was learned just how many handicapped children needed special education; the social, political, and economic turmoil resulting from the Civil War; the influence of Charles Darwin's theory of evolution, which led to the idea that handicapped people were inherently inferior and not amenable to improvement through education; the industrialization and urbanization of America; and the tremendous influx of immigrants whose cultures and personal attributes often clashed with what many considered to be the "American way of life."

It was not until after World War II that special education began to overcome the inertia of almost a century of neglect and regression. Great strides were made in many areas only after President Kennedy took office in 1961 and initiated his New Frontier programs. Much progress was made under the administration of President Johnson, and in recent years we have seen a return to a more optimistic attitude, although it is a guarded and realistic optimism. There is renewed interest in and respect for the legacies of the early leaders of special education (see, for example, Ball, 1971; Blatt and Morris, 1984; Lane, 1976). There is a trend away from needless institutional care and toward a community treatment focus. There is a recognition of the rights of exceptional individuals. In short, special education has made a comeback from the depths to which it sank a century ago.

Some individuals and institutions did not lose sight of the original high ideals of special education during the period of neglect—approximately 1860 to 1950. Important advances and milestones can be noted. There were shining examples—such as Grace Fernald (1879–1950), who developed remedial reading techniques—of what was right about special education. Our point is simply that the predominant tone, the prevailing attitude, the general drift of the field of special education, were not very positive during that period in American history.

Continued European Influence

Not only did special education begin with the work of European physicians, but European scholars and their ideas have continued to play an important role in special education in the United States (Juul, 1981). Two very clear examples are seen in the influence of Maria Montessori's methods and the work of the great developmental psychologist Jean Piaget. Another example is the emigration to the United States of educators of handicapped children when the Nazis came to power in Germany. Marianne Frostig, who had been a psychiatric social worker and rehabilitation therapist in Austria and Poland, came to the United States in 1938. Her subsequent training as a psychologist and her work with retarded, delinquent, and learning-disabled children had a strong influence on the development of special education, especially in the field of learning disabilities (see Frostig, 1976; Hallahan and Cruickshank, 1973; Hallahan et al., 1985). When Hitler gained control, Alfred A. Strauss, a neurologist, and Heinz Werner, a developmental psychologist, left Germany and joined the staff of the Wayne County Training School in Northville, Michigan. There they began a program of training and research that has influenced the course of special education from the late 1930s to the present (see Hallahan and Cruickshank, 1973; Hallahan et al., 1985; Kauffman, 1985a; Kauffman and Hallahan, 1976; Kavale and Forness, 1985).

In the 1960s Nicholas Hobbs, a distinguished psychologist and educator, was impressed by his observation of European *educateurs*—professional workers who play multifaceted roles in the care and education of troubled children. His observations of these European professionals greatly influenced the design of programs of special education for emotionally disturbed children in the United States (see Hobbs, 1974). Goldberg has noted that the Scandinavian countries have been at the forefront in providing care, education, and rehabilitation of mentally retarded children. Lippman summarizes his own observations this way: ". . . programs for the mentally retarded in Europe are better than in the United States—in part because attitudes are different. We in America can learn from Europe. We can modify our attitudes and, so doing, improve our programs" (1972, p. 68).

We do not want to leave a wrong impression here. The situation is not as simple as

"Europe, good—America, bad." But it is true that in some European countries the quality of services for handicapped people is well beyond that found in our own country. And it is still the case that some important ideas in special education find their way from other countries to America (see Csapo, 1984; Juul, 1981; Kugel and Wolfensberger, 1969).

Growth of the Discipline

Special education did not suddenly spring up as a new discipline, nor did it develop in isolation from other disciplines. Physicians were among the first professionals to become concerned about the welfare and education of exceptional children. In the twentieth century members of the medical profession have continued to play important roles in the field of special education, as exemplified by the work of Alfred Strauss and the contributions of other physicians to the contemporary literature on special education.

The emergence of the disciplines of psychology and sociology, and especially the beginning of widespread use of mental tests in the early years of the twentieth century, had enormous implications for the growth of special education. Psychologists' study of learning and their prediction of school failure or success by means of tests helped focus attention on children with special needs. Sociologists, social workers, and anthropologists drew attention to the ways in which exceptional children's families and communities responded to them and affected their learning and adjustment. As the education profession itself matured, and as compulsory school attendance laws became a reality, there was a growing realization among teachers and school administrators that a large number of children must be given something beyond the ordinary classroom experience. Thus contemporary special education is a professional field with roots in several academic disciplines—especially medicine, psychology, sociology, and social work—in addition to professional education. It is a discipline sufficiently different from the mainstream of professional education to require special training programs, but sufficiently like the mainstream to maintain a primary concern for schools and teaching.

Contemporary special education draws heavily on all disciplines concerned with child development (Blatt and Morris, 1984). Special educators must not only know the developmental characteristics of exceptional children, they must also understand how these characteristics differ from those of nonhandicapped children. In addition to an understanding of normal and delayed development, special educators must have a foundation of technical knowledge in the disciplines that involve a given exceptionality. For example, in order to be an adequate teacher of deaf children, one must have some knowledge of *audiology* (the science of hearing) and *otology* (the medical specialty of the ear and its diseases), as well as of communication and teaching techniques. We are not suggesting that an educator of deaf children must also be a developmental psychologist, an audiologist, and an otologist. But unless the educator of children with impaired hearing has the ability to communicate intelligently with professionals from these other disciplines, he or she will not be an effective teacher.

Becoming a special educator means preparing to *teach* exceptional children. It means preparing to spend one's time helping children change their behavior—grasp new concepts and perform new responses. Usually, but not always, it means working in public schools and classrooms. Always, it means working with other professionals and contributing to an interdisciplinary effort to help the child and the people the child lives with. Predictably, there is some confusion about exactly what role special educators should play. Kauffman has assessed the situation this way:

> As members and future members of the special-education profession, we are in many ways at an adolescent stage of development. We are being pulled in opposite directions, not really knowing whether we should separate ourselves from the educational mainstream and assert our independence or embrace and merge with the disciplines from which we spring. It is an awkward and painful stage that is full of conflicting urges and perplexing characteristics. We realize that our self-assurance is accompanied by self-doubt, that our growth is rapid and uneven, and that our desire to perform exceeds our knowledge and skill. We keenly sense our own tendency to be argumentative and we are constantly aware that our economic needs outstrip our ability to acquire financial support. (1974, p. iii)

We want to make one final point about the growth of the special education profession. Examine the histories of current leaders in the profession (see Blatt and Morris, 1984; Kauffman and Hallahan, 1976; Kauffman and Lewis, 1974; Kauffman and Payne, 1975; Kneedler and Tarver, 1977) and you will find that many of them did not receive formal training in special education, but earned their advanced degrees in psychology. It is only in relatively recent years that doctoral-level training programs in special education have expanded, so that now we are seeing a shift away from leaders trained in psychology toward those trained in special education. But another change also appears to be occurring in the leadership of the profession. As laws and court decisions have come to play a more prominent role, lawyers, judges, and government bureaucrats have taken leadership roles. The tremendous power wielded by legal-bureaucratic authority in decisions about special education is obvious. Not so obvious are the benefits and dangers of such authority (Kauffman, 1984, 1986b; Sarason and Doris, 1979; Weatherly, 1979).

Professional and Parent Organizations

Individuals and ideas have played crucial roles in the history of special education, but it is accurate to say that much of the progress made over the years has been achieved primarily by the collective efforts of professionals and parents. Professional groups were organized first, beginning in the nineteenth century. Effective national parent organizations have existed in the United States only since 1950.

The earliest professional organizations having some bearing on the education of handicapped children were medical associations founded in the 1800s. For example, the Association of Medical Officers of American Institutions for Idiotic and Feeble-Minded Persons, later to become what we know today as the American Association on Mental Deficiency (AAMD), and the Association of Medical Superintendents of American Institutions for the Insane, later to become the American Psychiatric Association, were organized before the turn of the century. Organization of a professional association devoted to special education did not occur until 1922, when the Council for Exceptional Children (first called the International Council for Exceptional Children) was founded. CEC and its divisions have become the primary professional organizations of special educators, although other professional groups, such as the American Orthopsychiatric Association (for teachers of emotionally disturbed children) and the American Association on Mental Deficiency (for teachers of retarded children) welcome special educators as members and work toward many of the same goals as CEC.

We cannot describe the growth of all the important professional organizations having to do with handicapped children; we concentrate here on CEC and its divisions. Elizabeth Farrell, the first president of CEC, described its organization in her president's address at the first annual CEC convention in 1923:

> The International Council was formed in August of last year, by teachers who were students in the Summer School of Teacher's College, Columbia University, and whose work was in the field of special education. In the Department of Special Education that summer about two hundred teachers representing practically every state in the union and five foreign countries joined in the organization meeting. When the word went out that a professional body of teachers interested in the teaching of exceptional children had been brought together, applications for membership were made by school administrators, superintendents, supervisors, school board members and others to the number of approximately five hundred. (Farrell, 1923, reprinted in Kirk and Lord, 1974, p. 16)

"International" was dropped from the title of CEC in 1956 because it was then a unit in the National Education Association and because the U.S. Congress was confused by the fact that an international organization was striving to deal with national problems (Kirk and Lord, 1974). From 1941 to 1974 CEC was affiliated with the National Education Association. It is now an independent organization that has launched the Foundation for Exceptional Children, a nonprofit foundation promoting research and innovation and working to protect the legal, educational, and human rights of children.

Today CEC has a national membership of over 50,000, including 10,000 students. There are state CEC organizations and hundreds of local chapters. The divisions of CEC (see Table 1.2) have been organized to meet the interests and needs of CEC members who specialize in a particular area.

Although the parent organizations offer membership to individuals who do not have handicapped or gifted children of their own, they are composed primarily of parents who do have such children and concentrate on issues of special concern to them. Parent organizations have typically served three essential functions: (1) providing an informal group for parents who understand one another's problems and needs and help one another deal with anxieties and frustrations; (2) providing information regarding services and potential resources; and (3) providing the structure for obtaining needed services for their children. Some of the organizations that came about primarily as the result of parents' efforts include the Association for Retarded Citizens (called the National Association for Retarded Children before 1973), the National Association for Gifted Children, the Association for Children and Adults with Learning Disabilities, and the National Society for Children and Adults with Autism.

Legislation and Litigation

Private schools and tutors have played a part in the education of handicapped children since the beginning of special education. Services supported by public funds began early in the nineteenth century. But as Martin (1976) points out, a national commitment to the right to a free public education for *every* individual, including every person with a handicap, represented a new level of maturity for America.

In the earliest years of special education in both Europe and America, government funds were first appropriated to support "experimental" schools to see whether or not children with handicaps could actually be educated. And early legislators or

Table 1.2 The Divisions of CEC

CASE	Council of Administrators of Special Education. Members are administrators, supervisors, or coordinators of special education programs and college faculty in the area of special education administration. Designed to deal with administrative and supervisory problems (organized 1952).
DVH	Division for the Visually Handicapped: Partially Seeing and Blind. Concerned with the education of children who are blind or partially sighted (organized 1952).
TED	Teacher Education Division. Designed to assist professionals who are involved in the education and training of teachers, such as the instructors of college courses and the supervisors of field experiences or student teaching, in all areas of special education (organized 1953).
DPH	Division for the Physically Handicapped. Concerned primarily with the education of crippled and health-impaired children (organized 1957).
TAG	The Association for the Gifted. Devoted to the education of gifted and talented children (organized 1958).
CEC–MR	Division on Mental Retardation. The division for educators of mentally retarded students (organized 1963).
CCBD	Council for Children with Behavioral Disorders. Deals with the problems of teaching behaviorally disordered and delinquent children and youths (organized 1964).
DCCD	Division for Children with Communication Disorders. Focuses on children with disorders of speech and language (organized 1968).
DLD	Division for Learning Disabilities. Designed to deal with the problems of teaching children who have learning disabilities (organized 1968).
DEC	Division for Early Childhood. Deals with the special concerns of those who are involved in the education of young handicapped children (organized 1973).
CEDS	Council for Educational Diagnostic Services. Concerned with problems and issues in testing and diagnosing exceptional children (organized 1974).
DCD	Division on Career Development. Founded to serve teachers who are involved in vocational training and job placement for exceptional children and youths (organized 1976).
TAM	Technology and Media Division. Organized to keep interested professionals informed of new technological developments related to the education of exceptional children (founded in 1984).
CEC–DR	Division for Research. Founded to promote research relating to the education of exceptional individuals (organized in 1987).

governors were often unbelievably stingy with public funds, even in the face of evidence of need and the efficacy of special education programs. Such was the case in 1857 when Henry J. Gardner, governor of Massachusetts, vetoed a bill calling for increased funds for the Massachusetts School for Idiotic and Feeble-Minded Youth, which had been opened in 1848. Dr. Samuel Gridley Howe wrote Governor Gardner a lengthy, brilliant, and scathing letter, part of which reads:

> The last paragraph of the Veto is as follows. "Under these circumstances an earnest desire to prevent any unnecessary expenses, constrains me to withhold my sanction from this resolve."

This is marvelous indeed!

When there are so many perennial leaks from the Treasury to be stopped, it is passing strange that a great pother should be made over such a driblet as this appropriation, to a Charitable Institution, of $2500 for a single year.

The Veto is a great State engine, and, when an enormous breach is made, which threatens to swamp the Treasury, then it may properly be brought out, like a great steam pump. To do this may be sublime, at least in sound; but to ring the alarm-bell, and get up steam merely to stop such a leak as three dollars and a quarter a week for supporting and educating fifteen idiotic children—that borders on the ridiculous. (Reprinted in Kirk and Lord, 1974, p. 13)

Examine the history of legislation for handicapped children and you will find that it was ever thus; public support in the form of legislation and appropriation of funds has been achieved and sustained only by the most arduous and persevering efforts of individuals who are advocates for exceptional children (see Martin, 1976; Melcher, 1976).

Legislation providing for special education may be of two types: permissive or mandatory. *Permissive* legislation states that schools *may* provide special education; *mandatory* legislation says they *must*. At the federal level, legislation has historically been permissive. The assumption has been that control over the education dollar is a state's right. Funds have been provided as incentives for the states to develop their own special education services with little federal control.

The most noteworthy legislative landmark of recent years, **PL 94-142,*** the Education for All Handicapped Children Act, contains a mandatory provision. It states that

in order to receive funds under the Act every school system in the nation must make provision for a free, appropriate public education for every child between the ages of 3 and 21 (unless state law does not provide free public education to children 3 to 5 or 18 to 21 years of age) regardless of how, or how seriously, he may be handicapped.

In 1986, PL 99-457 extended the requirements of PL 94-142 to children aged 3 to 5, even in states that do not provide free public education to children that young. To continue receiving federal special education funds, every state education agency must provide, by the 1990–91 school year, free and appropriate education and related services to all handicapped children 3 to 5 years of age. PL 99-457 also includes incentives for states to develop early intervention programs for handicapped infants and infants at risk, from birth to age 36 months.

Responsibility for implementing the provisions of PL 94-142 is shared by local, state, and federal governments. While PL 94-142 spells out what must be provided in the way of special education and related services, another law passed by the 93rd Congress (Section 504 of PL 93-112, the Rehabilitation Act of 1973) prohibits discrimination against handicapped people. Section 504 and PL 94-142 both require that every handicapped child be provided a free and appropriate education (Bateman and Herr, 1981).

PL 94-142, passed and signed into law in 1975, is the most significant bill in a long chain of federal enactments affecting the education of students with handicaps. We will not try to lead you through the thicket of that legislation here. Neither will we

---

* Legislation is typically designated PL (for Public Law), followed by a hyphenated numeral, the first set of digits representing the number of the Congress that passed the bill and the second set of numerals representing the number of that bill. Thus PL 94-142 is the 142nd Public Law passed by the 94th Congress.

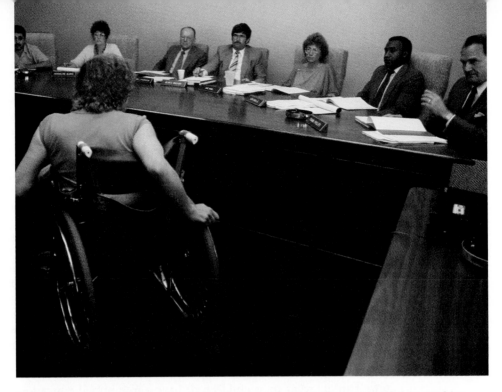

Handicapped people have increasingly been motivated to become skilled in working through government agencies at all levels to ensure their rights and obtain equal opportunities. (© Bob Daemmrich/Uniphoto)

try to give you a review of current litigation related to PL 94-142 and other special education laws. We will, however, discuss some general trends in law and special education.

Two general trends should be noted. First, legislation has been increasingly specific and mandatory. In the early 1980s, however, the renewed emphasis on states' rights and local autonomy in all matters of education, plus a general attempt at federal deregulation, gave rise to moves to repeal some of the provisions of PL 94-142 and to alter the federal rules and regulations related to the law. Second, although the U.S. Congress took the lead in mandating special education for handicapped children by passing PL 94-142, so far that body has legislated federal funding for only a small percentage of the cost. So while the demands of federal law are detailed, the federal contribution to the cost of educating students with handicaps is relatively small in comparison to state and local expenditures (U.S. Department of Education, 1986).

Legislation requires or gives permission to provide special education services. Whether or not the laws are administered properly is a legal question for the courts. That is, laws may have little or no effect on the lives of exceptional children unless there are court decisions regarding the meaning of those laws. Within the past few years there has been a flurry of litigation involving the special education activities of state and local education agencies. Exceptional children, primarily through the action of parent and professional organizations, are finally getting their day in court (Bateman and Herr, 1981).

Two general trends should be noted regarding this litigation. First, over the years court decisions have gone through three stages. As noted by Zelder (1953), school attendance has been seen as: (1) a *privilege* that may be awarded to or withheld from an individual child at the discretion of local school officials; (2) the *right* of every child, regardless of his or her handicap; and (3) a means of ensuring that every child receives an education *appropriate for his or her individual needs*. At the turn of the century the courts were still defending and protecting the majority of school-children against a handicapped minority. The courts typically found, during the nineteenth and early twentieth centuries, that disruptive or retarded children could be excluded from school for the sake of preserving order, protecting the teacher's time against excessive demands, and sparing children the "pain" of seeing others who are handicapped. But now the old excuses for excluding students with handicaps from school are no longer held to be valid.

The second trend to be noted is that litigation may involve legal suits filed for either of two reasons: because special education services are not being provided for children whose parents want them, or because children are being assigned to special education classes when their parents believe they should not be. Suits for inclusion in special education have been brought primarily by parents whose children are unquestionably handicapped and are being denied any education at all. Suits for exclusion have been brought primarily by parents of children whose handicaps are mild and who are already attending school. Thus the courts are being asked to make decisions that consider the individual child's characteristics, and local and state education agencies are being compelled to provide education *appropriate for every child*. Parents want their children to have a free public education that meets their needs, but does not stigmatize them unnecessarily. The burden of proof ultimately rests with local and state education specialists, who must show in every instance that the child's abilities and disabilities have been completely and accurately assessed and that the most effective educational procedures are being employed.

One court case of the 1980s deserves particular consideration. In 1982 the U.S. Supreme Court made its first interpretation of PL 94-142 in *Hudson* v. *Rowley,* a case involving a deaf child, Amy Rowley. The court's decision was that "appropriate" education for a child with a handicap does not necessarily mean education that will produce the maximum possible achievement. Amy's parents had contended that she might be able to learn more in school if she were provided with a sign language interpreter. But the court decided that because the school had designed an individualized educational program for Amy and she was achieving at or above the level of her nonhandicapped classmates, the school system had met its obligation under the law to provide an appropriate education. Additional cases will undoubtedly help to clarify what the law means by "appropriate" education and "least restrictive" environment (Yanok, 1986).

Legislation and litigation have brought tremendous progress, but the promise of appropriate education for every handicapped child has not yet been fulfilled. "Barriers to full implementation [of PL 94-142] remain, and continuing efforts are required at all levels of government to provide the full benefits of a free appropriate public education to all handicapped children and their parents" (Will, 1986, p. iii). Recent federal initiatives have focused on providing special education and related services to "traditionally underserved" populations, especially handicapped infants, secondary and postsecondary handicapped students, and seriously emotionally disturbed students. "A common factor among all of these groups is that they often have multiple, complex service needs that go beyond the bounds of education or educationally related services" (U.S. Department of Education, 1986, p. 18). Appropriate special education is a critical component of the service needs of these children, but

Major Provisions of PL 94-142

Each state and locality must have a plan to ensure:

Child identification	Extensive efforts must be made to screen and identify all handicapped children.
Full service, at no cost	Every handicapped child must be assured an appropriate public education at no cost to the parents or guardians.
Due process	The child's and parents' rights to information and informed consent must be assured before the child is evaluated, labeled, or placed, and they have a right to an impartial due process hearing if they disagree with the school's decisions.
Parent/parent surrogate consultation	The child's parents or guardian must be consulted about the child's evaluation and placement and the educational plan; if the parents or guardian are unknown or unavailable, a surrogate parent to act for the child must be found.
LRE	The child must be educated in the least restrictive environment that is consistent with his or her educational needs and, insofar as possible, with nonhandicapped children.
IEP	A written individualized education program must be prepared for each handicapped child. The plan must state present levels of functioning, long- and short-term goals, services to be provided, and plans for initiating and evaluating the services.
Nondiscriminatory evaluation	The child must be evaluated in all areas of suspected disability and in a way that is not biased by the child's language or cultural characteristics or handicaps. Evaluation must be by a multidisciplinary team, and no single evaluation procedure may be used as the sole criterion for placement or planning.
Confidentiality	The results of evaluation and placement must be kept confidential, though the child's parents or guardian may have access to the records.
Personnel development, in-service	Training must be provided for teachers and other professional personnel, including in-service training for regular teachers in meeting the needs of the handicapped.

There are detailed federal rules and regulations regarding the implementation of each of these major provisions. The definitions of some of these provisions—LRE and nondiscriminatory evaluation, for example—are still being clarified by federal officials and court decisions.

coordination and cooperation among a variety of professionals and social agencies is required.

Perspectives on Legislation and Litigation

PL 94-142 and court decisions related to it were greeted with enthusiasm by special educators, parents of handicapped children and other advocates for exceptional children. It seemed that a new day had dawned; finally, the law, the courts, and government agencies were on the side of students with handicaps. The new laws, court decisions, and rules and regulations of government agencies granted legal rights to exceptional individuals and set up requirements for their education that seemed reasonable and just. But it was not long before the limits of legal guarantees and the negative aspects of laws, judicial orders, rules, and regulations were questioned. We will comment briefly on just three questions some critics have raised about the law and its implementation.

1. Can educators do what the law requires?
2. Have the laws, rules, and regulations become ends in themselves?
3. Are lawyers and judges best qualified to establish educational policy?

How Much Can Educators Do?

The law makes certain requirements regarding a fair, nonbiased assessment of children, parental participation in and consent to educational placement and planning, individualized education plans, reevaluation of children, and so on. These requirements and the accompanying rules and regulations were instituted to protect handicapped children against abuses. PL 94-142 was a response to revelations that many children with handicaps were receiving no special education at all, were being placed in special programs without their parents' knowledge or consent, were being given little or nothing in the way of individual instruction, and were never reevaluated to see if they needed a different program. But the law requires meetings, forms, records, and reports of all teachers and school administrators regardless of their competence and the satisfaction of parents and children with the services they provide. Some teachers and other school personnel are now suggesting that the technicalities of the law have made it too demanding (Katzen, 1980).

One distinguished professor of special education describes the problem this way with reference to educating emotionally disturbed (behaviorally disordered) students:

> Part of the stress of teaching the emotionally disturbed comes from unwarranted assumptions that we can cure our pupils. The field as a whole and IEPs [individual education programs] in particular perpetuated these beliefs. We create expectations which are impossible to meet and make the teacher rather than the system accountable. We are guilty of oversell. Special education performs many miracles, but it promises more and demands that the teacher perform the miracles. (Morse, 1984, p. 121)

Certainly what the law requires seems to be nothing more than good educational practice. Yet the documentation and "safeguards" demanded are tremendously time-consuming. How to overcome the paperwork and legal roadblocks that keep good teachers from spending their time being good teachers, but at the same time ensure that the needs and rights of handicapped children are met, is one of the clear challenges of the future.

Section 504

Section 504 of the Rehabilitation Act of 1973 states:

> No otherwise qualified handicapped individual . . . shall, solely by reason of his/her handicap, be excluded from participation in, be denied the benefits of, or be subject to discrimination under any program or activity receiving federal financial assistance.

This means that if free public education is provided for nonhandicapped children, then it must also be provided for handicapped children. If free public education is denied to a handicapped child when it is available to others, then there is discrimination and federal funds to the program may be cut off. Section 504 is more general than PL 94-142 in its prohibition of discrimination. States must comply with Section 504 if they receive any form of federal financial assistance. They must meet the requirements of PL 94-142 only if they wish to receive funds specific to that act.

Are Laws and Regulations Their Own Ends?

The purpose of the law clearly was not to make more paperwork and set up meaningless requirements. Its purpose was to make certain that handicapped children are given an appropriate education. But rules and regulations do not in themselves make education better, even if they are followed to the letter. A case in point is the **individualized education program (IEP)** required by the law. There are many different ways of preparing an IEP (see Larsen and Poplin, 1980). The law and federal regulations do not specify how much detail must be included, only that the IEP must be a written statement developed in a meeting of the local education agency (LEA) representative, the teacher, the parents or guardian, and, whenever appropriate, the child, and that it must include:

> (A) a statement of the present levels of educational performance . . . , (B) a statement of annual goals, including short-term instructional objectives, (C) a statement of the specific educational services to be provided . . . , and the extent to which [the] child will be able to participate in regular educational programs, (D) the projected date for initiation and anticipated duration of such services, and appropriate objective criteria and evaluation procedures and schedules for determining, on at least an annual basis, whether instructional objectives are being achieved. (Education for All Handicapped Children Act of 1975, p. 3)

IEPs vary greatly in length, detail, and form from one school district to another. But regardless of the variance, it is easy to see how their preparation can become a ritual—a routine educators follow so they can say they have "educated" the child. Some people argue that short-term instructional objectives become ends in themselves and do not belong in most IEPs (Mann, 1980); others suggest that teachers must make IEPs routine just to survive the work load required of them by the education bureaucracy (Weatherly, 1979). We have already noted how the IEP may be related to unrealistic expectations of "miracles."

Figure 1.3 is a sample IEP. Again, IEPs vary greatly in format and detail from school district to school district, but the one in Figure 1.3 is probably about average in detail and specificity. While it does not, in our opinion, illustrate unreasonable demands on teachers' time or effort or unrealistic expectations of "miracles," you can see from the paperwork required by this example how the preparation of IEPs could become a task done simply for its own sake (to comply with regulations).

Figure 1.3A Individualized Education Program.

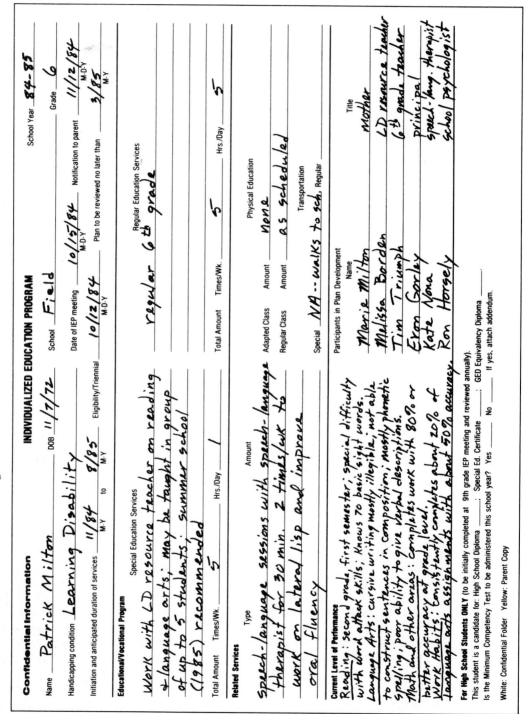

Confidential Information

INDIVIDUALIZED EDUCATION PROGRAM

School Year __84-85__

Name __Patrick Milton__   DOB __11/7/72__   School __Field__   Grade __6__

Handicapping condition __Learning Disability__

Date of IEP meeting __10/15/84__   Notification to parent __11/12/84__
                                          M-D-Y   M-D-Y

Initiation and anticipated duration of services __11/84__ to __9/85__   Eligibility/Triennial __10/12/84__   Plan to be reviewed no later than __3/85__
                                                   M-Y   M-Y   M-D-Y   M-Y

Educational/Vocational Program

Special Education Services   Regular Education Services

Work with LD resource teacher on reading   regular 6th grade
+ language arts; may be taught in group
of up to 5 students; summer school
(1985) recommended

Total Amount __5__ Times/Wk. __1__ Hrs./Day   Total Amount __5__ Times/Wk. __5__ Hrs./Day

Related Services

Type   Amount   Physical Education

Speech-language sessions with speech-language   Adapted Class   Amount __none__
therapist for 30 min. 2 times/wk to   Regular Class   Amount __as scheduled__
work on lateral lisp and improve
oral fluency   Transportation

                                                  Special __NA - walks to sch. Regular__

Current Level of Performance

Reading: second grade, first semester; special difficulty
with word attack skills; knows 70 basic sight words.
Language Arts: cursive writing mostly illegible; not able
to construct sentences in composition; mostly phonetic
spelling; poor ability to give verbal descriptions.
Math and other areas: completes work with 80% or
better accuracy at grade level.
Work habits: consistently completes about 20% of
language arts assignments with about 50% accuracy.

Participants in Plan Development

Name   Title

Marie Milton   Mother
Melissa Borden   LD resource teacher
Tim Triumph   6th grade teacher
Evan Gorley   Principal
Kate Nona   Speech-lang. therapist
Ron Horgely   School Psychologist

For High School Students ONLY (to be initially completed at 9th grade IEP meeting and reviewed annually).
This student is a candidate for: High School Diploma _____; Special Ed. Certificate _____; GED Equivalency Diploma _____
Is the Minimum Competency Test to be administered this school year? Yes _____ No _____ If yes, attach addendum.

White: Confidential Folder   Yellow: Parent Copy

Figure 1.3B

INDIVIDUALIZED EDUCATION PROGRAM

School Year **84-85**

ANNUAL GOAL: The student _Patrick Milton_ will:

SHORT TERM OBJECTIVES	Grading Periods	PROGRESS REPORTS COMMENTS
Objective: Given assigned work in resource room, Pat will complete all assignments on schedule with at least 80% accuracy. **Beginning Skill Level:** completes 20% of assignments with 50% accuracy **Date Initiated** 11/21/84	1. X 2. 12/84 M- 3. 3/85 M- 4.	
Objective: Note: See Ms. Nona's speech-language records for speech-language objectives and progress reports. **Beginning Skill Level:** **Date Initiated**	1. 2. 3. 4.	
Objective: **Beginning Skill Level:** **Date Initiated**	1. 2. 3. 4.	
Objective: **Beginning Skill Level:** **Date Initiated**	1. 2. 3. 4.	

Evaluation Procedures: Annual goals will be evaluated during the annual review. Short term objectives will be monitored at each nine week marking period. Beginning skill level indicates the student's performance prior to instruction.

Progress Key: No mark—Objective not initiated   **P**—Progressing on the Objective   **D**—Having difficulty with the objective (comment to describe difficulty)
M—Objective mastered   **M/R**—Objective mastered, but needs review to maintain mastery

White: Confidential Folder   Yellow: Parent Progress Report   Pink: Teacher Working Copy   Goldenrod: Parent Original

Figure 1.3C

INDIVIDUALIZED EDUCATION PROGRAM

School Year **84-85**

ANNUAL GOAL: The student **Patrick Milton** will: **complete all assigned work in language arts and reading with 90% or better accuracy at 5th grade level by Sept. 1985.**

PROGRESS REPORTS

SHORT TERM OBJECTIVES	Grading Periods	COMMENTS
Objective: Given 200 sight words from his reader, Pat will read them with 90% accuracy.	1. X	
	2. 12/84	P- learning average of 2 new sight wds./school day
Beginning Skill Level: 2² (Ginn); knows 70 Dolch words	3. 3/85	M- now knows all Dolch & all wds. in reader
Date Initiated 11/21/84	4.	
Objective: Given a topic with which he is familiar, Pat will write at least 5 complete sentences on the topic within 30 min.	1. X	
	2. 12/84	P- will write 2 or 3 sentences before refusing to continue; tells sentence from nonsentence with 75% accuracy
Beginning Skill Level: does not know sentence from nonsentence	3. 3/85	P-
Date Initiated 11/21/84	4.	
Objective: Given instructions to copy 5 lines of printed material from a book, Pat will write the material on lined paper using cursive letters so that another teacher can immediately decipher at least 90% of the material.	1. X	
	2. 12/84	P- most written work now 60% legible; 75% legible when copying
Beginning Skill Level: Only letters legible 86% of time are e, P, W	3. 3/85	M- nearly all written work is legible
Date Initiated 11/29/84	4.	
Objective: Given 50 sight wds from his reading book & 50 CVCG wds, Pat will read them with 90% accuracy; given the same wds from dictation, he will spell them with 95% accuracy.	1. X	
	2. 12/84	P- reads CVCE wds with 95% accuracy and writes them with 80% accuracy
Beginning Skill Level: tested spelling grade level = 2'	3. 3/85	M-
Date Initiated 11/21/84	4.	

Evaluation Procedures: Annual goals will be evaluated during the annual review. Short term objectives will be monitored at each nine week marking period. Beginning skill level indicates the student's performance prior to instruction.

Progress Key:
No mark—Objective not initiated   P—Progressing on the Objective   D—Having difficulty with the objective (comment to describe difficulty)
M—Objective mastered   M/R—Objective mastered, but needs review to maintain mastery

White: Confidential Folder   Yellow: Parent Progress Report   Pink: Teacher Working Copy   Goldenrod: Parent Original

Are Lawyers and Judges the Best Educational Policymakers?

Laws are not written by educators. And educators do not hand down judicial decisions. Lawyers and judges, often with advice from educators, make and interpret laws. We cannot argue that they should not, but we might ask how far they should go in deciding what constitutes reasonable, adequate, appropriate, or best educational practice. Some educators and psychologists have questioned the extent to which the legislative and judicial arms of government should intrude into educational practice and rehabilitation (Baumeister, 1981; Kauffman, 1981; Townsend and Mattson, 1981). Baumeister notes that courts and behavioral science operate in very different ways:

> It is doubtful . . . whether the procedures of the court are conducive to a scholarly presentation and resolution of issues, even by those credible scientists who are determined to provide evidence as fairly and impartially as possible. From a scientific point of view, the wrong questions are asked in court. Judicial proceedings are adversarial in nature and, as such, hardly constitute the ideal forum to address and resolve some of the complex theoretical, empirical, and professional issues involved in treatment of [handicapping conditions]. Under the white heat of the court room confrontation, people are inevitably forced to take sides, postures that tend to produce unwarranted generalizations and distorted presentation of information. (1981, p. 72)

Others have made similar observations about what happens to scientific information and professional judgment in the courtroom. "When social scientists are called upon to serve as expert witnesses, it is not uncommon for otherwise good scientists to throw cautious inferences based on probability out the courtroom window while they maintain a dogmatic insistence on the 'facts' that would never do in the classroom" (Edgerton, 1984, p. 142).

Critics argue that educational policy decisions are best left to educators. Or, if lawyers and judges have to be involved, perhaps they should pay more attention to the opinions of those who must live with their judicial decisions. Townsend and Mattson (1981), for example, suggest that lawyers and other advocates for handicapped people sometimes pursue legislation and litigation for their own purposes and according to their own biases, with little regard for the opinions of the educators, parents, and children involved. And Sarason and Doris state that "entrusting the welfare of people to centralized government is an invitation to social disaster"

Advocates of special education emphasize the rights of handicapped persons, including those rights guaranteed by the Bill of Rights. (© Russ Kinne/Photo Researchers)

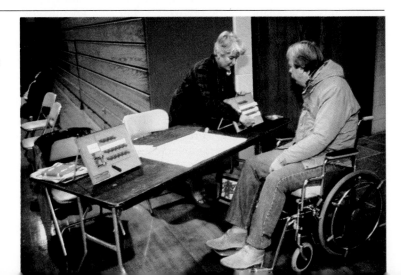

(1979, p. 81). One of the great issues in special education in the next decade will be the extent to which lawyers and judges should be involved in educational decision making.

Almost two centuries have passed since the beginnings of special education. We have gone a long way toward restoring the rights and dignity of exceptional individuals, but we still have a very long way to go. At the time of the bicentennial celebration of our country's Declaration of Independence, Edwin W. Martin wrote the following, perhaps in anticipation of the bicentennial of our Constitution:

> Special educators know that the promise of an appropriate education for every handicapped child or for each gifted child will not be fulfilled by the passage of a law, or by enrolling each youngster in a program. Special education is still evolving as a profession. It does not have all the knowledge it needs; it does not have all the answers. In trying to identify the major issues which should concern the special educator as a professional, the central theme of the Bill of Rights might offer direction. We must focus on the individual. (1976, p. 134)

It is with concern for the rights and needs of *all* children clearly in mind that we have written this book.

SUMMARY

Exceptional children are defined as those who require special education and related services if they are to realize their full human potential. *Special education* refers to specially designed instruction that meets the unique needs of exceptional children. There are many kinds of special education services available, depending on the extent to which the child differs from the average. The regular classroom teacher, provided he or she has the knowledge and training, may be able to handle certain types of exceptional students. But often consultation with special educators is needed in addition to special materials and methods. Itinerant teachers move from school to school, instructing handicapped children individually or in small groups, and are available to the regular teacher for advice on particular problems. Resource teachers typically serve only one school, providing educational intervention to the extent needed. Sometimes children are placed for a short time in a diagnostic-prescriptive center so their special needs can be determined. The special self-contained class is used for a small group of children, who are usually segregated all or most of the day from their nonhandicapped peers. Special day schools are for exceptional children whose handicaps necessitate special equipment and methods for care and education. Hospital and homebound instruction involves teaching programs within the hospital or at

home because the child is unable to go to regular classes. Finally, the residential school provides educational services and management of the daily living environment for severely handicapped children who must receive full-time care.

Present law requires that every exceptional child be placed in the least restrictive environment so that educational intervention will be consistent with individual needs and not interfere with individual freedom and potential. Today, therefore, most handicapped students are educated primarily in regular classes. Both special education and regular teachers may be involved in educating handicapped children by referring students for evaluation, evaluating academic abilities and disabilities, participating in eligibility conferences and in writing individual education plans, communicating with parents, and taking part in due process hearings and negotiations. In addition, special education teachers must have special expertise in instructing children with learning problems, managing serious behavior problems, using technological aids, and interpreting special education law.

Incidence refers to the number of new cases of exceptionality in a given period of time; *prevalence* has to do with the total number of existing cases at a given point in time. Determining the number of handicapped children with accuracy is difficult. For one thing, vague and changing definitions affect the number of individuals considered to fall within particular categories. Also, the classification of certain children may be problematical—for instance, one child may be blind, mentally retarded, *and* emotionally disturbed. Another factor making prevalence estimates difficult involves the accuracy of sampling methods. Still another is that a child may be considered exceptional according to a school definition (learning disabled, for example), but outside of school, or before entry into the educational system, may be classified as nonhandicapped. Finally, the stigma of identification may cause some cases of exceptionality to go unrecognized or unrecorded. Today, about 11 out of every 100 students in public schools are identified as handicapped. Most children and youth identified as handicapped are between the ages of 6 and 17, although identification of handicapped infants and youth past high school age is increasing. In all categories except one—learning disability—fewer students are identified as handicapped than one would expect on the basis of traditional prevalence estimates.

Concern for the special needs of exceptional children began in the early 1800s, when the first attempts were made to educate and protect "idiotic" and "insane" children. European physicians like Itard, Pinel, Seguin, and Montessori pioneered systematic efforts to treat and educate children who were handicapped by their differences. Their revolutionary ideas included individualized instruction, carefully sequenced series of educational tasks, emphasis on stimulation and awakening of the child's senses, meticulous arrangement of the child's environment, immediate reward for correct performance, tutoring in functional skills, and the belief that every child should be educated to the greatest extent possible.

Americans like Howe and Gallaudet brought special education techniques and ideas to this country. But there was a marked decline in special education efforts in the last part of the nineteenth century, and it was not until after World War II that there was a renewed interest in treating exceptional individuals as more than misfits to be ignored. The European influence continued, and educators such as Frostig, Strauss, Werner, and Hobbs developed new techniques and methods. Increasingly there was an interdisciplinary effort, as the fields of medicine, psychology, sociology, and special education began to cooperate to provide handicapped children with education beyond what the traditional system had been offering.

Much of the progress in the history of special education has resulted from the efforts of professional and parent organizations. The Council for Exceptional Children (CEC) is an influential group with many divisions devoted to such things as the study of specific exceptionalities; the administration, supervision, and implementation of special programs; and teacher training and placement. Organizations such as the Association for Retarded Citizens (ARC) provide parents, schools, and the public with information about exceptionalities and provide the structure for obtaining needed services for children.

The contemporary commitment to the principle that every individual has the right to as normal a life and education as possible has prompted greater involvement by the legal system in educational intervention. Two types of legislation have resulted: permissive, stating that schools may provide special education; and mandatory, stating that they must. PL 94-142, the Education for All Handicapped Children Act, mandates that, in order to receive funds under the act, *every school system in the country must make provision for a free, appropriate education for every handicapped child.* Laws regarding education of handicapped students have become increasingly specific and mandatory over the years. Today federal legislation takes the lead in mandating services for handicapped children, but federal funds account for only a small percentage of the cost of providing special education. The U.S. Supreme Court has refused to define appropriate education as that which will produce a student's maximum possible achievement. Future court cases will undoubtedly result in clarification of the term "appropriate" with reference to special education. Issues regarding special education law include the extent to which teachers can do what the law demands, the extent to which laws and rules becomes ends in themselves, and the qualifications of lawyers and judges for establishing educational policy.

REFERENCES

Algozzine, B., & Maheady, L. (Eds.) (1986). In search of excellence: Instruction that works in special education classrooms. *Exceptional Children, 52*(6), special issue.

Ball, T. S. (1971). *Itard, Seguin, and Kephart: Sensory education—A learning interpretation.* Columbus: Charles E. Merrill.

Ballard-Campbell, M. (Ed.) (1981). Bureaucracy, law, and litigation. *Exceptional Education Quarterly, 2*(2), entire issue.

Bateman, B. (1982). Legal and ethical dilemmas of special educators. *Exceptional Education Quarterly, 2*(4), 57–67.

Bateman, B. D., & Herr, C. M. (1981). Law and special education. In J. M. Kauffman & D. P. Hallahan (Eds.), *Handbook of special education.* Englewood Cliffs, N.J.: Prentice-Hall.

Baumeister, A. A. (1981). The right to habilitation: What does it mean? *Analysis and Intervention in Developmental Disabilities, 1,* 61–74.

Blackhurst, A. E. (Ed.). (1982). The special educator as a professional person. *Exceptional Education Quarterly, 2*(4), entire issue.

Blatt, B. (1975). Toward an understanding of people with special needs. In J. M. Kauffman & J. S. Payne (Eds.), *Mental retardation: Introduction and personal perspectives.* Columbus: Charles E. Merrill.

Blatt, B., & Morris, R. (Eds.) (1984). *Perspectives in special education.* Vol. 1: *Personal orientations.* Glenview, Ill.: Scott, Foresman.

Burbach, H. J. (1981). Labelling: Sociological issues. In J. M. Kauffman & D. P. Hallahan (Eds.), *Handbook of special education.* Englewood Cliffs, N.J.: Prentice-Hall.

Crane, S. J., & Iwanicki, E. F. (1986). Perceived role conflict, role ambiguity, and burnout among special education teachers. *Remedial and Special Education, 7*(2), 24–31.

Cruickshank, W. M. (1977). Guest editorial. *Journal of Learning Disabilities, 10,* 193–194.

Csapo, M. (1984). Special education in the USSR: Trends and accomplishments. *Remedial and Special Education 5*(2), 5–15.

Edgerton, R. B. (1984). Mental retardation: An anthropologist's changing view. In B. Blatt & R. Morris (Eds.), *Perspectives in special education.* Vol. 1: *Personal orientations.* Glenview, Ill.: Scott, Foresman.

Engelmann, S., & Carnine, D. W. (1982). *Theory of instruction.* New York: Irvington.

Farrell, E. E. (1974). President's address: First annual meeting of the International Council for Exceptional Children. In S. A. Kirk & F. E. Lord (Eds.), *Exceptional children: Educational resources and perspectives.* Boston: Houghton Mifflin.

Forness, S. R. (1985). Effects of public policy at the state level: California's impact on MR, LD, and ED categories. *Remedial and Special Education, 6*(3), 36–43.

Frostig, M. (1976). Marianne Frostig. In J. M. Kauffman & D. P. Hallahan (Eds.), *Teaching children with learning disabilities: Personal perspectives.* Columbus: Charles E. Merrill.

Goldberg, I. I. (1972). Foreword. In L. D. Lippman, *Attitudes toward the handicapped: A comparison between Europe and the United States.* Springfield, Ill.: Thomas.

Grossman, H. J. (Ed.) (1973). *Manual on terminology and classification in mental retardation.* Washington, D.C.: American Association on Mental Deficiency.

Hallahan, D. P., & Cruickshank, W. M. (1973). *Psychoeducational foundations of learning disabilities.* Englewood Cliffs, N.J.: Prentice-Hall.

Hallahan, D. P., Kauffman, J. M., & Lloyd, J. W. (1985). *Introduction to learning disabilities* (2nd ed.). Englewood Cliffs, N.J.: Prentice-Hall.

Hobbs, N. (1974). Nicholas Hobbs. In J. M. Kauffman & C. D. Lewis (Eds.), *Teaching children with behavior disorders: Personal perspectives.* Columbus: Charles E. Merrill.

Hobbs, N. (1975). *The futures of children.* San Francisco: Jossey-Bass.

Hoffman, E. (1975). The American public school and the deviant child: The origins of their involvement. *Journal of Special Education, 9,* 415–423.

Hungerford, R. H. (1950). On locusts. *American Journal of Mental Deficiency, 54,* 415–418.

Itard, J. M. G. (1962). *The wild boy of Aveyron.* (Trans. George & Muriel Humphrey). Englewood Cliffs, N.J.: Prentice-Hall.

Juul, K. (1981). Special education in Europe. In J. M. Kauffman & D. P. Hallahan (Eds.), *Handbook of special education.* Englewood Cliffs, N.J.: Prentice-Hall.

Kanner, L. (1964). *A history of the care and study of the mentally retarded.* Springfield, Ill.: Charles C Thomas.

Katzen, K. "A Teacher's View," *Exceptional Children, 48,* 1980, 582.

Kauffman, J. M. (1974). Series editor's foreword. In J. M. Kauffman & C. D. Lewis (Eds.), *Teaching children with behavior disorders: Personal perspectives.* Columbus: Charles E. Merrill.

Kauffman, J. M. (1976). Nineteenth century views of children's behavior disorders: Historic contributions and continuing issues. *Journal of Special Education, 10,* 335–349.

Kauffman, J. M. (1980). Where special education for emotionally disturbed children is going. A personal view. *Exceptional Children, 48,* 522–527.

Kauffman, J. M. (1981). Historical trends and contemporary issues in special education in the United States. In J. M. Kauffman & D. P. Hallahan (Eds.), *Handbook of special education.* Englewood Cliffs, N.J.: Prentice-Hall.

Kauffman, J. M. (1984). Saving children in the age of Big Brother: Moral and ethical issues in the identification of deviance. *Behavioral Disorders, 10,* 60–70.

Kauffman, J. M. (1985). *Characteristics of children's behavior disorders* (3rd ed.). Columbus: Charles E. Merrill.

Kauffman, J. M. (1986a). Growing out of adolescence: Reflections on change in special education for the behaviorally disordered. *Behavioral Disorders, 11,* 290–296.

Kauffman, J. M. (1986b). Educating children with behavior disorders. In R. Morris & B. Blatt (Eds.), *Special education: Research and trends.* New York: Pergamon.

Kauffman, J. M., & Hallahan, D. P. (Eds.) (1976). *Teaching children with learning disabilities: Personal perspectives.* Columbus: Charles E. Merrill.

Kauffman, J. M., & Lewis, C. D. (Eds.) (1974). *Teaching children with behavior disorders: Personal perspectives.* Columbus: Charles E. Merrill.

Kauffman, J. M., & Payne, J. S. (Eds.) (1975). *Mental retar-*

dation: *Introduction and personal perspectives.* Columbus: Charles E. Merrill.

Kavale, K. A., & Forness, S. R. (1985). The historical foundation of learning disabilities: A quantitative synthesis assessing the validity of Strauss and Werner's exogenous versus endogenous distinction in mental retardation. *Remedial and Special Education, 6*(5), 18–24.

Kerr, M. M., & Nelson, C. M. (1983). *Strategies for managing behavior problems in the classroom.* Columbus: Charles E. Merrill.

Kirk, S. A., & Lord, F. E. (Eds.) (1974). *Exceptional children: Educational resources and perspectives.* Boston: Houghton Mifflin.

Kneedler, R. D., & Tarver, S. G. (Eds.) (1977). *Changing perspectives in special education.* Columbus: Charles E. Merrill.

Kugel, R., & Wolfensberger, W. (1969). *Changing patterns in residential services for the mentally retarded.* Washington, D.C.: Government Printing Office.

Lane, H. (1976). *The wild boy of Aveyron.* Cambridge, Mass.: Harvard University Press.

Larsen, S. C., & Poplin, M. S. (1980). *Methods for educating the handicapped: An individualized education program approach.* Boston: Allyn & Bacon.

Lippman, D. (1972). *Attitudes toward the handicapped: A comparison between Europe and the United States.* Springfield, Ill.: Charles C. Thomas.

Lloyd, J. W., & Carnine, D. W. (Eds.) (1981). Structured instruction: Effective teaching of essential skills. *Exceptional Education Quarterly, 2*(1), entire issue.

Magliocca, L. A., & Stephens, T. M. (1980). Child identification or child inventory? A critique of the federal design of child-identification systems implemented under P.L. 94-142. *Journal of Special Education, 14,* 23–36.

Mann, L. (1980). Editorial: Divagations X. *Journal of Special Education, 14,* 127–129.

Martin, E. W. (1976). A national commitment to the rights of the individual—1776 to 1976. *Exceptional Children, 43,* 132–135.

Melcher, J. W. (1976). Law, litigation, and handicapped children. *Exceptional Children, 43,* 126–130.

Montessori, M. (1912). *The Montessori method.* (Trans. A. George). New York: Stokes.

Montessori, M. (1917). *The advanced Montessori method: Scientific pedagogy as applied to the education of children from seven to eleven years.* London: Heinemann.

Morris, R. J. (1985). *Behavior modification with exceptional children.* Glenview, Ill.: Scott, Foresman.

Morrison, G. M., Lieber, J., & Morrison, R. L. (1986). A multidimensional view of teacher perceptions of special education episodes. *Remedial and Special Education, 7*(2), 15–23.

Morse, W. C. (1984). Personal perspective. In B. Blatt & R. Morris (Eds.), *Perspectives in special education.* Vol. 1: *Personal orientations.* Glenview, Ill.: Scott, Foresman.

Murphy, D. M. (1986). The prevalence of handicapping conditions among juvenile delinquents. *Remedial and Special Education, 7*(3), 7–17.

Nelson, C. M. (1981). Classroom management. In J. M.

Kauffman & D. P. Hallahan (Eds.), *Handbook of special education.* Englewood Cliffs, N.J.: Prentice-Hall.

Polsgrove, L. (Ed.) (1983). Aversive control in the classroom. *Exceptional Education Quarterly, 3*(4), entire issue.

Roos, P. (1975). Parents and families of the mentally retarded. In J. M. Kauffman & J. S. Payne (Eds.), *Mental retardation: Introduction and personal perspectives.* Columbus: Charles E. Merrill.

Rosen, M., Clark, G. R., & Kivitz, M. S. (Eds.). (1975). *The history of mental retardation: Collected papers.* Vols. I & II. Baltimore: University Park Press.

Sarason, S. B., & Doris, J. (1866). *Educational handicap, public policy, and social history.* New York: Free Press, 1979.

Seguin, E. (1866). *Idiocy and its treatment by the physiological method.* New York: Wood.

Stowitschek, J. J. (Ed.) (1984). Technological advances in special education. *Exceptional Education Quarterly, 4,* entire issue.

Strain, P. S. (Ed.) (1981). Peer relations of exceptional children and youth. *Exceptional Education Quarterly, 1*(4), entire issue.

Townsend, C., & Mattson, R. (1981). The interaction of law and special education: Observing the emperor's new clothes. *Analysis and intervention in developmental disabilities, 1,* 75–90.

U.S. Department of Education. (1984). *Sixth annual report to Congress on the implementation of Public Law 94-142: The Education for All Handicapped Children Act.* Washington, D.C.: U.S. Government Printing Office.

U.S. Department of Education. (1986). *To Assure the Free Appropriate Public Education of All Handicapped Children. Eighth Annual Report to Congress on the Implementation of the Education of the Handicapped Act,* Volume 1. Washington, DC: U.S. Government Printing Office.

Weatherly, R. A. (1979). *Reforming special education.* Cambridge, Mass.: MIT Press.

Werner, E. E. (1986). The concept of risk from a developmental perspective. In B. K. Keogh (Ed.), *Advances in special education, Vol. 5: Developmental problems in infancy and the preschool years.* Greenwich, Conn.: JAI Press.

Will, M. (1986). Foreword to *To Assure the Free Appropriate Public Education of All Handicapped Children. Eighth Annual Report to Congress on the Implementation of the Education of the Handicapped Act,* Volume 1. Washington, DC: U.S. Government Printing Office.

Winzer, M. A. (1986). Early developments in special education: Some aspects of Enlightenment thought. *Remedial and Special Education, 7*(5), 42–49.

Yanok, J. (1986). Free appropriate public education for handicapped children: Congressional intent and judicial interpretation. *Remedial and Special Education, 7*(2), 49–53.

Zelder, E. Y. (1953). Public opinion and public education for the exceptional child—court decisions 1873–1950. *Exceptional Children, 19,* 187–198.

2

Mental Retardation

Everywhere, however, we hear talk of sameness. "All men are created equal" it is declared. And at the ballot box and the subway rush, in Hiroshima and Coney Island it almost seems that way. Moreover, coming back from Staten Island on the ferry, as you see an unkempt bootblack lift his head to gaze at the Manhattan skyline—you know these words of Jefferson are not mere snares for votes and popularity. But standing on the same boat with the hand of your idiot son in one of yours—with mingled love and distaste placing a handkerchief against his drooling mouth—you know that Jefferson's words are not easy to understand.

There is a difference in sameness. Perhaps the days of our years are for the bootblack. But assuredly the nights are for our idiot son.

(*Richard H. Hungerford, "On Locusts"*)

There is considerable danger in relying on Hungerford's portrayal (p. 43) for our only view of what it is like to have a retarded child. Such children may be heartbreakingly different from the children next door in some ways, but also like them in others. More and more research evidence indicates that retardation is quantitative rather than qualitative. In many areas, it seems, the retarded child functions like a nonhandicapped child—but a nonhandicapped child at a younger chronological age. Even the differences that do exist need not cause parents a lifetime of constant heartache. Hungerford's statement is valuable because it presents honest feelings. Unlike the romanticized portraits found in many TV dramas, movies, and books, retarded children can evoke agony, hatred, sorrow, and frustration, as well as love, in their parents.

The Hungerford quote, published in 1950, points up something else as well. It reflects the once-popular stereotype of the retarded person as a clumsy, drooling, helpless creature. Today we know this is simply not true. First, most children classified as mentally retarded are *mildly* retarded and look like the hypothetical average child living next door. Second, it can be misleading to characterize even the more severely retarded as helpless. With advanced methods of providing educational and vocational training, we are finding that many retarded people are capable of leading more independent lives than was previously thought possible. Given appropriate preparation, some are able to live and work with relatively small amounts of help from others.

The field of mental retardation has undergone a number of other exciting changes since the time Hungerford wrote. At one time, for example, minority children who functioned poorly in school were almost automatically labeled mildly retarded. The fact that they belonged to a cultural subgroup had much to do with this labeling. The trend today is to "de-label" such children.

Much of this change in attitude has come from changes in the definition of retardation. In this chapter we will discuss the movement toward applying more stringent criteria when identifying retarded children. The wave of criticism of labeling has also had an effect on other aspects of the education of retarded children. Terminology, for example, is changing. Whereas at one time the use of the label "idiot" would have been acceptable, today we use words that are less stigmatizing. Delivery of services, too, has been affected. The concept of mainstreaming mildly handicapped youngsters into the regular classroom had its beginnings in the area of mental retardation. Although it is not always carried out well, and is certainly not the solution many have claimed, mainstreaming does reflect a healthier attitude. It means we look upon mentally retarded people as individuals with human rights, just like all other members of society.

DEFINITIONS

In this century there have been a number of significant changes in the definition of mental retardation. The first descriptions of subnormal intelligence were concise and clear-cut, leaving relatively little room for debate. But the more we came to know about retardation, the more controversy arose about how to define it. The most recent definitions reflect a growing awareness of the negative consequences of mislabeling an individual.

For many years, the standard definition of mental retardation was that of Edgar Doll:

> Six criteria by statement or implication have been generally considered essential to an adequate definition and concept. These are (1) social incompetence, (2) due to mental

MISCONCEPTIONS
ABOUT MENTALLY RETARDED INDIVIDUALS

Myth	*Fact*
Once diagnosed as mentally retarded, a person remains within this classification for the rest of his or her life.	The level of mental functioning does not necessarily remain stable, particularly for those in the mild classification.
If a person achieves a low score on an IQ test, this means that his or her adaptive skills are also sure to be subnormal.	It is possible for a person to have a tested subnormal IQ and still have adequate adaptive skills. Much depends on the individual's training, motivation, experience, social environment, etc.
Children with Down syndrome are always happy, compliant, and pleasant to have around.	In general, although they are often tractable and good-natured, the idea that they are significantly more so than other children is exaggerated.
Retarded individuals go through different learning stages compared to nonhandicapped individuals.	Many studies indicate that the learning characteristics of retarded individuals, particularly those classified as mildly retarded, do not differ from those of nonhandicapped people. That is, retarded people go through the same stages, but at a slower rate.
Children classified as moderately retarded (once called "trainable") require a radically different curriculum from that appropriate for children classified as mildly retarded (once called "educable").	Although academic subjects are generally stressed more in classes for the mildly retarded, this generalization does not always hold true for individual children.
Most mental retardation can be diagnosed in infancy.	Because the vast majority of retarded children are mildly retarded, because infant intelligence tests are not as reliable and valid as those used in later childhood, and because intellectual demands on the child greatly increase upon entrance to school, most children eventually diagnosed as retarded are not so identified until they go to school.
Most mentally retarded children look different from nonhandicapped children.	The vast majority of mentally retarded children are mildly retarded, and most mildly retarded children look like nonhandicapped children.
In most cases, the cause of retardation can be identified.	In most cases (especially within the mild classification), the cause cannot be identified. For many of the children in the mild classification, it is thought that poor environment may be a causal factor. However, it is usually extremely difficult to document.
Severely retarded people are helpless.	With appropriate educational programming, many severely retarded people can lead relatively independent lives. In fact, with appropriate professional support, some can live in the community and even enter competitive employment.

subnormality, (3) which has been developmentally arrested, (4) which obtains at maturity, (5) is of constitutional origin, and (6) is essentially incurable. (1941, p. 215)

Thus, at one time mental retardation was viewed as a permanent condition. Evidence has considerably altered this pessimistic outlook of "incurability." Educators and other professionals now know that IQ scores can be raised, and many mentally retarded people can function efficiently and well in society.

Grossman's AAMD Definition

The definition currently accepted by most authorities is the one used by the American Association on Mental Deficiency (AAMD), the major professional organization in the field of mental retardation. It reads:

> **Mental retardation** refers to significantly subaverage general intellectual functioning resulting in or associated with impairments in adaptive behavior and manifested during the developmental period. (Grossman, 1983, p. 11)

The two most important elements of the AAMD definition are that, in order to be classified as retarded, a person must be well below average in both measured intelligence and adaptive behavior. Note that the AAMD definition makes no mention of incurability. Today mental retardation is not viewed as a condition with which an individual is necessarily saddled for life. Instead, according to current understanding, a person may be retarded at one time in his or her life, but not at another.

Adaptive Behavior

The AAMD definition gives much more weight to the role adaptive behavior plays in determining whether or not a person is retarded. A child can score low on a standardized intelligence test but have adequate adaptive skills; he or she may do poorly in school but still be "streetwise—able to cope, for example, with the subway system, with an after-school job, with peers. Much of the AAMD definition's emphasis on adaptive behavior can be traced to the 1970 report of the President's Committee on Mental Retardation entitled "The Six-Hour Retarded Child." It held that some children may function in the retarded range while they are in school for six hours of the day but behave normally—adjust and adapt competently—once they return to the home community for the other eighteen hours.

Adaptive behavior, however, encompasses more than the ability to survive outside school. Adaptive skills are age- and situation-specific. They are different for the preschooler and the adult. The inner-city teenager may need to be streetwise, but the teenager in a rural community requires a very different set of abilities. The AAMD specifies that in infancy and early childhood sensory-motor, communication, self-help, and socialization skills are important. In middle childhood and early adolescence, adaptive behavior makes use of abilities involving learning processes and interpersonal social skills. In late adolescence and adulthood, vocational skills and social responsibilities are important.

Intellectual Functioning

The words "subaverage general intellectual functioning" in the AAMD definition refer to scores more than two standard deviations below the mean on a standardized test of intelligence. One commonly used IQ is the Wechsler Intelligence Scale for

Adaptive behavior for preschoolers includes self-help skills, such as the ability to dress themselves.
(© Suzanne Szasz/Photo Researchers)

Children—Revised [WISC—R]. On this test, a score of 70 would be two standard deviations below the mean, or average, of 100.* In the AAMD manual, however, it does state that the score of 70 should be treated as a guideline and a cutoff of 75 might be warranted in some cases.

A cutoff score of 70 to 75 is more conservative than that which was once used. Before 1973 the AAMD recommended a cutoff as high as 85 (which is one standard deviation below the mean, or average, on the WISC—R and Stanford-Binet). The change to a more conservative cutoff is part of the same trend that has put more emphasis on adaptive behavior. Also, special educators and other professionals are responding to the belief that labeling children "retarded" may have a serious negative effect on their futures. And the lower cutoff score is felt to be less discriminatory against disadvantaged children, who tend to score lower than individuals from higher socioeconomic classes on standardized tests.

A Social System Definition

There is a related viewpoint consistent with the trend toward acknowledging the harmful effects of labeling. Sociologist Jane Mercer (1973) holds that *it is the individual's social system that determines whether he or she is retarded.* For example, most mentally retarded children, particularly those who are higher-functioning, do not "officially" become retarded until they enter school. The school as a social

* *Standard deviation* is a measure of the amount by which an individual test score differs from the mean (average) score. Standard deviations are statistical constructs that divide a normal distribution into areas, making it possible to predict the percentage of the distribution that falls above or below a score. *One* standard deviation refers to the range of IQ points that constitute one of these areas (see Figure 2.1).

system has a certain set of expectations some children just do not meet. As we have already noted, such children may not perform in a subaverage way within their own neighborhoods.

A Behavioral Definition

Some professionals use a definition that reflects a learning theory orientation. Sidney Bijou, for example, suggests that a *retarded individual is one who has a limited repertory of behavior shaped by events that constitute his history* (1966, p. 2). Further:

> In our view, retarded behavior is a *function of observable social, physical, and biological conditions, all with the status of independent variables.* In the traditional view, retarded behavior is said to be *caused* by either *hypothetical psychological concepts* (e.g., "defective intelligence") or *hypothetical biological concepts* (e.g., "constitutional defect"). (1966, p. 3)

The behavioral definition implies that some children's apparent retardation can be overcome by reinforcing appropriate behaviors.

CLASSIFICATION

Most professionals classify retarded individuals according to the severity of their problems. The most generally accepted approach is to consider retardation as existing on a continuum or scale of severity. The two most common systems are that of the AAMD and the one used primarily by educators.

The AAMD System

The AAMD system is depicted in Table 2.1. There are three reasons why most professionals agree that the AAMD system is the most useful:

1. The terms used—**mild, moderate, severe,** and **profound retardation**—do not carry the degree of negative stereotyping of earlier descriptions ("idiot," "feebleminded"). They are adjectives commonly applied to a vast array of other things or conditions besides retardation.

Table 2.1 Level of Retardation Indicated by IQ Range Obtained on Measure of General Intellectual Functioning

Term	IQ Range for Level
Mild mental retardation	50–55 to approx. 70
Moderate mental retardation	35–40 to 50–55
Severe mental retardation	20–25 to 35–40
Profound mental retardation	Below 20 or 25
Unspecified	

SOURCE: H. J. Grossman (Ed.), *Classification in Mental Retardation* (Washington, D.C.: American Association on Mental Deficiency, 1983), p. 13. Reprinted with permission.

2. The terms used emphasize the level of functioning of the individual.
3. The use of bands of IQ scores—for example 50–55 as the cutoff between mild and moderate retardation—leaves some room for clinical judgment and recognizes that IQ scores are not perfect predictors of a person's level of retardation. As the AAMD manual states:

. . . a narrow band at each end of each level was used to indicate that clinical judgment about all information, including the IQs, and more than one test, the information about intellectual functioning obtained from other sources, etc., is necessary in determining level. Thus, someone whose Full Scale Wechsler IQ is 53 might be diagnosed as either mild or moderate, depending on other factors, such as the relative difference in Performance and Verbal IQ or results of other tests. (Grossman, 1983, p. 13)

The Educators' System

Anyone who has been around school systems has no doubt heard of classes for "educable" and "trainable" retarded children. **Educable mentally retarded (EMR)** individuals are those with IQs between 75 or 70 (more and more school systems are now using 70 whereas previously they used 75) and 50. **Trainable mentally retarded (TMR)** persons have IQs between 50 and 25. Since the passage of PL 94-142, schools have been obligated to serve children with IQs below 25, and classes for these individuals are commonly referred to as classes for the **severely and profoundly handicapped (SPH).** The categories of educable and trainable have survived over the years among educators because they describe, albeit grossly, the educational needs of retarded children. In general, EMR persons can be taught some basic academic subjects. The curriculum for TMR individuals, on the other hand, concentrates more on functional academic subjects, with emphasis on self-help and vocational skills.

One disadvantage of this system is that some educators have at times taken the categories too literally. Some children labeled trainable retarded were denied access to learning academic subject matter within their intellectual reach. Intelligence test scores are not reliable and valid enough to be used to determine entirely different educational objectives for one child with an IQ of 51 (classified as educable) and another with an IQ of 49 (classified as trainable).

PREVALENCE

It is difficult to estimate how many retarded children there are in the United States. This is partly because definitions differ, as do methods of gathering data for prevalence studies.

The average (mean) score on an IQ test is 100. Theoretically, 2.27 percent of the population is expected to fall two standard deviations (IQ = 70 on the WISC–R) or more below this average. This expectation is based on the assumption that intelligence, like so many other human traits, is distributed along a "normal curve." Figure 2.1 shows the hypothetical normal curve of intelligence. This curve is split into eight areas by means of standard deviations. On the WISC–R, where one standard deviation equals 15 IQ points (the standard deviation for the Stanford-Binet is 16 IQ points), 34.13 percent of the population score between 85 and 100. Likewise, 2.14 percent score between 55 and 70, and 0.13 percent score below 55. Thus it would seem that 2.27 percent should fall between 0 and 70.

In keeping with the figure of 2.27 percent, the federal government for years

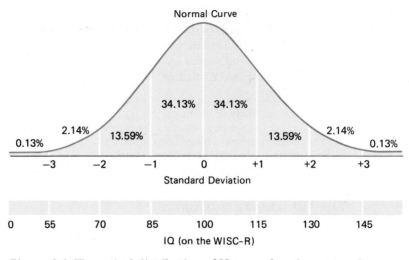

Figure 2.1 *Theoretical distribution of IQ scores based on normal curve.*

estimated the prevalence of retardation to be 2.3 percent. The U.S. Department of Education, however, has reported that 1.68 percent of individuals preschool through grade 12 are being served as mentally retarded. Authorities have pointed to three possible sources of the discrepancy between 2.3 and 1.68 percent. First, the fact that retarded children must now meet the dual criteria of low IQ *and* low adaptive behavior may have resulted in fewer children being identified. Second, litigation focusing on the improper labeling of minority students as mentally re-tarded may have made school personnel more cautious about identifying these children as retarded. Third, parents and school officials may be more likely to label children as learning-disabled rather than mentally retarded because it is perceived as a less stigmatizing label.

CAUSES

Classifying mental retardation according to causes is very difficult. In fact, many experts estimate that in only about 6 to 15 percent of cases can the cause be determined. MacMillan (1982) has noted that the set of causal factors for mild retardation tends to differ from those for the more severe levels of retardation (i.e., moderate, severe, and profound retardation). We will discuss the causal factors for mild retardation separately from those that often result in a more severe handicap. It is important to keep in mind, however, that this division is not absolute. In other words, some of the causal factors discussed under more severe retardation can also result in mild retardation.

Mild Retardation

Most individuals identified as retarded are classified as mildly retarded. They typi-cally do not differ in appearance from their nonhandicapped peers, and they are usually not diagnosed as mentally retarded until they enter school and begin to fall behind in schoolwork. In addition, in the vast majority of cases we are unable to specify the exact cause of retardation. Although there are no definitive data, the

Although it is usually difficult to pinpoint the environment as a cause of retardation, most authorities believe that poor social-environmental conditions can lead to mild retardation. Mild retardation presumed to be caused by poor environmental conditions is sometimes referred to as cultural-familial retardation. (© C. Vergara/Photo Researchers)

estimate of 6 to 15 percent noted above for identifiable causes of all retardation is undoubtedly even lower when just mildly retarded persons are considered.

Mildly retarded individuals are often referred to as having **cultural-familial retardation.** At one time the term was used for a person with a mild degree of retardation who had (1) no evidence of brain damage, (2) at least one parent who was retarded, and (3) at least one retarded sibling (if he or she had siblings) (Heber, 1959). The assumption was that the retardation was due to genetic or social-environmental factors.

More recently the term has come to be used when it is suspected that the retardation is caused by poor social-environmental conditions rather than heredity. Thus most professionals believe that a culturally-familially retarded person is one who (1) is mildly retarded, (2) has no evidence of brain damage, and (3) is being or has been raised in poor social-environmental conditions. Social-environmental conditions are presumed to cause the retardation because they produce such effects as inadequate learning opportunities and nutrition. But because these effects are difficult to pinpoint as causes, the classification of cultural-familial retardation tends to serve as a broad and rather vague catchall category—actually a "pseudo-causal" category. When authorities refer to the large numbers of retarded persons for whom no cause can be determined, most of the individuals they are talking about have been classified as culturally-familially retarded.

The Nature versus Nurture Controversy

How much of an individual's intelligence is determined by environmental factors and how much of it is decided by genetic makeup? This is one of the oldest debates in the fields of special education and psychology, and it will probably continue indefinitely because the variables are too complex to lend themselves to easy answers. Most authorities now agree that the question is not one of either/or. Rather, it is more logical to assume an interaction between hereditary and environmental factors. Heredity may set the limit one may reach in intellectual development, but the environment helps determine how close one will come to achieving this potential.

THE EARLY RESEARCH   The research used to argue that environment is important has been of two general types: (1) studies of stimulus deprivation in animals and (2) studies of early stimulation of human beings. Hunt (1961), having reviewed most of the animal literature, concluded that when animals are placed in a situation with little stimulation, there are negative effects on a variety of behaviors—nesting behavior and maze learning in rats, pecking in chicks, visual perception in chimpanzees. A number of ingenious experiments performed by Rosenzweig (1966) have done much to support the idea that stimulation is important for brain development. Rosenzweig and his colleagues placed some rats in cages that were empty except for food and water—the typical "living arrangement" for laboratory animals. Other rats were housed in cages furnished with "toys" and a treadmill. At the end of the experiment it was found that the rats from the stimulus-rich environment had thicker cortexes and higher levels of acetylcholine sterase (a brain chemical related to learning potential). The leap from results obtained with animals to implications for humans is obviously a large one—but the results of such tests are provocative.

Studies with human beings are not as easy to conduct or interpret. The strongest case for the importance of the environment is found in research in which some kind of intervention program has been set up for young children. The most famous study of this type, conducted by Skeels and Dye (1939), investigated the effects of stimulation on the development of infants and young children, many of whom were classified as mentally retarded, in an orphanage. One group of children remained in the typical orphanage environment, while the other group was given stimulation. For the latter group, nurturance was provided by retarded teenage girls who were institutionalized. The effects were clear-cut: Average IQs for members of the group given stimulation increased, while the other children's IQs decreased. Even more dramatic were the results of Skeels's follow-up study, done twenty-one years later:

> In the adult follow-up study, all cases were located and information obtained on them, after a lapse of 21 years. . . .
>
> All 13 children in the experimental group were self-supporting, and none was a ward of any institution. . . . In the contrast group of 12 children, one had died in adolescence following continued residence in a state institution for the mentally retarded, and four were still wards of institutions, one in a mental hospital, and the other three in institutions for the mentally retarded.
>
> In education, disparity between the two groups was striking. The contrast group completed a median of less than the third grade. The experimental group completed a median of the 12th grade. Four of the subjects had one or more years of college work, one received a B.A. degree and took some graduate training.
>
> Marked differences in occupational levels were seen in the two groups. In the experimental group all were self-supporting or married and functioning as housewives. The range was from professional and business occupations to domestic service, the latter the occupations of two girls who had never been placed in adoptive homes. In the contrast group,

four (36 percent) of the subjects were institutionalized and unemployed. Those who were employed, with one exception, were characterized as "hewers of wood and drawers of water." . . .

Eleven of the 13 children in the experimental group were married: nine of the 11 had a total of 28 children, an average of three per family. On intelligence tests, these second generation children had IQs ranging from 86 to 125, with a mean of 104. In no instance was there any indication of mental retardation or demonstrable abnormality. . . .

In the contrast group, only two subjects had married. One had one child and subsequently was divorced. Psychological examination of the child revealed marked mental retardation. . . . Another male subject had a nice home and a family of four children, all of average intelligence. (Skeels, 1966, pp. 54–55)

One of the strongest advocates of the idea of heredity of intelligence, Arthur Jensen, has used the failure of the Head Start program of the 1960s as a basic argument against environmental influence in intellectual development (Jensen, 1969). However, many experts believe the early programs of the 1960s failed because they were not structured well. As we will see, later programs that have been successful in increasing the intellectual capabilities of preschool children considered to be within the range of subnormality are quite structured. Rather than following a traditional nursery school model, which may be appropriate for middle-class normal preschoolers, these successful intervention programs are teacher directed: The teacher structures the child's learning experiences.

At one time Jensen's position seemed strong when he used data from studies comparing the IQs of individuals with varying degrees of "relatedness" such as siblings reared together versus those reared apart, identical versus fraternal twins, twins reared together versus those reared apart, and so on. But many of the twin studies Jensen cited were conducted by the British psychologist Sir Cyril Burt, whose work has been called into serious question. In a scandal that shook the usually staid world of academic psychology it was revealed in the 1970s that much of the now deceased Burt's work was simply made up (Hawkes, 1979; Hearnshaw, 1979). It is fair to say that Jensen's position, which had already been questioned on grounds of scientific merit (Layzer, 1974; Thoday and Gibson, 1970), was significantly weakened by heavy reliance on Burt's work to back up his own theories.

THE LATER RESEARCH   Beginning in the mid to late 1970s, more carefully controlled and sophisticated research on the effects of heredity and environment began to emerge. It is now held by most authorities in the area of behavioral genetics that *genetic factors are at least as important as environmental factors in determining intelligence* (Bouchard and McGue, 1981; Scarr-Salapatek, 1975).

An example of this more recent emphasis on the influence of genetics on intelligence is the theoretical position of Sandra Scarr (Scarr and McCartney, 1983). She maintains that some environmental differences among people are directed by genetic differences:

Differences among people can arise from both genetic and environmental differences, but the process by which differences arise is better described as genotype [a person's genetic makeup] → environment effects. . . . We propose that the genotype is the driving force behind development, because, we argue, it is the discriminator of what environments are actually experienced. The genotype determines the *responsiveness* of the person to those environmental opportunities. (Scarr and McCartney, 1983, p. 425)

And Scarr maintains that there are many different ways in which an individual's genetic makeup determines how he or she is influenced by the environment. One way involves the child's attention to selected aspects of his or her environment:

> People seek out environments they find compatible and stimulating. We all select from the surrounding environment some aspects to which we respond, learn about, or ignore. Our selections are correlated with motivational, personality, and intellectual aspects of our genotypes. (p. 427)

Even though Scarr posits that, in most instances, genetic factors determine the way in which the environment influences an individual's intellectual development, she does allow for the potentially powerful effects of the environment:

> Environments provided to children that are negatively related to their genotypes can have dramatic effects on average levels of development. Extrafamilial intervention that provides unusual enrichments or deprivations can alter the developmental levels of children from those that would be predicted by their family backgrounds and estimated genotypes. . . .

> Enriched day-care environments have been shown to enhance intellectual development of children from disadvantaged backgrounds (Ramey and Haskins, 1981; McCartney, Note 3). Similarly, less stimulating day-care environments can hamper children's intellectual and social development, even if they come from more advantaged families (McCartney, Scarr, Phillips, Grajek, and Schwarz, 1981; McCartney, Note 3). (pp. 429–430)

Further complicating the issue, Rowe and Plomin (1981) have drawn attention to the necessity of considering what they refer to as "within-family variation." Traditionally, the environmental influence attributed to being raised in a particular family was viewed as being equally distributed across family members. Rowe and Plomin, however, note that the environment can differentially affect the intellectual development of children within the same family. They posit that about 25 percent of variation in IQ is due to within-family experiential differences. The following scenario provides an example of how within-family variation can occur:

> Suppose a family with 16-year-old and 9-year-old boys visits the Space Center in Florida. The experience might have no effect whatsoever on the older child, who is heavily committed to basketball and dating. However, the younger boy, while showing aptitude in mathematics, has never really blossomed academically. He finds the Space Center fascinating. When he returns home he discovers his neighbor is a pilot, who shows the youngster about planes and takes him up for a ride. This ignites the child's interest in aviation. A unit on flight in a science class later that year reinforces it, and the child shows a marked increase in mental performance with this surge of motivation. (McCall, 1983, p. 414)

It should be obvious from the foregoing discussion that the study of the differential effects of heredity and environment on intellectual development has become more complex over the years. In other words, although we are now closer to an understanding of the potential effects of both environment and heredity, in individual cases we are far from knowing the exact contribution of each.

More Severe Retardation

Causes of retardation in individuals classified as moderately retarded through profoundly retarded are more easily determined than for those in the mild range of retardation. MacMillan (1982) divides causes for more severely retarded persons into two general categories—genetic factors and brain damage.

Genetic Factors

There are a number of genetically related causes of mental retardation. These are, generally, of two types—those that result from some damage to genetic material, such as chromosomal abnormalities, and those that are due to hereditary transmission. We will discuss three conditions—Down syndrome, which results from chromosomal abnormality, and PKU (phenylketonuria) and Tay-Sachs disease, both of which are inherited.

Estimated to account for approximately 10 percent of all moderate and severe cases of retardation, **Down syndrome** is sometimes, but less acceptably, referred to as *mongolism* because of the facial characteristic of thick epicanthal folds in the corners of the eyes, making them appear to slant upward slightly. Other common physical characteristics include small stature, decreased muscle tone (hypotonia), hyperflexibility of joints, speckling of the iris of the eye, small oral cavity which results in protruding of the tongue, short and broad hands with a single palmar crease, and a wide gap between the first and second toes (Batshaw and Perret, 1986; Blackman, 1984a). In addition, children with Down syndrome frequently have congenital heart defects, gastrointestinal malformations, and reduced resistance to respiratory infections (Blackman, 1984a).

Degree of retardation varies widely, with most individuals falling in the moderate range. Since the expansion of preschool programming for Down syndrome children in the 1970s, however, more and more of these children have been achieving IQ scores within the mildly retarded range (Rynders, Spiker, and Horrobin, 1978). Much has been said about the friendly, tractable nature of Down syndrome children. Although there is some evidence that they are generally more pleasant than many other retarded children (Belmont, 1971), reports of their happy disposition have often been exaggerated.

Individuals with Down syndrome are usually identifiable by their facial characteristics. (© Michael and Elvan Habicht/Taurus Photos)

Prenatal Diagnosis of Birth Defects

Beginning in the mid-1970s, there has been a dramatic increase in the availability of techniques for diagnosing defects in the unborn fetus. Three such methods are **amniocentesis, chorionic villus sampling (CVS),** and **sonography.**

Amniocentesis

In amniocentesis, the physician inserts a needle through the abdominal wall and into the amniotic sac of the pregnant woman and withdraws about one ounce of amniotic fluid from around the fetus. Fetal cells are separated from the fluid and allowed to grow in a culture medium for two to three weeks. The cells are then analyzed for chromosomal abnormalities. Although a variety of genetic disorders can be detected through amniocentesis, it is most often used to detect Down syndrome. In addition, amniocentesis allows one to analyze the amniotic fluid itself. Such analysis can detect about 90 percent of cases of spina bifida, a condition in which the spinal column fails to close during fetal development. In the fetus with spina bifida, certain proteins leak out of the spinal fluid into the surrounding amniotic sac. The elevation of these proteins enables this defect to be detected (see Chapter 8 for further discussion of spina bifida). Amniocentesis is most often performed at 16 to 18 weeks after the woman's last menstrual period.

Chorionic Villus Sampling

In chorionic villus sampling (CVS), the physician inserts a catheter through the vagina and cervix and withdraws about $\frac{1}{2000}$ of an ounce of villi, structures which will later become the placenta. Although first results are often available in two or three days, final verification takes two to three weeks. CVS can be used to detect a variety of chromosomal abnormalities. The major advantage of CVS over amniocentesis is that it can be performed much earlier, between the ninth to eleventh week of pregnancy. If the woman then elects to have an abortion, it can be done with less risk. Some physicians are more hesitant to conduct CVS, however, because, being a newer procedure, less is known about it. In addition, although neither amniocentesis nor CVS is risky, the incidence of miscarriage after CVS is higher than it is after amniocentesis.

Sonography

In sonography, high-frequency sound waves or ultrasound are converted into a visual picture of the fetus. This technique can be used to detect some major physical malformations such as spina bifida.

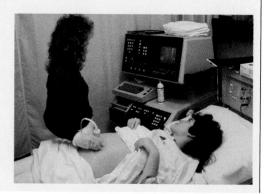

Sonography can be used to detect some major physical malformations, such as spina bifida, in the fetus. (© Russ Kinne/Photo Researchers)

Keeping Prenatal Testing in Perspective

There is little doubt that rapid advances in the field of prenatal testing are now allowing people to detect a number of heretofore unavoidable birth defects. As amazing as this technology is, however, it is well to keep in mind that it in no way guarantees a perfect baby. Many handicapping conditions cannot be detected by any available technique. In addition, as Pat Schnatterly, a genetic counselor in the University of Virginia's Department of Pediatrics, states:

> Prenatal testing is most appropriate when you know ahead of time what it is you're looking for. Thus, it is offered to couples who have specific known risks. This would include, for example, women 35 years of age and over, who have a higher risk for giving birth to a baby with Down syndrome. It would also include couples (for example, those of Ashkenazi Jewish descent who would be at risk for having a child with Tay-Sachs) whose ethnic backgrounds indicated they were at risk.

SOURCES: M. L. Batshaw and Y. M. Perret, *Children with Handicaps: A Medical Primer,* 2nd ed. (Baltimore: Paul H. Brookes Publishing Co. 1986); and M. Chitwood, "What's Past Is Prologue," *Helix,* 4(2) (1986). 4–7. The interested reader is encouraged to consult these sources for further information.

There are basically three different types of Down syndrome. In children with the **trisomy 21** type (by far the most common) there is an extra chromosome.* In this type the twenty-first set of chromosomes is a triplet rather than a pair, causing a condition called *trisomy*. The second type, **mosaicism,** results when, because of faulty development some of the individual's cells have this extra chromosome and others do not. In **translocation,** the third type, all or part of the extra chromosome of the twenty-first pair becomes attached to another of the chromosome pairs.

The likelihood of having a child with Down syndrome depends to a great extent on the age of the mother: More such children are born to women under 20 and, especially, over 40. For example, a woman between the ages of 20 and 30 has a 1 in 1300 chance of having a Down syndrome baby, a woman between 30 and 34 has a 1 in 600 chance, a woman between 35 and 39 has a 1 in 300 chance, and a woman between 40 and 44 has a 1 in 80 chance (Hansen, 1978). There are tests available whereby Down syndrome and some other birth defects can be diagnosed in the fetus during pregnancy. Such tests are sometimes recommended for older pregnant women because they are at higher risk for having a baby with Down syndrome.

More recently researchers are pointing to variables in addition to the age of the mother as possible causative factors in Down syndrome. Some of the factors being cited as potential causes are the age of the father, exposure to radiation, and exposure to some viruses (MacMillan, 1982).

PKU (phenylketonuria) involves the inability of the body to convert a common dietary substance—phenylalanine—to tyrosine; the accumulation of phenylalanine results in abnormal brain development. Screening tests for PKU can be given in the first few days after birth, and many states require that they be performed before an

---

* The nucleus of a normal human cell contains twenty-three pairs of **chromosomes,** making a total of forty-six chromosomes altogether. Chromosomes are composed of the essential genetic material— **genes.** Each gene within twenty-two of the chromosome pairs has a duplicate gene on the "matching" chromosome; the twenty-third pair is sex-linked, and its genes may be identical (XX for females) or different (XY for males).

infant leaves the hospital. Unless a special diet controlling the intake of phenyla-lanine is begun in infancy and continued into middle childhood, the child will usually develop severe retardation (Guthrie, 1984). And because some studies have shown that if the diet is stopped at middle childhood a decrease in IQ occurs, many authorities believe the diet should be maintained indefinitely (Batshaw and Perret, 1986). In addition to treating PKU once it has been detected, more and more emphasis is being placed on screening parents to determine if they are possible carriers of the PKU gene. Even though chances are slim (about 1 in 3600) of two carriers marrying, if this does occur, genetic counseling is highly advised.

Tay-Sachs disease, like PKU, can appear when both mother and father are carriers. It results in progressive brain damage and eventual death. It occurs almost exclusively among Ashkenazi Jews—that is, those of East European extraction. Genetic screening programs have been used to identify carriers. Also, the disease can be detected *in utero*.

Brain Damage

Brain damage can result from a host of factors that fall into two general categories— infections and environmental hazards.

INFECTIONS   Infections that may lead to mental retardation can occur in the mother-to-be or the infant or young child after birth. **Rubella** (German measles), **syphilis,** and **herpes simplex** in the mother can all cause retardation in the child. After rubella epidemics, more children are born with retardation (and/or other abnormalities). A new vaccine has dramatically reduced the incidence of this disease, and therefore the number of abnormal births because of it. Rubella is most dangerous during the first trimester (three months) of pregnancy. The venereal diseases, syphilis and herpes simplex, present a greater risk at later stages of fetal development (Hetherington and Parke, 1986). (Herpes simplex, which shows as cold sores or fever blisters, is not usually classified as a venereal disease unless it affects the genitals.)

Two examples of infections of the child that can affect mental development are meningitis and encephalitis. **Meningitis** is an infection of the covering of the brain that may be caused by a variety of bacterial or viral agents. Resulting more often in retardation and usually affecting intelligence more severely is **encephalitis,** an inflammation of the brain. Encephalitis may result in immediate retardation, or the effects may not occur until years later.

Infections, as well as other causative factors, can also result in microcephalus or hydrocephalus. **Microcephalus** is a condition characterized by a small head with a sloping forehead. It can be caused by infections such as rubella or by a genetic disorder. Retardation usually ranges from severe to profound. **Hydrocephalus** results from an accumulation of cerebrospinal fluid inside or outside the brain. Blockage of the circulation of the fluid, which results in a buildup of excessive pressure on the brain and enlargement of the skull, can occur for a variety of reasons—encephalitis, meningitis, malformation of the spine, or tumors. The degree of retardation depends on how early it is diagnosed and treated. Treatment consists of surgical implacement of a shunt (tube) that drains the excess fluid away from the brain and into a vein behind the ear or in the neck.

ENVIRONMENTAL HAZARDS   Examples of environmental hazards that can result in mental retardation are a blow to the head, poisons, radiation, malnutrition, prematurity or

Expectant mothers who consume large amounts of alcohol are at risk of giving birth to infants with fetal alcohol syndrome, a condition characterized by physical disabilities and mental retardation. (© Rhoda Sidney/Monkmeyer Press)

postmaturity, and birth injury. Although we are discussing these potential causal agents in this section, which deals with the causes of more severe forms of retardation, there is considerable evidence that in their milder forms each of these factors can result in mild retardation.

It should be obvious that a blow to a child's head can result in mental retardation. The obviousness of this connection, in fact, has served as an impetus for many of the mandatory laws pertaining to the use of child restraints in automobiles. Besides the usual accidents that can lead to brain damage, child abuse is being cited more and more often as a cause of brain damage that results in mental retardation and other disabilities (see Chapter 8).

Poisoning resulting in mental retardation can occur in the expectant mother or in the child. We are now much more aware of the harmful effects of a variety of substances, from obvious toxic agents such as heroin to more subtle potential "poisons" such as tobacco, alcohol, caffeine, and even food additives. In particular, research has shown that pregnant women who smoke and/or consume alcohol have a greater risk of having babies with behavioral and physical problems. For example, women who are heavy smokers are more likely than nonsmokers to have premature babies (Hetherington and Parke, 1986). And premature babies are at risk for a variety of developmental disabilities (see below).

The **fetal alcohol syndrome (FAS)** has been exposed as a significant health problem for expectant mothers who consume large quantities of alcohol and for their unborn children (Delaney and Hayden, 1977; Hetherington and Parke, 1986; Schultz, 1984); see also Chapter 8. Occurring in about one-third of the babies of pregnant alcoholic women, children with FAS are characterized by a variety of physical deformities as well as mental retardation.

Although pregnant women who drink moderately may not risk having children with FAS, there is evidence that even their infants will differ behaviorally from those born to women who do not drink during pregnancy. Among expectant mothers who drink moderately, there is evidence that the amount of alcohol they consume is related to their infants' arousal levels and central nervous system functioning (Streissguth, Barr, and Martin, 1983).

Some prescription drugs must also be avoided or used with caution by pregnant women. Research has linked some antibiotic, anticonvulsant, and anticancer medications to fetal malformations (Batshaw and Perret, 1986). And medication delivered to women during labor and delivery has also come under close scrutiny (Hetherington and Parke, 1986).

It is not always possible, of course, for expectant mothers to avoid using medication during pregnancy and labor. However, more and more authorities are questioning the high rates of drug ingestion by pregnant women—some studies have reported that expectant mothers in America ingest an average of six prescribed drugs and four over-the-counter drugs during their pregnancy. Given the potential for some of these drugs to be **teratogens**—substances that cause malformations in the fetus—many authorities have expressed caution about their use. Hetherington and Parke (1986) reflect a common view when they conclude:

> What can we conclude from the research on maternal drug intake and fetal development? The effects of drugs are difficult to predict. Many of the drugs which produce unfortunate effects have been tested on animals and nonpregnant adults and found to be harmless. We cannot make valid generalizations from tests performed on animals and human adults to the rapidly developing fetus since teratogens may affect different species at different stages of development in diverse ways. The problems in prediction are increased by the wide individual differences in infants and mothers in vulnerability to drug effects. In addition, there is little research on the long-term effects of maternal drug intake. However, it is apparent that great caution should be used in the ingestion of drugs by women during pregnancy and labor. (pp. 119–120)

Probably the most commonly referred to toxic agent affecting mental development in young children is lead-based paint. Although its use is now prohibited, infants, particularly in slum areas, still become poisoned by eating paint chips. Lead poisoning varies in its effect on the child; high levels can result in death. Robinson and Robinson (1976) point out some evidence suggesting that even low levels may trigger behavioral deviations in children who are already genetically susceptible. This possibility, along with other social considerations, has been an important factor in the federal government's requirement that automobile manufacturers produce cars using only lead-free gasoline.

The hazards of radiation to the unborn fetus have been recognized for some time. Physicians, for example, are cautious not to expose pregnant women to X rays unless absolutely necessary. Since the mid to late 1970s, however, the public has become even more concerned over the potential dangers of radiation from improperly designed or supervised nuclear power plants.

Retardation caused by improper nutrition can occur because the expectant mother is malnourished or because the child, once born, does not have a proper diet. Cravioto and DeLicardie (1975) and Hallahan and Cruickshank (1973) have reviewed research on both animals and human beings and have concluded it is much easier to show that poor nutrition leads to retardation in animal populations because the experimenter can control other possibly relevant variables. In studies with humans, it is difficult to separate poor nutrition from a poor home learning environment. But the evidence suggests that severe malnutrition can lead to abnormal brain development and thus mental retardation.

Disorders due to an abnormal length of pregnancy—either too short (prematurity) or too long (postmaturity)—can also result in retardation. The latter is not as likely to cause retardation, although it is possible that the fetus will suffer from poor nutrition if it is long overdue (Robinson and Robinson, 1976). Research on the effects of prematurity is complicated by the fact that it has sometimes been defined by the length of the pregnancy and sometimes by the weight of the infant at birth (5.5 pounds or lower is often used as an index of prematurity). The weight method results in the inclusion of some infants who may be small for reasons other than a short gestation period. Using length of pregnancy is also a problem because the length of gestation may have been inaccurately estimated. Both premature and small infants, however, are candidates for a variety of physical and behavioral abnormalities, including retardation (Blackman, 1984b). Prematurity itself is associated with a number of factors—poor nutrition, teenage pregnancy, drug abuse, excessive cigarette smoking, and socioeconomic level.

Brain injury can also occur during delivery if the child is not positioned properly in the uterus. One problem that sometimes occurs because of difficulty during delivery is **anoxia** (complete deprivation of oxygen).

MEASUREMENT

The two major areas that are measured in order to determine whether individuals are mentally retarded are intelligence and adaptive behavior. Methods of assessing intelligence have been in existence longer and for this reason are the better developed. Even though intellectual capability and the ability to adapt are related to a moderate degree (it is expected, for example, that the more intelligent child will usually be better able to adapt to the environment), there is enough difference between the two concepts to make it necessary to measure each area separately, using different techniques.

Intelligence Tests

There are many types of IQ tests. Because of their accuracy and predictive capabilities, individually administered tests are preferred over group tests. Individual tests are particularly valuable when a child must be diagnosed for placement in a special education program. Two of the most common individual IQ tests for children are the Stanford-Binet and the Wechsler Intelligence Scale for Children—Revised (WISC—R). The Wechsler Preschool and Primary Scale of Intelligence (WPPSI) and the Wechsler Adult Intelligence Scale (WAIS) are used with preschoolers and adults, respectively. Both the Stanford-Binet and the WISC—R are verbal, although the WISC—R is intended to assess both verbal and performance aspects of intelligence. It has a verbal and a performance scale with a number of subtests. The verbal and performance IQ measures are sometimes compared to scores on the subtests for purposes of educational programming. The "full-scale IQ," a statistical composite of the verbal and performance IQ measures, is used when a single overall score for a child is needed.

In general, a person's IQ is determined by dividing **mental age** (the age level at which a person is functioning) by **chronological age** and multiplying by 100 (to eliminate the decimal point). For example, a 10-year-old child who performs on an

IQ test as well as the *average* 8-year-old child (and thus has a mental age of 8 years) would have an IQ of 80.*

Compared to most psychological tests, IQ tests such as the Stanford-Binet and the WISC—R are among the most reliable and valid. By *reliability,* we mean that a child will obtain relatively similar scores if given the test on two separate occasions that are not too close nor far apart in time. *Validity* generally answers the question of whether or not the instrument measures what it is supposed to measure. A good indicator of the validity of an IQ test is its recognition as the best single index of how well a child will do in school. It is wise to be wary, however, of placing too much faith on any single score from a psychological test, even those as reliable and valid as the Stanford-Binet and WISC—R. There are at least four reasons for caution:

1. Estimates of reliability are based on statistical analysis of groups of children. This kind of statistical analysis masks the fact that an individual's IQ can change dramatically. McCall, Applebaum, and Hogarty (1973) have shown that in a group of middle-class normal children there was an average shift (in one direction or the other) of 28.5 IQ points between the ages of 2.5 and 17. Although it appears that this kind of shift is less likely with mentally retarded individuals (Robinson and Robinson, 1976), it nevertheless remains a possibility.

2. All IQ tests are culturally biased to a certain extent. Children from minority groups, largely because of differences in language and experience, are at a disadvantage in taking such tests.

3. The younger the child to whom the IQ test is administered, the less validity and reliability the test has. Infant intelligence tests are particularly questionable. However, as Robinson and Robinson (1976) point out, low scores on infant tests are much more valid than high scores. It is possible to identify retardation in infants, especially in the severe and profound ranges.

4. IQ tests are not the "be-all and end-all" when it comes to assessing an individual's ability to function in society. A superior IQ does not guarantee a successful life; a subnormal IQ does not doom a person to a miserable existence. Other variables are also important determiners of a person's coping skills in society (see box on p. 63).

Systematic Attempts to Reduce Cultural Bias in Intelligence Tests

Many professionals are concerned that minority groups are at a disadvantage when taking intelligence tests. They claim that such tests assess what is important in the dominant white culture in the United States but do not test those abilities that are stressed in certain minority groups (e.g., blacks and Hispanics). Two systems have been developed that attempt to eliminate this kind of bias—the SOMPA (System of Multicultural Pluralistic Assessment) (Mercer and Lewis, 1977) and the K-ABC (Kaufman Assessment Battery for Children) (Kaufman and Kaufman, 1983).

The SOMPA was developed by sociologist Jane Mercer. It attempts to eliminate as far as possible cultural and racial bias in intelligence testing. The most controversial aspect of SOMPA is its system for interpreting WISC—R scores. Mercer's assumption is that American society is composed of a dominant white, standard-English-

---

* This is the ratio method of determining IQ. The *deviation method* results in IQs that do not correspond exactly to the ratio method formula [$IQ = (MA/CA) \times 100$].

Keeping Tests in Perspective

Most professionals agree that tests, such as IQ tests and adaptive behavior instruments, are necessary. They can be helpful in making placement decisions and in evaluating program effectiveness. It is important to keep in mind, however, that they are far from perfect predictors about how a particular individual will function in the real world. The following two excerpts illustrate this point nicely. The first is from the renowned psychologist Seymour B. Sarason:

> The question I wish to discuss is: what is the relation between problem solving in test situations and in non-contrived, naturally occurring situations? I came to ask myself that question shortly after I took my first professional job testing individuals in a new institution for mentally retarded, a very innovative institution in the middle of nowhere. There was a certain problem with runaways. . . . Although I do not know how many of these runaways succeeded in not getting caught at all or only being found days later in their homes miles away, I did become aware that some of them had exhibited a kind and quality of problem-solving behavior that was simply not predictable from my testing of them. For example, I routinely administered the Porteus Mazes, which are scaled in difficulty from simple to complex. Some of the runaways who had done poorly on these mazes had managed to plan and execute their flights successfully, i.e., they demonstrated a level of planning and foresight quite at variance with their test performance. Part of my job was to make recommendations, on the basis of tests, for job placement within the institution. I began to learn that in a fair number of instances there was little relationship between the problem-solving behavior of an individual in testing and nontesting situations. I do not want to exaggerate the number of these instances; but their occurrence was frequent enough, and the discrepancies often dramatic enough, to make me wary of predicting from testing situations.

The following excerpt is from a case study of a mentally retarded woman by Oliver Sacks.

> Superficially she *was* a mass of handicaps and incapacities, with the intense frustrations and anxieties attendant on these; at this level she was, and felt herself to be, a mental cripple—beneath the effortless skills, the happy capacities, of others; but at some deeper level there was no sense of handicap or incapacity, but a feeling of calm and completeness, of being fully alive, of being a soul, deep and high, and equal to all others. Intellectually, then, Rebecca felt a cripple; spiritually she felt herself a full and complete being.

> When I first saw her—clumsy, uncouth, all-of-a-fumble—I saw her merely, or wholly, as a casualty, a broken creature, whose neurological impairments I could pick out and dissect with precision . . .

> The next time I saw her, it was all very different. I didn't have her in a test situation, "evaluating" her in a clinic. I wandered outside, it was a lovely spring day, with a few minutes in hand before the clinic started, and there I saw Rebecca sitting on a bench, gazing at the April foliage quietly, with obvious delight. Her posture had none of the clumsiness which had so impressed me before. Sitting there, in a light dress, her face calm and slightly smiling, she suddenly brought to mind one of Chekov's young women—Irene, Anya, Sonya, Nina—seen against the backdrop of a Chekovian cherry orchard. She could have been any young woman enjoying a beautiful spring day. This was my human, as opposed to my neurological, vision.

> As I approached, she heard my footsteps and turned, gave me a broad smile, and wordlessly gestured. "Look at the world," she seemed to say. "How beautiful it is."

And then there came out, in Jacksonian spurts, odd, sudden, poetic ejaculations: "spring," "birth," "growing," "stirring," "coming to life," "seasons," "everything in its time." I found myself thinking of Ecclesiastes: "To everything there is a season, and a time to every purpose under the heaven. A time to be born, and a time to die; a time to plant, and a time . . ." This was what Rebecca, in her disjointed fashion, was ejaculating—a vision of seasons, of times, like that of the Preacher. . . . She had done appallingly in the testing—which, in a sense, was designed, like all neurological and psychological testing, not merely to uncover, to bring out deficits, but to decompose her into functions and deficits. She had come apart, horribly, in formal testing, but now she was mysteriously "together" and composed.

Why was she so de-composed before, how could she be so re-composed now? I had the strongest feeling of two wholly different modes of thought, or of organisation, or of being. The first schematic—pattern-seeing, problem-solving—this is what had been tested, and where she had been found so defective, so disastrously wanting. But the tests had given no inkling of anything *but* the deficits, anything, so to speak, *beyond* her deficits.

They had given me no hint of her positive powers, her ability to perceive the real world—the world of nature, and perhaps of the imagination—as a coherent, intelligible, poetic whole: her ability to see this, think this, and (when she could) live this; they had given me no intimation of her inner world, which clearly *was* composed and coherent, and approached as something other than a set of problems or tasks. . . .

Our tests, our approaches, I thought, as I watched her on the bench—enjoying not just a simple but a sacred view of nature—our approach, our "evaluations," are ridiculously inadequate. They only show us deficits, they do not show us powers; they only show us puzzles and schemata, when we need to see music, narrative, play, a being conducting itself spontaneously in its own natural way.

Rebecca, I felt, was complete and intact as "narrative" being, in conditions which allowed her to organise herself in a narrative way; and this was something very important to know, for it allowed one to see her, and her potential, in a quite different fashion from that imposed by the schematic mode.

It was perhaps fortunate that I chanced to see Rebecca in her so-different modes—so damaged and incorrigible in the one, so full of promise and potential in the other—and that she was one of the first patients I saw in our clinic. For what I saw in her, what she showed me, I now saw in them all.

SOURCES: The first extract is from Seymour B. Sarason's book review of *Bias in Mental Testing* by Arthur Jensen in *Society,* Vol. 18, no. 1. Copyright © 1980 by Transaction, Inc. Reprinted by permission. The second is from O. Sacks, *The Man Who Mistook his Wife for a Hat: And Other Clinical Tales* (New York: Summit Books, 1985), pp. 170–173.) © 1970, 1981, 1983, 1984, 1985 by Oliver Sacks. Reprinted by permission of Summit Books, a division of Simon & Schuster, Inc.

speaking culture and a variety of other cultures. It is her contention that all these groups have the same innate ability. But because of different experiences associated with different cultures, individuals from some cultures are likely to score higher than individuals from other groups. For this reason, then, the SOMPA provides a method for converting a child's WISC—R score to an ELP (estimated learning potential) score based upon ethnic group as well as such things as size of the family, whether or not the child's family is on welfare, and how much the child's family engages in community activities. In essence, then, the SOMPA attempts to equalize all children's chances (no matter what their backgrounds) on the WISC—R. Using the SOMPA, a black child from a broken home on welfare who scores within the retarded range on the WISC—R may have an ELP score within the normal range. The SOMPA has generated much controversy; there have been questions about its scientific credibility as well as its underlying assumptions (Brown, 1979; Goodman, 1979; Oakland, 1979). Although numerous school districts have adopted it, the question of SOMPA's validity awaits further research.

The K-ABC has also been designed with cultural bias in mind. Although the fact that it has norms for blacks has contributed to its popularity, an even more compelling reason for its widespread use is that it purports to be based on the most current theories of cognitive processing. The K-ABC is based on the notion that cognitive tasks can be categorized primarily as requiring either simultaneous or sequential processing of information. Subtests of the K-ABC are thus designated as tapping simultaneous or sequential processing abilities. There have, however, been critics of the K-ABC who question whether (1) the theory of simultaneous versus sequential processing accounts adequately for how individuals process information and (2) the subtests of the K-ABC really do involve simultaneous and sequential skills (Das, 1984; Goetz and Hall, 1984; Sternberg, 1984).

Assessing Adaptive Behavior

Unfortunately, adequate measurement of adaptive behavior is more an ideal than a reality. Adaptive behavior tests are not as reliable and valid as IQ tests. To a certain extent, this situation is probably due to the rather fuzzy definitions of adaptive behavior. And although much has been said about the need to consider adaptive behavior as an important measure of mental ability, it is only since the early 1970s that serious efforts have been made to develop viable tests.

Numerous adaptive behavior measures are available, but the two that are probably used most commonly are the Adaptive Behavior Inventory for Children (ABIC) (Mercer and Lewis, 1977) and the AAMD Adaptive Behavior Scale—School Edition (Lambert and Windmiller, 1981).

The Adaptive Behavior Inventory for Children (ABIC)

The 242-item ABIC is designed to assess adaptive behavior in six different areas—family, community, peer relations, nonacademic school roles, earner/consumer, and self-maintenance. In the area of family, for example, the examiner asks the parent such things as how well the child gets along with brothers and/or sisters. For the community section, the child's relationships with people and events in the community are assessed. For peer relations, the interviewer asks questions regarding the child's ability to get along with peers. In the area of nonacademic school roles, the child's degree of involvement with the school is assessed. In the earner/consumer section, the examiner asks questions about the child's degree of knowledge about money and its management. In the area of self-maintenance, the questions address the child's ability to take care of his or her own daily living needs. Although it is too early for a final judgment on the value of the ABIC, many professionals believe it to be the best adaptive behavior instrument presently available for school-age children.

The AAMD Adaptive Behavior Scale—School Edition

The AAMD Adaptive Behavior Scale—School Edition is composed of two sections, one for daily living skills and one for personality and behavior. The nine domains assessed under Everyday Living Skills are: Independent Functioning, Physical Development, Economic Activity, Language Development, Numbers and Time, Prevocational Activity, Self-direction, Responsibility, and Socialization. The twelve domains assessed under Personality and Behavior are: Aggressiveness, Antisocial versus Social Behavior, Rebelliousness, Trustworthiness, Withdrawal versus Involvement, Mannerisms, Interpersonal Manners, Acceptability of Vocal Habits, Acceptability of Habits, Symptomatic Behavior, and Use of Medications.

PSYCHOLOGICAL AND BEHAVIORAL CHARACTERISTICS

It is important to know that statements about the psychological and behavioral characteristics of mentally retarded children are based on research studies comparing *groups* of intellectually subaverage children with nonretarded children. We cannot stress too strongly that *individual* mentally retarded children may not display all the characteristics mentioned. There is a great deal of variability in the behavior of retarded students, and each child must be considered as a unique and separate person. In this section we will discuss both the cognitive and personality characteristics of retarded individuals.

Cognitive Characteristics

The most obvious characteristic of retardation is a reduced ability to learn. There are a number of ways in which cognitive problems are manifested. Research has documented that retarded students are likely to have difficulties in at least four areas related to cognition*—attention, memory, language, and academics.

Attentional Abilities

The importance of attention for learning in general is obvious. A child must be able to attend to the task at hand before he or she can be expected to learn. Starting with the early research and theoretical formulations of Zeaman and House (1963), several authorities have posited that many of the cognitive problems of retarded individuals can be attributed to attentional difficulties. How retarded people allocate their attention is a particular problem (Brooks and McCauley, 1984; Sperber and McCauley, 1984). As Brooks and McCauley state:

Perhaps in older or more intelligent people some of the basic processes become automatic in much the same way as some motor skills such as bicycle riding or typing may become automatic. If a particular process is automatic one does not have to devote effort to directing or monitoring it. Attention not being used for some processes is then available to be focused on other cognitive activities.

Younger or less intelligent people would then be investing all of their attention on the simpler more basic processes, leaving less for more difficult or complicated processes. Thus, when asked to tell an examiner in what way a grape and an apple are alike, retarded people may not retrieve category information that they have available because they are expending so much of their attentional effort trying to keep the given examples in mind.

Other possibilities, again, with attention as the culprit, include the theory that retarded individuals simply have less attention to allocate to different processes or the theory that

---

* *Cognition* refers to the process of thinking.

retarded people cannot (or do not) efficiently assign the proper amount or quality of attention to the various aspects of a task. (pp. 481–482)

Memory

One of the most consistent findings in comparisons of the learning abilities of nonhandicapped and retarded individuals is that when the latter are asked to remember a list of words or sounds or a group of pictures presented a few seconds previously, they do more poorly than the nonhandicapped (Borkowski, Peck, and Damberg, 1983; Brown, 1974; Estes, 1970). Many authorities have conceptualized these memory problems within a theoretical framework that stresses the depth of processing that an individual must perform in order to remember certain material. The depth-of-processing approach is the brainchild of Craik and colleagues (Craik and Lockhart, 1972; Craik and Tulving, 1975). They maintain that we process incoming stimuli at various levels of analysis. At shallow levels only perceptual features are processed, whereas at deeper levels semantic features of the incoming stimuli are processed. For example, asking an individual to make judgments about whether a word just seen was in capital letters is an example of relatively shallow processing. Asking the person if the word would fit into a sentence that was presented just before the word is an example of deep processing (Craik and Tulving, 1975).

Research has demonstrated that the deeper the level of processing required, the larger the likelihood that mentally retarded individuals will have greater memory problems than their nonhandicapped peers (Schultz, 1983). In other words, the more complicated the memory task, the more likely it is that a retarded individual will have difficulties with it.

LEARNING STRATEGIES AND EXECUTIVE CONTROL PROCESSES (METACOGNITIVE PROCESSES) One of the primary reasons retarded individuals have problems on more complicated memory tasks is that they have difficulty using efficient learning strategies such as mediation and organization (Borkowski and Wanschura, 1974; Bray, 1979; Brown, 1974). An example of a mediation strategy is *rehearsal*. When given a list of words to remember, most individuals will rehearse the list aloud or to themselves in an attempt to "keep" the words in memory. Retarded students generally do not use rehearsal spontaneously (Borkowski and Cavanaugh, 1979).

One example of an organizing strategy is *clustering*. An example of clustering is the strategy of rehearsing serially presented items in groups. For instance, in trying to remember the digits 1, 7, 8, 5, 3, 4, it is easier to rehearse them in two clusters—178 and 534. There is a tendency, however, for retarded individuals not to do this spontaneously.

Many authorities have attributed retarded students' inefficient use of learning strategies such as rehearsal and clustering to the fact that their executive control processes are less well developed (Brown, 1974; Justice, 1985; Sternberg and Spear, 1985). **Executive control processes,** also called **metacognitive processes,** "are used to plan how to solve a problem, to monitor one's solution strategy as it is being executed, and to evaluate the results of this strategy once it has been implemented" (Sternberg and Spear, 1985, p. 303). Research has demonstrated that, when confronted with learning problems, retarded individuals frequently have trouble picking the best strategies to use, monitoring the use of the strategies (keeping track of their own performance), and evaluating the use of strategies (knowing whether or not the strategies are working).

But even though retarded individuals have been found to be deficient in the

Developmental versus Difference Theories of Cultural-Familial Retardation

There are two basic views of how culturally-familially retarded individuals differ from the nonretarded on cognitive tasks. Those who take a "difference" position (e.g., Ellis, 1982) maintain that retarded people learn in a way that is qualitatively different from that of the nonretarded. Some of these theorists attribute this different performance to inherent structural defects in the retarded individual's central nervous system.

Developmental theorists maintain that culturally-familially retarded individuals do not differ qualitatively from the nonretarded (Estes, 1970; Zigler and Balla, 1982). They believe that their differences are quantitative in nature in that they are slower to acquire knowledge or skills. They posit that culturally-familially retarded individuals go through the same stages of learning as do nonretarded persons, but at a slower rate. Thus they predict that mentally retarded and nonretarded individuals of the same developmental level (usually determined by mental age on an IQ test) will perform similarly. Zigler notes that when differences have been found in favor of the nonretarded of the same mental age, the retarded group has usually been institutionalized. He posits that the institutionalization, rather than the retardation, causes them to perform more poorly.

Although far from conclusive, the evidence tends to favor the developmental position. For thorough coverage of the developmental versus difference debate, see Zigler and Balla's *Mental Retardation: The Developmental-Difference Controversy* (Hillsdale, N.J.: Lawrence Erlbaum Associates, 1982).

spontaneous use of learning strategies and executive control processes, research has shown they can be taught to use such processes successfully (Borkowski and Cavanaugh, 1979; Borkowski, Peck, and Damberg, 1983; Glidden, 1985). More and more, authorities are recommending that teachers emphasize the use of executive control processes in their work with retarded students.

Language Problems

Language difficulties are frequent in mentally retarded children (MacMillan, 1982), and it is typical to find their language level below their general mental age level (Smith, 1974). Speech problems (difficulties in the formation of sounds, such as articulation errors) occur more frequently in retarded than in nonretarded children.

In addition to speech and language problems, four other generalizations regarding language and retarded individuals can be made:

1. The language of retarded children is structurally similar to that of nonhandicapped children (Lenneberg, 1967; O'Connor and Hermelin, 1963). As Lenneberg states, "The pathologically lowered IQ of the retarded does not result in bizarre use of language but merely in 'frozen' but normal primitive language stages" (p. 326).
2. There are data to indicate that particular kinds of speech defects are more common than others in retarded individuals. Articulation, voice, and stuttering problems are the most common (Spradlin, 1963).
3. The kinds of speech and language problems exhibited are not specific to the particular diagnostic categories of retardation (Keane, 1972). For example,

children with Down syndrome do not manifest disorders significantly different from those of PKU children.

4. Both the prevalence and the severity of speech and language handicaps are generally related to the severity of the retardation. Jordan (1976) has noted that among mildly retarded children, delay in beginning to talk is common, but mutism (absence of speech) is rare. Language of moderately retarded individuals is rarely free of defects and is commonly stereotypical: monotonous expressions are frequent. For severely retarded people, "mutism is common and primitive levels of language development such as babbling and jabbering are frequent" (Jordan, 1976, p. 308).

Academic Achievement

Because of the strong relationship between intelligence and achievement, it is not surprising that retarded children lag well behind their chronological age peers in all areas of achievement. They also tend to be underachievers in relation to expectations based on mental age. This underachievement is most pronounced in reading, especially reading comprehension (Dunn, 1973). Underachievement in arithmetic reasoning abilities is also evident, but arithmetic computation skill is relatively intact (Dunn, 1973; MacMillan, 1982). Dunn also notes very little basis for positing a relationship between type of retardation and kind or degree of academic retardation.

Personality Characteristics

Mentally retarded individuals are candidates for a variety of social and emotional problems. Simply being different undoubtedly influences the way a person is treated by others in social situations. Being referred to as the "dummy" in a group of children is almost certain to be detrimental to an individual's feelings of self-worth. In fact, research indicates that retarded people's self-concepts tend to be lower than those of nonretarded individuals (Leahy, Balla, and Zigler, 1982). In addition to lower self-esteem, retarded students are at risk for other behavior problems, such as disruptiveness and inattention (Polloway, Epstein, and Cullinan, 1985).

Among those who have pointed out the importance of personality characteristics in retarded individuals, Edward Zigler has been the most influential (Balla and Zigler, 1979; Zigler and Balla, 1982). He maintains that retarded behavior is the consequence not only of low intelligence, but also of personality and motivational factors. He believes that many retarded individuals, because of past experiences, have a high expectancy of failure. And this expectancy influences how they approach most situations that require cognitive skills.

The terms **outer-directed** (as opposed to **inner-directed**) and **external locus of control** (as opposed to **internal locus of control**) have been used to describe the lack of confidence some retarded people have in their own abilities. Research has shown that many retarded individuals do not believe they are in control of their own destinies; they believe they are controlled by external or outside forces. They tend to think that things happen to them by chance and that they themselves can do little to change anything. Given the regimentation of some institutions and the failure experiences of some mentally retarded children reared at home, it is not surprising that retarded people generally rely on others for help rather than on themselves. Along these lines, Harter and Zigler (1974) found that retarded individuals are less likely to engage in challenging tasks. Weisz (1981) found that when given negative feedback on cognitive tasks they were performing, retarded children stopped looking for effective strategies, whereas their nonretarded counterparts actually increased their search for effective solutions. Weisz (1982) characterizes the passive behavior of many retarded children as

the "pencil down" syndrome, in which children react to a problem they cannot solve quickly by placing pencil on desk and sitting passively, making no effort to persist at the puzzling problem, go on to another, or request assistance. One experienced teacher explained that these children "go into any new situation expecting to fail; when the going gets tough, they quit trying." (p. 28)

EDUCATIONAL CONSIDERATIONS

Education for Mildly Retarded Students

There are many ways of arranging the educational program for mildly retarded children, but most school systems have the following divisions: preschool classes, elementary primary classes, elementary intermediate classes, and secondary classes. In addition, many schools offer infant stimulation classes and postschool programs. The former focus on encouraging the sensory and intellectual development of the child from birth to 3 years, and the latter concentrate on providing the older teenager and young adult with skills for employment, independent living, and community adjustment.

Preschool Classes

The early childhood years are viewed by many educators and developmental psychologists as a critical time for the intellectual and social development of any child, especially one who is a likely candidate for identification as mentally retarded once he or she reaches elementary school age. When the possible degree of retardation is in the mild range, however, professionals prefer to take a conservative approach in identifying young children. They often refer to these children as "at risk," the idea being that they are at risk to become classified as mentally retarded once they attend elementary school.

Programs vary according to how services are delivered. Ramey and Bryant (1983) note that some of the most common forms of program delivery are educational home visitations, group educational day care, home visit/day-care combinations, and parent group sessions. Some programs have also offered job training for parents and medical care for children. Although all such programs have the ultimate goal of reducing the risk that infants and young children from disadvantaged backgrounds will become mentally retarded, they differ considerably with regard to curriculum emphasis. For example, some stress sensorimotor infant exercises; others focus on changing parent teaching styles (Ramey and Bryant, 1983).

Many classes for mildly retarded preschoolers emphasize what are commonly referred to as **readiness skills,** prerequisites for later learning. Kindergarten classes for nonhandicapped youngsters also focus on these types of activities, but preschool classes for mildly retarded children start at a lower level, and the training may take as long as two or three years. Readiness skills include the abilities to:

1. Sit still and attend to the teacher
2. Discriminate auditory and visual stimuli
3. Follow directions

4. Develop language
5. Increase gross- and fine-motor coordination (holding a pencil, cutting with a pair of scissors)
6. Develop self-help skills (tying shoes, buttoning and unbuttoning, zipping and unzipping, toileting)
7. Interact with peers in group situations

The preschool period is also a good time to begin to involve parents in the education of their children. Some research indicates that parents can be effective teachers of their preschool children. Karnes, Teska, Hodgins, and Badger (1970) trained mothers of disadvantaged preschoolers to stimulate cognitive and verbal development in their children. The IQs of these children averaged 16 points higher than the IQs of a control group whose mothers did not undergo training.

Elementary Primary Classes

Early primary classes are also heavily oriented toward providing mildly retarded children with readiness skills. With chronological ages from about 6 to 10 years and mental ages from about 4 to 6 years, most of these children need to be given classroom experiences typical for nonretarded kindergarten children. To a great extent, then, the curriculum of elementary primary classes is an extension of that of preschool classes, with continued emphasis on language development and concept formation. How much academic activities are stressed depends to a great degree on the quality and extent of the preschool programming the individual child has had. It is at this point that the rudiments of reading, math, and handwriting begin.

Education for mildly retarded children also provides training in socially adaptive behaviors. Researchers have formulated a number of techniques for improving the social skills of retarded students. Goldstein (1974), for example, has developed the Social Learning Curriculum, which is meant to be introduced as early as possible. Walker and his colleagues have published the ACCEPTS (A Curriculum for Children's Effective Peer and Teacher Skills) social skills curriculum for use with young

Readiness skills and socialization skills are important components of early elementary programming for mildly retarded children. (Titmus/Taurus Photos)

elementary children (Walker, McConnell, Holmes, Todis, and Golden, 1983). The ACCEPTS curriculum, a tightly structured and sequenced set of activities, focuses on five skill areas: (1) classroom skills (e.g., following directions), (2) basic interaction skills, (3) getting along, (4) making friends, and (5) coping skills.

Elementary Intermediate Classes

Intermediate classes for children between the ages of about 9 and 13 years (mental ages from about 6 to 9 years) are more common than primary classes for mildly retarded children (Robinson and Robinson, 1976). This is primarily because mildly retarded children are often not identified until they have been in school for a few years. Although readiness training may continue to some degree, the intermediate class is where academics assume a more important role. The academics taught, however, are frequently classified as functional academics. Whereas the nonretarded child is taught academics, such as reading, in order to learn other academic content, such as history, at a later stage, the retarded child is often taught reading in order to learn to function independently. In **functional academics** the individual is taught academics in order to do such things as read the newspaper, read the telephone book, read labels on goods at the store, make change, and fill out job applications.

Secondary School Classes

By the time the mildly retarded youngster reaches junior or senior high school, the need for readiness training should be almost entirely eliminated. At this point, the likelihood of a curriculum stressing functional academics is much greater than at younger age levels. Social and occupational education are also now very important. And **transitional programming,** or the preparation of retarded students for the world of work after secondary school, becomes critical. Figure 2.2 shows the relationship among readiness training, academic instruction, social and occupational

Figure 2.2 *Current conceptualization of the educational curriculum for mildly retarded students.*
SOURCE: The authors are indebted to Sandra B. Cohen for the conceptualization depicted in this figure.

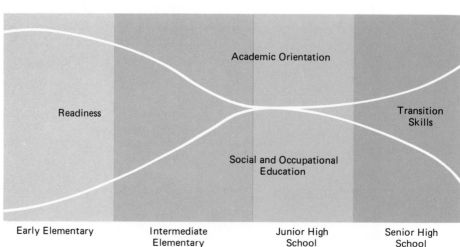

Table 2.2 Brolin's Career Education Model

Daily Living Skills
1. Managing family finances
2. Caring for home furnishings and equipment
3. Caring for personal needs
4. Raising children, family living
5. Buying and preparing food
6. Buying and making clothing
7. Engaging in civic activities
8. Using recreation and leisure
9. Getting around the community

Personal Social Skills
10. Achieving self-awareness
11. Acquiring self-confidence
12. Achieving socially responsible behavior
13. Maintaining good interpersonal skills
14. Achieving independence
15. Making good decisions, problem-solving
16. Communicating adequately with others

Occupational Guidance and Preparation
17. Knowing and exploring occupational opportunities
18. Making appropriate occupational decisions
19. Exhibiting appropriate work behaviors
20. Exhibiting sufficient physical and manual skills
21. Acquiring a specific salable job skill
22. Seeking, securing, and maintaining satisfactory employment

SOURCE: D. E. Brolin, Vocational Preparation of Persons with Handicaps, 2nd ed. Adapted from *A Competency-Based Career Special-Educa-
tion Curriculum Model, Grades 10–12* (Columbus, Ohio: Charles E. Merrill, 1982). © 1982 Merrill Publishing Company. Reprinted with permission of the publisher.

training, and transition programming for mildly retarded youngsters from early elementary through senior high school.

One of the keys to mentally retarded students' achieving a successful transition after secondary school is the degree to which they have developed appropriate social skills. Such skills allow them to form meaningful and lasting social friendships (see box, p. 76). Brolin's (1982) career education model is an example of how curriculum content at the secondary level stresses the development of personal-social skills, as well as the other "real world" skills related to daily living and occupational preparation (see Table 2.2).

WORK-STUDY PROGRAMS   One of the most frequent service delivery models for developing social, occupational, and transition skills in mildly retarded students is the **work-study program.** Students are placed in work situations in the community, and their academic program is oriented to supplement the work experience. Beirne-Smith, Coleman, and Payne (1986) conceptualize work-study programs as containing five phases: vocational exploration, vocational evaluation, vocational training, vocational placement, and follow-up. In *vocational exploration,* the goal is to acquaint students with a variety of occupations and their skill requirements. The *vocational evaluation* phase allows the teacher to determine abilities and prefer-

ONE PROFESSIONAL'S PERSPECTIVE

Patricia L. Pullen

B.A., Speech Pathology, University of Maryland
M.Ed., Special Education (MR), University of Virginia
Current Position: Teacher of a primary level EMR class, Charlottesville Public Schools, Virginia

Ms. Patricia L. Pullen taught mildly retarded fifth, sixth, and seventh graders in Lexington, Virginia, for two years and nonhandicapped children in private school in Charlottesville for two years before assuming her current position eleven years ago. Her class is comprised of 15 children from kindergarten through third grade. Their full-scale IQs place the children as a group squarely in the mildly retarded range—at least on paper. The class is quite varied in individual characteristics: 10 children are male, 5 are female; 6 are Caucasian, 9 are black; 12 qualify for free lunch; 9 receive services from a speech-language pathologist; 1 receives adaptive physical education. One child had no exposure to school until the age of seven; another has had instruction since the age of one. Two children take Ritalin. One wears bilateral hearing aids, and three have significant vision problems. Ms. Pullen describes her position at Jackson-Via Elementary School as "idyllic and not representative of the real world of special education in some respects." She has a full-time aide, a large classroom with two bathrooms, a water fountain, and a sink. And she considers herself "privileged to work with a staff who support the edict of the least restrictive environment."

We asked Ms. Pullen the following questions:

Why did you decide to become a teacher of the mentally retarded? I grew up with a deaf grandmother and decided at an early age to devote my life to educating the hard-of-hearing. My first job after completing my undergraduate degree was in a private school for preschool multiply handicapped rubella victims in Washington, D.C. But when I returned to my home town of Lexington, Virginia, I had a choice: become a peripatetic speech therapist with a case load of 70 students in six different schools or teach a self-contained class of mildly retarded students. I found the prospect of teaching the EMR class, which had a part-time aide *and* a hard-of-hearing child, more attractive. My experiences in Lexington convinced me of the challenge of improving education for retarded students, and I subsequently entered the graduate program in special education at UVA. When I started teaching in Lexington, I had little information about my students—no *confidential* folders, only one psychological assessment (five years old and showing that the child had a full-scale IQ of 93!), no educational assessments, no minutes of staffing or eligibility meetings, no data to tell me who had declared these children

eligible for special education or *why*. After laborious digging through files I discovered that 10 of my 12 students had been retained in grade at least once. They had all been behavior problems. One comment from a classroom teacher was, "John is impotent in the classroom." I wondered if he was potent *outside* the class, until it dawned on me that the teacher had meant "impudent." IEPs hadn't been invented yet. Special education for retarded students was still a waste basket for all the misfits—ill-behaved and otherwise difficult children who were considered the garbage of the schools. No one expected you to teach them anything, just make them happy. Some of my colleagues of the 1970s were hired for special education because they were music or art teachers. You were expected to cut, paste, sing, but not teach reading or math skills. I thought these children deserved more.

If you could change one thing about your job, what would it be? I'd have more time for all the various things I do.

What major changes have occurred in your field since you began teaching? I've already described the lack of information about my students when I started teaching. Probably the biggest changes are those brought about by the law. I complain bitterly about the overwhelming paperwork involved in complying with PL 94-142. And sometimes I do not agree with the placement of a child. But I do at least know *who* was responsible for the placement and *why* the decision was made, and I know whether or not the parents agreed with the placement. Even more important, I know the procedures for having a child reevaluated and for considering a change in placement. I am relieved that children can no longer be placed in special education classes or removed from them by merely trading cumulative folders in the office file cabinet.

With what one student in your career have you had the most success, and how did you work with him or her? I've taught a lot of difficult children, but none has been the trial that Earl presented when he arrived in my class three years ago. Baseline data showed that he could stay seated for 30 seconds and could attend to direct instruction for 6 seconds. His fine motor skills were almost nonexistent (he thought pencils were to put up his nose), and he could not tolerate any free time. He was defiant, unaware of appropriate behavior, and would steal everything that was not nailed down. If he wanted to go from point A to point B, he made an unswerving line and bulldozed everything in his path—teachers, children, toys, or furniture. He hit, kicked, scratched anybody and everybody without apparent motive.

One afternoon, he became angry and began to demolish the room. He tore around the room, turned over chairs, scooped the contents out of the shelves, scraped materials off tables and ripped down two bulletin boards before I finally caught him. He accomplished this destruction in about 30 seconds.

He had difficulty sitting close to others because he would unbutton their clothing, examine their scalps, or put his hands in their pockets. I have never seen a child so impulsive, so totally out of control. The school psychologist felt that the low scores she got when she tested him were invalid but recommended Earl for my class anyway. I felt totally overwhelmed. No one in my class was learning anything. We felt lucky to survive each day. I first made a list of all Earl's aberrant behavior, then picked two that were dangerous. I discovered that he sat very still for a story, and that he loved food.

So I bought a ton of sunflower seeds and started every lesson with a lapful of seeds. Everybody in his group earned a seed for correct responses. He soon began to attend so that he could answer correctly and earn a seed. I also arranged for fifth graders to read stories to him contingent upon his showing a minimal amount of self-control.

Gradually, his attention span increased and he attended to instruction for 20 minutes by the end of the year. He could also listen to a story in the regular classroom by June. Earl repeated kindergarten, is now in the first grade, and is mainstreamed 70 percent of the day, including reading instruction. He works for praise and stickers and can usually postpone tangible rewards until the end of the day. He is still very hyperactive, but his medication (Ritalin) helps. And he still steals. We have to frisk him regularly to recover pencils, pens, erasers, paper clips, toys, and occasionally we stumble on a lunch from a classmate's lunch box. But he's learning, and many of his skills are on grade level. In fact, there is some concern that he may not qualify for my program when he is reevaluated in a few months.

Describe the most interesting student with whom you've worked. Earl awarded me the most success, but Ben is the most interesting child I have ever taught. He is also the most beautiful child I have ever taught—dark wavy hair, large brown eyes, with eye lashes that curl above his eyebrows. He has delicate features even for a kindergarten child, and teachers and students often comment, "Ben is pretty." The educational and psychological assessments show a wide range of skills and potential, from trainable to slightly above average. The examiners on both assessments felt the scores were depressed and probably not valid. But he has such a serious attention deficit that it

was almost impossible to obtain valid scores.

Sometimes he struggles to attend. He will turn his head toward the book or my face, but his eyes are still gazing to the right or left. I have to wait for his eyes to catch up with his head before I instruct him. It's like waiting for the fruit to stop spinning on a slot machine. Sometimes he refuses to try to attend and becomes defiant and disruptive. His attention deficits and stubbornness are not the only blocks to achieving valid test scores. He also has a strange sense of humor and often appears emotionally disturbed. He talks to magic markers and walls and complains that his chair is hot. He refers to inanimate objects as if they were people or pets. He will misname pictures of objects that I am sure he can name. He tells children that they have turned green.

When I asked Ben's mother about these behaviors, she related that she had been a drama major and often played with her children by altering her voice and speaking for objects. There have been days when he laughed maniacally or screamed for hours. There have also been times when he threw himself on the floor with a sickening thud.

We have discovered in the last six months that Ben has a lot of age appropriate skills. He knows the alphabet, eight sounds, can count to 20, and name numerals to five. There is only one consistency with Ben. He loves music. But it has to be live music. Record players and tapes won't do. He is trying to control his behavior, to attend to lessons so that he may go to music class after lunch. The music teacher has either a kindergarten or a first grade class after lunch every day and permits Ben to attend. Ben usually earns four extra lessons a week. What is extraordinary is that the music teacher says that Ben is a pleasure to have in the class.

The Importance of Friendship

In being concerned about improving the cognitive and work skills of retarded individuals, professionals often overlook the importance of an area as fundamental as friendship. The following extract highlights the important role friendship can play in the lives of retarded people.

A sense of belonging, of feeling accepted, and of having personal worth are qualities brought to life through friendship. Friendship creates an alliance and a sense of security. It is a vital human connection.

Mentally retarded people want and need friendship like everyone else. Yet they are often denied opportunities to form relationships or to develop the skills necessary to interact socially with others. Their exposure to peers may be limited because they live and work in sheltered or isolated environments. They typically lack a history of socializing events such as school clubs, parties, or sleepovers that help to develop or refine personal skills. They may not know how to give of themselves to other people and may be stuck in an egocentric perspective. Retarded persons may also respond inappropriately in social situations unless instructed otherwise. Many people shun retarded individuals who freely hug or kiss strangers when greeting them. Some retarded persons have speech problems, making communication difficult. Other factors may further hinder their ability to attract and keep friends. Mildly retarded individuals often avoid associating with other retarded persons for fear of emphasizing their own stigma. The normal community, however, may be reluctant to incorporate these retarded individuals within their smaller social circles, given what are often real differences in interests.

With few contacts and opportunities, retarded persons may attempt to befriend strangers or unwitting individuals. Many attempt to become social acquaintances with their professional contacts. In their effort to maintain those contacts and relationships they have developed, some retarded individuals will overcompensate: calling their friend too many times, talking too long on the phone, demanding attention, and not being able to let up. Unfortunately, these behaviors tend to make people uncomfortable and hesitant to interact with retarded persons for fear that they will have to "hurt their feelings" at some later date. Some mentally retarded persons have also been victimized or exploited by some "friends"—a situation which unfortunately may be a normal risk.

A friend can play a vital role in the adjustment of a retarded individual to community living, by providing emotional support and guidance through the exigencies of daily life. Certain organizations have begun to address the mentally retarded adult's need for friends by constructing social opportunities with realistic peer groups. Examples of these include the Mohawks and Squaws, a social club for retarded adults in which members plan their own parties and projects, and Citizen Advocacy programs which sponsor one-to-one relationships between a community volunteer and a retarded individual for the purpose of aiding adjustment. Researchers in behavior training have also begun to devise strategies for teaching retarded individuals appropriate social skills, such as how to address strangers, initiate conversations, and respond in various social situations.

SOURCE: J. R. Patton and J. L. Spears, "Adult and Community Issues," in J. R. Patton, J. S. Payne, and M. Beirne-Smith (Eds.), *Mental Retardation,* 2nd ed. (Columbus, Ohio: Charles E. Merrill, 1986), pp. 470–471). © 1986 Merrill Publishing Company. Reprinted by permission.

ences for different jobs. In *vocational training,* the goal is to develop specific job skills in a general area of preference. To ensure broad-based training, the training at this stage involves a variety of job skills (usually at the semi-skilled level). *Vocational placement* consists of placing students in jobs after graduation from high school. During *follow-up,* former students having difficulty are counseled. In addition, this phase may involve retraining and/or placement in other jobs.

Education for Moderately Retarded Students

Preschool Classes

Because moderate retardation is easier to diagnose than mild retardation, preschool programs are relatively common for moderately retarded children. Unlike preschool programs for at-risk children, in which the goal is to prevent retardation from developing, programs for moderately retarded preschoolers are designed to enable them to achieve as high a level as possible. A great deal of emphasis is placed on language and conceptual development. In addition, because these children often have multiple disabilities, other professionals—for example, speech therapists and physical therapists—are frequently involved. Also, many of these programs include opportunities for parent involvement. MacMillan (1982) has reviewed these programs and is cautiously optimistic about their success:

> Programs like the ones we have described have been successful in preparing established risk children to enter public school programs. Their goal has been not so much to make the children "normal," but to optimize their development through early stimulation. . . . The preliminary finding—that these children are capable of higher levels of functioning than was formerly thought—indicates that early intervention holds some promise for established risk children. (p. 512)

Elementary and Secondary Classes

The educational program for moderately retarded individuals is in general less academically oriented than that for the mildly retarded, and the academics that are taught are even more likely to fall under the rubric of functional academics. Much more emphasis is placed on providing students with skills that will enable them to function independently in a social and work environment. Two very important curriculum content areas are self-help skills and vocational skills.

SELF-HELP SKILLS   Authorities agree that the teaching of self-help skills is vital. Self-help skills vary in complexity. They include such things as toileting, self-feeding, dressing, and grooming. In a sense, these are the rudiments upon which other aspects of the curriculum are built. In order for an individual to be employable, for example, he or she will need to have attained a great many self-help skills.

Reid, Wilson, and Faw (1983) note that most approaches to training self-help skills have been based on behavioral principles. Since the 1960s there has been a long line of investigations using behavior modification to train self-help skills in the retarded. Reid et al. note that such self-help skills as toileting, self-feeding, dressing, and personal hygiene have been successfully taught to severely and profoundly retarded as well as moderately retarded individuals.

VOCATIONAL SKILLS   In order for moderately retarded individuals to become independent, functioning members of society, they must learn skills that will enable them to obtain and keep a job. The kinds of jobs available vary according to each individual's adaptive behavior skills and mental age level. The potential variety and number of jobs that moderately retarded individuals can fill is limited to a great degree by their training and motivation and the cooperation and understanding of the nonhandicapped population.

Education for Severely and Profoundly Retarded Students

In the history of educational programming for mentally retarded individuals there has been a marked neglect of the needs of severely and profoundly retarded students. It was not until the mid-1970s that the federal government made a serious commitment to provide services for severely and profoundly retarded children. The passage of Public Law 94-142, assuring every handicapped child a right to instruction, formalized the obligation to provide an appropriate educational program for many children who had previously been ignored by the schools.

The Needs of Severely and Profoundly Retarded Students

Because of the low level of functioning of severely and profoundly retarded children, training begins with basic survival and self-help skills. Table 2.3 provides a summary of some of the basic areas in which these individuals need special educa-

Participation in such events as the Special Olympics can do much to further the physical coordination of mentally retarded individuals. It can also enable them to experience the joy of accomplishment.
(© Peter Glass/Monkmeyer Press)

Table 2.3 Suggested Areas of Program Emphasis for Profoundly Retarded Students

Preschool	School	Adult
Sensorimotor Stimulation	*Sensorimotor Development*	*Sensorimotor Integration*
1. Stimulating sight, hearing, touch, smell, and muscular response 2. Enriching environment and encouraging exploration of interesting and attractive surroundings	1. Identifying shapes, colors, sizes, locations, and distances 2. Identifying sound patterns, locations, tonal qualities, rhythms 3. Identifying textures, weights, shapes, sizes, temperatures 4. Identifying familiar aversive and pleasant odors	1. Sorting, transferring, inserting, pulling, folding 2. Responding to music activities, signals, warnings 3. Making personal choices and selections 4. Discriminating sizes, weights, colors, distance, locations, odors, temperatures, etc.
Physical Development	*Physical Mobility and Coordination*	*Physical Dexterity and Recreation*
1. Body positioning 2. Passive exercising 3. Rolling, creeping, and crawling 4. Balancing head and trunk 5. Using hands purposefully 6. Standing practice 7. Training for mobility	1. Practicing ambulation 2. Overcoming obstacles; walking on ramps and stairs, running, skipping, jumping, balancing, climbing 3. Using playground equipment 4. Participating in track and field events	1. Riding vehicles; participating in gymnastic-like activities and track and field events 2. Marking with pencil; cutting with scissors; stringing beads; pasting; and assembling 3. Swimming and water play 4. Using community parks, and other recreational resources
Pre–Self-Care	*Self-Care Development*	*Self-Care*
1. Taking nourishment from bottle and spoon; drinking from cup and finger feeding 2. Passive dressing; accommodating body to dressing; partially removing clothing 3. Passive bathing; handling soap and washcloth; participating in drying 4. Passive placement on toilet; toilet regulating	1. Self-feeding with spoon and cup; eating varied diet; behaving appropriately while dining 2. Removing garments; dressing and undressing with supervision; buttoning, zipping, and snapping 3. Drying hands and face; partially bathing 4. Toilet scheduling; indicating need to eliminate; using toilet with supervision	1. Eating varied diet in family dining situation; using eating utensils; selecting foods 2. Dressing with partial assistance or supervision 3. Bathing with partial assistance or supervision 4. Using toilet independently with occasional supervision

(table continues)

Preschool	School	Adult
Sensorimotor Stimulation	*Sensorimotor Development*	*Sensorimotor Integration*
Language Stimulation	*Language Development*	*Language and Speech Development*
1. Increasing attention to sounds	1. Recognizing own name, names of familiar objects, and body parts	1. Listening to speaker
2. Encouraging vocalization	2. Responding to simple commands	2. Using gestures, words, or phrases
3. Responding to verbal and nonverbal requests	3. Initiating speech and gestures	3. Following uncomplicated directions
4. Identifying objects	4. Using gestures, words, or phrases	
Interpersonal Response	*Social Behavior*	*Self-Direction and Work*
1. Recognizing familiar persons	1. Requesting personal attention	1. Using protective skills
2. Requesting attention from others	2. Playing individually alongside other residents	2. Sharing, taking turns, waiting for instructions
3. Occupying self for brief periods	3. Using basic self-protective skills	3. Traveling with supervision
4. Manipulating toys or other objects	4. Playing cooperatively with other residents	4. Completing assigned tasks
		5. Participating in work activity center programs

SOURCE: *Action Guidelines: Evaluating and Monitoring Education Services for Mentally Retarded Persons* (Arlington, Tex.: National Association for Retarded Citizens). Reprinted by permission.

tion. As the table shows, the emphasis is on training functional daily living skills. In addition, as Balthazar (1975) notes, severely and profoundly retarded people often exhibit undesirable behaviors, such as stereotypical acts (rocking, scratching, eyerubbing). The elimination of such behaviors should also be a major consideration in training procedures.

Appropriate Program Characteristics

Bates, Renzaglia, and Wehman (1981) maintain that there are twelve essential characteristics of an appropriate educational program for severely and profoundly handicapped individuals. They are:

1. Age-appropriate curriculum and materials
2. Specific objectives
3. Functional activities
4. Consistent cue hierarchy
5. Regular data collection
6. Periodic IEP (individualized education program) revision
7. Detailed classroom schedule

8. Instruction outside the classroom
9. Integrated therapy
10. Small-group instruction
11. Interaction with the nonhandicapped
12. Family involvement

AGE-APPROPRIATE CURRICULUM AND MATERIALS   In the past there was a tendency to "baby" even older severely and profoundly retarded persons because of their intellectual limitations. Authorities now agree that this is not only demeaning, but also educationally harmful. Using infantile materials works against the goal of fostering as much independent behavior as possible in severely and profoundly retarded students.

SPECIFIC OBJECTIVES   Although all special educators are aware of the value of specific teaching objectives, those who work with lower-functioning individuals are particularly appreciative of the need to specify as precisely as possible the objectives of instruction.

FUNCTIONAL ACTIVITIES   Activities need to be practical. Learning to dress oneself by practicing on a doll, for example, is not as effective as practice using one's own clothes.

CONSISTENT CUE HIERARCHY   A consistent cue hierarchy using cues or prompts (such as pointing) is necessary to help the person make correct discriminations. As Bates et al. (1981) state: "When instructing a child to 'pick up the cup,' a teacher may accompany the instructions with a gesture towards the cup. This gestural cue is an extra stimulus or prompt which facilitates the student's correct response" (p. 145).

REGULAR DATA COLLECTION   The more often the teacher evaluates a student's progress, the better able he or she will be to determine whether the teaching objectives are being met.

PERIODIC IEP REVISION   Because many severely and profoundly retarded individuals have quite variable learning rates, it is difficult to predict very far in advance how much they can be expected to achieve. Therefore Bates et al. recommend frequent revision of IEPs.

DETAILED CLASSROOM SCHEDULE   The teacher needs to maintain a consistent classroom schedule. This structure not only benefits the students, it also helps the teacher keep track of the myriad activities he or she needs to plan for each child.

INSTRUCTION OUTSIDE THE CLASSROOM   Because many of the skills being taught to severely and profoundly retarded students are for use in settings outside the classroom, such as public transportation or the grocery store, instruction in such activities has proved more effective when done in the natural setting (Snell, 1982). As Brown and his colleagues have stated:

> There are many severely handicapped students in this country who are being taught important skills, but only in artificial or simulated environments. Included are those adolescents who are being taught telephone skills using a telephone that functions only

between the classroom and hallway; those who are being taught to "ride" the cardboard bus in the school cafeteria; those who are being taught to tell time only on clocks made from paper plates; and those who are being taught to "grocery shop" for empty boxes in the classroom store.

One major assumption underlying such training, of course, is that if a student is being taught to perform a functional skill in a simulated environment (e.g., a public school), he/she then will be able to perform the same skill in a natural environment. Where severely handicapped students are concerned, however, one can have little confidence in such an inference (Stokes and Baer, 1977). Unfortunately, we cannot infer that because they perform important skills in simulated environments, they will perform the same skills in natural environments. (Brown, Branston, Hamre-Nietupski, Pumpian, Certo, and Gruenewald, 1979, p. 84)

INTEGRATED THERAPY   Many severely and profoundly retarded persons have multiple disabilities, necessitating the services of a variety of professionals, such as speech therapist, physical therapist, and occupational therapist. The student will benefit most when the goals of all these professionals are integrated so that each can contribute to the student's overall development.

SMALL-GROUP INSTRUCTION   Bates et al. (1981) note that in the past a great deal of the instruction of severely and profoundly retarded students took place on a one-to-one basis. Some group instruction, however, may contribute to the student's social development.

INTERACTION WITH NONHANDICAPPED INDIVIDUALS   Most authorities agree that it is beneficial for both severely and profoundly retarded individuals and the nonhandicapped population to interact in some way. One method some schools are trying involves having nonhandicapped students act as tutors or classroom helpers in classes for severely and profoundly handicapped students.

FAMILY INVOLVEMENT   Because many of the skills being taught to these students are for use in the home, Bates et al. (1981) recommend that families be involved in some way in the education of their children. The involvement can range from simply informing parents about the progress of their children to having them act as classroom aides.

Behavior Modification

Although behavior modification is used with virtually every type of handicapping condition, many authorities have noted its particular usefulness with severely and profoundly retarded individuals. It seems to have been successful where other methods have failed. And its emphasis on specific task analysis is particularly well suited to the problems of this population. Specific behavioral objectives are needed, for example, in order to teach a person to carry out instructional sequences in such tasks as using a fork, tying shoes, using a telephone, saying "Hello." Behavior modification has thus become one of the primary methods for instruction for most practitioners working with severely and profoundly retarded people.

A good example of a behaviorally based program that has gained wide acceptance and has helped to eliminate a persistent problem is Foxx and Azrin's (1973) program for toilet training the retarded. The Foxx and Azrin program, unlike traditional approaches, is based on the premise that bladder and bowel control is a complex social process. Typically, children learn to control themselves in order to avoid embarrassment. Foxx and Azrin's program emphasizes the socialization aspect of toileting by advocating the use of immediate praise for successful eliminations and immediate rebukes for accidents.

Other educational techniques for training severely and profoundly retarded individuals are being developed. These programs have progressed beyond basic self-help skills attainment to social abilities (recreation and group interaction skills), minimal work training (packaging, sorting), speech and language training, and the rudiments of academics. Bricker and Bricker have developed a number of behaviorally based approaches to teaching basic receptive and productive language skills to severely and profoundly retarded children (Bricker and Bricker, 1969, 1970, 1974). Brown and his colleagues have pioneered in teaching a number of basic skills to very low-functioning children (Brown, Williams, and Crowner, 1974). Using a highly structured approach and emphasizing the use of imitation, they have taught such things as visual discrimination, sight vocabulary, basic math skills, and speech articulation.

Administrative Arrangements

We have already mentioned most of the kinds of administrative placements for mentally retarded children. The most common types are regular classes, resource rooms, special classes, special day schools, and residential facilities. The degree of retardation will have a lot to do with which situation is most appropriate. Generally, this list is ordered from the least to the most severe. In other words, severely and profoundly retarded individuals are more likely than mildly retarded students to be placed in residential facilities, whereas mildly retarded children are more likely than severely retarded students to be found in resource rooms or regular classes.

As is true for the other areas of special education, resource room placement for retarded children is becoming more and more common. In this type of arrangement the child is kept for part of the day or week in the regular classroom and is seen by a resource teacher for the rest of the time. For the most part, the resource room has been used with children in the mildly retarded range. There are, however, those who have pointed out that mainstreaming of some mildly retarded students may be causing unanticipated problems for those who reside in special classes (see box, p. 84).

Because the academic program of the typical moderately retarded child is generally restricted, it is quite uncommon for children at that level or below to be placed in a resource room setting. If there is any integration for moderately retarded students, it is usually in nonacademic activities such as physical education, music, or art. Probably the most common placement for these youngsters is the special class. Sheltered workshops for older individuals are also common. At the preschool level moderately retarded children are sometimes provided with services in a special day school setting. Some moderately retarded children are also found in residential facilities. Residential placement for the moderately retarded child may be appropriate when other handicaps (such as deafness) are present and severe or when the family situation is undesirable.

The traditional placement for the severely and profoundly retarded individual has been the institution. With increased sophistication in dealing with the special problems of severely retarded individuals and the growing public commitment to their education, more and more of these children are being kept in the home, and large

The Changing Face of Mental Retardation

Professionals working with mentally retarded individuals have had to adjust to a number of population shifts since the early and mid-1970s. Because of definitional changes and the advent of deinstitutionalization and mainstreaming, the characteristics of mentally retarded students in certain placements have changed significantly. Perhaps the most dramatic changes have occurred in the institutional population and self-contained classes for mildly retarded students.

The residential institution population is now much more severely handicapped than was once the case. Many mentally retarded people have been moved back into the community in group homes or public school classes. In general, those who have been integrated into the community have tended to be higher functioning than those who have not. This shift in the characteristics of mentally retarded individuals in institutions has meant that professionals in those settings now need different skills than they did when more of the residents were classified as moderately and even mildly retarded.

Today's typical student enrolled in a class for the mildly retarded is different from the typical student who would have been placed in that class in the early or mid-1970s (Forness and Kavale, 1984; Polloway, 1985). Students in today's mildly retarded classes have greater learning and behavior problems than did their predecessors; they are what MacMillan and Borthwick (1980) have termed "a more patently disabled group" (p. 155). There are at least two reasons for the change in the characteristics of students identified as mildly retarded. First, the definition of mental retardation has changed from including those with IQs below 85 to including those with IQs below 70 who also have deficits in adaptive behavior. Thus, children in classes for the mildly retarded now have IQs between 50 and 70, whereas previously they could, and often did, have IQs between 70 and 85. Second, there is an emphasis on placing as many mildly retarded students as possible in general education classrooms. Because those who are mainstreamed tend to be higher functioning, those who remain in self-contained classes tend to be the lower functioning of those identified as mildly retarded.

Virtually all professionals agree with the changes in the definition of mental retardation and the concept of mainstreaming. Some authorities, however, are concerned that the needs of mildly retarded students in self-contained classes are being neglected. As Forness and Kavale (1984) state:

> Preoccupation with the 30 percent or more of mentally retarded children who are mainstreamed may have caused us to neglect somewhat the large majority of mentally retarded children who may not be able to be mainstreamed. This may have, unfortunately, caused us to limit our efforts to improve special class instruction for such children. As a profession, then, we may not be planning as realistically as we might for those mentally retarded who remain in special classrooms. As MacMillan has shown, those children remaining in EMR classes are a relatively impaired group of youngsters compared to those on whom our previous research on educable mentally retarded was carried out (MacMillan & Borthwick, 1980; MacMillan, Meyers, & Morrison, 1980). The legacy of heroic biomedical efforts (Sells & Bennett, 1977) may be that countless numbers of mentally retarded children now survive into the school years, possibly a more multihandicapped group than those who formerly made up the population of our special classes or special schools. A recent survey of referrals to interdisciplinary hospitals and clinics of over 3400 developmentally disabled school children reveals over 60 percent with two or more handicapping conditions (Forness, et al., 1983). Mildly mentally retarded children, in particular, may now be a group of pupils for whom our previous developmental and instructional assumptions no longer apply, as they once did. The point has been made that special class EMR children may need a much broader range of instructional interventions than was the case even *prior* to mainstreaming (Polloway & Smith, 1983).

SOURCE: S. R. Forness and K. A. Kavale, "Education of the Mentally Retarded: A Note on Policy," *Education and Training of the Mentally Retarded, 19* (1984), p. 241.

institutions are being depopulated. Although virtually all educators agree that severely and profoundly retarded individuals should be integrated as much as possible into the mainstream of special education, there is considerable debate over the degree of integration that is possible. Burton and Hirshoren (1979), for example, advocate nonresidential community centers because they have

> the benefits of homogeneous grouping, flexibility in scheduling, the concentration of ancillary services, efficiency in the maintenance of a barrier free educational environment, and programming in an accepting environment for a population of children and adults who are handicapped. (p. 602)

Sontag, Certo, and Button (1979), on the other hand, argue that community centers, like traditional institutions, do not allow enough interaction with nonhandicapped peers.

One of the biggest difficulties with debates like this one is that for the individual case, they are relatively meaningless. The most appropriate placement for a particular child depends on a variety of factors. Although integration into the mainstream should always be the ultimate goal, the appropriate placement for a particular child may, in reality, be a community center or perhaps even an institution. The stress on a family that keeps and cares for a severely disabled child is tremendous. Parents should not be forced to feel that the only morally right thing to do is to care for the individual at home.

The Community Residential Facility or Group Home

One administrative arrangement growing in popularity is the **community residential facility (CRF)** or group home. With the movement toward depopulation of large residential institutions, many formerly institutionalized individuals are now placed in small groups (three to ten people) in houses under the direction of house parents (Bruininks, Hauber, and Kudla, 1980). The level of retardation of individuals in these homes ranges from mild to severe. Group homes have been established to accommodate children, adolescents, and adults, with each home focused on a specific age range. Placement in a CRF can be permanent or, with higher-functioning individuals, a temporary living arrangement in order to prepare the person for independent living (Sitkei, 1980). In either case, the purpose of the CRF is to teach independent living skills in a more normal setting. For many parents of retarded individuals, the CRF provides a positive and less stigmatized alternative to institutional placement.

The Activity Center

Another type of arrangement that is becoming more popular is the activity center. Primarily for severely and profoundly retarded individuals, the activity center is a place where parents can take their children for a portion of the day. Activities are usually related to recreation and crafts. The emphasis of the program in such facilities is to provide socialization experiences rather than formal training. They are designed for individuals functioning at a level so low that they would not be able to profit from a sheltered workshop setting. An activity center, however, can be a steppingstone to placement in a sheltered workshop.

SPECIAL CONSIDERATIONS IN EDUCATING THE PRESCHOOL CHILD

The 1960s witnessed the birth of infant and preschool programs for at-risk children and their families. Since the late 1970s, when many of the young children placed in these programs were reaching their teenage years, we have been able to assess the effects of these programs. Investigators from twelve such projects decided to pool their data in 1976 when their original children ranged in age from 9 to 19 years (Lazar and Darlington, 1982). This collaborative effort demonstrated that those who had attended one of the early childhood programs were significantly less likely to have been retained in grade or to have been assigned to a special education class.

In 1984 a further follow-up study was done of one of the twelve projects, the Perry Preschool Project (Berrueta-Clement, Schweinhart, Barnett, Epstein, and Weikart, 1984). Begun in the early 1960s, the Perry Preschool Project was designed to answer the question, "Can high-quality early childhood education help improve the lives of low-income children and their families and the quality of life of the community as a whole?" A sample of 123 3- and 4-year-old black children, from impoverished backgrounds and having IQs between 60 and 90, were randomly assigned to an experimental group that received two years of a cognitively oriented curriculum or to a control group that received no preschool program. When studied again at 19 years of age, a number of differences favored those who had received the preschool program over those who had not:

- They scored significantly higher on a test designed to measure skills needed for educational and economic success.
- They were more likely to complete high school and almost twice as likely to attend college or receive other postsecondary training (38 versus 21 percent).
- They were less likely to have been classified as handicapped, especially mentally retarded (15 versus 35 percent).
- They were more likely to be employed (50 versus 32 percent).
- They had a median annual income three times higher.
- They were more likely to report high levels of job satisfaction (42 versus 26 percent).
- They had a lower teenage pregnancy rate.
- They were less likely to be receiving welfare (19 versus 32 percent).

One of the best-known infant stimulation programs among those started more recently is the Abecedarian Project (Ramey and Campbell, 1984). Potential participants were identified before birth by selecting a pool of pregnant women living in poverty. For example, the typical child in this study came from a home headed by a single 20-year-old black woman who had less than a high school education and no earned income. After birth, half of the identified infants were randomly assigned to a day-care program and half were not. The program provided them with experiences to promote perceptual-motor, intellectual, language, and social development. The families were also given a number of social and medical services. Results reported through second grade of the Abecedarian Project indicate that preschool educational programming can improve the IQ and achievement test scores of children at-risk for eventually being identified as mildly retarded.

SPECIAL CONSIDERATIONS IN EDUCATING THE ADOLESCENT AND ADULT

For many years there was relatively little programming for mentally retarded adults. Beginning in the late 1970s, however, there has been a significant change in philosophy. The increased emphasis on integrating retarded individuals, even those classified as severely and profoundly retarded, into the community has resulted in much more attention to the needs of mentally retarded adults.

In the mid-1980s, the U.S. Department of Education made transition programming a priority (Rusch and Phelps, 1987). **Transition programming** is the educational process of preparing students to move from high school to the workforce. Transition programs are of three basic types: (1) those with no special services, (2) those with time-limited services, and (3) those with ongoing services (U.S. Department of Education, 1986). These three options are roughly related to severity of retardation, with more severely retarded individuals requiring more intensive services. Some retarded individuals, usually those classified as mildly retarded, are able to find and hold jobs with no special services. Those classified as more severely retarded usually need at least short-term services, if not ongoing support services. Regardless of which type of service is required, authorities have noted that the delivery of good-quality transition programming requires complex coordination of a variety of agencies and services.

In developing transition programs for mentally retarded individuals, professionals are preparing those individuals to enter the world of work. Two very different kinds of employment arrangements are usually available—the sheltered workshop or the nonsheltered work environment, or competitive employment.

Sheltered Workshops

The traditional job training environment for mentally retarded adults, especially those classified as moderately or more severely retarded, has been the sheltered workshop.

A **sheltered workshop** is:

> a structured environment which enables retarded people to learn necessary work habits, receive training in particular skills, and eventually gain salaried employment either within

Professionals and students alike recognize the importance of transition programming—preparing handicapped students to move from high school to the workforce. (Mimi Forsyth/Monkmeyer Press)

the workshop itself or through placement in the community. Of course, each sheltered workshop is unique to the characteristics of the people served, the local community, and the administration and workers. (Mercer and Payne, 1975, p. 121)

Gold (1973) notes that there are basically three different kinds of sheltered workshops, the transitional shop, the extended care or terminal shop, and the comprehensive shop. The *transitional* shop is a temporary placement for the individual in which he or she learns skills before entering the competitive job market. The *extended care* shop is usually a final placement for the retarded person who is viewed as incapable of ever achieving enough independence and skill to enter the competitive job market. The *comprehensive* shop, the most common kind, deals with both types of clients.

A good workshop should provide opportunities for people to learn a variety of new skills. Since the moderately retarded population is heterogeneous with regard to kinds and levels of abilities, the ideal workshop should provide a wide spectrum of jobs. Gold believes that one of the major flaws in many sheltered workshop programs is that they offer only limited job experiences. He lists the following five characteristics of the ideal workshop:

> (1) It requires skills that must be taught rather than skills which the clients already have. This includes some skills learned and transferred from other contracts. (2) There must be sufficient lead time to set up production and training to allow for client considerations and not just production considerations. (3) The contract should be heavy on labor. That is, the amount of shop space taken up by the contract should be in proportion to the number of clients employed on the job. If a contract takes up 40% of the shop floor, it should provide full-time work for at least 40% of the clients. This emphasis is the opposite for industry, where labor is kept at a minimum. (4) The contract should have enough different operations to allow for a variety of job stations. A simple contract has only simple operations. A complex contract has the potential for a range of different operations. (5) The contract should be profitable for both the shop and the clients. (1973, p. 104)

Regarding the last point, it should be noted that sheltered workshops are rarely self-sufficient (Beirne-Smith et al., 1986). Since the major purpose is training rather than profits, funding by federal, state, and local governments and/or private sources is almost always necessary.

Nonsheltered Work Environments

Since the early 1980s, some authorities have recommended the use of nonsheltered work environments, or competitive employment, rather than sheltered workshops (Brown et al. 1986; Rusch, Martin, and White, 1985; Stodden and Browder, 1986; Wehman et al., 1985). Professionals have proposed two definitions of **nonsheltered work environments.** Brown et al. (1986) define these settings as "those in which almost all workers are nonhandicapped" (p. 133). Wehman et al. (1985) define them as situations in which the person is "working for at least the federal minimum wage . . . with no subsidized wages of any kind" (p. 275).

Brown et al. (1986) present the following rationale for the use of nonsheltered instead of sheltered work environments:

> In sum, severely handicapped adults who work in nonsheltered environments have a greater probability of experiencing a more enhanced quality of life than [those who are] in sheltered environments in that there are experiences that can be realized in nonsheltered environments that cannot be realized in sheltered environments. Some of these include:

- Interactions with nondisabled persons;
- The rich array of sounds and sights offered in the real world;
- Friendships with nondisabled persons that extend beyond the work time and space;
- Feelings of self-worth when a severely disabled person understands that his work is valuable and that if he did not do it, nondisabled persons would have to;
- The respect offered by parents/guardians and nondisabled coworkers when one makes a contribution in a nonsheltered environment;
- The sense of accomplishment associated with being allowed to take calculated risks and overcome initial obstacles and failures; and
- The pride that comes from being in a position to help nondisabled persons. (pp. 173–174)

Although research on the effectiveness of nonsheltered settings does not have a long history, results thus far are encouraging. Retarded workers have been able to hold down jobs with a good deal of success, as measured by such things as attendance, employer satisfaction, and length of employment (Brown et al., 1986; Martin, Rusch, Tines, Brulle, and White, 1985; Stodden and Browder, 1986; Rusch, Martin, and White, 1985; Wehman et al., 1985). In general, these studies involved workers with IQ scores ranging from mild to severe levels, although the majority fell within the moderate classification.

When retarded adults within both the mild and moderate ranges do fail on the job, the evidence is overwhelmingly consistent in pointing to personality or social adaptation factors as the cause. Rather than competence, such things as work habits and interpersonal interaction patterns with other employees are more likely to be at the root of job failure (Cunningham and Presnall, 1978; Domino and McGarty, 1972; Edgerton, 1967; Gold, 1973; Malgady, Barcher, Tonner, and Davis, 1979; McCarver and Craig, 1974; Schalock and Harper, 1978; Schalock and Lilley, 1986). Research has shown, however, that it is not enough to train the retarded individual in daily living skills and social skills that are not work related and hope that these skills will automatically help the person hold a job successfully (Reiter and Levi, 1980). There is often little overlap between the skills the retarded individual needs to live successfully in the neighborhood and the skills needed to function successfully on the job. The retarded person should be trained both to achieve appropriate work habits and to interact in a socially acceptable manner with other employees and with an employer. That such interpersonal skills can be taught has been demonstrated by LaGreca, Stone, and Bell (1983). They provided groups of three to five mildly and moderately retarded persons with training in twelve one-hour sessions over four weeks. Trainers worked with participants on difficult work-related hypothetical interpersonal situations involving supervisors as well as co-workers. An example of a potential problem situation with a supervisor was this:

> You need to get a drink of water (or use the toilet). You walk up to your supervisor to tell him/her and see that he/she's working at the desk. *Inappropriate:* leave work area without permission; talk to co-workers until supervisor notices. *Appropriate:* politely ask permission. (La Greca et al., 1983, p. 272)

An example of a potential problem situation with a co-worker was this:

> You are working in the morning and the person next to you is being very loud, talking and laughing. You are finding it hard to concentrate on your work because of the noise. *Inappropriate:* yell at co-worker to "shut up"; throw something at co-worker; insult co-worker; threaten co-worker. *Appropriate:* politely request quiet behavior; ignore co-worker. (La Greca et al., 1983, p. 272)

The training consisted of (1) the trainers describing the hypothetical situation and then modeling the inappropriate responses, (2) the group discussing why the responses were inappropriate and trying to come up with alternatives, (3) the trainers modeling the appropriate responses, (4) each participant role-playing the appropriate response with a trainer, (5) participants role-playing the appropriate responses with each other, after which (6) the trainers and other participants provided feedback on their performance. After training, the participants worked in a sheltered workshop setting on tasks that included assembling screens, loading and unloading boxes, and assembling paper kites. For six weeks there were weekly meetings in which participants could present actual problem situations for discussion and role-playing. The regimen, although time-consuming, proved highly beneficial. Compared with a group that did not receive such training, the trained group was rated as having better interpersonal skills and social competence as well as fewer behavior problems in the work setting. In addition, they were employed for a longer period of time.

Community Survival Skills

In order for mentally retarded persons to adjust to living in the community, they need to acquire a number of skills, many of which are in the area of self-help. Schalock and colleagues (Schalock and Harper, 1978; Schalock, Harper, and Carver, 1981; Schalock and Lilley, 1986), for example, found that successful living in the community was dependent on such things as ability to manage money, prepare meals, maintain a clean house, and keep one's clothing and oneself groomed. In addition, research has found that the degree of family involvement is important for the work and living adjustment of retarded individuals (Schalock and Lilley, 1986). Successful community placement is easier when the retarded person's family becomes actively involved in the integration process. In a review of the research Martin, Rusch, and Heal (1982) concluded that attempts to train community survival skills have been encouraging, especially when the training occurred within the actual setting in which the individuals were to live.

Even though the research can help us to predict which skills should be fostered in retarded individuals so that they will have the best possible chance of adjusting to the community, it is important to keep in mind that a particular person's adjustment is not always easy to predict. Edgerton and Bercovici's examples point this out:

Other predictions were wildly wrong. For example, a man (Hal, No. 2a, aged 49, IQ 82) was a relatively competent member of the cohort, but his incendiary temper and the wretched conditions under which he worked seemed to suggest that the future would bring marked changes. In 1960–61, he was married to another cohort member with whom he regularly fought, often physically. His job required 50 to 60 hours per week of dreary labor in a foundry in return for a small wage. Given that this man was originally institutionalized for alleged rape and murder, it seemed likely that he would "explode" in the same way at some point in the future. In fact, however, he was found in 1972–1973 in exactly the same job, for the same pay, without having fallen into any serious trouble. The only change was divorce which was amicably carried out. Another surprise was provided by a woman (Bertha, No. 22b, aged 38, IQ 57) who was greatly dependent upon her cohort member husband, 11 years her senior and 27 IQ points her superior. Both worked in a restaurant, but he was the dominant partner who apparently gave their life stability and success. Without him she would assuredly be unable to cope, or so it was predicted. In 1967, he suffered a fatal heart attack. Since that time, she had been entirely self-supporting in other jobs (currently as a maid), had a rewarding leisure life, was considering remarriage, and seemed much more competent and independent than she was in 1960–1961. (1976, pp. 488–489)

MANAGING THE CHILD IN SCHOOL

With the trend toward mainstreaming mildly retarded pupils into the regular classroom, it is imperative that teachers know the proper techniques for working with them. Although each child has individual learning problems, a few general suggestions can be made:

1. The teacher should constantly attempt to sequence learning tasks for the retarded child. Relatively complex activities, if taken one step at a time, can be taught to most retarded children.
2. Many retarded children learn facts best by drill and repetition. Repeated exposure to the same material often makes the difference between success and failure.
3. Verbal mediation should be encouraged in the student. This strategy helps in concept learning and problem solving. Having the child verbally rehearse what he or she is to learn has also been shown to be an effective way of helping retarded students to remember. Much of the research we have reviewed in this chapter indicates that retarded children lack appropriate learning strategies as much as or more than they lack the ability to learn itself.
4. Since there is some research suggesting that many retarded individuals lack motivation, the teacher should look for ways in which to increase motivation. Novelty is one such method. The retarded child, however, needs a sense of structure and familiarity; too much novelty can be confusing.
5. Many mildly retarded children come from an environment in which little reinforcement has been or will be given to school-related behaviors. Therefore a program of consistent reinforcement applied to the development of skills associated with "learning to learn" is necessary. For example, the idea of numerical grades as a reinforcer needs to be structured to be rewarding. Task completion and independent work habits need to be developed.
6. The child's level of functioning should be continually assessed. This assessment may be formal or informal, but the teacher should keep some record of progress, because it is likely to be erratic—up one day, down the next.
7. Continual and immediate feedback should be provided for all learning activities in order to help the child learn basic discriminations among responses.

SUMMARY

Professionals are generally more cautious about identifying students as retarded than they once were. Current definitions of mental retardation reflect a concern for the consequences of mislabeling. Doll's definition, which was accepted for many years, assumed that retardation was a permanent, incurable condition. Today we know that, with appropriate educational programming, this need not be the case, especially for those classified as mildly retarded. Doll's definition also assumed that people who are subnormal in intelligence are also socially incompetent. Today we know that individuals can learn and use adaptive behaviors that enable them to function well in society, even though they may have low intelligence as measured by an IQ test. The AAMD definition of mental retardation—the definition accepted by most professionals—posits that *both* intellectual functioning and adaptive ability are important; indeed, if adequate adaptive behavior exists, a person is not considered retarded.

The most commonly accepted approach to classification is to consider retarded people along a continuum of degree of severity. Most professionals favor using the AAMD classification system, which uses the terms "mild," "moderate," "severe," and "profound." These words help minimize negative stereotyping. Some educators also use the classifications "educable mentally retarded," "trainable mentally retarded," and "severely and profoundly handicapped."

From a purely statistical-theoretical viewpoint, 2.27 percent of the population should score low enough on an IQ test (below about 70) to qualify as retarded. Most recent figures indicate, however, that only 1.68 percent of the school-age population is identified as retarded. Authorities point to three possible reasons for this discrepancy. First, low adaptive behavior as well as low tested IQ is needed to consider an individual retarded. Second, school personnel tend to be cautious about mislabeling minority children. Third, parents and school officials may prefer to have children labeled "learning disabled" rather than "mentally retarded" because they perceive it as a less stigmatizing label.

Mental retardation can be caused by a variety of factors, but in very few cases can we actually specify the cause for a specific individual. And the less severe the retardation, the more difficult it is to identify causes. Most mildly retarded persons are considered culturally-familially retarded, a kind of catchall category of unknown causes possibly relating to poor environmental and/or hereditary factors. In the case of persons identified as moderately to severely retarded, causes are more easily determined. We can categorize these causes as due to genetic factors or to brain damage. Down syndrome, PKU, and Tay-Sachs disease are all examples of retardation due to genetic factors. Down syndrome is due to chromosomal abnormalities and is linked to the age of the mother and possibly other factors, such as the age of the father. PKU and Tay-Sachs are due to hereditary factors. Brain damage can be the result of infectious diseases—for example, meningitis, encephali-

tis, and rubella—or environmental hazards and accidents. Much attention is being paid to alcohol and drugs as environmental hazards. Research indicates that alcohol consumed by expectant mothers, perhaps even in moderate quantities, may cause central nervous system damage to the fetus. And research has shown that certain drugs should be avoided during pregnancy.

Using amniocentesis, chorionic villus sampling, or sonography, physicians are now able to detect a variety of defects in the unborn fetus. Although these methods do not guarantee a perfect baby, they are often recommended for women who are at risk—for example, older women because they have a greater likelihood of giving birth to a Down syndrome child or couples who because of their ethnic backgrounds may have a child with severe defects.

The debate about whether intelligence is determined primarily by the environment or by genetic makeup continues. Most authorities believe there is an interaction between the two, with heredity being at least as important as environment.

Although there are now tests that purportedly minimize cultural bias—for example, the SOMPA and the K-ABC—The Wechsler Intelligence Scale for Children—Revised (WISC—R) and the Stanford-Binet continue to be two of the most commonly used intelligence tests. Although they are considered reliable and valid, it is important to remember these points: (1) An individual's test score can change; (2) IQ tests, being heavily verbal in nature, are culturally biased to a certain extent; (3) although it is possible to test infants, the younger the child, the less reliable the results; and (4) IQ should not be considered the only basis for judging a person's ability to live a successful and fulfilling life.

Several adaptive behavior scales are available. Two commonly used ones are the Adaptive Behavior Inventory for Children (ABIC) of the SOMPA and the AAMD Adaptive Behavior Scale—School Edition. Probably because of the vaguer definitions of adaptive behavior, these assessments are generally less reliable and valid than those of intelligence tests.

Of all the behavioral and psychological characteristics of retarded individuals, the most obvious is reduced ability to learn. They are likely to have difficulties in at least four areas of cognition: attention, memory, language, and academics. Two important concepts when considering the cognitive problems of retarded students are *depth of processing* and *executive control* or *metacognitive processes.* Depth of processing refers to how much cognitive activity a person has to undergo in order to perform a task; it is related to the perceptual features of the information to be processed by the person. For example, perceptual features require shallower levels of processing than semantic features. In general, the deeper the level of processing a task requires, the more likely it is that retarded students will do poorly on it. Executive control or metacognitive processes are also found to be deficient in many retarded individuals. They refer to ability in (1) planning how to solve problems, (2) monitoring the execution of problem-solving strategies, and (3) evaluating the results of the implementation of strategies.

In addition to cognitive problems, mentally retarded students often have behavioral and personality problems. They sometimes exhibit disruptive and inattentive behavior. And they are at risk to develop low self-esteem and an external locus of control—a perception that they do not have control over their own lives.

For mildly retarded students in preschool and early elementary school, the emphasis is on readiness skills such as following directions and developing language and self-help skills. Learning socially adaptive behaviors is also important for children at this age. On the intermediate level, there is increased emphasis on academics, frequently *functional* academics—that is, those taught for the purpose of enabling the person to function independently. At the secondary level there is strong emphasis on academic skills, social and occupational skills, and transition skills. The latter refer to social and vocational skills students specifically need once they leave school and enter the workforce. One of the most popular service delivery models at the secondary level is the work-study program.

For moderately retarded individuals, the educational program is generally less academically oriented, and the academics taught are even more likely to be functional. Unlike programming for mildly retarded students, in which the goal is to prevent the development of retardation in children judged to be "at risk," programming for moderately retarded preschoolers aims to get them to develop to the highest possible level. Self-help and vocational skills are emphasized at the elementary and secondary levels.

PL 94-142 has brought about a change in attitude regarding the education of severely and profoundly retarded persons. More and more, they are being educated in public school settings. For the most part, these individuals need to be provided with basic survival and self-help skills. Behavior modification has been especially useful in the training of these skills.

Depending to a large extent on the degree of severity of retardation, individuals may be placed in general education classrooms, resource rooms, special classes, special day schools, or residential facilities. The first two are generally recommend for mildly retarded children; moderately retarded youngsters are most often placed in special classes. Severely and profoundly retarded individuals are now enjoying more latitude in terms of possible placement, with many now being taught in special classes rather than in institutions. As large residential facilities wane in popularity, they are being replaced by community residential facilities or group homes.

Preschool programming differs in its goals according to the intellectual impairment evidenced by the children enrolled. For moderately, severely, and profoundly retarded children, the emphasis is on developing their skills as far as possible, especially self-help skills and language. Because of the reluctance to mislabel children, there are usually no programs called "mildly retarded preschool classes." Many programs for children who are considered "at risk" to be placed in classes for the retarded once they enter elementary school, however, were started in the 1960s and 1970s. Two notable examples are the Perry Preschool Project and the Abecedarian Project. Their benefits are now being documented in follow-up studies of their graduates.

Programming for retarded adolescents and adults has received a great deal of emphasis. In the mid-1980s it became a priority of the federal government. Transition programming, preparing students to hold jobs when they leave school, is of three different types. It can be done with (1) no special services, (2) time-limited services, or (3) ongoing services. In general, the greater the degree of severity of retardation, the more likely the second or third option will be used. Two basic types of work settings are used in training students in job skills—sheltered workshops and nonsheltered work environments. Sheltered workshops are places where individuals can learn job skills under close supervision. Since the early 1980s, some professionals have begun to place mildly, moderately, and even severely retarded individuals in nonsheltered settings. Nonsheltered settings, sometimes referred to as competitive employment, allow the retarded person to work alongside nondisabled co-workers and, in some cases, earn at least the minimum wage. Thus far, research on the success of nonsheltered placements has been encouraging.

One index of how well retarded adults have woven themselves into the fabric of society is occupational adjustment. It is generally accepted that, with proper education, many retarded people can hold jobs. When occupational failures do occur, they can usually be traced to personality and/or social factors rather than incompetence. In addition to holding a job, the retarded person also needs to acquire a number of community survival skills. Research has demonstrated that many retarded persons can be trained to do such things as manage money, prepare meals, maintain a clean house, and keep themselves and their clothes neat. This research also indicates that they more easily attain these skills if they receive their training in the actual setting in which they will use them.

REFERENCES

Balla, D., & Zigler, E. (1979). Personality development in retarded persons. In N. R. Ellis (Ed.), *Handbook of mental deficiency: Psychological theory and research* (2nd ed.). Hillsdale, N.J.: Lawrence Erlbaum Associates.

Balthazar, E. E. (1975). *General programs for the mentally retarded.* Monograph No. 3 of Programs for the Developmentally Disabled: A Multidisciplinary Approach. State of Wisconsin Department of Health and Social Services.

Bates, P., Renzaglia, A., & Wehman, P. (1981). Characteristics of an appropriate education for severely and profoundly handicapped students. *Education and Training of the Mentally Retarded, 16,* 142–149.

Batshaw, M. L., & Perret, Y. M. (1986). *Children with handicaps: A medical primer* (2nd ed.). Baltimore: Paul Brookes Publishing Co.

Beirne-Smith, M., Coleman, L. J., & Payne, J. S. (1986). Career and vocational planning. In J. R. Patton, J. S. Payne, & M. Beirne-Smith, *Mental retardation* (2nd ed.) (pp. 384–407). Columbus, Ohio: Charles E. Merrill.

Belmont, J. M. (1971). Medical-behavioral research in retardation. In N. R. Ellis (Ed.), *International review of research in mental retardation,* Vol. 5. New York: Academic Press.

Berrueta-Clement, J. R., Schweinhart, L. J., Barnett, W. S., Epstein, A. S., & Weikart, D. P. (1984). *Changed lives: The effects of the Perry Preschool Program on youths through age 19.* (Monograph of the High/Scope Educational Research Foundation No. 8.) Ypsilanti, Mich.: The High/Scope Press.

Bijou, S. W. (1966). A functional analysis of retarded development. In N. R. Ellis (Ed.), *International review of research in mental retardation,* Vol. 1. New York: Academic Press.

Blackman, J. A. (1984a). Down syndrome. In J. A. Blackman (Ed.), *Medical aspects of developmental disabilities in children birth to three.* Revised first edition (pp. 92–95). Rockville, Md.: Aspen Systems Corp.

Blackman, J. A. (1984b). Low birth weight. In J. A. Blackman (Ed.), *Medical aspects of developmental disabilities in children birth to three.* Revised first edition (pp. 143–146). Rockville, Md.: Aspen Systems Corp.

Borkowski, J. G., & Cavanaugh, J. C. (1979). Maintenance and generalization of skills and strategies by the retarded. In N. R. Ellis (ed.), *Handbook of mental deficiency: Psychological theory and research* (2nd ed.). Hillsdale, N.J.: Lawrence Erlbaum Associates.

Borkowski, J. G., Peck, V. A., & Damberg, P. R. (1983). Attention, memory, and cognition. In J. L. Matson & J. A. Mulich (Eds.), *Handbook of mental retardation* (pp. 479–497). New York: Pergamon Press.

Borkowski, J. G., & Wanschura, P. B. (1974). Mediational processes in the retarded. In N. R. Ellis (Ed.), *International review of research in mental retardation,* Vol. 7. New York: Academic Press.

Bouchard, T. J., & McGue, M. (1981). Familial studies of intelligence: A review. *Science, 212,* 1055–1059.

Bray, N. W. (1979). Strategy production in the retarded. In N. R. Ellis (Ed.), *Handbook of mental deficiency: Psychological theory and research* (2nd ed.). Hillsdale, N.J.: Lawrence Erlbaum Associates.

Bricker, W. A., & Bricker, D. D. (1969). Four operant procedures for establishing auditory control with low-functioning children. *American Journal of Mental Deficiency, 73,* 981–987.

Bricker, W. A., & Bricker, D. D. (1970). A program of language training for the severely language handicapped child. *Exceptional Children, 37,* 101–111.

Bricker, W. A., & Bricker, D. D. (1974). An early language

training strategy. In R. Schiefelbusch & L. Loyd (Eds.), *Language perspectives—acquisitions, retardation, and intervention.* Baltimore: University Park Press.

Brolin, D. E. (1982). *Vocational preparation of persons with handicaps* (2nd ed.). Columbus, Ohio: Charles E. Merrill.

Brooks, P. H., & McCauley, C. (1984). Cognitive research in mental retardation. *American Journal of Mental Deficiency, 88,* 479–486.

Brown, A. L. (1974). The role of strategic behavior in retardate memory. In N. R. Ellis (Ed.), *International review of research in mental retardation,* Vol. 7. New York: Academic Press.

Brown, F. (1979). The SOMPA: A system of measuring potential abilities. *The School Psychology Digest, 8,* 37–46.

Brown, L., Branston, M. B., Hamre-Nietupski, S., Pumpian, I., Certo, N., & Gruenewald, L. (1979). A strategy for developing chronological-age-appropriate and functional curricular content for severely handicapped adolescents and young adults. *Journal of Special Education, 13,* 81–90.

Brown, L., Shiraga, B., Ford, A., Nisbet, J., Van Deventer, P., Sweet, M., York, J., & Loomis, R. (1986). Teaching severely handicapped students to perform meaningful work in nonsheltered vocational environments. In R. J. Morris & B. Blatt (Eds.), *Special education: Research and trends* (pp. 131–189). New York: Pergamon.

Brown, L., Williams, W., & Crowner, T. (1974). *A collection of papers and programs related to public school services for severely handicapped students.* Madison, Wisc.: Madison Public Schools, Department of Vocational Education.

Bruininks, R., Hauber, F. A., & Kudla, M. J. (1980). National survey of community residential facilities: A profile of facilities and residents in 1977. *American Journal of Mental Deficiency, 84,* 470–478.

Burton, T. A., & Hirshoren, A. (1979). The education of severely and profoundly retarded children: Are we sacrificing the child to the concept? *Exceptional Children, 45,* 598–603.

Chitwood, M. (1986). What's past is prologue. *Helix, 4*(2), 4–7.

Craik, F. I. M., & Lockhart, R. S. (1972). Levels of processing: A framework for memory research. *Journal of Verbal Learning and Verbal Behavior, 11,* 671–684.

Craik, F. I. M., & Tulving, E. (1975). Depth of processing and the retention of words in episodic memory. *Journal of Experimental Psychology: General, 104,* 268–294.

Cravioto, J., & DeLicardie, E. R. (1975). Environmental and nutritional deprivation in children with learning disabilities. In W. M. Cruickshank & D. P. Hallahan (Eds.), *Perceptual and learning disabilities in children.* Vol. 2: *Research and theory.* Syracuse, N.Y.: Syracuse University Press.

Cunningham, T., & Presnall, D. (1978). Relationship between dimensions of adaptive behavior and sheltered workshop productivity. *American Journal of Mental Deficiency, 82,* 386–393.

Das, J. P. (1984). Simultaneous and successive processes and K-ABC. *The Journal of Special Education, 18,* 229–238.

Delaney, S., & Hayden, A. (1977). Fetal alcohol syndrome: A review. *American Association for the Education of the Severely and Profoundly Handicapped, 2,* 164–168.

Doll, E. A. (1941). The essentials of an inclusive concept of mental deficiency. *American Journal of Mental Deficiency, 46,* 214–219.

Domino, G., & McGarty, M. (1972). Personal and work adjustment of young retarded women. *American Journal of Mental Deficiency, 77,* 314–321.

Dunn, L. M. (1973). Children with mild general learning disabilities. In L. M. Dunn (Ed.), *Exceptional children in the schools* (2nd ed.). New York: Holt, Rinehart and Winston.

Edgerton, R. B. (1967). *The cloak of competence: Stigma in the lives of the mentally retarded.* Berkeley: University of California Press.

Edgerton, R. B., & Bercovici, S. M. (1976). The cloak of competence: Years later. *American Journal of Mental Deficiency, 80,* 485–497.

Ellis, N. R. (1982). A behavioral research strategy in mental retardation: Defense and critique. In E. Zigler & D. Balla (Eds.), *Mental retardation: The developmental-difference controversy* (pp. 189–202). Hillsdale, N.J.: Lawrence Erlbaum Associates.

Estes, W. K. (1970). *Learning theory and mental development.* New York: Academic Press.

Forness, S. R., & Kavale, K. A. (1984). Education of the mentally retarded: A note on policy. *Education and Training of the Mentally Retarded, 19,* 239–245.

Foxx, R. M., & Azrin, N. H. (1973). *Toilet training the retarded: A rapid program for day and nighttime independent toileting.* Champaign, Ill.: Research Press.

Glidden, L. M. (1985). Semantic processing, semantic memory, and recall. In N. R. Ellis (Ed.), *International review of research in mental retardation,* Vol. 13. (pp. 247–278). New York: Academic Press.

Goetz, E. T., & Hall, R. J. (1984). Evaluation of the K-ABC Battery for Children from an information processing perspective. *The Journal of Special Education, 18,* 281–296.

Gold, M. W. (1973). Research on the vocational habilitation of the retarded: The present, the future. In N. R. Ellis (Ed.), *International review of research in mental retardation,* Vol. 6. New York: Academic Press.

Goldstein, H. (1974). *Social learning curriculum: Teacher's guide.* Columbus, Ohio: Charles E. Merrill.

Goldstein, H. (1975). Importance of social learning. In J. M. Kauffman & J. S. Payne (Eds.), *Mental retardation: Introduction and personal perspectives.* Columbus, Ohio: Charles E. Merrill.

Goodman, J. F. (1979). Is tissue the issue? A critique of SOMPA's models and tests. *The School Psychology Digest, 8,* 47–62.

Grossman, H. J. (Ed.). (1983). *Classification in mental retardation.* Washington, D.C.: American Association on Mental Deficiency.

Guthrie, R. (1984). Explorations in prevention. In B. Blatt & R. Morris (Eds.), *Perspectives in special education: Personal orientations* (pp. 157–172). Glenview, Ill.: Scott Foresman.

Hallahan, D. P., & Cruickshank, W. M. (1973). *Psychoeducational foundations of learning disabilities.* Englewood Cliffs, N.J.: Prentice-Hall.

Hansen, H. (1978). Decline of Down's Syndrome after abortion reform in New York State. *American Journal of Mental Deficiency, 83,* 185–188.

Harter, S., & Zigler, E. (1974). The assessment of effective motivation in normal and retarded children. *Developmental Psychology, 10,* 169–180.

Hawkes, N. (1979). Tracing Burt's descent to scientific fraud. *Science, 205,* 673–675.

Hearnshaw, L. S. (1979). *Cyril Burt, psychologist.* Ithaca: Cornell University Press.

Heber, R. F. (1959). A manual on terminology and classification in mental retardation. *American Journal of Mental Deficiency Monograph.*

Hetherington, E. M., & Parke, R. D. (1986). *Child psychology: A contemporary viewpoint* (3rd ed.). New York: McGraw-Hill.

Hunt, J. (1967). *MCV. Intelligence and experience.* New York: Ronald Press.

Jensen, A. R. (1969). How much can we boost IQ and scholastic achievement? *Harvard Educational Review, 39,* 1–123.

Jordan, T. E. (1976). *The mentally retarded* (4th ed.). Columbus, Ohio: Charles E. Merrill.

Justice, E. M. (1985). Metamemory: An aspect of metacognition in the mentally retarded. In N. R. Ellis (Ed.), *International review of research in mental retardation,* Vol. 13 (pp. 79–107). New York: Academic Press.

Karnes, M. B., Teska, J. A., Hodgins, A. S., & Badger, E. D. (1970). Educational intervention at home by mothers of disadvantaged infants. *Child Development, 41,* 925–935.

Kaufman, A. S., & Kaufman, N. L. (1983). *The Kaufman Assessment Battery for Children.* Circle Pines, Minn.: American Guidance Service.

Keane, V. E. (1972). The incidence of speech and language problems in the mentally retarded. *Mental Retardation, 10,* 3–8.

LaGreca, A. M., Stone, W. L., & Bell, C. R., III. (1983). Facilitating the vocational-interpersonal skills of mentally retarded individuals. *American Journal of Mental Deficiency, 88,* 270–278.

Lambert, N., & Windmiller, M. (1981). *AAMD Adaptive Behavior Scale—School Edition.* Washington, D.C.: American Association of Mental Deficiency.

Layzer, D. (1974). Heritability analyses of IQ scores: Science or numerology? *Science, 183,* 1259–1266.

Lazar, I., & Darlington, R. (1982). Lasting effects of early education: A report from the Consortium for Longitudinal Studies. *Monographs of the Society for Research in Child Development, 47,* (2–3, Serial No. 195).

Leahy, R., Balla, D., & Zigler, E. (1982). Role taking, self-image, and imitation in retarded and non-retarded individuals. *American Journal of Mental Deficiency, 86,* 372–379.

Lenneberg, E. H. (1967). *Biological foundations of language.* New York: Wiley.

Lent, J. R. (1975). Teaching daily living skills. In J. M. Kauffman & J. S. Payne (Eds.), *Mental retardation: Introduction and personal perspectives.* Columbus, Ohio: Charles E. Merrill.

MacMillan, D. L. (1982). *Mental retardation in school and society* (2nd ed.). Boston: Little, Brown.

MacMillan, D. L., & Borthwick, S. (1980). The new educable mentally retarded population: Can they be mainstreamed? *Mental Retardation, 18,* 155–158.

Malgady, R. G., Barcher, P. R., Tonner, G., & Davis, J. (1979). Language factors in vocational evaluation of mentally retarded workers. *American Journal of Mental Deficiency, 83,* 432–438.

Martin, J. E., Rusch, F. R., Tines, J. J., Brulle, A. R., & White, D. M. (1985). *Mental Retardation, 23*(3), 142–147.

Martin, J. E., Rusch, F. R., & Heal, L. W. (1982). Teaching community survival skills to mentally retarded adults: A review and analysis. *The Journal of Special Education, 16,* 243–267.

McCall, R. B. (1983). Environmental effects on intelligence: The forgotten realm of discontinuous nonshared within family factors. *Child Development, 54,* 408–415.

McCall, R. B., Appelbaum, M. I., & Hogarty, P. S. (1973). Developmental changes in mental performance. *Monographs of the Society for Research in Child Development, 38,* (Ser. No. 150).

McCartney, K., Scarr, S., Phillips, D., Grajek, S., & Schwarz, J. C. (1981). Environmental differences among day care centers and their effects on children's development. In E. F. Zigler & E. W. Gordon (Eds.), *Day care: Scientific and social policy issues.* Boston: Auburn House.

McCarver, R. B., & Craig, E. M. (1974). *Placement of the retarded in the community: Prognosis and outcome. In N. R. Ellis (Ed.), International review of research in mental retardation,* Vol. 7. New York: Academic Press.

Mercer, C. D., & Payne, J. S. (1975). Programs and services. In J. M. Kauffman & J. S. Payne (Eds.), *Mental retardation: Introduction and personal perspectives.* Columbus, Ohio: Charles E. Merrill.

Mercer, J. R. (1973). *Labelling the mentally retarded.* Berkeley: University of California Press.

Mercer, J. R., & Lewis, J. F. (1977). *Adaptive behavior inventory for children, parent interview manual: System of multicultural pluralistic assessment.* New York: The Psychological Corporation.

Oakland, T. (1979). Research on the adaptive behavior inventory for children and the estimated learning potential. *The School Psychology Digest, 8,* 63–70.

O'Connor, N., & Hermelin, B. (1963). *Speech and thought in severe subnormality.* Elmsford, N.Y.: Pergamon Press.

Patton, J. R., & Spears, J. L. (1986). Adult and community issues. In J. R. Patton, J. S. Payne, & M. Beirne-Smith (Eds.), *Mental retardation* (2nd ed.) (pp. 445–486). Columbus, Ohio: Charles E. Merrill.

Polloway, E. A. (1985). Identification and placement in mild retardation programs: Recommendations for professional practice. *Education and Training of the Mentally Retarded, 20,* 218–221.

Polloway, E. A., Epstein, M. H., & Cullinan, D. (1985). Prevalence of behavior problems among educable mentally retarded students. *Education and Training of the Mentally Retarded, 20,* 3–13.

President's Committee on Mental Retardation. (1970). *The six-hour retarded child.* Washington, D.C.: U.S. Government Printing Office, 1970.

Ramey, C. T., & Bryant, D. M. (1983). Early intervention. In J. L. Matson & J. A. Mulich (Eds.), *Handbook of mental retardation* (pp. 467–478). New York: Pergamon Press.

Ramey, C. T., & Campbell, F. A. (1984). Preventive education for high-risk children: Cognitive consequences of the Carolina Abecedarian Project. *American Journal of Mental Deficiency, 88,* 515–523.

Ramey, C. T., & Haskins, R. (1981). The modification of intelligence through early experience. *Intelligence, 5,* 5–19.

Reid, D. H., Wilson, P. G., & Faw, G. D. (1983). Teaching self-help skills. In J. L. Matson & J. A. Mulich (Eds.), *Handbook of mental retardation* (pp. 429–442). New York: Pergamon Press.

Reiter, S., & Levi, A. M. (1980). Factors affecting social integration of noninstitutionalized mentally retarded adults. *American Journal of Mental Deficiency, 85,* 25–30.

Robinson, N. M., & Robinson, H. B. (1976). *The mentally retarded child: A psychological approach* (2nd ed.). New York: McGraw-Hill.

Rosenzweig, M. R. (1966). Environmental complexity, cerebral change, and behavior. *American Psychologist, 21,* 321–332.

Rowe, D. C., & Plomin, R. (1981). The importance of non-shared (E.) environment influences in behavioral development. *Developmental Psychology, 17,* 517–531.

Rusch, F. R., Martin, J. E., & White, D. M. (1985). Competitive employment: Teaching mentally retarded employees to mention their work behavior. *Education and Training of the Mentally Retarded, 20,* 182–189.

Rusch, F. R., & Phelps, L. A. (1987). Secondary special education and transition from school to work: A national priority. *Exceptional Children, 53*(6), 487–492.

Rynders, J. E., Spiker, D., & Horrobin, J. M. (1978). Underestimating the educability of Down's syndrome children: Examination of methodological problems in recent literature. *Journal on Mental Deficiency, 82,* 440–448.

Sacks, O. (1985). *The man who mistook his wife for a hat: And other clinical tales.* New York: Summit Books.

Sarason, S. B. (1984). Unlearning and learning. In B. Blatt & R. Morris (Eds.), *Perspectives in special education: Personal orientations* (pp. 1–24). Glenview, Ill.: Scott Foresman.

Scarr, S., & McCartney, K. (1983). How people make their own environments: A theory of genotype-environmental effects. *Child Development, 54,* 424–435.

Scarr-Salapatek, S. (1975). Genetics and the development of intelligence. In F. D. Horowitz (Ed.), *Review of child development research,* Vol. 4. Chicago: University of Chicago Press.

Schalock, R. L., & Harper, R. S. (1978). Replacement from community-based mental retardation programs: How well do clients do? *American Journal on Mental Deficiency, 83,* 240–247.

Schalock, R. L., Harper, R. S., & Carver, G. (1981). Independent living placement: Five years later. *American Journal of Mental Deficiency, 86,* 170–177.

Schalock, R. L., & Lilley, M. A. (1986). Placement from community-based mental retardation programs: How well do clients do after 8 to 10 years? *American Journal of Mental Deficiency, 90*(6), 669–676.

Schultz, E. E., Jr. (1983). Depth of processing by mentally retarded and MA-matched nonretarded individuals. *American Journal of Mental Deficiency, 88,* 307–313.

Schultz, F. R. (1984). Fetal alcohol syndrome. In J. A. Blackman (Ed.), *Mental aspects of developmental disabilities in children birth to three.* Revised first edition (pp. 109–110). Rockville, Md.: Aspen Systems Corp.

Sitkei, E. G. (1980). After group home living—what alternatives? Results of a two year mobility follow-up study. *Mental Retardation, 18,* 9–13.

Skeels, H. M. (1966). Adult status of children with contrasting early life experiences. *Monographs of the Society for Research in Child Development, 31,* Ser. No. 105.

Skeels, H. M., & Dye, H. B. (1939). A study of the effects of differential stimulation on mentally retarded children. *Convention Proceedings,* American Association on Mental Deficiency, *44,* 114–136.

Smith, R. M. (1974). *Clinical teaching: Methods of teaching for the retarded* (2nd ed.). New York: McGraw-Hill.

Snell, M. (1982). Education and habilitation of the profoundly retarded. In P. T. Cegelka & H. J. Prehm (Eds.),

Mental retardation: From categories to people (pp. 309–350). Columbus, Ohio: Charles E. Merrill.

Sontag, E., Certo, N., & Button, J. E. (1979). On a distinction between the education of the severely and profoundly handicapped and a doctrine of limitations. *Exceptional Children, 45,* 604–616.

Sperber, R. D., & McCauley, C. (1984). Semantic processing efficiency in the mentally retarded. In P. H. Brooks, R. D. Aperber, & C. McCanley (Eds.), *Learning and cognition in the mentally retarded* (pp. 141–163). Hillsdale, N.J.: Lawrence Erlbaum Associates.

Spradlin, J. E. (1963). Language and communication of mental defectives. In N. R. Ellis (Ed.), *Handbook of mental deficiency: Psychological theory and research.* New York: McGraw-Hill.

Sternberg, R. J. (1984). The Kaufman Assessment Battery for Children: An information-processing analysis and critique. *The Journal of Special Education, 18,* 269–280.

Sternberg, R. J., & Spear, L. C. (1985). A triarchic theory of mental retardation. In N. R. Ellis (Ed.), *International review of research in mental retardation,* Vol. 13 (pp. 301–326). New York: Academic Press.

Stodden, R. A., & Browder, P. M. (1986). Community-based competitive employment preparation of developmentally disabled persons: A program description and evaluation. *Education and Training of the Mentally Retarded, 21,* 43–53.

Stokes, T., & Baer, D. M. (1977). An implicit technology of generalization. *Journal of Applied Behavior Analysis, 10,* 349–367.

Streissguth, A. P., Barr, H. M., & Martin, D. C. (1983). Maternal alcohol use and neonatal habituation assessed with the Brazelton Scale. *Child Development, 54*(5), 1109–1118.

Thoday, J. M., & Gibson, J. B. (1970). Environmental and genetic contributions to class differences: A model experiment. *Science, 167,* 990–992.

U.S. Department of Education. (1986). To assure the free appropriate public education of all handicapped children. *Eighth Annual Report to Congress on the Implementation of the Education of the Handicapped Act,* Vol. *1.* Washington, D.C.: U.S. Government Printing Office.

Walker, H. M., McConnell, S., Holmes, D., Todis, B., Walker, J., & Golden, N. (1983). *The Accepts Program.* Austin, Tex.: Pro-Ed.

Wehman, P., Hill, M., Hill, J. W., Brooke, V., Pendleton, P., & Britt, C. (1985). Competitive employment for persons with mental retardation: A follow-up six years later. *Mental Retardation, 23*(6), 274–281.

Weisz, J. R. (1981). Learned helplessness in black and white children identified as retarded and nonretarded. *Developmental Psychology, 17,* 499–508.

Weisz, J. R. (1982). Learned helplessness and the retarded child. In E. Zigler & D. Balla (Eds.), *Mental retardation: The developmental-difference controversy* (pp. 27–40). Hillsdale, N.J.: Lawrence Erlbaum Associates.

Zeaman, D., & House, B. J. (1963). The role of attention in retardate discrimination learning. In N. R. Ellis (Ed.), *Handbook of mental deficiency.* New York: McGraw-Hill.

Zigler, E., & Balla, D. (1982). Introduction: The developmental approach to mental retardation. In E. Zigler & D. Balla (Eds.), *Mental retardation: The developmental-difference controversy* (pp. 3–8). Hillsdale, N.J.: Lawrence Erlbaum Associates.

3

Learning Disabilities

and report cards I was always afraid to show
Mama'd come to school
and as I'd sit there softly cryin'
Teacher'd say he's just not tryin'
Got a good head if he'd apply it
but you know yourself
it's always somewhere else

I'd build me a castle
with dragons and kings
and I'd ride off with them
As I stood by my window
and looked out on those
Brooklyn roads

(*Neil Diamond, "Brooklyn Roads"*)

eil Diamond's "Brooklyn Roads" (see page 99) expresses the frustrations often experienced by the learning-disabled child. Such children, as usually defined, have learning problems in school even though they may be no less intelligent than their "normal" classmates. They have difficulty in one or more skill areas. Reading, in particular, looms as a major stumbling block. Learning-disabled children are also apt to be hyperactive and inattentive. In the early school years their parents may see them as simply overenergetic. Later this unconcern may turn to desperation when, unlike their playmates, these children fail to outgrow their ungovernable ways and poor school performance.

It is such desperation that has led many parents of learning-disabled children to seek miracle cures. Professionals also sometimes fall for what seem to be quick and easy solutions to the array of problems presented by the learning-disabled child. In no other area of special education have so many fads been so intensely embraced. But the field of learning disabilities is unusual because it is a blend of the old and the new. Even though it is the most recent formal category of special education, its roots lie deep in other areas of the field, particularly mental retardation. It is for this reason that the discipline of learning disabilities has often served as a testing ground for new ideas and a battleground for old wars. Issues debated years ago concerning other exceptionalities have frequently resurfaced in slightly different forms in the learning disabilities area. It has been encouraging to see the renewal of some of these controversies, for they have taught us something. And it is refreshing to see a positive response to innovation. Though many of the methods and approaches introduced to the field of learning disabilities have eventually been discarded as unworkable, others have not.

The lyrics of Diamond's song might well apply to children in other categories of exceptionality, particularly emotionally disturbed/behaviorally disordered children, with whom learning-disabled children have much in common. This recalls the old chicken-and-egg dilemma: Does the learning disability cause the emotional disturbance, or vice versa? How realistic *is* it to attempt to determine causes? How can we tell whether a child really has a learning problem or is "just not tryin'"? It is to the critical questions of definition that we turn first.

DEFINITIONS

The field of learning disabilities is the newest category of special education. It was at a 1963 parents' meeting in New York City that Samuel Kirk proposed this term as a compromise because of the confusing variety of labels then being used to describe the child with relatively normal intelligence who was having learning problems. Such a child was likely to be referred to as being *minimally brain injured,* a *slow learner, dyslexic,** or *perceptually disabled.* But parents as well as teachers knew that the label "brain injured" was virtually useless because brain damage is difficult to determine. And even when it was proved, the diagnosis offered little real help in planning and implementing treatment. The term "slow learner" described the affected child's performance in some areas but not in others—and besides, intelligence testing indicated that the *ability* to learn existed. "Dyslexic," too, fell short as a definitive term because it dealt with a symptom that could have any number of causes, from brain injury to environmental disadvantage. To describe a child as "perceptually disabled" just confused the issue further, for perceptual problems might be only part of a puzzling inability to learn. So it was finally around the

---

* **Dyslexia** refers to an impairment of the ability to read.

MISCONCEPTIONS
ABOUT LEARNING-DISABLED INDIVIDUALS

Myth	Fact
All learning-disabled children have brain damage or dysfunction.	Although more learning-disabled children are found to have central nervous system damage or dysfunction than "normal" children, it is possible to have a learning problem without any evidence of brain damage.
A child who is mixed-dominant (e.g., right-handed, left-eyed, left-footed, and right-eared) will have a learning disability.	While there is a slight *tendency* for mixed dominance to occur more frequently in learning-disabled children, many children who are mixed-dominant learn normally.
All learning-disabled children have perceptual problems.	While perceptual problems are more frequent in learning-disabled children, many do not show perceptual problems.
The diagnosis of brain injury is foolproof.	Diagnosing brain injury is often very difficult, particularly if the suspected damage is subtle.
It is valuable for the teacher to know whether or not the child's learning disability is due to brain damage.	While the diagnosis of brain injury may be important for the medical professional, educators gain no useful information from such a diagnosis.
Hyperactive children's most serious problem is excessive motor activity.	Although hyperactive children do exhibit excessive motor activity, most authorities now believe their most fundamental problems lie in the area of inattention.
Using drugs to control hyperactivity is simply a matter of the physician prescribing the right pill.	To use drugs effectively is a highly complex affair. The parents, physician, teacher, and child must maintain close communication in order to monitor the drug's effects.
Learning-disabled students exhibit disorders of language, reading, and writing much more than they do problems in math.	Math problems are more prevalent than was once thought. It has been estimated that two out of three learning-disabled youngsters receive special instruction in math and one out of four receives special education services primarily because of math problems.
Perceptual and perceptual-motor training will automatically lead to academic gains (e.g., in reading).	There is very little research to support the notion that such training will automatically lead to academic gains. The most that can be said, and the research is equivocal even on this, is that perceptual training may increase perceptual skills, which can then serve as the basis for academic remediation.

educationally oriented term *learning disabilities* that the New York parents' group rallied to found the Association for Children with Learning Disabilities (ACLD), now known as the Association for Children and Adults with Learning Disabilities. Following the lead of the parents, a few years later the professionals officially recognized the term by forming the Division for Children with Learning Disabilities (DCLD), now called the Division for Learning Disabilities, of the Council for Exceptional Children (CEC), the major professional organization concerned with the education of exceptional children.

The interest in learning disabilities evolved as a result of a growing awareness that a large number of children were not receiving needed educational services. Because they were within the normal range of intelligence, these children did not qualify for placement in classes for retarded children. In addition, although many of them did show inappropriate behavior or personality disturbances, some of them did *not*. Thus it was felt that placement in emotionally disturbed classes was inappropriate. Learning-disabled students actually do have a great deal in common with mildly retarded and emotionally disturbed students, but at the time the concept of "learning disabilities" was born, classes for emotional disturbance were primarily oriented toward social adjustment problems, and classes for retarded children were often vocationally oriented or involved a "watered-down" curriculum. Parents of children who were not achieving at their expected potential—*learning-disabled* youngsters—wanted their children's *academic achievement* problems corrected.

Factors to Consider in Definitions of Learning Disabilities

Numerous definitions of learning disabilities have been proposed. Although they share a number of commonalities, each of these definitions provides a slightly different slant on what the individual with learning disabilities looks like. There are four factors, each of which is included in some definitions but not all, that have caused a great deal of controversy:

1. IQ–achievement discrepancy
2. Presumption of central nervous system dysfunction
3. Psychological processing disorders
4. Learning problems not due to environmental disadvantage, mental retardation, or emotional disturbance

We will discuss these factors briefly, and then we will present the most commonly accepted definition, the federal definition, as well as two other definitions.

IQ–Achievement Discrepancy

An **IQ–achievement discrepancy** means that the child is not achieving up to potential as measured, usually, by a standardized intelligence test. The child with an IQ–achievement discrepancy or *academic* retardation, then, is one who fails to achieve at the level of his or her intellectual abilities. For many years, most professionals agreed that an IQ–achievement discrepancy was the least debatable characteristic of learning-disabled children. Recently, however, some have begun to question the notion of such a discrepancy, especially with respect to how it is measured.

A number of methods have been used to determine academic retardation. For many years, professionals used a very simple method of comparing the mental age obtained from an intelligence test to the grade-age equivalent taken from a standardized achievement test. A difference of two years between the two was frequently used as an indicator of academic retardation. One problem with this method is that two years below expected grade level is not equally serious at all grade levels. For example, a child who tests two years below grade 8 has a less severe deficit than one who tests two years below grade 4. This is why formulas that take into account the relative ages of the children being assessed were developed.

Starting in the late 1970s and early 1980s, many states and school divisions began to adopt different formulas for identifying IQ–achievement discrepancies. Authorities have pointed out, however, that most of the formulas professionals use are statistically flawed (Cone and Wilson, 1981; McKinney, 1987b; Reynolds, 1984–85). They do not take into account the strong relationship between tested intelligence and tested achievement. The one type of statistically adequate formula, referred to as the **regression-based discrepancy formula,** does take into account the strong correlation between IQ and achievement. However, practitioners have criticized it because it is difficult and expensive to implement (McKinney, 1987b).

Authorities also have questioned the wisdom of using formulas on other grounds than statistical inadequacy or ease of implementation. For example, the Board of Trustees of the Council for Learning Disabilities, one of the largest professional organizations in learning disabilities, came out with a position statement against the use of formulas (Board of Trustees of the Council for Learning Disabilities, 1986). It cited the following reasons for opposing the use of formulas:

1. Discrepancy formulas tend to focus on a single aspect of learning disabilities (e.g., reading, mathematics) to the exclusion of other types of learning disabilities;
2. Technically adequate and age-appropriate assessment instruments are not currently available for all areas of performance, especially for preschool and adult populations;
3. Discrepancy formulas may contribute to inaccurate conclusions when based on assessment instruments that lack adequate reliability or validity;
4. Many learning disabled individuals' intelligence test scores are depressed so that the resulting difference between intelligence and achievement test scores may not be large enough to meet the discrepancy criterion. Therefore, such individuals may be denied access to, or may be removed from, needed services;
5. Many underachieving individuals obtain significant discrepancies between intelligence and achievement test scores for reasons other than the presence of a learning disability;
6. The use of discrepancy formulas often creates a false sense of objectivity and precision among diagnosticians who feel that their decisions are statistically based when formulas are employed;
7. In practice, discrepancy formulas are often used as the sole or primary criterion for determining legal eligibility for learning disability services;
8. Although promoted as a procedure for increasing accuracy in decision-making, discrepancy formulas often represent a relatively simplistic attempt to reduce incidence rates of learning disabilities. (p. 245)

Central Nervous System Dysfunction

Historically this is the area in definitions of learning disabilities that has stimulated the greatest debate. Many of the theoretical concepts and teaching methods associated with the field of learning disabilities grew out of work done in the 1930s and

1940s with brain-injured, mentally retarded children. When the field of learning disabilities was being established, it was noted that many low-achieving children displayed behavioral characteristics similar to those exhibited by children known to have brain damage (distractibility, hyperactivity, perceptual disturbances). In the case of learning-disabled children, however, there was little neurological evidence that brain damage had occurred. Some professionals have been content to attribute brain damage to learning-disabled children on the basis of behavioral characteristics alone. More recently, however, there has been a trend away from considering a child brain damaged unless the results from a neurological examination are unquestionable. The term "dysfunction" has come to replace "injury" or "damage." Thus a child with learning disabilities is now more likely to be referred to as having brain dysfunction than brain injury. The change in terminology reflects the awareness of how hard it is to diagnose brain damage. "Dysfunction" does not necessarily mean tissue damage; it signifies a malfunctioning of the brain.

Psychological Processing Disorders

The field of learning disabilities was originally developed on the assumption that learning-disabled children have deficits in abilities to perceive and interpret stimuli—that is, they have psychological processing problems. Advocates of this viewpoint might assume, for example, that a child who was not learning to read had problems in perceiving and integrating visual information. Proponents of the psychological processing position believe that many learning-disabled children need specific training in processing information in order to learn academic skills such as reading. Over the years a strong opposition has developed to the idea that learning-disabled children exhibit psychological processing problems that can be remediated for the benefit of academic performance. As we will discuss later in the chapter, critics have noted the lack of solid evidence that psychological processing can be accurately measured and that training in processing information can lead to academic improvement.

Environmental Disadvantage, Mental Retardation, or Emotional Disturbance

Most definitions state that a child with learning problems that can be traced to environmental disadvantage is not to be included in the learning disabilities category. Some special educators, however, have seriously questioned this exclusion. They claim that environmentally disadvantaged children are likely to have learning problems similar to those of middle-class learning-disabled children (Cravioto and DeLicardie, 1975; Hallahan, 1975; Hallahan and Cruickshank, 1973), and believe it is illogical to exclude children from learning disabilities services simply because they happen to be poor (Hallahan, Kauffman, and Lloyd, 1985).

Most definitions try to distinguish between the learning-disabled child and the mentally retarded or emotionally disturbed child. Some authorities have pointed out, however, that many mildly emotionally disturbed and mildly mentally retarded children are similar to learning-disabled youngsters in that they too do not achieve up to their potential (Hallahan and Kauffman, 1977; Hallahan, Kauffman, and Lloyd, 1985). They also maintain that the behavioral characteristics of children in all three areas are quite similar (see, for example, Cullinan and Epstein, 1985), and teaching strategies and materials for many of these students are comparable.

We turn now to three definitions that have been offered.

The Federal Definition

The most commonly accepted definition is that endorsed by the federal government in 1977:

> "Specific learning disability" means a disorder in one or more of the basic psychological processes involved in understanding or in using language, spoken or written, which may manifest itself in an imperfect ability to listen, think, speak, read, write, spell, or to do mathematical calculations. The term includes such conditions as perceptual handicaps, brain injury, minimal brain dysfunction, dyslexia, and developmental aphasia. The term does not include children who have learning problems which are primarily the result of visual, hearing, or motor handicaps, of mental retardation, of emotional disturbance, or of environmental, cultural, or economic disadvantage. (*Federal Register,* December 29, 1977, p. 65083)

The National Joint Committee for Learning Disabilities Definition

In 1981 the National Joint Committee for Learning Disabilities (NJCLD), composed of representatives of the American Speech-Language-Hearing Association, the Association for Children and Adults with Learning Disabilities, the Council for Learning Disabilities, the Division for Children with Communication Disorders, the International Reading Association, and the Orton Dyslexia Society, issued an alternative definition. This definition reads:

> Learning disabilities is a generic term that refers to a heterogeneous group of disorders manifested by significant difficulties in the acquisition and use of listening, speaking, reading, writing, reasoning, or mathematical abilities. These disorders are intrinsic to the individual and presumed to be due to central nervous system dysfunction. Even though a learning disability may occur concomitantly with other handicapping conditions (e.g., sensory impairment, mental retardation, social and emotional disturbance) or environmental influences (e.g., cultural differences, insufficient-inappropriate instruction, psychogenic factors), it is not the direct result of those conditions or influences. (Hammill, Leigh, McNutt, and Larsen, 1981, p. 336)

Authors of the NJCLD definition believe that their definition has several advantages over the federal definition (Hammill, Leigh, McNutt, and Larsen, 1981): (1) It is not concerned exclusively with children; (2) it avoids the phrase "basic psychological processes," which has been so controversial; (3) spelling is not included because it is logically subsumed under writing; (4) it avoids mentioning ill-defined conditions (e.g., perceptual handicaps, dyslexia, minimal brain dysfunction) that have caused much confusion; and (5) it clearly states that learning disabilities may occur concomitantly with other handicapping conditions.

Another important distinction between the federal and the NJCLD definition is that the latter presumes learning disabilities are due to central nervous system dysfunction. This presumption, as we have already mentioned, is not held by all authorities in the field (Hallahan, Kauffman, and Lloyd, 1985).

The Association for Children and Adults with Learning Disabilities Definition

Another definition which presumes that learning disabilities have a neurological origin is the one adopted by the ACLD in 1984. A distinctive feature of this definition is that it broadens the scope of potentially affected areas beyond academics. The definition reads:

Specific Learning Disabilities is a chronic condition of presumed neurological origin which selectively interferes with the development, integration, and/or demonstration of verbal and/or non-verbal abilities.

Specific Learning Disabilities exists as a distinct handicapping condition in the presence of average to superior intelligence, adequate sensory and motor systems, and adequate learning opportunities. The condition varies in its manifestations and in degree of severity.

Throughout life the condition can affect self-esteem, education, vocation, socialization, and/or daily living activities.

PREVALENCE

Estimates of the prevalence of learning disabilities have varied widely, from as low as 1 percent to as high as 30 percent. This is understandable in view of the confusion regarding definition. For many years the federal estimate of learning disabilities in the school-age population hovered around 2 to 3 percent. In the late 1970s and early 1980s, however, there was a rapid growth in the number of students being identified as learning disabled. The most recent prevalence figures indicate that the number of children identified as learning disabled has more than doubled since 1976. Indicative of the expansion of the learning disabilities category is the fact that for the 1976–77 school year, about 23 percent of all handicapped children were identified as learning disabled, whereas by the 1985–86 school year, this figure had risen to approximately 43 percent. Prevalence figures kept by the U.S. Department of Education indicate that during the 1985–86 school year, 4.73 percent of the school-age population was receiving learning disabilities services in the public schools.

Debate abounds about whether this dramatic increase in identification of the learning disabled is entirely warranted or whether it reflects poor diagnostic practices (Algozzine and Ysseldyke, 1983). Concern has been expressed, especially by officials in the federal government (General Accounting Office, 1981; *Report on Education Research,* 1983), that the learning disabilities category has grown larger than it should. Many believe that the field of learning disabilities is now at a crossroads over the issue of who does and does not get identified as learning disabled. They fear that continued expansion of the category will seriously erode federal and public support of educational services for learning-disabled students.

CAUSES

In most cases the cause of a child's learning disabilities remains a mystery. Possible causes fall into three general categories—organic and biological, genetic, and environmental.

Organic and Biological Factors

We have already mentioned that some believe brain injury is at the root of learning disabilities. Because the learning problems were not severe and because the neurological evidence was far from convincing, affected children were frequently referred to as "minimally brain injured" or "minimally brain damaged." While these terms (and the term **minimal brain dysfunction***) are still used today, particularly within the medical profession, special educators have protested strongly against their use. They have pointed out, for example, that the term "minimal" is quite

---

* A term used to describe a child who shows behavioral but not neurological signs of brain injury.

misleading. Parents and teachers can attest to the fact that the problem presented by these children is far from small. In addition, the label of brain injury often carries with it a note of finality; it and its behavioral consequences are frequently viewed as irreversible. It is not known how often teachers have used the label of brain injury as a reason not to teach a child. Some people have a similar reaction to the term learning disabled, but for most people it does not appear to connote permanence or hopelessness.

Besides these criticisms based on subjective reactions to the label, there is a more objective rationale for questioning the use of any label denoting brain damage or dysfunction, and that is there is little certain scientific evidence that the typical learning-disabled child has an injured or malfunctioning brain. In the majority of cases the evidence is equivocal at best. The concept of **mixed dominance** is an example of a construct that some have used inappropriately to attribute brain injury to learning-disabled children. Mixed dominance is a term applied to a person whose preferred anatomical sides are mixed. For example, such a person may be right-handed, left-eyed, and left-footed. An early neurological theorist, Samuel Orton (1937), developed a theory that relied heavily on mixed dominance as an indicator that brain pathology was the cause of reading disabilities. According to the theory, "mixedness" reflects an abnormal development of the brain. It has been shown that there is little scientific validity to this hypothesis (Belmont and Birch, 1965; Tinker, 1965).

Although the term "dysfunction" is now used rather than "injury" or "damage," the label "minimal brain dysfunction" carries with it some of the same problems as "minimal brain injury" or "minimal brain damage." There is a paucity of solid evidence to indicate that all, or even most, learning-disabled children have malfunctioning brains.

Even though research on brain dysfunction as a possible cause of learning disabilities has not been very fruitful, there is still hope that future research will uncover brain dysfunction as a significant cause of learning disabilities. Scientists are increasingly capable of harnessing advanced technology for the purpose of studying the brain. John and Ahn and their colleagues at New York University, for example, have conducted some promising research which suggests that many learning-disabled students have abnormal brain waves as measured by digitally computerized recording and analysis of EEGs (Ahn et al., 1980; John et al., 1980). An **EEG,** or **electroencephalogram,** is a recording of electrical activity in the brain. It is obtained by placing electrodes at various locations on the person's head.

Similar to the claim that learning-disabled children suffer from a malfunctioning brain is the notion that they exhibit a minimal brain dysfunction *syndrome*. Proponents of this position claim that a variety of behavioral (poor visual-motor coordination, hyperactivity) and neurological (abnormal EEG) indicators tend to cluster in these children. Again, there is no evidence to support this claim. The research data that are available indicate that a syndrome of minimal brain dysfunction does not exist (Nichols and Chen, 1981; Routh and Roberts, 1972b).

Some evidence, however, suggests biological factors as causal agents in some learning-disabled children. Waldrop and Halverson (1971) have reported a series of studies that link the presence of minor physical anomalies with hyperactivity in children ranging in age from preschool to early elementary years. (It is likely that many of these hyperactive children were also candidates for being identified as learning disabled because hyperactivity and learning problems often go together.) These studies show hyperactive children tend to possess minor physical anomalies (fine "electric" hair, low-seated ears, abnormal head circumference, webbing of the two middle toes) more often than nonhandicapped children. Since such anomalies are often associated with congenital defects such as Down syndrome, Waldrop and Halverson suggest that some hyperactive children may have a subtle chromosomal irregularity or may have had an impediment to proper embryological development. However, the relationship between minor physical anomalies and learning disabilities has been questioned by others (Krouse and Kauffman, 1982).

Genetic Factors

Today it is acknowledged that learning disabilities tend to "run in families" (Owen, Adams, Forrest, Stolz, and Fisher, 1971; Walker and Cole, 1965). Whether this is due to hereditary factors or similar learning environments is a matter to be resolved by further research. Studies of twins (Hallgren, 1950; Norrie, 1959) suggest that at least *some* cases of learning disabilities may be inherited. These studies generally show that when one twin has a reading disability, the other one is more likely to also have a reading disability if he or she is an identical (monozygotic—from the same egg) twin rather than a fraternal (dizygotic—two eggs) twin.

Environmental Factors

Environmental causes are difficult to document. There is much evidence showing that environmentally disadvantaged children are more prone to exhibit learning problems. It is still not certain if this is due strictly to inadequate learning experiences or to biological factors such as brain damage or nutritional deprivation (Cravioto and DeLicardie, 1975; Hallahan and Cruickshank, 1973).

Another factor that has been named as a possible environmental cause of learning disabilities is poor teaching (Engelmann, 1977; Lovitt, 1977). Engelmann, in fact, has estimated that perhaps as many as 90 percent of learning-disabled students are so identified because they have been mistaught. Unfortunately there are no adequate data to determine the validity of Engelmann's 90 percent figure. Although not all authorities agree with his high estimate, many do believe that if teachers were better prepared to handle the special learning problems of children in the early school years, many learning disabilities could be avoided.

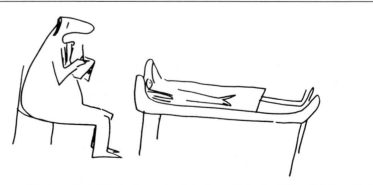

"Your feelings of insecurity seem to have started when Mary Lou Gurnblatt said, 'Maybe I don't have a learning disability—maybe you have a teaching disability.'"

SOURCE: J. H. Crouse and P. T. McFarlane, "Monopoly, Myth, and Convivial Access" to the Tools of Learning, *Phi Delta Kappan, 56,* (9) (1975), 593. Drawn by Tony Saltzman.

MEASUREMENT

It is now a commonly accepted idea that psychological and educational testing must be oriented toward providing relevant information for educational programming. Scores on a test are meaningless unless they can be translated into educational recommendations. This "diagnosis for teaching" rather than for identification is associated with *prescriptive teaching,* a concept originated by Laurence J. Peter, the creator of the Peter Principle (Peter, 1965). The medical analogy here refers to the practice of diagnosing a physical illness and then prescribing medicine on the basis of the diagnosis. *Prescriptive teaching,* then, is the writing of an educational prescription in the form of educational tasks on the basis of diagnostic information gained from testing and observing the child.

Four methods of testing are popular in the field of learning disabilities:

1. Standardized achievement tests
2. Process tests
3. Informal reading inventories
4. Formative evaluation methods

Standardized Achievement Tests

The most common test used with the learning-disabled child is the standardized achievement test. This is because achievement deficits are the primary characteristic of these children. The fact that the test is standardized means it has been administered to a large group of children so that any one child's score can be compared to the norm, or average. Most of these tests are relatively easy and inexpensive to administer. Standardized achievement tests can be designed to assess either multiple areas or just one area of achievement. Some examples of general achievement batteries are the California Achievement Test, the Iowa Test of Basic Skills, the Stanford Achievement Test, the Peabody Individual Achievement Test, and the Woodcock-Johnson Psychoeducational Battery. Some examples of reading achievement tests are the Stanford Diagnostic Reading Test, the Roswell-Chall Diagnostic Test of Word Analysis Skills—Revised and Extended, the Diagnostic Reading Scales, and the Woodcock Reading Mastery Tests. Some examples of math achievement tests are the Key Math Diagnostic Arithmetic Test and the Stanford Diagnostic Mathematics Test.

Standardized test information can be used intelligently or it can be misused. The teacher who goes no further than simply obtaining a grade- or age-level score has not gained much useful data on the child. To gain more insight into the "whys" of a particular student's failure, it is necessary to inspect the particular kinds of errors he or she has made. Some achievement tests are designed to be used this way. The Key Math Diagnostic Arithmetic Test, for instance, provides an extensive list of instructional objectives keyed to test items so the teacher can plan instruction accordingly.

Process Tests

The use of tests of psychological processes to diagnose underlying processing* deficiencies is one of the innovations brought to the field of special education by the discipline of learning disabilities. Some have not viewed this practice as a blessing

---

* Processing refers to what takes place after an individual has perceived something by means of the senses—how he or she interprets or puts the perception to meaningful use intellectually.

(e.g., Newcomer and Hammill, 1976). *Process testing* is the assessment of those psychological (usually perceptual or linguistic) processes, one or more of which the tester assumes is (are) the cause(s) of the child's academic problem. With this approach, the child with a reading difficulty is not treated simply for his or her reading problems. Tests are given in order to identify the particular psychological process in which the child is deficient. Remediation is then planned accordingly. The educational program focuses on the underlying process problem rather than directly on the reading problem.

Opponents of process testing note that these tests tend to be low in their predictive validity for academic failure. Predictive validity here refers to whether or not one can predict the level of score a child will obtain on an achievement test on the basis of his or her score on the process test. It is obviously important that a test have good predictive validity if it is to be educationally useful. Reviews of the literature (e.g., Coles, 1978; Hallahan and Cruickshank, 1973; Hammill and Larsen, 1974; Newcomer and Hammill, 1976) indicate that some of the most popularly used instruments in this area have *not* been demonstrated to be good predictors of academic achievement.

Two typical process tests are the Illinois test of Psycholinguistic Abilities (Kirk, McCarthy, and Kirk, 1961, 1968) and the Marianne Frostig Developmental Test of Visual Perception (Frostig, Lefever, and Whittlesey, 1964). We will briefly discuss these two tests since they cover the two major areas of psychological processes—linguistics and visual perception—and are among the most commonly used.

Illinois Test of Psycholinguistic Abilities (ITPA)

Probably more than any other instrument, the ITPA is the test that made process testing popular. It can even be said that the ITPA itself helped to generate interest and growth in the field of learning disabilities as a whole.

First published in 1961 and revised in 1968, the ITPA tests three categories:

1. Channels of communication (auditory-vocal and visual-motor)
2. Psycholinguistic processes (reception, organization, and expression)
3. Levels of organization (representational and automatic)

Channels are the various sensory modalities through which information can come or go (visual, auditory, motor, vocal). In psycholinguistic processes *reception* refers to the ability to take in information; *organization* refers to the internal manipulation of concepts and linguistic information; *expression* has to do with the transmission of information. The *representational level* is concerned with symbolic thought, whereas the *automatic level* deals with habit chains.

Each of the twelve subtests of the ITPA is classified within the three general categories listed above. For example, the auditory reception subtest requires the child to answer "yes" or "no" to questions such as "Do airplanes fly?" "Do cars talk?" This subtest involves the auditory-vocal channel, the reception process, and the representational level.

Even though research has not substantiated the predictive validity of the ITPA, its development has had at least one positive impact on the field of special education. The ITPA was built primarily to be used in gathering educationally relevant information, and it has helped to bring about an awareness that psychological and educational testing should be sensitive to the educational needs of the child.

Marianne Frostig Developmental Test of Visual Perception (DTVP)

Developed by Marianne Frostig and her colleagues, the DTVP assesses aspects of visual perception that are considered by some to be crucial to reading. Like the ITPA's attempt to assess different areas of psycholinguistic functioning, the DTVP purports to measure relatively specific aspects of visual perception. On the basis of the test's results, the examiner is supposed to be able to pinpoint a child's particular kind(s) of perceptual deficit(s). There are five subtests, each designed to test a different kind of ability:

1. *Eye-Motor Coordination.* A test of eye-hand coordination involving the drawing of continuous straight, curved, or angled lines between boundaries of various width or from point to point without guidelines.
2. *Figure-Ground.* A test involving shifts in perception of figures against increasingly complex grounds. Intersecting and "hidden" geometric forms are used.
3. Constancy of Shape. A test involving the recognition of certain geometric figures presented in a variety of sizes, shadings, textures, and positions in space, and their discrimination from similar geometric figures. Circles, squares, rectangles, ellipses, and parallelograms are used.
4. *Position in Space.* A test involving the discrimination of reversals and rotations of figures presented in series. Schematic drawings representing common objects are used.
5. *Spatial Relationships.* A test involving the analysis of simple forms and patterns. These consist of lines of various lengths and angles that the child is required to copy, using dots as guide points. (Frostig, Lefever, and Whittlesey, 1964, p. 5)

Informal Reading Inventories

A common method of assessment used by teachers in the area of reading ability is an informal reading inventory (IRI). An IRI is

> a series of reading passages or word lists graded in order of difficulty. A student reads from the series of lists or passages, beginning with one that the teacher thinks is likely to be easy. As long as the reading does not become too difficult, the student continues to read from increasingly harder lists or passages. As the student reads, the teacher monitors performance and may record the kinds of reading errors a student makes (e.g., omitted word, mispronunciation, reversal). When an IRI is made up of passages, the teacher may ask questions after each one to help estimate the student's comprehension of the material. Depending on the student's accuracy in reading and answering questions, various levels of reading skill can be ascertained. . . . In general, the kind of material that a student can read with a certain degree of ease is considered to be at his or her *independent, instructional,* or *frustration level.* (Hallahan, Kauffman, and Lloyd, 1985, p. 210)

Because of the growing disenchantment with formal, or standardized, tests, particularly those that are process oriented, there has been a trend toward the greater use of informal inventories. The major drawback to using IRIs is that their reliability and validity depend on the skills of the teachers constructing them. In the hands of a skilled teacher, however, they can be invaluable. They can be useful for determining what level of reading material the student should be working on (Lovitt and Hansen, 1976), as well as for pinpointing specific reading skill deficits.

Formative Evaluation Methods

Although some authorities have espoused them since the 1960s, formative evaluation methods began receiving a great deal of attention beginning in the early 1980s (e.g., Deno, 1985; Fuchs, 1986; Fuchs and Fuchs, 1986; Germann and Tindal, 1985; Marston and Magnusson, 1985; White and Haring, 1980). Although there are a variety of different formative evaluation models, at least five features are common to all of them:

1. The assessment is usually done by the child's teacher, rather than a school psychologist or diagnostician.
2. The teacher assesses behaviors directly relevant to classroom functioning. Whereas process testing involves behaviors that are purported to be related to behaviors relevant to classroom success, formative evaluation involves observation and recording of such behaviors directly. For instance, if the teacher is interested in measuring the child's pronunciation of the letter "l," he or she looks at that particular behavior and records whether the child can pronounce that letter.
3. The teacher observes and records the child's behavior frequently and over a period of time. Most other kinds of tests are given once or twice a year at the most. Formative evaluation involves measuring performance at least two or three times a week.
4. The teacher uses formative evaluation to assess the child's progress toward educational goals. After an initial testing, the teacher establishes goals for the child to reach in a given period of time. For example, if the child can orally read 25 words correctly in one minute out of a certain book, the teacher may set a goal, or criterion, of being able to read 100 words correctly per minute after one month. This aspect of formative evaluation is sometimes referred to as **criterion-referenced testing.**
5. The teacher uses formative evaluation to monitor the effectiveness of educational programming. For instance, in the example above, if after a few days the teacher realizes the child's progress makes it unlikely that he or she will reach the goal of 100 words, he or she can try a different educational intervention.

Curriculum-Based Assessment

Curriculum-based assessment (CBA) is a particular model of formative evaluation that has received a great deal of attention. In fact, an entire issue (November 1985) of *Exceptional Children,* one of the major professional journals in special education, was devoted to CBA. Although drawing heavily upon earlier research (e.g., Carnine and Silbert, 1979; Haring and Lovitt, 1969; White and Liberty, 1976), CBA was largely developed by Deno and his colleagues at the University of Minnesota (Deno, 1985; Deno, Marston, and Mirkin, 1982; Deno, Mirkin, and Chiang, 1982; Fuchs, Deno, and Mirkin, 1984; Marston, Mirkin, and Deno, 1984).

Because it is a type of formative evaluation, CBA has the five features noted above. In addition, it has two other distinguishing characteristics. First, it is designed to measure children's performance on the particular curriculum they are exposed to. In the area of spelling, for example, a typical CBA assessment strategy is to give children two-minute spelling samples using dictation from a random selection of words from the basal spelling curriculum, with the number of words or letter sequences correctly spelled serving as the performance measure. In the case of math, the teacher may give children two minutes to compute samples of problems from the basal text and record the number of digits computed correctly. Proponents of CBA state that this reliance on the curriculum is an advantage over commercially available standardized achievement tests, which are usually not keyed to the curriculum being used in any particular school.

Second, CBA compares handicapped children's performance to that of their peers in their own school or school division. Deno and his colleagues advocate that CBA measures be taken on a random sample of nonhandicapped students so that this comparison can be made. Comparison with a local reference group is seen as more relevant than comparison with national norming groups used in commercially developed standardized tests.

Research on the Effectiveness of Formative Evaluation

Several studies have focused on the effectiveness of using formative evaluation. In general, they have demonstrated that students whose teachers use formative evaluation make more progress than those whose teachers do not. These studies also demonstrate that the effectiveness of formative evaluation is enhanced if the teacher: (a) writes goals for the children that focus on generalization and maintenance of skills, (b) writes goals that promote task persistence, (c) measures student performance at least twice weekly, (d) graphs the data taken on the students, and (e) uses prescribed rules for deciding when to change a student's educational program because it is not working (Fuchs, 1986).

PSYCHOLOGICAL AND BEHAVIORAL CHARACTERISTICS

A variety of characteristics have been attributed to learning-disabled children. A national task force, recognizing the proliferation of terms and labels in this area, found ninety-nine characteristics reported in the literature (Clements, 1966). The ten most frequently found symptoms were these:

1. Hyperactivity
2. Perceptual-motor impairments
3. Emotional lability (frequent shifts in emotional mood)
4. General coordination deficits
5. Disorders of attention (short attention span, distractibility, preservation)
6. Impulsivity
7. Disorders of memory and thinking
8. Specific academic problems (reading, arithmetic, writing, spelling)
9. Disorders of speech and hearing
10. Equivocal neurological signs and electroencephalographic (EEG) irregularities

We shall cover each of these characteristics in the following discussion, but for purposes of organization we shall group similar ones together.

It is important to keep in mind that not all these characteristics are found in every learning-disabled child; any individual student is likely to exhibit only a few. The broad range of disabilities displayed by these children makes it exceedingly difficult for practitioners and researchers alike to work with and study learning-disabled children. Researchers are beginning to make progress, however, in breaking this heterogeneous population into discrete subgroups (see box on p. 114).

Coping with the Heterogeneity of the Learning-Disabled Population: The Search for Subtypes

For years the wide range of problems displayed by learning-disabled students has stymied teachers and researchers. Teachers have found it difficult to plan educational programs for the diverse group of children they find in their classrooms. And the heterogeneity of the learning-disabled population has produced nightmares for researchers, who worry about whether inconsistent results from study to study are indeed real or are caused by variations in children selected for one study versus another.

Since the inception of the learning disabilities field, investigators have searched for the existence of subgroups, or subtypes, of learning disabilities (e.g., Bateman, 1968; Boder, 1973; Ingram, 1969; Johnson and Myklebust, 1967; Kinsbourne and Warrington, 1963). The research of these early investigators, who relied on clinical intuition to direct their research efforts, was methodologically flawed; but it did provide the impetus for more objective endeavors (McKinney, 1987a).

Using more sophisticated statistical techniques, researchers began in the late 1970s to make progress on documenting subtypes of learning disabilities. There are now a number of research teams focused on the task of discovering the most useful ways to subtype learning-disabled children (e.g., Feagans and Appelbaum, 1986; Lyon, 1985; Lyon and Watson, 1981; Lyon, Stewart, and Freedman, 1982; McKinney and Feagans, 1984; McKinney, Short, and Feagans, 1985; McKinney and Speece, 1986; Rourke, 1978; Satz and Morris, 1981; Speece, McKinney, and Appelbaum, 1985; Watson, Goldgar, and Ryschon, 1983). Perhaps the most fruitful of all these teams has been the one led by McKinney at the University of North Carolina's Frank Porter Graham Child Development Center.

McKinney's Carolina Longitudinal Project has continued to follow a sample of 63 first- and second-graders who were first identified as learning disabled in 1978. As part of the project, investigators have documented the existence of subtypes within three different domains: (a) perceptual-cognitive, (b) language, and (c) behavioral. Thus far, most of their research has focused on subtypes within the behavioral area. Using teacher ratings on four bipolar dimensions (task orientation/distractibility; independence/dependence; introversion/extroversion; considerateness/hostility), they have found evidence for seven different behavioral subtypes:

Subtype 1. Attention Deficit: This subtype is characterized by inattention and dependent behavior. It is also the largest group, representing about 29 percent of the sample.

Subtype 2. Normal Behavior: Although this subtype has slightly elevated ratings on considerateness and introversion, all behaviors are within normal limits. This subtype comprised about 25 percent of the sample.

Subtype 3. Conduct Problems: Representing about 14 percent of the sample, this subtype is characterized by mild attention deficits and high hostility and distractibility.

Subtype 4. Withdrawn Behavior: Comprised mostly of girls, this subtype exhibits dependent and introverted behavior. Eleven percent of the sample fall into this subtype.

Subtype 5. Normal Behavior: Although this subtype has slightly elevated ratings on hostility, like Subtype 2 all of the ratings are within the normal range. It contains about 10 percent of the sample.

Subtype 6. Low Positive Behavior: Children in this subtype are characterized by low ratings on all of the positive behaviors—i.e., task orientation, independence, extroversion, considerateness—but without high ratings on the negative counterparts of those behaviors—i.e., distractibility, dependence, introversion, hostility. This subtype contains about 6 percent of the sample.

Subtype 7. Global Behavior Problems: Representing only about 5 percent of the sample, this subtype is characterized by extremely negative ratings on all the behaviors.

McKinney and his colleagues have come up with a number of educationally relevant findings relative to these subtypes. Two of their most important findings have been these:

1. There was some movement in classification from one subtype to another. However, if a child was originally classified in one of the maladaptive subtypes, he or she was five times more likely to still be classified in a maladaptive subtype than to move into an adaptive one. One of the most important trends was for children in the attention deficit subtype to move into one of the problem behavior subtypes.
2. Although children in the various subtypes did not differ from each other in achievement at the beginning of the study when they were in the first and second grades, over the next two years there were different achievement outcomes based on subtype membership. Students in the normal behavior and withdrawn subtypes progressed well academically, but those in the attention deficit subtype and the behavior problem subtypes (3, 6, and 7) deteriorated academically.

These findings hold promise for helping educators plan educational programs for learning-disabled children. For example, McKinney (1987a) speculates that, since all of the learning-disabled students in the sample were receiving resource room services over the course of the two years, this type of service may not be appropriate for those with attention deficits and behavior problems. They may require more intensive services. There is also the related question of whether particular types of teaching approaches, for example those emphasizing behavioral principles, are more or less effective with certain behavioral subtypes. McKinney and his colleagues are currently designing research to answer questions related to whether certain subtypes are more or less responsive to different educational strategies.

Perceptual, Perceptual-Motor, and General Coordination Problems

Those involved in determining causes, treatment, and educational programs for brain-damaged mentally retarded children were oriented toward looking for perceptual, particularly visual, disturbances. Many professionals in learning disabilities have a similar interest in perceptual problems in learning-disabled children.

In the 1930s and 1940s Heinz Werner and Alfred Strauss, at the Wayne county Training School in Northville, Michigan, found in clinical studies and experimental investigations that a variety of perceptual abnormalities were characteristic of some mentally retarded children. At the time they believed that the children who had perceptual problems were brain injured. The methodology of their studies has since been seriously questioned, and it is now believed that the assumption cannot be made that these children were unquestionably brain damaged. Nevertheless, Werner and Strauss *did* identify perceptual abnormalities in some of the children, brain damaged or not. Individuals associated with Werner and Strauss, such as Newell Kephart, popularized the notion that learning-disabled children also have perceptual and perceptual-motor problems.

Visual Perceptual Disabilities

Many studies indicate that reading-disabled children are more likely to exhibit visual perceptual problems (problems in organizing and interpreting visual sensory stimuli) than children who are average or above-average readers. While some of the studies can be criticized on methodological grounds, the "evidence strongly suggests that learning-disabled children, as a group, perform poorly on tasks designed to assess visual perceptual abilities" (Hallahan, 1975, p. 31).

Auditory Perceptual Disabilities

Although fewer in number, there have been some investigations of the auditory perceptual abilities of children with learning disabilities. These studies indicate that auditory perceptual difficulties are more often found in learning-disabled than in nonhandicapped children (Hallahan, 1975). Numerous professionals have pointed out that this relationship is logical, since reading requires the individual to associate visual units with their auditory equivalents.

A Cautionary Note

Despite empirical evidence indicating that visual and auditory perceptual skills are associated with the academic ability of reading, caution must be maintained in considering the significance of these results. The studies mentioned above are based on groups of children. In other words, not all children with reading problems have perceptual deficits, and some children who have perceptual deficits can read adequately. Furthermore, merely because perceptual skills are correlated or associated with reading problems does not necessarily mean that they cause them. Many practitioners, unfortunately, have prescribed visual perceptual training activities for *all* learning-disabled children. As we will note in a later section of this chapter, we do not know that perceptual training by itself will help learning-disabled children who do have perceptual problems, let alone those who do not have these deficits.

Perceptual-Motor and General Coordination Problems

It has been observed clinically that learning-disabled children often have difficulty in physical activities involving the use of motor skills. They are frequently described by parents, teachers, and peers as having "two left feet" or "ten thumbs." The difficulties ascribed to them involve both fine-motor (small motor muscles) and gross-motor (large motor muscles) skills. Fine-motor skills often involve the coordination of the visual and motor systems. Theories and programs concerned with perceptual-motor and physical coordination are closely related to those concerned with perceptual disabilities. The same cautions noted for perceptual training are in order for these areas.

Disorders of Attention and Hyperactivity

Also stemming from the work of Werner and Strauss (1941) with retarded children is the great interest in the attentional problems and hyperactivity of learning-disabled children. In addition to finding a variety of perceptual disturbances in some mentally retarded children, Werner and Strauss discovered that some of these children exhibited attentional difficulties and hyperactivity. William Cruickshank, who at one time worked with Werner and Strauss, was instrumental in bringing the attentional and hyperactivity problems of learning-disabled children to the attention of special educators.

Numerous studies have documented the existence of hyperactivity in a large percentage of learning-disabled youngsters. These estimates have ranged from a low of about 33 percent to as high as 80 percent (Shaywitz and Shaywitz, 1987). Even the lowest estimates suggest that hyperactivity is a frequently encountered problem in learning-disabled students.

The Relationship between Attentional Problems and Hyperactivity

Professionals and laypeople alike often use the terms "attentional problems" and "hyperactivity" interchangeably. And they do this with good reason, for research has shown the relationship between the two is a strong one. In addition, most authorities agree that attentional problems are more basic than hyperactivity problems (Hallahan, Kauffman, and Lloyd, 1985; Shaywitz and Shaywitz, 1987). In other words, the major problems of most children labeled "hyperactive" lie more in the area of attention difficulties than in the area of excessive motor activity.

The psychiatric profession also recognizes the prominence of attentional problems in hyperactive children. Its members do not clinically refer to children as "hyperactive" without also attaching the label "attention deficit," and in their diagnostic terms, the words "attention deficit" precede the word "hyperactive." In 1980 the American Psychiatric Association's *Diagnostic and Statistical Manual of Mental Disorders* (*DSM-III*) included categories of "Attention Deficit Disorder With Hyperactivity" and "Attention Deficit Disorder Without Hyperactivity." Because clinicians have not classified many youngsters in the latter category, current plans for revision of the manual include collapsing the two categories into one: "Attention

Hyperactivity is one of the most frequently mentioned characteristics of learning-disabled children. Most experts agree that attentional problems are at the heart of most hyperactive children's problems. (Bohdan Hrynewych/Southern Light)

The Use and Misuse of Drugs for Hyperactivity: What the Research Tells Us

Of all the controversies in the area of learning disabilities (and there are many), the issue of whether or not drugs should be used to help control hyperactivity is one of the most hotly debated. Questions of possible drug abuse, harmful side effects, hidden plots to control the behavior of America's youth, and inappropriate advertising practices have been raised. Although a variety of drugs have been prescribed to control hyperactive and inattentive behavior, the three most commonly recommended are the psychostimulants Ritalin, Dexedrine, and Cylert. As one might expect in such a highly controversial area, research has not yet provided many definitive answers. Comprehensive reviews (Gadow, Torgesen, Greenstein, and Schell, 1986; Henker and Whalen, 1980; Kauffman and Hallahan, 1979; Pelham, 1983; Pelham and Murphy, 1986; Shaywitz and Schaywitz, 1987; Sroufe, 1975; Whalen and Henker, 1980) of the available research, however, point to the following 10 cautions:

1. Psychostimulants produce inconsistent effects on intelligence and achievement test scores—some studies have found gains, others have not.
2. Possibly related to the first point is the conclusion that drugs do not appear to have much, if any, effect on the child's acquisition of new skills, but do influence academic productivity—the child's ability to produce more of the kind of academic work with which he or she is already familiar.
3. The time course for many of these drugs is relatively brief, meaning that optimal response to the medication may only last a few hours.
4. Side effects are common. The most frequent are a decrease in appetite and an increase in sleeplessness.
5. Psychostimulants do not affect all children in the same way. Some experience side effects; others do not. Researchers estimate that around 60 to 70 percent who receive psychostimulants show improvement on teacher ratings of their behavior. The remainder either do not improve or actually get worse.
6. There are little data to support the long-term benefits of psychostimulant use. Although some have speculated that there may be a causal relationship between psychostimulant use in childhood and later substance abuse, researchers have not yet conducted definitive studies on this possibility.
7. There is the possibility that the taking of medication leads to undesirable motivational changes for the child. The child may come to rely on the medicine rather than himself or herself to change his or her behavior.
8. The medication of children may also lead to motivational changes on the part of adults. It may be that in some cases drugs are too effective in the sense that they appear to offer an apparently quick and easy solution to a problem that needs to be approached on a variety of fronts. Drugs *can,* for example, afford an easy excuse for teachers to shirk their duties.
9. Teachers need to be aware that dosage levels that lead to a lessening of motor activity may be so high as to lead to impaired performance on cognitive tasks. The result can be a situation in which, while the child's behavior seems better to the teacher, he or she is actually on too high a dosage level to gain any benefits in academic performance.
10. Medication alone is rarely, if ever, enough. There is little research indicating that drugs are more effective than *educational* treatments such as behavior modification or cognitive training. In other words, a child whose behavioral problems are severe enough to warrant the administration of psychostimulants will almost always also need to be provided with strong educational programming. Some clinicians believe that a combination of drug therapy with behavior or cognitive training is better than either one alone. Research on this matter thus far, however, is inconclusive.

Does this list of cautions mean that drugs should never be used with hyperactive children? No. But all these cautions should be kept in mind before drugs are administered, and it should never be forgotten that these drugs are powerful substances. Again, this does not mean that drugs should never be used. *Many authorities recommend that when educational efforts have been tried and have failed, drugs may be attempted, in combination with educational programming.* Research does indicate that for many hyperactive and distractible children, psychostimulants lead to improvements in goal-directed and attentional behavior. When drugs are used, however, it should be obvious from the 10 points above that it is crucial they be monitored extremely closely. To reap the maximum benefit of the drugs and to reduce any harmful side effects, it is essential that close communication be maintained among parents, physician, teacher, and child.

Deficit-Hyperactivity Disorder" (Shaywitz and Shaywitz, 1987). It is evident that attention is considered the primary problem in children whom parents and teachers have traditionally called "hyperactive."

Three Types of Attention Problems

Since the early 1970s, a wide variety of studies have indicated that learning-disabled children are more inattentive than their nonhandicapped peers (see Hallahan, 1975, and Hallahan and Reeve, 1980, for a review of some of these early studies). Researchers have found these attentional problems in a variety of settings, both in the laboratory and in the classroom. Keogh and Margolis (1976) have analyzed these problems as falling into three categories: *coming to attention, decision making,* and *maintaining attention.*

Inattention comes in many forms, such as daydreaming. (Bob Adelman/Magnum)

COMING TO ATTENTION   Many learning-disabled students have poor task-approach skills; they are slow to get actively involved in the assignments set before them. It has been hypothesized that they have difficulty in picking out the important information to which they should be attending (Keogh and Margolis, 1976).

DECISION MAKING   Many learning-disabled children's inattentiveness has been linked to impulsivity. Numerous researchers and practitioners have noted that these children tend to be impulsive decision makers. When confronted with problem-solving situations, they are likely to choose one of the first alternatives they come upon rather than considering other possibilities before responding.

MAINTAINING ATTENTION   Numerous investigators have found that learning-disabled youngsters have difficulty once they begin a task (Pelham, 1981). When given relatively long tasks, for example, their performance is apt to deteriorate more quickly than that of nonhandicapped students.

Disorders of Memory and Thinking

Memory

Learning-disabled children, in general, demonstrate memory deficits for both auditory and visual stimuli (Hallahan, 1975; Hallahan, Kauffman, and Lloyd, 1985; Torgesen and Kail, 1980). Joseph Torgesen and his colleagues have provided us with the clearest reasons why learning-disabled children do poorly on memory tasks. Torgesen and Kail (1980) have presented the following conclusions:

1. Learning-disabled children are deficient in their use of *strategies* nondisabled children use to learn. For example, nondisabled children, when presented with a list of words to memorize, will rehearse the names to themselves. They will also make use of categories by rehearsing words in groups that go together. Learning-disabled children, however, do not generally use these strategies spontaneously.
2. The poor memory performance of learning-disabled children may also be due to their poor language skills, which make verbal material particularly difficult for them to remember.

Thinking

Thinking can be defined in a number of ways. Among other things, thinking involves the ability to solve problems and to conceptualize. The ability to think, broadly considered, is what is generally thought of as making up "intelligence." So it is not surprising that very little consideration was originally given to the thought processes of learning-disabled children because they are, by definition, commonly regarded as being of normal intelligence.

IMPULSIVITY-REFLECTIVITY   The earliest work in this area involved investigations into "cognitive styles," or *how* people go about thinking when solving problems (Blackman and Goldstein, 1982). An example of a cognitive style dimension that has received a lot of attention in the field of learning disabilities is *impulsivity-reflectivity*. Using a task—the Matching Familiar Figures Test—developed by Jerome Kagan and his colleagues (Kagan, Rosman, Day, Albert, and Phillips, 1964), researchers have consistently found learning-disabled children to be more impulsive than their nonhandicapped peers. When presented with a problem-solving task, instead of reflecting on various alternatives, they tend to respond quickly and make many errors (Hallahan, Kauffman, and Ball, 1973; Heins, Hallahan, Tarver, and Kauffman, 1976).

It is easy to see how impulsivity interferes with learning. School activities so frequently require a student to select among competing choices that an impulsive problem-solving style is a great drawback.

METACOGNITION   Learning-disabled children also have problems in what are called metacognitive skills. **Metacognition** involves two components:

> (1) An awareness of what skills, strategies, and resources are needed to perform a task effectively and (2) the ability to use self-regulatory mechanisms to ensure the successful completion of the task, such as planning one's moves, evaluating the effectiveness of one's ongoing activities, checking the outcomes of one's efforts, and remediating whatever difficulties arise (Baker and Brown, 1984). (Baker, 1982, pp. 27–28)

Several investigators have found that learning-disabled students often have problems in using metacognitive skills (See Hallahan, Kneedler, and Lloyd, 1983; Hallahan, Lloyd, Kauffman, and Loper, 1983; Kneedler and Hallahan, 1984; Ryan, Short, and Weed, 1986; and Wong, 1985, for reviews of this literature). There are several different aspects of metacognition (e.g., metamemory, metalistening, and metacomprehension) that researchers have studied.

A study by Torgesen (1979) found learning-disabled children deficient in metamemory capabilities. For example, when asked the question "Suppose you lost your jacket while you were at school, how would you go about finding it?" learning-disabled students could not produce as many alternative strategies as their nondisabled peers.

Most teachers of learning-disabled students note that many of them are poor listeners. Corroborating this anecdotal information is a study of metalistening skills (Kotsonis and Patterson, 1980) in which an adult told children that they were going to play a game involving several rules. She then stated one rule at a time, stopping after each rule to ask if the children thought they had enough information to play the game. Learning-disabled students were ready to play the game well before their nondisabled peers, even though by objective standards they had not yet heard enough rules to know how to play the game appropriately.

Metacomprehension in reading, sometimes referred to as **comprehension monitoring,** is also a problem for many learning-disabled youngsters (Anderson, 1980; Baker and Anderson, 1982; Baker and Brown, 1980; Brown, 1980; Forrest and Waller, 1981; Paris and Myers, 1981; Wong, 1982). See the box on p. 122 for a discussion of comprehension monitoring and its implications for educational practice.

Social Adjustment

Emotional lability—frequent changes in mood—can be viewed as a particular aspect of personality and social maladjustment. The learning-disabled child frequently exhibits behaviors characteristic of emotional disturbance. There are at least four sources of evidence for the notion that learning-disabled individuals exhibit signs of social maladjustment—ratings by peers, teachers, parents, and learning-disabled students themselves.

How often have you been reading along in a novel, a magazine, or some other material and suddenly realized that for the past few seconds, maybe even minutes, you've not really been comprehending it? Perhaps thoughts of tomorrow's meeting with the principal intruded. Or maybe you were thinking of more important matters, such as whether or not you should go to a movie this evening. Or maybe you weren't thinking of anything in particular — your mind just wandered. You needn't be overly concerned if you have experienced these lapses of concentration. Even the best readers tune out on occasion. Actually, the very fact that you recognize that you're not comprehending is a strong indication that you are a good reader. By catching yourself in the act of not paying attention, you are displaying a skill that researchers are finding of utmost importance in reading comprehension. You are demonstrating *comprehension monitoring skills.* The learning disabled, however, are apparently more susceptible than most of us to those stray thoughts of what movie to watch tonight. Researchers believe their problem is due to their lack of a repertoire of skills that help them organize their approach to the task of reading.

Critical Comprehension Monitoring Skills Pinpointed

In the last few years there has been an explosion of interest in comprehension monitoring. The results of recent studies (by individuals from a wide geographical range such as Thomas Anderson and Ann Brown at the University of Illinois, Linda Baker at the University of Maryland, Candace Bos at the University of Arizona, Scott Paris at the University of Michigan, and Bernice Wong at Simon Fraser University in Canada) have led to a number of important conclusions regarding the comprehension monitoring skills needed to be a good reader. These researchers have summarized their findings with the following points:

— *Clarifying the Purposes of Reading.* Before efficient readers begin to read, they have a mind-set regarding the general purpose of their reading. They approach reading to obtain the gist of a news article with a different mind-set than the one they use for reading to gain information from a textbook on which they will be tested. Learning-disabled children, however, are not as adept at adjusting their reading style to fit the purpose or the difficulty level of the reading material.

— *Focusing Attention on Important Parts of Text.* Learning-disabled children have problems in picking out the main idea of a paragraph. Good readers spend more time and effort focusing on the major ideas contained in the text they read.

— *Monitoring One's Level of Comprehension.* It isn't yet known exactly what tips them off, but efficient readers can sense when it is that they are not understanding what they're reading. Timing is apparently a key. They pick up quickly, before they've covered a lot of material, that something's not quite right, that they're losing the meaning.

— *Rereading and Scanning Ahead.* So what do efficient readers do when they realize that they're not comprehending? Researchers have identified a couple of strategies used by good readers, but not by poor ones. These strategies are neither mysterious nor complex. Good readers often stop and reread portions of the passage and/or scan ahead looking for clues that will help them understand what they're reading.

— *Consulting External Sources.* Another way in which good readers have a leg up on the learning-disabled is that they know when to use external sources for help; they realize that they can use the written language system to their advantage. For example, they realize that consulting a dictionary, asking others for help, and using contextual cues are good ways of helping them figure out specific words that give them difficulty.

Successful Teaching Techniques Identified

Investigators are just beginning to devise teaching techniques designed to short-circuit comprehension monitoring difficulties. One of the most active researchers in this area has been Dr. Bernice Wong of Simon Fraser University in Canada. In one of her studies, she tested the effects of a set of teaching procedures that are designed to help learning-disabled children improve their reading comprehension. Before each paragraph of a story the children were reading, the teacher read aloud questions pertaining to the main ideas of the paragraph. The same questions were printed in the children's copies of the stories. This simple and straightforward procedure resulted in the students recalling more of the story on a subsequent test. In particular, they improved their comprehension of the most thematically important ideas in the story.

In another investigation, Wong developed an even more streamlined instructional procedure. She improved the comprehension of learning-disabled students by having them:

—ask themselves, "What am I studying the passage for?";

— find the main ideas and underline them;

— think of a question about the main idea and write it;

— look back at questions and answers to see how they provide them with more information.

The development of instructional techniques for attacking the comprehension monitoring deficits of learning-disabled students is still in its infancy. The future holds great promise for the development of yet other teaching strategies. One of the striking aspects of curriculum development in this area is that it is so "commonsensical". The teaching techniques developed by Wong and others are, at once, powerful and simple — simple in the sense that their rationale can be easily understood by learning-disabled students themselves. It's a good bet that the inherent understandability of these techniques is what makes them work so well. [T]

SOURCE: *Special Education Today,* November, 1983, pp. 4–5. Reprinted with permission.

Peer Ratings

When children are asked on sociometric questionnaires to name children they would most like to "play with" or "be friends with," the learning-disabled child is almost always overlooked (Bryan, 1974; 1976; Gottlieb, Gottlieb, Berkell, and Levy, 1986; Gresham and Reschly, 1986; Scranton and Ryckman, 1979). And evidence indicates that learning-disabled girls are even more at risk for social rejection and isolation than are learning-disabled boys.

Teacher Ratings

Numerous studies demonstrate that teachers rate learning-disabled children as having more social adjustment difficulties than their nonhandicapped peers (Center and Wascom, 1986; Cullinan, Epstein, and Lloyd, 1981; Epstein, Cullinan, and Lloyd,

1986; Perlmutter, Crocker, Cordray, and Garstecki, 1983). There is evidence that teachers rate the types of problems displayed differently depending upon the age of the learning-disabled child. For example, they perceive younger learning-disabled children as having attentional problems and older students as evidencing predelinquent behavior problems (Epstein et al., 1986).

Parent Ratings

There has been comparatively little research on parental perceptions of learning-disabled children's social behavior. What little research has been done, however, suggests that parents too view their learning-disabled children as having social behavior problems (McConaughy and Ritter, 1986; Owen, Adams, Forrest, Stolz, and Fisher, 1971).

Self-Ratings

Several researchers have investigated how learning-disabled children feel about themselves. These studies of self-concept have been consistent in showing that learning-disabled children have negative self-concepts relative to their academic abilities. However, they apparently do not suffer from poor self-esteem relative to nonacademic performance (Bryan and Bryan, 1986).

Possible Explanations for Socialization Problems

Several explanations have been forwarded for why learning-disabled children have such difficulties in social situations. According to Bryan and Bryan (1986), investigators have posited as many as five different areas as possible causes of social problems for learning-disabled children: (a) social norm violation, (b) social cognition, (c) role-taking skills, (d) referential communication, and (e) classroom behavior.

SOCIAL NORM VIOLATION Investigators have found that, even though learning-disabled students are aware of social norms, they are more willing than nonhandicapped peers to violate them. For example, they admit to being more willing to commit antisocial acts (Bryan, Werner, and Pearl, 1982). And they tend to use inappropriate ways of getting others to like them (Bryan, Sonnefeld, and Greenberg, 1981).

SOCIAL COGNITION Several authorities believe that learning-disabled children elicit negative reactions from others because they lack social comprehension skills (Bryan, 1977; Horowitz, 1981; Wong and Wong, 1980; Weiss, 1984). They often exhibit difficulties in reading social cues and may misinterpret the feelings and emotions of others. For example, one study compared them to their nonhandicapped peers in ability to judge the feelings of soap opera characters (Pearl and Cosden, 1982b). Segments of soap operas were chosen because they are often laden with emotion. The learning-disabled group's understanding of the social interchanges was less accurate than that of the nonhandicapped group.

ROLE-TAKING SKILLS There is a great deal of evidence that learning-disabled students have difficulty understanding and taking the perspective of others. Authorities have noted that this is not surprising, because being able to put oneself in another's shoes is a complex cognitive-affective task (Bryan and Bryan, 1986).

REFERENTIAL COMMUNICATION   The learning-disabled child's tendency to have trouble communicating with others, both as a listener and a speaker, put that child at risk to have social difficulties. One can readily imagine how easy it would be to misinterpret inattentiveness in a social interchange as disinterest or negativism.

CLASSROOM BEHAVIOR   Although teachers *rate* learning-disabled children as engaging in a variety of negative behaviors, researchers who have directly observed classroom interactions have not been able to tease out exactly what it is they actually do that evokes these negative ratings (Bryan and Bryan, 1986). One interesting hypothesis is that their nonverbal behavior contributes in some way to negative reactions. In one clever laboratory study, adults were shown brief videotapes of learning-disabled and nondisabled children (Bryan and Perlmutter, 1979). After just a few minutes of exposure to the tapes, adults judged the learning-disabled child as less socially desirable than the nondisabled child. What is even more amazing, adults were able to make these judgments even when the sound was turned off! The particular nonverbal behaviors that elicit such immediate negative reactions remain a mystery, although a subsequent study suggests it may be that learning-disabled children do not make appropriate eye contact with other people in conversations (Bryan, Sherman, and Fisher, 1980).

Motivational Difficulties

Another source of social adjustment problems for learning-disabled students is their motivation, or feelings about their own abilities to deal with life's many problems. Numerous authorities have pointed out that many learning-disabled individuals lack motivation; they appear content to let events happen without attempting to "take charge" of their own destinies. The importance of feelings of self-determination is well articulated by Deci and Chandler (1986):

> We believe that self-determination as a quality of behavior should be a goal of *all* education. In other words, we would like the education of all children, including LD [learning disabled] and other special population children, to be organized by principles that promote self-determined functioning. Such functioning would capitalize on intrinsically motivated behavior—behavior that is organized by interest and the desire to take on new challenges—and it would also facilitate the internalization and eventual integration of external regulations that are necessary for effective functioning in the social world. As pointed out by Connell and Ryan (1984), many of the activities that children are asked to do in schools are lacking in inherent interest, so an internalization of the motivation (Chandler, 1981) for doing such activities is one of the most important educational outcomes. (p. 589)

That learning-disabled children are more extrinsically than intrinsically motivated is supported by a wealth of literature (Bryan and Bryan, 1986). Much of this research has focused on learning-disabled children's **locus of control,** with much support for the notion that they are more likely to possess an external rather than an internal locus of control (Hallahan, Gajar, Cohen, and Tarver, 1978). For example, when asked a question such as "Suppose you did a better than usual job in a subject at school. Would it probably happen (1) because you tried harder, or (2) because someone helped you?" the learning-disabled child is more likely to choose (2). In other words, these children view themselves as controlled by external rather than internal factors. To put it more dramatically for the sake of emphasis, they do not view themselves as in control of their own destiny.

Closely related to the work on locus of control is the research on attributions. **Attributions** refer to what people think are the causes of their successes and failures. The findings on attributions of learning-disabled children are consistent with what one would expect, given their propensity for an external locus of control. Bryan and Bryan (1986) provide the following summary of attribution research:

> Across ages, then, learning-disabled children and adolescents are unlikely to take pride in their successes and are particularly prone to minimize or discount whatever successes they achieve. They are not so reluctant, however, to minimize their responsibilities for failure. Further, they appear to be more pessimistic than nondisabled peers with regard to future success. (p. 203)

Given the motivational profile of an external locus of control and pessimistic attributions, it is no wonder that authorities have also tagged learning-disabled children as at risk for developing **learned helplessness.** This refers to a person's belief that his or her efforts will not result in desired outcomes (Seligman, 1975). The person learns to expect failure no matter how hard he or she tries; therefore, he or she tends to "give up" or to lose motivation. For example, it has been found that when learning-disabled children fail on a task, they are less likely than nondisabled children to blame the failure on a lack of effort (Pearl, Bryan, and Donahue, 1980). In other words, learning-disabled children tend to devalue effort, to believe that no amount of effort on their part will help them achieve. They tend to view themselves as helpless in the academic situation.

Whether the learned helplessness causes the academic problems of the learning-disabled child or vice versa is an unanswerable question at this point. It is logical to assume, however, that there is a kind of vicious circle: The learning-disabled child who exhibits problems in certain areas learns to expect failure in any new situation. This expectancy of failure, or learned helplessness, may cause the child to give up readily in the face of a task that is not easily solvable. The result is failure. A child who has experienced years of this failure–expectancy of failure–failure chain will likely need, as Pearl et al. (1980) state, to be taught coping strategies for dealing with failure.

The Learning-Disabled Child as an Inactive Learner with Strategy Deficits

Many of the psychological and behavioral characteristics we have described can be summed up by saying that the learning-disabled child is a passive individual who lacks strategies for attacking academic problems. Specifically, research points to the learning-disabled child as one who does not believe in his or her own abilities (learned helplessness), has an inadequate grasp of what strategies are available for problem-solving (poor metacognitive skills), and is unable to produce appropriate learning strategies spontaneously. *The picture we get is of a child who does not actively involve himself or herself in the learning situation.*

These observations have led Torgesen (1977) to refer to the learning-disabled child as an inactive learner. Hallahan has also concluded that a major difficulty many learning-disabled children have, and one that affects how they go about attempting to learn in a variety of situations, is their inability to use task-approach skills spontaneously (Hallahan and Bryan, 1981; Hallahan, Kauffman, and Lloyd, 1985; Hallahan and Reeve, 1980). But there is a bright side to the generalization that many learning-disabled children are inactive, passive learners: This inactivity can be overcome.

Given appropriate experiences, learning-disabled children can be taught to use appropriate task-approach strategies. (We will discuss this in more detail in the section on Cognitive Training.)

Neurological Problems

We have already noted that not all children with learning disabilities show definitive signs of neurological abnormalities. However, a larger percentage of learning-disabled children show such signs than is true for the general population. It surprises many parents, teachers, and others outside the medical profession to find that neurological diagnostic methods are still fairly limited. The tests are not as accurate as many believe, particularly when used on children. Moreover, it is not unusual for an otherwise perfectly normal and healthy child to display one or more of the behavioral signs of brain damage. Called "soft signs," such characteristics

> include poor fine motor coordination, impaired visual motor coordination, poor balance, clumsiness, strabismus [crossed eyes], choreiform movements [uncontrollable movements], and "poor speech." . . . Such signs are referred to as "soft" because—unlike the "hard" signs of classical neurology, paresis and paralysis, anesthesia, and reflex changes— the "soft" signs are slight, inconsistently present, and not clearly associated with localized neuro-anatomical lesions. Dysfunctions such as clumsiness may represent "normal" variation and be totally unassociated with central nervous system pathology. (Wender, 1971, p. 27)

The greatest danger in considering the neurological aspects of learning disabilities is that the existence of brain injury will be affirmed solely because soft signs are present. This practice can be very misleading. Too many parents of learning-disabled children have been needlessly alarmed by the ominous diagnosis of "minimal brain injury." This term convinces them that their child's problem is irreversible. Fortunately, learning-disabled children are far from being "beyond hope" in terms of correction of their problems.

Academic Achievement

There is little disagreement among professionals concerning the presence of academic deficits in learning-disabled children. Indeed, such deficits are the hallmark of learning disabilities. In fact, by definition, if there is no academic problem, a learning disability does not exist. Some children have deficits in all scholastic areas—reading, spoken language, written language, and mathematics; others have problems in only one or two academic subjects.

Spoken Language Problems

Language problems of learning-disabled students can be divided into five different areas: phonology, syntax, morphology, semantics, and pragmatics (see Chapter 5).

PHONOLOGY **Phonology** is the study of how individual sounds make up words. There is evidence that learning-disabled children have difficulties both in breaking words down into their component sounds and in blending individual sounds together in order to make words (Ackerman, Anhalt, and Dykman, 1986; Kass, 1966;

Kavale, 1981; Liberman, Shankweiler, Liberman, Fowler, and Fischer, 1977; Tarver and Ellsworth, 1981; Vellutino, 1979; Wagner, 1986).

SYNTAX   **Syntax** refers to how words are put together in sentences according to established rules. It is often called *grammar*. A number of studies indicate that learning-disabled students are likely to make syntactical or grammatical errors in language usage (Bryan and Pflaum, 1978; Fayne, 1981; Simms and Crump, 1983; Wiig, Semel, and Abele, 1981).

MORPHOLOGY   **Morphology** is the study of how adding or deleting parts of words can change their meaning (*chase* = present tense, *chased* = past tense; *boy* = one boy, *boys* = more than one boy). Learning-disabled youngsters make more morphological errors than their nondisabled peers (Kass, 1966; Vogel, 1977; Wiig, Semel, and Crouse, 1973).

SEMANTICS   **Semantics** refers to the meaning of language. Research indicates that many learning-disabled children demonstrate semantic problems (Denckla and Rudel, 1976; Perfetti and Lesgold, 1978; Wiig and Semel, 1974). For example, when required to say rapidly the names of common objects, words, letters, colors, and numerals, reading-disabled children and adolescents took longer and made more errors than their nondisabled peers (Denckla and Rudel, 1976; Wiig and Semel, 1974).

PRAGMATICS   **Pragmatics** refers to the child's knowledge of how to use language in social settings. It deals less with the mechanics of language and more with how individuals use language to communicate. Studies indicate that they have problems in the use of language in social situations (Bryan, Donahue, and Pearl, 1981; Bryan, Donahue, Pearl, and Herzog, 1984; Bryan, Donahue, Pearl, and Sturm, 1981; Kotsonis and Patterson, 1980; Noel, 1980). These deficiencies are manifested both in the production of language and in listening to the language of others.

In their review of learning-disabled children's pragmatic language skills, Bryan and Bryan (1986) note that they are unskilled conversationalists. When conversing with others, such children are often agreeable and cooperative, but they are unpersuasive and deferential. In addition, they tend to make task-irrelevant comments and make those with whom they are talking feel uncomfortable. In one often-cited study, for example, learning-disabled and nonhandicapped children took turns playing the role of host in a simulated television talk show (Bryan, Donahue, Pearl, and Sturm, 1981). Analysis of the verbal interactions revealed that, in contrast to when nonhandicapped children were hosts, learning-disabled children playing the host role allowed their nonhandicapped guests to dominate the conversation. And their guests also exhibited more signs of discomfort during the interview than did the guests of nonhandicapped hosts.

Reading Problems

One of the most common problems attributed to learning-disabled children is reading disabilities (Norman and Zigmond, 1980). Most teachers of learning-disabled youngsters, in fact, spend more time teaching reading than any of the other academic areas (Kirk and Elkins, 1975).

Reading difficulties are manifested in a variety of ways. Since reading problems are related to many spoken language problems, some of the most common reading errors reflect difficulties in phonology, syntax, morphology, and semantics.

A variety of terms are used to refer to students with reading problems. Hallahan, Kauffman, and Lloyd (1985) note that three of the most common are *dyslexic, corrective reader,* and *remedial reader:*

Dyslexia   The term *dyslexia* comes from Greek and means "difficulty with reading." A dyslexic is a person who has dyslexia. It has medical connotations and is more often used by physicians and by those who believe that reading problems are the result of biological (particularly neurological) problems. Dyslexia also suggests a severe reading disability, perhaps because students with quite serious deficits are more likely to be taken to medical clinics than are other students.

Corrective Reader   The term *corrective reader* is more educational in origin than dyslexic and is usually used to refer to students whose reading difficulties are not so severe that intensive remedial efforts are warranted. The difficulties experienced by a student labeled a corrective reader might be less persistent and might involve problems only in reading accuracy, fluency, rate, or comprehension.

Remedial Reader   The term *remedial reader* is also more educational than dyslexic. It is used to indicate students who need extensive and intense remedial education in the area of reading. Students considered remedial readers are likely to have serious difficulties both with accuracy, fluency, and rate of reading and with understanding what they have read. The reading problems of students with learning disabilities are more similar to the reading problems of remedial readers than to those of corrective readers. (p. 202)

Written Language Problems

Written language can be divided into handwriting, spelling, and composition. Learning-disabled students often have difficulties in one or more of these areas.

HANDWRITING   Although even the best students can have less than perfect handwriting, the kinds of problems manifested by some learning-disabled students are much more severe. Their written products are frequently illegible. In addition to problems in legibility, learning-disabled students are sometimes very slow writers.

SPELLING   Spelling involves the ability to learn the correspondence between phonemes (sounds) and graphemes (written letters). Phoneme-grapheme correspondence is a skill that is poorly developed in some learning-disabled children (Carpenter and Miller, 1982; Gerber and Hall, 1981). And the high prevalence of spelling problems is no doubt related to the fact that the English language consists of a wide variety of graphemes for individual phonemes (Hallahan, Kauffman, and Lloyd, 1985).

COMPOSITION   Although virtually all teachers of learning-disabled students attest to the fact that they have problems in composition, little research has actually been done on the topic. The research that does exist indicates that learning-disabled students' problems in composition range from grammatical errors to stylistic deficiencies (Morris and Crump, 1982; Poplin, Gray, Larsen, Banikowski, and Mehring, 1980; Thomas, Englert, and Gregg, 1987).

Mathematical Problems

Although disorders of language, reading, and writing have traditionally received more emphasis than problems in mathematics, the latter are now gaining a great deal more attention. For example, when learning disabilities teachers were asked about why their students were receiving services, they stated that two out of three were receiving special instruction for arithmetic disabilities and more than one in four were getting special education services primarily because of problems in math (McLeod and Armstrong, 1982).

Learning-disabled students who exhibit problems in math do so for a variety of reasons. Some of their problems in math are caused indirectly by difficulties in other related areas, such as attention and reading. Learning-disabled children have particular difficulty in solving "story problems" (Larsen, Trenholme, and Parker, 1978). There is considerable evidence, however, that many children's math difficulties are not restricted to story problems. They also exhibit computational errors. The kinds of errors they make, rather than being random, are usually the result of applying incorrect problem-solving strategies (Cox, 1975; Ginsberg, 1977).

EDUCATIONAL CONSIDERATIONS

There are several possible orientations for planning treatment programs for learning-disabled children. The following seven categories reflect what the majority of professionals recognize as the major approaches:

- Process training
- Multisensory approaches
- Structure and stimulus reduction
- Medication
- Cognitive training
- Behavior modification
- Direct instruction

In practice, one often finds a combination of two or more of these approaches. With the possible exceptions of process training and behavior modification or process training and direct instruction, which seem mutually exclusive, it is not uncommon to find a blend of several.

Process Training

There are advocates and opponents of the idea that one must consider underlying psychological processes in planning educational programs for learning-disabled children. Proponents of process training assume that underlying processes involved in learning academic subjects can be specified. When they are identified, children are trained to improve the processes themselves. For example, a child believed to have reading problems because of difficulties in visual perception would be given visual perception training before being given reading instruction.

A number of programs have been developed for training visual and visual-motor skills as well as psycholinguistic processes. In the realm of visual perception training, some of the more popular approaches are those of Barsch (1965), Frostig (Frostig and Horne, 1964), Getman (Getman, Kane, and McKee, 1968), and Kephart (1960, 1971). For psycholinguistic training, teaching strategies have been developed by Kirk and Kirk (1971) and Minskoff, Wiseman, and Minskoff (1974). A number of these strategies were devised specifically to be used with information from tests. Frostig's is to be used with the Frostig DTVP test; the Kirk and Kirk and the Minskoff, Wiseman, and Minskoff materials are designed for use with the ITPA. The other approaches are constructed around theoretical frameworks of one kind or another. All these training approaches are quite similar in that there is a great deal of overlap with regard to activities and materials. We will briefly discuss one approach—that of Kephart—as a general example of process training.

Newell Kephart's Approach

Kephart, in his classic book *The Slow Learner in the Classroom* (Kephart, 1960, 2nd ed., 1971), presented his theoretical rationale and remedial procedures for children with visual and visual-motor difficulties. His training activities were based on what he termed the **perceptual-motor match**:

> This process of establishing a perceptual-motor correspondence has been called the perceptual-motor match. It normally occurs in three stages best illustrated by the development of eye-hand coordination. In the first stage, the hand leads and generates most of the information. In this stage, the process is hand–eye, the hand leading and the visual information being matched to it. As this matching becomes more complete, the rapid, extensive nature of the visual data becomes apparent and the child learns to monitor and let **kinesthesis** [the sensation of bodily movements as perceived through muscles, tendons, joints] control the response while he uses the visual data for more remote predictions. He has entered the second stage: eye–hand. Here the greatest reliance is upon vision, the hand being used only to confirm or to solve complex or confusing situations. Finally, the match is close enough that he can depend upon vision alone. He can explore with eyes in the same way and get the same information as he originally did with his hand. This shift is possible because of a firm, accurate perceptual-motor match. The child has entered the third stage and become perceptual. (Kephart, 1975, pp. 65–66)

Kephart's contention that motor development precedes visual development led him to devise training activities that first stress motor skills. Visual training is matched to the learned motor experiences. Many developmental psychologists disagree. They maintain that visual development is chronologically ahead of motor skills. That visual and motor development interact and should therefore probably be combined in correction of visual, motor, or visual-motor disabilities, however, has been substantiated (Hetherington and Parke, 1986).

The Effectiveness of Process Training

There is very little solid research evidence to support the use of process training. Many critics of process testing have noted that there is little in the literature to support the position that perceptual and psycholinguistic training will enhance academic performance. Hammill and Larsen (1974), for example, reviewed the early research on psycholinguistic training and found little support for its effectiveness. Hallahan and Cruickshank (1973) found the same was true for visual and visual-motor training. Most research, in fact, casts doubt on the worth of any process training (Liberman and Shankweiler, 1979; Vellutino, 1977). There are strong indications that the responsibility for demonstrating the efficacy of process training still rests with the developers of these programs.

Search for Aptitude-Treatment Interactions

Closely related to the issue of process training is the debate over the existence of evidence for aptitude-treatment interactions (ATIs). As Haring and Bateman (1977) have noted:

Teachers have long been taught, "There is no way to teach all children—some need one method, others need another." The often unspoken assumption is that somehow we can consistently and accurately identify those children who need technique A and those who need B. Presumably the secret of this successful matching is in some identifiable characteristics of the children. (p. 144)

A hypothetical example of an ATI would be if one were to find that children diagnosed as having a visual perceptual deficit benefited from a phonics approach to reading, whereas children with auditory perceptual deficits profited from a sight-word approach. There are also those who believe that one should teach to the deficits rather than the strengths of the child. These individuals would advocate focusing efforts on the visual deficits of the child weak in visual perception rather than presenting him or her with a phonics approach. In either case, the teacher is assuming the existence of an ATI, since he or she is tailoring the remediation approach to the particular strengths and weaknesses of the child.

Those who believe in an ATI approach are similar to those who advocate process training in that both look at strengths and weaknesses in order to plan educational strategies. In fact, since the bulk of ATI advocates are concerned with comparing the child's auditory and visual perceptual capabilities, they frequently use process tests such as the ITPA and Marianne Frostig Developmental Test of Visual Perception. The difference is that ATI proponents often recommend working educationally with academic materials (e.g., phonics) rather than with psychological processes directly.

In general, evidence does not support the notion of an ATI approach (Lloyd, 1984; Tarver and Dawson, 1978). Most studies have not found that it is particularly helpful to know the psychological strengths and weaknesses of the child. It may be that the basic idea behind the ATI orientation is a valid one, but that the tests used to diagnose problems lack reliability and validity (Meyers, 1980).

Multisensory Approaches

Although they include some of the same activities found in process training, programs classified as being multisensory are more likely to emphasize working with academic materials directly (Fernald, 1943; Gillingham and Stillman, 1956; McGinnis, 1963). Multisensory methods involve correction of a child's problems by using a combination of the child's sensory systems in the training process. The assumption is that the child will be more likely to learn if more than one sense is involved in learning experiences.

The prototype of most multisensory approaches is Fernald's VAKT method (*V* stands for visual, *A* for auditory, *K* for kinesthetic, and *T* for tactual). In the first step of this method the child tells the teacher a story. The teacher writes down the words of the story, which serves as the material as the child learns to read. (Advocates point out that using a student's own story is a particularly good motivator, especially for older children.) In learning the words, the child first sees the word (visual), then hears the teacher say the word (auditory). Next the child says the word (auditory), and finally, the child traces the word (kinesthetic and tactual).

Structure and Stimulus Reduction for Hyperactivity and Distractibility

For the distractible, hyperactive mentally retarded child, Strauss and Werner recommended a structured program with a minimum of extraneous stimulation. Cruickshank extended these ideas for use with learning-disabled children who are also inattentive and hyperactive. Cruickshank presented his recommendations in *A Teaching Method for Brain-Injured and Hyperactive Children* (Cruickshank, Bentzen, Ratzeburg, and Tannhauser, 1961), a publication on his Montgomery County Project. This project was designed around three principles:

1. Structure
2. Reduction of environmental stimulation
3. Enhancement of intensity of teaching materials

Basically, a **structured program** is one that is almost totally teacher directed—that is, most activities are determined by the teacher. The rationale for this approach is that the hyperactive and distractible child cannot make his or her own decisions until carefully educated to do so.

Because of the child's susceptibility to distraction, irrelevant stimuli are reduced. What the teacher wants the child to attend to is increased in intensity (often through the use of bright colors). **Stimulus reduction** is achieved by some of the following modifications:

- Soundproofing of walls and ceilings
- Carpeting
- Opaque windows
- Enclosed bookcases and cupboards
- Limited use of bulletin boards
- Use of cubicles and three-sided work areas

The Effectiveness of Stimulus Reduction

Cruickshank and his colleagues reported some evidence that the Montgomery County program had been successful in bringing about better attentional abilities in the children. Academic gains, however, were not forthcoming. Cruickshank (1975) has since pointed out the problems he and his associates encountered in this field-based program. In general, however, studies investigating the use of stimulus-reduction procedures that have been conducted since Cruickshank's project have reached the same conclusions: Attending skills have been improved, but achievement gains have not been automatic (Hallahan and Kauffman, 1975).

The Use of Medication with Hyperactive Children

There has been considerable controversy about the use of drugs to control hyperactivity and distractibility in children (see box on p. 118). Claims have been made, for example, that the use of drugs represents a conspiracy of the middle class to keep the lower class docile and oppressed, and that drug usage in childhood will automatically lead to drug abuse in the teenage years.

There is very little question about the effectiveness of drugs in changing the behavior of many learning-disabled children. Medication, particularly with stimulant drugs such as Ritalin, is often successful in reducing hyperactive behavior and increasing attending skills (see Henker and Whalen, 1980; Kauffman and Hallahan, 1979; Pelham, 1983; Whalen and Henker, 1980 for reviews of this literature). The concern many have is that teachers and parents will come to rely too heavily on drugs. As one parent has said, parents and teachers can also become "addicted" to Ritalin. Drugs cannot substitute for good teaching. Another fear is that drugs may be given to children who do not really need them. It is not always an easy matter to determine when the overactivity warrants medication. When drugs *are* prescribed, it is important that physician, teacher, parent, and child be in close communication in order to monitor the dosage. Side effects are not uncommon, and determination of the proper dosage requires medical expertise.

Cognitive Training

Traditional behavior modification focuses on modifying overt behavior. The focus of **cognitive training** is on changing covert thoughts. Pioneered by Meichenbaum at the University of Waterloo in Canada, cognitive training has gained widespread popularity as an intervention approach for learning-disabled students (Borkowski, Weyhing, and Turner, 1986; Hall, 1980; Hallahan, Kauffman, and Lloyd, 1985; Hallahan, Kneedler, and Lloyd, 1983; Kneedler, 1980; Kneedler and Hallahan, 1984; Lloyd, 1980; Palincsar, 1986; Paris and Oka, 1986; Wong, 1979, 1986). Authorities give at least three reasons why cognitive training is particularly appropriate for learning-disabled youngsters:

1. It stresses self-initiative by involving the child as much as possible as his or her own teacher. In this way, it is aimed at helping the child overcome motivational problems of passivity and learned helplessness.
2. It provides the child with specific learning strategies for solving problems.
3. Many of the techniques appear particularly well suited for attentional and impulsivity problems.

Cognitive training is sometimes given different names, largely depending upon the particular orientation of the practitioner or researcher. Some have used the term **cognitive behavior modification** to stress the distinction between *cognitive* versus *behavior* modification. Others have used the term **metacognitive strategy instruction** to emphasize providing the child with strategies for understanding and regulating thought processes. Although there are sometimes some distinctions in practice among these approaches, they are often so subtle that the terms "cognitive training," "cognitive behavior modification," and "metacognitive strategy instruction" can be used synonymously.

A variety of specific techniques fall under the heading of cognitive training. Here we present three that have been found to be particularly useful with learning-disabled students: self-instruction, self-monitoring, and reciprocal teaching. Another cognitive training approach, the Learning Strategies Curriculum, will be discussed later in our section on secondary educational programming.

Self-Instruction

Teachers have often combined **self-instruction training** with modeling. **Modeling** refers to the use of adults or peers to demonstrate appropriate solution strategies. In this strategy, the child observes the model using self-instruction.

Meichenbaum has been a major proponent of the use of self-instructional training for impulsive children (Meichenbaum, 1975; Meichenbaum and Goodman, 1971). The idea behind this approach is to encourage the child to learn to develop verbal control of behavior. The training regimen has been described by Meichenbaum in the following way:

1. An adult model performed a task while talking to himself out loud (cognitive modeling);
2. The child performed the same task under the directions of the model's instruction (overt self-guidance);
3. The child whispered the instructions to himself as he went through the task (faded, overt self-guidance); and finally
4. The child performed the task while guiding his performance via private speech (covert self-instruction). (1975, pp. 16–17)

Self-instructional training has also been used successfully in academic situations. Kosiewicz, Hallahan, Lloyd, and Graves (1982), for example, found a self-instructional routine beneficial in improving the handwriting performance of a learning-disabled boy. The particular steps they used were these:

1. The child said the word to be written aloud.
2. Next he said the first syllable of the word.
3. Then he named each of the letters in the syllable three times.
4. Next he said each letter as he wrote it.
5. The child repeated steps 2 through 4 for each succeeding syllable.

Self-Monitoring

Self-monitoring refers to procedures that require the individual to keep track of whether or not he or she engages in particular behaviors. For example, Hallahan and colleagues have taught learning-disabled children to self-monitor when they are displaying attentive behaviors (Hallahan, Lloyd, Kosiewicz, Kauffman, and Graves, 1979; Lloyd, Hallahan, Kosiewicz, and Kneedler, 1980). The procedure is a simple one. A tape recorder is placed near the child. While the child is engaged in some kind of academic activity, a tape containing tones (the time between tones varies randomly) is played. Whenever he or she hears a tone, the child is to stop work and ask the question, "Was I paying attention?" He or she then records on a separate score sheet, a "Yes" or "No" depending on his or her own assessment of attentional behavior. This technique has been successful in aiding learning-disabled children to increase attentive behavior and academic productivity. Presumably, it helps children to become more aware of and in control of their own attentional processes. Here is a set of sample instructions:

"Johnny, you know how paying attention to your work has been a problem for you. You've heard teachers tell you, 'Pay attention,' 'Get to work,' 'What are you supposed to be doing' and things like that. Well, today we're going to start something that will help you help yourself pay attention better. First we need to make sure that you know what paying attention means. This is what I mean by paying attention." (Teacher models immediate and sustained attention to task.) "And this is what I mean by not paying attention." (Teacher models inattentive behaviors such as glancing around and playing with objects.)

"Now you tell me if I was paying attention." (Teacher models attentive and inattentive behaviors and requires the student to categorize them.) "Okay, now let me show you what we're going to do. While you're working, this tape recorder will be turned on. Every once in a while, you'll hear a little sound like this:" (Teacher plays tone on tape.) "And when you hear that sound quietly ask yourself, 'Was I paying attention?' If you answer 'yes,' put a check in this box. If you answer 'no,' put a check in this box. Then go right back to work. When you hear the sound again, ask the question, answer it, mark your answer, and go back to work. Now, let me show you how it works." (Teacher models entire procedure.) "Now, Johnny, I bet you can do this. Tell me what you're going to do everytime you hear a tone. Let's try it. I'll start the tape and you work on these papers." (Teacher observes student's implementation of the entire procedure, praises its correct use, and gradually withdraws her presence.) (Hallahan, Lloyd, and Stoller, 1982, p. 12)

Reciprocal Teaching

Developed by Brown at the University of Illinois and Palincsar at Michigan State University, **reciprocal teaching** focuses on metacognitive skills for fostering and monitoring reading comprehension. Researchers have shown it to be a highly effective technique (Brown and Campione, 1984; Brown and Palincsar, 1982; Palincsar, 1986; Palincsar and Brown, 1984). Reciprocal teaching is based on the Soviet psychologist Vygotsky's theory of the importance of social context in children's learning. Vygotsky's theory states that children learn from their elders in ways that are similar to apprentices who learn their craft from masters. In translating this theory to the teaching situation, Brown and Palincsar believe that good teaching involves the teacher providing a structure or "scaffolding" with which children can gradually learn. In other words, the teacher at first structures the teaching situation but then gradually gives more and more responsibility to the students. This requires teachers to monitor children's level of understanding so that they can judge how much structure to provide. The teaching situation is called "reciprocal" because there is a dialogue between teacher and students "for the purpose of jointly constructing the meaning of the [reading] text" (Palincsar, 1986, p. 119).

The reciprocal situation consists of four activities: (a) summarizing, (b) question generating, (c) clarifying, and (d) predicting. In the first, the child or teacher summarizes the main ideas in the text. In the second, comprehension questions are generated. In the third, if there is a breakdown in comprehension, steps are taken to correct the situation—such as rereading. In the fourth, hypotheses are generated about what the content of the next paragraph(s) of the text will be.

Here is the basic procedure:

> The adult teacher assigned a segment of the passage (usually a paragraph) to be read and either indicated that it was her turn to be the teacher or assigned one of the students to teach that segment. The adult teacher and the students then read the assigned segment silently. After reading the text, the teacher (student or adult) for that segment summarized (reviewed) the content, discussed and clarified any difficulties, asked a question that a teacher or test might ask on the segment, and, finally, made a prediction about future content. All of these activities were embedded in as natural a dialogue as possible, with the teacher and other students giving feedback to one another. (Brown and Campione, 1984, p. 174)

Behavior Modification

For years, behavior modification has been used successfully to work with inattention and hyperactivity (Hallahan and Kauffman, 1975) as well as with specific academic behaviors (Kauffman, 1975; Lovitt, 1975a, b). Here the work of Thomas Lovitt and colleagues at the University of Washington is particularly relevant. Lovitt has used behavior modification to improve arithmetic performance (Lovitt and Curtiss, 1968; Smith and Lovitt, 1975; Smith, Lovitt and Kidder, 1972) and linguistic skills (Lovitt and Smith, 1972).

Frank Hewett's Santa Monica Project is important as an example of behavior modification applied to children with attentional problems (Hewett, 1967, 1968). Hewett devised the "engineered classroom," in which the teacher reinforces children with tokens or checkmarks that can be turned in for prizes such as candy or trinkets. The program is based on building a developmental hierarchy of skills in the child, beginning with attending abilities. The child with attentional problems is given a number of highly structured activities that require attending skills. A special section of the room is set aside for this. Once the student becomes relatively successful at attending to the task at hand, he or she is moved up to the next level in the hierarchy. Hewett's program has been found to be successful in increasing task attention.

Another classic study that is an example of the use of reinforcement to increase attending skills is that of a very disruptive first-grader named Levi (Hall, Lund, and Jackson, 1968). Hall and associates demonstrated that Levi's "on-task" behavior could be increased dramatically if the teacher simply ignored nonattending responses and responded only to on-task behavior.

Direct Instruction

Direct instruction is similar to behavior modification. It differs, however, in that it focuses specifically on the instructional process. Advocates of direct instruction stress a logical analysis of the concept to be taught, rather than the characteristics of the student. As stated by Hallahan, Lloyd, Kauffman, and Loper (1983):

> The Direct Instruction model shares many features with the Behavior Analysis model. Among these are the following: (a) emphasis on the importance of increasing the probability of correct responses recurring by rewarding correct responses, (b) concern with frequent measurement of progress as a means of determining whether instruction should be altered, (c) dependence on systematic structuring of the instructional environment in order to maintain task-oriented teacher and student behaviors, and (d) emphasis on directly teaching specific skills required by academic tasks.
>
> The Direct Instruction model differs from the Behavior Analysis model in the amount of emphasis placed on (a) the structure among solution strategies taught to students and (b) the selection of examples to be used during instruction. In the Direct Instruction model, students are taught systems for operating on and solving problems, and these systems are selected and developed in ways that take advantage of relationships among problems. For example, the means of analyzing and solving ratio problems is related to the means for handling fractional equivalencies; the commonalities of all basic arithmetic computation tasks (e.g., equality) are made apparent by the instructional programs; skills for understanding what one reads are systematically related to skills for understanding what one hears. Selection of examples to be used in presenting concepts and solution strategies is particularly unique. Examples are selected so that only one interpretation of a series of examples is possible. Crucial to designing such sequences is the use of examples that are and are not instances of the concept at hand and organization of them so that competing interpretations are discredited. Critical differences between concepts must be shown, and features of examples that are not critical to discriminating the concept at hand from other concepts (i.e., irrelevant features) must be varied in such a way that learners do not "attend" to them. (Hallahan, Lloyd, Kauffman, and Loper, 1983, pp. 113–114.)

One of the most popular direct instruction programs is *Corrective Reading* (Engelmann, Becker, Hanner, and Johnson, 1978). The program consists of highly structured, scripted daily lesson plans for the teacher to follow. Research has shown it to be very effective for improving the reading skills of learning-disabled students, especially those whose deficits are severe (Lloyd, Epstein, and Cullinan, 1981; Maggs and Maggs, 1979; Pflaum and Pascarella, 1980).

Administrative Arrangements

Although residential programs and special classes are sometimes used with learning-disabled children, the resource room is the most common arrangement. Because the learning-disabled child, as usually defined, is of at least near-normal intelligence and may have deficits in only a few areas of academic achievement, he or she is often seen as a good candidate for such placement.

The resource room is not the solution for all the ills of special education. A major consideration in the success of any resource room plan is how capable the regular class teacher is and how well equipped he or she is to deal with the special needs of the exceptional child. That we should always be striving toward reintegrating the learning-disabled child into the regular class is evidenced in the following anecdote related by Hewett:

> The patient was having delusions about people tapping his telephone and hiding tape recorders in his room. The therapist continually called the patient's attention to the fact that these beliefs were unlikely to be true and that they were simply not reality. After many sessions during which he heard the term, reality, over and over again the patient angrily confronted the therapist with, 'Tell me, Doc, what's so good about this reality?" The therapist looked him straight in the eye and calmly stated, "I never said it was good. I only said it was there." Whatever else the contemporary American public school regular classroom may be, it most certainly is "there." (1974, p. 397)

SPECIAL CONSIDERATIONS IN EDUCATING THE PRESCHOOL CHILD

There is very little preschool programming for learning-disabled children because of the difficulties in identifying learning-disabled children at such an early age (Keogh and Glover, 1980; Mercer, Algozzine, and Trifiletti, 1979). As Keogh and Glover point out, when we talk about testing the learning-disabled preschool child, we are really talking about prediction rather than identification. In other words, because preschool children do not ordinarily engage in academics, it is not possible, strictly speaking, to say that they are behind academically. Unfortunately, all other things being equal, prediction is always less precise than identification.

At least two factors make prediction at preschool ages of later learning disabilities particularly difficult:

1. In many cases of learning disabilities, we are talking about relatively mild problems. Many of these children seem bright and competent until faced with a particular academic task such as reading or spelling. Unlike many other handicapped children, learning-disabled children are not so immediately noticeable.
2. It is often difficult to determine what is a true developmental delay and what is merely a maturational slowness (Mercer et al., 1979). Many nondisabled children show slow developmental progress at this young age, but they soon catch up with their peers.

ONE PROFESSIONAL'S PERSPECTIVE

Donna J. Staggers

B.A., Elementary Education,
Waynesburg College

M.Ed., Special Education for the
Emotionally Disturbed, University of Virginia

Current Position: Teacher of
self-contained, learning disabilities class at Walker Middle School, Charlottesville
City Schools, Virginia

Ms. Donna Staggers has been a first and third grade regular class teacher, a learning disabilities resource teacher at the elementary level, and a self-contained learning disabilities teacher at the middle school level. Since she began teaching in 1970, she has also taught in five different school districts in three states—Pennsylvania, Texas, and Virginia. Her present learning disabilities, self-contained class contains 11 middle school students, 9 boys and 2 girls. Six of the youngsters are black and 5 are white. Their IQs range between 67 and 100, with an average of 85. Their reading achievement grade levels range between 2.2 and 6.2, with an average of 4.0. Math achievement grade levels range between 2.8 and 6.4, with an average of 4.3. And their language achievement grade levels range between 2.8 and 6.2, with an average of 4.2.

We asked Ms. Staggers the following series of questions:

What influenced your decision to be a teacher of learning-disabled children? I majored in education in college because it seemed like the thing to do, not because I had a burning desire

to teach. At the time I was in school women were not entering the fields of business and science. I really liked languages but had no idea what I would do with a major in French or Spanish.

Two of my sisters were teachers, and they seemed to be enjoying their classroom experiences. My parents were convinced that I too should become a teacher. They grew up during the Depression and remembered that teachers held jobs and managed nicely during those hard times. They believed that the teaching field offered stability and would be a wise career choice.

After a very positive student teaching experience in a first grade class of underprivileged children, I felt that teaching was the profession for me. My first year of teaching was pleasant enough (in spite of my shortcomings) to keep me interested in working with children. I found that I enjoyed teaching and organizing materials for my classroom and never thought about doing anything but teaching.

There have always been opportunities for me to change grade levels so that I could continue to grow and improve my skills. This is important for me and has enabled me to have

some wonderful experiences during my career.

If you could change one thing about your job, what would it be? The more specialized we become, the more interference there is in a student's day. For example, students who are underachieving have many needs and are often found eligible for resource, speech, counseling, or volunteer tutoring services. It looks great on paper to say that a child's needs are being met by these ancillary services when in fact the classroom schedule has to be juggled to accommodate the support personnel. Reading and math groups sometimes are forced to take a back seat to the extra help provided for students. This is even more true in a self-contained special education classroom. Ideally, these classes are set up with small numbers so instruction can be more individualized and beneficial to the students. By the time schedules have been set to include physical education, related arts, and speech, however, it is difficult to organize math and reading groups satisfactorily. If any pupils are mainstreamed there are more scheduling problems in addition to the burden of maintaining contact with the regular teacher and the home to communicate progress. All teachers are aware that students need time on task, but some days that is not always possible due to schedule changes or other unexpected disruptions.

What major changes have occurred in your field since you began teaching? In my first few years in the field, there was an emphasis on open classrooms and individualizing instruction. Learning centers were encouraged rather than paper and pencil tasks which might discourage students. Public Law 94-142 gave handicapped students the right to a formal education and parents of gifted children began to seek special programs for their children too. By the late 1970s parents and teachers alike were crying out that schools needed to get back to the basics. Students were graduating without being proficient in reading and math. Test scores were falling and the schools were blamed.

Presently, many teachers are being instructed on how to teach using the directive teaching model. Students are expected to be engaged in learning activities at all times. Writing across the curriculum is stressed—not just to improve language skills, but to assess understanding of concepts in content areas. Vocational assessments and training are being considered to help underachieving kids and keep them in school. In addition, computers are widely used in classrooms to aid instruction.

There has also been a noticeable change in student behavior since I began teaching. Virtually all classrooms have to deal with some difficult behaviors, and the general attitude of many students is not very positive. It is no longer a given that children come to school ready to learn or that they have respect for the school. The stress of dealing with behavior problems has led to an increasing rate of teacher burnout, a term which has been coined since I began teaching.

Pick the one student in your career with whom you've had the most success and describe your involvement with him or her. In Odessa, Texas, I taught a desegregation class of 15 underachieving third graders who were not eligible for any special education services. The class was in a minority school of black and Mexican children. All of them were very pleasant and had a respect for the school although education was not a priority for many of them.

One of the most delightful students I have ever taught was an 8-year-old Mexican boy who was in the "Room of 15." Roberto entered my class reading on a K-9 grade level. Math and language skills were high first- or second-grade level.

Robert came from a broken home and received very little encouragement or supervision for his schoolwork. I worried that he did not get enough to eat and that he was left alone or had to fend for himself. Many days he expressed concern about circumstances at home.

In spite of these conditions, there was a sweetness and sensitivity about him that I have yet to encounter in any other child that I have taught. Roberto's success in the classroom had a lot to do with his disposition. He seemed to thrive in the small group and appreciated the help he was given. As he became more confident, he initiated more conversations which helped his English (Spanish was spoken at home). He was attentive and receptive to the instruction given. He wanted to do well and worked hard to improve. By April, his reading scores were at a 4.2 grade level and his math scores were at a 5.0 grade level.

I tried to capitalize on Roberto's positive attitude and desire to learn by offering as much structure and positive reinforcement as possible. Every day we had a full schedule of work and repeated out loud that our goal was to be on grade level. He and the other students worked well together and applauded each other as daily gains were made. The principal and other teachers were invited to admire the good work being done. Recognition was given for all progress.

Teaching this special class was truly one of the highlights of my career. The conditions were not perfect, but I felt that I had the right to teach and that my students had come to learn. The results were wonderful!

Describe the most challenging student you've ever had and what made him or her so difficult. One of the most difficult students I have had to teach was a 13-year-old student who had been identified in first grade as learning disabled. For six years he was in a special education class and by the time he entered my class I felt the services had been wasted. I honestly believed that any disability that child may have had was secondary to his poor attitude and street behavior.

He was very sensitive and insecure but hid the fact by mocking others before they could see through him. He was afraid of failing and could not handle making mistakes. If he made an error in writing he would tear up the paper rather than erase.

When faced with a daily schedule he almost fell apart. He had to be given one direction and one assignment at a time or else he became very hyperactive. Even with lots of individual attention he had to be coaxed and coddled to complete his work. Any change in procedure would throw him out of whack.

This child was also obsessed with cleanliness. If he thought another child was unclean, he would make a point of walking around his desk to avoid him or her. I remember in particular how he instructed student nurses to clean the dummy's mouth when they demonstrated artificial respiration.

The real challenge in teaching this child was to overcome his negative attitude and the lack of support from the home. The extra effort I put in with this child exhausted me. I gave him rides home from school dances and made time so I could get to know him. Once he trusted me, he really settled down and made some progress.

The most accurate predictors of later academic problems are preacademic skills, such as counting. (Richard Hutchings/Photo Researchers)

Although most professionals hesitate to program for learning-disabled children at the preschool level, ideally it would be good to do so. Thus we greatly need research into better predictive tests at the preschool level. At present we know that the most accurate predictors are preacademic skills (Mercer et al., 1979). **Preacademic skills** are behaviors that are needed before formal instruction can begin, such as identification of letters, numbers, shapes, and colors. Further refinement of tests of these skills will be necessary before an increase in preschool programming for the learning-disabled child is feasible.

SPECIAL CONSIDERATIONS IN EDUCATING THE ADOLESCENT AND ADULT

In considering the older learning-disabled individual, definition and identification are almost as great a problem as with the younger child. As Deshler (1978) points out, the learning-disabled adult tends to blend in with other individuals who are experiencing similar problems for other reasons. One problem we face in identifying the older learning-disabled individual stems from the fact that until the late 1970s and early 1980s relatively little learning disabilities programming extended beyond the elementary school years. Thus we are somewhat in the dark when it comes to describing the specific behavioral characteristics of the learning-disabled adolescent and adult and educational programs that would be appropriate for them.

We do know, however, that just as with younger learning-disabled children, academic achievement problems are the trademark of older individuals. In an extensive review of the long-term consequences of learning disabilities, Kavale (1987) concluded that learning-disabled adults are not likely to overcome their problems in reading and spelling. In addition, they are at risk for behavior problems, especially low self-esteem. Kavale is quick to point out, however, that it is impossible to predict the future adjustment of any particular child with any great accuracy. Such things as parental attitudes, intensity of educational interventions, and the individual's motivation can increase or decrease an adult's chances of coping with learning disabilities.

Secondary Programming

There are a variety of approaches to educating learning-disabled students at the secondary level. Zigmond and Sansone (1986) note that these models differ with regard to: (a) how much time students spend with special versus general education teachers, and (b) the degree to which their curriculum is "special," or different from the general curriculum. Models can differ on each of these two dimensions. At the one extreme are approaches in which the student spends little or no time with special educators and does not have a special curriculum. An example of this kind of approach would be the *consultation model,* in which the special education teacher works with general education teachers in order to help them adjust their teaching to accommodate learning-disabled students in their classes. Another example of an approach requiring both a minimum of direct service from a special educator and change in the regular curriculum would be a *resource room–tutoring model.* In this kind of arrangement, the special educator works with learning-disabled students on subjects in which they are having difficulty in order to help them make passing grades.

At the other extreme on the two dimensions are approaches that require intensive involvement with special educators and the use of a different type of curriculum. An example of this kind of model is what Zigmond and Sansone (1986) call the *self-contained class–novel curriculum.* This approach is characterized by a **functional academics** curriculum similar to what is often used with mildly retarded students (see Chapter 2). The curriculum is oriented more toward preparing students for the job market than toward achieving higher levels of academic preparation. Another example of a model that is special educator-intensive and requires considerable modification of the regular curriculum is the *work-study model,* again similar to what is used with mildly retarded students (see Chapter 2). In this model, students spend part of their time working on actual jobs.

Because these models represent the extremes on two continua—special educator intensity and special curriculum—they are probably most appropriate for students at the extreme ends of the severity continuum. The consultation and resource room–tutoring models would probably be appropriate for students with mild learning disabilities. The self-contained class–novel curriculum and work-study models would appear most appropriate for students with severe disabilities. There are a number of learning-disabled students, however, whose difficulties fall somewhere toward the middle of the severity continuum. For these students, approaches falling in the middle of Zigmond and Sansone's two continua are perhaps most appropriate. These approaches fall under the heading of *resource room–novel curriculum* model. They are characterized by a modest amount of special educator involvement, up to two hours per day, and some use of different curricula. Two examples are the Learning Strategies Curriculum and the School Survival Skills Curriculum.

Learning Strategies Curriculum

Donald Deshler, Jean Schumaker, and their colleagues at the University of Kansas have developed a curriculum for secondary learning-disabled students called the Learning Strategies Curriculum (Schumaker, Deshler, Alley, and Warner, 1983; Schumaker, Deshler, and Ellis, 1986). The idea behind this approach is that learning-disabled adolescents need strategies to learn how to learn more than they need specific subject content. This emphasis on strategies allows us to categorize the Learning Strategies Curriculum as a type of cognitive training. As Deshler and Schumaker (1986) state:

> Three major rationales underlie a learning strategies intervention approach for adolescents. First, the development and application of learning strategies or metacognitive skills is significantly related to age; that is, older students consistently are more proficient in the use of such behaviors (Armbruster, Echols, & Brown, 1984). Second, adolescents who "learn how to learn" in secondary schools will be in a much better position to learn new skills and to respond to rapidly changing information and conditions in the future (Deshler & Schumaker, 1984). Third, a learning strategies instruction approach requires students to accept major responsibility for their learning and progress (Wong, 1985). Such a commitment must be made by students if they are to truly become independent. (p. 584)

The organization of the Learning Strategies Curriculum is determined by what the Kansas group sees as the major demands of the secondary curriculum. It is therefore comprised of three strands. One is devoted to helping students acquire information from written materials. It includes strategies for such things as word identification, reading comprehension, and interpretation of diagrams and charts. A second strand is designed to help students remember important information and facts. It contains strategies for such things as taking notes and using mnemonics. A third strand involves aid in improving written expression. It includes strategies for such things as writing sentences and paragraphs. Another feature of this strand is that it includes strategies for completing assignments on time and test taking.

Multipass is an example of one set of the strategies used in the strand designed for getting information from written materials (Schumaker, Deshler, Alley, Warner, and Denton, 1982). Based on the SQ3R method (Robinson, 1946), Multipass involves having the student make many "passes" (hence the name) through the reading material. The three major passes are the Survey, the Size-Up, and the Sort-Out. These three passes are embedded in a context of highly individualized programming and a heavy reliance on ensuring that the child achieves certain performance goals before moving on to the next stage. Here is a description of Multipass:

> The purpose of the Survey Pass was to familiarize the student with main ideas and organization of the chapter. Thus, this previewing pass required the student to: (a) read the chapter title, (b) read the introductory paragraph, (c) review the chapter's relationship to other adjacent chapters by perusing the table of contents, (d) read the major subtitles of the chapter and notice how the chapter is organized, (e) look at illustrations and read their captions, (f) read the summary paragraph, and (g) paraphrase all the information gained in the process.
>
> The Size-Up Pass was designed to help students gain specific information and facts from a chapter without reading it from beginning to end. This pass required the student to first

read each of the questions at the end of the chapter to determine what facts appeared to be the most important to learn. If the student was already able to answer a given question as a result of the Survey Pass, a check mark ($\sqrt{}$) was placed next to the question. The student now progressed through the entire chapter following these steps: (a) look for a textual cue (e.g., bold-face print, subtitle, colored print, italics); (b) make the cue into a question (e.g., if the cue was the italicized vocabulary word *conqueror,* the student asked, "What does conqueror mean?"; if the cue was the subtitle "The Election of 1848," the student might ask, "Who won the election of 1848?" or "Why was the election of 1848 important?"; (c) skim through the surrounding text to find the answer to the question; and (d) paraphrase the answer to yourself without looking in the book. When the student reached the end of the chapter using these four steps for each textual cue, he/she was required to paraphrase all the facts and ideas he/she could remember about the chapter.

The Sort-Out Pass was included to get students to test themselves over the material presented in the chapter. In this final pass, the student read and answered each question at the end of the chapter. If the student could answer a question immediately, he/she placed a checkmark next to it. If the student was unable to answer a question, however, the answer was sought by (a) thinking in which section of the chapter the answer would most likely be located, (b) skimming through that section for the answer, (c) if the answer was not located, thinking of another relevant section, and (d) skimming that section, and so on until the student could answer the question. A checkmark was then placed next to the question, and the student moved on to answer the next question. (Schumaker, Deshler, Alley, Warner, and Denton, 1982, pp. 298–299)

School Survival Skills Curriculum

As any parent of a teenager can attest, the adolescent years are a difficult period. Peer acceptance is of paramount importance to most high school students. Wearing the right clothes, hanging out with the "right" crowd, and the like are perceived as important ingredients of happiness. For the learning-disabled student, who adds to these relatively normal feelings an additional set of learning and social problems, the secondary school years can be a devastating experience.

Recognizing the magnitude of social problems for the learning-disabled adolescent, Zigmond and colleagues have developed a comprehensive curriculum—the School Survival Skills Curriculum (Zigmond and Brownlee, 1980). It involves four steps: (1) assessing what social skills need to be taught, (2) teaching social perception skills, (3) teaching socially appropriate behaviors, and (4) involving significant adults in the youngster's program. The following is a brief description of how such steps are integrated into the curriculum:

In the School Survival Skills Curriculum the emphasis is on exploring and developing coping skills essential to survival in high school. Working with groups of four to six students at a time, teacher and students together assess the extent to which students are able to control disruptive behaviors and to conform to teacher and school expectations (step 1: assessment). Certain particularly troublesome behaviors are identified as targets for change. Then students learn to be more sensitive to cues in their environment that could help them define what would be appropriate behaviors (step 2: social perception training). Next, students practice new behaviors, first in a resource room setting under simulated conditions, and then in the mainstream of the school. Practice sessions employ role playing, modeling, discussion, and corrective feedback to help students master new behaviors (step 3: teaching new behaviors). Finally, teachers are alerted to the new behavior patterns students are learning, and then cooperation in mainstreaming these new behaviors is arranged (step 4: working with significant others). (Zigmond and Brownlee, 1980, p. 81)

Learning Disabilities and Juvenile Delinquency: Is There a Causal Connection?

Many investigators have found a higher prevalence of learning disabilities among juvenile delinquents than is ordinarily found in the general population. A review of these prevalence studies (Murphy, 1986) found that, although the particular prevalence rates vary widely from a low of 9 percent to a high of 36.5, even the most conservative figures contrast sharply with what is usually found in the population at large.

The reason for the high rate of learning disabilities among juvenile delinquents has been a topic of debate for years. Although it is tempting simply to assert that learning disabilities cause juvenile delinquency, most authorities agree that even if there is such a causal relationship, it is undoubtedly a very complex one. They have posited several feasible explanations for the association between the two categories, some of which specify a direct causal link between the two, and some of which do not. In a review of this literature funded by the U.S. Department of Justice's Office of Juvenile Justice and Delinquency Prevention, Keilitz and Dunivant (1986) found five theoretical explanations. The first three theories are causal, while the last two are not:

Causal Theories

1. *School Failure Theory:* This theory posits that learning disabilities directly result in school failure, which then results in juvenile delinquency. There are five hypothesized ways in which this can happen. These students may:
    1.1 become angry at their inability to learn and "strike back at society in anger and retaliation" (Keilitz and Dunivant, 1986, p. 19);
    1.2 be influenced by other delinquency-prone students with whom they are grouped in school, for example behavior disordered youngsters;
    1.3 because of their school failure become disenchanted with teachers and other symbols of the school as an institution, and this disenchantment may diminish their commitment to socially accepted behavior;
    1.4 perceive that their academic failure will prohibit them from obtaining a job leading to adequate financial resources and prestige, and this, in turn, leads them to try to obtain money and prestige through illegal means;
    1.5 because of their lack of success in school blame others rather than themselves for negative events.
2. *Susceptibility Theory:* According to this theory, learning-disabled children have certain personality and cognitive attributes that make them susceptible to delinquent behavior. These characteristics include such things as poor impulse control, problems in reading social cues, and suggestibility.
3. *Differential Treatment Theory:* This theory posits that there may not actually be any difference in how often learning-disabled and nonhandicapped youngsters commit delinquent acts. Instead, there is a difference in whether they are caught for their delinquent acts and/or how they are treated by the juvenile justice system. This theory has three hypotheses:
    3.1 *Differential arrest hypothesis:* This hypothesis holds that learning-disabled youngsters are more likely than the nonhandicapped to be apprehended by the police for the same activities. Differential arrest rates may occur for a variety of reasons—for example, learning-disabled students' inability to use strategies for not being caught or their inability to talk their way out of arrest.
    3.2 *Differential adjudication hypothesis:* This hypothesis posits that learning-disabled youths, after being arrested, are more likely to have their cases settled judicially. A variety of explanations for this higher incidence of adjudication have been forwarded—for example, their lack of self-control and

social ineptness may cause the authorities to be more likely to bring them to trial.

3.3 *Differential disposition hypothesis:* For some of the same reasons noted under the above two hypotheses, this hypothesis holds that learning-disabled youths receive harsher treatment by the juvenile court.

Noncausal Theories

4. *Sociodemographic Characteristics Theory:* This theory holds that learning disabilities and juvenile delinquency frequently occur together because they are both caused by social factors such as parents' education level and socioeconomic status.

5. *Response Bias Theory:* This theory holds that learning-disabled adolescents do not commit more delinquent acts than their nonhandicapped peers. However, when asked in surveys or questionnaires to reveal their delinquent behaviors, they are less likely to conceal them.

If we look at these five theories and some of the subtheories, it should be apparent just how complicated the relationship between learning disabilities and juvenile delinquency is. No wonder there has been so much debate about whether there is a causal connection. Although much more research on this issue is needed, Keilitz and Dunivant (1986) have conducted two large-scale studies that support the three causal theories above. From these results, they have concluded:

Generally, the data are consistent with causal theories that describe the contribution learning disabilities makes to delinquent behavior. Of course, LD is only one among many causes of delinquency. Only a relatively small proportion of the youth population is affected by LD. Within this group, however, learning disabilities appear to be one of the important causes of delinquency. (Keilitz and Dunivant, 1986, p. 24)

Postsecondary Programming

More and more colleges and universities are establishing special programs and services for learning-disabled students. There is very little agreement in the field, however, on how these programs should be arranged because so little is currently known about the specific needs of the learning-disabled college student. What research has been done indicates that these students are likely to exhibit problems in reading, effective study habits, written language skills, and note taking (Vogel, 1982). With regard to the last, Vogel notes:

For many LD [learning-disabled] adults, the task of taking notes in lectures is overwhelming, nor is it any wonder. Note-taking requires simultaneous listening, comprehending, and synthesizing and/or extracting main ideas while retaining them long enough to formulate a synopsis and write it down. The writing act, in turn, requires automaticity and speed in letter formation and sufficient legibility and spelling ability to decipher what has been written at a later time. (p. 523)

For those learning-disabled individuals who do make it through the rigors of college, there is evidence suggesting that their career choices are limited (Gottfredson, Finucci, and Childs, 1984). For example, researchers who followed up graduates of a private college preparatory school for reading-disabled boys found these men to be overrepresented in managerial and sales positions and underrepresented

Some authorities are now pointing to previously unrecognized learning disabilities as a possible cause of college failure. (Michael Philip Manheim/Southern Light)

in professions such as law, medicine, and college teaching (Gottfredson, Finucci, and Childs, 1984). The researchers hypothesize that their results were based on the different skills required for sales and managerial versus professional positions. When asked what skills are necessary for performance in their occupations, professionals ranked reading and writing among the highest skills, whereas managers and salesmen stressed personality attributes such as being persuasive and taking the initiative.

MANAGING THE CHILD IN SCHOOL

The child with learning disabilities needs individual tutoring in one or more areas of disability. Whether or not there is a resource teacher available will determine to a great extent how much of this instruction will be assumed by the regular class teacher. It cannot be stressed too much that the general classroom and resource teachers should have a cooperative working relationship. The general education teacher should be sure to work out with the resource teacher exactly what the duties of each will be. *Who will be responsible for what* is a basic question that is sometimes never decided. This can only lead to frustration for both teachers and for the child.

The learning-disabled child, as usually defined by public schools, has at least near-normal intelligence. So there are special considerations the teacher needs to keep in mind:

1. In particular, the teacher should be careful to *have the child work on a level commensurate with his or her abilities.* Because the child has a relatively high

IQ, the teacher may assume the child can do more than he or she is actually capable of doing. Especially in the early stages of working with the child, it is important that the teacher find a level at which the child can gain a number of success experiences. Failure experiences are probably "old hat" to the learning-disabled child; tolerance for failure is likely to be quite low.

2. It is also important to be careful to provide *clear instructions* for the child. Furthermore, the teacher should be attuned to the possibility that directions may not be understood. Learning-disabled children are notorious for looking as if they understand what is being said when in fact they are confused.

3. If the child proves to be highly distractible and hyperactive, the teacher may wish to consider making *special physical arrangements* in the room. Placing the youngster's desk in a corner, using the walls to form a "cubicle," may be enough. If not, it may be wise to look into the possibility of using partitions. (The teacher must be sure to communicate to the student that this is not a punitive arrangement.) Also, to reduce overstimulation, the child's desk should be clear of extraneous materials that are not pertinent to the task he or she is presently working on.

4. The teacher should not be surprised if the child displays *signs of emotional disturbance.* The teacher should not be willing to tolerate bizarre behavior, but should be aware that disturbed behavior is not unlikely. In this respect, our recommendations for working with the disturbed are very much in order for the teacher of learning-disabled children (see Chapter 4).

SUMMARY

The term "learning disabled" was coined in 1963 to describe children who in spite of normal or near-normal intelligence have a puzzling array of learning and behavior problems. What prompted the birth of this newest area of special education was the realization that many children with learning problems were simply not receiving needed educational services.

Numerous definitions of learning disabilities have been proposed. The four most common factors in these definitions are: IQ–achievement discrepancy; presumption of central nervous system dysfunction; psychological processing problems; learning problems not due to environmental disadvantage, mental retardation, or emotional disturbance. Much controversy has surrounded the inclusion of each factor. Some have questioned the IQ–achievement discrepancy, especially when it is measured by the use of formulas. Some have been critical of the search for central nervous system dysfunction as a causal agent, stating that such evidence is usually largely speculative. Others have stated that psychological processing disorders are irrelevant to academic learning, and training

of psychological processes does not result in academic benefits. Still others have claimed that it is often illogical to treat learning disabilities as separate from mild emotional disturbance and mild mental retardation because the characteristics of children in each of these categories are quite similar. Regardless of these controversies, however, the most common definition—the one used by the federal government—includes the above four factors.

The prevalence of students receiving learning disabilities services has increased dramatically. There are now more than twice as many children identified as learning disabled than there were in 1976. During the 1985–86 school year, 4.73 percent of the school age population received such services. Many are concerned about this rapid growth, especially federal officials.

Causal factors for learning disabilities fall generally into three groups: organic and biological, genetic, and environmental. There is as yet no solid evidence to indicate that a learning-disabled child necessarily has brain injury or malfunction. Scientists, however, continue to research possible organic factors. Learning disabilities do tend to run in families—but whether this is due to genetic factors or similar learning environments is yet to be determined. Environmental causes are hard to pinpoint, although it appears that children from lower income areas tend to exhibit more learning problems. Poor teaching can be another environmental factor contributing to academic difficulties.

Learning disabilities professionals use tests of several different types: standardized achievement tests, process tests, informal reading inventories, and formative evaluation methods. The standardized achievement test is most often used. It is important that the teacher inspect the particular kinds of errors a child makes on such a test in order to gain insight into that child's learning problems.

Some have devised process tests to assess the child's psychological processes, one or more of which are assumed to be the cause(s) of the academic problems. Remediation is aimed at correcting the faulty process rather than the academic problem. Among the more commonly used process tests are the Illinois Test of Psycholinguistic Abilities (ITPA) and the Marianne Frostig Developmental Test of Visual Perception (DTVP). The ITPA investigates the channels of communication, psycholinguistic processes, and levels of organization. This particular test succeeded in bringing about an awareness that psychological and educational testing should be sensitive to the educational needs of the child. The DTVP assesses aspects such as eye-motor coordination, figure-ground perception, and position in space in order to pinpoint perceptual deficits.

An informal reading inventory is usually developed by the teacher to appraise level of competence on a test without reference to other children. The teacher sometimes uses it to determine the child's independent learning level, instructional level, and frustration level.

Formative evaluation methods are characterized by five features. First, the teacher usually does the assessment. Second, the focus of the assessment is on behaviors that are directly relevant to classroom performance. Third, the teacher measures the child's behavior fre-

quently and over a period of time. Fourth, the assessment is used in conjunction with the setting of educational goals. (This aspect is sometimes referred to as criterion-referenced testing.) Fifth, the teacher uses the assessment information to decide whether the educational program for an individual student is effective. If it is not, then the teacher tries an alternative intervention strategy.

Curriculum-based assessment is an example of a formative evaluation method. In addition to the five features above, it is designed to measure performance in the curriculum to which the child is exposed and to compare his or her performance with that of peers.

The 10 most frequently cited characteristics attributed to learning-disabled children are hyperactivity, perceptual-motor impairments, emotional lability, general coordination deficits, disorders of attention, impulsivity, disorders of memory and thinking, specific academic problems, disorders of speech and hearing, and equivocal neurological signs and EEG irregularities. The evidence is strong that many learning-disabled children perform poorly on visual and auditory perceptual abilities. It is wrong, however, to assign learning disabilities solely to perceptual problems, because some children do quite well despite such problems.

In general, many learning-disabled individuals demonstrate memory deficits for both visual and auditory stimuli. The reasons for these memory problems may be linked to the deficient use of learning strategies such as verbal rehearsal. Likewise, the ability to conceptualize and use problem-solving strategies has been found to be deficient in learning-disabled children.

Some have conceptualized the attention problems of learning-disabled children as being of three different types: coming to attention, decision making, or maintaining attention. Attentional problems are intimately connected with hyperactivity. In fact, many authorities maintain that the basic problem of most children labeled hyperactive is that they have attentional difficulties. Impulsivity, like hyperactivity and distractibility, interferes with the ability to develop adequate problem-solving capabilities.

Problems in metacognition interfere with the

learning-disabled student's awareness of learning strategies and ability to regulate use of such strategies. Learning-disabled children can exhibit a variety of different types of metacognitive problems, such as metamemory, metalistening, and metacomprehension. The latter, when it is applied to reading, is sometimes called comprehension monitoring and has received a great deal of research attention. Critical comprehension monitoring skills involve being able to clarify the purposes of reading, to focus on important parts of the text, to monitor one's level of comprehension, to know when to reread and scan ahead, and to consult external sources.

Social adjustment problems are frequent in learning-disabled students. Ratings by peers, teachers, and parents are consistent in demonstrating that learning-disabled youngsters are not well liked. Learning-disabled children themselves have poor self-esteem relative to their academic abilities. And they are poorly motivated; they frequently show signs of external rather than internal sources of motivation. In the area of "attributions," they fail to acknowledge that their own efforts can lead to success, but are quick to attribute their failures to their own inabilities. These pessimistic attributions of the causes of their successes and failures make them at risk for developing "learned helplessness," a perception that no matter what one does, one will still fail.

Neurological problems are also more likely to occur in learning-disabled than in nonhandicapped children. But for most learning-disabled children, there is only scant evidence that they indeed have central nervous system dysfunction. One of the most frequent methods for attributing neurological problems to such children—soft signs—is often unreliable because it is based on behavioral rather than neurological indicators.

Needless to say, scholastic difficulties exist in all learning-disabled children to some extent. Although in general their greatest areas of academic difficulties are related to language and reading, the possibility of problems in math should not be ignored.

Some authorities believe that a composite of the above characteristics indicates that many learning-disabled children are passive rather than active learners. Many of their problems can be attributed to the fact that they often lack the ability to use appropriate task-approach strategies spontaneously.

Given the great deal of heterogeneity of behavioral characteristics exhibited by learning-disabled students, some researchers are attempting to document subtypes of learning disabilities. One research team, for instance, has provided evidence for the existence of behavioral subtypes based on teacher ratings. They suggest that these subtypes have educational relevance. For example, children in an attention deficit subtype and subtypes characterized by behavioral problems are at risk to deteriorate over time academically.

There are many approaches to educating learning-disabled children. In process training, as in process testing, the learning processes themselves are a focus. Newell Kephart based his process training methods on the "perceptual motor match," in which the rationale is that motor development precedes visual development. With this method, a person is first taught appropriate motor skills, with visual training later matched to the learned motor experiences. This theory has been criticized by current developmental psychologists.

Multisensory approaches attempt to remedy learning problems by using a combination of the sensory systems in the training process. In the VAKT method, the student's own words and ideas in a story provide the material for the subsequent learning procedure.

Cruickshank's Montgomery County Project is an example of an approach built upon the notion that inattentive and hyperactive children need to have irrelevant stimuli reduced and a great deal of structured teaching. In this project, classroom activities were strongly teacher-directed. In addition, the teacher reduced irrelevant stimuli to enhance the intensity of the educational materials.

Cognitive training differs from traditional behavior modification in that thought processes are the object of change, rather than strictly observable behaviors. It is sometimes referred to as cognitive-behavior modification to highlight this contrast with behavior modification.

Many professionals advocate cognitive training because such techniques: (a) stress self-initiative on the part of the child, (b) provide the child with specific learning strategies, and (c) appear particularly well-suited for attentional and impulsivity problems. Three types of cognitive training that have been successfully applied to learning-disabled students are self-instructional training, self-monitoring, and reciprocal teaching. Self-instruction involves having the student talk about what it is he or she is doing. Self-monitoring involves the individual evaluating and recording his or her own behavior. For example, teachers have taught children to monitor their own attentional behavior. In reciprocal teaching, the teacher gently structures the learning situation so that children gradually take over more and more responsibility for their own instruction.

Behavior modification is an educational approach that has been used effectively with learning-disabled students, particularly those who are hyperactive and/or easily distracted. In this procedure the teacher specifies goals, carefully monitors behavior, and provides reinforcement for successful learning.

Direct instruction is similar to behavior modification, but it focuses more on what the teacher should be doing in the instructional process than on the characteristics of the learners. Research on the effectiveness of direct instruction has been very positive.

The resource room is the most common type of placement for learning-disabled children, primarily because as traditionally defined they are of at least near-normal intelligence, and may have learning problems in only a few academic areas. The goals of such an arrangement are to move the child back into the general education classroom for more and more of the day and to gear teaching methods to the needs of the individual student.

Most professionals are cautious about establishing programs for learning-disabled preschoolers because it is hard to predict at that age level which children will develop academic difficulties. More research is needed in this area. We do know that certain preacademic skills such as letter, number, shape, and color recognition are the best predictors of later academic learning.

The importance of educational programming at the secondary level and beyond is underscored by evidence indicating that learning-disabled individuals as adults do not outgrow their academic deficiencies and are at risk to have behavior problems, especially low self-esteem. There is considerable evidence indicating a higher prevalence of learning disabilities among juvenile delinquents. There is, however, considerable debate over whether learning disabilities contribute causally to juvenile delinquency. Most authorities agree that, if there is a link between the two, the connection is indeed complex.

It was not until the late 1970s that educators paid much attention to how to program for learning-disabled adolescents and adults. There are now a variety of approaches for serving learning-disabled youngsters at the secondary level. Some approaches are for students with relatively mild disabilities. Examples of these approaches are the consultation model and resource room–tutoring model, which stress having students stay with their general education teacher and work with the general education curriculum as much as possible. Other approaches are for youngsters with relatively severe disabilities. Examples of these are the self-contained class–novel curriculum model and the work-study model, which involve a great deal of student contact with special education professionals and much more involvement with an alternative curriculum. For students whose disabilities fall in the middle range of severity, there is the resource room–novel curriculum model, in which students receive a moderate amount of contact with special educators and some use of different curricula. Two such programs, which have gained widespread acceptance, are the Learning Strategies Curriculum and the School Survival Skills Curriculum.

More and more colleges and universities are offering educational services for learning-disabled students. Some of these programs emphasize such things as helping students improve skills in reading, writing, note taking, and forming effective study habits.

REFERENCES

Ackerman, P. T., Anhalt, J. M., & Dykman, R. A. (1986). Inferential word-decoding weakness in reading disabled children. *Learning Disability Quarterly, 9*(4), 315–324.

Ahn, H., Prichep, L., John, E. R., Baird, H., Trepetin, M., & Kaye, H. (1980). Developmental equations reflect brain dysfunctions. *Science, 210*(12), 1259–1262.

Algozzine, B., & Ysseldyke, J. (1983). Learning disabilities as a subset of school failure: The oversophistication of a concept. *Exceptional Children, 50,* 242–246.

American Psychiatric Association. (1980). *Diagnostic and statistical manual of mental disorders* (3rd ed.). Washington, D.C.: American Psychiatric Association.

Anderson, T. H. (1980). Study strategies and adjunct aids. In P. J. Spiro, B. C. Bruce, & W. F. Brewer (Eds.), *Theoretical issues in reading comprehension* (pp. 483–502). Hillsdale, N.J.: Erlbaum.

Armbruster, B. B., Echols, C. H., & Brown, A. L. (1984). The role of metacognition in reading to learn: A developmental perspective. *The Volta Review, 84*(5), 79–101.

Baker, L. (1982). An evaluation of the role of metacognitive deficits in learning disabilities. *Topics in Learning and Learning Disabilities, 2*(1), 27–35.

Baker, L., & Anderson, R. I. (1982). Effects of inconsistent information on text processing: Evidence for comprehension monitoring. *Reading Research Quarterly, 17,* 281–294.

Baker, L., & Brown, A. L. (1980). *Metacognitive skills and reading* (Tech. Rep. No. 188). Champaign, Ill.: University of Illinois Center for the Study of Reading.

Baker, L., & Brown, A. L. (1984). Cognitive monitoring in reading. In J. Flood (Ed.), *Understanding reading comprehension.* Newark, Del.: International Reading Association.

Barsch, R. H. (1965). *A movigenic curriculum.* Madison, Wis.: Department of Public Instruction, Bureau for the Handicapped.

Bateman, B. D. (1968). *Interpretations of the 1961 Illinois Test of Psycholinguistic Abilities.* Seattle: Special Child Publications.

Belmont, L., & Birch, H. G. (1965). Lateral dominance, lateral awareness, and reading disability. *Child Development, 34,* 57–71.

Blackman, S., & Goldstein, K. M. (1982). Cognitive styles and learning disabilities. *Journal of Learning Disabilities, 15,* 106–115.

Board of Trustees of the Council for Learning Disabilities (1986). Use of discrepancy formulas in the identification of learning disabled individuals. *Learning Disability Quarterly, 9*(3), 245.

Boder, E. (1973). Developmental dyslexia: A diagnostic approach based on three atypical reading-spelling patterns. *Developmental Medicine and Child Neurology, 15,* 663–687.

Borkowski, J. G., Weyhing, R. S., & Turner, L. A. (1986). Attributional retraining and the teaching of strategies. *Exceptional Children, 53*(2), 130–137.

Brown, A. L. (1980). Metacognitive development and reading. In R. J. Spiro, B. C. Bruce, & W. F. Brewer (Eds.), *Theoretical issues in reading comprehension* (pp. 453–481). Hillsdale, N.J.: Erlbaum.

Brown, A. L., & Campione, J. C. (1984). Three faces of transfer: Implications for early competence, individual differences, and instruction. In M. E. Lamb, A. L. Brown, & B. Rogoff (Eds.), *Advances in developmental psychology,* (Vol. 3, 143–192). Hillsdale, N.J.: Lawrence Erlbaum.

Brown, A. L., & Palincsar, A. S. (1982). Inducing strategic learning from text by means of informed, self-control training. *Topics in Learning and Learning Disabilities, 2,* 1–17.

Bryan, J. H., & Perlmutter, B. (1979). Immediate impressions of learning disabled children by female adults. *Learning Disability Quarterly, 2,* 80–88.

Bryan, J. H., & Sonnerfeld, J., & Greenberg, F. (1981). Children's and parent's views about integration tactics. *Learning Disability Quarterly, 4,* 170–179.

Bryan, T. H. (1974). Peer popularity of learning disabled children. *Journal of Learning Disabilities, 7,* 621–625.

Bryan, T. H. (1976). Peer popularity of learning disabled children. A replication. *Journal of Learning Disabilities, 9,* 307–311.

Bryan, T. H. (1977). Learning disabled children's comprehension of nonverbal communication. *Journal of Learning Disabilities, 10,* 501–506.

Bryan, T. H., & Bryan, J. H. (1986). *Understanding learning disabilities.* Palo Alto, Calif.: Mayfield Publishing Company.

Bryan, T. H., Donahue, M., & Pearl, R. (1981). Learning disabled children's peer interactions during a small group problem solving task. *Learning Disability Quarterly, 4,* 13–22.

Bryan, T., Donahue, M., Pearl, R., & Herzog, A. (1984). Conversational interactions between mothers and their learning disabled children during a problem-solving task. *Journal of Speech and Hearing Disorders, 49,* 64–71.

Bryan, T. H., Donahue, M., Pearl, R., & Strum, C. (1981). Learning disabled children's conversational skills—The "TV Talk Show." *Learning Disability Quarterly, 4*(3), 250–260.

Bryan, T. H., & Pflaum, S. (1978). Social interactions of learning disabled children: A linguistic, social, and cognitive analysis. *Learning Disability Quarterly, 1,* 70–79.

Bryan, T. H., Sherman, R., & Fisher, A. (1980). Learning disabled boy's nonverbal behaviors with a dyadic interview. *Learning Disability Quarterly, 3,* 65–72.

Bryan, T., Werner, M. A., & Pearl, R. (1982). Learning disabled students' conformity responses to prosocial and antisocial situations. *Learning Disability Quarterly, 5,* 344–352.

Carnine, D., & Silbert, J. (1979). *Direct instruction reading.* Columbus, Ohio: Charles E. Merrill.

Carpenter, D., & Miller, L. J. (1982). Spelling ability of reading disabled LD students and able readers. *Learning Disability Quarterly, 5,* 65–70.

Center, D. B., & Wascom, A. M. (1986). Teacher perceptions of social behavior in learning disabled and socially normal children and youths. *Journal of Learning Disabilities, 19*(7), 420–425.

Chandler, C. (1981). The effects of parenting techniques on the development of motivational orientations in children. Unpublished doctoral dissertation, University of Denver.

Clements, S. D. (1966). *Minimal brain dysfunction in children: Terminology and identification*. NINDB Monograph No. 3. Washington, D.C.: U.S. Department of Health, Education and Welfare.

Coles, G. (1978). The learning-disabilities test battery—empirical and social issues. *Harvard Educational Review, 48,* 313–340.

Cone, T. E., & Wilson, L. R. (1981). Quantifying a severe discrepancy: A critical analysis. *Learning Disability Quarterly, 4,* 359–371.

Connell, J. P., & Ryan, R. M. (1984). A developmental theory of motivation in the classroom. *Teacher Education Quarterly, 11*(4), 64–77.

Conners, C. K., Goyette, C. H., Southwick, D. A., Lees, J. M., & Andrulonis, P. A. (1976). Food additives and hyperkinesis: A controlled double-blind experiment. *Pediatrics, 58,* 154–166.

Cox, L. S. (1975). Diagnosing and remediating systematic errors in addition and subtraction computations. *The Arithmetic Teacher, 22,* 151–157.

Cravioto, J., & DeLicardie, E. R. (1975). Environmental and nutritional deprivation in children with learning disabilities. In W. M. Cruickshank & D. P. Hallahan (Eds.), *Perceptual and learning disabilities in children. Vol. 2: Research and Theory*. Syracuse: Syracuse University Press.

Cruickshank, W. M. (1975). The learning environment. In W. M. Cruickshank & D. P. Hallahan (Eds.), *Perceptual and learning disabilities in children. Vol. 1: Psychoeducational practices*. Syracuse: Syracuse University Press.

Cruickshank, W. M., Bentzen, F. A., Ratzeburg, F. H., & Tannhauser, M. T. (1961). *A teaching method for brain-injured and hyperactive children*. Syracuse: Syracuse University Press.

Cullinan, D., & Epstein, M. H. (1985). Adjustment problems of mildly handicapped and nonhandicapped students. *Remedial and Special Education, 6*(2).

Cullinan, D., Epstein, M. H., & Lloyd, J. (1981). School behavior problems of learning disabled and normal girls and boys. *Learning Disability Quarterly, 4,* 163–169.

D'Alonzo, B. J., & Wiseman, D. E. (1978). Actual and desired roles of the high learning disability resource teachers. *Journal of Learning Disabilities, 11,* 390–397.

Davol, S. H., & Hastings, M. L. (1967). Effects of sex, age, reading ability, SES, and display position on measures of spatial relationships of children. *Perceptual and Motor Skills, 24,* 375–387.

Deci, E. L., & Chandler, C. L. (1986). The importance of motivation for the future of the LD field. *Journal of Learning Disabilities, 19*(10), 587–594.

Denckla, M., & Rudel, R. (1976). Naming of object drawings by dyslexic and other learning disabled children. *Brain and Language, 3,* 1–16.

Deno, S. L. (1985). Curriculum-based measurement: The emerging alternative. *Exceptional Children, 52*(3), 219–232.

Deno, S. L., Marston, D., & Mirkin, P. (1982). Valid measurement procedures for continuous evaluation of written expression. *Exceptional Children, 48*(4), 368–371.

Deno, S., Mirkin, P. K., & Chiang, B. (1982). Identifying valid measures of reading. *Exceptional Children, 49*(1), 36–45.

Deshler, D. D. (1978). Issues related to the education of learning disabled adolescents. *Learning Disability Quarterly, 1,* 2–10.

Deshler, D. D., & Schumaker, J. B. (1984). *Strategies instruction: A new way to teach*. Salt Lake City: Worldwide Media, Inc.

Deshler, D. D., & Schumaker, J. B. (1986). Learning strategies: An instructional alternative for low-achieving adolescents. *Exceptional Children, 52*(6), 583–590.

Englemann, S. E. (1977). Sequencing cognitive and academic tasks. In R. D. Kneedler & S. G. Tarver (Eds.), *Changing perspectives in special education*. Columbus, Ohio: Charles E. Merrill.

Englemann, S., Becker, W. C., Hanner, S., & Johnson, G. (1978). *Corrective reading* (series guide). Chicago: Science Research Associates.

Epstein, M. H., Cullinan, D., & Lloyd, J. W. (1986). Behavior-problem patterns among the learning disabled: III-replication across age and sex. *Learning Disability Quarterly, 9*(1), 43–54.

Fayne, H. R. (1981). A comparison of learning disabled adolescents with normal learners on an anaphoric pronominal reference task. *Journal of Learning Disabilities, 14,* 597–599.

Feagans, L., & Appelbaum, M. I. (1986). Validation of language subtypes in learning disabled children. *Journal of Educational Psychology 78*(5), 358–364.

Federal Register. (1977). Procedures for evaluating specific learning disabilities. Washington, D.C.: Department of Health, Education and Welfare, December 29.

Feingold, B. F. (1975). *Why your child is hyperactive*. New York: Random House.

Fernald, G. M. (1943). *Remedial techniques in basic school subjects*. New York: McGraw-Hill.

Forrest, D. L., & Waller, T. G. (1981). *Reading ability and knowledge of important information*. Paper presented at the meeting of the Society for Research in Child Development, Boston, Mass., April.

Frostig, M., & Horne, D. (1964). *The Frostig program for the development of visual perception. Teacher's guide*. Chicago: Follett.

Frostig, M., Lefever, D. W., & Whittlesey, J. R. B. (1964). *The Marianne Frostig developmental test of visual perception*. Palo Alto: Consulting Psychology Press.

Fuchs, L. S. (1986). Monitoring progress among mildly handicapped pupils: Review of current practice and research. *Remedial and Special Education, 7*(5), 5–12.

Fuchs, L., Deno, S. L., & Mirkin, P. K. (1984). The effects of frequent curriculum-based measurement and evaluation of pedagogy, student achievement and student awareness of learning. *American Educational Research Journal, 24*(2), 449–460.

Fuchs, L. S., & Fuchs, D. (1986). Effects of systematic formative evaluation: A meta-analysis. *Exceptional Children, 53*(3), 199–208.

Gadow, K. D., Torgesen, J. K., Greenstein, J., & Schell, R. (1986). Learning disabilities. In M. Hersen (Ed.), *Pharmacological and behavioral treatment: An integrative approach* (pp. 149–177). New York: John Wiley & Sons.

General Accounting Office. (1981). *Disparities still exist in who gets special education*. Report to the Chairman, Subcommittee on Select Education, Committee on Education and Labor, House of Representatives of the United States. Gaithersburg, Md.: GAO.

Gerber, M. M., & Hall, R. J. (1981). *Development of spelling in learning disabled and normally-achieving children*.

Unpublished manuscript, University of Virginia Learning Disabilities Research Institute, Charlottesville.

Germann, G., & Tindal, G. (1985). An application of curriculum-based assessment: The use of direct and repeated measurement. *Exceptional Children, 52*(3), 244–265.

Getman, G. N., Kane, E. R., & McKee, G. W. (1968). *Developing learning readiness programs.* Manchester, Mo.: McGraw-Hill.

Gillingham, A., & Stillman, B. (1956). *Remedial training for children with special disability in reading, spelling, and penmanship.* Cambridge, Mass.: Educators Publishing Service.

Ginsberg, H. (1977). *Children's arithmetic: The learning process.* New York: D. Van Nostrand.

Gottlieb, B. W., Gottlieb, J., Berkell, D., & Levy, L. (1986). Sociometric status and solitary play of LD boys and girls. *Journal of Learning Disabilities, 19*(10), 619–622.

Gottfredson, L. S., Finucci, J. M., & Childs, B. (1984). Explaining the adult careers of dyslexic boys: Variations in critical skills for high-level jobs. *Journal of Vocational Behavior, 24,* 355–373.

Gresham, F. M., & Reschly, D. J. (1986). Social skill deficits and low peer acceptance of mainstreamed learning disabled children. *Learning Disability Quarterly, 9*(1), 23–32.

Hall, R. J. (1980). Cognitive behavior modification and information-processing skills of exceptional children. *Exceptional Education Quarterly, 1,* 9–15.

Hall, R. V., Lund, D., & Jackson, D. (1968). Effects of teacher attention on study behavior. *Journal of Applied Behavior Analysis, 1,* 1–12.

Hallahan, D. P. (1975). Comparative research studies on the psychological characteristics of learning disabled children. In W. M. Cruickshank & D. P. Hallahan (Eds.), *Perceptual and learning disabilities in children.* Vol. 1: *Psychoeducational practices.* Syracuse: Syracuse University Press.

Hallahan, D. P., & Bryan, T. H. (1981). Learning disabilities. In J. M. Kauffman & D. P. Hallahan (Eds.), *Handbook of special education.* Englewood Cliffs, N.J.: Prentice-Hall.

Hallahan, D. P., & Cruickshank, W. M. (1973). *Psychoeducational foundations of learning disabilities.* Englewood Cliffs, N.J.: Prentice-Hall.

Hallahan, D. P., Gajar, A. H., Cohen, S. B., & Tarver, S. G. (1978). Selective attention and locus of control in learning disabled and normal children. *Journal of Learning Disabilities, 4,* 47–52.

Hallahan, D. P., & Kauffman, J. M. (1975). Research on the education of distractible and hyperactive children. In W. M. Cruickshank & D. P. Hallahan (Eds.), *Perceptual and learning disabilities in children.* Vol. 2: *Research and theory.* Syracuse: Syracuse University Press.

Hallahan, D. P., & Kauffman, J. M. (1977). Labels, categories, behaviors: ED, LD, and EMR reconsidered. *The Journal of Special Education, 11,* 139–149.

Hallahan, D. P., Kauffman, J. M., & Ball, D. W. (1973). Selective attention and cognitive tempo of low achieving and high achieving sixth grade males. *Perceptual and Motor Skills, 36,* 579–583.

Hallahan, D. P., Kauffman, J. M., & Lloyd, J. W. (1985). *Introduction to learning disabilities.* Englewood Cliffs, N.J.: Prentice-Hall.

Hallahan, D. P., Kneedler, R. D., & Lloyd, J. W. (1983). Cognitive behavior modification techniques for learning disabled children: Self-instruction and self-monitoring. In J. D. McKinney & L. Feagans (Eds.), *Current topics in learning disabilities Vol. 1.* Norwood, N.J.: Ablex.

Hallahan, D. P., Lloyd, J. W., Kauffman, J. M., & Loper, A. B. (1983). Academic problems. In R. J. Morris & T. R. Kratochwill (Eds.), *Practice of child therapy: A textbook of methods* (pp. 113–141). New York: Pergamon Press.

Hallahan, D. P., Lloyd, J., Kosiewicz, M. M., Kauffman, J. M., & Graves, A. W. (1979). Self-monitoring of attention as a treatment for a learning disabled boy's off-task behavior. *Learning Disability Quarterly, 2,* 24–32.

Hallahan, D. P., Lloyd, J. W., & Stoller, L. (1982). *Improving attention with self-monitoring: A manual for teachers.* Charlottesville, Va.: University of Virginia Learning Disabilities Research Institute.

Hallahan, D. P., & Reeve, R. E. (1980). Selective attention and distractibility. In B. K. Keogh (Ed.), *Advances in special education.* Vol. 1: *Basic constructs and theoretical orientations.* Greenwich, Conn.: J.A.I. Press.

Hammill, D. D., & Larsen, S. (1974). The effectiveness of psycholinguistic training. *Exceptional Children, 41,* 5–15.

Hammill, D. D., Leigh, J. E., McNutt, G., & Larsen, S. C. (1981). A new definition of learning disabilities. *Learning Disability Quarterly, 4,* 336–342.

Haring, N., & Lovitt, T. (1969). The application of functional analysis of behavior by teachers in a natural setting. Unpublished manuscript, University of Washington, Experimental Education Unit, Seattle.

Harley, J. P., Ray, R., Matthews, C. G., Cleeland, C. S., Tomasi, L., Eichman, P., & Chun, R. (1976). Food additives and hyperactivity in children. Paper presented at the annual meeting of the Nutrition Foundation, Naples, Florida.

Heins, E. D., Hallahan, D. P., Tarver, S. G., & Kauffman, J. M. (1976). Relationship between cognitive tempo and selective attention in learning disabled children. *Perceptual and Motor Skills, 42,* 233–234.

Henker, B., & Whalen, C. K. (1980). The changing faces of hyperactivity: Retrospect and prospect. In C. K. Whalen & B. Henker (Eds.), *Hyperactive children: The social ecology of identification and treatment.* New York: Academic Press.

Hetherington, E. M., & Parke, R. D. (1986). *Child psychology: A contemporary viewpoint* (3rd ed). New York: McGraw-Hill.

Hewett, F. M. (1967). Educational engineering with emotionally disturbed children. *Exceptional Children, 33,* 459–467.

Hewett, F. M. (1968). *The emotionally disturbed child in the classroom.* Boston: Allyn & Bacon.

Hewett, F. M. with Forness, S. R. (1974). *Education of exceptional learners.* Boston: Allyn & Bacon.

Horowitz, E. C. (1981). Popularity, decentering ability and role-taking skills in learning disabled and normal children. *Learning Disability Quarterly, 4,* 23–30.

Ingram, T. T. S. (1969). Developmental disorders of speech. In P. J. Vinken & G. W. Bruyn (Eds.), *Handbook of clinical neurology* (Vol. 4). Amsterdam: North Holland.

John, E. R., Ahn, H., Prichep, L., Trepetin, M., Brown, D., & Kaye, H. (1980). Developmental equations for the electroencephalogram. *Science, 210*(12), 1255–1258.

Johnson, D. J., & Myklebust, H. (1967). *Learning disabilities: Educational principles and practices.* Orlando, Fla.: Grune & Stratton.

Kagan, J., Rosman, B., Day, D., Albert, J., & Phillips, W. (1964). Information processing in the child: Significance of analytic and reflective attitudes. *Psychological Monographs. 78* (Whole No. 578).

Kass, C. E. (1966). Psycholinguistic disabilities of children with reading problems. *Exceptional Children, 32,* 533–539.

Kauffman, J. M. (1975). Behavior modification. In W. M. Cruickshank & D. P. Hallahan (Eds.), *Perceptual and learning disabilities in children.* Vol. 2: *Research and theory.* Syracuse: Syracuse University Press.

Kauffman, J. M., & Hallahan, D. P. (1979). Learning disability and hyperactivity (with comments on minimal brain dysfunction). In B. B. Lahey & A. E. Kazdin (Eds.), *Advances in clinical child psychology, Vol. 2.* New York: Plenum.

Kavale, K. (1981). The relationship between auditory perceptual skills and reading ability: A meta-analysis. *Journal of Learning Disabilities, 14,* 539–546.

Kavale, K. A. (1987). The long-term consequences of learning disabilities. In M. C. Wang, M. C. Reynolds, & H. J. Walberg (Eds.), *Handbook of special education: Research and practice.* New York: Pergamon.

Keilitz, I., & Dunivant, N. (1986). The relationship between learning disability and juvenile delinquency: Current state of knowledge. *Remedial and Special Education, 7*(3), 18–26.

Keogh, B. K., & Glover, A. T. (1980). Research needs in the study of early identification of children with learning disabilities. *Thalamus, Newsletter of the International Academy for Research in Learning Disabilities,* November.

Keogh, B. K., & Margolis, J. (1976). Learn to labor and wait: Attentional problems of children with learning disorders. *Journal of Learning Disabilities, 9,* 276–286.

Kephart, N. C. (1960). *The slow learner in the classroom.* Columbus, Ohio: Charles E. Merrill.

Kephart, N. C. (1975). The perceptual-motor match. In W. M. Cruickshank & D. P. Hallahan (Eds.), *Perceptual and learning disabilities in children.* Vol. 1: *Psychoeducational practices.* Syracuse: Syracuse University Press.

Kinsbourne, M., & Warrington, E. K. (1963). Developmental factors in reading and writing backwardness. *British Journal of Psychology, 54,* 145–156.

Kirk, S. A., & Elkins, J. (1975). Characteristics of children enrolled in the Child Service Demonstration Centers. *Journal of Learning Disabilities, 8,* 630–637.

Kirk, S. A., & Kirk, W. D. (1971). *Psycholinguistic learning disabilities: Diagnosis and remediation.* Urbana: University of Illinois Press.

Kirk, S. A., McCarthy, J. J., & Kirk, W. D. (1961). (1968). *Illinois test of psycholinguistic abilities.* Urbana: University of Illinois Press.

Kneedler, R. D. (1980). The use of cognitive training to change social behaviors. *Exceptional Education Quarterly, 1,* 65–73.

Kneedler, R. D., & Hallahan, D. P. (1984). Self-monitoring as an attentional strategy for academic tasks with learning disabled children. In B. Gholson & T. Rosenthal (Eds.), *Applications of cognitive development theory.* New York: Academic Press.

Kosiewicz, M. M., Hallahan, D. P., Lloyd, J. W., & Graves, A. W. (1982). Effects of self-instruction and self-correction procedures on handwriting performance. *Learning Disability Quarterly, 5,* 71–78.

Kotsonis, M. E., & Patterson, C. J. (1980). Comprehension-monitoring skills in learning-disabled children. *Developmental Psychology, 16,* 541–542.

Krouse, J. & Kauffman, J. M. (1982). Minor physical anomalies and exceptional children: A review and critique of research. *Journal of Abnormal Child Psychology, 10*(2), 247–264.

Larsen, S. C., Trenholme, B., & Parker, R. (1978). The effects of syntactic complexity upon arithmetic performance. *Learning Disability Quarterly, 1*(4), 80–85.

Liberman, I. Y., & Shankweiler, O. (1979). Speech, the alphabet, and teaching to read. In L. Resnick & P. Weaver (Eds.), *Theory and practice of early reading,* Vol. 1 (pp. 109–132). Hillsdale, N.J.: Lawrence Erlbaum Associates.

Liberman, I. Y., Shankweiler, D., Liberman, A. M., Fowler, C., & Fischer, F. W. (1977). Phonetic segmentation and recoding in the beginning reader. In A. S. Reber & D. Scarborough (Eds.), *Toward a psychology of reading.* Hillsdale, N.J.: Lawrence Erlbaum Associates.

Lloyd, J. (1980). Academic instruction and cognitive behavior modification: The need for attack strategy training. *Exceptional Education Quarterly, 1,* 53–63.

Lloyd, J. W. (1984). How shall we individualize instruction—Or should we? *Remedial and Special Education, 5,* 7–15.

Lloyd, J., Epstein, M. H., & Cullinan, D. (1981). Direct teaching for learning disabilities. In J. Gottlieb & S. S. Strichart (Eds.), *Developmental theory and research in learning disabilities.* (pp. 278–309). Baltimore, Md.: University Park Press.

Lloyd, J., Hallahan, D. P., Kosiewicz, M. M., & Kneedler, R. D. (1980). *Self-assessment versus self-recording: Two comparisons of reactive effects on attention to task and academic productivity.* University of Virginia Learning Disabilities Research Institute, Technical Report No. 29.

Lovitt, T. C. (1975a). Applied behavior analysis and learning disabilities—Part I: Characteristics of ABA, general recommendations, and methodological limitations. *Journal of Learning Disabilities, 8,* 432–443.

Lovitt, T. C. (1975b). Applied behavior analysis and learning disabilities—Part II: Specific research recommendations and suggestions for practitioners. *Journal of Learning Disabilities, 8,* 504–518.

Lovitt, T. C. (1977). *In spite of my resistance . . . I've learned from children.* Columbus, Ohio: Charles E. Merrill.

Lovitt, T. C., & Curtiss, K. A. (1968). Effects of manipulating an antecedent event on mathematics response rate. *Journal of Applied Behavior Analysis, 1,* 329–333.

Lovitt, T. C., & Hansen, C. (1976). Round one: Placing the child in the right reader. *Journal of Learning Disabilities, 9,* 347–353.

Lovitt, T. C., & Smith, J. O. (1972). Effects of instructions on an individual's verbal behavior. *Exceptional Children, 38,* 685–693.

Lyon, G. R. (1985). Identification and remediation of learning disability subtypes: Preliminary findings. *Learning Disabilities Focus, 1*(1), 21–35.

Lyon, G. R., Stewart, N., & Freedman, D. (1982). Neuropsychological characteristics of empirically derived subgroups of learning disabled readers. *Journal of Clinical Neuropsychology, 4,* 343–365.

Lyon, G. R., & Watson, B. (1981). Empirically derived subgroups of learning disabled readers: Diagnostic characteristics. *Journal of Learning Disabilities, 14,* 256–261.

Maggs, A., & Maggs, R. (1979). Review of direct instruction, research in Australia. *Journal of Special Education Technology, 2*(3), 26–34.

Marston, D., & Magnusson, D. (1985). Implementing curriculum-based measurement in special and regular education settings. *Exceptional Children, 52*(3), 266–276.

Marston, D., Mirkin, P. K., & Deno, S. (1984). Curriculum-based measurement of academic skills: An alternative to traditional screening, referral, and identification of learning disabled students. *Journal of Special Education, 18,* 109–118.

McConaughy, S. H., & Ritter, D. R. (1986). Social competence and behavioral problems of learning disabled boys. *Journal of Learning Disabilities, 19*(1), 39–45.

McGinnis, M. (1963). *Aphasic children: Identification and education by the association method.* Washington, D.C.: Volta Bureau.

McKinney, J. D. (1987a). Research on conceptually and empirically derived subtypes of specific learning disabilities. In M. C. Wang, M. C. Reynolds, & H. J. Walberg (Eds.), *Handbook of special education: Research and practice.* New York: Pergamon.

McKinney, J. D. (1987b). Research on the identification of LD children: Perspectives on changes in educational policy. In S. Vaughn & C. Bos, *Future directions and issues in research for the learning disabled.* San Diego: College-Hill Press.

McKinney, J. D., & Feagans, L. (1984). Academic and behavioral characteristics: Longitudinal studies of learning disabled children and average achievers. *Learning Disability Quarterly, 7,* 251–265.

McKinney, J. D., Short, E. J., & Feagans, L. (1985). Academic consequences of perceptual-linguistic subtypes of learning disabled children. *Learning Disabilities Research, 1*(1), 6–17.

McKinney, J. D., & Speece, D. L. (1986). Academic consequences and longitudinal stability of behavioral subtypes of learning disabled children. *Journal of Educational Psychology, 78*(5), 365–372.

McLeod, T. M., & Armstrong, S. W. (1982). Learning disabilities in mathematics—skill deficits and remedial approaches at the intermediate and secondary level. *Learning Disability Quarterly, 5,* 305–311.

Meichenbaum, D. H. (1975). Cognitive factors as determinants of learning disabilities: A cognitive-functional approach. Paper presented at the NATO Conference on "The Neuropsychology of Learning Disorders: Theoretical Approaches," Korsor, Denmark, June.

Meichenbaum, D. H., & Goodman, J. (1971). Training impulsive children to talk to themselves: A means of developing self-control. *Journal of Abnormal Psychology, 77,* 115–126.

Mercer, C. D., Algozzine, B., & Trifiletti, J. (1979). Early identification—an analysis of the research. *Learning Disability Quarterly, 2,* 12–24.

Meyers, M. J. (1980). The significance of learning modalities, modes of instruction, and verbal feedback for learning to recognize written words. *Learning Disability Quarterly, 3,* 62–69.

Minskoff, E. H., Wiseman, D. E., & Minskoff, J. G. (1974). *The MWM Program for Developing Language Abilities.* Ridgefield, N.J.: Educational Performance Associates.

Mori, A. (1983). Career education for the learning dis-

abled—Where are we now? *Learning Disability Quarterly, 3,* 91–101.

Morris, N. T., & Crump, W. D. (1982). Syntactic and vocabulary development in the written language of learning disabled and non-learning disabled students at four age levels. *Learning Disability Quarterly, 5,* 163–172.

Murphy, D. M. (1986). The prevalence of handicapping conditions among juvenile delinquents. *Remedial and Special Education, 7*(3), 7–17.

Newcomer, P. L., & Hammill, D. D. (1976). *Psycholinguistics in the schools.* Columbus, Ohio: Charles E. Merrill.

Nichols, P. L., & Chen, T. C. (1981). *Minimal brain dysfunction: A prospective study.* Hillsdale, N.J.: Lawrence Erlbaum.

Noel, M. (1980). Referential communication abilities of learning disabled children. *Learning Disability Quarterly, 3,* 70–75.

Norman, C., & Zigmond, N. (1980). Characteristics of children labeled and served as learning disabled in school systems affiliated with Child Service & Demonstration centers. *Journal of Learning Disabilities, 13,* 542–547.

Norris, E. (1959). Ordblindness. In S. J. Thompson (Ed.), *Reading disability.* Springfield, Ill.: Charles C Thomas.

Orton, S. (1937). *Reading, writing, and speech problems in children.* New York: Norton.

Owen, F. W., Adams, P. A., Forrest, T., Stolz, L. M., & Fisher, S. (1971). Learning disorders in children: Sibling studies. *Monographs of the Society for Research in Child Development, 36,* (4, Ser. No. 144).

Palincsar, A. S. (1986). Metacognitive strategy instruction. *Exceptional Children, 53*(2), 118–124.

Palincsar, A. S., & Brown, A. L. (1984). The reciprocal teaching of comprehension fostering and comprehension monitoring activities. *Cognition and Instruction, 1,* 117–175.

Paris, S. G., & Myers, M. (1981). Comprehension monitoring, memory, and study strategies of good and poor readers. *Journal of Reading Behavior, 13,* 5–22.

Paris, S. G., & Oka, E. R. (1986). Self-regulated learning among exceptional children. *Exceptional Children, 53*(2), 103–108.

Pearl, R., Bryan, T., & Donahue, M. (1980). Learning disabled children's attributions for success and failure. *Learning Disability Quarterly, 3,* 3–9.

Pearl, R., & Cosden, M. (1982a). Sizing up a situation: LD children's understanding of social interactions. *Learning Disability Quarterly, 5,* 371–373.

Pearl, R., & Cosden, M. (1982b). Sizing up a situation: LD children's understanding of social interactions. *Learning Disability Quarterly, 5,* 371–373.

Pelham, W. E. (1981). Attention deficits in hyperactive and learning-disabled children. *Exceptional Education Quarterly, 2*(3), 13–23.

Pelham, W. E. (1983). The effects of psychostimulants on academic achievement in hyperactive and learning-disabled children. *Thalamus* (Newsletter of the International Academy for Research in Learning Disabilities), *3*(1), 2–48.

Pelham, W. E., & Murphy, H. A. (1986). Attention deficit and conduct disorders. In M. Hersen (Ed.), *Pharmacological and behavioral treatment: An integrative approach* (pp. 108–148). New York: John Wiley & Sons.

Perfetti, C. A., & Lesgold, A. M. (1978). Discourse comprehension and sources of individual differences. In M. A.

Just & P. A. Carpenter (Eds.), *Cognitive processes in comprehension*. Hillsdale, N.J.: Lawrence Erlbaum Associates.

Perlmutter, B. F., Crocker, J., Cordray, D., & Garstecki, D. (1983). Sociometric status and related personality characteristics of mainstreamed learning disabled adolescents. *Learning Disability Quarterly, 6,* 20–30.

Peter, L. J. (1965). *Prescriptive teaching*. New York: McGraw-Hill.

Pflaum, S. W., & Pascarella, E. T. (1980). Interactive effects of prior reading achievement and training in context on the reading of learning disabled children. *Reading Research Quarterly, 16,* 138–158.

Poplin, M. S., Gray, R., Larsen, S., Banikowski, A., & Mehring, R. (1980). A comparison of components of written expression abilities in learning disabled and non-learning disabled students at three grade levels. *Learning Disability Quarterly, 3*(4), 46–53.

Report on Education Research. (1983). Number of handicapped students leveling off, ED official says. July 6, *15*(14), 5–6.

Reynolds, C. R. (1984–1985). Critical measurement issues in learning disabilities. *Journal of Special Education, 18,* 451–476.

Robinson, F. P. (1946). *Effective study*. New York: Harper & Brothers.

Rourke, B. P. (1978). Reading, spelling, arithmetic disabilities: A neuropsychological perspective. In H. R. Myklebust (Ed.), *Progress in learning disabilities* (Vol. 4). New York: Grune & Stratton.

Routh, D. K., & Roberts, R. D. (1972a). Minimal brain dysfunction in children: Failure to find evidence of a behavioral syndrome. *Psychological Reports, 31,* 307–314.

Routh, D. K., & Roberts, R. D. (1972b). Minimal brain dysfunction in children: Failure to find evidence of a behavioral syndrome. *Psychological Reports, 31,* 307–314.

Ryan, E. B., Short, E. J., & Weed, K. A. (1986). The role of cognitive strategy training in improving the academic performance of learning disabled children. *Journal of Learning Disabilities, 19*(9), 521–529.

Satz, P., & Morris, R. (1981). Learning disability subtypes: A review. In F. J. Pirozzolo & M. C. Wittrock (Eds.), *Neuropsychological and cognitive processes in reading*. New York: Academic Press.

Schumaker, J. B., Deshler, D. D., Alley, G. R., Warner, M. M., & Denton, P. H. (1982). Multipass: A learning strategy for improving reading comprehension. *Learning Disability Quarterly, 5*(3), 295–304.

Schumaker, J. B., Deshler, D. D., Alley, G. R., & Warner, M. M. (1983). Toward the development of an intervention model for learning disabled adolescents: The University of Kansas Institute. *Exceptional Education Quarterly, 4*(1), 45–74.

Schumaker, J. B., Deshler, D. D., & Ellis, E. S. (1986). Intervention issues related to the education of LD adolescents. In J. K. Torgeson & B. Y. L. Wong (Eds.), *Learning disabilities: Some new perspectives*. New York: Academic Press.

Scranton, T. R., & Ryckman, D. A. (1979). Disabled children in an integrative program: Sociometric status. *Journal of Learning Disabilities, 2,* 402–407.

Seligman, M. E. (1975). *Helplessness: On depression, developmental, and death*. San Francisco: W. H. Freeman.

Shaywitz, S. E., & Shaywitz, B. A. (1987). *Attention Deficit Disorder: Current perspectives*. Paper presented at National Conference on Learning Disabilities, Bethesda, MD: National Institutes of Child Health and Human Development (NIH).

Simms, R. B., & Crump, W. D. (1983). Syntactic development in the oral language of learning disabled and normal students at the intermediate and secondary level. *Learning Disability Quarterly, 6,* 155–165.

Smith, D. D., & Lovitt, T. C. (1975). The use of modeling techniques to influence the acquisition of computational arithmetic skills in learning disabled children. In E. Ramp & G. Semb (Eds.), *Behavior analysis and education—1973*. Englewood Cliffs, N.J.: Prentice-Hall.

Smith, D. D., Lovitt, T. C., & Kidder, J. D. (1972). Using reinforcement contingencies and teaching aids to alter subtraction performance of children with learning disabilities. In G. Semb (Ed.), *Behavior analysis and education—1972*. Lawrence: Kansas University Department of Human Development.

Speece, D. L., McKinney, J. D., & Appelbaum, M. I. (1985). Classification and validation of behavioral subtypes of learning-disabled children. *Journal of Educational Psychology, 77*(1), 67–77.

Spring, C., & Sandoval, J. (1976). Food additives and hyperkinesis: A critical evaluation of the evidence. *Journal of Learning Disabilities, 9,* 560–569.

Sroufe, L. A. (1975). Drug treatment of children with behavior problems. In F. D. Horowitz (Ed.), *Review of child development research*, Vol. 4 (pp. 347–407). Chicago: University of Chicago Press.

Swanson, J. M., & Kinsbourne, M. (1980). Food dyes impair performance of hyperactive children on a laboratory learning test. *Science, 207,* 1485–1487.

Tarver, S. G., & Dawson, M. M. (1978). Modality preference and reading. An assessment of the research and theory. *Journal of Learning Disabilities, 11,* 5–17.

Tarver, S. G., & Ellsworth, P. S. (1981). Written and oral language for verbal children. In J. M. Kauffman & D. P. Hallahan (Eds.), *Handbook of special education* (pp. 491–511). Englewood Cliffs, N.J.: Prentice-Hall.

Thomas, C. C., Englert, C. S., & Gregg, S. (1987). An analysis of errors and strategies in the expository writing of learning-disabled students. *Remedial and Special Education, 8*(1), 21–30, 46.

Tinker, K. J. (1965). The role of laterality in reading disability. In *Reading and inquiry*. Newark, Del.: International Reading Association.

Torgesen, J. K. (1977). The role of nonspecific factors in the task performance of learning disabled children: A theoretical assessment. *Journal of Learning Disabilities, 10,* 27–34.

Torgesen, J. K. (1979). Factors related to poor performance on memory tasks in reading disabled children. *Learning Disability Quarterly, 2,* 17–23.

Torgesen, J. K., & Kail, R. V. (1980). Memory processes in exceptional children. In B. K. Keogh (Ed.), *Advances in special education*. Vol. 1: *Basic constructs and theoretical orientations*. Greenwich, Conn.: J.A.I. Press.

Vellutino, F. R. (1977). Alternative conceptualizations of dyslexia: Evidence in support of a verbal-deficit hypothesis. *Harvard Educational Review, 47,* 334–354.

Vellutino, F. R. (1979). *Dyslexia: Theory and research*. Cambridge, Mass.: MIT Press.

Vogel, S. A. (1977). Morphological ability in normal and

dyslexic children. *Journal of Learning Disabilities, 10,* 41–49.

Vogel, S. A. (1982). On developing LD college programs. *Journal of Learning Disabilities, 15,* 518–528.

Wagner, R. K. (1986). Phonological processing abilities and reading: Implications for disabled readers. *Journal of Learning Disabilities, 19*(10), 623–630.

Waldrop, M. F., & Halverson, C. F. (1971). Minor physical anomalies and hyperactive behavior in young children. In J. Hellmuth (Ed.), *Exceptional infant.* Vol. 2, *Studies in abnormalities.* New York: Brunner/Mazel.

Walker, L., & Cole, E. M. (1965). Familial patterns of expression of specific reading disability in a population sample. *Bulletin of the Orton Society, 15.*

Watson, B. V., Goldgar, D. E., & Ryschon, K. L. (1983). Subtypes of reading disability. *Journal of Clinical Neuropsychology, 5*(4), 377–399.

Weiss, E. (1984). Learning disabled children's understanding of social interactions of peers. *Journal of Learning Disabilities, 17,* 612–615.

Wender, P. H. (1971). *Minimal brain dysfunction in children.* New York: Wiley.

Werner, H., & Strauss, A. A. (1941). Pathology of figure-background relation in the child. *Journal of Abnormal and Social Psychology, 36,* 236–248.

Whalen, C. K. (1983). Hyperactivity, learning problems, and attention deficit disorders. In T. H. Ollendick & M. Hersen (Eds.), *Handbook of child psychopathology* (pp. 151–199). New York: Plenum.

Whalen, C. K., & Henker, B. (1980). The social ecology of psychostimulant treatment: A model for conceptual and empirical analysis. In C. K. Whalen & B. Henker (Eds.), *Hyperactive children: The social ecology of identification and treatment.* New York: Academic Press.

White, O., & Haring, N. (1980). *Exceptional teaching.* Columbus, Ohio: Charles E. Merrill.

White, O. R., & Liberty, K. A. (1976). Behavioral assessment and precise educational measurement. In N. G. Haring & R. L. Schiefelbusch (Eds.), *Teaching special children.* New York: McGraw-Hill.

Wiig, E. H., & Semel, E. M. (1974). Productive language abilities in learning disabled adolescents. *Journal of Learning Disabilities, 8,* 578–588.

Wiig, E. H., Semel, E. M., & Abele, E. (1981). Perception of ambiguous sentences by learning disabled twelve-year-olds. *Learning Disability Quarterly, 4,* 3–12.

Wiig, E. H., Semel, E. M., & Crouse, M. A. B. (1973). The use of English morphology by high-risk and learning disabled children. *Journal of Learning Disabilities, 6,* 457–465.

Wong, B. Y. L. (1979). Increasing retention of main ideas through questioning strategies. *Learning Disability Quarterly, 2,* 42–47.

Wong, B. Y. L. (1982). Understanding the learning disabled student's reading problems: Contributions from cognitive psychology. *Topics in Learning and Learning Disabilities, 1*(4), 43–50.

Wong, B. Y. L. (1985). *Metacognition: Why should special educators attend to it?* Montreal: Canadian Society for the Study of Education.

Wong, B. Y. L. (1986). A cognitive approach to teaching spelling. *Exceptional Children, 53*(2), 169–173.

Wong, B. Y. L., & Wong, R. (1980). Role-taking skills in normal achieving and learning disabled children. *Learning Disability Quarterly, 3,* 11–18.

Zigmond, N., & Brownlee, J. (1980). Social skills training for adolescents with learning disabilities. *Exceptional Education Quarterly, 1,* 77–83.

Zigmond, N., & Sansone, J. (1986). Designing a program for the learning disabled adolescent. *Remedial and Special Education, 7*(5), 13–17.

Emotional Disturbance/ Behavioral Disorder

Young child with dreams
Dream every dream on your own.
When children play,
Seems like you end up alone.
Papa says he'd love to be with you,
If he had the time,
So you turn to the only friend
You can find,
There in your mind.

(*Neil Diamond, "Shilo"*)

Children who are emotionally disturbed or behaviorally disordered are not good at making friends. In fact, their most obvious problem is failure to establish close and satisfying emotional ties with other people. As Neil Diamond's song suggests (see p.159), the only friends they may be able to find are imaginary ones. Other children are not attracted to them, and adults do not find them pleasant to be around.

Some of these children are withdrawn. Other children or adults may try to reach them, but their efforts are usually met with fear or disinterest. In many cases, this kind of quiet rejection continues until those who are trying to make friends simply give up. Because close emotional ties are built around reciprocal social responses, people naturally lose interest in someone who simply does not respond.

Many disturbed children, however, are isolated from others not because they withdraw from friendly advances, but because they strike out with hostility and aggression. They are abusive, destructive, unpredictable, irresponsible, bossy, quarrelsome, irritable, jealous, defiant—anything but pleasant to be with. Naturally, other children and adults choose not to spend time with this kind of child unless they have to. And understandably, others tend to strike back at a child who shows these characteristics. It is no wonder, then, that these children seem to be embroiled in a continuous battle with everyone.

Where does the problem start? Does it begin with behavior that angers or irritates other people? Or does it begin with a social environment so uncomfortable or inappropriate for the child that the only reasonable response is withdrawal or attack? These questions cannot be answered fully on the basis of current research. The best thinking today is that the problem is not just in the child's behavior or just in the environment. The problem arises because *the social interactions and transactions between the child and the social environment are inappropriate.* This is an *ecological* perspective—an interpretation of the problem as a negative aspect of the child and of the environment in which he or she lives.

Special education for these students is in many ways both confused and confusing (Kauffman, 1986). The terminology of the field is inconsistent, and there is much dissatisfaction with current definitions. Meaningful classifications of children's behavior problems have only recently begun to emerge from research. The large number of different theories regarding the causes and the best treatments of emotional and behavioral disorders makes it difficult to sort out the most useful concepts. Thus the study of this area of special education demands more than the usual amount of perseverance and critical thinking.

TERMINOLOGY

Many different terms have been used to designate children who have extreme social-interpersonal and/or intrapersonal problems. For example, many terms have been used to designate students or problems, such as: emotionally handicapped, emotionally impaired, behaviorally impaired, socially/emotionally handicapped, emotionally conflicted, personal and social adjustment problems, and seriously behaviorally disabled. These terms do not designate distinctly different types of disorders. They do not refer to clearly different types of children and youth. Rather, the different labels appear to represent personal preferences for terms, and perhaps slightly different theoretical orientations. The terminology of the field is so variable and confused that you can pick a label of choice simply by matching words from Column A with Column B on p. 161 (and, if it seems appropriate, adding other qualifiers such as "seriously").

MISCONCEPTIONS ABOUT EMOTIONALLY DISTURBED/ BEHAVIORALLY DISORDERED CHILDREN

Myth	_Fact_
Most ED/BD children escape the notice of people around them.	Although it is difficult to identify the types and causes of problems, most disturbed children, whether aggressive or withdrawn, are quite easy to spot.
Disturbed children are usually very bright.	Relatively few disturbed children have above-average intelligence; in fact, most mildly or moderately disturbed children are low normal in IQ. Most severely or profoundly disturbed children, when they can be tested, have scores in the retarded range—the average is around 50.
Children who exhibit shy, anxious behavior are more seriously impaired than children whose behavior is hyperaggressive.	Children with aggressive, acting-out behavior patterns have less chance for good social adjustment and mental health in adulthood. Neurotic, shy, anxious children have a better chance of getting and holding jobs, overcoming their problems, and staying out of jails and mental hospitals unless their withdrawal is extreme. This is especially true for boys.
Most ED/BD children need a permissive environment in which they feel accepted and can accept themselves for what they are.	Research shows that a firmly structured and highly predictable environment is of greatest benefit to most disturbed children.
Only psychiatrists, psychologists, and social workers are able to help disturbed children overcome their problems.	Most teachers and parents can learn to be highly effective in helping ED/BD children, often without extensive training or professional certification.
The undesirable behaviors we see a disturbed child perform are only symptoms; the real problems are hidden deep in the child's psyche.	There is no sound scientific basis for belief in hidden causes; the child's behavior and its social context are the problems. Causes may involve a child's thoughts, feelings, and perceptions, however.

Column A	_Column B_
EMOTIONAL	DISTURBANCE
SOCIAL	DISORDER
BEHAVIORAL	MALADJUSTMENT
PERSONAL	HANDICAP
	IMPAIRMENT

"Seriously emotionally disturbed" was the term used when PL 94-142 was passed; today, that term is criticized as inappropriate (Kauffman, 1986). "Behaviorally disordered" is consistent with the name of the Council for Children with Behavioral Disorders (CCBD, a division of the Council for Exceptional Children) and has the advantage of focusing attention on the most obvious problems of these children—disordered behavior (Huntze, 1985). Because the terminology of this area of special education is in transition, we have chosen to use "emotionally disturbed/behaviorally disordered" (or ED/BD) to designate the children in question. We also use the simple term "disturbed" to refer to the same general population.

DEFINITION

There is no universally accepted definition of ED/BD children. Professional groups and experts dealing with these children have felt free to construct individual working definitions to fit their own professional purposes. For practical reasons, we might say that children are disturbed whenever an adult authority says they are. It may seem cynical to suggest such a vague and subjective definition, but as yet no one has come up with an objective standard that is understandable and acceptable to a majority of professionals.

Definition Problems

There are valid reasons for the lack of consensus regarding definition. Defining the disturbed child is somewhat like defining a familiar experience—anger, loneliness, or happiness, for example. We all have an intuitive grasp of what these experiences are, but their objective definition is far from simple. The factors that make it particularly difficult to arrive at a good definition of emotional disturbance in children are these:

- Lack of an adequate definition of mental health and normal behavior
- Differences among conceptual models
- Difficulties in measuring emotions and behavior
- Relationships between ED/BD and other handicapping conditions
- Differences in the functions of socialization agents who categorize and serve children

We will discuss each of these in turn.

Mental Health and Normal Behavior

Mental health specialists agree that the mentally healthy child is happy most of the time, builds lasting and positive relationships with other people, has an accurate perception of reality, is able to organize thoughts and actions to accomplish reasonable goals, achieves academically at a level close to his or her potential, has mostly good feelings about himself or herself, and behaves as expected for a child of a given age and sex. Mental illness is revealed by opposite characteristics—unhappiness, trouble getting along with others, disorganization, underachievement, feelings of worthlessness and inadequacy, and inappropriate behavior.

But recognizing the characteristics of mental health and mental illness does not resolve the problem of categorizing a certain child as emotionally healthy or mentally ill. When individual children are examined, it becomes obvious that all children exhibit *some* of the characteristics of mental illness *some* of the time. Mental health, then, is judged by estimating the *degree* to which a child's consistent characteristics fit those of an abstract definition. Today's definitions of mental health give us an idea of what to look for, but they are not good enough to separate clearly the healthy from the ill.

It is a truism that everyone has emotional ups and downs. Children who exhibit certain behaviors are more or less likely to be judged disturbed depending on age, sex, and the particular circumstances. For example, a 16-year-old boy who cries when he is asked a question in history class is more likely to be considered disturbed than a 4-year-old girl who cries in response to a scolding by her older brother. The point is that the child's developmental level and the particular circumstances surrounding a given act, plus the child's *typical* emotional state, must be taken into account.

Too often, adults fail to recognize that people of every age often experience great stress in everyday life. Stress and ways of managing it are not the exclusive problems of grownups. Certainly different events produce stress at different developmental levels. But we tend to forget that stressful events (the ones we've mastered or forgotten, at least) are defined from a highly personal viewpoint, as Harry Reasoner illustrates in his commentary on "Childish Concerns—and Stress" (see p. 164). One cannot make adequate judgments about individual children's mental health without understanding the points of stress in their lives.

Normal variations in emotions and behavior complicate the problem of definition because we can almost never say that an act itself indicates emotional disturbance or behavioral disorder. It is "normal" for children to do almost anything occasionally and under certain conditions. In addition, there is a nearly infinite number of ways to be ED/BD. A child may be too aggressive or too withdrawn, too euphoric or too sad, preoccupied with religion, unable to achieve at school, unable to communicate with others, and so on. An adequate definition must allow for an extremely wide range of behaviors. Finally, ED/BD may vary all the way from mild, almost insignificant deviations to profoundly handicapping behavior. It is difficult to formulate a definition that takes such a wide range into account.

Behavior that conforms to a pattern expected by the child's social or cultural group is not considered disturbed—except perhaps when the child is not a member of the dominant culture. Behavior that is considered normal and adaptive in a subculture may be looked upon as deviant or inadequate by members of the dominant group. The child may thus be defined as disturbed or healthy, depending on whose expectations are used as the reference point. Even within the same culture, there are different expectations in different social classes. It is clear that social and cultural expectations must be taken into account in defining ED/BD, but there is often a problem in deciding whose expectations should be the standard.

Conceptual Models

Treatment methods and special educational programs for ED/BD children are based on many different models. That is, there are many different theories regarding the origin, nature, and cure of disturbance in children. (For a detailed analysis of several conceptual models, see McDowell, Adamson, and Wood, 1982.) The following are some of the major models, which we will discuss later in the chapter.

1. *The Biological Approach:* the view that genetic, neurological, and biochemical factors may cause disturbed behavior.

Childish Concerns—and Stress

Children, we think, are carefree. They have freckles and puppies and pockets full of little cars and chewing gum, and they do; but they have problems, too, as the town of Derby Line, Vermont, has recognized. Derby Line has established a stress management program for its grade-school kids on the theory that we all have stress, and it's better to learn how to deal with it. I made an informal survey around here, running this news by some colleagues and, invariably, they rolled their eyes and shrugged, as if to say, "What next?" I think I can explain the reaction.

We adults think we have a lock on stress. We live in the rough, tough world without freckles and puppies and pockets full of comforting toys, and we won't have anyone diminishing our supply of stomach acids. We figure, arrogantly, that when the big dinner party goes bad, that's stress, whereas being knocked down by the school bully in front of all your friends, why, that's just part of growing up. And then, stress, well, stress is having an hour left to do two hours' worth of work, with the boss flying in from the coast and the accountants on their way across town. On the other hand, to be lying awake with your thumb in your mouth because you think there's an alligator under the bed, that's childish. Nah, kids don't know about stress. Stress is what you feel when you're stuck in a cab and you're already 20 minutes late for an important meeting. Not having done your homework because you found stunning evidence that your new baby brother is from Mars and you spent the night trying to warn your parents, so that you've got to tie your shoelaces all morning in class to keep the teacher from calling on you, that's just getting what you deserve.

We are parsimonious about stress, I think. It is a badge these days between adults, as well; but just think how you'd feel, now, if you were truly convinced that there was an alligator under your desk.

SOURCE: Originally broadcast December 20, 1983, over the CBS Radio Network on the CBS Radio News, Harry Reasoner: Newsnotes and Comments. © CBS Inc. 1983. All rights reserved.

2. *The Psychoanalytic Approach:* the view that traditional psychoanalytic concepts can be used to find the underlying causes of disturbance.
3. *The Psychoeducational Approach:* the view that discovering why children behave as they do is important, but so is the acquisition of academic and daily living skills.
4. *The Humanistic Approach:* the view that behavioral disorders are symptomatic of a child's being out of touch with self and feelings.
5. *The Ecological Approach:* the view that ED/BD results from poor interaction of the child with elements of the social environment.
6. *The Behavioral Approach:* the view that all behavior is learned; therefore, ED/BD represents inappropriate learning.

Measurement

In the field of mental retardation, the intelligence test serves as a measurement device (along with judgment of adaptive behavior) for purposes of definition. Learning disability has been defined primarily on the basis of discrepancies between children's scores on two types of standardized measurement devices—intelligence and achievement tests. But there are no valid, reliable, generally accepted tests that can be used to measure ED/BD. Personality tests and behavior rating scales are simply not precise enough. Even with precise and reliable measures of behavior obtained by direct observation (so that it can be stated, for example, that the child being observed spends 78 percent of the time playing alone and hits another child an average of thirteen times per day), the problem is still not solved. There are no norms or criteria for determining that the child who exhibits a behavior at a certain frequency is disturbed. The determination that a child is ED/BD is made on the basis of "clinical" judgment. It may be derived in part from the test scores or direct observation and measurement of the child's behavior, but such tests and measures are by themselves inadequate bases for definition (Walker, Severson, Haring, and Williams, 1986).

Other Handicapping Conditions

Children can be ED/BD and at the same time be handicapped in other ways. There is, for example, a considerable body of literature regarding those who are both emotionally disturbed and mentally retarded (Barrett, 1986; Epstein, Cullinan, and Polloway, 1986). The combination of ED/BD and other handicaps confuses the issue because it is often impossible to tell what one handicapping condition contributes to the other: Is mental retardation a contributing factor in the child's disturbance, or does ED/BD contribute to the child's mental retardation? Which handicap is the *primary* one? "Children may have a complex of socioemotional problems and still have another primary special education label" (Morse, 1985, p. 48).

Socialization Agents

The socialization agents responsible for children's well-being (school personnel, police officers, officials of the juvenile court, clinical psychologists, and other mental health experts) tend to view behavior according to the services they render to children and their parents. A definition constructed by court officials will emphasize deviance in terms of the law; a definition written by educators will focus on school failure; and a definition offered by a mental health clinic will highlight psychological problems. So definitions of ED/BD children vary because a definition must serve the purposes of those who have a reason to identify and label children.

All these problems make defining ED/BD difficult for everyone—novice and expert. Furthermore, the problems become harder to overcome when one considers specific children. Many definitions seem quite adequate in the abstract. Confronted with living, breathing children, however, one often wonders how an apparently clear and crisp definition has suddenly become so vague and imprecise.

Current Definitions

But although the terminology used and the relative emphasis given to certain points vary considerably from one definition to another, it is possible to extract several common features of current definitions. There is general agreement that ED/BD refers to

- Behavior that goes to an extreme—behavior that is not just slightly different from the usual.
- A problem that is chronic—one that does not quickly disappear.
- Behavior that is unacceptable because of social or cultural expectations.

One definition that must be considered is the one included in the federal rules and regulations governing the implementation of PL 94-142. Section 121a.5 of the rules and regulations defines "seriously emotionally disturbed" as follows:

(i) The term means a condition exhibiting one or more of the following characteristics over a long period of time and to a marked extent, which adversely affects educational performance:
  (A) An inability to learn which cannot be explained by intellectual, sensory, or health factors;
  (B) An inability to build or maintain satisfactory relationships with peers and teachers;
  (C) Inappropriate types of behavior or feelings under normal circumstances;
  (D) A general pervasive mood of unhappiness or depression; or
  (E) A tendency to develop physical symptoms or fears associated with personal or school problems.
(ii) The term includes children who are schizophrenic or autistic.* The term does not include children who are socially maladjusted unless it is determined that they are seriously emotionally disturbed. (*Federal Register,* Vol. 42, No. 163, Tuesday, August 23, 1977, p. 42478)

The federal definition is modeled after one proposed by Bower (1981). Bower's definition, however, does *not* include the statements found in part ii of the federal definition. These inclusions and exclusions are, as Bower (1982) and Kauffman (1985, 1986) have pointed out, unnecessary; common sense tells us that Bower's five criteria for emotional disturbance indicate that "autistic" and "schizophrenic" children *must be included* and that "socially maladjusted" children *cannot be excluded*. Furthermore, the clause "which adversely affects educational performance" makes reasonable interpretation of the definition extremely difficult.

> Note that a definition including educational performance leaves out those who have no school problems or problems that do not affect achievement, and this can be a significant number. The idea that all disturbed children must have an educational problem in behavior or achievement is a significant error. The other error lies in implying that even when children have problems in school these problems are primarily school-related. The fact is that problems are often generated outside of the school environment and brought to school (Morse, 1985, p. 43).

Thus the federal definition, though based on one that is frequently cited by professionals as helpful and reasonable, is flawed. Furthermore, the federal definition, like all others, is not entirely adequate for deciding just who is and who is not ED/BD.

CLASSIFICATION

Given the fact that there are many ways to be disturbed, it seems reasonable to expect that disturbed individuals could be grouped into subcategories according to the types of problems they have. Still, there is no generally agreed upon system for classifying ED/BD children.

---

* The U.S. Department of Education later decided that autistic children will no longer be included under the category of seriously emotionally disturbed. They are now considered "other health impaired." See Bower (1982) for comment on this change.

Classification Problems

The specific problems encountered in classifying ED/BD children are these:

- Lack of reliability and validity of the classification system
- Significance of etiology
- Special legal considerations
- Differences between classification systems for adults and children

Reliability and Validity

A reliable classification system is one in which a certain child or behavior is classified the same way over a span of time, under different conditions, and by different classifiers. In such a system a child will not be placed in one category today and a different one next week; in one category if classified at home and a different one if classified at school; or in one category by psychologist A and a different one by psychologist B. Unfortunately, most classification systems for disturbed children are quite unreliable. Evidence of this has been presented by Achenbach and Edelbrock (1983). A valid classification system is one in which a child's assignment to a certain category is predictable using other reliable and valid devices, or is predictable on the basis of theory and has sound implications for how the child's behavior should be managed. The validity of most systems is very poor; a child's placement in a certain category means almost nothing as far as treatment or education is concerned.

Significance of Etiology

Psychiatry places great emphasis on identifying the etiology (cause) of mental "disease." The hope of psychiatrists and other mental health professionals is that identification of the causal factors underlying emotional disturbance will result in a classification system. Then assignment of a child to the proper category might lead directly to a prescription for treatment. It is true that finding the causes of children's emotional disturbances would be a significant accomplishment. It is also true that in the vast majority of cases one can only guess why a child is disturbed. That is, even though many mental health specialists have attached supreme importance to the task of finding out why children become disturbed, and even though a vast amount of research has been aimed at the problem of etiology, there is still no sound empirical evidence linking most cases of ED/BD to specific causes (Kauffman, 1985). Therefore, classification according to causes is not possible at present (Achenbach, 1985).

Legal Considerations

Because some ED/BD children exhibit behaviors that involve violations of the law, certain labels are used specifically to allow the courts to intervene. A child or adolescent may be involuntarily committed to an institution if he or she is judged to fall into the categories of *psychotic* or *criminally insane. Runaway* or *incorrigible* are other classifying labels used within the legal system. Legal definitions are sometimes at odds with or become entangled with psychiatric definitions and clinical judgments. It is not surprising, therefore, that legal considerations often confuse the issue of classification (Murphy, 1986).

Adult Classification Systems

Classification of adult psychiatric disorders has been an issue for a longer period of time than classification of children's disorders. Many of the attempts to devise classifications for children have been efforts to scale down or adapt systems proposed for adults. This has not worked very well because the same type of behavior (such as talking to imaginary friends or throwing temper tantrums) may have very different meanings for an adult and for a young child. Children pass through developmental stages in which certain types of behavior are to be expected; behavior considered normal for a child of a certain age may be viewed as abnormal for a person much older or younger. What is needed is a system that takes into account the behavior that is to be expected and the behavior that signifies significant problems at various developmental stages (Achenbach, 1985).

Current Classification Systems

Psychiatric classification systems have been widely criticized. Hobbs has commented: "It is important to note that competent clinicians would seldom use for treatment purposes the categories provided by diagnostic manuals; their judgment would be more finely modulated than the classification schemes, and more sensitive than any formal system can be to temporal, situational, and developmental changes" (1975, pp. 58–59). Clearly the usual diagnostic categories—for example, those found in publications of the American Psychiatric Association—have little meaning for teachers. Some psychologists and educators have recommended relying more on individual assessment of the child's behavior and situational factors than on traditional diagnostic classification (Morse, 1985).

An alternative to traditional psychiatric classifications is the use of statistical analyses of behavioral characteristics to establish clusters or *dimensions* of disordered behavior. Using sophisticated statistical procedures, researchers look for patterns of behavior that characterize children who have emotional/behavioral disorders. By using these methods, researchers have been able to derive descriptive categories that are less susceptible to bias and unreliability than the traditional psychiatric classifications (Achenbach, 1985). Quay (1979) and others have used behavior ratings by teachers and parents, children's life history characteristics, and the responses of children to questionnaires to derive four "dimensions" or clusters of interrelated traits: conduct disorder, anxiety-withdrawal, immaturity, and socialized aggression.

Children whose behavior fits the conduct disorder category are likely to exhibit such characteristics as disobedience, destructiveness, jealousy, and boisterousness. The life history characteristics associated with conduct disorder include defiance of authority and inadequate feelings of guilt. Children with conduct disorders frequently give questionnaire responses indicating that they do as they like regardless of what other people think, that they do not trust other people, and that they like to think of themselves as "tough."

Anxiety-withdrawal is characterized by feelings of inferiority, self-consciousness, social withdrawal, anxiety, depression, expressions of guilt and unhappiness. Immaturity, a third dimension, is associated with short attention span, clumsiness, passivity, daydreaming, preference for younger playmates, and other behavioral characteristics of children lagging behind their agemates in social development. The dimension of socialized aggression is made up of characteristics such as associating with and being loyal to bad companions, being active in a delinquent group, stealing, and habitual truancy. In addition, these children exhibit behavior traits like fighting and destructiveness that result in violation of the law.

Achenbach and his colleagues also have described various dimensions of disordered child behavior (Achenbach, 1985; Achenbach and Edelbrock, 1983; Edelbrock and Achenbach, 1984). They have found two broad dimensions which they refer to as *externalizing* and *internalizing*. Children characterized by the externalizing dimension exhibit aggressive, acting-out behavior quite similar to Quay's descriptions of conduct disorder and socialized aggression; those characterized by the internalizing dimension exhibit immature, withdrawn behavior similar to Quay's anxiety-withdrawal and immaturity descriptions. These two dimensions—externalizing (aggressive, acting-out) and internalizing (immature, withdrawn)—seem to be the most consistently recognized and reliable categories of disordered child behavior.

It is important to recognize that individual children may show behaviors characteristic of more than one dimension; that is, the dimensions are not mutually exclusive. A child might exhibit several of the behaviors associated with the immaturity dimension (messy, sloppy, inattentive, short attention span) and perhaps several of those defining conduct disorder as well (fighting, hitting, disobedient, defiant, for example). Still, behavioral dimensions are a way of describing types of problems that tend to co-occur.

Behavioral dimensions do not by themselves provide an entirely satisfactory system of classification; they merely describe the major types of behavior ED/BD children may exhibit. Therefore they are not an adequate basis for designing intervention programs. Similar dimensions have, however, been found with remarkable consistency in many samples of children, so the dimensions do provide a reliable basis for description (Achenbach, 1985, Achenbach and Edelbrock, 1983; Cullinan, Epstein, and Kauffman, 1984).

All those who propose schemes for classifying ED/BD children recognize that severity of the disorder is a significant factor. In traditional psychiatric terms, children with mild or moderate disorders have most often been referred to as having a **neurosis** or **psychoneurosis;** children with severe or profound disorders are usually said to have **psychosis, schizophrenia,** or **autism.** When a child is called "severely neurotic" or "a borderline psychotic," this adds to the bewildering array of labels and categories employed in the field. As we use the terms in this chapter, the mildly and moderately disturbed child exhibits behavior that can be effectively managed by parents and teachers if they are given consultation with a mental health specialist. Usually there is no need to remove such a child from the home or regular class for an extended period of time. The term "severely and profoundly disturbed" indicates children for whom intensive and prolonged intervention is required. Typically such children will need to be taught at home or in a special class, special day school, or residential institution for a considerable period of time.

It is dangerous to establish categories on the basis of the type of services required because the quality and effectiveness of intervention vary from one locality to another. The distinction between the mild-moderate and severe-profound levels of disturbance cannot be made entirely clear in any classification system presently being used. The distinction we are making here is educationally relevant and assumes that the intervention provided is appropriate and effective.

PREVALENCE

Estimates of the prevalence of ED/BD in children and youth have varied tremendously because there has been no standard and reliable definition or screening instrument. For decades the federal government estimated that 2 percent of the school-age population was "seriously emotionally disturbed." The government's estimate was *extremely* conservative. Rather consistently, credible studies in the United States and many other countries of the world have indicated that at least 6 to 10 percent of children and youths of school age exhibit serious and persistent emotional/behavioral problems (see Juul, 1986; Kauffman, 1984, 1985, 1986; Morse, 1985). Data published by the U.S. Department of Education (1986), however, show that only about 1 percent of schoolchildren in the United States are identified as seriously emotionally disturbed. The Department of Education (1986) now recognizes the ED/BD as a "traditionally underserved" category of special education students whose needs are particularly complex.

The most common type of problem exhibited by students in special education for ED/BD is conduct disorder (aggressive, acting-out behavior). Most of the students identified as ED/BD are not considered *severely* disturbed—that is, they are not diagnosed as psychotic. Boys outnumber girls by a ratio of 5 to 1 or more. Overall, boys tend to exhibit more aggression and conduct disorder patterns than girls do (Cullinan and Epstein, 1985; Cullinan, Epstein, and Kauffman, 1984; Kazdin, 1987).

Juvenile delinquency presents a problem in estimating the prevalence of ED/BD. One point of view is that *all* delinquent youth should be considered to have emotional/behavioral disorders. But some authorities argue that many delinquents are "socially maladjusted," but not "seriously emotionally disturbed" for special education purposes. Clearly, handicapping conditions, including emotional disturbance, are much more common among juvenile delinquents than among the general population (Murphy, 1986).

Delinquency itself is a very serious problem in the United States. About 3 percent of American youths are referred to a juvenile court in a given year (see Achenbach, 1982; Arnold and Brungardt, 1983). There is no doubt that juvenile crime is increasing at a rapid rate and that it is becoming more violent and destructive (Arnold and Brungardt, 1983). More arrests and juvenile court appearances are made in the lower socioeconomic groups, but the relationship between socioeconomic level

Delinquency can result in a child or youth being referred to the juvenile court, but not all rebellious or defiant juvenile behavior is delinquent, and not all delinquent behavior is known to juvenile authorities. (Leo deWys)

and delinquent acts is not known. There has been a sharp increase in arrest rates beginning at the junior high school age, and it appears that younger children are committing more serious and violent crimes than in previous decades. Crimes involving aggression have characterized male delinquents, and sex-related crimes have characterized female delinquents, but there appears to be a trend toward more violent crimes committed by girls (see Moore and Arthur, 1983).

CAUSES

The causes of ED/BD have been attributed to four major factors: biological disorders and diseases, pathological family relationships, negative cultural influences, and undesirable experiences at school. Although in the vast majority of cases there is no conclusive empirical evidence that any one of these factors is directly responsible for disordered behavior, it is apparent that some may give a child a predisposition to exhibit problem behavior, and others may precipitate or trigger such behavior. That is, some factors, such as genetics, influence behavior over a long period of time and increase the likelihood that a given set of circumstances will trigger maladaptive responses. Other factors (for example, observing one parent beating the other) may have a more immediate effect and may trigger maladaptive responses in an individual who is already predisposed to develop problem behavior.

Another concept important in all theories of ED/BD is the idea of *contributing factors*. It is extremely unusual to find a single cause that has led directly to disturbed behavior. Usually several factors together contribute to the development of a problem. In almost all cases the question of what specifically has caused a child to become disturbed cannot be answered; no one really knows.

The roles biological disorders, pathological family relationships, negative cultural influences, and undesirable school experiences play in determining how children behave are important in the conceptual models that guide educational intervention. The role played by each factor also has important implications for preventive efforts.

Causes and Conceptual Models

Conceptual models differ considerably in the importance they attach to finding the causes of ED/BD. At one extreme, the psychoanalytic model gives higher priority to identifying the underlying causes of the child's behavior than to resolving the problem. The rationale for this arrangement of priorities is that unless the underlying psychodynamic causes are found and removed, only the symptom of mental disease is being treated. And if only the symptom is eradicated, the underlying pathology will show itself in some new form. At the other extreme, the behavioral model sets a higher priority on resolving the problem than on identifying the root cause. The rationale for the behavioral approach is that underlying, hidden, or historical causes can never be confirmed by direct observation and measurement. If the child's environment can be arranged so that the behavior problem is resolved, there simply are no other causes worth seeking. These contrasting views are illustrated in classic cases presented by Bettelheim (1970) and Wolf, Risley, and Mees (1964).

Bettelheim described a 4-year-old girl who had been diagnosed as psychotic. This child attempted to smash people's eyeglasses, and her behavior became extremely wild whenever she was prevented from doing so. In order to discover the underlying cause of this compulsion, Bettelheim simply accepted the breaking of glasses for three years, until the child was able to reveal the hidden psychological meaning of her behavior in terms that could be understood. The little girl's mother was a chronic schizophrenic; when the child had tried on her mother's glasses at an early age, she had had difficulty seeing clearly because her own eyesight was normal. She then, according to Bettelheim's interpretation, became infuriated at the injustice of the situation. Other people could see better when they put on glasses, but when she tried to see better (that is, understand her mother) by putting on glasses, her vision was distorted. Finding and understanding the cause underlying the girl's insistent attempts to break people's glasses, Bettelheim felt, was crucial in enabling the student ultimately to resolve her behavior problem.

Wolf and his colleagues described a 3-year-old boy diagnosed as a childhood schizophrenic. The boy threw severe temper tantrums, frequently injuring himself purposely, and was tyrannical with his parents. He had developed cataracts at 9 months of age, and both lenses had been removed from his eyes. His rages and other problem behaviors had begun at about the time his cataracts were discovered, and his parents were not able to get him to wear his glasses (which were necessary to prevent him from losing his vision). Wolf and his associates placed the child in his room for 10 minutes (or longer, if he was still having a tantrum at the end the "time-out") every time he had a tantrum or threw off his glasses. He was given frequent small rewards (bites of food) for positive behavior—first for holding the empty frames, then for putting them up to his eyes, and then for doing the same with plain lenses, then for looking through prescription lenses, and so on. The Wolf group concentrated on manipulating the environment, especially the consequences of certain of the boy's responses, to produce specific desirable outcomes. They were successful in treating the boy's behavioral disorder (he stopped his tantrums and wore his glasses) without dealing with the underlying causes of his behavior.

All conceptual models show concern for the cause of the problem, but models vary in their emphasis on historical and symbolic causal factors versus current and observable factors. In the discussion here of biological, family, cultural, and school influences on behavior, it is important to remember that views regarding the causal significance of conditions and events differ. One fact is becoming increasingly clear as research data are accumulated: Causal factors are exceedingly complex, and the usual psychoanalytic (or developmental) and behavioral analyses are oversimplifications. As Rutter (1985) notes:

> The implication is that we need to re-think our concepts of the ways in which life experiences influence socio-behavioral development. Developmental theories that postulate a "structure" of personality that is established during the course of the developmental process do not fit the empirical findings. Equally, however, behaviorist theories that conceptualize effects entirely in terms of the here-and-now without the need to invoke developmental considerations are inconsistent with the evidence (p. 361).

Biological Factors

Behavior may be influenced by genetic, neurological, or biochemical factors, or by combinations of these. Certainly there is a relationship between body and behavior, and it would therefore seem reasonable to look for a biological causal factor of some kind for certain emotional/behavioral disorders. The fact is, though, that only rarely is it possible to demonstrate a relationship between a specific biological factor and ED/BD. Many disturbed children have no detectable biological flaws that could account for their actions, and many behaviorally normal children have serious biological defects. For mildly and moderately ED/BD children as a group, there simply is no real evidence that biological factors alone are at the root of the problem. For the severely and profoundly disturbed, however, there is evidence to suggest that biological factors may contribute to the condition (Achenbach, 1982; Werry, 1979).

All children are born with a biologically determined behavioral style or **temperament.** Although children's inborn temperaments may be changed by the way they are reared, some believe that children with "difficult" temperaments are predisposed to become disturbed (Thomas and Chess, 1984; Thomas, Chess, and Birch, 1968). There is no one-to-one relationship between temperament and disturbance, however. A "difficult" child may be handled so well or a child with an "easy" temperament so poorly that the final outcome is quite different from what one might predict on the basis of initial behavioral style. Other biological factors besides temperament—disease, malnutrition, and brain trauma, for example—may predispose children to develop emotional problems. But except in extremely rare instances it is not possible to determine that these factors are direct causes of problem behavior.

As is the case in mental retardation, there is more often evidence of a biological cause among severely and profoundly disabled children. Psychotic (autistic or schizophrenic) children frequently, but not always, show signs of neurological defects (see Achenbach, 1982; Werry, 1979). There is convincing evidence that genetic factors contribute to schizophrenia (Nicol and Erlenmeyer-Kimling, 1986). But even when there is severe and profound disturbance, the role of specific biological factors often remains a mystery (Kauffman, 1985; Ornitz, 1986; Werry, 1979).

Family Factors

Mental health specialists have been tempted to blame behavioral difficulties primarily on parent-child relationships because it is obvious that the nuclear family—father, mother, and children—has a profound influence on early development. In fact, some advocates of psychoanalysis, such as Bettelheim (1967), believe that almost all severe problems of children stem from early negative interactions between mother and child. However, empirical research on family relationships indicates that the influence of parents on their children is no simple matter, and that deviant children may influence their parents as much as the parents influence them. It is increasingly clear that family influences are interactional and transactional, and that the effects of parents and children on one another are reciprocal (Martin, 1981). Even in cases of severe and profound disturbance in children, it is not possible to find consistent and valid research findings that allow the blame for the children's problem behavior to be placed primarily on their parents (Sameroff, Seifer, and Zax, 1982).

The outcome of parental discipline depends not only on the particular techniques used, but also on the characteristics of the child (Rutter, 1985). Generalizations about the effects of parental discipline are difficult to make, for, as Becker (1964) commented long ago, "There are probably many routes to becoming a 'good parent' which vary with the personality of both the parents and children and with the pressure in the environment with which one must learn to cope" (p. 202). Nevertheless, sensitivity to children's needs, love-oriented methods of dealing with misbehavior, and reinforcement (attention and praise) for appropriate behavior unquestionably tend to promote desirable behavior in children. Parents who are generally lax in disciplining their children but are hostile, rejecting, cruel, and inconsistent in dealing with misbehavior are likely to have aggressive, delinquent children (Patterson, 1982). Broken, disorganized homes in which the parents themselves have arrest

How parents deal with their children's exasperating behavior may contribute to behavior disorders; however, parental discipline alone is not the cause of most behavior problems. (Bill Binzen/Photo Researchers)

records or are violent are particularly likely to foster delinquency (Arnold and Brungardt, 1983) and lack of social competence (Wolfe, Zak, Wilson, and Jaffe, 1986).

Cultural Factors

Children and their families are embedded in a culture that influences their behavior. Aside from family and school, many environmental conditions affect adults' expectations of children and children's expectations for themselves and their peers. Values and behavioral standards are communicated to children through a variety of cultural conditions, demands, prohibitions, and models. Several specific cultural influences leap to mind: the level of violence in the media (especially television and motion pictures), the use of terror as a means of coercion, the availability of recreational drugs and the level of drug abuse, changing standards for sexual conduct, religious demands and restrictions on behavior, and the threat of nuclear accidents or war.

Undoubtedly, the culture in which children are reared exerts an influence on their emotional, social, and behavioral development. Case studies of rapidly changing cultures bear this out. In Khartoum, for example, Sudan boys of school age showed three times the number of behavioral problems in 1980 as had boys of the same age in that culture in 1965 (Rahim and Cederblad, 1984). Rahim and Cederblad suggest that rapid urbanization, including exposure of young males to cultural values conflicting with those of their homes, was a significant factor in this increase.

Other studies suggest cultural influences on anxiety, depression, and aggression (Chivian, Mack, Waletzky, Lazaroff, Doctor, and Goldenring, 1985; Goldstein, 1983a,b). The fear of nuclear holocaust contributes to depression for some children and youth. The level of violence depicted on TV and in movies is almost certainly a contributing factor in the increasing level of violence in our society (Gelfand, Ficula, and Zarbatany, 1986). Particularly troubling is the finding that television violence seems more "real" to disturbed than to nondisturbed children. This finding suggests that disturbed children may be more likely than most youngsters to perform aggressive acts after watching televised violence (Sprafkin, Gadow, and Dussault, 1986).

In short, social and cultural conditions or changes may have a marked effect on children's behavior. As Morse observes:

> Sexual mores have changed, placing new responsibilities on adolescents. The consequence of these and many other societal changes are reflected in more than half-a-million teenage mothers each year; the increase in depression and suicide; and the prevalence of delinquency, alcoholism, and drug abuse. Currently, a million youths run away each year. Although youth violence is a mirror image of adult behavior, it has reached epidemic proportions in some schools. . . . It is a sad commentary that over half of the robberies and assaults on youngsters actually occur in school! (1985, pp. ix–x)

Clearly, cultural influences on behavior are significant; just as clearly, they are not the only contributing factor in children's emotional or behavioral problems.

School Factors

Some children are already ED/BD when they begin school; others develop emotional disorders during their school years, perhaps in part because of damaging experiences in the classroom itself. Children who are disturbed when they enter school may become better or worse because of how they are managed in the classroom. School experiences are no doubt of great importance to children; but like biological and family factors, we cannot justify many statements regarding how such experiences contribute to the child's behavioral difficulties. A child's temperament and social competence may interact with classmates' and teachers' behavior in contributing to emotional/behavioral problems (Paget, Nagle, and Martin, 1984; Pullis and Cadwell, 1985). When a child with an already difficult temperament enters school lacking the skills for academic and social success, he or she is likely to get negative responses from peers and teachers.

There is a very real danger that such a child will become trapped in a spiral of negative interactions in which he or she becomes increasingly irritating to and irritated by teachers and peers. The school can contribute to the development of emotional problems in several rather specific ways. Teachers may be insensitive to children's individuality; they may require a mindless conformity to rules and routines. Educators and parents alike may hold too high or too low expectations for the child's achievement or conduct, and communicate to the child who disappoints these expectations that he or she is inadequate or undesirable.

Discipline in the school may be too lax, too rigid, or inconsistent. Instruction may be offered in skills for which the child has no real or imagined use. The school environment may be such that the misbehaving child is rewarded with recognition and special attention (even if that attention is criticism or punishment), while the child who behaves is ignored. Finally, teachers and peers may be models of misconduct—the child may misbehave by imitating them (Kauffman, 1985; Kauffman, Pullen, and Akers, 1986).

Prevention

If the specific causes of ED/BD could be clearly identified, prevention would be greatly simplified. At our current level of knowledge, however, there is more error than accuracy in predicting children's emotional/behavioral disorders on the basis of any of the factors known to contribute to them. Preventive efforts are limited to attempts to control elements thought to increase the risk that children will become disturbed. We now know that some rather obvious factors are part of children's emotional/behavioral problems; poverty, malnutrition, neglect, abuse, family conflict, and failure at school, for example, are known to increase a child's chances for abnormal development. There may be other important factors more subtle and complex than these, but only intensive longitudinal research on large numbers of children will reveal what they are. Longitudinal studies may soon tell us much about the development of serious behavior problems (Campbell, Breaux, Ewing, and Szumowski, 1986; Walker, Shinn, O'Neill, and Ramsey, in press). These and other studies may also suggest ways to prevent emotional and behavioral disorders in children.

There is a chance too that once children begin exhibiting disturbed or disordered behavior, their interactions with the environment set off a downward spiral. As we have already mentioned, inappropriate behavior tends to elicit negative responses from peers and adults (see Kauffman et al., 1986). These negative reactions further increase the chance that children will behave in undesirable ways. Therefore early identification of ED/BD children and early intervention are important in preventing further difficulties.

A particularly important feature of prevention is identifying and teaching the social skills and adaptive interpersonal behavior that help children make and keep friends and get along with adults (Weissberg and Allen, 1986). Some prevention programs involve attempts to teach very specific skills, such as making positive comments about a peer during an invitation to play, through modeling, role playing, rehearsal, and direct coaching. Other programs involve teaching more general social problem-solving skills, such as thinking before acting, generating alternative responses, and considering the consequences of various types of behavior. Weissberg and Allen's review indicates that a combination of direct coaching in specific skills and instruction in general problem-solving strategies is probably the most effective approach.

IDENTIFICATION

It is much easier to identify disturbed/disordered *behaviors* than it is to define and classify types and causes of ED/BD. Most ED/BD children do not escape the notice of their teachers. Occasionally a disturbed child will not be a bother to anyone and thus be "invisible," but it is usually easy for experienced teachers to tell when a child needs help. The most common type of ED/BD children—those with conduct disorders—attract attention with their behavior, so there is seldom any real problem in identifying them. Immature children and those with personality problems may be less obvious, but they are not difficult to recognize. ED/BD children are so readily identified by school personnel, in fact, that few schools bother to use systematic screening procedures. Another reason for not using systematic procedures is that special services for disturbed children lag so far behind the need. There is not much point in screening children for problems when there are no services available to treat these problems.

What we have just said should not be interpreted to mean that there is never any question about whether or not a child is ED/BD. The younger the child, the more difficult it is to judge whether or not that child's behavior signifies a serious problem. And some ED/BD children do go undetected because teachers are not sensitive to their problems or because they do not stand out sharply from other children in the environment who may be even more disturbed. Furthermore, even sensitive teachers sometimes make errors of judgment. Finally, some disturbed children do not exhibit problems at school.

Formal screening and accurate early identification for the purpose of planning educational intervention are complicated by the problems of definition we have already discussed. In general, however, informal teacher judgment has served as a fairly valid and reliable means of screening children for emotional/behavioral problems (as compared with judgments of psychologists and psychiatrists). When more formal procedures are used, teacher ratings of behavior have turned out to be quite accurate (Edelbrock and Achenbach, 1984). Children's ratings of their peers and their own behavior have also proved helpful (Bower, 1981).

Walker and his colleagues have devised a screening system for use in elementary schools based on the assumption that teacher judgment is a valid and cost-effective though greatly underused method of identifying ED/BD children (Walker et al., 1986). Although teachers tend to over-refer students who exhibit externalizing behavior problems (those with conduct disorders), they tend to under-refer students with internalizing problems (those who are characterized by anxiety-withdrawal). To make certain that children are not overlooked in screening, but that a lot of time and effort is not wasted, a three-step process is used.

First, the teacher lists and rank-orders students with externalizing and internalizing problems. Those who best fit descriptions of students with externalizing problems and those who best fit descriptions of those with internalizing problems are listed. Then they are rank-ordered from most like to least like the descriptions. Second, the teacher completes two checklists for the three highest-ranked pupils on each list. One checklist asks the teacher to indicate whether or not each pupil exhibited specific behaviors during the past month (such as "steals," "has tantrums," "uses obscene language or swears"). The other checklist requires that the teacher judge how often (never, sometimes, frequently) each pupil shows certain characteristics (e.g., "follows established classroom rules," "cooperates with peers in group activities or situations"). Third, pupils whose scores on these checklists exceed established norms are observed in the classroom and on the playground by a school professional other than the classroom teacher (a school psychologist, counselor, or resource teacher).

Classroom observations indicate the extent to which the pupil meets academic expectations; playground observations assess the quality and nature of social behavior. These direct observations of behavior, in addition to teacher ratings, are then used to decide whether or not the child has problems that warrant classification for special education. Carefully researched screening systems like the one devised by Walker et al. may lead to improved services for children with ED/BD. Systematic efforts to base identification on teacher judgment *and* careful observation should result in services being directed to those most clearly in need.

PSYCHOLOGICAL AND BEHAVIORAL CHARACTERISTICS

Intelligence and Achievement

The idea that ED/BD children tend to be bright youngsters is a myth. Research clearly shows that the average mildly or moderately disturbed child has an IQ in the dull-normal range (around 90) and that very few score above the bright-normal range. Compared to the normal distribution of intelligence, many more ED/BD children fall into the slow learner and mildly retarded categories. Although severely and profoundly disturbed children are often untestable, those who can be tested are likely to have IQs in the retarded range; the average for these children is about 50. On the basis of a review of the research on the intelligence of ED/BD children, Kauffman (1985) has hypothesized distributions of intelligence as shown in Figure 4.1. Of course, we have been referring to ED/BD children as a group. ED/BD children, even some who are severely or profoundly disturbed, can be extremely bright and score very high on intelligence tests. But they are not representative of ED/BD children as a group.

There are pitfalls in assessing the intellectual characteristics of a group of children by examining the distribution of the IQs. Intelligence tests are not perfect instruments for measuring what we mean by "intelligence." And it can be argued that emotional/behavioral difficulties may prevent children from scoring as high as they could. That is, it might be argued that intelligence tests are biased against ED/BD children and that their "true" intelligence is higher than the test scores indicate. Still, the lower-than-normal IQs for disturbed children do indicate lower ability to perform tasks other children can perform successfully, and the lower scores are consistent with impairment in other areas of functioning (academic achievement and social skills, for example). IQ is a relatively good predictor of how far a child will progress academically and socially, even in cases of severe and profound disturbance (DeMyer, 1975).

Most ED/BD children are also underachievers at school, as measured by standardized tests (Kauffman, 1985). A disturbed child does not usually achieve at the level expected for his or her mental age; it is relatively seldom that one finds such a child to be academically advanced. Many severely and profoundly ED/BD children lack even the most basic reading and arithmetic skills; and the few who seem to be

Figure 4.1 *Hypothetical frequency distributions of IQ for mildly to moderately and severely to profoundly disturbed compared to normal frequency distribution.*
SOURCE: J. M. Kauffman, *Characteristics of Children's Behavior Disorders,* 3rd ed. (Columbus, Ohio: Charles E. Merrill, 1985), p. 142. Reprinted with permission.

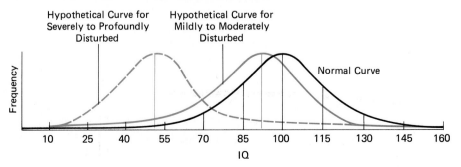

competent in reading or math are often unable to apply their skills to everyday problems. Some severely and profoundly disturbed youngsters do not even possess basic self-care or daily living skills, such as toileting, grooming, dressing, and feeding.

Social and Emotional Characteristics

Earlier we described two major dimensions of disordered behavior based on analyses of behavior ratings: externalizing and internalizing. The externalizing dimension is characterized by aggressive, acting-out behavior; the internalizing dimension is characterized by anxious, withdrawn behavior. Our discussion here will focus on the aggressive and withdrawn types of behavior typically exhibited by mildly and moderately disturbed children.

Although both aggressive and withdrawn behaviors are commonly seen in severely and profoundly as well as in mildly and moderately ED/BD children, we will discuss the characteristics of the severely and profoundly disturbed in a separate section. Severely and profoundly disturbed children may be qualitatively as well as quantitatively different from others, for certain behavioral features set these children apart. Remember too that a given child might, at different times, show both aggressive and withdrawn behaviors.

At the beginning of this chapter we said that most ED/BD children are not well liked by their peers. Studies of the social status of students in regular elementary and secondary classrooms have indicated that those who are identified as ED/BD are seldom socially accepted by peers (Sabornie, 1985; Sabornie and Kauffman, 1985). Given what we know about the behavioral characteristics of ED/BD students and the behavioral characteristics that support social acceptance, this should come as no surprise: "The research indicates that children—whether normal or exceptional— who are in frequent conflict with authority, who fight or bother others a great deal, and who demonstrate verbal aggression are rarely the objects of social acceptance" (Drabman and Patterson, 1981, p. 53). Children who show these characteristics are actively rejected, not just neglected, by their peers (Gelfand et al., 1986).

Aggressive, Acting-Out Behavior (Externalizing)

As we noted earlier, conduct disorders are the most common problems exhibited by ED/BD children. Hitting, fighting, teasing, yelling, refusing to comply with requests, crying, destructiveness, vandalism, extortion—these behaviors, if exhibited often, are very likely to earn a child the label "disturbed." Normal children cry, scream, hit, fight, become negative, and do almost everything else disturbed children do, only not so impulsively and so often. Children of the type we are discussing here drive adults to distraction. They are not popular with their peers either, unless they are socialized delinquents who do not offend other social deviants. And they typically do not respond quickly and positively to well-meaning adults who care about them and try to be helpful.

Some of these children are considered hyperactive or brain injured; some are called **sociopathic** because they appear to hurt others deliberately and without any sense of doing wrong. Their behavior is not only extremely troublesome, but also appears to be resistant to change through the usual discipline. Often they are so frequently scolded and punished that punishment means little or nothing to them. Because of adult exasperation with them and their own deviousness, they get away with misbehavior a lot of the time. We are talking about children who behave horribly not once in a while, but so often that the people they must live with or be

Aggressive children are frequently in conflict with others. Fighting, teasing, or causing pain and discomfort for no socially acceptable purpose are aggressive behaviors.
(Ken Gaghan/Jeroboam, Inc.)

with cannot stand them. Of course, aggressive, acting-out children typically cannot stand the people they have to live and be with either, and usually for good reason. Such children are screamed at, criticized, and punished a lot. The problem, then, is not just the child's behavior. What must be examined if the child or anyone else is to be helped is the *interaction between the child's behavior and the behavior of other people in his or her environment.*

Aggression has been analyzed from many different viewpoints. The analyses of aggression that have the strongest support in empirical research are those of social learning theorists such as Bandura (1973) and behavioral psychologists such as Patterson (Patterson, 1982; Patterson, Reid, Jones, and Conger, 1975). Their studies take into account the child's experience and his or her motivation, based on the anticipated consequences of aggression. In brief, they view aggression as *learned* behavior, and they assume that it is possible to identify the conditions under which aggressive behavior will be learned. The following statements about learned aggression are supported by research (see Bandura, 1973; Goldstein, 1983a; Goldstein, Carr, Davidson, and Wehr, 1981).

Children learn many aggressive behaviors by observing parents, siblings, playmates, and people portrayed on television and in movies. Individuals who model aggression are more likely to be imitated by children if they are high in social status and if they are observed to receive rewards and escape punishment for their aggression, especially if they experience no unpleasant consequences or obtain rewards by overcoming their victims. If children are placed in an unpleasant situation and they cannot escape from the unpleasantness or obtain rewards except by aggression, they are more likely to be aggressive, especially if this behavior is tolerated or encouraged by others.

Aggression is encouraged by external rewards (social status, power, suffering of the victim, obtaining desired items), vicarious rewards (seeing others obtain desirable consequences for their aggression), and self-reinforcement (self-congratulation or enhancement of self-image). If children can justify aggression in their own minds (by comparison to the behavior of others or by dehumanizing their victims), they are more likely to be aggressive. Punishment may actually increase aggression under some circumstances: when it is inconsistent or delayed, when there is no positive alternative to the punished behavior, when it provides an example of aggression, or when counterattack against the punisher seems likely to be successful.

Teaching aggressive children to be less obnoxious is no simple matter, but social learning theory and behavioral research do provide some general guidelines (see Bandura, 1973; Goldstein et al., 1981; Patterson, 1982). In general, research does not support the notion that it is wise to let children "act out" their aggression freely. The most helpful techniques include providing examples (models) of nonaggressive responses to aggression-provoking circumstances, helping the child rehearse or role-play nonaggressive behavior, providing reinforcement for nonaggressive behavior, preventing the child from obtaining positive consequences for aggression, and punishing aggression in ways that involve as little counteraggression as possible (using "time-out" or brief social isolation rather than spanking or yelling).

The seriousness of ED/BD children's aggressive, acting-out behavior should not be underestimated. As noted earlier, it has been a popular idea for decades that although these children cause a lot of trouble, they are not as seriously disturbed or handicapped as children who are shy, anxious, neurotic types. The work of Robins (1966, 1979) and others (Kazdin, 1987; Loeber, 1982; Patterson, 1982) has exploded this myth. When combined with school failure, aggressive, antisocial behavior in childhood generally means a gloomy future in terms of social adjustment and mental health, especially for boys. Neurotic, shy, anxious children are much more likely to be able to get and hold a job, overcome their emotional problems, and stay out of jails and mental hospitals than are adults who were conduct problems and delinquent as children.

Of course, there are exceptions to the rule. But there is a high probability that the aggressive child who is a failure in school will become more of a social misfit as an adult than the withdrawn child. And when we consider that conduct disorders and delinquency are highly correlated with school failure, the importance of meeting the needs of acting-out and underachieving children is obvious.

Immature, Withdrawn Behavior (Internalizing)

In noting the seriousness of aggressive, acting-out behavior, we do not intend to downplay the handicaps of immaturity and withdrawal. In their extreme forms, withdrawal and immaturity are characteristics of the severe and profound disorders known as childhood schizophrenia and infantile autism. Such disorders (sometimes called childhood psychoses) are not only extremely damaging to individuals in their childhood years, but carry a very poor prognosis for adult mental health. Even the mildly or moderately disturbed child whose behavior fits a pattern of immaturity and withdrawal cannot develop the close and satisfying human relationships that characterize normal development. Such a child will find it difficult to meet the pressures and demands of everyday life.

All children exhibit immature behavior and act withdrawn once in a while. ED/BD children who fit the withdrawn-immature description, however, are typically infantile in their ways or reluctant to interact with other people. They are social isolates who have few friends, seldom play with children their own age, and lack the social skills necessary to have fun. Some retreat into fantasy or daydreaming; some develop fears that are completely out of proportion to the circumstances; some complain constantly of little aches and pains and let their "illness" keep them from participating in normal activities; some regress to earlier stages of development and demand constant help and attention; and some become depressed for no apparent reason.

As in the case of aggressive, acting-out behavior, withdrawal and immaturity may be interpreted in many different ways. Proponents of the psychoanalytic approach are likely to see internal conflicts and unconscious motivations as the underlying causes. Behavioral psychologists tend to interpret such problems in terms of failures in social learning. The social learning view is supported by more empirical research data than other views (see Kauffman, 1985). A social learning analysis attributes withdrawal and immaturity to an inadequate environment. Causal factors may include overrestrictive parental discipline, punishment for appropriate social responses, reward for isolate behavior, lack of opportunity to learn and practice social skills, and models (examples) of inappropriate behavior. It is possible to teach immature or withdrawn children the skills they lack by arranging opportunities for them to learn and practice appropriate responses, showing models engaging in appropriate behavior, and providing rewards for improved behavior (see, for example, Strain, 1981; Twardosz, Nordquist, Simon, and Botkin, 1983).

A particularly important aspect of immature, withdrawn behavior is depression. Only very recently have mental health workers and special educators begun to realize that depression is a widespread and serious problem among children and

Depression, which often includes social withdrawal in various forms, is now recognized as a frequent and serious problem of youth. (Richard Hutchings/Photo Researchers)

adolescents (Earls, 1984; Epstein, Kauffman, and Cullinan, 1985; Kaslow and Rehm, 1983; Petti, 1983). Today the consensus of psychologists is that the nature of depression in children and youths is quite similar to that of depression in adults (Gelfand et al., 1986). The indications of depression include disturbances of mood or feelings, inability to think or concentrate, lack of motivation, and decreased physical well-being. A depressed child or youth may act sad, lonely, and apathetic; exhibit low self-esteem, excessive guilt, and pervasive pessimism; avoid tasks and social experiences; and/or have physical complaints or problems in sleeping, eating, or eliminating. Sometimes depression is accompanied by such problems as bed-wetting (nocturnal enuresis), fecal soiling (encopresis), extreme fear of or refusal to go to school, failure in school, or talk of suicide or suicide attempts (see p. 184 for a list of the primary signs of depression).

Suicide has increased dramatically during the past decade among those between the ages of 15 and 24; it is now among the leading causes of death in this age group. Depression, especially when it is severe and accompanied by a sense of hopelessness, is linked to suicide and suicide attempts. Therefore it is important that all those who work with young people be able to recognize the signs of depression.

Depression sometimes has a biological cause, and antidepressant medications have at times been successful in helping depressed children and youths overcome their problems. In many cases, however, no biological cause can be found. Depression can also be caused by environmental or psychological factors, such as the death of a loved one, separation of one's parents, school failure, rejection by one's peers, or a chaotic and punitive home environment. Interventions based on social learning theory—instructing children in social interaction skills and self-control techniques and teaching them to view themselves more positively, for example—have often been successful in such cases (see Cantwell, 1982; Kaslow and Rehm, 1983; Petti, 1983).

Special Characteristics of Severely and Profoundly Disturbed Children

Children whose behavior is grossly different from normal are generally considered severely disturbed, severely retarded, or in some other way severely or profoundly handicapped. We have avoided using a particular label such as autistic for these children because there is still confusion about exactly what the common labels mean. We know that these children are extremely different from other youngsters, but diagnosticians often disagree about the most appropriate label in the individual case. Generally, however, **schizophrenia** refers to psychotic behavior manifested by loss of contact with reality, bizarre thought processes, and extremely inappropriate behavior. **Autism** is characterized by extreme social withdrawal, self-stimulation, cognitive deficits, and language disorders that are apparent before the age of 30 months. Childhood schizophrenia typically does not manifest itself until the child is at least 5 years old, and the onset often occurs in later childhood or adolescence, whereas autism (sometimes called *early infantile autism*) is a disorder beginning before the child is 2½ years old.

We will describe briefly the types of behavior that set these children apart from the mildly and moderately disturbed. Remember that not every severely disturbed child exhibits all these characteristics (see Schreibman, Charlop, and Britten, 1983; Schreibman and Mills, 1983).

Primary Indications of Depression

When a person, regardless of age, exhibits several of the following characteristics consistently over a period of two weeks or longer, he or she is almost certain to be considered depressed by a psychologist or psychiatrist. Teachers should be on the lookout for children who show these signs of depression and refer them to the school psychologist or counselor:

- Sudden change in appetite or significant change in weight
- Disturbance of sleep (complaints about not being able to sleep or being always sleepy)
- Agitated activity or extremely low activity level
- Inability to have fun, to experience pleasure and happiness
- Loss of energy, constant feelings of fatigue
- Feelings of worthlessness, self-reproach, or excessive or inappropriate guilt
- Inability to concentrate or think or to make decisions
- Ideas of suicide or suicide threats or attempts

Lack of Daily Living Skills

One of the reasons severely disturbed and retarded children are often confused is that children fitting both descriptions frequently lack basic self-care skills. They may be unable to dress and feed themselves and not be toilet trained at the age of 5 or even 10 years. Unable to communicate with others and take care of their daily needs, they present a picture of helplessness characteristic of infancy.

Perceptual Deviations

Severely disturbed children are sometimes mistakenly thought to be deaf or blind. They may seem deaf or blind to the casual observer because at first they appear to be oblivious of what is going on around them: They ignore people and do not seem to be affected by conversation or loud noises or bright lights. In short, they are not responsive to visual and auditory stimuli in the same way as ordinary children with vision and hearing. Yet closer observation shows that such a child does respond to some auditory and visual stimuli, perhaps sights and noises that are insignificant or uninteresting to most children. It is as if the child cannot make sense of what he or she sees and hears.

Cognitive Deficits

Some severely disturbed children are untestable. Those who can be given intelligence and achievement tests frequently score in the mentally retarded range. Some of these children may seem intellectually competent because they can carry on a conversation. But after a while it is obvious that there is only one topic they can converse about, or that their conversation soon turns to meaningless jargon and bizarre statements or questions. Many severely disturbed children "look" intelligent and some can perform amazing feats of memory or computation, but their "intelligence" is deceptive—they cannot apply their skills or seeming brilliance to everyday tasks.

Unrelatedness to Other People

One of the most disconcerting aspects of severely disturbed children's behavior is that they tend to react to other people, including their parents and siblings, as physical objects. Often these children ignore or resist their parents and others when they try to show love and affection. They do not adapt their posture to their parents' when they are being held and they do not develop an anticipatory posture when being picked up. There is no exchange of warmth and gratification between adults and such children.

Language and Speech Deviations

Some severely disturbed children do not speak at all or do not seem to understand language. Some show **echolalia**—that is, they parrot back whatever they hear but do not say anything else (see Chapter 5). Misuse of pronouns ("he" or "you" for "I" or "her" for "you") and meaningless jargon are common. Some of these children have an extremely strange vocal quality (such as an extraordinarily low- or high-pitched voice) or repeat questions or statements incessantly.

Self-Stimulation

Behavior that is stereotyped, repetitive, and useful only for obtaining sensory stimulation is common in severely disturbed children. Such self-stimulation can take a nearly infinite variety of forms (swishing saliva, twirling an object, patting one's cheeks, flapping one's hands, staring at lights). Severely disturbed children often exhibit such behavior so constantly that it is extremely difficult to engage them in any other activity.

Self-stimulation may range from relatively mild forms, such as thumb-sucking, to stereotypic behaviors that are incompatible with normal activity and learning. (Marion Bernstein)

Self-Injurious Behavior

Some severely disturbed children injure themselves purposely and repeatedly to such an extent that they must be kept in restraints so they will not mutilate and/or slowly kill themselves. They seem impassive to the self-inflicted pain. The ways such children can injure themselves include biting, scratching, poking, bumping, or scraping various parts of their bodies.

Aggression Toward Others

It is not unusual for severely disturbed children to throw severe temper tantrums in which they strike out at others or to treat others in calculatedly cruel ways. Biting, scratching, and kicking others are common characteristics of these children.

Prognosis without Early Intensive Intervention

The undesirability of these characteristics is obvious. Not so obvious is the fact that the prognosis for these children is poor. They are likely to function at a retarded level and require supervision and care even after years of the most effective treatment known today, unless the intensive treatment is begun while they are still very young. Recent research has shown that if intensive treatment (forty hours or more of one-to-one teaching per week) is begun before an autistic child is 3½ years of age, about 50 percent of these children may recover completely—that is, become indistinguishable from other children by the time they are in the first or second grade (Lovaas, 1982). With less intensive treatment, and when treatment is started after autistic children are 3½ years old, the prognosis is much more guarded. They are likely to continue showing severely handicapping behaviors, and many of them will probably be considered psychotic as adults (Lovaas, Koegel, Simmons, and Long, 1973; Petty, Ornitz, Michelman, and Zimmerman, 1984).

EDUCATIONAL CONSIDERATIONS

If you ask special educators and mental health professionals how disturbed children should be educated, you will get many different answers. This is partly because the general category of ED/BD embraces so many different behavior problems, ranging from aggression to withdrawal, and degrees of disturbance, ranging from mild to profound. But the major reason for differing views goes back to something first mentioned in our discussion of definition—the problem of different conceptual models or theories.

Conceptual Models and Education

Conceptual models are just theories until they are put to use to guide educational practices; then the essential differences among models can be tested empirically. The differences among recommended practices and their outcomes, therefore, should provide the basis for evaluation of conceptual models. But although it would seem to be relatively simple to compare them, the job is actually quite difficult because it is not always apparent whether a difference between practices is a real one or just a matter of terms. For example, is the difference between the "planned ignoring" technique (a practice associated with the psychoeducational model) and "extinction" (a practice associated with the behavioral model) a real one? Does the teacher actually do different things? In reading the statements of those who propose different theoretical models, one gets the impression that the differences are often more words than deeds (see Kauffman and Lewis, 1974).

Of course, there are some real differences between conceptual models. For example, the proponents of a psychoanalytic model purposely encourage acting-out behavior in some circumstances, on the assumption that the child must work through underlying conflicts before more desirable behavior can be expected. In contrast, behaviorists discourage misbehavior because they believe it only makes the problem worse. They consistently try to suppress inappropriate behavior and reward desirable responses. The substantive differences between some conceptual models may make them incompatible, for under some circumstances they suggest directly opposite actions and cannot be used in combination.

Our purpose here is merely to point out that there are many different views regarding the education of ED/BD children and to provide brief sketches of the major features of several different approaches (see Table 4-1). Rhodes and Tracy (1972a, b) and McDowell et al. (1982) provide a more detailed analysis of various approaches and their theoretical underpinnings. Some concepts are common to several approaches, and in practice we seldom find a really "pure" single viewpoint. But as we have pointed out, the ideas of one model can be incompatible with those of another. There is a limit to the extent to which a teacher can pick and choose techniques without its becoming self-defeating.

The Psychoanalytic Approach

This particular approach to education was formulated primarily by psychiatrists and clinical psychologists who believe that the guiding principles of **psychoanalysis** can be used in education. The problem of ED/BD is viewed as a pathological imbalance among the dynamic parts of the mind: id, ego, and superego. Educational practices are designed to help uncover the underlying mental pathology in an effort to improve psychological functioning, as well as behavior and achievement.

The emphasis is on building a teacher-pupil relationship in which the child feels accepted and free to act out his or her impulses in a permissive environment. The primary concern of the teacher is to help the child overcome underlying mental conflicts, not to change the surface behavior or to teach academic skills. Usually the child and the parents receive therapy, and the psychotherapist is relied upon to help the child "work through" problems in therapy sessions. The work of Bettelheim (1950, 1967) and Berkowitz and Rothman (1960) is representative of this approach (see also Tuma and Sobotka, 1983).

The Psychoeducational Approach

Those who developed the psychoeducational approach (such as Fagen, 1979; Fenichel, 1974; Long, Morse, and Newman, 1980; Rezmierski, Knoblock, and Bloom, 1982) have tried to interweave psychiatric and educational concerns. Since the problems of disturbed children are assumed to involve both underlying psychiatric disorders and the observable misbehavior and underachievement of the child, there is a balance between therapeutic goals and goals for achievement in the recommended educational practices. Unconscious motivation and underlying pathology are taken into account. But there is also concern for the management of surface

Table 4-1 Approaches to Educating ED/BD Children

	Psychoanalytic Approach	Psychoeducational Approach	Humanistic Approach	Ecological Approach	Behavioral Approach
The problem	A pathological imbalance among the dynamic parts of the mind (id, superego, ego).	Involves both underlying psychiatric disorders and the readily observable misbehavior and underachievement of the child.	The ED/BD child is out of touch with his or her own feelings and can't find fulfillment in traditional educational settings.	The child interacts poorly with the environment; child and environment affect each other reciprocally and negatively.	The child has learned inappropriate responses and failed to learn appropriate ones.
Purpose of educational practices	Use of psychoanalytic principles to help uncover underlying mental pathology.	Concern for unconscious motivation/underlying conflicts *and* academic achievement/positive surface behavior.	Emphasis on enhancing child's self-direction, self-evaluation, and emotional involvement in learning.	Attempt to alter entire social system so that it will support desirable behavior in child when intervention is withdrawn.	Manipulation of child's immediate environment and the consequences of behavior.
Characteristics of teaching methods	Reliance on individual psychotherapy for child and parents; little emphasis on academic achievement; highly permissive atmosphere.	Emphasis on meeting individual needs of the child; reliance on projects and creative arts.	Use of nontraditional educational settings in which teacher serves as resource and catalyst rather than as director of activities; nonauthoritarian, open, affective, personal atmosphere.	Involves all aspects of a child's life, including classroom, family, neighborhood, and community, in teaching the child useful life and educational skills.	Involves measurement of responses and subsequent analyses of behaviors in order to change them; emphasis on reward for appropriate behavior.

behavior and academic achievement. There is emphasis on meeting the individual needs of children, and teaching is often done through projects or the creative arts (music, art, dance).

The Humanistic Approach

The humanistic approach to educating disturbed children grew out of humanistic psychology (Maslow, 1962; Rogers, 1969), the open education movement, and the revolt against traditional concepts of education beginning in the late 1960s. The basic problem, as humanistic educators see it, is that ED/BD children are out of touch with their own feelings and cannot find meaning and self-fulfillment in traditional educational settings. The recommended educational practices are designed to enhance children's self-direction, self-evaluation, and emotional involvement in learning in nontraditional settings. The teacher functions as a resource and catalyst for children's learning rather than as a director of activities. Children and teachers work together as learners, pursuing areas of interest to themselves and sharing information. "Nonauthoritarian," "self-directed," "self-evaluative," "affective," "open," and "personal" are words used to describe humanistic education for disturbed children. Dennison (1969), Knoblock (1973), and Schultz, Heuchert, and Stampf (1973) have written descriptions of the humanistic approach (see also Morse, Ardizzone, MacDonald, and Pasick, 1980).

The Ecological Approach

Proponents of the ecological approach (Hobbs, 1966, 1974; Rhodes, 1967, 1970; Swap, 1978; Swap, Prieto, and Harth, 1982) believe that the problem of ED/BD is one of the child in interaction with the various elements of the environment (school, family, community, and social agencies). The child is viewed as a *disturber* of the environment, and his or her behavior is considered as disturbing as it is disturbed. Borrowing concepts from biological ecology and ecological psychology, these theorists suggest that educational practices must be part of a strategy to alter the entire social system in which the child is enmeshed. The goal of this approach is not just to intervene in the child's behavior, but to change the environment enough so that it will continue to support desirable behavior in the child once the intervention is over. There is concern not only for effective teaching of the child in the classroom, but also for work with the child's family, neighborhood, and community agencies. The ecological approach requires teachers who are able to teach children specific useful skills (including academics, recreation, and everyday living skills) and to work with adults in the child's environment.

The Behavioral Approach

In the 1960s Haring and Phillips (1962), Haring and Whelan (1965), Hewett (1968), Lovaas (1967), Whelan (1966) and others presented an approach to the education of ED/BD children based on the principles of operant and respondent conditioning. The assumption was that behavioral problems represent inappropriate learning and that ED/BD children can be helped when their observable behavior is modified. Modification of behavior can be accomplished by manipulation of the child's immediate environment—the classroom setting and the consequences of the child's behavior. Since it is the child's behavior that is the focus of concern, recommended educational practices include precise measurement of the child's responses.

Because behavior is assumed to be learned, educational practices are clearly specified and analyzed for their effects on the behaviors being measured. The focus of the behavioral approach, then, is on precise definition and measurement of the observable behaviors that are a problem and manipulation of the consequences of these behaviors in order to change them. The behavioral approach has been described by Bornstein and Kazdin (1985), Gelfand and Hartmann (1984), Kerr and Nelson (1983), Morris (1985), Morris and McReynolds (1986), and many others.

Current Synthesis of Conceptual Models

Within the past decade, psychologists of all theoretical persuasions have placed new emphasis on the self. Morse (1985) describes a "metamorphosis" in psychologists' thinking about why individuals behave and perceive things as they do: "This metamorphosis is a result of the blending of developmental and learning psychology with a balanced attention to both the affective and cognitive aspects, which is sometimes called social cognition" (p. 4). The synthesis of developmental and learning perspectives is called **individual psychology** by Morse and other writers. **Cognitive-behavior modification** is not exactly the same as individual psychology, but it is also an attempt to blend learning theory with concern for the individual's thoughts, feelings, and perceptions (see Harris, Wong, and Keogh, 1985, and Meichenbaum, 1977; see also Chapter 3).

People change their behavior, most psychologists now agree, for multiple reasons. They do not change simply because they obtain new understandings about themselves or because they resolve their troubled feelings. Neither do they change simply because someone arranges different consequences for their behavior or shows them appropriate behavioral models. The most effective methods of changing behavior typically require attention to the child as a thinking, feeling person *and* to the consequences of the child's behavior. Attempts to blend learning and developmental theories often result in getting the child involved in self-management. This may mean self-monitoring (keeping track of one's own behavior), self-instruction (talking one's way through a problem), self-evaluation (judging one's own performance), self-reinforcement (complimenting oneself or allowing oneself a reward for good performance), and so on.

Setting goals for oneself is an example of a behavior change strategy involving self-control. Such a strategy may be used in conjunction with other behavior modification techniques. The outcome of an experimental study involving goal setting is shown in Figure 4.2. Lyman (1984) worked with six boys, ages 11 to 13, who were considered emotionally disturbed and attended a school in a residential treatment facility. The boys exhibited conduct disorders, including such problem behaviors as noncompliance with teacher directions, aggression, truancy, and destruction of property. All of them were considerably behind their agemates academically and had difficulty staying on task in the classroom. Lyman defined "on-task" behavior as looking at one's workbook or paper, asking a question related to the assigned work, or listening to the teacher. Each student's on-task behavior was observed systematically during one hour of the school day, and the percentage of time each student was observed to be on task was recorded and plotted on a graph, as shown in Figure 4.2. After obtaining observational data under baseline conditions in which specific goals were not set by the students, Lyman experimented with the effects of private and public goal setting. In the private goal-setting phase each student was called to the teacher's desk and given the following instructions individually:

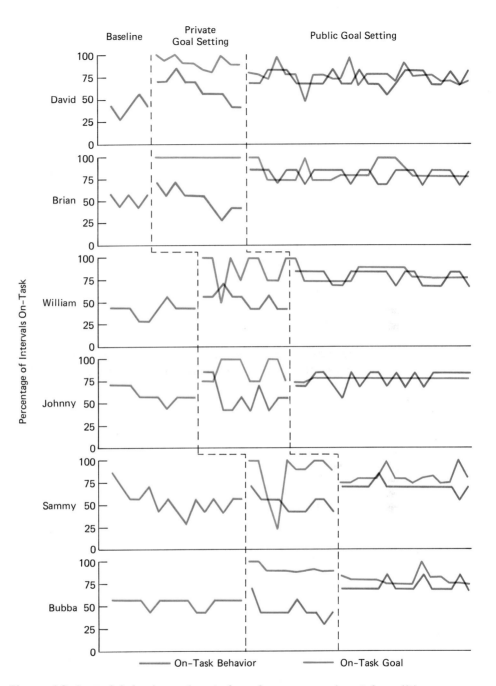

Figure 4.2 *On-task behavior and on-task goals across experimental conditions.*
SOURCE: R. D. Lyman, "The Effect of Private and Public Goal Setting on Classroom On-task Behavior of Emotionally Disturbed Children," *Behavior Therapy, 15,* 398–99. Copyright 1984 by the Association for Advancement of Behavior Therapy. Reprinted by permission of the publisher and the author.

We're going to try something to help you work better in class. I want you to pick a goal for yourself for a percentage of time you're going to work for the next hour. Working means looking at your workbook or response sheet, asking a question about your work, or listening to the teacher. This should be a level that you can try for and that you think is a fair goal for yourself. Try to challenge yourself but don't set a goal that would be unfair to you. Now I want you to pick a percent of time for your goal. I'll write it down on this card and give it to you to remind you of your goal. (Lyman, 1984, p. 398)

In the public goal-setting phase the teacher gave students the same individual instructions, but instead of saying "'I'll write it [the goal] down on this card and give it to you to remind you of your goal,' the teacher said, 'I'll write it down on this card and put it up here on this chart to remind you of your goal'" (Lyman, 1984, p. 298). The student's card was then placed beside his name on a bulletin board at the front of the class under the heading "Work Goals." As shown in Figure 4.2, the students all performed better (i.e., spent more time on task) when their goal setting was public than when it was private. Note that the private and public goal-setting phases were started at different points in time for pairs of students. This was done to show that the goal setting, not some other uncontrolled factor, was responsible for the observed changes in behavior.

Administrative Arrangements

It is estimated that a relatively small proportion of ED/BD children receive any special education services at all (Kauffman, 1986; Morse, 1985). Most programs are designed for mildly and moderately disturbed children, and most serve children in the primary and middle grades. Relatively few provisions are made for ED/BD children at the secondary level. In the past the most common type of program was the special self-contained class, but there is a trend toward consultant or "crisis" teacher and resource arrangements for mildly and moderately disturbed students. Here a special educator works with the regular class teacher to try to keep the child in the mainstream as much as possible.

It is an unfortunate fact that coherent, comprehensive descriptions of educational programs for ED/BD students are rare in the professional literature (Grosenick and Huntze, 1983; Noel, 1982). Analysis of the few program descriptions one can find shows that a high percentage lack adequate details about the following elements: philosophy, goals, definition of the population to be served, criteria for entry into and exit from the program, educational methods, evaluation, and operational procedures (Grosenick and Huntze, 1983). One of the greatest needs in the field today is for an adequate literature to guide program development and improvement.

Severely and Profoundly Handicapped Students

For the most part, severely and profoundly ED/BD children must be instructed individually. They simply do not learn in a group without having had intensive individual instruction first because of their great difficulty in responding, paying attention, and behaving within an interactive situation. It is not possible to integrate them into regular classes until they have learned the needed skills. Although one must maintain hope for the improvement of every child, it is a sad reality that some severely and profoundly disturbed children cannot reasonably be expected, with today's educational and therapeutic procedures, to progress to the point where they can be integrated into classes with their nonhandicapped peers.

The trend now is away from placing severely and profoundly disturbed youngsters in residential institutions and toward the establishment of day schools and special public school classes. Since 1953, when Carl Fenichel established the League School (the first day school for seriously emotionally disturbed children in the United States—see Fenichel, 1974) in Brooklyn, it has become clear that such children do not always need to be removed from their homes and communities in order to be helped. And since the emergence of behavior modification techniques in the early 1960s, more and more educators are becoming convinced that they can approach extreme behavioral problems directly and effectively, without long years of probing into unconscious, underlying causes (see Schreibman et al., 1983; Schreibman and Mills, 1983; Koegel, Rincover, and Egel, 1982).

The teacher of severely and profoundly ED/BD children must have more than empathy and a desire to help seriously handicapped children. Unless the teacher is equipped with specific teaching skills, the time he or she spends with these children will amount to little more than custodial care. A permissive environment maintained under the fiction of "therapy" is not likely to be effective and may in fact be detrimental to the child's progress. Empathy and humanistic concern are to be encouraged, but skill in using behavior modification techniques is essential for teachers who work with such children. The curriculum for most severely and profoundly ED/BD youngsters must be extremely basic—in fact, a lot like the curriculum for the severely retarded. It will involve teaching daily living skills, language, and beginning academic skills. A teacher who works with these children has to be willing to spend countless hours of patient labor to achieve small gains. And he or she must be ready to persist in working with youngsters whose behavior is extremely unpleasant and who will often reject efforts to help them (see Koegel et al., 1982).

Mildly and Moderately Handicapped Students

Paralleling the movement away from custodial institutional placement for severely and profoundly ED/BD children is a trend toward less frequent use of institutions, day schools, and segregated special classes for the less seriously handicapped. In those cases in which it simply is not possible to keep the child in a regular class with normal peers, the currently popular strategy is to remove the child to a resource room for part of the school day or to a special class or special school for a brief period of time, with the goal of quick reintegration into the mainstream.

The curriculum for most mildly and moderately ED/BD children will parallel the curriculum for most youngsters. The basic academic skills have a great deal of survival value for any child in our society; failure to teach a disturbed child to read, write, and perform basic arithmetic is like depriving him or her of any reasonable chance for successful adjustment. Two points need emphasis here: First, new methods may be needed to teach basic academic skills to disturbed youngsters; and second, social skills and affective experiences are as crucial as academic skills. How to manage one's own feelings and behaviors and how to get along with other people are essential features of the curriculum for ED/BD children. These children cannot be expected to learn such skills without instruction, for the ordinary processes of socialization obviously have failed with them.

The teacher of mildly and moderately ED/BD children must be able to tolerate a great deal of unpleasantness and rejection without becoming counteraggressive or withdrawing. Most of the children he or she will teach are social rejects: if kindness

ONE PROFESSIONAL'S PERSPECTIVE

Winfield L. Chadwick

B.A., English, Arizona State University
M.A., Special Education (ED), Arizona State University
Current Position: Teacher, McKemy Junior High School, Tempe, Arizona

Mr. Win Chadwick played professional baseball for the New York Yankees for three years before beginning his teaching career. For the past five years he has been a homeroom 8th grade teacher (civics, language, spelling, composition, and reading). Before assuming his present position, he taught a self-contained class for emotionally handicapped students at McKemy Junior High for seven years. He has also taught graduate level classes for ASU and the Arizona Department of Education on a part-time basis. He has two reading classes and two homeroom classes per day. His morning reading group is small and composed of students who are having a difficult time academically. His afternoon reading class is on grade level but has a high percentage of "behavior problem" students. His two homeroom classes are composed of students with a wide range of abilities, with once again a high percentage of "behavior problems" (as well as a hearing impaired student or two). All the students are 12–14 years old. Many have been selected specifically for his class because of his ability and experience as a special education teacher. A majority of his students are male.

Mr. Chadwick's daily schedule is as follows:

8:10   Arrive at school (late, generally, so he can miss at least 10 minutes of the faculty meeting if there is one!); open classroom.
8:10–8:50   Available to students; check mailbox in office; interact with other teachers; occasional teachers' meetings or parent conferences.
8:50–9:40   Reading class (below grade level students).
9:40–9:45   Check attendance (or lack thereof); send roll to office; all-school announcements, etc.
9:45–10:30   Preparation period (a very valuable 45 minutes): copy materials, adjust materials for individuals, grade papers.
10:30–11:20   Homeroom class (civics).
11:20–11:25   Monitor halls during break.
11:25–12:10   Homeroom class (language, spelling, composition).
12:15–12:45   Study hall (AM homeroom students); tutor students who are having difficulty.
12:45–1:10   Lunch; Mr. Chadwick doesn't particularly enjoy smoky teachers' lounges, so he goes to the cafeteria to interact with students on a nonacademic basis.
1:10–1:15   Monitor halls during break.
1:15–2:00   Reading class (on grade level, but a high percentage of "bad dudes").

2:00–2:05   Monitor halls during break.
2:05–2:45   Homeroom class (spelling, language, composition).
2:45–2:50   Monitor halls during break.
2:50–3:30   Homeroom class (civics).
3:30–5:30   Activities vary from day to day.

We asked Mr. Chadwick to respond to the following questions:

What made you decide to choose the profession you're in?   I made the decision to enter the field of education for many different reasons. Initially, I had intended to become a professional baseball superstar and earn megabucks for little or no effort. Unfortunately, that failed to materialize, but my parents had counseled me to remain in college in the event that what happened might happen—a debilitating injury might force me to actually *work* for a living! While in high school I had an outstanding sophomore English teacher, Richard Kirkpatrick, who influenced me greatly. I thought it might be wonderful to be a competent teacher, making education challenging yet fun for my students. I enrolled in secondary education courses at ASU. After teaching "regular" education for two years, I didn't feel challenged. I met Ken Howell, the special education teacher at the school, and *he seemed challenged!*

I made the decision to do my masters work in special education with emphasis on the emotionally handicapped. I became obsessed with the challenge of having kids in my class that no one could handle, systematically applying learning theory, and teaching them appropriate behavior that would allow them to return to the mainstream. To me, it is the most challenging, stimulating, interesting, and frustrating job in the world.

If you could change one thing about your job, what would it be? I wouldn't change much about the job *per se.* Instead, I'd change the attitudes of the majority of those who hold the job—the regular classroom teachers who erroneously believe that they are hired to educate only a certain kind of child, the one who can do the work and not present any problems along the way. Too many teachers exclude kids with learning and/or behavior problems. By neglecting to modify education to benefit the children least able to function without academic or behavioral assistance, many teachers systematically excise these students from their classes and force them to spend precious minutes that could be used for education sitting outside their classrooms or in the vice-principal's office. If I had a "magic wand," I'd wave it over these teachers and chant an incantation of modification, education, tolerance, and sensitivity.

What are the major changes you've seen in your field since you entered teaching? Most of the changes I've seen have been positive. Regular classroom teachers have been made more aware of the exceptional child, but I'm nonetheless convinced that most of these teachers *really don't know* what to do about him or her. The nation as a whole has been made more aware of the importance of education (and good educators), yet salary structures haven't really changed to lure the "best and the brightest" into the education profession or to reward the teachers who demonstrate exceptional abilities in the classroom. Reinforcement in education remains a function of "keeping one's nose clean" and "producing a pulse" at the beginning and end of each school year. Even so, I view education as changing for the better, and I hope it continues to do so.

Pick the one student in your career with whom you've had the greatest success and describe your involvement with him or her. During my second year of teaching emotionally handicapped students, I was assigned an 8th grader whose problem could be best described as "math phobia." He had violent reactions (tantrums, vomiting, etc.) to any and all math assignments. After much counseling and a variety of other interventions, he was turned over to me to "cure." We began at rock bottom; we discussed the problem and possible solutions. But we were getting nowhere. The plan I decided to employ involved implementation of successive approximations of the final goal—to complete a 35-problem math assignment without any complications in the regular classroom. By beginning with just writing numbers, then doing one problem, then two problems, then three, and so on, he eventually was able to complete a 35-problem worksheet in *my* classroom. But he was still unable to complete an assignment of even 1 or 2 problems in a regular class, so the entire process had to be replicated in the "new" environment as well. All the while, through good and bad times, he was given the support and reinforcement he needed to reach the goal. It took us 3½ months to finally reach our goal, but we did it! The day Robert sat in that 8th grade math class and successfully completed his assignment was a great day for both of us. It seemed like such a small step to most people, but Robert and I knew what a giant leap it actually was for him. Robert eventually graduated from high school, and I have since lost track of him. Such is the life of a teacher. . . .

Think of the most difficult student you have ever had. What made him or her so difficult? Every student one encounters in a classroom for emotionally handicapped students is difficult in his or her own way. But an 8th grade boy comes to mind. During my fourth year of teaching a self-contained class, I received a student who exhibited a wide variety of inappropriate behaviors ranging from severe tantrums to fire-setting. Along with these "talents," he was extremely charismatic, and he used this attribute to influence the behavior of all the other students in my class. He would randomly threaten other students with physical harm if they did not act out when he gave a special signal. For example, class would be proceeding as planned when suddenly, for no apparent reason, one student would stand on top of his desk and begin screaming at the top of his lungs. I would respond by withdrawing the student's behavior points, placing him in time out, or using another intervention—all to no avail. I was at a loss to explain why these behaviors were occurring daily, at random, in my carefully structured classroom. One day, after observing Gino intimidate a student at the bus stop, it dawned on me . . . maybe he was, in fact, the maestro of these shenanigans. I instituted a plan to "dethrone" Gino. I informed him that any time anyone in the class acted out, I would remove *his* behavior points and/or put *him* in time out. The tranquility of my classroom returned and "Gino's class" had a good year. It may seem like an easy problem and an easy solution, but until you have lived with it you can't hope to understand the befuddlement and frustration I went through during those months of turmoil. Sometimes all the spitting, scratching, profanity, and physical abuse one endures during a school year can't hold a candle to the frustration one feels when he applies techniques he knows are effective but for unexplained reasons are not working.

were the only thing required to help these children, they probably would not be considered handicapped. The teacher cannot expect caring and decency always to be returned by pupils. Teachers must be sure of their own values and confident of their teaching and living skills. They must be able and willing to make wise choices for children when the children choose to behave unwisely. Hobbs described the ideal "teacher-counselor" (the term applied to teachers in Project Re-ED, an ecological approach to helping disturbed children) as follows:

> But most of all a teacher-counselor is a decent adult; educated, well-trained; able to give and receive affection, to live relaxed, and to be firm; a person with private resources for the nourishment and refreshment of his own life; not an itinerant worker but a professional through and through; a person with a sense of the significance of time, of the usefulness of today and the promise of tomorrow; a person of hope, quiet confidence, and joy; one who has committed himself to children and to the process of reeducation. (1966, pp. 1106–1107)

SPECIAL CONSIDERATIONS IN EDUCATING THE PRESCHOOL CHILD

Early identification and prevention are basic goals of intervention programs for any category of handicap. For ED/BD students, these goals present particular difficulties—yet they hold particular promise. The difficulties are related to definition and measurement of ED/BD, especially in young children; the particular promise is that young children's social-emotional behavior is quite flexible, so preventive efforts seem to have a good chance of success.

As we mentioned previously, defining ED/BD in such a way that children can be reliably identified is a difficult task. Definition and identification in preschool children are complicated by several additional factors. First, the developmental tasks that young children are expected to achieve are much simpler than those expected of older children, so the range of normal behaviors to be used for comparison is quite restricted. Infants and toddlers are expected to eat, sleep, perform relatively simple motor skills, and respond socially to their parents. School-age children must learn much more varied and complex motor and cognitive skills and develop social relations with a variety of peers and adults. Second, there is wide variation in the child-rearing practices of good parents and in family expectations for preschool children's behavior in different cultures, so we must guard against inappropriate norms used for comparison. "Immature," "withdrawn," or "aggressive" behavior in one family may not be perceived as such in another. Third, in the preschool years children's development is rapid and often uneven, making it difficult to judge what spontaneous improvements might occur.

Fourth, the most severe types of ED/BD often are first observed in the preschool years. But it is frequently difficult to tell the difference between ED/BD and other conditions, like mental retardation or deafness. Often the first signs of disturbance are difficulty with basic biological functions (for example, eating, sleeping, eliminating) or social responses (for example, responding positively to a parent's attempts to offer comfort, "molding" to the parent's body when being held). Difficulty with these basic areas or in achieving developmental milestones like walking and talking indicate that the child may be disturbed. But these difficulties may also be indicators of other conditions such as mental retardation, sensory impairment, or physical disability (see Kauffman, 1983).

The patterns of behavior that signal difficulty for the preschool child are those that bring them into frequent conflict with or keep them aloof from their parents or caretakers and their siblings or peers. Infants or toddlers who exhibit a very "difficult temperament"—who are irritable; have irregular patterns of sleeping, eating, and eliminating; have highly intense responses to many stimuli and negative reactions toward new situations—are at risk for developing serious behavior problems unless their parents are particularly skillful at handling them. Children of preschool age are likely to elicit negative responses from adults and playmates if they are much more aggressive or much more withdrawn than most youngsters their age. (Remember the critical importance of same-age comparisons. *Normal* toddlers frequently grab what they want, push other children down, throw things and kick and scream when they don't get their way; *normal* toddlers do not have much finesse at social inter-course and often hide from strangers.)

Because children's behavior is quite responsive to conditions in the social envi-ronment and can be shaped by adults, the potential for *primary prevention*—preventing serious behavior problems from occurring in the first place—would seem to be great. If parents and teachers could be taught effective child management skills, perhaps many or most cases of ED/BD could be prevented. Furthermore, one could imagine that if parents and teachers had such skills, children who are already ED/BD could be prevented from getting worse (*secondary prevention*). But, as Bower (1981) notes, the task of primary prevention is just not that simple. For one thing, the tremendous amount of money and personnel needed for training in child management are not available. For another, even if the money and personnel could be found, professionals would not always agree on what patterns of behavior should be prevented or on how undesirable behavior could be prevented from developing (see Gelfand et al., 1986).

All preschoolers engage in behavior that could be considered emotionally disturbed or behaviorally disordered in older children or adults. Young children must be taught socially appropriate ways of interacting with their peers and adults. (Suzanne Szasz/Photo Researchers)

Assuming that overly aggressive or withdrawn behavior has been identified in a preschooler, what kind of intervention program is most desirable? Our experience and reading of the literature lead us to the conclusion that behavioral interventions are most effective. A behavioral approach implies defining and measuring the child's behaviors and rearranging the environment (especially adults' and other children's responses to the problem child) to teach and support more appropriate conduct. In the case of aggressive children this usually involves preventing their aggression from winning them social rewards. For example, hitting another child or throwing a temper tantrum might result in brief social isolation or time-out instead of adult attention or getting one's own way. In all cases of aggression, rewards for desirable, nonaggressive behavior must be provided.

Sometimes prompts for appropriate behavior and models of good conduct are also needed. Socially withdrawn preschoolers have responded well to several behavioral techniques: providing peer models (either live or filmed) of social interaction, training the withdrawn child's peers to initiate social interactions, and encouraging preschoolers to play games in which affectionate behaviors are shown (see Strain and Fox, 1981; Twardosz et al., 1983). Early intervention with preschoolers, whether they are aggressive or withdrawn, has the potential to make many such children "normal"—that is, indistinguishable from their peers—by the time they are in the elementary grades (Lovaas, 1982; Strain, Steele, Ellis, and Timm, 1982).

SPECIAL CONSIDERATIONS IN EDUCATING THE ADOLESCENT AND ADULT

As we mentioned earlier, special education programs for ED/BD students are not common at the secondary level. Furthermore, there is no convincing evidence that any of the program models that have been tried with this population is effective (Nelson and Kauffman, 1977; Safer, 1982).

The programs tried with disturbed adolescents have varied widely in aims and structure. Nelson and Kauffman (1977) have described the following types and commented on the effectiveness of each: regular public high school classes, consultant teachers who work with the regular teacher to provide individualized academic work and behavior management, resource rooms and special self-contained classes to which students may be assigned for part or all of the school day, work-study programs in which vocational education and job experience are combined with academic study, special private or public schools that offer the regular high school curriculum in a different setting, alternative schools that offer highly individualized programs that are nontraditional in both setting and content, and private or public residential schools (see also Knoblock, 1979).

Incarcerated ED/BD youths are an especially neglected group in special education (Rutherford, Nelson, and Wolford, 1986; Wolford, 1983). One suspects that the special educational needs of many (or most) ED/BD teenagers who are in prisons are neglected because incarcerated youths are defined as "socially maladjusted" rather than "seriously emotionally disturbed." The current federal definition appears to allow the denial of special education to a very large number of young people who exhibit extremely serious misbehavior and have a long history of school failure.

One of the reasons it is difficult to design special education programs for ED/BD students at the secondary level is that this category of youth is so varied. Adolescents categorized for special education purposes as "seriously emotionally disturbed" may have behavioral characteristics ranging from autistically withdrawn to aggressively delinquent, intelligence ranging from severely retarded to highly gifted, and academic skills ranging from preschool to college level. Therefore it is hardly realistic to suggest that any single type of program or model will be appropriate for all such youths. In fact, ED/BD youths, perhaps more than any other category of exceptionality, need a highly individualized, creative, and flexible education. Programs may range from teaching daily living skills in a sheltered environment to advanced placement in college, from regular class placement to institutionalization, and from the traditional curriculum to unusual and specialized vocational training.

Outlook for Adulthood

Many seriously disturbed children and youths grow up to be adults who have real difficulties in leading independent, productive lives. The outlook is especially grim for children and adolescents fitting two classifications: psychotic and conduct disordered. With today's typical treatment, many psychotic children, whether labeled autistic or schizophrenic, are likely to be considered bizarre as adults, and some will be institutionalized. Some will make a successful adjustment to community living and hold jobs that allow them to be self-sufficient. But, as follow-up studies show, the majority are unlikely ever to get rid of all the troublesome characteristics they showed during the developmental period (Kanner, 1971; Kanner, Rodriguez, and Ashenden, 1972; Petty, Ornitz, Michelman, and Zimmerman, 1984).

Contrary to popular opinion, the child or youth who is shy, anxious, or neurotic is not the most likely to have psychiatric problems as an adult. It is, rather, the conduct-disordered (hyperaggressive) child or youth whose adulthood is most likely to be characterized by socially intolerable behavior (Kazdin, 1987). About half the children who are hyperaggressive will have problems that require legal intervention or psychiatric care when they are adults (Robins, 1979).

One of the frustrating things about the prognosis for ED/BD children is that it is impossible to predict which psychotic or hyperaggressive children will make a successful adult adjustment and which will not. That is, we can only predict a *percentage* of cases that will improve, not point to the *individuals* who will improve. Painstaking research will be required to find out what characteristics of individual children and their treatments or environments make the critical difference in adult outcomes.

MANAGING THE CHILD IN SCHOOL

Since most ED/BD children apparently are not receiving special education services, most must be in regular classrooms taught by regular teachers (Kauffman, 1985, 1986). Therefore, it is obvious that if the goals of preventing ED/BD and mainstreaming cases that cannot be prevented are to be realized anytime soon, regular classroom teachers must be prepared to recognize and deal more effectively with problem behavior.

The advice given to regular classroom teachers by special educators and mental health professionals varies considerably because of differences in theoretical orientation. But the following general suggestions should help (see also Kerr and Nelson, 1983):

1. If there is a child in the regular classroom who has received special education services (resource or crisis help, special class or special school), the teacher should ask the special education teacher for advice concerning behavior management and teaching techniques. If a psychologist, psychiatrist, or other men-

tal health worker has been working with the child, that person's advice should be sought regarding the child's management.

2. The teacher should let the child know from the first contact that he or she expects a reasonable standard of conduct to be maintained. The sooner the child knows the limits of permissible conduct, the better.

3. It is essential that the teacher communicate his or her expectations to the child clearly and firmly. Nothing is to be gained by beating around the bush or keeping the child guessing what the teacher has in mind regarding behavior and goals. The child should know what is expected at all times.

4. There must be consistent, appropriate consequences for behavior. The child's desirable behavior should be immediately recognized and rewarded with praise and other signs of approval. Inappropriate behavior is to be consistently ignored or, if necessary, met with mild punishment. Recognition and praise for good behavior should be given publicly so that other students can see and hear. But if it is necessary to correct or reprimand the child, this should be done as quietly and privately as possible.

5. The teacher must have realistic expectations concerning the child's behavior and academic performance; tasks should be well within the child's capacity, but still a challenge. If the child is unable to perform academic tasks with 90 percent accuracy, the work is too difficult. The child must feel success and pride in what he or she accomplishes.

6. It is important that the teacher empathize with the child and understand how negative aspects of the social environment (abuse at home, peers who tease and taunt, teachers who criticize) may contribute to inappropriate behavior. If negative influences can be identified, the teacher should try to change them.

7. Good behavior management for disturbed children has a lot in common with good behavior management for all children. The best preventive action any teacher can take is to make sure that the classroom is a happy place where children take pride in their work and learn to treat others with respect. The school psychologist or books on behavior management (e.g. Gelfand and Hartmann, 1984; Morris, 1985; Morse, 1985; Smith, 1984; Walker, 1979) can be consulted for specific techniques.

SUMMARY

ED/BD is used here to designate those children called "seriously emotionally disturbed" in PL 94-142 because the terminology of the field is in transition. Most ED/BD children are isolated from others either because they withdraw from all social contact themselves or because they behave in an aggressive, hostile way and others withdraw from them. The problem is seen as the result of negative social interactions and transactions between the child and the environment. There is no one accepted definition of emotional disturbance or behavioral disorder for a number of reasons. But despite the many differences in orientation and terminology, it is generally agreed that ED/BD refers to behavior that goes to an extreme, is unacceptable be-cause of social or cultural expectations, and represents a problem that is chronic.

The current federal definition lists five char-acteristics, one or more of which may indicate that a child is disturbed if such behavior is ex-hibited to a marked extent and over a long pe-riod of time and results in an adverse effect on educational performance: (1) inability to learn that cannot be explained by intellectual, sen-sory, or health factors; (2) inability to build or maintain satisfactory relationships with peers and teachers; (3) inappropriate behavior or feelings under normal conditions; (4) a perva-sive mood of unhappiness or depression; and (5) physical symptoms, pains, or fears associ-ated with personal or school problems. Such characteristics obviously include schizophrenic and autistic children, although children with autism have been excluded from the category of seriously emotionally disturbed by federal regulation.

Determining subcategories of ED/BD is also difficult. Most authorities today agree that it is necessary to rely upon individual assessment of each child's behavior and situational factors rather than on traditional diagnostic classification. Dimensional approaches use clusters of interrelated behaviors to classify behavior problems among children. Four dimensions—conduct disorder, anxiety-withdrawal, immaturity, and socialized aggression—provide a fairly reliable, empirically derived basis for the description of the major types of problem behavior. Two broader dimensions have also been described: externalizing (aggressive, acting-out) and internalizing (immature, withdrawn).

In any scheme to classify ED/BD, the severity of the disorder is significant. Children with mild or moderate disorders may be referred to as neurotic or psychoneurotic; those with severe or profound disorders may be labeled psychotic, schizophrenic, or autistic. For the latter group, intensive and prolonged intervention is necessary. Mildly and moderately ED/BD children can usually be managed within the home and regular classroom, with the aid of mental health specialists.

Estimates of the prevalence of ED/BD among children vary greatly because of the absence of standard definitions or screening instruments. Most such children fall into the mild-moderate category, and most are characterized by conduct disorder. Most are boys. About 3 percent of American youth are referred to juvenile courts in a given year, and juvenile crime appears to be on the increase. Although most prevalence estimates suggest that 6 to 10 percent of schoolage children have serious emotional/behavioral problems, only about 1 percent receive special education in the "seriously emotionally disturbed" category under PL 94-142. The U.S. Department of Education now recognizes ED/BD as a "traditionally underserved" category.

Although it is extremely difficult to assign specific causes to ED/BD in children, four major factors predispose one to or trigger maladaptive behavior: biological disorders and diseases, pathological family relationships, negative cultural influences, and undesirable experiences at school. Longitudinal studies may soon reveal much about the development of disordered behavior. Efforts to prevent the development of ED/BD include reducing risk factors, such as neglect, abuse, family conflict, and school failure, as well as teaching the social skills that allow children to make and keep friends and get along well with adults.

Because it is fairly easy for teachers to identify problem behaviors, and also because adequate services for treating disorders are not generally available, most schools do not use systematic screening procedures. Teachers' ratings, combined with children's judgments of their own and their peers' behavior, can be helpful in determining which children need help. Screening systems that involve multiple ratings plus direct observation of children in the classroom and on the playground may prove to be the most cost-effective and lead to improved services for ED/BD students.

Research has shown that the average mildly/moderately ED/BD child is likely to have an IQ in the dull-normal range. It is sometimes impossible to test severely or profoundly ED/BD children, but those who can be tested usually fall within the retarded range. Although it is admittedly difficult to determine the intellectual and achievement abilities of ED/BD children, IQ is still a fairly good predictor of how far a child is likely to progress academically and socially. Most disturbed children lack in varying degrees the ability to apply their knowledge and skills to the demands of everyday living.

Those children who express their problems in aggressive, acting-out behavior are involved in a vicious cycle. Their behavior alienates others, so that positive interactions with adults and peers become less and less likely. Children whose behavior is consistently aggressive have less chance of learning to make social adjustments and of achieving mental health in adulthood than do those who are shy, anxious, or neurotic.

Severely or profoundly disturbed children usually lack the basic self-care skills, may appear to be perceptually handicapped, and have serious cognitive deficits. Especially evident and important is their inability to relate to other people. In addition, deviations in speech and language abilities, the presence of self-stimulatory or self-injurious behaviors, and the tendency to injure others deliberately combine to give these children a poor prognosis. Some of them function permanently at a retarded level and require continued supervision and care, although recent research shows that many may become "normal" with early intensive intervention.

There are many different views regarding the education of ED/BD children. The psychoanalytic approach is characterized by a high degree of permissiveness, little emphasis on academic achievement, and reliance on individual psychotherapy for the child and parents to resolve the underlying causes of the disturbance. The psychoeducational approach recognizes the existence and importance of underlying causes, but also stresses the importance of academic achievement and learning to cope with the reality of everyday demands. In the humanistic approach disturbed children are considered to be out of touch with their own feelings and unable to find meaning and self-fulfillment in traditional educational settings. Educational practices are characterized by a nonauthoritarian atmosphere in which the teacher functions as a resource and catalyst rather than as a director of activities. Those who subscribe to the ecological approach see ED/BD as a problem of the child in interaction with the various elements of the environment. Educational intervention is aimed at altering the child's relationships with school, family, community, and social agencies. The behavioral approach sees ED/BD as representing inappropriate learning. The focus of this approach is on observation and measurement of maladaptive behaviors and manipulation of the consequences of these behaviors in order to change them. Today, a synthesis of conceptual models, variously termed "individual psychology" or "cognitive-behavior modification," is often suggested. These current approaches, which blend developmental and learning theories, place new emphasis on the development of the child's self. Behavior change strategies intended to teach self-control are now commonly suggested.

Apparently, only a small percentage of ED/BD children receive any special educational services. Where these are given, there is a trend toward "alternative education." Most severely or profoundly disturbed children must be instructed individually; they are seldom integrated into the regular classroom. The educational emphasis for these children is on teaching daily living skills, language, and beginning academic skills. The curriculum for mildly or moderately disturbed children is similar to that used for most youngsters; the aim is to reintegrate them as fully as possible into the regular classroom. Equally important in educational intervention plans for the mildly ED/BD is acquisition of social skills and affective experiences.

Special considerations for preschool ED/BD children include the goals of early identification and prevention. These goals hold particular promise because children's behavior is quite flexible, but they pose particular difficulties because ED/BD is so hard to define precisely in preschoolers and because different conceptual models suggest different goals and intervention methods. Special education for disturbed adolescents and young adults must be highly individualized because of the wide differences in intelligence, behavioral characteristics, and achievement of the students involved. The outlook for adulthood is particularly poor for children and youths who are categorized as psychotic or as hyperaggressive (conduct disordered).

REFERENCES

Achenbach, T. M. (1985). *Assessment and taxonomy of child and adolescent psychopathology.* Beverly Hills, Calif.: Sage.

Achenbach, T. M. (1982). *Developmental psychopathology* (2nd ed.). New York: Ronald Press.

Achenbach, T. M., & Edelbrock, C. S. (1983). Taxonomic issues in child psychopathology. In T. H. Ollendick & M. Hersen (Eds.), *Handbook of child psychopathology* (pp. 65–93). New York: Plenum.

Arnold, W. R., & Brungardt, T. M. (1983). *Juvenile misconduct and delinquency.* Boston: Houghton Mifflin.

Bandura, A. (1973). *Aggression: A social learning analysis.* Englewood Cliffs, N.J.: Prentice-Hall.

Barrett, R. P. (Ed.). (1986). *Severe behavior disorders in the mentally retarded.* New York: Plenum.

Becker, W. C. (1964). Consequences of different kinds of parental discipline. In M. L. Hoffman & L. W. Hoffman (Eds.), *Review of child development research* (Vol. 1). New York: Russell Sage Foundation.

Berkowitz, P. H., & Rothman, E. P. (1960). *The disturbed child.* New York: New York University Press.

Bettelheim, B. (1950). *Love is not enough.* New York: Macmillan.

Bettelheim, B. (1967). *The empty fortress.* New York: Free Press.

Bettelheim, B. (1970). Listening to children. In P. A. Gallagher & L. L. Edwards (Eds.), *Educating the emotionally disturbed: Theory to practice.* Lawrence: University of Kansas.

Bornstein, P. H., & Kazdin, A. E. (Eds.). (1985). *Handbook of clinical behavior therapy with children.* Homewood, Ill.: Dorsey Press.

Bower, E. M. (1981). *Early identification of emotionally handicapped children in school* (3rd ed.). Springfield, Ill.: Charles C Thomas.

Bower, E. M. (1982). Defining emotional disturbance: Public policy and research. *Psychology in the Schools, 19,* 55–60.

Campbell, S. B., Breaux, A. M., Ewing, L. J., & Szumowski, E. K. (1986). Correlates and predictors of hyperactivity and aggression: A longitudinal study of parent-referred problem preschoolers. *Journal of Abnormal Child Psychology, 14,* 217–234.

Cantwell, D. P. (1982). Childhood depression: A review of current research. In B. B. Lahey & A. E. Kazdin (Eds.), *Advances in clinical child psychology* (Vol. 5, pp. 39–94). New York: Plenum.

Chivian, E., Mack, J. E., Waletzky, J. P., Lazaroff, C., Doctor, R., & Goldenring, J. M. (1985). Soviet children and the threat of nuclear war: A preliminary study. *American Journal of Orthopsychiatry, 55,* 484–502.

Cullinan, D., & Epstein, M. H. (1985). Teacher-rated adjustment problems of mildly handicapped and nonhandicapped students. *Remedial and Special Education, 6*(2), 5–11.

Cullinan, D., Epstein, M. H., & Kauffman, J. M. (1984). Teachers' ratings of students' behaviors: What constitutes behavior disorder in school? *Behavioral Disorders, 10,* 9–19.

DeMyer, M. K. (1975). The nature of neuropsychological disability in autistic children. *Journal of Autism and Childhood Schizophrenia, 5,* 109–128.

Dennison, G. (1969). *The lives of children.* New York: Random House.

Drabman, R. S., & Patterson, J. N. (1981). Disruptive behavior and the social standing of exceptional children. *Exceptional Education Quarterly, 1,* 45–55.

Earls, F. (1984). The epidemiology of depression in children and adolescents. *Pediatric Annals, 13,* 23–31.

Edelbrock, C. S., & Achenbach, T. M. (1984). The teacher version of the Child Behavior Profile: I. Boys aged 6–11. *Journal of Consulting and Clinical Psychology, 52,* 207–217.

Epstein, M. H., Cullinan, D., & Polloway, E. A. (1986). Patterns of maladjustment among the mentally retarded. *American Journal of Mental Deficiency, 91,* 127–134.

Epstein, M. H., Kauffman, J. M., & Cullinan, D. (1985). Patterns of maladjustment among the behaviorally disordered: II. Boys aged 6–11, boys aged 12–18, girls aged 6–11, and girls aged 12–18. *Behavioral Disorders, 10,* 125–135.

Fagen, S. A. (1979). Psychoeducational management and self-control. In D. Cullinan & M. Epstein (Eds.), *Special education for adolescents: Issues and perspectives.* Columbus: Charles E. Merrill.

Fenichel, C. (1974). Carl Fenichel. In J. M. Kauffman & C. D. Lewis (Eds.), *Teaching children with behavior disorders: Personal perspectives.* Columbus, Ohio: Charles E. Merrill.

Gelfand, D. M., Ficula, T., & Zarbatany, L. (1986). Prevention of childhood behavior disorders. In B. A. Edelstein & L. Michelson (Eds.), *Handbook of prevention.* New York: Plenum.

Gelfand, D. M., & Hartmann, D. P. (1984). *Child behavior analysis and therapy* (2nd ed.). New York: Pergamon.

Goldstein, A. P. (Ed.). (1983a). *Prevention and control of aggression.* New York: Pergamon.

Goldstein, A. P. (1983b). United States: Causes, controls, and alternatives to aggression. In A. P. Goldstein & M. H. Segall (Eds.), *Aggression in global perspective.* New York: Pergamon.

Goldstein, A. P., Carr, E. G., Davidson, W. S., & Wehr, P. (Eds.). (1981). *In response to aggression.* New York: Pergamon.

Grosenick, J. K., & Huntze, S. L. (1983). *More questions than answers: Review and analysis of programs for behaviorally disordered children and youth.* Columbia, Mo.: Department of Special Education, University of Missouri.

Haring, N. G., & Phillips, E. L. (1962). *Educating emotionally disturbed children.* New York: McGraw-Hill.

Haring, N. G., & Whelan, R. J. (1965). Experimental methods in education and management. In N. J. Long, W. C. Morse, & R. G. Newman (Eds.), *Conflict in the classroom.* Belmont, Calif.: Wadsworth.

Harris, K. R., Wong, B. Y. L., & Keogh, B. K. (Eds.). (1985). Cognitive-behavior modification with children: A critical review of the state-of-the-art. *Journal of Abnormal Child Psychology, 13,* special issue.

Hewett, F. M. (1968). *The emotionally disturbed child in the classroom.* Boston: Allyn & Bacon.

Hobbs, N. (1966). Helping disturbed children: Psychological and ecological strategies. *American Psychologist, 21,* 1105–1115.

Hobbs, N. (1974). Nicholas Hobbs. In J. M. Kauffman & C. D. Lewis (Eds.), *Teaching children with behavior disorders: Personal perspectives.* Columbus, Ohio: Charles E. Merrill.

Hobbs, N. (1975). *The futures of children.* San Francisco: Jossey-Bass.

Huntze, S. (1985). A position paper of the Council for Children with Behavioral Disorders. *Behavioral Disorders, 10,* 167–174.

Juul, K. D. (1986). Epidemiological studies of behavior disorders in children: An international survey. *International Journal of Special Education, 1,* 1–20.

Kanner, L. (1971). Follow-up study of eleven autistic children originally reported in 1943. *Journal of Autism and Childhood Schizophrenia, 1,* 119–145.

Kanner, L., Rodriguez, A., & Ashenden, B. (1972). How far can autistic children go in matters of social adaptation? *Journal of Autism and Childhood Schizophrenia, 2,* 9–33.

Kaslow, N. J., & Rehm, L. P. (1983). Childhood depression. In R. J. Morris & T. R. Kratochwill (Eds.), *The practice of child therapy.* New York: Pergamon.

Kauffman, J. M. (1983). Emotional disturbance. In S. G. Garwood (Ed.), *Educating young handicapped children: A developmental approach* (2nd ed.) (pp. 373–406). Rockville, Md.: Aspen.

Kauffman, J. M. (1984). Saving children in the age of big brother: Moral and ethical issues in the identification of deviance. *Behavioral Disorders, 10,* 60–70.

Kauffman, J. M. (1985). *Characteristics of children's behavior disorders* (3rd ed.). Columbus, Ohio: Charles E. Merrill.

Kauffman, J. M. (1986). Educating children with behavior disorders. In R. J. Morris & B. Blatt (Eds.), *Special education: Research and trends.* New York: Pergamon.

Kauffman, J. M. & Lewis, C. D. (Eds.). (1974). *Teaching children with behavior disorders: Personal perspectives.* Columbus, Ohio: Charles E. Merrill.

Kauffman, J. M., Pullen, P. L., & Akers, E. (1986). Classroom management: Teacher-child-peer relationships. *Focus on Exceptional Children, 19*(1), 1–12.

Kazdin, A. E. (1987). *Conduct disorders in childhood and adolescence.* Beverly Hills, Calif., Sage.

Kerr, M. M., & Nelson, C. M. (1983). *Strategies for managing behavior problems in the classroom.* Columbus, Ohio: Charles E. Merrill.

Knoblock, P. (1973). Open education for emotionally disturbed children. *Exceptional Children, 39,* 358–365.

Knoblock, P. (1979). Educational alternatives for adolescents labeled emotionally disturbed. In D. Cullinan & M. Epstein (Eds.), *Special education for adolescents: Issues and perspectives.* Columbus, Ohio: Charles E. Merrill.

Koegel, R. L., Rincover, A., & Egel, A. L. (1982). *Educating and understanding autistic children.* San Diego: College Hill Press.

Loeber, R. (1982). The stability of antisocial and delinquent behavior: A review. *Child Development, 53,* 1431–1446.

Long, N. J., Morse, W. C., & Newman, R. G. (Eds.). (1980). *Conflict in the classroom* (4th ed.). Belmont, Calif.: Wadsworth.

Lovaas, O. I. (1967). A behavior therapy approach to the treatment of childhood schizophrenia. In J. P. Hill (Ed.), *Minnesota symposia on child psychology.* Minneapolis: University of Minnesota Press.

Lovaas, O. I. (1982). An overview of the Young Autism Project. Paper presented at the annual convention of the American Psychological Association, Washington, D.C., September.

Lovaas, O. I., Koegel, R. L., Simmons, J. Q., & Long, J. S. (1973). Some generalization and follow-up measures on autistic children in behavior therapy. *Journal of Applied Behavior Analysis, 6,* 131–166.

Lyman, R. D. (1984). The effect of private and public goal setting on classroom on-task behavior of emotionally disturbed children. *Behavior Therapy, 15,* 395–402.

Martin, J. A. (1981). A longitudinal study of the consequences of early mother-infant interaction: A microanalytic approach. *Monographs of the Society for Research in Child Development, 46* (Serial No. 190).

Maslow, A. (1962). *Toward a psychology of being.* New York: Van Nostrand.

McDowell, R. L., Adamson, G. W., & Wood, F. H. (Eds.). (1982). *Teaching emotionally disturbed children.* Boston: Little, Brown.

Meichenbaum, D. (1977). *Cognitive-behavior modification: an integrative approach.* New York: Plenum.

Moore, D. R., & Arthur, J. L. (1983). Juvenile delinquency. In T. H. Ollendick & M. Hersen (Eds.), *Handbook of child psychopathology* (pp. 357–388). New York: Plenum.

Morris, R. J. (1985). *Behavior modification with exceptional children.* Glenview, IL: Scott Foresman.

Morris, R. J., & McReynolds, R. A. (1986). Behavior modification with special needs children: A review. In R. J. Morris & B. Blatt (Eds.), *Special education: Research and trends.* New York: Pergamon.

Morse, W. C. (1985). *The education and treatment of socio-emotionally impaired children and youth.* Syracuse, N.Y.: Syracuse University Press.

Morse, W. C., Ardizzone, J., MacDonald, C., & Pasick, P. (1980). *Affective education for special children and youth.* Reston, Va.: Council for Exceptional Children.

Murphy, D. M. (1986). The prevalence of handicapping conditions among juvenile delinquents. *Remedial and Special Education, 7*(3), 7–17.

Nelson, C. M., & Kauffman, J. M. (1977). Educational programming for secondary school age delinquent and maladjusted pupils. *Behavior Disorders, 2,* 102–113.

Noel, M. M. (1982). Public school programs for the emotionally disturbed: An overview. In M. M. Noel & N. G. Haring (Eds.), *Progress or change: Issues in educating the emotionally disturbed.* Vol. 8. *Service delivery* (pp. 1–28). Seattle, Wash.: Program Development Assistance System, University of Washington.

Nicol, S. E., & Erlenmeyer-Kimling, L. (1986). Genetic factors in psychopathology: Implications for prevention. In B. A. Edelstein & L. Michelson (Eds.), *Handbook of prevention.* New York: Plenum.

Ornitz, E. M. (1986). Prevention of developmental disorders. In B. A. Edelstein & L. Michelson (Eds.), *Handbook of prevention.* New York: Plenum.

Paget, K. D., Nagle, R. J., & Martin, R. P. (1984). Interrelationships between temperament characteristics and first-grade teacher-student interactions. *Journal of Abnormal Child Psychology, 12,* 547–560.

Patterson, G. R. (1982). *Coercive family process.* Eugene, Ore.: Castalia.

Patterson, G. R., Reid, J. B., Jones, R. R., & Conger, R. E. (1975). *A social learning approach to family intervention.* Vol. 1, *Families with aggressive children.* Eugene, Ore.: Castalia Publishing Co.

Petti, T. A. (1983). Depression and withdrawal in children. In T. H. Ollendick & M. Hersen (Eds.), *Handbook of child psychopathology.* New York: Plenum.

Petty, L. K., Ornitz, E. M., Michelman, J. D., & Zimmerman, E. G. (1984). Autistic children who become schizophrenic. *Archives of General Psychiatry, 41,* 129–135.

Pullis, M., & Cadwell, J. (1985). Temperament as a factor in the assessment of children educationally at risk. *Journal of Special Education, 19,* 91–102.

Quay, H. C. (1979). Classification. In H. C. Quay & J. S. Werry (Eds.), *Psychopathological disorders of childhood* (2nd ed.). New York: Wiley.

Rahim, S. I. A., & Cederblad, M. (1984). Effects of rapid urbanisation on child behavior and health in a part of Khartoum, Sudan. *Journal of Child Psychology and Psychiatry,* (1986). 629–641.

Rezmierski, V. E., Knoblock, P., & Bloom, R. B. (1982). The psychoeducational model: Theory and historical perspective. In R. L. McDowell, G. W. Adamson, & F. H. Wood (Eds.), *Teaching emotionally disturbed children* (pp. 47–69). Boston: Little, Brown.

Rhodes, W. C. (1967). The disturbing child: A problem of ecological management. *Exceptional Children, 33,* 637–642.

Rhodes, W. C. (1970). A community participation analysis of emotional disturbance. *Exceptional Children, 36,* 309–314.

Rhodes, W. C., & Tracy, M. L. (Eds.) (1972a). *A study of child variance.* Vol. 1, *Theories.* Ann Arbor: University of Michigan Press.

Rhodes, W. C., & Tracy, M. L. (Eds.) (1972b). *A study of child variance.* Vol. 2, *Interventions.* Ann Arbor: University of Michigan Press.

Robins, L. N. (1966). *Deviant children grown up.* Baltimore: Williams & Wilkins.

Robins, L. N. (1979). Follow-up studies. In H. C. Quay & J. S. Werry (Eds.), *Psychopathological disorders of childhood* (2nd ed.). New York: Wiley.

Rogers, C. (1969). *Freedom to learn.* Columbus, Ohio: Charles E. Merrill.

Rutherford, R. B., Nelson, C. M., & Wolford, B. I. (1986). Special education programming in juvenile corrections. *Remedial and Special Education, 7*(3), 27–33.

Rutter, M. (1985). Family and school influences on behavioral development. *Journal of Child Psychology and Psychiatry, 26,* 349–368.

Sabornie, E. J. (1985). Social mainstreaming of handicapped students: Facing an unpleasant reality. *Remedial and Special Education, 6*(2), 12–16.

Sabornie, E. J., & Kauffman, J. M. (1985). Regular classroom sociometric status of emotionally disturbed adolescents. *Behavioral Disorders, 10,* 268–274.

Safer, D. J. (Ed.). (1982). *School programs for disruptive adolescents.* Baltimore: University Park Press.

Sameroff, A. J., Seifer, R., & Zax, M. (1982). Early development of children at risk for emotional disorder. *Monographs of the Society for Research in Child Development, 47* (Ser. No. 199).

Schreibman, L., Charlop, M. H., & Britten, K. R. (1983). Childhood autism. In R. J. Morris & T. R. Kratochwill (Eds.), *The practice of child therapy* (pp. 221–252). New York: Pergamon.

Schreibman, L., & Mills, J. I. (1983). Infantile autism. In T. H. Ollendick & M. Hersen (Eds.), *Handbook of child psychopathology* (pp. 123–150). New York: Plenum.

Schultz, E. W., Heuchert, C. M., & Stampf, S. W. (1973). *Pain and joy in school.* Champaign, Ill.: Research Press.

Smith, D. D. (1984). *Effective discipline: A positive approach to discipline for educators in all settings.* Austin, Tex.: Pro-Ed.

Sprafkin, J., Gadow, K. D., & Dussault, M. (1986). Reality perceptions of television: A preliminary comparison of emotionally disturbed and nonhandicapped children. *American Journal of Orthopsychiatry, 56,* 147–152.

Strain, P. S. (1981). Peer-mediated treatment of exceptional children's social withdrawal. *Exceptional Education Quarterly, 1,* 93–105.

Strain, P. S., & Fox, J. E. (1981). Peers as behavior change agents for withdrawn classmates. In A. E. Kazdin & B. B. Lahey (Eds.), *Advances in clinical child psychology* (Vol. 4, pp. 167–198). New York: Plenum.

Strain, P. S., Steele, P., Ellis, T., & Timm, M. (1982). Long-term effects of oppositional child treatment with mothers

as therapists and therapist trainers. *Journal of Applied Behavior Analysis, 15,* 163–169.

Swap, S. (1978). The ecological model of emotional disturbance in children: A status report and proposed synthesis. *Behavioral Disorders, 3,* 186–196.

Swap, S., Prieto, A. G., & Harth, R. (1982). Ecological perspectives on the emotionally disturbed child. In R. L. McDowell, G. W. Adamson, & F. H. Wood (Eds.), *Teaching emotionally disturbed children* (pp. 70–98). Boston: Little, Brown.

Thomas, A., & Chess, S. (1984). Genesis and evolution of behavioral disorders: From infancy to early adult life. *American Journal of Psychiatry, 141,* 1–9.

Thomas, A., Chess, S., & Birch, H. G. (1968). *Temperament and behavior disorders in children.* New York: New York University Press.

Tuma, J. M., & Sobotка, K. R. (1983). Traditional therapies with children. In T. H. Ollendick & M. Hersen (Eds.), *Handbook of child psychopathology* (pp. 391–426). New York: Plenum.

Twardosz, S., Nordquist, V. M., Simon, R., & Botkin, D. (1983). The effect of group affection activities on the interaction of socially isolate children. *Analysis and Intervention in Developmental Disabilities, 3,* 311–338.

U.S. Department of Education. (1986). "To assure the free appropriate public education of all handicapped children." *Eighth Annual Report to Congress on the Implementation of the Education of the Handicapped Act.* Washington, DC: U.S. Government Printing Office.

Walker, H. M., Severson, H., Haring, N. G., & Williams, G. (1986). Standardized screening and identification of behavior disordered pupils in the elementary age range: A multiple gating approach. *Direct Instruction News, 5*(3).

Walker, H. M., Shinn, M. R., O'Neill, R. E., & Ramsey, E. (in press). A longitudinal assessment of the development of antisocial behavior in boys: Rationale, methodology, and first year results. *Remedial and Special Education.*

Weissberg, R. P., & Allen, J. P. (1986). Promoting children's social skills and adaptive interpersonal behavior. In B. A. Edelstein & L. Michelson (Eds.), *Handbook of prevention.* New York: Plenum.

Werry, J. S. (1979). The childhood psychoses. In H. C. Quay & J. S. Werry (Eds.), *Psychopathological disorders of childhood* (2nd ed.). New York: Wiley.

Whelan, R. J. (1966). The relevance of behavior modification procedures for teachers of emotionally disturbed children. In P. Knoblock (Ed.), *Intervention approaches in educating emotionally disturbed children.* Syracuse: Syracuse University Press.

Wolf, M. M., Risley, T. R., & Mees, H. (1964). Application of operant conditioning procedures to the behavior problems of an autistic child. *Behavior Research and Therapy, 1,* 305–312.

Wolfe, D. A., Zak, L., Wilson, S., & Jaffe, P. (1986). Child witnesses to violence between parents: Critical issues in behavioral and social adjustment. *Journal of Abnormal Child Psychology, 14,* 95–104.

Wolford, B. I. (1983). Correctional education and special education—an emerging partnership; or "Born to lose." In R. B. Rutherford (Ed.), *Monograph in Behavioral Disorders* (pp. 13–19). Tempe, Ariz.: Arizona State University.

5

Speech and Language Disorders

What I remember most acutely about my stuttering is not the strangled sound of my own voice but the impatient looks on other people's faces when I had trouble getting a word out. And if their eyes happened to reflect some of the pain and frustration I was feeling, that only made me more uneasy. There was nothing they could do to help me, and I certainly didn't want their sympathy. I was nine or ten at the time. Like most people with a stuttering problem, I had already learned to live by my wits in a way that normally fluent people cannot begin to appreciate. Whenever I opened my mouth, I mentally glanced ahead at the sentence I wanted to say, to see if there was any word I was likely to stutter on. For me, speaking was like riding down a highway and reading aloud from a series of billboards. I knew that to speak normally I had to keep moving forward at a steady pace. Yet every once in a while I became aware of an obstacle, like an enormous boulder, blocking the road some five or six billboards ahead of me. I knew that when I got to that particular word I would be unable to say it.

(Gerald Jonas, *Stuttering: The Disorder of Many Theories*)

S peech and language are such natural parts of our everyday lives that we seldom stop to think about them. Social conversation with families, friends, and casual acquaintances is normally so effortless and pleasant that it is hard to imagine anyone having difficulty with it. Most of us have feelings of uncertainty about the adequacy of our speech or language only in stressful or unusual social situations, like talking to a large audience or being interviewed for a job. If we always had to worry about our speech or language, we would worry about every social interaction we had.

Not every type of **speech disorder** is so handicapping in social interactions as **stuttering,** nor is stuttering the most common disorder of speech. The problem Jonas describes (see p. 207) affects only about one person in a hundred, and then usually just during childhood. But stuttering is a mystery. Its causes and cures remain largely unknown, although for many years it captured a large share of speech-language pathologists' attention. In one sense, then, stuttering is a poor example to use in introducing a chapter on disorders of speech and language. It is not the most representative disorder; it is difficult to define precisely; its causes are not fully understood; and few suggestions about how to overcome it can be made with confidence (Curlee, 1984; Shames, 1986). But in another sense stuttering is the best example. When people think of speech and language disorders, they tend to think first of stuttering (Owens, 1986). It is a disorder we all have heard and recognized (if not experienced) at one time or another; the social consequences are obvious; it *appears* to be a simple problem with obvious "logical" solutions ("Just slow down," "Relax, don't worry," "Think about how to say it"); but these seemingly commonsense approaches do not work.

Our points here are simply these: First, speech and **language disorders** carry social penalties. Second, speech and language are among the most complex human functions, and disorders of these functions do not always yield to intuitive or commonsense "solutions."

DEFINITION

Speech and language are tools used for purposes of communication. Communication requires *encoding* (sending in understandable form) and *decoding* (receiving and understanding) messages. Communication always involves a sender and a receiver of messages, but it does not always involve language. Animals communicate through movements and noises, for example, but their communication does not qualify as a true language. We are concerned here only with communication involving language.

Language is the communication of ideas through an arbitrary system of symbols that are used according to certain rules that determine meaning. When people think of language, they typically think of the oral language most of us use. **Speech**—the behavior of forming and sequencing the sounds of oral language—is the most common symbol system used in communication between humans. Some languages, however, are not based on speech. For example, American Sign Language does not involve speech sounds; it is a manual language used by many people who cannot hear speech. Moreover, **augmentative communication** for people with disabilities involving the physical movements of speech may consist of alternatives to the speech sounds of oral language.

The American Speech-Language-Hearing Association provides definitions of disor-

MISCONCEPTIONS
ABOUT SPEECH AND LANGUAGE DISORDERS

Myth	*Fact*
Children with language disorders always have speech difficulties as well.	It is possible for a child to have good phonology, voice, and speech flow and yet not make any sense when he or she talks; however, most children with language disorders have speech disorders as well.
Individuals with speech or language disabilities are always emotionally disturbed or mentally retarded.	Some children with speech and/or language disorders are normal in cognitive, social, and emotional development.
How children learn language is now well understood.	Although recent research has revealed quite a lot about the sequence of language acquisition and led to theories of language development, exactly how children learn language is still unknown.
Stuttering is primarily a disorder of people with extremely high IQs. Children who stutter become stuttering adults.	Stuttering can affect individuals at any level of intellectual ability. Some children who stutter continue stuttering as adults; most, however, stop stuttering before or during adolescence with help from a speech-language pathologist. Stuttering is primarily a childhood disorder and it is found much more often in boys than in girls.
Disorders of phonology (or articulation) are never very serious and are always easy to correct.	Disorders of phonology can make speech unintelligible; it is sometimes very difficult to correct phonological or articulation problems, especially if the individual is retarded, disturbed, or cerebral palsied.
A child with a cleft palate always has defective speech.	The child born with a cleft palate may or may not have a speech disorder, depending on the nature of the cleft, the medical treatment given, and other factors such as psychological characteristics and speech training.
There is no relationship between intelligence and disorders of speech and language.	Speech and language disorders of all types occur more frequently among individuals of lower intellectual ability, although it is possible for these disorders to occur in individuals who are extremely intelligent.
There is not much overlap between language disorders and learning disabilities.	Problems with verbal skills—listening, reading, writing, speaking—are often a central feature of a learning disability. The definitions of learning disability and language disorder are overlapping.

ders of communication, including **speech disorders, language disorders,** and variations in communication (differences or dialects and augmentative systems) that are not disorders (see box on p. 211). Note that language disorders include problems in the comprehension and use of language for communication, regardless of the symbol system used (spoken, written, or other). The *form, content,* and/or *function* of language may be involved. The form of language includes sound combinations **(phonology),** construction of word forms such as plurals and verb tenses **(morphology),** and construction of sentences **(syntax).** The content of language refers to the intentions and meanings people attach to words and sentences **(semantics).** Language function is the use to which language is put in communication, and it includes nonverbal behavior as well as vocalizations that form the pattern of language use **(pragmatics).**

Speech disorders are impairments in the production and use of oral language. They include disabilities in producing voice, making speech sounds **(articulation),** and producing speech with a normal flow **(fluency).**

Differences in speech or language that are shared by people in a given region, social group, or cultural/ethnic group should not be considered disorders. For example, black English (or Ebonics), Appalachian English, and the New York dialect are varieties of English, not disorders of speech or language (ASHA, 1983). Augmentative communication systems do not imply that a person has a language disorder. Rather, such systems are used by those who have a temporary or permanent inability to use speech satisfactorily for communication. Those who use augmentative communication systems may or may not have a language disorder in addition to their inability to use speech.

Before discussing the disorders of speech and language, we will provide a brief description of how speech is produced and a brief discussion of normal language development. It is not possible to appreciate the complexity of speech disorders without considering the intricate and carefully coordinated movements required to produce intelligible speech. Likewise, language disorders cannot be understood and corrected without knowledge of normal language development (Owens, 1984; Shames and Wiig, 1986; Starkweather, 1983; Wallach and Butler, 1984).

SPEECH PRODUCTION

Production of speech requires an airstream that can be passed over and shaped by *phonatory, resonatory,* and *articulatory* processes. Intelligible speech also requires that speech sounds be produced in sequence and with a rhythm that may be referred to as **speech flow.** Thus the organs involved in respiration are necessarily involved in the act of speaking.

The basic process in speech production is the phonatory process. **Phonation** involves controlling the breath stream to produce speech sounds. Some speech sounds are made with the **larynx** open, as in normal breathing (see Figure 5.1). These *voiceless* speech sounds (consonants such as [t], [p], and [s]) are made by stopping and releasing the breath flow in pulses or by causing turbulence in the airstream as it passes through the **pharynx** and oral cavity. Other speech sounds are *voiced* (vowels such as [i] and [a]). That is, sound waves are generated as the breath stream passes through the larynx, which opens and closes rapidly as a result of the air moving through it. Phonation is a result of this vibration of the vocal cords. The frequency of vibration of the vocal cords determines the **pitch** of the sound that is

Definitions of the American Speech-Language-Hearing Association

Communicative Disorders

A. A SPEECH DISORDER is an impairment of voice, articulation of speech sounds, and/or fluency. These impairments are observed in the transmission and use of the oral symbol system.

1. A VOICE DISORDER is defined as the absence or abnormal production of vocal quality, pitch, loudness, resonance, and/or duration.
2. An ARTICULATION DISORDER is defined as the abnormal production of speech sounds.
3. A FLUENCY DISORDER is defined as the abnormal flow of verbal expression, characterized by impaired rate and rhythm which may be accompanied by struggle behavior.

B. A LANGUAGE DISORDER is the impairment or deviant development of comprehension and/or use of a spoken, written, and/or other symbol system. The disorder may involve (1) the form of language (phonologic, morphologic, and syntactic systems), (2) the content of language (semantic system), and/or (3) the function of language in communication (pragmatic system) in any combination.

1. Form of Language
   a. PHONOLOGY is the sound system of a language and the linguistic rules that govern the sound combinations.
   b. MORPHOLOGY is the linguistic rule system that governs the structure of words and the construction of word forms from the basic elements of meaning.
   c. SYNTAX is the linguistic rule governing the order and combination of words to form sentences, and the relationships among the elements within a sentence.
2. Content of Language
   a. SEMANTICS is the psycholinguistic system that patterns the content of an utterance, intent and meanings of words and sentences.
3. Function of Language
   a. PRAGMATICS is the sociolinguistic system that patterns the use of language in communication which may be expressed motorically, vocally, or verbally.

Communicative Variations

A. COMMUNICATIVE DIFFERENCE/DIALECT is a variation of a symbol system used by a group of individuals which reflects and is determined by shared regional, social, or cultural/ethnic factors. Variations or alterations in the use of a symbol system may be indicative of primary language interferences. A regional, social, or cultural/ethnic variation of a symbol system should not be considered a disorder of speech or language.

B. AUGMENTATIVE COMMUNICATION is a system used to supplement the communicative skills of individuals for whom speech is temporarily or permanently inadequate to meet communicative needs. Both prosthetic devices and/or non-prosthetic techniques may be designed for individual use as an augmentative communication system.

SOURCE: American Speech-Language-Hearing Association, *Definitions: Communicative Disorders and Variations, ASHA,* 1982, *24,* 949–950.

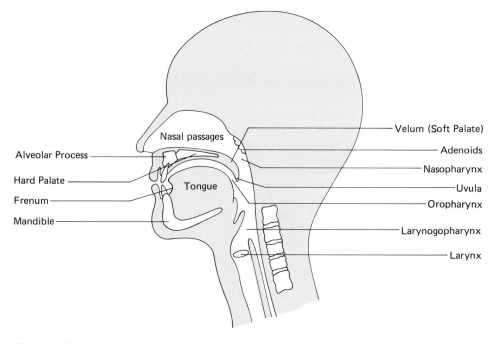

Figure 5.1 *Location of some of the major organs of speech.*

heard. Other phonatory processes include those that determine the loudness and quality of the voice.

Sound waves generated by the phonatory process are *resonated* and *articulated* into the sounds of speech as they pass through the throat, mouth, and nose. That is, the sound waves are *modulated* into speech sounds. **Articulation** refers to the movements the vocal tract makes during production of speech sounds; **resonance** has to do with the quality of the sound imparted by the size, shape, and texture of the organs in the vocal tract. Articulation and resonance are closely linked processes because as the pharynx, tongue, lips, and other parts of the vocal tract are moved to articulate sounds, the size and shape of the vocal tract, and hence its resonance characteristics, also change.

Articulation and resonance have to do with the way individual phonemes are produced. The speech-flow process, on the other hand, refers to movement from sound to sound, syllable to syllable, word to word, phrase to phrase, and sentence to sentence. Intelligible speech requires that limits be placed on the order, length, and speed with which speech sounds and pauses between units of speech (syllables, words, phrases) are made. The rhythm or **prosody** of speech—its patterns of stress and rate—also help give meaning to speech.

Our extremely simplified description of the basic speech production process does not mean that the act of speaking is a simple one. Intelligible speech requires an extremely fast, coordinated sequence of many movements. Speech scientists are still striving to measure and unravel exactly what happens physiologically when speech is produced. It is much easier to describe what intelligible speech sounds like than to specify how one speaks intelligibly (see Costello, 1984; and Zemlin, 1986, for more detailed descriptions of speech production).

LANGUAGE DEVELOPMENT

The newborn makes few sounds other than cries. The fact that within a few years the human child can form the many complex sounds of speech, understand spoken and written language, and express meaning verbally is one of nature's great miracles. The major milestones in this "miraculous" ability to use language are fairly well known by child development specialists. The underlying mechanisms that control the development of language are still not well understood, however. What parts of the process of learning language are innate, and what parts are controlled by the environment? What is the relationship between cognitive development and language development? These and many other questions about the origins and uses of language cannot yet be answered definitively; scholarly research is guided by a variety of theoretical models. A discussion of language learning models is beyond the scope of this chapter (see Leonard, 1986; McCormick and Schiefelbusch, 1984; Owens, 1984, 1986). Here we will present only a brief summary of the sequence in which milestones in the development of oral language are reached.

Recent research has demonstrated that infants are much more adept at communication than was previously thought. They receive and give messages to their caretakers in ways that were not formerly understood. Mothers and other caretakers approach babies as if they can communicate. This is significant in understanding early language learning, because it highlights the social nature of the process. Interaction of infants and caregivers includes joint reference to objects (e.g., "Oh look!"), joint action (e.g., games such as peek-a-boo), turn taking (often during joint action), and situational variations (e.g., games played during bathing or diaper changing, but not when the infant is being put to sleep in the crib). It is the need to communicate—to exchange meanings involving social interactions—that sets the stage for the development of language. Recognition of this principle has led to intense interest in the social contexts and uses of language. As you read the description of the emergence of oral language, you should keep in mind the social use of language for children at various stages of development.

At about 2 to 3 months of age babies begin "gooing," and by 4 to 6 months they are babbling. That is, they make some of the vowel and consonant sounds and other noises over and over, often apparently just to explore their vocal apparatus and to entertain themselves. Sometimes they babble when they are alone and will stop abruptly if an adult attends to them. Sometimes babbling occurs when they are being cared for or played with. These vocalizations may be social—that is, used to communicate with their caretakers.

Babbling soon turns into vocal play. The sounds children are able to make gradually increase in variety. They begin to string sounds together ("da-da-da") and, toward the end of the first year, to put different syllables together ("duh-buh"). They make vocal sounds more frequently and seem to take delight in their own performance. But they also begin to take an interest in listening to the speech of adults and to carry on "conversations" by "answering" when spoken to. Now they begin to use intonations, changing the pitch and intensity of their vocal productions to make them sound like adults' commands, questions, or exclamations. They experiment with rhythm and intonation patterns.

What they are "saying" is still meaningless gibberish if taken out of its social context—but it sounds as if they are talking. Their vocalizations may be a form of effective communication with adults who know them well. Mother and child may make their desires and intentions mutually understood even though other adults

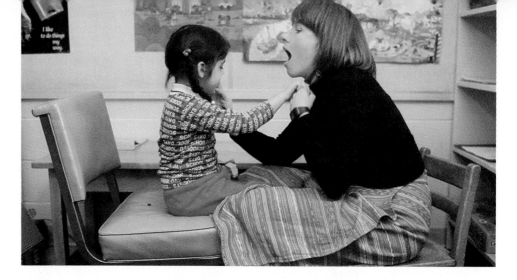

Nonhandicapped children quickly learn that language is a means of influencing others and obtaining what they want. Children with language disabilities, however, may need a specific program of instruction if they are to use language effectively. (Alan Carey/The Image Works)

may be unable to interpret the child's "speech." Children play delightedly (and delightfully) with vocalizations, and may continue this kind of vocal play for a few years, even though by that age they have acquired a vocabulary of several hundred words and may be putting two and three words together in simple sentences (see Kuczaj, 1983). An important thing to note here is that at more advanced stages of normal language development, there is greater variation in the age at which milestones are reached. For example, there is greater variation in the age at which children usually speak their first words than there is in the age at which children normally begin to babble.

At about the same time children learn to walk and to feed themselves—roughly between 10 and 18 months—they normally say their first words. Actually, it is not at all easy to pinpoint when a child starts to use words because approximations of words often occur in an infant's vocalizations and it is often impossible to judge their communicative intent (Rees, 1980). Even before they have started to say what everyone would agree are words, babies have begun to exhibit an understanding of simple questions and commands. During the second year vocal play continues. Children may utter unintelligible strings of syllables with occasional understandable words mixed in. They may sometimes be *echolalic* (i.e., repeat what they have heard without understanding it or being able to use it appropriately in conversation). Many of their words are idiosyncratic or poorly articulated. They may use a single word in place of an entire phrase or sentence ("sue" to indicate "Put on my shoe"). The listener has to rely on intonations, facial expression, gestures, and the social context to interpret the meaning of these single-word expressions (Rees, 1980; Wood, 1976). Children may also use one word to indicate a single, undifferentiated class of objects ("doggie" to indicate all animals).

After age 2 children's language develops rapidly. Their single-word utterances are replaced by speech more closely approximating the syntax used by adults when they speak to each other. At the age of 2 years, children ordinarily use expressions that average about two words in length; by the time they are 5 years old, their average sentence is up to about six words in length (see Winitz, 1971). At age 2, they may have a vocabulary of several hundred words; by the age of 5, they know many more, and their vocabulary continues to increase at a rapid rate. By the time they are about 5, their speech is readily understandable by anyone. By the time they begin school, they are fluent speakers and have mastered most of the basic *morphological* characteristics of language (they can construct word forms such as plurals, verb tenses, and compound words correctly). By the time they are 8 or 9 years old, they have mastered all the *phonemic* components of language (their articulation of the speech sounds is correct).

We repeat: There is great variability in the age at which children will demonstrate a particular level of speech or language performance (Owens, 1984; Schwartz, 1984). The statements we have made may be used as guidelines for judging the adequacy of an individual's language development, but only as very general guidelines. For example, one should not jump to the conclusion that an 8-year-old who still makes a few errors in articulation and constructs a few incorrect plurals is significantly slow in speech or language development.

The How and Why of Language Learning

Although no one knows exactly how or why children learn language, we do know that language development is related in a general way to physical maturation, cognitive development, and socialization. But the details of the process—the particulars of what happens physiologically, cognitively, and socially in the learning of language—are still being studied. Schiefelbusch and McCormick (1981) reviewed language acquisition research that addresses three important questions:

1. *What do children talk about when they are learning to talk (what is the relationship between emerging language and the child's sensorimotor and conceptual abilities)?* They talk about things, events, and relationships in their environment. In particular, they tend to talk about things they see often and can act upon or interact with frequently. Many children will first learn object names like "ball," "blanket," or "cookie," people's names like "mommy" or "kitty," personal-social words like "no" and "please," and action words like "bye-bye," "gone," or "down." Their learning of names for new objects seems to be based primarily on the perceptual features (shape, color, size, sound, texture, taste) of things (Tomikawa and Dodd, 1980). Early language serves to help children communicate about what they see, do, and can understand.

2. *How do children learn the forms and structures they produce when they first learn to talk (how do they become competent language users)?* Infants' sound making, which is initially adequate for communication, gradually changes into the language of adults. The child must learn to use conventional words and sentences for more complex and sophisticated communication. Mothers' and fathers' speech to their children is generally tuned to the child's cognitive level. Parents constantly provide "language lessons" for their children by talking to them about what they (children and parents) are doing. And parents gradually expand the child's knowledge and linguistic competence by changing the way they talk to the child, keeping their language matched to his or her cognitive development.

3. *How do children learn to use language (how do they learn to make language meet their communicative needs)?* This question deals with the *pragmatic* side of language—how to make it serve a useful purpose. In their

earliest interactions with parents children find that they can influence parents' behavior by their vocalizations. They are also influenced by their parents' vocalizations to them. As children learn the role of vocalization in social interactions with their parents, they begin to communicate intentionally, to make reference to objects and direct the actions of others. They learn that their language is involved in cause-effect relations. Most children as young as 2 years of age learn basic rules of *discourse,* that taking turns in talking and repeating or clarifying is necessary for effective communication (Wilcox and Webster, 1980).

Schiefelbusch and McCormick go on to say that the sensorimotor and cognitive, linguistic, and pragmatic aspects of language are all cognitive in the broad sense of the term, and that they are interactive and interdependent in the process of language learning (see also McCormick and Schiefelbusch, 1984). Language learning is an active process in which the child stimulates others verbally and responds to others' verbalizations. Language development cannot be explained adequately by examining the structure of language or by analyzing only the environmental forces that act on the child. It must be studied from the perspective of what children do to meet their needs for communication. We turn now to the disorders of speech and language.

SPEECH DISORDERS

As we noted at the beginning of the chapter, speech disorders include disorders of voice, articulation, and fluency. We will discuss each of these, as well as disorders associated with defects of the mouth and face (orofacial defects) and those associated with neurological damage. Remember that an individual may have more than one disorder of speech and that speech and language disorders sometimes occur together.

Voice Disorders

People's voices are perceived as having pitch, loudness, and quality. Changes in pitch and loudness are part of the stress patterns of speech. Vocal quality is related not only to production of speech sounds, but also to the nonlinguistic aspects of speech. Together, the three dimensions of voice are sufficient to reveal a person's identity, and often a good deal about the individual's physical and emotional status as well. *Voice disorders,* though difficult to define precisely, are characteristics of pitch, loudness, and/or quality that are abusive of the larynx, hamper communication, or are perceived as markedly different from what is customary for someone of a given age, sex, and cultural background. Voice disorders that involve a dysfunction within the larynx are referred to as *disorders of phonation.* Disorders having to do with the dysfunction of the oral and nasal air passageways are called *disorders of resonance.*

Pitch

The adult's voice is generally lower in pitch than the child's, and after puberty the male's voice is generally lower in pitch than the female's. If a person's voice is markedly lower or higher in pitch than is expected, considering age and sex, that person may experience social censure, and communication may be less than opti-

The voice must be modulated according to the demands of a given situation. But disorders of voice sometimes involve inappropriate use, such as speaking in a voice much louder or softer than necessary. Prolonged abuse of the vocal mechanism, such as screaming at an athletic competition, can result in temporary or permanent problems in voice production. (Bill Weems/Woodfin Camp & Associates)

The Speech-Language Pathologist

A speech-language pathologist is a highly trained professional capable of assuming a variety of roles in assisting persons who have speech and language disorders. Entering the profession requires rigorous training and demonstration of clinical skills under close supervision. Certification requires completion of a master's degree in a program approved by the American Speech-Language-Hearing Association (ASHA). You may want to write to ASHA, 10801 Rockville Pike, Rockville, MD 20852 for a free booklet, *Careers in Speech-Language Pathology and Audiology.*

About 50 percent of the practicing speech-language pathologists in the United States are members of ASHA. It is estimated that about 40 percent are employed in elementary or secondary schools, about 10 percent in universities, about 20 percent in nonuniversity clinics in hospitals, rehabilitation centers, and so on, and about 5 percent in private practice. About 5 percent are voluntarily unemployed (Matthews, 1986).

Because of the emphasis on *least restrictive environment* or mainstreaming (see Chapter 1), speech-language pathologists are doing more of their work in regular classrooms and are spending more time consulting with classroom teachers than they have in the past. Matthews (1986) predicts that the school-employed speech-language pathologist of the future will need more knowledge of classroom procedures and the academic curriculum, especially in the areas of reading, writing, and spelling, and will be more involved in the overall education of children with communication disorders. More emphasis will be placed on working as a team member in the schools to see that handicapped children obtain an appropriate education. Because of legislation and changing population demographics, speech-language pathologists of the future will also probably be more involved with preschool children and those with learning disabilities and severe, multiple disabilities. There will be broader concern for the entire range of communication disorders, including both oral and written communication.

mal. During normal speech there are smooth transitions of pitch to higher and lower tones. These transitions or intonations help to provide emphasis and make speech more interesting to listen to. It can be extremely distracting to listen to a person who never changes pitch (someone who speaks in a monotone), speaks with stereo-typed inflections (uses a "sing-song" voice or constant dogmatic emphasis), or uses a voice that constantly cracks or breaks into falsetto. Pitch breaks (either to higher or lower pitch) are common experiences of adolescents entering puberty. If they persist, they can be a serious problem (see Eisenson and Ogilvie, 1983).

Loudness

Too soft or weak a voice can make it difficult or impossible to understand the speaker at a reasonable distance and with a reasonable level of background noise. When a person cannot use the voice at all (because of laryngitis or for any other reason) he or she is said to have *aphonia*. A voice that is too loud is irritating to the listener, especially if it has an unpleasant vocal quality. Communication may also be hampered if a person begins statements with adequate loudness but lets his or her voice trail off at the ends of phrases, or if he or she uses a stereotyped pattern of loudness for emphasis.

Quality

Defining voice quality in objective, quantitative terms is extremely difficult, though it is easy to recognize and describe subjectively the qualitative differences among individuals' voices. "Sweet," "mellow," "thin" "rough," and other words with tactual or visual referents are often used to describe the auditory perceptions created by the timbre of speech.

The appropriateness of a person's vocal quality must be judged according to age, sex, and physical status, and according to the demands of the situation. That is, voice disorders are not definable by their acoustic characteristics alone, but by the re-quirements and expectations of the speaker's environment as well. A loud, harsh voice may be required in order to make oneself heard during an athletic competi-tion. But this vocal quality may be inappropriate and may stigmatize the speaker in everyday conversation.

Prevalence

Estimates of the prevalence of voice disorders depend on what age group is sur-veyed and what criteria are used to define abnormalities (Eisenson and Ogilvie, 1983). Children in the lower grades tend to have more voice problems than older children (Moore, 1986), and one would expect to find more voice problems among children with other disabilities than among the general population. Moore (1986) estimates that voice problems affect 6 percent of children of school age.

Causes

Voice disorders can be the result of a variety of biological and nonbiological causes. Growths in the larynx (such as nodules, polyps, or cancerous tissue), infections of the larynx (laryngitis), damage to the nerves supplying the larynx, or accidental bruises or scratches on the larynx can cause disorders. Misuse or abuse of the voice also can lead to a voice that is judged to be abnormal. Disorders resulting from misuse or abuse can lead to damage to the tissues of the larynx. Sometimes a person has psychological problems that lead to complete loss of voice (aphonia) or to severe voice abnormalities. Voice disorders having to do with resonance may be caused by physical abnormalities of the oral cavity (such as cleft palate) or damage to the brain or nerves controlling the oral cavity. Infections of the tonsils, adenoids, or sinuses can also influence how the voice is resonated. Most people who have a severe hearing loss typically have problems in achieving a normal or pleasingly resonant voice. Finally, sometimes a person simply has not learned to speak with an appropriately resonant voice. There are no biological or deep-seated psychological reasons for the problem; rather, it appears that the person has learned faulty habits of positioning the organs of speech (Moore, 1986; Starkweather, 1983).

Assessment and Intervention

When children are screened for speech and language disorders, the speech-language pathologist is on the lookout for problems in voice quality, resonance, pitch, and loudness (Eisenson and Ogilvie, 1983). If a problem is found, then referral for examination by a physician is indicated. A medical report may indicate that surgery or other treatment is needed because of a growth or infection. Aside from the medical evaluation, the pathologist will evaluate when the problem began and how the individual uses his or her voice in everyday situations and under stressful circumstances. Besides looking for how voice is produced and structural or functional problems, the pathologist looks for signs of infection or disease that may be contributing to the disorder or be an indication of serious illness.

Therapy for voice problems usually involves these steps when the problem is misuse or abuse of the voice:

1. Identify vocal misuses and abuses.
2. Reduce vocal misuses and abuses.
3. Search with the patient for the best voice he or she can produce.
4. Employ various approaches to maintain the optimum voice. (Boone, 1980, p. 339)

Articulation Disorders

Distinctions between articulation disorders and phonological disorders are sometimes difficult to make. *Phonology* refers to the study of the rules for using the sounds of language. When a person has difficulty communicating because he or she does not use speech sounds according to standard rules, the disorder is phonological. *Articulation* refers to the "movements of the articulators in production of the speech sounds that make up the words of our language" (McReynolds, 1986, p. 142). The distinction between articulation and phonological disorders is a technical one, and even speech-language pathologists may disagree about how a given individual's problem should be classified. In general, however, the problem is considered to be an articulation (speech) problem if the individual cannot or does not understand *how to make the speech sound*; it is considered a phonological (language) problem if the individual does not understand *how to use the speech sounds according to linguistic rules or to communicate meaning accurately* (see Locke, 1983; Newman, Creaghead, and Secord, 1985; Shames and Wiig, 1986; Shriberg, 1980).

Whether the disorder is one of speech (articulation) or language (phonology), the individual may make one or more of several types of errors in producing words: Word sounds may be omitted, substituted, distorted, or added.

Omissions

In omission errors, only parts of words are pronounced. For example, [t] may be consistently omitted ("ie my shoes igh" for "tie my shoes tight"), or [l] may be omitted except when it is the ending sound of a word ("I ove my ittle o-ipop" for "I love my little lollipop").

Substitutions

These include such errors as substituting [w] for [r] or [l] (e.g., "wed" for "red" or "wike" for "like"). Common substitutions are [b] for [v] ("bery" for "very"), [t] for [k] ("tate the rate" for "take the rake"), [f] for [θ] ("baf" for "bath"), and [ʒ] or [θ] for [s] ("thith thide" for "this side"). Substitution of [θ] for [ʃ] or [s] ("thunthine" or "shunshine" for "sunshine") is often referred to as a lisp. But lisping may include a variety of other substitutions or distortions involving [s] and [z].

Distortions

Sounds may approximate what is acceptable but not be quite "right." There are many ways of producing an approximation of what an [s] or some other phoneme should sound like. For example, a distorted [w] may be produced if the tip of the tongue is high in the mouth, making it close to but not exactly like [r].

Additions

Sounds may be added to or inserted within a word (e.g., "He's my fuhriend" for "He's my friend").

When are articulation or phonological errors a disorder? Deciding that errors represent a disorder really depends on a clinician's subjective judgment. That judgment will be influenced by the clinician's experience, the number and types of errors, the consistency of these errors, the age and developmental characteristics of the speaker, and the intelligibility of the person's speech.

Young children make many errors in speech sounds when they are learning to talk. Many children do not master all the phonological rules of the language and learn to produce all the speech sounds correctly until they are 8 or 9 years old. Furthermore, most children make frequent errors until after they enter school. Age of the child is thus a major consideration in judging the adequacy of articulation. Another major consideration is the phonological characteristics of the child's community because children learn speech largely through imitation. A child reared in the Deep South may have speech that sounds peculiar to residents of Long Island, but that does not mean that the child has a speech disorder.

Prevalence

Detailed information about the prevalence of articulation and phonological disorders in children is not readily available. It is estimated that 10 percent of the population has some type of problem communicating and that about 75 percent of these problems involve articulation or phonology (Newman et al., 1985). The number of children experiencing difficulty in producing word sounds decreases markedly during the first three or four years of elementary school. Among children with other disabilities, especially mental retardation and neurological disorders like cerebral palsy, the prevalence of articulation disorders is higher than in the general population.

Causes

Lack of ability to articulate speech sounds correctly can be caused by biological factors. For example, brain damage or damage to the nerves controlling the muscles used in speech may make it difficult or impossible to articulate sounds. Furthermore, gross abnormalities of the oral structures, such as a cleft palate, may make normal speech difficult or impossible. Relatively minor structural changes, such as loss of teeth, may produce temporary errors. Delayed phonological development may also result from a hearing loss. But most children's articulation disorders are not the result of biological factors. Nor can one say with confidence that they are the result of perceptual-motor problems or psychosocial factors. There simply is no satisfactory explanation for the fact that some children whose development appears to be normal in every other way persist in making articulation errors (Bernthal and Bankson, 1984; McReynolds, 1986; Shriberg, 1980).

Assessment and Intervention

Parents of preschool children may refer their child for assessment if he or she has speech that is really difficult to understand. Most schools screen all new pupils for speech and language problems, and in most cases a child who still makes many articulation errors in the third or fourth grade will be referred for evaluation. Older children and adults sometimes seek help for themselves when their speech draws negative attention. A speech-language pathologist will assess not only phonological characteristics, but also the child's social and developmental history, hearing, general language ability, and speech mechanism. Assessment of articulation may involve giving commercially prepared tests and/or using materials the clinician has devised. Testing to compare the child's phonology to that of others is done by having the child say words, count, name or describe pictures, and so on. Judgment of whether or not a particular sound is correctly articulated rests with the trained ear of the pathologist.

The decision whether or not to include the child in an intervention program will depend on the child's age, other developmental characteristics, and the type and consistency of the articulatory errors. The decision will also depend on the pathologist's assessment of the likelihood that the child will self-correct the errors and of the social penalties, such as teasing and shyness, the child is experiencing. If the child misarticulates only a few sounds but does so consistently and suffers social embarrassment or rejection as a consequence, an intervention program is usually called for.

Intervention for a child who has severely delayed speech usually begins in the preschool or early elementary grades. Children who have a developmental phonological disorder—one not known to be caused by or associated with other developmental problems—may not be included in an intervention program until the middle grades. The pathologist will teach the child the auditory, visual, and tactile cues involved in producing sounds correctly. This will be done by providing models, giving instructions, having the child listen to differences in sounds, and helping the child understand the movements of the tongue and lips in producing sounds.

Once sounds are reliably produced correctly in a clinical setting, the focus of intervention shifts to transfer of the training to the everyday environment (see Spradlin and Siegel, 1982; McReynolds, 1986). To make it likely that the child will articulate the correct sounds in ordinary conversation, the clinician may enlist the aid of parents and teachers. Parents and teachers may give the child reminders, provide special practice sessions, or be asked to change the ways they respond to the child's errors and correct sound productions.

Fluency Disorders*

Normal speech is characterized by some interruptions in speech flow. All of us occasionally get speech sounds in the wrong order ("revalent" for "relevant"), speak too fast to be understood, pause at the wrong place in a sentence, use an inappropriate pattern of stress, or become *disfluent*—that is, stumble and backtrack, repeating syllables or words, and fill in pauses with "uh" while trying to think of how to finish what we have to say. It is only when the speaker's efforts are so intense or the interruptions in the flow of speech are so frequent or pervasive that they keep the speaker from being understood or draw extraordinary attention that they are considered disorders. Besides, listeners have a greater tolerance for some types of disfluencies than others. Most of us will more readily accept speech-flow disruptions we perceive as necessary corrections of what the speaker has said or is planning to say than disruptions that appear to reflect the speaker's inability to proceed with the articulation of what he or she has decided to say (Perkins, 1980).

Stuttering

The most frequent type of fluency disorder is stuttering. As we noted at the opening of the chapter, stuttering remains one of the greatest puzzles in speech pathology (Andrews, Craig, Feyer, Hoddinott, Howie, and Neilson, 1983). There is no agreement among speech-language pathologists regarding even its definition. A "stutterer" is not just one who stutters (we all sometimes exhibit the same disfluencies as stutterers), but one who is considered by others and/or himself or herself to be a stutterer (Perkins, 1983).

PREVALENCE Fluency disorders affect millions of Americans. About 1 percent of children and adults are considered stutterers. More boys than girls stutter. Most stutterers are identified by at least age 5 (Andrews et al., 1983). However, parents sometimes perceive their child as stuttering as early as 20 to 30 months of age (Yairi, 1983).

CHARACTERISTICS AND TREATMENT The majority of stutterers begin to show an abnormal speech pattern between 2 and 5 years of age. Many children outgrow their childhood disfluencies. These children generally use regular and effortless disfluencies, appear to be unaware of their hesitancies, and have parents and teachers who are unconcerned about their speech patterns (Shames and Rubin, 1986).

Advances in the diagnosis of young stutterers have made possible the distinction between children who will outgrow the disfluency without intervention and chil-

---

* We are grateful to Susan C. Meyers, Ph.D., for her substantial contributions to this section of the chapter.

dren who will require therapy (Adams, 1977, 1980; Gregory, 1986; Meyers, 1986). *Quantitatively,* stutterers have a higher percentage of disfluent speech than children who experience normal speech hesitation. Adams (1982), Culp (1984), and Meyers (1986) have reported that over 10 percent of a stutterer's conversational speech is characterized by disfluency. Stutterers, compared to children with normal interruptions of speech flow, have different types of disfluency—they show *qualitative* as well as quantitative differences. For example, young stutterers emit more part-word repetitions (e.g., "cuh . . . cuh . . . cuh . . . candy"), prolongations (e.g., "s————something"), broken words (e.g., "Push————ing"), and tense pauses (e.g., lip posturing, rapid eye blinks, and other distracting mannerisms when attempting to say a word). Children with normal disfluencies emit whole word and phrase repetitions (e.g., "I . . . I . . . I like . . . I like candy"), revisions or incomplete phrases (e.g., "I wanna suh . . . Do you think I can have a soda?"), interjections (fillers such as, "um," "like," "er," "well"), and unfilled pauses (taking excessive pause time to think about what you intend to say (e.g., "I want a [pause] cookie").

Three additional characteristics differentiate stutterers from nonstutterers. First, stutterers struggle, strain, and exhibit more visible effort when talking (Adams, 1980; Meyers, 1986; Starkweather, 1982). Second, when trying to speak fluently, stutterers speak at a much slower pace to maintain fluency (Cross and Luper, 1979; Meyers and Freeman, 1985c). Third, there appears to be a genetic predisposition to stutter (Brutten, 1986; Kidd, 1984; Wingate, 1986).

Research has shown that parents of stutterers and parents of nonstutterers are quite similar (Meyers and Freeman, 1985a). For instance, listening partners tend to talk faster (Meyers and Freeman, 1985c), interrupt disfluency frequently (Meyers and Freeman, 1985b), and use more negative statements and complex questions when talking to stutterers (Mordecai, 1979). It is possible to differentiate between parents of stutterers and those of nonstutterers in one major area, however. Parents of stutterers are genuinely concerned about their child's fluency development. They are much more anxious about their child's disfluencies. Living day in and day out with a child who is struggling to speak can produce feelings of helplessness and despair. Some intervention programs, such as the one at the University of Virginia Fluency Development Clinic, teach parents to interrupt less often, focus on the child's fluent speech, and make more positive comments about their child's fluent speech. Working with parents may be just as important as teaching the child to speak in a more natural, effortless way.

A child who is thought to stutter should be evaluated by a speech-language pathologist. Early diagnosis is important if the development of chronic stuttering is to be avoided. Unfortunately, many educators and physicians do not refer potential stutterers for in-depth assessment because they are aware that disfluencies are a normal part of speech-language development. But nonreferral is extremely detrimental to children who are at risk to stutter. If their stuttering goes untreated, it typically results in a lifelong disorder which affects their ability to communicate, develop positive feelings about self, and pursue certain educational and employment opportunities.

Cluttering

Cluttering is a fluency disorder that is much less well defined and understood than stuttering. There appear to be few differences between stuttering and cluttering except that the clutterer seems indifferent to the problem, which involves speaking in an extremely fast, disorganized, and often unintelligible way (Perkins, 1980).

Disorders Associated with Orofacial Defects

A wide variety of abnormalities of the mouth and face can interfere with speech and language (McWilliams, 1984; 1986). Nearly all of these defects are present at birth. A few are acquired through accident or disease in which part of the facial tissues must be removed surgically. The defects can involve the tongue, lips, nasal passages, ears, teeth and gums, and hard and soft palates. Any defect in the mechanisms of hearing and speaking can affect the development and use of speech and language. By far the most common orofacial defect seen in children is an orofacial cleft—a rift or split in the upper part of the oral cavity or the upper lip (Ewanowski and Saxman, 1980). (Cleft lip is sometimes referred to inappropriately by uninformed or insensitive individuals as "harelip.") We will discuss only orofacial clefts, although all types of craniofacial abnormalities may have implications for speech and language (see also McWilliams, 1984; 1986; McWilliams, Morris, and Shelton, 1984; and Chapter 8).

Clefts of the **prepalate** (the upper lip and the upper gum ridge) may be unilateral or bilateral (see Figure 5.1). Some children have clefts that involve only the lip; some clefts extend from the lip all the way to the back of the roof of the mouth to include the hard and soft palates; other clefts involve only the palate. Clefts of the **palate** (the roof of the mouth) may involve both the hard palate and the soft palate, the soft palate only, or just the **uvula,** the suspended "tail" of the soft palate. When only the uvula is involved, the condition is known as **bifid uvula.** Figure 5.2 shows models of some of the many types of clefts. In addition to those shown in Figure 5.2, there are submucous clefts. That is, a child may have a cleft in the soft or hard palate that is covered by the mucous linings of the top of the oral cavity. These submucous clefts sometimes go undetected until the child shows a persistent speech problem.

Clefts of the palate are, in general, more serious than clefts of the prepalate. An infant or older child may have difficulty managing food because the food escapes into the nasal passage when he or she tries to swallow. Because the function of the **eustachian tube** (the tube connecting the middle ear and the throat) is usually impaired when there is a cleft in the palate, the child may be prone to impaired hearing. By far the most important consideration for speech, however, is the difficulty the child with a cleft palate experiences in building up sufficient air pressure in the oral cavity and in preventing air from escaping through the nasal cavity while articulating most sounds—i.e., **velopharyngeal closure.** In English only three sounds—[m], [n], and [K] (as in thing)—require nasal resonance; all other sounds are made with the soft palate closing off the flow of air through the nose. If air is allowed to escape through the nasal cavity during the production of most speech sounds, the speaker will probably be perceived as having a hypernasal voice.

Velopharyngeal closure, the ability to close off the passage of air into the nasal cavities during speech, may be lacking for reasons other than a cleft in the palate. In some cases the palate is not cleft but the **velum** (soft palate) is too short to make good contact with the back of the throat. In such cases of a "short palate" surgery of various types may be successful in narrowing the gap to allow complete closure.

Clefts of the prepalate are virtually always correctable by surgery; such repair usually is made soon after birth. Figure 5.3 shows how effective surgery can be in repairing a cleft lip. Even children who are much more severely disfigured by clefts than the one shown here can be made very normal in appearance (see Ewanowski and Saxman, 1980; McWilliams, 1986).

Surgery and clinical correction of defective speech have made great advances in recent years. But they are not yet so advanced that speech problems can be elimi-

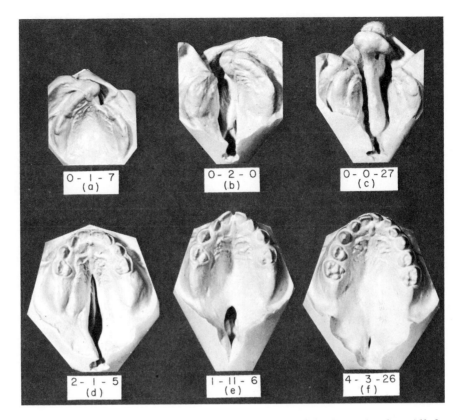

Figure 5.2 *Representations of the most common clefts of the lip and palate. All these casts of the upper surface of the mouth were obtained from infants prior to any surgery. The numbers refer to the child's age in years, months, and days. They may be interpreted as follows: (a) complete unilateral cleft of the lip and alveolar process; (b) complete unilateral cleft of both the lip and palate; (c) complete bilateral cleft of the lip and palate; (d) cleft of the hard and soft palate; (e) cleft of the soft palate; (f) bifid uvula.*
SOURCE: S. Pruzansky, "Description, Classification and Analysis of Unoperated Clefts of the Lip and Palate," *American Journal of Orthodontics 1953,* 39:595.

nated in all cases. Whether or not a child will have a speech defect depends on much more than the presence or absence of certain speech structures or the condition of these structures. General intelligence, hearing acuity, environmental stimulation, and dental characteristics, in addition to the condition of the palate and prepalate, affect the adequacy of speech (McWilliams, 1986).

The language of children with orofacial clefts appears to lag during the early years. But by the time they approach adulthood, the difference between their language development and that of individuals without clefts tends to disappear (Ewanowski and Saxman, 1980). The reasons for this lag in early language development might be that children with clefts (1) experience many disruptions in early experience and oral sensation, (2) receive insufficient language stimulation, or (3) perceive negative reactions from their listeners.

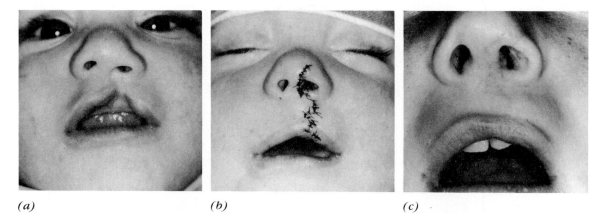

(a)   *(b)*   *(c)*

Figure 5.3 *Preoperative and postoperative photos of a unilateral cleft lip. The preoperative photo (a) shows the unrepaired cleft and an associated asymmetry of the nose. The postoperative photos (b) and (c) show the extent to which the cleft was closed and the nose made symmetrical.*
SOURCE: Courtesy of Dr. Milton T. Edgerton, Chairman, Department of Plastic Surgery, University of Virginia School of Medicine.

Prevalence

The prevalence of clefts varies from one racial group to another. It is about 1 in 750 to 1000 births for Caucasians, but about 1 in 500 for Orientals and about 1 in 2000 or 3000 for blacks. More boys than girls are born with clefts (McWilliams, 1986).

Causes

Orofacial clefts may result from genetic inheritance, mutant genes, abnormalities in chromosomes, or damage to the embryo during development. The external and internal features of the face develop very quickly during the first 9 weeks of embryological growth. As Ewanowski and Saxman have explained:

> Embryological development of the orofacial complex is exquisitely timed. Each structure of the face develops on schedule and at prearranged times the structures fuse and continue to grow as one. The direction and timing of this growth and development is uncompromising: Even a slight deviation from schedule can result in a profound orofacial disorder. (1980, p. 359)

As McWilliams (1986) notes regarding the causes of clefts, much more is known about *what* happens than *why* it happens. Cleft palate should not be attributed to some fault of the parents. Because genetic factors are clearly involved, genetic counseling is appropriate for people with clefts before they have families of their own.

Assessment and Intervention

Assessment of orofacial defects and their implications for speech and language requires an interdisciplinary team of specialists. Intervention too must be an interdisciplinary effort. A pediatrician and a plastic surgeon are typically involved from the beginning. Frequently a child with an orofacial defect has health problems requiring consultation with other medical specialists. Dentists, audiologists, psychologists, and speech-language pathologists are part of the team required for adequate assessment and intervention.

The work of the speech-language pathologist with a child who has an orofacial defect will be similar in many respects to work with children who have phonological, voice, or other disorders, but no defect of the speech mechanism. That is, the goal will be to teach the child how to use appropriate voice, articulate sounds so that they can be understood, and use language skillfully. The difference is that in working with the child who has an orofacial defect it is necessary to collaborate closely with other specialists. In cases where the defect prevents normal articulatory movement, the pathologist must teach the child alternative ways of making speech sounds.

Disorders Associated with Neurological Damage

The muscles that make speech possible are under voluntary control. When there is damage to areas of the brain controlling these muscles or to the nerves leading to them, there is a disturbance in the ability to speak normally. These disorders may involve articulation of speech sounds **(dysarthria)** or selecting and sequencing speech **(apraxia).** The difficulties in speaking are due to the fact that the muscles controlling breathing, the larynx, the soft palate and pharynx, the tongue, the jaw, and/or the lips cannot be controlled precisely. Depending on the nature of injury to the brain, perceptual and cognitive functions may also be affected; the individual may have a language disorder in addition to a speech disorder (see LaPointe, 1986; Mysak, 1986).

Causes

In Chapter 8 we discuss the many possible causes of brain injury. Among them are physical trauma, oxygen deprivation, poisoning, diseases, and strokes. Any of these, naturally, can be the cause of dysarthria or apraxia. Probably the condition that most frequently accounts for dysarthria and apraxia in children is *cerebral palsy*— brain injury before, during, or after birth that results in muscular weakness or paralysis.

Assessment and Intervention

The speech-language pathologist will assess the neurologically impaired individual's ability to control breathing, phonation, resonation, and articulatory movements. This will be done by listening to the person's speech and inspecting the speech mechanism. Medical, surgical, and rehabilitative specialists in the treatment of neurological disorders also must evaluate the person's problem and plan a management strategy. As in the case of orofacial disorders, surgical or mechanical interventions may be possible. Even after all possible medical-surgical treatment has been exhausted, the speech-language pathologist is still called upon to aid the person in learning or relearning more intelligible speech. In cases where the neurological impairment makes the person's speech unintelligible, alternative communication systems, such as communication boards, may be required (Aronson, 1980; Jaffe, 1984).

LANGUAGE DISORDERS

During the past decade, there has been a shift in concern among speech-language pathologists away from speech disorders. Much more interest is now shown in the disorders of language (Butler, 1986a,b). Estimates are that today 50 to 80 percent of the children seen by speech-language pathologists have language disorders (Wiig, 1986). The language problems of adolescents and young adults have been relatively neglected, however, in comparison to the language problems of young children (see box pp. 231–233).

The primary reason for the shift in focus from speech to language is the recognition that disorders of language are much more debilitating—they are much more at the center of difficulties in communication. The distinction between speech and language disorders is significant. It is possible for a child to have normal speech—to have acceptable voice, articulation, and fluency—yet not make sense when he or she talks or to misinterpret the meaning of what is heard or read. Speech has to do with intelligible vocal encoding of messages; language has to do with the formulation and interpretation of meaning. It involves listening and speaking, reading and writing, technical discourse and social interaction. Language problems are basic to many of the disabilities discussed in this text, especially mental retardation and learning disability.

Classification of Language Disorders

Language disorders can be classified according to several criteria. The ASHA definitions included in Table 5-1 provide one classification scheme: *phonology* (sounds), *morphology* (word forms), *syntax* (word order and sentence structure), *semantics* (word and sentence meanings), and *pragmatics* (social use of language). Difficulty with one of these dimensions of language is virtually certain to be accompanied by difficulty with one or more of the others. However, children with language disorders often have particular difficulty with one dimension.

A second scheme for classifying language disorders is comparison to the normal developmental schedule and sequence (Leonard, 1986). The language-disordered child may follow the same sequence of development as most children, but achieve each skill or milestone at a later age. Some children whose language development is delayed will catch up and achieve all the language characteristics of nonhandicapped children, but at a later age. Others reach a final level of development significantly below that of their nonhandicapped peers. Still other children are generally delayed in language development but show great discrepancies in the rate at which certain features of language are acquired. Differences in the development of a language-disordered and a normally developing child are outlined in Table 5-1. Notice that, in general, the sequence of development is similar for the two children, but the language-disordered child's development is slower. Careful examination of the table will reveal, however, that the children show different relationships among certain linguistic features. For example, the normally developing child uses the suffix *-ing* when the mean length of her sentences is 2.00 words, but the language-disordered child does not use *-ing* when her average sentences are the same length.

A third way of classifying language disorders is based on the presumed cause or related conditions. Leonard (1986) notes that during the past 20 years efforts have been made to describe the language characteristics of children with mental retardation, autism, hearing impairments, and various other conditions. This classification scheme has not worked very well because the language problems of children with

Table 5-1 Pattern of Development Shown by a Language-Disordered Child and a Nonhandicapped Child

Language-Disordered Child			Nonhandicapped Child		
Age	Attainment	Example	Age	Attainment	Example
27 months	First words	this, mama, bye bye, doggie	13 months	First words	here, mama, bye bye, kitty
38 months	50-word vocabulary		17 months	50-word vocabulary	
40 months	First two-word combinations	this doggie more apple this mama more play	18 months	First two-word combinations	more juice here ball more T.V. here kitty
48 months	Later two-word combinations	Mimi purse Daddy coat block chair dolly table	22 months	Later two-word combinations	Andy shoe Mommy ring cup floor keys chair
52 months	Mean sentence length of 2.00 words		24 months	Mean sentence length of 2.00 words	
55 months	First appearance of -ing	Mommy eating		First appearance of -ing	Andy sleeping
63 months	Mean sentence length of 3.10 words		30 months	Mean sentence length 3.10 words First appearance of is	My car's gone!
66 months	First appearance of is	The doggie's mad	37 months	Mean sentence length of 4.10 words First appearance of indirect requests	Can I have some cookies?
73 months	Mean sentence length of 4.10 words				
79 months	Mean sentence length of 4.50 words First appearance of indirect requests	Can I get the ball?	40 months	Mean sentence length of 4.50 words	

SOURCE: L. Leonard, "Early Language Development and Language Disorders," in G. H. Shames and E. H. Wiig (Eds.), *Human Communication Disorders,* 2nd ed. (Columbus, Ohio: Charles Merrill, 1986), p. 294. © 1986 Charles Merrill Publishing Company. Reprinted by permission of the publisher.

different diagnostic labels are often similar, and the problems of those in a given diagnostic category are often extremely varied.

Yet another classification scheme has been suggested by Naremore (1980), who relies on description of the language and related behaviors of the child. It is important to know: (1) what language and nonlanguage behaviors the child imitates, since much language learning is based on imitation; (2) what the child comprehends, since receptive language is important in early learning; and (3) what language the child produces spontaneously, since communication is the ultimate goal. With this in mind, four general types of language disorders can be considered (see Table 5-2):

Table 5-2   Types of Language Disorders

Type	Commonly Suspected Causative Factors or Related Conditions
No Verbal Language:	
Child does not show indications of understanding or spontaneously using language by age 3.	Congenital or early acquired deafness
	Gross brain damage or severe mental retardation
	Childhood psychosis
Qualitatively Different Language:	
Child's language is different from that of nonhandicapped children at any stage of development—meaning and usefulness for communication are greatly lessened or lost.	Inability to understand auditory stimuli
	Childhood psychosis
	Learning disability
	Mental retardation
	Hearing loss
Delayed Language Development	
Language follows normal course of development, but lags seriously behind that of most children who are the same chronological age.	Mental retardation
	Experiential deprivation
	Lack of language stimulation
	Hearing loss
Interrupted Language Development:	
Normal language development begins but is interrupted by illness, accident, or other trauma; language disorder is acquired.	Acquired hearing loss
	Brain injury due to oxygen deprivation, physical trauma, or infection

SOURCE: Summarized from R. C. Naremore, "Language Disorders in Children," in T. J. Hixon, L. D. Shriberg, and J. H. Saxman (Eds.), *Introduction to Communication Disorders* (Englewood Cliffs, N.J.: Prentice-Hall, 1980).

1. Child has not developed any verbal language.
2. Child's language is qualitatively different from normal language.
3. Child's language follows normal pattern of development but is delayed.
4. Child's language development is interrupted.

We will describe some of the major features of each of these types.

Absence of Verbal Language Development

Some children 3 years of age or older show no signs that they understand language and do not use language spontaneously. They may make noises, but they use these for communication in only the most primitive way (for example, by grunting, crying, or screaming to get what they want). Often these children are clearly abnormal in other ways besides their lack of language. Some of them are known to be deaf or deaf and blind; some are developmentally disabled in obvious ways (that is, profoundly retarded or brain damaged and/or physically disabled); some show bizarre patterns of behavior characteristic of childhood psychosis. A few of the children who fall into this category are normal in physical development, relate to other people in normal

An Interview with Dr. Elisabeth H. Wiig

Dr. Elisabeth H. Wiig is an eminent scholar, professor, and clinician. She has authored or coauthored over 50 professional publications, including numerous journal articles, standardized tests, intervention programs, and college textbooks dealing with research and applications in the area of language and language-learning disabilities. A frequent presenter at state and national meetings, Dr. Wiig has been an important participant on many national committees and has served on the editorial boards of several scholarly journals. Among her more recent publications are *Language Assessment and Intervention for the Learning Disabled* (Merrill, 1984), and *TLC: Test of Language Competence* (Psychological Corporation, 1986). This interview was conducted in Boston, Massachusetts on July 15, 1986, by Wayne A. Secord, Coordinator, School Speech-Language Pathology, at The Ohio State University.

Your more recent writings have taken a different perspective toward language assessment and intervention. Could you tell why?

Yes, I can. Language problems in older school-age children, adolescents, and college students are frequently different from those encountered in very young children. We're not doing enough to respond to the changing nature of language deficits in this population, especially in young adults of college age. A number of things are missing—in assessment, and in intervention.

What do you think is missing?

Let me say first that in general we're doing an adequate job in assessing and training linguistic skills and repertories . . . Unfortunately intervention focuses almost exclusively on skills, especially syntactic and vocabulary skills and very little on strategies. We have simply not done an adequate job in assessing strategic language use or in other terms metalinguistics, nor have we begun to teach it.

Before we go on, you've used some terms with regard to language that I would like you to explain. They are: skills, repertories, and strategies.

A *linguistic skill* can be defined as a response given in a unique one-to-one relationship to a stimulus. We see this kind of response when we show a person a picture and say "What is this?" and get the response "A zebra." This is a one-to-one relationship between the label and the referent. A *repertory,* on the other hand, can be defined as a family of related responses given to a set of related stimuli. We see many examples of repertories in the area of morphology.

For example, the phonological conditioning rules can be thought of as repertory. Here is an example. I say to you, "Here is a cat. Here are two ———." If you know your repertory, you should answer, "cats." . . . You have learned the rules for the one-to-one response to a set of related stimuli . . . If I were to say, "Here's a mouse. These are two ———." I would test for a skill.

Because there is only one acceptable response, responses to irregular cases in morphology are skills, whereas phonological conditioning can be thought of as a linguistic repertory.

Now finally to *strategy.* A strategy is a set of available responses from which one response is chosen on the basis of a decision making process. The decision making process is made in stages or in steps. The first step is "What's significant in this situation?" The second step is to hypothesize about the level of significance and to decide which pattern you should react to. After you've made that decision, you might say, "What skills and repertories do I have that I can use in responding to this pattern?" You choose a response or an action set or a way to go and say, "I'll try it to see if it works". You evaluate yourself as you give the chosen response. Finally, if you need to, you revise and reevaluate the situation, and formulate new hypotheses. This is a dynamic decision making process.

There are numerous examples. Consider this, you're having an interview with somebody you never saw before. You size up the situation and you say, "There are three phones on this desk. Must be important. He's wearing Nike's . . . I don't know how to react. Some signals are formal. Some signals are casual, informal. What am I going to do?" So you might step back and say to yourself, "I'm not going to initiate this interaction, because I don't know what the level of formality should be" . . . In interpersonal interactions, people constantly make such decisions. They stand back and watch the situation, evaluate it, and decide on responses more or less automatically.

Many of us are aware that students employ different strategies in learning, but are linguistic or language strategies related to learning strategies?

That's right. Learning strategies and linguistic strategies are related. They are related in that the thinking processes involved may not differ at all. But the *content* against which you have to apply the process does. For example, in response to some linguistic materials you have to perceive alternatives either in meaning or alternatives in ways of responding. If I said to you, "He wiped the glasses", you might go through a decision process that said first of all, "I can target the word *glasses*. It has two meanings—eyeglasses or drinking glasses. Therefore what he wiped could be either one or the other." You formulate alternative interpretations and wait to see how the context could help you in resolving the ambiguity. That would be an example of a linguistically based strategy.

Another example comes from figurative language. Take the expression, "She cast a spell over me." In this case, you would target *'cast a spell'* and apply linguistic strategies to it that might say, "It's not meant literally. She's not turning me into a toad"— which, by the way, is what language-learning disabled adolescents often say . . . Then you formulate hypotheses about whether or not they are used literally or figuratively. Next you transform the expression into the figurative domain, in this case affection, and say, "The most likely interpretation is that he is in love with her." Then you utilize contextual and other cues to assist you in deciding on the right interpretation.

How does one utilize language strategies in communication?

Assume you and I interact in discourse. In that case, you could show your communicative competence by predicting what I might be saying next. Let me show you how this works. Pretend I come in from my back yard and say, "I just saw a beautiful butterfly." If you say, "Really?", what would I tell you about? 99% of my audiences have predicted that I would tell about color. A few people say, "Well, you could also talk about design." Yet we have never learned that the word *beautiful,* applied to butterflies, refers to color. We've learned that from experience.

Another area where we see linguistic strategy is in planning for production. One example is reconstructing what somebody could have said. Pretend you're in conversation with somebody, and there's a third person talking to a fourth person at a cocktail party. You're talking to Person 2, but you're really listening to Person 3 and Person 4. You're, of course, not hearing every single word they say. Instead you are reconstructing and making hypotheses about what was said. Every time you listen in, you're actually verifying or rejecting hypotheses formulated on the basis of incomplete information . . .

When do we see the ability to use linguistic strategies emerge?

There seems to be a critical transition period in a child's development. Children who are preoperational, that is, the preschool child, are really not strategists. They do not stand back from the task and make decisions about it. The emerging ability to look at a task strategically occurs in the concrete operational period of development—that period during which children learn ordinal seriation, hierarchical classification, conservation principles, all logical operations. The age range from 6–7, to 11–12 years seems critical for the acquisition of linguistic strategies. Children do not seem to apply strategies before they can de-center from a task, that is, before they can take several attributes of a task into account at one time. Preschool children tend to react to one attribute or aspect of a situation or a message. It is only with the emerging logical growth and linguistic competence that the child can take care of integrating several dimensions or several attributes of situations and messages.

So you're saying, I would imagine, that language deficits in school age children and adolescents involve much more than simply skills and repertories.

Yes. There is evidence that the language learning disabled student does not move to a spontaneous development of linguistic strategies and application of these strategies. They seem to function at the level of skills and repertories. Let me give an example. If I gave two language learning disabled adolescents the sentence, "He wiped the glasses," the student, who wore glasses, might say "He was wiping the eyeglasses." The student without eyeglasses, might say, "He is wiping drinking glasses." A typical pattern in these students is that they can give only one interpretation. They do not perceive the alternatives or formulate alternative hypotheses.

Another example would be from the figurative language. I'll use the expression, "She casts a spell over me." In research, language learning disabled adolescents often say, "Well, she kissed him and he turned into a toad or a prince." They often refer to magic stories.

What impact does this have on the student?

I'd like to give you an illustration of a fifth grader who received language intervention since grade two. When first identified, his vocabulary was deficient. He didn't know a number of morphological rules, and he didn't have adequate sentence structure. In other words, he was deficient at the level of linguistic skills and repertories. In therapy, he was taught vocabulary, so that his vocabulary matched his chronological age and grade level. He was also taught morphological rules for plurals, possessives, and verb tenses until his morphological rules matched age and grade level expectations. He was taught how to form and use different types of sentences so that his syntactic acquisition level matched what was expected for his age and grade. He was then phased out of language intervention and put back into the regular fifth grade classroom. In that classroom, however, he was still an oddball. He did not understand the more subtle aspects of language and communication. For example, when a joke was told in the classroom and he did not catch it. When students were asked to interact with riddles he could not grasp them. Metaphoric and other figurative expressions were used in the classroom and in texts and he couldn't interpret them. He could not understand sarcasms. This student was, in a way, "out to lunch" in the classroom. His interpersonal communication skills were grossly inadequate. This student had not acquired some of the higher level linguistic repertories, and he could not interact strategically with spoken or written language. He was not a communicatively competent speaker or language user. Yet this communicative-linguistic inadequacy existed in the presence of scores on traditional language tests which showed no discrepancy between his chronological age and his language age and he was excluded from language intervention.

SOURCE: *The Directive Teacher,* 1986, *8*(1), pp. 10–11. © 1986 The Ohio State University.

ways except for lack of language, and are alert to visual stimuli. These children seem to have a problem in processing or making sense of auditory stimuli. The reason for their disability is not clear, but the suspicion is that they have suffered neurological damage.

Children who have little or no useful language by the time they are 3 years old are usually considered to be severely mentally retarded or severely emotionally disturbed (unless it is found that they are deaf). The absence of useful language is a major handicap. So teaching these children to speak is one of the first goals in their education. Without functional language, they cannot become truly social beings (Lane, 1976). Because nonverbal children are typically found in institutions or in special classes for severely retarded or disturbed students, teachers of these children must have a working knowledge of how speech and language skills can be taught. The task is not one that can be made the sole responsibility of the speech-language pathologist.

The earliest contemporary systematic efforts to teach language to nonverbal children consisted of the use of operant conditioning methods. That is, a step-by-step sequence of behaviors approximating functional language was established, and the child's responses at each step in the sequence were rewarded. The rewards typically consisted of praise, hugs, and food given by the teacher immediately following the child's performance of the desired behavior. At the earliest step in the sequence the child might be reinforced for establishing eye contact with the teacher. The next step might be making any vocalization while looking at the teacher; next making a vocalization approximating a sound made by the teacher; then imitating words spoken by the teacher; and finally replying to the teacher's questions. Of course, this description is a simplification of the procedures that were employed, but through such methods nonverbal children were taught basic oral language skills (see Devany, Rincover, and Lovaas, 1981; Koegel, Rincover, and Egel, 1982).

A major problem of early research on these methods was that few of the children acquired truly functional language, even after intensive and prolonged training. Their speech tended to have a stereotyped, mechanical quality and often was used for a restricted range of purposes. A current trend in language training for nonverbal children is to try to make their language *functional*. The goal is to give the child a tool for communication—a means of influencing and interacting with the environment. Instead of training the child to imitate words in isolation or to use syntactically and grammatically correct forms, we might train him or her to use a language structure to obtain a desired result. For example, the child might be taught to say "I want juice" (or a simplified form: "juice" or "want juice") in order to get a drink of juice. The goal is to train the child to use language in a functional way in social contexts—to train *communicative competence* (Goetz, Schuler, and Sailor, 1981; McCormick and Schiefelbusch, 1984; Schiefelbusch and McCormick, 1981).

The first consideration in such training is the arrangement of an environment that will give the child many opportunities to use language and that will provide immediate reinforcement for steps toward communication. Naturally this requires that parents and teachers work closely with a communication specialist. A second consideration in training is how to combine structure, content, and function— what is said and what is talked about or intended. Training in the structure of language is of little value without training in how to use language for communication. But the uses of language cannot be taught successfully without attention to its structure.

Qualitatively Different Language

Some children can make speech sounds with no difficulty and acquire an extensive oral vocabulary. The way they use words, however, is very different from normal speech. These language-impaired children do not use speech effectively in communication. We will give a few examples of qualitative differences in language that impair its value for communication.

Some children are echolalic (they repeat, parrotlike, what they've heard). An attempted conversation with an echolalic child might go like this:

Adult:	Are you Johnny?
Child:	Johnny?
Adult:	Yes.
Child:	Yes.
Adult:	I'm Jim.
Child:	Jim.
Adult:	Right.
Child:	Right.
Adult:	What's your name?
Child:	Your name?
Adult:	No, *your* name.
Child:	*Your* name.
Adult:	Johnny.
Child:	Johnny.
Adult:	I'm Jim.
Child:	I'm Jim.
Adult:	No, *I'm* Jim.
Child:	*I'm* Jim.
Adult:	. . . Forget it.
Child:	Forget it.

Other children may speak jargon or nonsense words that fail to meet the demands of social situations. Sometimes we find that a child understands what is said to him or her but almost never imitates speech or spontaneously produces it. Or, when asked to imitate a sentence, a child may not be able to convey the meaning of the sentence as most children could. Naremore (1980, p. 156) gives this example: "When asked to repeat the sentence, 'The little boy's dump truck is broken,' a nonhandicapped two-year-old said, 'Dump truck broke,' whereas a language-impaired six-year-old responded with, 'Boy is break.'" The nonhandicapped child did not imitate precisely but chose words that preserved the meaning of the sentence. The language-impaired child, however, could not convey the meaning.

The qualitative differences we have mentioned so far are most frequently associated with severe emotional disturbance or mental retardation. Recently there has been interest in the language disorders of children with learning disabilities (Stark and Wallach, 1980; Wiig, 1986; see also Chapter 3). The research to date has not pinpointed the ways in which the language of learning-disabled children is different from other children's language, but it appears that these children are less capable than nonhandicapped children of making themselves understood (Hallahan and Bryan, 1981; Hallahan, Kauffman, and Lloyd, 1985). They do not seem to comprehend language well or be able to adapt their language usage to the social context so that meaning is communicated. In talking to younger children, for example, they may fail to make their language appropriately simple. They may not understand instructions or the meaning of another person's statements. They may say things in social situations that most children would know are inappropriate. Finally, they may fail to understand or produce written language, even though their oral language skills are adequate (see Butler, 1986a; Tarver and Ellsworth, 1981).

Language is always embedded in a social context. Its meanings and nuances can easily be lost by the producer or interpreter so that no communication takes place. Qualitative differences in language can seriously distort or obscure meaning or pragmatic value. These differences often occur in the language abilities of children whose social behavior and academic achievement are impaired. In fact, language disabilities appear to be closely connected with learning disabilities of all types. The implications of qualitative differences in language for remediation strategies are not presently clear. However, it is likely that an emphasis on the *functions* of language and *strategies* for comprehension and production will be most helpful in this area (Fey, 1986: Hubbell, 1981).

Delayed Language

A child may progress through the stages of language development with one principal exception: He or she does so at a significantly later age than most children. Many of the children whose language development is delayed show a pervasive developmental lag. Frequently they are diagnosed as mentally retarded or "developmentally disabled." Sometimes they come from environments where they have been deprived of many experiences, including language stimulation from adults, required for normal development.

It may be difficult in some cases to tell the difference between delayed and qualitatively different language. This is true because not much is known about the normal development of language and because qualitative differences may be very subtle. In general, we would expect that a child with delayed language will learn language in the same way most children do, and that his or her level of language learning will approximate his or her level of general intellectual ability.

Language learning may be delayed for a variety of reasons. This child's learning of oral language is delayed because of her hearing impairment. A special teaching program is necessary to help her learn to produce the sounds of oral language. (Irene Bayer/Monkmeyer Press)

Interrupted Language Development

Children can *acquire* a language disorder after a period of normal development if their hearing or brain functioning is seriously damaged. Deprivation of oxygen, accident, or infection, for example, can result in damage to the mechanisms of hearing or the brain (see Chapters 6 and 8). The specific effects of acquired hearing loss or brain injury depend not only on the nature and extent of the loss or injury, but also on the age of the child when the loss or injury occurs. A child deafened before he or she learns oral language will not learn language as easily as one who has learned language before the deafness was acquired; and the more language experience a child has acquired before being deafened, the better his or her communication skills are likely to be. On the other hand, damage to the brain generally has more serious consequences when it occurs later in the development of language. The younger child's nervous system is generally more "plastic"—it compensates more easily for loss of or damage to its tissues.

Children whose language development has been interrupted by illness or accident causing damage to the brain are sometimes said to have **acquired aphasia** (Leonard, 1986). The terms *severely language impaired* and *severe language disability* are also used to designate the disabilities of children who have extreme difficulties in acquiring or using language, especially when the disabilities are known or thought to be the result of brain damage.

COMMUNICATION SYSTEMS
FOR SEVERELY HANDICAPPED INDIVIDUALS

For some individuals, oral language is out of the question; they are too severely disabled to learn to communicate through speech. Alternative or augmentative communication systems must be designed for them. Those for whom nonspeech communication systems must be devised range in intelligence from gifted to severely retarded, but all of them are unable to communicate effectively through speech because of physical (motor) impairment. Some may be unable to make any speech sounds at all; others need a system to augment their speech when they cannot make themselves understood because of environmental noise, difficulty in producing certain words or sounds, or unfamiliarity with the person they are trying to communicate with.

In some cases manual communication used by hearing impaired persons (e.g., signing—see Chapter 6) may be useful. But many individuals with severe physical limitations are unable to use their hands to communicate through gestures or signs; they must use another means of communication, usually involving special equipment. The problem to be solved in helping these individuals communicate is how to give them an effective, efficient means of indicating elements in their vocabularies. This problem may be solved in a variety of ways, some of which involve relatively simple or "low-technology" solutions and some of which require complex or "high-technology" solutions (Vanderheiden, 1984).

There are many different ways to provide an individual with a means to indicate the elements of his message, all of which are elaborations on combinations of two fundamental approaches: *direct selection* and *scanning*. With direct selection, the individual points directly to his selection in some fashion. With scanning, someone or something points to the items for the individual one item at a time. When the item the individual desires is

Alternative or augmentative communication systems must be designed for individuals whose motor disabilities preclude their use of oral language.
(Jonathan Fisher/Jeroboam, Inc.)

indicated, he or she gives some type of signal. The game "Twenty Questions" is an example of the scanning approach. Another example is a rotating arrow that the individual could stop. A person pointing to items one at a time until signaled by the handicapped individual would be another example of scanning. (Vanderheiden, 1984, p. 41)

An extremely wide variety of direct-selection and scanning methods have been devised for alternative communication systems, depending on the capabilities of the individual. The system used may involve indication by pointing with the hand or a headstick (see Chapter 8, Figure 8.9), eye movements, or operation of a microswitch by foot, tongue, head movement, or breath control. Sometimes the individual can use a typewriter or computer terminal if it is fitted with a key guard so that keys are not likely to be pressed accidentally or if an alternative means is devised for selecting key strokes. Often communication boards are used. A communication board is an array of pictures, words, or other symbols that can be used with either a direct-selection or scanning strategy. The content and arrangement of the board will vary, depending on the capabilities of the handicapped person. An example of a communication board is shown in Figure 5.4.

Speed, reliability, portability, cost, and overall effectiveness in helping a person communicate independently are factors to be considered in designing and evaluating an alternative communication system (Calculator and Luchko, 1983; Fairweather, Haun, and Finkle, 1983; Musselwhite and St. Louis, 1982; Vanderheiden, 1984). A communication board will not necessarily be useful just because it is available. And the most sophisticated technological solution to communication is not always the one that will be most useful in the long run. Today increasingly innovative and creative technological solutions to the problem of nonvocal communication for the severely handicapped are being found. At the same time, the importance of making decisions on a highly individual basis in selecting the mode of indicating and the code for expressing meaning is being recognized (McCormick and Schiefelbusch, 1984; Owens and House, 1984).

PREVALENCE

No trustworthy estimates of the prevalence of language disorders in children and youths are available. Estimating prevalence is extremely difficult because the procedures for definition and assessment still lack precision. Moreover, language disorders

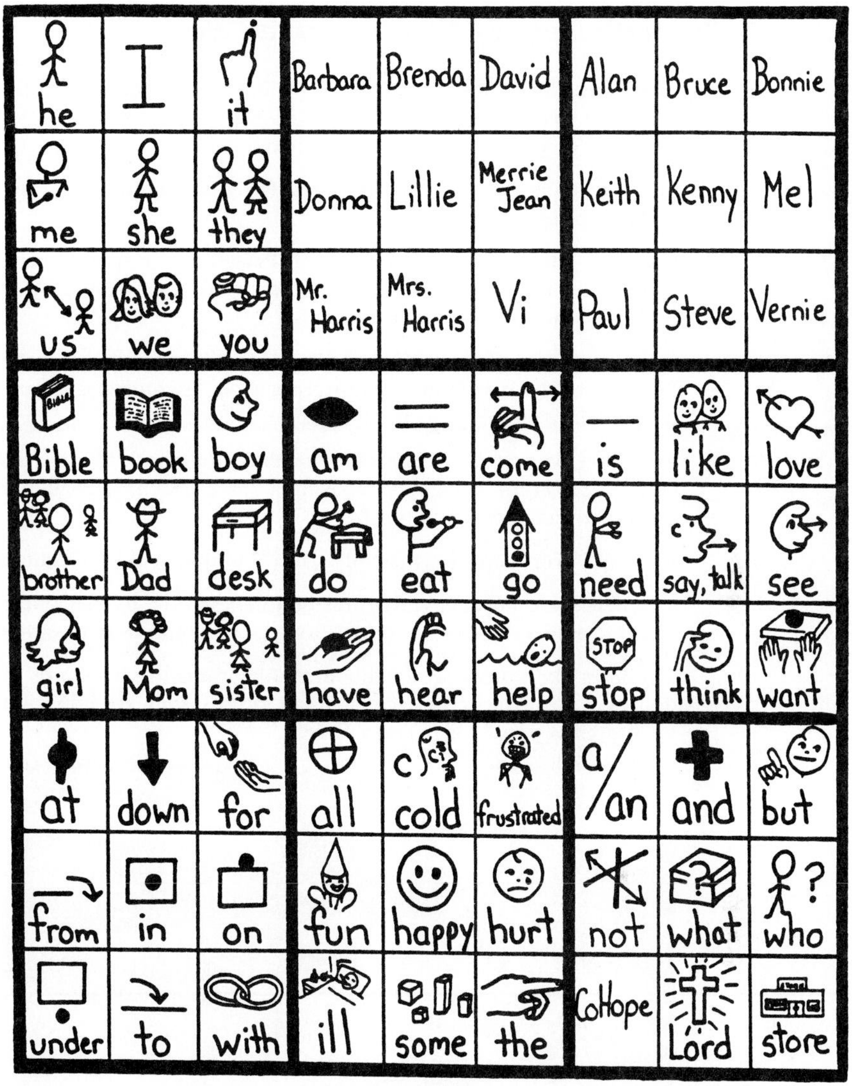

This "9-in-9" system has been used extensively by four of our students. The student must be able to indicate nine (9) numbers, using various identification systems such as those discussed in Section II. The student first identifies the number of the primary cell which contains the desired word. A second number is then given, which identifies the specific word within the primary cell. (eg. - 1,2 is the word "I," 6,3 is the word "love," 1,9 is "you"). It is helpful if the listener verbally confirms the indicated numbers.

Figure 5.4 *An example of a communication board utilizing encoding.*
SOURCE: B. C. Fairweather, D. H. Haun, and L. J. Fikle, *Communication Systems for Severely Handicapped Persons* (Springfield, Ill.: Charles C Thomas, 1983), p. 22. Reprinted with permission.

typically occur in combination with other handicapping conditions, such as hearing impairment, learning disability, cerebral palsy, emotional disturbance, and mental retardation. If this overlap is considered and if language is defined to include speaking, listening, reading, and writing, then probably 5 to 10 percent of the child population could be considered to have a language disorder.

Youth 'Talks' with Help of Computerized Box

Charlottesville—Tracy Fewell, 14, a beaming teen-ager with a big smile, has big plans. He wants to be a race car driver. He wants to make millions. He wants to win the heart of a certain girl in the sixth grade.

But just saying hello to that girl was a fairly insurmountable task. Tracy has spastic cerebral palsy. . . .

Last year, a local Kiwanis club bought Fewell a new voice box. It is literally a box that sits upon a personal computer in a classroom at Henley Middle School, in the Blue Ridge foothills near Crozet.

Soon after receiving the gift, Fewell gave his first oral book report to classmates. Before long, he was churning out reports on Alabama and about the ponies on Assateague Island.

And there was more. The machine enabled the youth to ask questions in class. He could type on the keyboard choosing a voice "pitch," and then speak by switching on the Votrax speech synthesizer.

He could even make new friends. They'd understand him right away.

Teachers were impressed that this child knew how to spell, after all; and that he could proofread his own work, as long as he could hear it, rather than read it.

Machines like Votrax are readily available at electronics stores for several hundred dollars. Easily attached to personal computers, they are improving the quality of life for scores of people like Tracy Fewell.

Paula Cochran, speech-language pathologist at the University of Virginia, said:

"These people have intact intellectual functioning. They just haven't found a way to express themselves. But by using synthetic speech, we've found people we never thought were such a wit—so humorous."

For his part, Fewell is becoming more talkative all the time, said University of Virginia Professor Glen Bull, who programmed his "voice."

"It's made such a difference in his life," added Fewell's teacher, Kendall Young. "Now I just wish we could get him one of these at home."

And yet, for all the voice synthesizer's advantages, when it comes to the handicapped, it is not without glitches or imperfections. Computer scientists and speech pathologists are trying to devise ways to make using the computerized voice as easy as it is, normally, to use the human voice.

Unfortunately, the disabled still must type what they wish to say, which is slow. Speeding the process, say, by pointing at positions on a screen, would be impossible with most personal computers, because they have too limited a memory.

Worse still, speech synthesizers don't sound very natural. The monotone makes them sound like robots and the syntax is often wrong.

By far the worst dilemma, however, is not technological, say advocates for the handicapped. Society, complained Ms. Cochran, puts more emphasis on commercial applications than making the technology available to those who really need it.

SOURCE: *Richard Times Dispatch,* November 18, 1984. Photo by Keith Epstein. Reprinted with permission.

STRATEGIES FOR ASSESSMENT AND INTERVENTION

We have already mentioned some of the considerations for assessing and correcting various types of language disorders. Here we provide a thumbnail sketch of the general features of language assessment and intervention. Only a brief sketch is possible here because the assessment, classification, and treatment of language disorders are complex and changing rapidly. Several alternative theoretical approaches to language assessment and intervention can be found in the current professional literature of speech-language pathology (see, for example, Arwood, 1983; Fey, 1986; Lund and Duchan, 1983; Wallach and Butler, 1984). Although much research is under way, relatively little is understood about the disorders of this most complex of all human activities.

Two general strategies of language assessment are to determine in as much detail as possible what the child's current language abilities are and to observe the ease and speed with which the child learns new language skills. The first strategy typically involves standardized testing, nonstandardized testing, use of developmental scales, and behavioral observations. Standardized testing has many dangers and is not always useful in planning an intervention program. But it can sometimes be helpful in making crude comparisons of the child's abilities in certain areas (Fey, 1986; Miller and Prutting, 1979; Schiefelbusch and McCormick, 1981). Developmental scales are ratings of observations that may be completed by direct observation, or based on memory or records of developmental milestones. Nonstandardized tests and behavioral observations are non-normative in nature, but they may yield the most important assessment information. As Schiefelbusch and McCormick (1981) point out, the subjective judgment of an experienced clinician based on observation of the child's language in a variety of environments and circumstances may provide the most useful basis for intervention. Because language disorders vary widely in nature and are seen from early childhood through old age, assessment and intervention are never simple and are always idiosyncratic.

An intervention plan must take into consideration the content, form, and use of language (Fey, 1986; Schiefelbusch and McCormick, 1981). That is, one must consider: (1) what the child talks about and should be taught to talk about; (2) how the child talks about things and how he or she could be taught to speak of those things more intelligibly; and (3) how the child uses language and how his or her use of it could be made to serve the purposes of communication and socialization more effectively. In arranging a training sequence, one might base instruction on the normal sequence of language development. Other sequences of instruction might be more effective, however, since language-disordered children obviously have not learned in the normal way and since research is beginning to indicate that different sequences of learning may be more effective (Devany, Rincover, and Lovaas, 1981). And it is more and more apparent that effective language intervention must occur in the child's natural environment and involve parents and classroom teachers, not just the speech-language pathologist (Spradlin and Siegel, 1982).

PSYCHOLOGICAL AND BEHAVIORAL CHARACTERISTICS

Taken as a group, speech- and language-handicapped children appear to be generally inferior to nonhandicapped children on measures of intelligence, achievement, and adaptive social behavior. But this is so primarily because of the large percentage of retarded, disturbed, physically disabled, and learning-disabled children who have speech and language disorders. Not counting those who have serious handicaps in addition to defective speech and language, we are left with a group about which we can make few valid generalizations. One thing that can be said, however, is that in our society people with speech disorders sometimes pay a heavy price in terms of rejection, exclusion, attack, overprotection, condescension, and so on—and these penalties are sufficient to evoke frustration, anxiety, guilt, and hostility in the speaker (Van Riper, 1978).

Although having a speech or language disorder can be extremely traumatic, it is possible for the psychological damage, under the right conditions, to be very slight. A child's life will not necessarily be miserable nor will he or she become maladjusted just because of a speech or language problem. We should point out here that a few generalizations can be made about several particular groups of children with speech and/or language handicaps. First, children with markedly deviant or delayed speech and language are almost always severely retarded, severely disturbed, or have severely impaired hearing and are thus functioning at a very early developmental level. Second, although research has indicated that children with cleft palates tend to be underachieving and to show more personality problems, such as shyness, inhibition, and social withdrawal, than nonhandicapped children do (Richman, 1976), there is not much evidence that children with clefts are psychologically or emotionally maladjusted or that there is anything like a "cleft-palate personality" (Ewanowski and Saxman, 1980). Third, severe stutterers often show a lot of anxiety and tend to have a low opinion of themselves (Travis, 1971; Van Riper, 1971, 1978). Finally, language problems may underlie nearly all severe problems in academic learning and may tend to persist from early childhood through adolescence (Aram, Ekelman, and Nation, 1984; Lee and Shapero-Fine, 1984).

EDUCATIONAL CONSIDERATIONS

Helping children overcome speech and language disorders is not the responsibility of any single profession. Identification is the joint responsibility of the classroom teacher, the speech-language pathologist, and the parents. The teacher can carry out specific suggestions for individual cases. By listening attentively and empathetically when children speak, providing appropriate models of speech and language for children to imitate, and encouraging children to use their communication skills appropriately, the classroom teacher can help not only to improve speech and language, but also to prevent disorders from developing in the first place.

Role of the Teacher in Language Use (Pragmatics)

The primary role of the special education teacher is to facilitate the *social use of language*. Phonology, morphology, syntax, and semantics are certainly important. Yet the fact that a student has a language disorder does not necessarily mean that the teacher or clinician must intensify efforts to teach the student about the form, structure, or content of language:

> Rather, the aim is to foster the *use* of language by the child, in both comprehension and expression. The use of language involves active problem solving. Children have to decide what the utterances they hear mean; in addition, they have to decide what to say themselves, and how to say it. (Hubbell, 1981, p. 197)

This use of language is fostered in human relationships in which the ability to communicate is important. The circumstances under which children learn to use language effectively must include at least three elements:

> First, children must have opportunities to use and hear language. . . . Second, they must participate in communicative situations that provide sufficient input and feedback. . . . Third, they must have the ability and opportunity to participate in human relationships in what might be called a constructive manner. (Hubbell, 1981, p. 266)

The classroom offers many possibilities for language learning. It should be a place in which there are almost continuous opportunities for students and teachers to employ language and obtain feedback in constructive relationships. Language is the basic medium through which most academic and social learning takes place in school (see Nelson, 1984; Silliman, 1984, 1986). Nevertheless, the language of schools, including that found in classrooms and textbooks, is often a problem for both students and teachers (Butler, 1986b).

School language is more formal than the language many children use at home and with playmates. It is structured discourse in which listeners and speakers or readers and writers must learn to be clear and expressive, to convey and interpret essential information quickly and easily. Without skill in using the language of school, a child is certain to fail academically and virtually certain to be socially unsuccessful as well.

The box on pp. 244–245 illustrates four of the many types of language problems special education teachers might encounter. Helping students like those described here learn to use language as a tool for academic learning and social relations is particularly difficult, because their language disorders seem to reflect basic problems in cognition. Their language appears to be related to basic problems in understanding or thinking. Teachers must use their own cognitive and language skills to devise ways to help such children learn more effective use of language.

Teachers need the assistance of speech-language specialists in assessing their students' language disabilities and in devising interventions. Part of the assessment and intervention strategy, however, must examine the language of the teacher.

The Language of School: How Children Can Fail

1. *Student, age 17:1, in a transitional classroom; resource room and speech therapy provided.*

EXAMINER: How would you change a tire?
STUDENT: . . . Well . . . um . . . I change a wheel Saturday night coz when I went outside, the wheel was flat. An' me an' my frien', we hadda change it.
EXAMINER: Can you tell me exactly what you did?
STUDENT: Well . . . um . . . first my frien', he got the . . . um . . . thing that you use . . . un the thing for puttin' under the um . . . *(20 second pause)* . . .
EXAMINER: *(Prompting)* Jack?
STUDENT: Yeah, that's it. I knowed what it was but I just couldn't think of it.

2. *Student, age 4:3, in an early childhood program, enrolled at age 2:6 in speech therapy.*

EXAMINER: What is a bicycle?
STUDENT: Ride it.
EXAMINER: What's a chair?
STUDENT: I donno.
EXAMINER: What's a stove?
STUDENT: I have to go potty. It's a cooking.

3. *Student, age 10:7, in a self-contained special education class, enrolled following a sledding accident and temporal-parietal damage of the brain; speech therapy, occupational therapy, physical therapy.*

EXAMINER: Say these sentences after me: The girl likes walking by herself.
STUDENT: Girl walk herself.
EXAMINER: Mommy is playing because it is fun.
STUDENT: Mommy play.
EXAMINER: *(Shows picture of fireman putting out a fire)* What is the fireman doing?
STUDENT: Fire . . . fireplace . . . hose . . . puttin' on hose . . . drink'n beer.

4. *Student, age 7:11, in a pre-first grade special classroom, English is the child's second language.*

EXAMINER: Tell me a story . . . anything you like . . . take your time.
STUDENT: Richard's goin' on the hill. And he's goin' to jump on the snow with his friend, C. P. And he do somethin' with him and Richard. They have fun with the snow and they make a big hill with lots of snow so they won't get kill. We have to go under the snow. Richard me and Charlie. Mens doesn't get us. They got a gun on their hand so they won't shoot us cause we go under there, under the snow. 'Cause they won't know where we are. *(The narrative continues but with diverse elements embedded.)* Then Richard and me and Charlie went and get my new sneakers . . . and I don't have tie them 'cause they got blue on the bottom with three things. *(Topic returns to playing in the snow, followed by a series of new topics, including walking the dog, skiing, going to McDonald's, and the presence of "company.")* . . . We ate dinner for 'sert. And it's jello. And we dinner for 'sert 'cause we have to stay outside so we won't get bother them. . . . We go under the snow . . . Than means we won't get hurt and we, we, we won't get kill.

It can be easily seen that each of the four student's attempts to respond to the examiner epitomizes the inability of the language disordered individual to be clear and expressive. It is also clear that language does not come either quickly or easily. The impact of their language difficulties is further exemplified when one considers their current or future problems:

- Student 1, already the father of two children, has been unable to benefit thus far from the vocational training or to find work. Past employers have complained that he cannot follow directions.
- Student 2, born at risk and developmentally delayed, exhibits semantic and processing difficulties. Fortunately, early language intervention may ameliorate some of those difficulties.
- Student 3 is 18 months post-trauma. In those months, speech and language have returned, although the structure of the language remains telegraphic in nature. It is not possible at this point to predict the degree of recovery from aphasia, but it is likely that there will be some residual deficits.
- Student 4 has been retained twice in school. His language problems, noted on school entry, appear to be above and beyond that which might be anticipated from a bilingual child. He has had little or no success in mastering the decoding skills required for reading

It is clear that children such as these will have difficulty in processing the language of instruction. Their failure to do so indicates that they have not yet been able to employ the cognitive or linguistic strategies necessary for success in school.

SOURCE: K. G. Butler, "Language Research and Practice: A Major Contribution to Special Education," in R. J. Morris and B. Blatt (Eds.), *Special Education: Research and Trends* (New York: Pergamon, 1986), pp. 284–285. © 1986 Pergamon Books Ltd. Reprinted with permission.

Problems in classroom discourse involve how teachers talk to students, as well as how students use language. Learning how to be clear, relevant, and informative and how to hold listeners' attention is not only a problem for students with language disorders—it's also a problem for their teachers.

One example of the role of the teacher's language in classroom discourse is in asking questions. Blank and White (1986) note that teachers often ask students questions in areas of their identified weakness. For example, a teacher might ask a preschooler who does not know colors to identify colors repeatedly. Unfortunately, teachers may not know how to modify their questions to teach a concept effectively, so their questions merely add to the child's confusion.

The following exchange between a teacher and a child diagnosed as having difficulties with problem solving and causal reasoning illustrates this point.

Teacher: How could grass in a jungle get on fire?
Child: 'Cause they *(referring to animals)* have to stay in the jungle.
Teacher: *(in an incredulous tone)* You mean the grass gets on fire because the animals stay in the jungle?
Child: Yeah.
Teacher: I don't think so. What if there was a fire in somebody's house—
Child: *(interrupting)* Then they're dead, or hurt.
Teacher: Yeah, they'd be hurt. But how would a fire start in somebody's house?
Child: By starting something with matches.
Teacher: A match, okay. Now do you think this fire could have started with a match?

Child: Yeah.
Teacher: This fire in the jungle? Who would have a match in the jungle? The animals?
Child: A monkey.
Teacher: A monkey would have a match in the jungle?
Child: (*nodding*) I saw that on TV . . . .

After seventeen more exchanges, the teacher gave up (Blank and White, 1986, p. 4).

Alternative question-asking strategies can be used to help students think through problems successfully. When students fail to answer a higher-order question because it is beyond their level of information or skill, the teacher should reformulate the problem at a simpler level. After the intermediate steps are solved, the teacher can return to the question that was too difficult at first, as illustrated by the following dialogue:

Adult: Why do we use tape for hanging pictures?
Child: 'Cause it's shiny.
Adult: *Here's a shiny piece of paper and here's a shiny piece of tape. Let's try them both. Try hanging the picture with the shiny paper.*
Child: (*does it*)
Adult: Does it work?
Child: No, it's falling.
Adult: Now, try the tape.
Child: (*does it*)
Adult: Does it work?
Child: Yeah, it's not falling.
Adult: So, why do we use the tape for hanging pictures?
Child: It won't fall. (Blank and White, 1986, p. 5)

Teachers sometimes do not clearly express their intent in questioning students or fail explicitly to delimit the topic of their questions. Consequently, students become confused. Teachers must learn to clarify the problem under such circumstances. As Blank and White (1986) have noted: "Teachers do not establish psychological comfort and eagerness to learn by making students spend as much, if not more, energy deciphering the intent than the content of their questions" (p. 8).

Teachers must also give unambiguous feedback to students' responses to their questions. Too often, teachers do not tell students explicitly that their answers are wrong, for fear of showing nonacceptance. Lack of accurate, explicit feedback, however, prevents students from learning the concepts involved in instruction.

Our points here are these: First, the teacher's role is not merely to instruct students *about* language, but to teach them *how to use it.* More specifically, the teacher must help students learn *how to use language in the context of the classroom.* Second, the teacher's own use of language is a key factor in helping students learn effectively, especially if students have language disorders.

SPECIAL CONSIDERATIONS IN EDUCATING THE PRESCHOOL CHILD

Preschoolers who require intervention for a speech or language disorder are typically multiply handicapped, often severely or profoundly so. Language is closely tied to cognitive development, so impairment of general intellectual ability is likely to have a retarding influence on language development. Because speech is dependent on neurological and motor development, any neurological or motor problem might impair ability to speak. Normal social development in the preschool years is dependent on the emergence of language, so a language-impaired child is at a disadvantage in social learning. Therefore it is seldom that the preschool child's language is the only target of intervention (see Allen, Holm, and Schiefelbusch, 1978; Fey, 1986).

The goals of early language intervention will be guided to some extent by what is known today about normal language development (McCormick and Schiefelbusch, 1984). The specific teaching goals and techniques employed will depend on the individual case: age, physical characteristics, and current language repertoire of the child, for example. Initial goals will be chosen on the basis of the child's knowledge of objects and relations. Specifically, one needs to know the extent of the child's knowledge about:

- Objects and object classes
- Relations between objects of the same and different classes
- Relations between an object or event and the speaker
- Relations between events

Intervention is likely to be based on assessment of the child's behavior related to the content, form, and especially the use of language in social interaction. For the child who has not yet learned language, assessment and intervention will focus on imitation, ritualized and make-believe play, play with objects, and functional use of objects. At the earliest stages in which the content and form of language are interactive, it is important to evaluate the extent to which the child looks at or picks up an object when it is referred to, does something with an object when directed by an adult, and uses sounds to request or refuse things and call attention to objects. When the child's use of language is considered, the earliest objectives involve the child's looking at the adult during interactions, taking turns in and trying to prolong pleasurable activities and games, following the gaze of an adult and directing the behavior of adults, and persisting in or modifying gestures, sounds, or words when an adult does not respond.

Much of the language intervention activity for preschoolers will involve playing the part of the good parent. This means a lot of simple play with accompanying verbalizations. It means talking to the child about objects and activities in the way most mothers talk to their babies. But it also means choosing objects, activities, words, and consequences for the child's vocalizations with great care so that the chances that the child will learn functional language are enhanced (Goldstein and Wetherby, 1984; McMorrow, Foxx, Faw, and Bittle, 1986).

SPECIAL CONSIDERATIONS IN EDUCATING THE ADOLESCENT AND ADULT

In the past, adolescents and adults who were the targets of speech and language intervention programs generally fell into three categories: the self-referred, those with other health problems, and the severely handicapped. Adolescents or adults may refer themselves to a speech-language pathologist because their phonology, voice, or stuttering is causing them social embarrassment and/or interfering with occupational pursuits. These are generally persons with problems of long standing who are highly motivated to change their speech and obtain relief from the social penalties their differences impose.

ONE PROFESSIONAL'S PERSPECTIVE

Joye L. McLeod

B.A., Psychology, University of Nebraska at Omaha
M.S., Speech Pathology, University of Nebraska at Omaha
Current Position: Speech-language pathologist serving two elementary schools in the Papillion-LaVista Public Schools, Nebraska

Ms. Joye McLeod has been in her current position for 12 years. For three years after earning her B.A. degree, she was a psychometrist in a psychiatrist's office. Since completing her master's degree, she has had a part-time private practice, held summer positions in other school districts, worked with an outreach diagnostic team for a local rehabilitation institute, and been appointed as an adjunct instructor at the University of Nebraska. Her caseload as a speech-language pathologist includes children ages 4 to 14. She serves 2 to 3 times more boys than girls. The children range in intelligence from moderately retarded to gifted. Many of the children are learning disabled, some are acoustically handicapped, some are physically disabled, and a few are visually impaired. Many are also receiving other special services. Both of the elementary schools she serves draw primarily from suburban areas in which families are highly mobile due to their association with a major military base. Some of the children she serves have lived in many different places in the United States and foreign countries. Her caseload is predominantly Caucasian.

Ms. McLeod's typical workday begins at 7:10 A.M. and ends between 4:15 and 5:45 P.M. One

day of the week does not conform to the previous description. On that day, Ms. McLeod has large blocks of time for new evaluations, and she schedules children for therapy whom she sees less frequently (weekly, monthly, quarterly, etc.). She also uses this time for in-depth planning, for IEP preparation, for parent conferences, for development of materials, and for the bulk of the mundane paperwork her job requires.

We asked Ms. McLeod the following questions:

Why did you choose to become a speech-language pathologist? I became interested in speech pathology when I was in high school. I don't remember how the interest was first sparked. I do, however, remember visiting a public school speech-language pathologist in a nearby city on my senior "Career Day." The first college I attended on scholarships had no speech pathology program. I chose a major in elementary education. I was not comfortable working with large groups of children. My niche was with one-to-one and small group interactions. I changed schools and changed majors. Psychology had been my minor, so it seemed the logical choice. I earned a degree in psychology and found a job I enjoyed, but I

hadn't found a career. I still carried my old dream of a career in speech pathology, so I applied to graduate school in speech pathology. I loved the demanding, scientific framework of the field and the intellectual challenges of problem solving involved in diagnosis and therapy planning. I was comfortable with the intense interpersonal clinical interaction, and I valued the opportunities to make significant contributions in the lives of others.

If you could choose to change one thing about your job, what would it be? Professional isolation is one problem and caseload size is another. I'll focus on isolation because I believe it affects most public school speech-language pathologists (SLPs). The isolation takes many forms. The SLP is isolated because his or her role is so distinctly different from the general academic mission of the public schools. This leads to a lack of clear understanding of the value of the speech-language pathology program by the higher administration, with a resulting lack of value placed upon it, a lack of commitment to its quality, and a lack of financial support. Even though other special education programs also differ from the regular curriculum, it can readily be seen that their missions still remain primarily academic. It is less easy to see how voice therapy, for example, ties in.

Another aspect of isolation has to do with a lack of opportunity for consultations or cooperative problem solving. Most teachers (with the exception of those in remote, one room schools) are members of a staff of other teachers who share a common background and common problems. The SLP typically has no one in the school building with a common background regarding the problems with which he or she is dealing. There is no readily accessible avenue for getting a "second opinion."

Since, with high caseload demands, time for cooperative work doesn't appear forthcoming (at least not in my position), some considerations for a public school SLP position become apparent. One, a prerequisite, is to have a very independent nature. Another is to maintain involvement in professional organizations. A third is to develop a relationship with another SLP in order to share professional concerns.

What are the most significant changes you've observed in your field since you entered the profession? During the past ten years, the major change in my field has been the evolution in the area of assessment of and intervention for language disordered children. Certainly, language has always been a part of the speech pathology domain; however, our role with language disorders has expanded and our information base has mushroomed. Because of the explosive increase in interest in language and the consequent explosion in research, publications, workshops, and commercial programs related to language, one has to be cautious and critically evaluate what one reads and hears in order to discriminate fads from approaches based upon sound theoretical principles.

Another change has resulted from the passage of PL 94-142. Through the public schools, the SLPs are now serving many more children. The age range served by the public schools has been expanded as has the severity range. Many children are mainstreamed into the public schools who previously would have been seen in more restrictive, often residential, environments. The changes resulting from PL 94-142 are essentially positive. One negative point, however, comes from conflicts in values in our society. There are conflicts between the demands on the public schools to be all things to all

people, to help children develop as total individuals to the best of their potentials, and to minimize the hardships of their environments on the one hand and the inconsistent demands for a return to the basics, for taxation freezes, and for financial cutbacks on the other.

What has been the greatest success experience you've had as a professional? One of my most exciting success stories is about a girl I will call Jennifer. She moved into my district in November of her kindergarten year having had no previous therapy. Jennifer was totally unintelligible, with severe articulation and moderate language disorders. Only one person in her world could understand her, and that was an older brother who "interpreted" for her within her family. Jennifer's parents had been told by a physician just to wait, "She'll outgrow it by the time she's five." They anguished over having followed that recommendation.

Because Jennifer's articulation system was so extensively disordered, I used an approach in which the entire phonological system is taught at the child's level of comprehension. Jennifer was a good learner and her family was very supportive, providing excellent home followthrough on practice assignments. By the end of her kindergarten year, she had mastered an understanding of all phonemes and their production in isolation at age appropriate levels. During the next school year, application of her newly learned phonological system was integrated with syntactic and morphologic language expansion. By the end of her first grade year, Jennifer was a moderately intelligible communicator, more outgoing, and the delight of her family. Her mother once jokingly asked if, now that I had started her talking, I could tell them how to turn her off!

During second grade, intelligibility was very high. Jennifer

continued in therapy, working on /r/, the only remaining articulation error, and on decreasing noun-verb agreement inconsistencies in her expressive language.

Describe the most difficult, challenging, or complicated case with which you've worked. One of my children who had incredibly complicated problems I will call Ann. Ann was in kindergarten and first grade during the time I worked with her. She was a frail child, born with chronic hereditary anemia, a heart disorder, a severe seizure disorder, a cleft palate, and digit webbing. She was from a single-parent family and her mother had a highly demanding career. Ann had had private therapy prior to enrolling in public school. She had unintelligible speech with a severe articulation disorder and extreme hypernasality. I determined that she had velopharyngeal sufficiency so she could begin working on oral air flow for speech. I used a distinctive feature approach for her articulation work. After a few months of slow but steady progress, Ann had a serious episode of recurring seizures for which she was hospitalized. When she returned to school after six weeks, she had not only lost all she had gained that year but she had regressed even further. She had a hemiparesis which involved her palate, tongue, and lips. We started all over again. With depressing regularity, her progress would be wiped out by repeated neurological episodes. After Ann's first grade year she had brain surgery. The physicians had determined that she had only a capillary system feeding the brain, so she underwent an experimental procedure to attempt to construct a sufficient blood flow system. Ann moved away that summer. I understand that she is now in fourth grade and continues in therapy.

Those with other health problems have suffered damage to speech or language capacities as a result of disease or injury. They may have lost part of their speech mechanism through injury or surgical removal. Treatment of these individuals always demands an interdisciplinary effort. In some cases of progressive disease, severe neurological damage, or loss of tissues of the speech mechanism, the outlook for functional speech is not good. However, surgical procedures, medication, and prosthetic devices are making it possible for more people to speak normally.

Severely handicapped individuals may need the services of a speech-language pathologist to help them achieve more intelligible speech. They may also need to be taught an alternative to oral language. One of the major problems in working with severely handicapped adolescents and adults is setting realistic goals for speech and language learning. Teaching simple, functional language such as social greetings, naming objects, and making simple requests may be realistic goals for some severely handicapped adolescents and adults (McMorrow et al., 1986).

Today much more emphasis is being placed on the language disorders of adolescents and young adults who do not fit into any of the categories just described. Many of these individuals were formerly seen as having primarily academic and social problems that were not language-related, but now it is understood that underlying many or most of the school and social difficulties experienced by adolescents and adults are basic disorders of language (see Wiig, 1986, and box, pp. 231–233). These language disorders are a continuation of difficulties experienced earlier in the person's development.

By providing many opportunities for children to speak and listen, the classroom teacher can foster language development. Of primary importance is the child's understanding and mastery of the social uses of language. (Michal Heron/Woodfin Camp & Associates)

There is strong evidence now . . . that many young language impaired children will continue to encounter difficulties in acquiring more advanced language skills in later years and that these problems will be manifested in both social and academic realms. Thus children's understanding of figurative language affects both their ability to use slang correctly with peers and their ability to recognize metaphors that appear in language arts or English literature texts. (Stephens, 1985, p. v)

Some adolescents and adults with language disorders are excellent candidates for *strategy training* that teaches them how to select, store, retrieve, and process information (see Hallahan et al., 1985, and Chapter 3). Others, however, do not have the required reading skills, symbolic abilities, or intelligence to benefit from the usual training in cognitive strategies.

Whatever techniques are chosen for use with adolescents and older students, the teacher or speech-language pathologist should be mindful of the principles that apply to intervention with these individuals. Larson and McKinley (1985) note the importance of understanding the theoretical basis of intervention and summarize several additional principles as follows:

Clinicians must treat their adolescent clients like the maturing adults they are, engaging them as full partners committed to the intervention enterprise. Clinicians should recognize that many adolescents will need and will benefit from counseling regarding the impact of their language disorders on academic progress, personal and social growth, and the achievement of vocational goals. Finally, adolescents seem to function best in natural group settings, in which peers talk to peers and learn from each other. (p. 77)

MANAGING THE CHILD IN SCHOOL

We have already suggested several ways in which the classroom teacher should assist the speech-language pathologist in identifying, correcting, and preventing speech and language disorders. One of the most important aspects of the teacher's role is making it enjoyable and useful for children to talk and listen. There are at least three basic ways in which talking and listening can be made fun:

1. The teacher can provide enjoyable activities for children to talk about (see Berry, 1980; Lindfors, 1980; McCormick and Schiefelbusch, 1984; Rousey, 1984; and Wood, 1976, for many specific suggestions).
2. Talking appropriately can be made to "pay off" for the child if social rewards (and, in some cases, material rewards) are provided for desirable speech and language.
3. The teacher can be a receptive audience for what the child has to say by establishing eye contact with the child when he or she speaks and responding appropriately to the affective and cognitive content of the child's speech.

For the disfluent or stuttering child it is important that the teacher be patient, listen attentively, let the child finish what he or she has to say (not say things for the child), and avoid any form of ridicule. We are *not* saying that the teacher should avoid talking to these children about their difficulty; ignoring or denying the problem provides no basis for change. It is important for the teacher to let these children know that he or she recognizes their difficulty and to avoid becoming anxious or tense when they speak.

In order to learn to use correct articulation and voice, children need to attend carefully to other people's speech and to the sounds of words. Some children have not had guided practice in listening to other people's speech and identifying its characteristics. The teacher can plan activities in which children identify well-known personalities by voice alone and then describe the distinguishing features of that voice. Children can be helped to isolate certain speech sounds and then practice making these sounds.

Children can do relatively little to improve their speech if they do not listen to themselves talk. Ultimately, children must learn to monitor their own voices when they are speaking. Some children have never been encouraged to listen to themselves and so need experiences that will help them recognize their articulation, voice, and speech-flow characteristics. They often can be taught to listen to each other and to themselves very effectively with the aid of a tape recorder. The speech-language pathologist will be able to provide specific suggestions about taping children's speech. Once the child recognizes the difference between his or her own speech and that of a desirable model and can correct speech productions, the teacher should find ways to let the child practice these new skills.

In making a referral to a speech-language pathologist, teachers are most effective if they can describe the relevant features of the child's speech and language precisely. The following questions should be kept in mind as the child is observed:

1. How much does the child talk? Is he or she comfortable talking only to the teacher, to one other child, to a small informal group of classmates?
2. How do other children react to the child's speech? Is the child ignored, ridiculed, or mimicked? Do other children understand the meaning and intentions of the child's language?
3. How well does the child listen to others? Is it necessary to repeat things for the child? Under what conditions, if any, does he or she seem to hear or understand? Does he or she seem to understand what is being said as well as other children?
4. How intelligible is the child's speech? Does he or she make more phonological errors than most children of the same age? Is it possible to identify the sounds that are consistently misarticulated?
5. How fast does the child talk? Does he or she exhibit peculiar speech rhythms or make any repetitions, prolongations, or pauses when speaking?
6. How well modulated is the child's voice? Does it have a peculiar or unpleasant quality? (Remember that a chronically hoarse voice may be indicative of a health-related problem.) Are the pitch and loudness of the child's voice appropriate for age, sex, and circumstances? Does the child use appropriate emphasis and intonation?
7. How well can the child express himself or herself? Does he or she have an age-appropriate vocabulary? Does the child use proper grammar, syntax, and inflections? Can he or she tell a story or give directions in sequence? Does the child make sense when he or she talks?
8. Is the child's language appropriate for its context? Does the child understand the social uses of language?
9. Does the child have difficulty with written language, oral language, or both?

Because the majority of children with speech and language problems are in regular classrooms, the teacher has an important responsibility in helping them achieve effective communication skills.

SUMMARY

Communication requires sending and receiving meaningful messages. *Language* is the communication of ideas through an arbitrary system of symbols that are used according to certain rules. *Speech* is the behavior of forming and sequencing the sounds of oral language. Speech disorders include disorders of *voice* (phonation), *articulation* (movements resulting in speech sounds), and *fluency* (the flow of speech); language disorders include disorders of *phonology* (the sound system of language), *morphology* (construction of word forms), *syntax* (sentence construction), *semantics* (word and sentence meanings), and *pragmatics* (the pattern of social use of language). Phonology, morphology, and syntax constitute the *form* of language; semantics refers to language *content;* pragmatics refers to the *function* of language. *Communicative variations* that should not be considered disorders of speech or language include *dialects* and *augmentative communication* systems.

Speech production requires *phonation* (control of the breath stream to produce speech sounds), *articulation* (movements of the vocal tract during phonation), and *resonation* (quality of the sound produced according to the size, shape, and texture of the organs in the vocal tract). All three—phonation, articulation, and resonation—are required for intelligible speech. Speech flow or *fluency* is the production of speech sounds in a sequence and rhythm that allows words to be understood. The patterns of stress and rate at which words are produced *(prosody)* are also important in giving meaning to speech.

Infants are much more adept at communication than was previously thought. Their caretakers typically treat them as if they had communication skills and are able to interpret their communicative intent. When children learn to talk, they first talk about things, events, and relationships in their environment. Parents' and other caretakers' speech to children is an important factor in the development of language. Children gradually learn that language can control the actions of other people. Even though the structure and development of language have been carefully studied and described, relatively little is known about *how* or *why* children attain the ability to handle language. The exact relationship between cognitive development and language development is not understood.

Children may have more than one type of speech disorder, speech disorders may occur in combination with language disorders. *Voice disorders* are characteristics of pitch, loudness, and quality perceived as markedly different from what is customary for someone of a given age, sex, and cultural background. It is often difficult to distinguish an *articulation disorder* from a *phonological disorder,* but articulation refers to the making of sounds, and phonology refers to the use of sounds in oral language. Articulation and phonological disorders involve omissions, substitutions, distortions, and additions of speech sounds. *Fluency disorders* include stuttering and cluttering. Youngsters who are likely to continue to stutter are characterized by a struggle to speak, qualitative and quantitative differences in disfluencies, and a genetic predisposition to stutter.

Some speech disorders are associated with *orofacial defects.* The most common types are orofacial clefts. Conditions in which there is a rift or split in the upper part of the oral cavity or the upper lip are referred to as *cleft palate* and *cleft lip.* The major speech problem of children with cleft palate is inability to close off the passage of air into the nasal cavities while speaking. Most clefts can be repaired by surgery. Interdisciplinary cooperation is required to address the speech problems of children with orofacial defects.

Some speech disorders are associated with

neurological damage. These may involve articulation *(dysarthria)* or selection and sequencing of speech *(apraxia)*. Difficulties in speaking result from lack of precise control of the muscles involved in speech and/or the cognitive processing required for language. Augmentative communication systems, such as communication boards, are often required for those whose speech is disordered by neurological damage.

Language disorders can be classified in a variety of ways. One way is (1) no verbal language development, (2) language qualitatively different from normal, (3) delayed language development, and (4) interrupted language development. In all types of language disorders, the focus of intervention today tends to be on the *social* use of language (pragmatics).

Augmentative communication systems must be devised for those whose physical disabilities preclude oral language. These systems give the disabled person a means of selecting or scanning an array of pictures, words, or other symbols. A communication board is one type of alternative communication system, but technology is making many other approaches possible.

Assessment of speech and language disorders may involve standardized and nonstandardized testing, use of developmental scales, and direct observation under a variety of circumstances. Much depends on the subjective judgment of a highly skilled and experienced speech-language pathologist. The initial assessment should reveal the extent of the child's current language abilities, and an ongoing assessment should show how quickly the child responds to intervention. An intervention plan should take into account the content, form, and use of language. Currently, increasing emphasis is being placed on making language serve a useful function for the child in everyday life.

There is no particular personality type or set of psychological or behavioral characteristics associated with speech and language disorders. One cannot assume that a speech or language disorder of a particular type will necessarily be accompanied by psychological or behavioral problems.

The teacher plays a critical role in helping students learn to use language effectively. The formal language of school is often difficult for students and for teachers. Students may be unable to use language clearly and expressively to convey and interpret information quickly and easily in oral or written form. Teachers are sometimes not sufficiently skilled in classroom discourse to help students with language disorders. Asking questions is an area in which teachers themselves sometimes do not have sufficient language skills.

Intervention programs for preschoolers focus on the earliest stages of language acquisition. Many of the teaching activities involve language interactions similar to those between parents and children. Adolescents and adults with speech and language problems may be self-referred, have other health problems, or be severely handicapped. However, language disorders are now believed to be the underlying problem in the academic and social difficulties many adolescents and young adults have in school.

REFERENCES

Adams, M. (1977). A clinical strategy for differentiating the normally nonfluent child and the incipient stutterer. *Journal of Fluency Disorders, 2,* 141–148.

Adams, M. (1980). The young stutterer: Diagnosis, treatment, and assessment of progress. *Seminars in Speech, Language, and Hearing, 1*(4), 289–299.

Adams, M. (1982). Fluency, nonfluency, and stuttering in children. *Journal of Fluency Disorders, 7,* 171–185.

Allen, K. E., Holm, V. A., & Schiefelbusch, R. L. (Eds.) (1978). *Early intervention—A team approach.* Baltimore: University Park Press.

American Speech-Language-Hearing Association. (1982). Definitions: Communicative disorders and variations. *ASHA, 24,* 949–950.

American Speech-Language-Hearing Association. (1983). Position of the American Speech-Language-Hearing Association on social dialects. *ASHA, 25,* 23–25.

Andrews, G., Craig, A., Feyer, A., Hoddinott, S., Howie, P., & Neilson, M. (1983). Stuttering: A review of research findings and theories circa 1982. *Journal of Speech and Hearing Disorders, 48,* 226–246.

Aram, D. M., Ekelman, B. L., & Nation, J. E. (1984). Preschoolers with language disorders: 10 years later. *Journal of Speech and Hearing Research, 27,* 232–244.

Aronson, A. E. Dysarthria. In T. J. Hixon, L. D. Shriberg, & J. H. Saxman (Eds.), (1980). *Introduction to communication disorders.* Englewood Cliffs, N.J.: Prentice-Hall.

Arwood, E. L. *Pragmaticism: Theory and application.* Rockville, Md.: Aspen Systems.

Bernthal, J. E., & Bankson, N. W. (1984). Phonological disorders: An overview. In J. M. Costello (Ed.), *Speech disorders in children: Recent advances* (pp. 3–24). San Diego: College Hill Press.

Berry, M. F. (1980). *Teaching linguistically handicapped children.* Englewood Cliffs, N.J.: Prentice-Hall.

Blank, M., & White, S. J. (1986). Questions: A powerful form of classroom exchange. *Topics in Language Disorders, 6*(2), 1–12.

Boone, D. R. (1980). Voice disorders. In T. J. Hixon, L. D. Shriberg, & J. H. Saxman (eds.), *Introduction to communication disorders.* Englewood Cliffs, N.J.: Prentice-Hall.

Brutten, G. (1986). Two-factor behavior theory and therapy. In G. Shames & H. Rubin (Eds.), *Stuttering: Then and now* (pp. 143–183). Columbus, Ohio: Merrill.

Butler, K. G. (1986a). *Language disorders in children.* Austin, Tex.: Pro-Ed.

Butler, K. G. (1986b). Language research and practice: A major contribution to special education. In R. J. Morris & B. Blatt (Eds.), *Special education: Research and trends* (pp. 272–302). New York: Pergamon.

Cairns, C. E., & Williams, F. (1973). Language: In F. D. Minifie, T. J. Hixon, & F. Williams (Eds.), *Normal aspects of speech, hearing, and language.* Englewood Cliffs, N.J.: Prentice-Hall.

Calculator, S., & Luchko, C. D. (1983). Evaluating the effectiveness of a communication board training program. *Journal of Speech and Hearing Disorders, 48,* 185–191.

Costello, J. M. (Ed.) (1984). *Speech disorders in children: Recent advances.* San Diego: College Hill Press.

Cross, D., & Luper, H. (1979). Voice reaction time of stuttering and nonstuttering children and adults. *Journal of Fluency Disorders, 4,* 59–77.

Culp, D. (1984). The preschool fluency development program. In M. Peins (Ed.), *Contemporary approaches to stuttering therapy* (pp. 39–69). Boston: Little, Brown.

Curlee, R. F. (1984). Stuttering disorders: An overview. In J. M. Costello (Ed.), *Speech disorders in children: Recent advances* (pp. 227–260). San Diego: College Hill Press.

Devany, J. M., Rincover, A., & Lovaas, O. I. (1981). Teaching speech to nonverbal children. In J. M. Kauffman & D. P. Hallahan (Eds.), *Handbook of special education.* Englewood Cliffs, N.J.: Prentice-Hall.

Eisenson, J., & Ogilvie, M. (1983). *Communicative disorders in children* (5th ed.). New York, Macmillan.

Ewanowski, S. J., & Saxman, J. H. (1980). Orofacial disorder. In T. J. Hixon, L. D. Shriberg, & J. H. Saxman (Eds.), *Introduction to communication disorders.* Englewood Cliffs, N.J.: Prentice-Hall.

Fairweather, B. C., Haun, D. H., & Finkle, L. J. (1983). *Communication systems for severely handicapped persons.* Springfield: Ill.: Charles C Thomas.

Fey, M. E. (1986). *Language intervention with young children.* San Diego: College-Hill Press.

Goetz, L., Schuler, A. L., & Sailor, W. (1981). Functional competence as a factor in communication instruction. *Exceptional Education Quarterly, 2*(1), 51–60.

Goldstein, H., & Wetherby, B. (1984). Application of a functional perspective on receptive language development to early intervention. *Remedial and Special Education, 5*(2), 48–57.

Gregory, H. (1986). Environmental manipulation and family counseling. In G. Shames & H. Rubin (Eds.), *Stuttering: Then and now* (pp. 273–291). Columbus, Ohio: Merrill.

Hallahan, D. P., & Bryan, T. H. (1981). Learning disabilities. In J. M. Kauffman & D. P. Hallahan (Eds.), *Handbook of special education.* Englewood Cliffs, N.J.: Prentice-Hall.

Hallahan, D. P., Kauffman, J. M., & Lloyd, J. W. (1985). *Introduction to learning disabilities* (2nd ed.). Englewood Cliffs, N.J.: Prentice-Hall.

Hixon, T. J., & Abbs, J. H. (1980). Normal speech production. In T. J. Hixon, L. D. Shriberg, & J. H. Saxman (Eds.), *Introduction to communication disorders.* Englewood Cliffs, N.J.: Prentice-Hall.

Hubbell, R. D. (1981). *Children's language disorders: An integrated approach.* Englewood Cliffs, N.J.: Prentice-Hall.

Jaffe, M. B. (1984). Neurological impairment of speech production: Assessment and treatment. In J. M. Costello (Ed.), *Speech disorders in children: Recent advances* (pp. 157–186). San Diego: College Hill Press.

Jonas, G. (1977). *Stuttering: The disorder of many theories.* New York: Farrar, Straus & Giroux.

Koegel, R. L., Rincover, A., & Egel, A. L. (1982). *Educating and understanding autistic children.* San Diego: College Hill Press.

Kidd, K. (1984). Stuttering as a genetic disorder. In R. Curlee & W. Perkins (Eds.), *Nature and treatment of stuttering: New directions.* San Diego: College-Hill.

Kuczaj, S. A. (1983). *Crib speech and language play.* New York: Springer-Verlag.

Lane, H. (1986). *The wild boy of Aveyron.* Cambridge, Mass.: Harvard University Press.

LaPointe, L. L. (1986). Neurogenic disorders of speech. In G. H. Shames & E. H. Wiig (Eds.), *Human communication disorders* (2nd ed.) (pp. 495–530). Columbus, Ohio: Merrill.

Larson, V. L., & McKinley, N. L. (1985). General intervention principles with language impaired adolescents. *Topics in Language Disorders, 5*(3), 70–77.

Lee, A. D., & Shapero-Fine, J. (1984). When a language problem is primary: Secondary school strategies. In G. P. Wallach & K. G. Butler (Eds.), *Language learning disabilities in school-age children* (pp. 338–359). Baltimore: Williams & Wilkins.

Leonard, L. (1986). Early language development and language disorders. In G. H. Shames & E. H. Wiig (Eds.), *Human communication disorders* (2nd ed.) (pp. 291–330). Columbus, Ohio: Merrill.

Lindfors, J. W. (1980). *Children's language and learning.* Englewood Cliffs, N.J.: Prentice-Hall.

Locke, J. L. (1983). *Phonological acquisition and change.* New York: Academic Press.

Lund, N. J., & Ducha, J. F. (1983). *Assessing children's language in naturalistic contexts.* Englewood Cliffs, N.J.: Prentice-Hall.

Matthews, J. (1986). The professions of speech-language pathology and audiology. In G. H. Shames & E. H. Wiig (Eds.), *Human communication disorders* (2nd ed.) (pp. 3–26). Columbus, Ohio: Merrill.

McCormick, L., & Schiefelbusch, R. L. (1984). *Early language intervention.* Columbus, Ohio: Merrill.

McMorrow, M. J., Foxx, R. M., Faw, G. D., & Bittle, R. G.

(1986). *Looking for the words: Teaching functional language strategies.* Champaign, Ill.: Research Press.

McReynolds, L. V. (1986). Functional articulation disorders. In G. H. Shames & E. H. Wiig (Eds.), *Human communication disorders* (2nd ed.) (pp. 139–182). Columbus, Ohio: Merrill.

McWilliams, B. J. (1984). Speech problems associated with craniofacial anomalies. In J. M. Costello (Ed.), *Speech disorders in children: Recent advances* (pp. 187–223). San Diego: College Hill Press.

McWilliams, B. J. (1986). Cleft palate, In G. H. Shames & E. H. Wiig (Eds.), *Human communication disorders* (2nd ed.) (pp. 445–482). Columbus, Ohio: Merrill.

McWilliams, B. J., Morris, H. L., & Shelton, R. L. (1984). *Cleft palate speech.* Philadelphia: Decker.

Meyers, S. (1986). Qualitative and quantitative differences and patterns of variability in disfluencies emitted by preschool stutterers. *Journal of Fluency Disorders, 11,* 293–306.

Meyers, S., & Freeman, F. (1985a). Are mothers of stutterers different? An investigation of social-communicative interaction. *Journal of Fluency Disorders, 10,* 193–209.

Meyers, S., & Freeman, F. (1985b). Interruptions as a variable in stuttering and disfluency. *Journal of Speech and Hearing Research, 28,* 428–435.

Meyers, S., & Freeman, F. (1985c). Mother and child speech rates as a variable in stuttering disfluency. *Journal of Speech and Hearing Research, 28,* 436–444.

Miller, C. E., & Prutting, C. A. (1979). Inconsistencies across the language comprehension tests for specific grammatical features. *Language, Speech, and Hearing Services in Schools, 10,* 162–168.

Moore, P. (1986). Voice disorders. In G. H. Shames & E. H. Wiig (Eds.), *Human communication disorders* (2nd ed.) (pp. 183–229). Columbus, Ohio: Merrill.

Mordecai, D. (1979). An investigation of the communicative styles of mothers and fathers of stuttering versus nonstuttering preschool children. *Dissertation Abstracts International, 40,* 4759–B.

Musselwhite, C. R., & St. Louis, K. W. (1982). *Communication programming for the severely handicapped: Vocal and nonvocal strategies.* San Diego: College Hill Press.

Mysak, E. D. (1986). Cerebral palsy. In G. H. Shames & E. H. Wiig (Eds.), *Human communication disorders* (2nd ed.) (pp. 531–560). Columbus, Ohio: Merrill.

Naremore, R. C. (1980). Language disorders in children. In T. J. Hixon, L. D. Shriberg, & J. H. Saxman (Eds.), *Introduction to communication disorders.* Englewood Cliffs, N.J.: Prentice-Hall.

Nelson, N. W. (1984). Beyond information processing: The language of teachers and textbooks. In G. P. Wallach & K. G. Butler (Eds.), *Language learning disabilities in school-age children* (pp. 154–178). Baltimore: Williams & Wilkins.

Newman, P. W., Creaghead, N. A., & Secord, W. (1985). *Assessment and remediation of articulatory and phonological disorders.* Columbus, OH: Merrill.

Owens, R. E. (1986). Communication, language, and speech. In G. H. Shames & E. H. Wiig (Eds.), *Human communication disorders* (2nd ed.) (pp. 27–79). Columbus, Ohio: Merrill.

Owens, R. E., & House, L. I. (1984). Decision-making processes in augmentative communication. *Journal of Speech and Hearing Disorders, 49,* 18–25.

Perkins, W. H. (1980). Disorders of speech flow. In T. J. Hixon, L. D. Shriberg, & J. H. Saxman (Eds.), *Introduction to communication disorders.* Englewood Cliffs, N.J.: Prentice-Hall.

Perkins, W. H. (1983). The problem of definition: Commentary on "stuttering." *Journal of Speech and Hearing Disorders, 48,* 245–249.

Rees, N. S. (1980). Learning to talk and understand. In T. J. Hixon, L. D. Shriberg, & J. H. Saxman (Eds.), *Introduction to communication disorders.* Englewood Cliffs, N.J.: Prentice-Hall.

Richman, L. C. (1976). Behavior and achievement of cleft palate children. *The Cleft Palate Journal, 13,* 4–10.

Rousey, C. G. (1984). *A practical guide to helping children with speech and language problems: For parents and teachers only.* Springfield, Ill.: Charles C Thomas.

Schiefelbusch, R. L., & McCormick, L. P. (1981). Language and speech disorders. In J. M. Kauffman & D. P. Hallahan (Eds.), *Handbook of special education.* Englewood Cliffs, N.J.: Prentice-Hall.

Schwartz, R. G. (1984). The phonological system: Normal acquisition. In J. M. Costello (Ed.), *Speech disorders in children: Recent advances* (pp. 25–74). San Diego: College Hill Press.

Shames, G. H. (1986). Disorders of fluency. In G. H. Shames & E. H. Wiig (Eds.), *Human communication disorders* (2nd ed.) (pp. 243–289). Columbus, Ohio: Merrill.

Shames, G., & Rubin, H. (1986). Overview of part two: Theory, research, and clinical management—a system of interactions. In G. Shames & H. Rubin (Eds.), *Stuttering: Then and now* (pp. 23–46). Columbus, Ohio: Merrill.

Shames, G. H., & Wiig, E. H. (Eds.) (1986). *Human communication disorders* (2nd ed.). Columbus, Ohio: Merrill.

Shriberg, L. D. (1980). Developmental phonological disorders. In T. J. Hixon, L. D. Shriberg, & J. H. Saxman (Eds.), *Introduction to communication disorders.* Englewood Cliffs, N.J.: Prentice-Hall.

Silliman, E. R. (1984). Interactional competencies in the instructional context: The role of teaching discourse in learning. In G. P. Wallach & K. G. Butler (Eds.), *Language learning disabilities in school-age children* (pp. 288–317). Baltimore: Williams & Wilkins.

Silliman, E. R. (Ed.) (1986). Interdisciplinary perspectives on classroom discourse. *Topics in Language Disorders, 6(2),* special issue.

Spradlin, J. E., & Siegel, G. M. (1982). Language training in natural and clinical environments. *Journal of Speech and Hearing Disorders, 47,* 2–6.

Stark, J., Wallach, G. P. (1980). The path to a concept of language learning disabilities. *Topics in Language Disorders, 1(1),* 1–14.

Starkweather, C. W. (1983). *Speech and language: Principles and processes of behavior change.* Englewood Cliffs, N.J.: Prentice-Hall.

Starkweather, C. (1982). *Counseling stutterers.* Memphis: Speech Foundation of America.

Stephens, M. I. (Ed.) (1985). Language impaired youth: The years between 10 and 18. *Topics in Language Disorders, 5(3),* special issue.

Tarver, S. G., & Ellsworth, P. S. (1981). Written and oral language for verbal children. In J. M. Kauffman & D. P. Hallahan (Eds.), *Handbook of special education.* Englewood Cliffs, N.J.: Prentice-Hall.

Tomikawa, S. A., & Dodd, D. H. (1980). Early word meanings: Perceptually or functionally based? *Child Development, 51,* 1103–1109.

Travis, L. E. (1971). The unspeakable feelings of people with special reference to stuttering. In L. E. Travis (Ed.), *Handbook of speech pathology and audiology.* Englewood Cliffs, N.J.: Prentice-Hall.

Vanderheiden, G. C. (1984). High and low technology approaches in the development of communication systems for severely physically handicapped persons. *Exceptional Education Quarterly, 4*(4), 40–56.

Van Riper, C. (1971). *The nature of stuttering.* Englewood Cliffs, N.J.: Prentice-Hall.

Van Riper, C. (1973). *The treatment of stuttering.* Englewood Cliffs, N.J.: Prentice-Hall.

Van Riper, C. (1978). *Speech correction: Principles and methods* (6th ed.). Englewood Cliffs, N.J.: Prentice-Hall.

Wallach, G. P., & Butler, K. G. (Eds.) (1984). *Language learning disabilities in school-age children.* Baltimore: Williams & Wilkins.

Wiig, E. H. (1986). Language disabilities in school-age children and youth. In G. H. Shames & E. H. Wiig (Eds.), *Human communication disorders* (2nd ed.) (pp. 331–383). Columbus, Ohio: Merrill.

Wilcox, M. J., & Webster, E. J. (1980). Early discourse behavior: An analysis of children's responses to listener feedback. *Child Development, 51,* 1120–1125.

Wingate, M. (1986). Physiological and genetic factors. In G. Shames & H. Rubin (Eds.), *Stuttering: Then and now* (pp. 49–69). Columbus, Ohio: Merrill.

Wingate, M. E. (1983). Speaking unassisted: Comments on a paper by Andrews et al. *Journal of Speech and Hearing Disorders, 48,* 255–263.

Winitz, H. (1971). Psycholinguistic considerations in language development. In L. E. Travis (Ed.), *Handbook of speech pathology and audiology.* Englewood Cliffs, N.J.: Prentice-Hall.

Wood, B. S. (1976). *Children and communication: Verbal and nonverbal language development.* Englewood Cliffs, N.J.: Prentice-Hall.

Yairi, E. (1983). The onset of stuttering in two- and three-year-old children: A preliminary report. *Journal of Speech and Hearing Disorders, 48,* 171–178.

Zemlin, W. R. (1986). Anatomy and physiology of speech. In G. H. Shames & E. H. Wiig (Eds.), *Human communication disorders* (2nd ed.) (pp. 81–133). Columbus, Ohio: Merrill.

6

Hearing Impairment

No deaf child who has earnestly tried to speak the words which he has never heard—to come out of the prison of silence, where no tone of love, no song of bird, no strain of music ever pierces the stillness—can forget the thrill of surprise, the joy of discovery which came over him when he uttered his first word. Only such a one can appreciate the eagerness with which I talked to my toys, to stones, trees, birds and dumb animals, or the delight I felt when at my call Mildred ran to me or my dogs obeyed my commands. It is an unspeakable boon to me to be able to speak in winged words that need no interpretation.

(The Story of My Life, Helen Keller)

A lthough Helen Keller's achievements were unique in the truest sense of the word, the emotions she conveys here are not (see page 259). The deaf child who does acquire the ability to speak must certainly experience a "joy of discovery" similar to Keller's. Hearing impairment is a great barrier to the normal development of language. As we will see, even if the impairment is not severe enough for the child to be classified as "deaf" but rather as "hard of hearing," the hearing-impaired child is at a distinct disadvantage in virtually all aspects of language development. The importance of language in our society, particularly in school-related activities, is obvious. A significantly large group of educators of deaf individuals believe that many of the problems of hearing-impaired people related to social and intellectual development are primarily due to their deficiencies in language. We will explore this issue in some depth in this chapter.

Another related controversy inherent in Keller's words is the debate concerning whether the hearing-impaired child should be educated to communicate orally or through manual **sign language.** Keller's opinion is that the ability to speak offers a richer means of communication. But she was extraordinary; few deaf individuals have attained her level of fluency. The oral versus manual approach debate has raged for years. For many years there was no middle ground. Although some still debate the merits of each, since the late 1960s and 1970s, many educators have begun to use a method of "total communication" that involves a combination of both orientations.

DEFINITION AND CLASSIFICATION

There are many definitions and classification systems of hearing impairment. By far the most common division is between deaf and hard of hearing. This would seem simple enough, except that the two categories are defined differently by different professionals. The extreme points of view are represented by those with a physiological orientation and those with an educational orientation. Those maintaining a strictly physiological viewpoint are interested primarily in the *measurable degree* of hearing loss. Children who cannot hear sounds at or above a certain intensity (loudness) level are classified as deaf; others with a hearing loss are considered hard of hearing. Hearing sensitivity is measured in **decibels** (units of relative loudness of sounds). Zero decibels (0 dB) designates the point at which people with normal hearing can detect the faintest sound. Each succeeding number of decibels indicates a certain degree of hearing loss. Those who maintain a physiological viewpoint generally consider those with hearing losses of about 90 dB or greater to be deaf, those with less to be hard of hearing.

People with an educational viewpoint are concerned with how much the hearing loss is likely to affect the child's ability to speak and develop language. Because of the close causal link between hearing loss and delay in language development, these professionals categorize primarily on the basis of spoken language abilities.

The most commonly accepted set of definitions reflecting this educational orientation are those of the Executive Committee of the Conference of Educational Administrators Serving the Deaf. Their Ad Hoc Committee has put forth the following definitions:

> *Hearing impairment:* A generic term indicating a hearing disability which may range in severity from mild to profound: it includes the subsets of *deaf* and *hard of hearing.*

MISCONCEPTIONS
ABOUT HEARING-IMPAIRED INDIVIDUALS

Myth	*Fact*
Deafness leads automatically to inability to speak.	Even though hearing impairment, especially with greater degrees of hearing loss, is a barrier to normal language development, most deaf people can be taught some understanding of oral language and the ability to speak.
Deafness is not as great a handicap as blindness.	Although it is impossible to predict the exact consequences of a handicap on a person's functioning, in general deafness is a greater handicap than blindness. This is due to a large degree to the effects hearing loss can have on the ability to understand and speak oral language.
The deaf child is inherently lower in intellectual ability.	It is generally believed that, unless they are born with additional handicaps, deaf infants have the same intellectual capacities as hearing infants. Deaf individuals, however, may perform more poorly on some tasks because of their difficulty in communicating with those who hear.
In learning to understand what is being said to them, deaf individuals concentrate on reading lips.	*Lipreading* refers only to visual cues arising from movement of the lips. Deaf people not only learn to lipread, they also learn to make use of a variety of other visual cues, such as facial expressions and movements of the jaw and tongue. Deaf individuals thus engage in what is referred to as *speechreading,* a term that covers all visual cues associated with speaking.
Teaching American Sign Language is harmful to a child and may hamper development of oral language.	Most educators today acknowledge that a combination of the manual and oral methods, according to the needs of the individual child, is the best approach to teaching communication skills.
American Sign Language is a loosely structured group of gestures.	American Sign Language is a true language in its own right with its own set of grammatical rules.
American Sign Language can only be used to convey concrete ideas.	American Sign Language can be used at any level of abstraction.
A hearing aid is of no use to a person with sensorineural hearing loss.	While not as useful as with conductive hearing losses, hearing aids almost always help people with sensorineural impairments.

Myth	*Fact*
Hearing aids should not be used for hearing losses that are very mild or very severe.	There are no hearing losses too mild or too severe to prevent a person from trying a hearing aid.
Hearing losses in the high-frequency range can't be corrected by a hearing aid.	This was true at one time of hearing aids that were worn on the body because, in rubbing against clothing, the aids created low-frequency sounds that drowned out higher frequencies. Today, however, body aids can be equipped with special microphones that virtually eliminate this problem.

A *deaf* person is one whose hearing disability precludes successful processing of linguistic information through audition, with or without a hearing aid.

A *hard of hearing* person is one who, generally with the use of a hearing aid, has residual hearing sufficient to enable successful processing of linguistic information through audition. (Brill, MacNeil, and Newman, 1986, p. 67)

Educators are extremely concerned about the *age of onset* of the hearing impairment. Again, the close relationship between hearing loss and language delay is the key here. The earlier the hearing loss manifests itself in a child's life, the more handicapped he or she will be in terms of developing language. For this reason, professionals working with hearing-impaired children frequently use the terms **congenitally deaf** (those who were born deaf) and **adventitiously deaf** (those who acquire deafness at some time after birth). Two other frequently used terms are even more specific in pinpointing language acquisition as critical: **Prelingual deafness** is "deafness present at birth, or occurring early in life at an age prior to the development of speech or language"; **postlingual deafness** is "deafness occurring at an age following the development of speech and language" (Brill, MacNeil, and Newman, 1986, p. 67). Because linguists are emphasizing more and more the importance of receptive language in the early months and years, the dividing point between prelingual and postlingual deafness has been moving down over the years. Whereas some years ago the age for prelingual deafness was considered to be before 3 years, it is now considered to be before 18 months, and many believe it should be adjusted even further to 12 months or even 6 months (Meadow-Orlans, 1987).

In addition, Brill et al. specify the following hearing threshold classifications: mild (26–54 dB), moderate (55–69 dB), severe (70–89 dB), and profound (90 dB and above). These levels of severity according to loss of hearing sensitivity cut across the broad classifications of "deaf" and "hard of hearing." The broader classifications are not directly dependent on hearing sensitivity. Instead, they stress the degree to which speech and language are affected.

Some experts object to following any of the various classification systems too strictly. These definitions, because they deal with events that are difficult to measure and that occur in variable organisms, are not precise. It is best not to form any hard-and-fast opinions about an individual's ability to hear and speak solely on the basis of a classification of his or her hearing disability.

PREVALENCE

Estimates of the numbers of children with hearing impairment vary considerably. Such things as differences in definition, populations studied, and accuracy of testing contribute to the varying figures. The U.S. Department of Education has reported that .17 percent of individuals preschool through grade 12 are being served as deaf or hard of hearing. Although the U.S. Department of Education does not report separate figures for the categories of deaf and hard of hearing, some authorities believe that many hard-of-hearing children who could benefit from special education services are not being served.

ANATOMY AND PHYSIOLOGY OF THE EAR

The ear is one of the most complex organs of the body. The many elements that make up the hearing mechanism are divided into three major sections: the outer, middle, and inner ear. The outer ear is the least complex and least important for hearing; the inner ear is the most complex and most important for hearing. Figure 6.1 shows these major parts of the ear.

The Outer Ear

The outer ear consists of the auricle and the external auditory canal. The canal ends with the **tympanic membrane** (eardrum), which is the boundary between the outer and middle ear. The **auricle** is the part of the ear that protrudes from the side of the head. As Martin (1981) notes, the auricle is the one part of the ear visible to all, but it is the least important in terms of hearing. The external auditory canal

---

Figure 6.1 *Illustration of the outer, middle, and inner ear.*
SOURCE: H. L. Davis and S. R. Silverman (Eds.), *Hearing and Deafness,* 4th ed. (New York: Holt, Rinehart and Winston, 1978). Copyright © 1947, 1960, 1970, 1978 by Holt, Rinehart and Winston, Inc. Reprinted by permission.

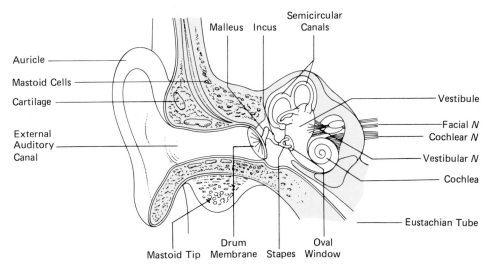

contains coarse hairs and **cerumen** (earwax), which aid in protecting the deeper structures from insects and dust particles. The bitter taste of the cerumen repels insects; the hairs "wave" unwanted objects away. The part that the outer ear plays in the transmission of sound is relatively minor. Sound is "collected" by the auricle and is funneled on to the eardrum, which vibrates, sending the sound waves on to the middle ear.

The Middle Ear

The middle ear is composed of the eardrum and three very tiny bones **(ossicles)** called the **malleus** (hammer), **incus** (anvil), and **stapes** (stirrup) contained within an air-filled space. It is here that the transmission of sound begins to get sophisticated. The chain of the malleus, incus, and stapes conducts the vibrations of the eardrum along to the **oval window,** which is the connecting link between the middle and inner ear. To prevent a significant loss of energy between the vibration of the eardrum and the vibration of the oval window, the chain of bones is constructed in such a way that it takes advantage of the physical laws of leverage. Because of this there is an efficient transfer of energy from the air-filled cavity of the middle ear to the dense, fluid-filled inner ear (Davis, 1978a; Goodhill and Guggenheim, 1971; Martin, 1981).

The Inner Ear

About the size of a pea, the inner ear is an intricate mechanism of thousands of moving parts (Martin, 1981). Because it looks like a maze of passageways and because of its complexity, this part of the ear is often called a *labyrinth*. The inner ear can be divided into two sections according to function: The **vestibular mechanism** and the **cochlea.** These sections, however, do not function totally independently of each other.

The Vestibular Mechanism

The vestibular mechanism, located in the upper portion of the inner ear, is responsible for the sense of balance. Its most prominent organs are three soft, fluid-filled semicircular canals. The solution in these canals and two other small organs connected to them is extremely sensitive to such things as acceleration, head movement, and head position. Information regarding movement is fed to the brain through the vestibular nerve.

The Cochlea

By far the most important organ for hearing is the cochlea. Lying below the vestibular mechanism, this snail-shaped organ contains the parts necessary to convert the mechanical action of the middle ear into an electrical signal in the inner ear that is transmitted to the brain. In the normally functioning ear, sound causes the malleus, incus, and stapes of the middle ear to move. When the stapes moves, it pushes the oval window in and out, causing the fluid in the cochlea of the inner ear to flow. The movement of the fluid in turn causes a complex chain of events in the cochlea ultimately resulting in excitation of the cochlear nerve. With stimulation of the cochlear nerve, an electrical impulse is sent to the brain, and the sound is heard.

MEASUREMENT OF HEARING ABILITY

Hearing ability can be measured in several ways, some more precise than others. For example, someone who suspects a hearing problem in a child can place himself or herself behind the child and softly whisper the child's name to try to find out how well the youngster can hear. Another example of a crude measure of hearing is the "watch test." Here an examiner slowly moves a watch toward each of the child's ears, and the child is asked to tell when he or she first hears ticking. Besides the chance that the "whisper test" will cause the child to wonder at the weird behavior of the adult, both tests lack accuracy. Most important, they lack an appropriate standard with which responses can be compared. Whispering or the ticking of a watch can vary considerably, as can background noise. Furthermore, the child's responses cannot be compared with those of other children.

Audiologists* use tests of hearing that are considerably more accurate. Their methods are also relatively uniform, so that results would be about the same even if several examinations were conducted by different audiologists.

There are three different general types of scientific hearing tests: pure-tone audiometry, speech audiometry, and specialized tests for very young children. Depending upon the characteristics of the examinee and the use to which the results will be put, the audiologist may choose to give any number of tests from any one or a combination of these three categories.

Pure-Tone Audiometry

Pure-tone audiometry is designed to establish the individual's threshold for hearing at a variety of different frequencies. (Frequency, measured in **Hertz (Hz) units,** has to do with the number of vibrations per unit of time of a sound wave; the pitch is higher with *more* vibrations, lower with *fewer*.) A person's threshold for hearing is simply the level at which he or she can first detect a sound; it refers to how *intense* a sound must be before the person can detect it. Intensity is measured in units known as decibels (dB).

Pure-tone audiometers are designed to present tones of various intensities (dB levels) at various frequencies (Hz). Audiologists are usually concerned with measuring sensitivity to sounds ranging from 0 to about 110 dB. A person with average-normal hearing is barely able to hear sounds at a sound pressure level of 0 dB. The zero decibel level is frequently called the zero hearing threshold level (HTL) or **audiometric zero.**

Hertz are usually measured from 125 Hz ("low" sounds) to 8000 Hz ("high" sounds). Sounds below 125 Hz or above 8000 Hz are not measured because most speech does not fall within this range. (The whistle designed to call dogs, for example, has a frequency too high to be heard by human beings.) Frequencies contained in speech range from 80 to 8000 Hz, but most speech sounds have energy in the 500 to 2000 Hz range. Therefore the child's sensitivity within this latter range is particularly important.

The procedure for testing a person's sensitivity to pure tones is relatively simple. Each ear is tested separately. The audiologist presents a variety of tones within the range of 0 to about 110 dB and 125 to 8000 Hz until he or she establishes at what level of intensity (dB) the individual can detect the tone at a number of frequencies—125 Hz, 250 Hz, 500 Hz, 1000 Hz, 2000 Hz, 4000 Hz, and 8000 Hz. For each of

---

* **Audiology** is the science of hearing impairments, their detection, and their correction.

Testing with a pure-tone audiometer. The child is indicating by raising her hand that she hears the tone. (David R. Frazier/Photo Researchers)

these frequencies there is a measure of degree of hearing impairment. A 50 dB hearing loss at 500 Hz, for example means the individual is able to detect the 500 Hz sound when it is given at an intensity level of 50 dB, whereas the normal person would have heard it at 0 dB.

Speech Audiometry

Because the ability to detect and understand speech is of prime importance, a technique called **speech audiometry** has been developed to test a person's detection and understanding of speech. Speech detection is defined as the lowest level (in dB) at which the individual can detect speech without understanding. More important is the determination of the dB level at which one is able to *understand* speech. This is known as the **speech reception threshold (SRT).** One way to measure SRT is to present the person with a list of two-syllable words, testing each ear separately. The dB level at which he or she can understand half the words is often used as an estimate of SRT level.

Tests for Young and Hard to Test Children

A basic assumption of pure-tone and speech audiometry is that the person being tested understands what is expected of him or her. The individual must be able to comprehend the instructions and to show with a head nod or raised hand that he or she has heard the tone or word. He or she must also be cooperative. None of this may be possible for very young children (under about 4 years of age) or for children with other handicaps. Because the problem of testing is about the same for very young children and those with certain handicaps—inability to respond *voluntarily*—the tests we will describe are frequently used with both the very young non-handicapped child and the multihandicapped youngster.

Play Audiometry

This technique is primarily used to establish rapport with the child and to motivate him or her to respond. The examiner sets the testing situation up as a game. Using pure tones or speech, the examiner teaches the child to do various activities whenever he or she hears a signal. The activities are designed to be attractive to the young child. For example, the child may be required to pick up a block, squeeze a toy, or open a book. Davis (1978b) has recommended **play audiometry** as particularly suitable for children about 2½ years of age.

Reflex Audiometry

Infants normally possess some reflexive behaviors to loud sounds, which are useful for the testing of hearing. Present at birth is the *Moro reflex,* which is defined as a movement of the face, body, arms, and legs and a blinking of the eyes (Davis, 1978b). Another response that may be used to determine hearing ability is the *orienting response.* This response is evident when the infant turns his or her head and body toward the source of a sound. Davis (1978b) believes the orienting response is the best method of **reflex audiometry** and points out that it is at its most accurate between the ages of 6 and 12 months, when identification of hearing problems is crucial.

Evoked-Response Audiometry

Another method designed to measure hearing in a person unable to make voluntary responses is **evoked-response audiometry.** This technique involves measuring changes in brain-wave activity by using an electroencephalograph (EEG). All sounds heard by an individual result in electrical signals within the brain, so this method has become more popular with the development of sophisticated computers. Although very expensive and difficult to interpret, evoked-response audiometry has certain advantages. It can be used during sleep, and the child can be sedated and thus not be aware he or she is being tested.

School Screening

Before a child even reaches the audiologist for an extensive evaluation using any combination of the tests described above, he or she must usually be identified as having a potential problem. This task frequently falls upon the schools. Although children with severe hearing losses are easily identified, those with mild losses are likely to go undetected for years without some routine screening procedures (Newby, 1971).

Screening tests are administered either individually or in a group. In the group setting the examiner may present pure tones to children one at a time or to more than one child at a time. Each child has a pair of earphones and is instructed to keep his or her eyes closed and to raise his or her hand upon hearing a tone.

As with any kind of testing, group tests are less accurate than individual tests. So individual tests are generally preferred, even though this means the testing will be more time-consuming. The most common individual screening test is the **sweep test** performed with a portable audiometer (Newby, 1971). Each child is presented with a tone at about 20 to 25 dB for the frequencies of 500 Hz, 1000 Hz, 2000 Hz, 4000 Hz, and 6000 Hz. Children with problems detected in this procedure are referred for more extensive evaluation.

CAUSES

Conductive, Sensorineural, and Mixed Impairments

The most common way to classify the causes of hearing loss is on the basis of the location of the problem within the hearing mechanism. There are three major classifications: conductive hearing losses, sensorineural hearing losses, and mixed hearing losses (a combination of the first two). A *conductive loss* refers to impairments that interfere with the transfer of sound along the conductive pathway of the ear. Anatomically, conductive losses are the result of problems of the outer and/or middle ear. *Sensorineural impairments* involve problems confined to the inner ear.

One of the most important functions of the audiologist is to determine the specific site of the hearing loss. The first problem to be solved is whether the impairment is conductive, sensorineural, or mixed. The first clue may be the severity of the hearing loss. A general rule of thumb is that any hearing loss greater than 60 or 70 dB involves some inner-ear malfunctioning.

A more precise way of categorizing the hearing problem is to administer a pure-tone test by earphones (**air conduction**) and compare this with the results obtained by the use of a vibrator placed on the forehead (**bone conduction**). An individual with a conductive loss will exhibit normal hearing by bone conduction but abnormal hearing by air conduction. A sensorineural loss is indicated if the air and bone conduction tests show a nearly equal abnormality. A mixed loss is indicated when impairment is shown with both tests, but more with the air test. In addition, there is a relatively greater loss of sensitivity for the higher compared to the lower frequencies in sensorineural and mixed impairments. An **audiogram** is a graphic representation of the weakest (lowest dB) sound that the individual being tested can hear at each of several frequency levels (Hz).

Impairments of the Outer Ear

As we indicated earlier, the auricle and external auditory canal of the outer ear are less important than the middle and inner ear for hearing. This does not mean, however, that problems associated with the outer ear will not cause real educational difficulties. Several conditions of the outer ear, particularly the external auditory canal, can result in the child's being hard of hearing.

In some children, for example, the external auditory canal does not form, resulting in a condition known as **atresia.** Children are also subject to hearing losses produced by the presence of foreign objects in the external ear. They may also suffer from **external otitis,** or "swimmer's ear," an infection of the skin of the external auditory canal. Tumors of the external auditory canal, if large enough, are another source of impairment. Excessive buildup of cerumen, or earwax, can result in hearing problems. Finally, perforation of the eardrum, resulting from any of a number of causes ranging from a blow to the head to excessive pressure in the middle ear, also produces hearing impairment.

Impairments of the Middle Ear

Hearing losses resulting from abnormalities of the middle ear are generally more serious than those of the external ear. But middle-ear problems rarely result in deafness; children with impairments arising from middle-ear problems are usually classified as hard of hearing. Another factor that makes middle-ear impairments less devastating than inner-ear problems is that most of them are correctable with medical or surgical treatment. Most middle-ear hearing losses occur because the mechanical action of the ossicles is interfered with in some way.

Probably the most common problem of the middle ear is **otitis media**—an infection of the middle-ear space. Although otitis media can affect individuals of any age, it is primarily a disease of childhood, occurring most commonly in children under the age of 2 years (Pelton and Whitley, 1983). Estimated to occur in about 5 percent of all children before the age of 10 years (Martin, 1981), otitis media is even more common among children with Down syndrome or cleft palate. The reason for the high incidence among children with these congenital conditions is linked to physical abnormalities of the eustachian tube (Castiglia, Aquilina, and Kemsley, 1983), where the infection usually begins before spreading to the middle ear. Otitis media can result in a temporary conductive hearing loss and, if left untreated, can eventually lead to rupture of the tympanic membrane (Martin, 1981).

More subtle in its effects, but still a childhood middle-ear problem of some significance, is **nonsuppurative otitis media,** or **serous otitis media.** Nonsuppurative otitis media, which can occur without infection, also usually results from a disruption of the functioning of the eustachian tube such that negative pressure occurs in the middle ear, which causes the blood serum of the middle-ear lining to be "sucked" into the middle-ear cavity. Nonsuppurative otitis media is generally preceded by a bout with infectious otitis media (Castiglia et al., 1983). In addition, some authorities hold that allergies, by leading to eustachian tube malfunctioning, can cause nonsuppurative otitis media (Bluestone, 1978; Castiglia et al., 1983).

Besides the more common problems resulting from otitis media, there are a number of other less frequent middle-ear disorders. **Otosclerosis,** which occurs rarely in children, is a disease of the bone that causes the stapes to become abnormally attached to the oval window. Otosclerosis is generally believed to be hereditary (Goodhill and Guggenheim, 1971). Tumors may also interfere with the mechanism of the middle ear, and a blow to the head is also obviously a potential cause of middle-ear malfunction. Middle-ear problems may also be the result of congenital defects.

Impairments of the Inner Ear

The most severe hearing impairments are associated with the inner ear. Unfortunately, inner-ear hearing losses present the greatest problems for both education and medicine. Troubles other than those related to loss of threshold sensitivity are frequent. For example, sound distortion often occurs. People with sensorineural impairments often have difficulties in understanding speech—a condition known as **dysacusis.** Disorders of the inner ear frequently result in problems of balance and vertigo along with hearing loss. Also, **tinnitus**—roaring or ringing noises—is evident in some individuals with inner-ear impairments.

Causes of inner-ear disorders can be hereditary or acquired. The most frequent cause of childhood deafness is heredity (Hoemann and Briga, 1981; Moores, 1978; Schildroth, 1986). Acquired hearing losses of the inner ear include those due to bacterial infections (such as meningitis, the second most frequent cause of childhood deafness—Schildroth, 1986—and encephalitis), viral infections (such as mumps and measles), anoxia (deprivation of oxygen) at birth, prenatal infections of the mother (such as maternal rubella, congenital syphilis, and cytomegalovirus), Rh incompatibility (which can now usually be prevented with proper prenatal care of the mother), blows to the head, unwanted side effects of some antibiotics, and excessive noise levels.

Congenital cytomegalovirus (CMV) has, beginning in the late 1970s and early 1980s, received a great deal of attention as a potential cause of hearing impairment as well as other handicapping conditions (Hanshaw, 1982; Williamson, et al., 1982). CMV is the most frequently occurring congenital virus among newborns, but there

Cochlear Implants

A new surgical procedure now allows some profoundly deaf individuals to hear previously unheard sounds. An internal electromagnetic coil, with an electrode that runs into the cochlea of the inner ear, is placed in the mastoid bone behind the ear. An external coil is fitted on the skin right over the internal coil. Sounds are picked up by a microphone worn on the clothing and are sent on to the cochlear nerve in the inner ear by way of the external coil, internal coil, and electrode in the inner ear.

Although the implant allows deaf individuals to hear a number of environmental sounds such as ringing phones and car horns, Paul Lambert, an otolaryngologist at the University of Virginia who has done the surgery, notes its limitations. It does not automatically enable a patient to understand speech, although it does make speechreading easier and the speech of the deaf person more understandable. After the surgery the patient needs to be seen by a therapist in order to learn how to differentiate the sounds he or she is now hearing for the first time.

SOURCE: *Special Education Today,* November 1984, p. 15.

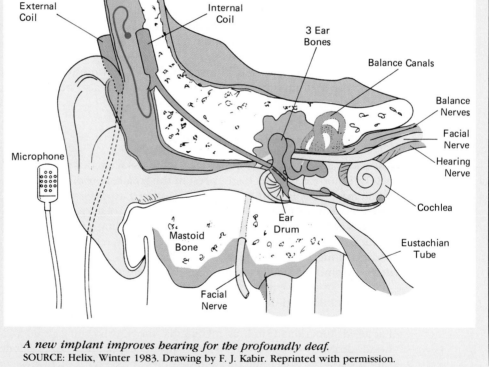

A new implant improves hearing for the profoundly deaf.
SOURCE: Helix, Winter 1983. Drawing by F. J. Kabir. Reprinted with permission.

are as yet no definitive data on the prevalence of hearing impairments due to CMV. One survey conducted in the state of Texas identified 1.1 percent of those students who had known causes of hearing loss as having hearing problems due to CMV. Unfortunately, there is as yet no treatment or vaccine for CMV (Thomas, 1985).

Also starting in the late 1970s and early 1980s, more attention has been given to noise as a possible contributor to hearing loss. With overcrowded living conditions, individuals are exposed for longer periods of time to loud noises. Davis (1978c) has listed jet engine roar, skeet shooting, and tractor noise as particular hearing hazards. Others believe that playing portable cassette players with headphones at loud levels can lead to hearing problems.

There is a relationship between the cause of the hearing impairment and the degree of hearing loss. The most devastating losses occur because of meningitis, maternal rubella, and hereditary factors. At least 50 percent of school-age children who have impairments due to one of these three causes have hearing losses in the profound range (exceeding 90 dB) (Karchmer, Milone, and Wolk, 1979).

PSYCHOLOGICAL AND BEHAVIORAL CHARACTERISTICS

Hearing loss can have profound consequences for some aspects of a person's behavior and little or no effect on other characteristics. Everyone knows the question, "If you were forced to choose, which would you rather be—blind or deaf?" On first impulse most of us choose deafness, probably because we rely upon sight for mobility and because many of the beauties of nature are visual. But in terms of functioning in a language-oriented society, the deaf person is at a much greater disadvantage. Let us see why.

Language and Speech Development

By far the most severely affected areas of development in the hearing-impaired person in the United States are the comprehension and production of the *English* language. We stress here the fact that it is the English language because that is the predominant language in the United States of those who can hear. In other words, hearing-impaired people are generally deficient in the language used by most people of the "hearing" society in which they live. The distinction is important because the hearing-impaired people can be expert in their own form of language. The current opinion is that hearing-impaired individuals who use manual sign language are taking part in the production and comprehension of a true language. We will return to this point later in this chapter.

Regarding English, however, it is an unfortunate but undeniable fact that hearing-impaired individuals are at a distinct disadvantage. This is true in terms of language comprehension, language production, and speech. With regard to speech, for example, a nationwide survey (Jensema, Karchmer, and Trybus, 1978) of teachers of hearing-impaired students found that they rated the speech of their students in the following way: very intelligible, 15.4 percent; intelligible, 29.4 percent; barely intelligible, 21.9 percent; not intelligible, 20.5 percent; would not speak, 12.8 percent.

As disconcerting as these figures are, they still point out that the vast majority of hearing-impaired people do have some speech. The old term deaf-mute reflected the attitude that deafness automatically meant an inability to speak. The current view is that although hearing impairment is a great barrier to normal speech development, very few deaf individuals cannot be taught some speech. One of the reasons for this change is the growing body of evidence that almost no children are born with absolutely no hearing sensation.

Regardless of the successes that can be cited, the fact remains that without extensive training (and many would claim even *with* extensive training), the hearing-impaired child will not develop normal English language comprehension and production. Carhart (1970) notes that the child who is totally deaf *will* grow up mute unless given special training.

Why are hearing-impaired people so prone to poor English language and speech ability? First of all, the earlier the hearing loss occurs, the worse the English language deficit will be. In Lenneberg's words:

> Those who lose hearing after having been exposed to the experience of speech, even for as short a period as one year, can be trained much more easily in all language arts, even if formal training begins some years after they have become deaf. . . . It seems as if even a short exposure to language, a brief moment during which the curtain has been lifted and oral communication established, is sufficient to give a child some foundation on which much later language training can be based. (1966, pp. 237–239)

Many factors cause the child born with a hearing impairment to have a more difficult time with English language acquisition than the child who acquires an impairment after a period of time. Three of the most obvious disadvantages hearing-impaired children face are that they:

1. Receive inadequate auditory feedback when they make sounds
2. Receive inadequate verbal reinforcement from adults
3. Are unable to hear adequately an adult language model

Inadequate auditory feedback and verbal reinforcement are often cited as reasons for the deaf child's particular pattern of babbling as an infant (Ling and Ling, 1978; Schow and Nerbonne, 1980). The deaf infant enters the babbling stage at the same time as the hearing infant, but soon abandons it. By as early as 8 months of age, and possibly earlier, hearing-impaired babies babble less than nonhandicapped infants. And the babbling they do is of a qualitatively different nature: Hearing-impaired infants produce a smaller variety of consonants in their babbling than do hearing infants (Stoel-Gammon and Otomo, 1986). It is thought that these differences occur because hearing infants are reinforced by hearing their own babbling and by hearing the verbal responses of adults. Deaf children, unable to hear either themselves or others, are not reinforced.

The lack of feedback has also been named as a primary cause of deaf children's poor speech production. As Fry (1966) states, hearing children learn to associate the sensations they receive when they move their jaws, mouth, and tongue with the auditory sounds these movements produce. Hearing-impaired children are obviously handicapped in this process. In addition, they have a difficult time hearing the sounds of adult speech, which other children hear and imitate, so they are deprived of an adequate adult model.

Table 6-1 gives general examples of the effects various degrees of hearing loss may have on English language development. This is only a general statement of these relationships, since many factors interact to influence language development in the hearing-impaired child.

Intellectual Ability

The intellectual ability of hearing-impaired children, particularly those classified as deaf, has been a subject of much controversy over the years. Traditionally there have been two very different points of view. One states that hearing impairment results in

Table 6-1   Relationship of Degree of Impairment* to Understanding of Language and Speech

Average of the Speech Frequencies in Better Ear	Effect of Hearing Loss on Understanding of Language and Speech
SLIGHT 27–40 dB (ISO)	May have difficulty hearing faint or distant speech. May experience some difficulty with language arts subjects.
MILD 41–55 dB (ISO)	Understands conversational speech at a distance of 3–5 feet (face to face). May miss as much as 50 percent of class discussions if voices are faint or not in line of vision. May exhibit limited vocabulary and speech anomalies.
MARKED 56–70 dB (ISO)	Conversation must be loud to be understood. Will have increased difficulty in group discussions. Is likely to have defective speech. Is likely to be deficient in language usage and comprehension. Will have limited vocabulary.
SEVERE 71–90 dB (ISO)	May hear loud voices about one foot from the ear. May be able to identify environmental sounds. May be able to discriminate vowels but not all consonants. Speech and language defective and likely to deteriorate.
EXTREME 91 dB or MORE (ISO)	May hear some loud sounds but is aware of vibrations more than tonal patterns. Relies on vision rather than hearing as primary avenue for communication. Speech and language defective and likely to deteriorate.

SOURCE: Adapted from *Report of a Committee for a Comprehensive Plan for Hearing-Impaired Children,* May 1968, Office of the Superintendent of Public Instruction, Title VI, Elementary and Secondary Education Act, and the University of Illinois, Division of Services for Crippled Children.
* Medically irreversible conditions and those requiring prolonged medical care.

deficient conceptual ability because thought depends on language (Vygotsky, 1962). The other states that thought is possible without language, so only language-related concepts are difficult for hearing-impaired individuals (Furth, 1964, 1971). A more recent point of view is that hearing-impaired individuals have in sign language a true language. Any difficulty they may have on conceptual tasks is therefore due not to poor language ability itself, but rather to inadequate communication with those around them (Liben, 1978).

Thought Depends on Language

Because the influence of hearing loss on English language development is great, many have assumed that cognitive or intellectual development must also be affected. This belief has been kept alive primarily because some psychologists and educators have equated language with cognitive abilities. Vygotsky (1962), for instance, theorized that the early speech of children becomes interiorized as inner speech, and inner speech is the equivalent of cognitive thought. According to this view, the intellectual growth of a person parallels language development, and a severely hearing-impaired individual is also handicapped in cognitive ability.

Thought Does Not Depend on Language

Hans Furth is the strongest advocate of the position that thought is possible without language. He believes that deaf children are not necessarily slower intellectually than hearing children. Besides conducting his own studies, Furth (1964, 1971) has reviewed experiments designed to compare the concept development of deaf and hearing children. His conclusion is that the cognitive abilities of deaf children are essentially unimpaired except in cases in which the particular concept is dependent on language experience. He believes, moreover, that the occurrence of language-dependent concepts is low enough so that overall cognitive development need not be retarded in deaf children. In addition, Furth stresses that when deaf children do perform less well than hearing children on intellectual tasks, it may be because they have not received adequate parental stimulation or educational instruction. Ross and Hoemann agree with Furth in the conclusions they draw from their study of probability concepts in deaf and hearing adolescents:

> It can be concluded that adolescent deaf subjects do, in general, show a lag in performance on probability problems when compared with like-aged hearing peers. This lag is small when balanced against the twin advantages of the hearing comparison groups of a greatly superior mastery of language and more advanced mathematical instruction. That unselected deaf subjects made significant progress with classroom training and that deaf adolescents who had a prior short-course in logic performed as well as hearing adolescents suggests that a severe language deficit by itself is not a handicap; obtained differences appear to be the result of experience and teaching differences. (1975, pp. 112–113)

Hearing-Impaired Individuals Have a True Language

In the late 1970s professionals began to question Furth's position that language and therefore language-related concepts are deficient in deaf people. More and more professionals are recognizing that manual sign language is a true language with its own rules of grammar (Baker and Bathson, 1980; Klima and Bellugi, 1979; Meadow, 1980; Wilbur, 1979). They now believe that Furth's position on language must be qualified to mean *English* language. Any problems hearing-impaired children may have on conceptual tasks are due to the relative lack of communication between them and the "hearing" society, which uses only standard spoken English (Liben, 1978).

Intelligence Testing

Besides experimental investigations of concept development, there is also a long tradition of controversy over results of intelligence testing of hearing-impaired children. Years ago, the prevailing opinion was that hearing impairment led to lower intelligence scores. These notions, however, were based on studies using IQ tests that were heavily verbal. Today, most authorities agree that, if nonverbal intelligence tests are used and especially if these tests are administered using sign language, hearing-impaired students are not intellectually retarded (Sullivan, 1982). And those who do score in the retarded range tend to be among the 20 to 40 percent of deaf individuals who have additional handicaps—visual impairment, learning disabilities, and so forth (Meadow, 1984).

An example of a study showing hearing-impaired children to be equal to hearing children in nonverbal IQ is the Annual Survey of Hearing Impaired Children and Youth of Gallaudet College as reported by McConnell (1973). This survey of 19,698 hearing-impaired children, the majority of whom were deaf, found the average nonverbal IQ to be 100.38. Lenneberg agrees, saying:

In my experience with preschool deaf children (screened for psychiatric and nervous disorders), I have found the individual performances on the Leiter scale (1936–1955), which is a largely language-free concept formation test, to differ in no respect from those of hearing children. In this test, pictures have to be sorted in accordance with given criteria. . . . Toys with toys, musical instruments with musical instruments, four symbols with four symbols. The sorting criteria go from the simple to the complex and require both conceptualization as well as reasoning. . . .

My colleagues also have used this test on many deaf and hearing children . . . [and] have found that successful performance even of older children than those tested by myself does not depend on the demonstrable language skills of the individual. (1967, pp. 360–361)

There are several nonverbal intelligence tests available for use with hearing-impaired students. Four of the most popular are the Performance Scale of the Wechsler Intelligence Scale for Children-Revised (WISC-R), the Leiter International Performance Scale, the Raven's Progressive Matrices, and the Hiskey-Nebraska Test of Learning Aptitude. There is some evidence that the Hiskey-Nebraska may be the best predictor of how well hearing-impaired pupils will do academically (Watson, Goldgar, Kroese, and Lotz, 1986).

Academic Achievement

Unfortunately, hearing-impaired children are frequently handicapped in varying degrees in educational achievement. Reading ability, which relies heavily on language skills and is probably the most important aspect of academic achievement, is the most affected. A number of surveys over the years, taken as a whole, paint a gloomy picture of the academic progress of hearing-impaired students, particularly deaf youngsters. And the situation does not appear to be improving. So it is difficult to argue with Furth's (1973) claim that only a small percentage of deaf individuals understand language well enough to read a college-level textbook.

Using a special 1973 edition of the Stanford Achievement Test (SAT-HI) that was standardized on 6,871 hearing-impaired children, Trybus and Karchmer (1977) found severe underachievement in reading. By age 20, only about half of the students were able to read at mid-fourth-grade level—that is, barely at newspaper literacy level. In addition, in arithmetic, a subject that is one of the highest areas of achievement for hearing-impaired youngsters, less than half of the students were able to work at an eighth-grade level by age 20.

The 1973 adaptation of the SAT was used widely until 1983, when a new version of the SAT-HI was introduced (Allen, White, and Karchmer, 1983). Though it is too early to tell what effect this new edition will have on the tested achievement levels of hearing-impaired students, it is doubtful that it will show they have achievement levels comparable to those of hearing individuals. This does not mean that hearing-impaired students are inherently incapable of achieving much higher levels than they ordinarily do. It is fair to say, however, that hearing-impaired students are in need of much more intensive instruction than they typically receive in order to make up for the disadvantage of their hearing loss. Moog and Geers (1985), for example, found that a three-year program of intensive and systematic instruction for profoundly hearing-impaired children started when they were 6 to 8 years of age resulted in the students being only one year behind their hearing peers in reading achievement.

Social Adjustment

Social and personality development in the general population depends heavily on communication. Social interaction, by definition, is the communication of ideas between two or more people. In the hearing population, language is by far the most common way messages move between people. Because of society's heavy dependence on language, it is no wonder that many investigators have found hearing-impaired individuals to have personality and social characteristics different from those of people who have normal hearing ability (see McConnell, 1973; Meadow, 1975, 1984; and Myklebust, 1964, for reviews of this literature). The personality problems to which we refer are not severe. As Meadow (1975) has pointed out, severe emotional disturbance is no more prevalent in deaf individuals than in those with hearing. Rather, deaf people have more "problems of living"—higher arrest rates, and more marital, social, and vocational problems. There is also some evidence suggesting that it is the 20 to 40 percent of deaf children who have additional handicaps—for example, visual impairment and learning disabilities—who are likely to exhibit social maladjustment (Meadow, 1984).

Whether a hearing-impaired child will develop behavioral problems depends on how well those in the child's environment accept the disability (Hoemann and Briga, 1981; Moores, 1982). Just as with other physical and sensory impairments, it is not the hearing impairment itself, but how individuals in the child's environment—particularly parents—respond that largely determines whether the child will show behavioral problems. As Hoemann and Briga point out, the family climate is critical:

> When there is only one deaf child among the family of hearing persons, it often happens that the deaf child is excluded from the affairs of the family. It is tedious for a hearing member of the family to explain things to the deaf child, and it is easy to leave the deaf child out of family discussions and decision making. Meanwhile, hearing children not only hear, they overhear much of what goes on in the home, even the fights that their parents have and their telephone conversations with personal and business associates. The deaf child does not benefit from this informal education about the affairs of living, and such an experiential deficit can have long-lasting effects on the child's social adjustment and development of social competence. (1981, p. 232)

Because they are frequently cut off from communicating with the population at large, hearing-impaired children can grow up in relative isolation. They sometimes have difficulty making friends, and are perceived by teachers as excessively shy (Loeb and Sarigiani, 1986). This tendency toward withdrawn behavior can be even more pronounced if they do not have hearing-impaired parents or peers with whom they can interact nonverbally.

It is probably the need for social interaction and acceptance that is most influential in leading many hearing-impaired individuals to associate primarily with other hearing-impaired persons. Hard-of-hearing, and especially deaf individuals, more than any other handicapped group, tend to mix socially with people who have the same handicap.

This preference for isolation from the hearing community on the part of some deaf persons can be viewed as beneficial or not. Furth is one who stresses the worth of what he calls "the deaf community":

> Of all physical disabilities, deafness is the only one that makes its members part of a natural community. Therefore, although we do not find blind or crippled subgroups in society, we are justified in referring to a deaf community as a societal subgroup. This major difference

More than any other disabled population, deaf people tend to socialize with others who share the same disability. This is due to the special role that communication plays in social interaction. (Bob Nickelsberg/Gamma Liaison)

between deafness and other disabilities must never be forgotten. In the United States deaf persons are perhaps better organized than in other parts of the world, but regardless of country, deafness creates an underlying community that provides for all but a few individuals a social-psychological basis of belonging. This belonging to a community is probably the single most important factor working in favor of the deaf individual. (1973, pp. 1–2)

This strong inclination toward isolation and socializing only with other hearing-impaired individuals poses special problems for mainstreaming hearing-impaired students. Some authorities recommend training these students in specific social skills, such as conversational skills, asking and answering questions, accepting and responding to criticism, and accepting and giving compliments (Smith, Schloss, and Schloss, 1984).

EDUCATIONAL CONSIDERATIONS

The problems facing the educator of hearing-impaired children are formidable ones. As we would expect, one major dilemma is communication. Teachers of hearing-impaired pupils face the challenge of communicating with their students and teaching them how to communicate with others. There are three general approaches to teaching communication:

1. Auditory training
2. Speechreading
3. Sign language and fingerspelling

Before describing each of these methods and their combinations in the total communication approach, we should say something about a major controversy concerning the teaching of communication skills: the oralism-manualism debate.

Oralism versus Manualism

Auditory training and speechreading are associated with what has traditionally been known as the oral approach; the sign language and fingerspelling methods have traditionally been called the manual approach. For many years the oral and manual methods were viewed as two radically different schools of thought. Some schools using the oral method prohibited gesturing by the children. The overriding philosophy was that it is crucial for the deaf child to learn to develop what remaining hearing he or she has and to learn to speak well enough to communicate with hearing individuals. Advocates of manualism believed, however, that very few persons classified as deaf have enough hearing ability to enable them to be trained to communicate with the rest of society. Their emphasis was on methods like sign language that would provide the deaf child with a code for communicating with other deaf individuals and with teachers.

Manualism was the preferred method until the middle of the nineteenth century, when oralism started to gain in popularity. Oralism then predominated until the late 1960s and early 1970s, when it became obvious that a combination of the two approaches was the most logical choice. At the end of the 1960s the Maryland School, a residential facility, developed what has come to be known as the **total communication approach.** Although there are still advocates of oral- and manual-only approaches, total communication is now the most frequent method used in classes for hearing-impaired students.

As Moores and Maestas y Moores (1981) point out, the shift from oral-only instruction to an approach that combines manual methods and oral techniques was brought about by two factors:

1. A number of research studies (Meadow, 1968; Stuckless and Birch, 1966; Vernon and Koh, 1970, 1971) found that deaf children of deaf parents who had been exposed to manual methods, when compared to deaf children of hearing parents who had not been so exposed, were superior in English skills, academic achievement, writing, reading, and social maturity. In addition, there were no differences in speech between the two groups.
2. In the late 1960s there was a growing dissatisfaction with the effectiveness of oral-only methods, particularly at the preschool level.

Williams (1985) also provides the following rationale for the use of total communication over the once-predominant oralism:

In my 50 years of involvement in services to deaf people, the widespread failure of the expensive educational program for this special population of normal intelligence has resisted change until the past two decades. I believe that the beginning of this change occurred in the National Leadership Training Program at California State University at Northridge where future heads of schools for the deaf were in close daily contact with deaf fellow students. These future school superintendents learned from sources higher than textbooks or ideological lectures, specifically deaf leaders of the deaf. They learned that a methodology of teaching the deaf, oralism, which largely ignored the primary strength of deaf people, their normal intelligence, in favor of its inherent psychological incredibility was the probable main cause of the disordered language of prelingual deaf people.

It is now recognized that sign language can convey the expression of abstract concepts. (Mimi Forsyth/Monkmeyer Press)

The Maryland School for the deaf got the message and courageously pioneered total communication which has since swept the country. The word "courageously" is used advisedly, for the poor logic of the established system was known to many, but none spoke out before. One cannot say that courage was lacking elsewhere. It was more likely a question of timing in a state school whose board of trustees was able to agree that something else needed to be done in the face of the continuing and pervasive language problems of prelingually deaf persons.

And so today we have practically universal adherence to total communication throughout the country. In the words of Mary E. Switzer, great champion of deaf people, on our way to talk with Supreme Court Justice Tom Clark, she remarked in effect that the methodology battle was ridiculous in view of the pressing need for deaf children to have every possible cue (lipreading, speech, signs, writing, amplification) in order to understand what was being discussed. Total communication is just that. Moreover, it is for deaf people the equal opportunity that the Constitution of the United States guarantees them. . . .

In closing, please let me assure you that I, and the mass who think as I have stated, are very pro-speech. However, we are first prolanguage. We are aware that language is the main goal, that speech is one method of language manifestation, that signs are another method, and that all are attainable and conditions for effective living for most deaf people. We are deeply concerned that the methodology conform to the logic of human development. We are firm in our believe [sic] that total communication is the way to improve language and secure better speech among deaf people, the way to their better emotional and mental health, the way to their capabilities for higher level training and consequently, the way to more challenging and satisfying employment and community involvement (Williams, 1985, pp. 2–3).

Oral Techniques— Auditory Training and Speechreading

Auditory training is the procedure of teaching the deaf or hard-of-hearing child to make use of what hearing he or she possesses. Advocates claim that all but a very few totally deaf children are able to benefit from auditory training. The benefits of auditory training have been augmented by rapid technological advances in the development of hearing aids.

Speechreading—sometimes inappropriately called lipreading—involves teaching hearing-impaired children to use visual information to understand what is being said to them. Speechreading is a more accurate term than lipreading because the latter refers only to the use of visual cues arising from movement of the mouth in speaking. Other visual stimuli in the environment, however, can help the hearing-impaired person to understand spoken messages.

There is a controversy among those advocating the oral approach about how much to stress auditory training versus speechreading. One popular view is that the teacher should first concentrate on getting the hearing-impaired child to use his or her residual hearing (Sanders, 1982). Accordingly, visual cues associated with speechreading should not be denied the child, but the teacher should focus attention on them only when the student needs more information than can be gained from auditory stimulation alone.

Auditory Training

Auditory training frequently involves three major goals:

1. Development of awareness of sound

2. Development of the ability to make gross discriminations among environmental sounds
3. Development of the ability to discriminate among speech sounds

DEVELOPMENT OF AWARENESS OF SOUND   The first task facing the teacher of a hearing-impaired child is to be sure the child knows there is a variety of sounds, including speech, in his or her environment. This goal will be especially difficult if the child's parents have inadvertently ignored this important area. Helping severely affected children to realize that speech is a means of communication can be a major task. Children who are profoundly deaf from birth, for example, may have great difficulty in adjusting to the use of hearing aids if they are not introduced early in infancy (Sanders, 1982). The sounds they are hearing for the first time may seem so overwhelming that they learn to "tune them out." Thus most advocates of auditory training underscore the importance of using amplification as soon as possible so the young child develops an awareness of the function of sound in his or her environment.

GROSS DISCRIMINATIONS OF ENVIRONMENTAL SOUNDS   Once the child is aware of sound, the process of teaching gross discriminations of environmental sounds begins. This training usually starts at about 3 years of age and often involves requiring children to match prerecorded environmental sounds with their corresponding pictures. The following is an example of how the teacher works with children in the early stages of learning to discriminate among environmental sounds:

> Your first task is to ensure that the children are aware of the sounds you have recorded and to check that each child is familiar with them. In the first session present each sound three or four times with a short pause between each presentation. For example, the first sound may be a telephone ringing. As you play and repeat the recording, show the children a picture of a telephone. You listen, point to the picture and say, "telephone—the telephone's ringing—telephone." If you have any doubts whether a particular child can hear the sound, play the game with that child alone. "John—listen, point to the telephone when it rings—that's right, it's ringing—listen again—good boy." Repeat the procedure for a small group of different sounds which you should present one by one—for example, telephone ringing, dog barking, fire engine clanging, vacuum cleaner going. These then constitute the sounds for a first lesson in listening and watching. . . .

> Some children entering the preschool program late, particularly those with limited residual hearing, may need to work with actual noisemakers rather than taped sounds. Drums, bells, keys, or rattles may prove more stimulating initially than recorded sounds, because the child experiences the actual noise source, can see and hold it, and can make the sounds himself or herself. (Sanders, 1982, pp. 296–297)

DISCRIMINATION AMONG SPEECH SOUNDS   Once the child can identify gross environmental sounds, he or she is taught to discriminate speech sounds. The discrimination of speech sounds requires much more sophisticated learning on the part of the child than does the discrimination of gross environmental sounds. One of the reasons why speech discrimination training is so complicated is that everyday speech frequently occurs among a variety of factors, referred to as "noise," that can reduce the discriminability of the speech sounds.

Noise used in this sense has a broader meaning than mere audible noise. Noise can occur within the speaker, the environment, or the listener. An example of noise within the speaker would be poor syntax. An example within the environment would be sound reverberation. An example of noise within the listener would be his or her high distractibility (Sanders, 1982). Thus, although speech discrimination training in the early stages may take place under optimum, low-noise conditions, the child must gradually be trained to cope with discriminating speech under more natural conditions that are relatively high in noise.

There is also evidence indicating that speech discrimination training should go hand in hand with speech production. Research suggests that hearing-impaired individuals trained to listen and produce speech sounds make better progress in both speech production and speech discrimination than do those whose training only involves listening (Novelli-Olmstead and Ling, 1984).

Silverman provides several guidelines that are useful in setting up auditory training procedures:

1. Most deaf children have a small but useful portion of the auditory area that lies above the range of useful audiometry. Consequently, many children who have been termed "totally deaf" as a result of audiometric tests actually can hear properly amplified sound. Audiograms may not tell the whole story of a child's ability to appreciate speech by his hearing. Formal auditory training is essential, however, to teach the deaf child to make use of this remnant of hearing. The hearing aid alone is not enough.

2. Auditory training appears to be more effective, through mutual reinforcement, when hearing is combined with vision and/or touch. There are times when hearing alone is used to teach a child to concentrate on specified information-bearing cues.

3. The techniques of auditory training should be geared to a child's auditory capabilities. This requires frequent assessment of his hearing.

4. Auditory training, even without a hearing aid, should be begun as soon as it is determined that a child is deaf.

5. Formal instruction can make hearing aids more acceptable to children by giving them experiences that are meaningful. Such instruction should teach children to discriminate, even though grossly, various environmental sounds, and, within the limits of their hearing, teach them to understand speech by hearing. (1971, p. 420)

Speechreading

Speechreading (sometimes called lipreading) involves teaching hearing-impaired children to use visual information to understand what is being said to them. There are two general approaches to teaching speechreading. The *analytic* method emphasizes teaching the person to perceive small segments of speech, such as syllables, and then to recognize them when they are put together in words and sentences. The *synthetic* approach promotes the idea that the person should concentrate on the meaning of speech rather than on individual sounds.

Sanders (1982) lists three different kinds of visual stimuli that need to be considered in the training of the hearing-impaired child:

1. Stimuli arising from the environment in which the communication occurs.

2. Stimuli associated directly with the message, but not part of speech production.

3. Stimuli directly associated with the production of speech sounds. (1982, p. 76)

ONE PROFESSIONAL'S PERSPECTIVE

Susan Davidoff Gershowitz

B.S., Education of the Deaf and Elementary Education, University of Illinois
M.Ed., Special Education with minor in Counseling, University of Pittsburgh
Current Position: Teacher of a total communication class of first and second grade deaf children, Montgomery County Public Schools, Maryland

Ms. Susan Davidoff Gershowitz has been a resource and self-contained class teacher of the deaf since 1974. The students she is currently teaching have a wide range and multiplicity of problems. In general, her students have severe to profound bilateral sensorineural hearing losses. Though some have good to excellent speech, a large proportion of her children have speech that is unintelligible to those unfamiliar with speech of deaf individuals. All students in Ms. Gershowitz's class use sign language. And approximately half come from families in which the parents are deaf. Most of her students have normal intelligence, but some tend to have learning disabilities, possibly as a consequence of their hearing problems.

In addition, Ms. Gershowitz, herself deaf, is the founder and director of "Deaf Dimensions—A Hearing and Deaf Dance Company," and is one of the 15 dancers in the company. This group combines different dimensions of the arts—music, dance, song, and mime—with expressive sign language.

We asked Ms. Gershowitz the following series of questions:

What influenced your decision to be a teacher of hearing impaired children?   From my childhood, I had always wanted to be a teacher, later narrowing my specific interest in teaching to physical education. After losing my hearing at 16 years of age, however, I was forced to reassess my situation. Rather than abandoning the idea of teaching completely, I came to realize that I could fulfill my lifelong goals by teaching the deaf.

After extensive investigation, I identified the University of Illinois' Deaf Education program as most appropriate to my interests. The program, however, was restricted to students with normal hearing. Though I applied for admission, I was denied entrance. Because I had a long-standing love for and interest in dance, with the advice and counsel of the rehabilitation-education center at the University, I enrolled in the University's Dance Education program, with the eventual, though much narrower, objective of teaching dance to deaf students.

As a freshman dance major, I took untold hours of dance classes, music history, and choreography. Because I simply could not hear the instructors, I disliked the classes intensely. (Ironically, I received As in music classes—not bad for a deaf person!) But my determination to gain admission into the Deaf Education program was strengthened. To this end, I did what I could to gain experience. I learned sign language on my own, did volunteer work, worked as a teacher's aide in a summer school auditory program, and armed myself with numerous recommendations from persons in the field who had seen my work with deaf people. Finally, a year and a half later, I was admitted to the program—the first deaf person to be accepted into the University of Illinois' Deaf Education program. I then came to realize that what I really wanted was to teach deaf children *everything*—language, math, science, reading—whatever was necessary to teach them to communicate and ultimately to fulfill their potential.

What major changes have occurred in your field since you began teaching?   In the past several years, the most noticeable change in the field stems from the fact that the use of Total Communication in the classroom has become more acceptable and widespread. In the past, Total Communication was considered to be the appropriate choice only for those deaf children who failed in oral classes where speaking, amplification, and speechreading were emphasized. It was felt that using sign language would impede speech development. The increasing acceptance of sign language is, additionally, reflected by its integration into school systems, the media, and the broader community. It is even now offered as an elective in high schools. And more parents are, in fact, now choosing Total Communication classes as the most effective teaching approach for their children.

There have been other changes, too. For example, cued speech has grown in popularity. The Montgomery County's Auditory Program now has classes using three modalities—Total

Communication, Oralism, and Cued Speech.

Pick the one student in your career with whom you've had the most success and describe your involvement with him or her. Picture a Puerto Rican boy, 9 years old, who had apparently received only the most insignificant education in the Puerto Rican day care center where he had been kept all his life. He had no language, only a crude gesture system he had invented. He had no speech, only animal-like sounds came from his mouth. When he entered the classroom for the first time, he ran to the board and wrote his first name. And that was all he knew. He was wild and uncontrollable, rolling on the floor, climbing up to the windows, running around the room, totally without discipline. It took me two weeks just to get him to sit in a chair!

Where to begin? For four months, we worked on colors—not reading colors, *identifying* them. I wondered if he was color blind. Then one day the learning clicked—he ran around, identifying the color of everything he touched. His response was reminiscent of Helen Keller's learning the word "water."

At the same time, we worked on numbers, ABCs, language and communication. I started to teach him to count to 5, then 10, using signed numbers, though he fought me because he did not like contorting his fingers to make the numbers. It was several months before he could sign the "names" of things around him, but in time he "soaked up" everything and began to love to learn. He did not like to *do* work, however. Many times he refused to do the written work he was given. Rather than sit and write, he wanted to sit and learn by interacting with the teacher. But I taught him the concept of "stubborn." Though he did not fully understand the word, he knew it

was not flattering. Whenever I said, "Don't be stubborn," he would look embarrassed and proceed to work.

By the end of two years in my class, this boy was doing third-grade math and reading primers with great zest. His signed communication, though lacking correct sentence structure, was clear and meaningful. He could write simple sentences, usually following fixed patterns, could answer questions, use a few pronouns and negations, differentiate between singular and plural forms, and make noun-verb agreements for the verb "be."

There is an ironic ending to this story. After two years with a foster family in this area, the youngster returned to Puerto Rico to live with his parents. Though I doubt Puerto Rico offers special education for deaf children in any way comparable to what we offer in Montgomery County, I like to think that our efforts were not wasted, that this student did not totally lose his new skills and desire to learn, and that he has continued to build upon the educational foundation—fragile though it was—that had been established during the two-year period that we worked together.

Describe the most challenging student you've ever had and what made him or her so difficult. The multiple problems of a child that I began to teach when he was 16 years old were so overwhelming that his family had not been able to find him an educational program. He was deaf, diabetic, autistic, hyperactive, and more. He lived in his own world, in a room with nothing but toys to play with. Without language or a communication system, whenever he was tested, the results always indicated mental retardation. In combination with all his other problems, the mental retardation label kept this youngster from being accepted into school.

By a stroke of luck, however, for the first time at age 16 he was admitted to a Montgomery County school for retarded students. Because he was autistic as well as deaf, had no language or sign language system and no one to help, he sat in the class day after day unaware of what was happening. Moreover, from time to time, from frustration, boredom, or whatever other reason, this tall, strong 16-year-old would simply explode—he kicked through the walls, broke desks, threw chairs.

When I was assigned as this student's first auditory resource teacher, with some hesitation I undertook the difficult task of teaching him language, communication, and later math skills. Because he was so big, I must admit I was somewhat afraid at first. But I tried to keep his level of frustration at a minimum as I taught him the most basic skills. At the end of the first year, when retested, this youngster was found to have an IQ of 125! Because of his late start in school and his autism, however, he continued to be functionally retarded.

Planning ways to teach this student presented a continuing challenge. The results were, however, tremendously gratifying. Significantly, during the period when I served as this youngster's resource teacher, his status changed so dramatically that he was able to be placed in a foster home with a hearing-impaired man who worked in the school system. In the four years he was in the school system (he reached the maximum limit at age 20), he learned functional life skills and social behavior. In addition to low-level communication skills, he learned basic math, money management, and enough functional language for daily living. Six years later he still lives with his foster father, who continues to teach him at home.

ENVIRONMENTAL STIMULI   The training of hearing-impaired children depends greatly on their ability to pay attention to and obtain meaning from the environment. In the first phase of training the teacher concentrates on making children aware of situational cues that accompany spoken messages. This involves teaching children to expect certain kinds of messages in certain kinds of situations. These expectancy predictions can rarely be completely accurate, though, and it is important that the teacher realize this. A significant goal of this stage of therapy is simply to help the young child to an awareness of his or her visual surroundings. One way of sharpening this awareness is to show the child pictures and then ask questions about them.

NONVERBAL STIMULI DIRECTLY RELATED TO THE SPEAKER   Training in this area involves teaching the child that some actions of the speaker are more likely to be connected with certain messages. Facial expressions are the best example of nonverbal cues directly related to the content and tone of the words the speaker is using. It would, for instance, be unlikely that a person would be smiling while talking about a serious car accident he or she had seen.

SPEECH STIMULI   This phase of training involves teaching the child to discriminate among visible stimuli arising from the production of speech. Such discrimination is not easy; it requires a great deal of concentration and hard work on the part of the individual with a hearing loss. The speechreader must learn to rely on visual cues from the lips, tongue, and jaw to differentiate various sounds from one another. For example, in order to discriminate among vowels, the speechreader learns to rely on cues related to the degree of jaw opening and lip shaping (see Figure 6.2).

A number of factors can influence the visibility of speech movements. Four mentioned by Sanders (1982) are these:

1. The degree of visibility of the movement.
2. The rapidity of articulatory movements.
3. The similarity of the visual characteristics of the articulatory movements involved in the production of different speech sounds.
4. Intersubject variations in the visible aspects of articulatory movements involved in the production of any given sound. (1982, pp. 78–79).

Regarding the visibility of speech movements, many sounds are produced with little obvious movement of the mouth. This adds to the difficulty of speechreading.

Figure 6.2 *Differentiation among vowels is made on the basis of jaw opening and lip shaping. The contrast between /a/ (as in "father") and /i/ (as in "he") is shown here.*
SOURCE: D. A. Sanders, *Aural Rehabilitation,* 2nd ed. (Englewood Cliffs, N.J.: Prentice-Hall, 1982), p. 128.

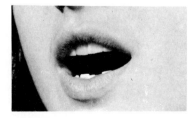
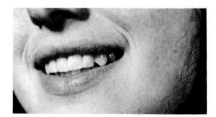

[ɑ]   [i]

Furthermore, as Silverman (1971) points out, the amount of light on the speaker's face is important.

The rapidity with which one speaks can also be crucial. Sanders cites data showing that the average speaker makes about thirteen articulatory movements per second during normal conversation—and the average person can visually record only eight or nine movements per second. If the speechreader encounters a fast talker, the problem becomes worse.

Although each sound has its own particular articulatory patterns, the visible ("revealing") movements are not unique to each sound. There are many **homophenes,** sounds that are identical in terms of revealing movements. For example, the speechreader cannot distinguish when the speaker pronounces [p], [b], or [m].

Intersubject variation (differences among individuals) also causes difficulty for the speechreader. No two people pronounce sounds exactly alike. One example of this is the noticeable difference between a speaker from the southeastern United States and a native of Boston, Massachusetts. Intrasubject variation (differences within individuals) refers to the fact that even the same person changes to some extent the way he or she pronounces sounds from time to time.

Manual Techniques— Sign Language and Fingerspelling

As we indicated earlier, manual approaches have a long history. For example, Socrates in the third century B.C. referred to deaf individuals as using their hands, head, and other parts of their bodies to signify meaning (Bender, 1981). And there is evidence that in the seventeenth and eighteenth centuries signs were used to communicate by monastic orders of priests who were not allowed to speak because of vows of silence (Bender, 1981). In fact, the priest who opened the first school for deaf children in Paris in 1775 used many Trappist gestures to establish communication with his pupils (Furth, 1973).

There have been, and are, a variety of signing systems. Today a standard set of signs known as **American Sign Language (Ameslan)** is used by many deaf people. Because the system lacks some of the grammatical features of oral English, it was formerly not considered a true language. However, beginning in the 1970s (Bellugi and Klima, 1978; Meadow, 1975; Wilbur, 1979) there was a change in attitude. Ameslan today is considered by most professionals to be a true language. In fact, Ameslan "grammarians" speak of the same types of grammatical errors as traditional grammarians do when referring to spoken and written English. They even speak of "slips of the hand" (the equivalent of "slips of the tongue"). Another myth that has been exploded in recent years is that Ameslan is merely a system for conveying concrete ideas. It is now recognized that Ameslan can be used to express any level of abstraction (Bellugi and Klima, 1978).

Whereas sign language is a system of gestures, **fingerspelling** is a "spelling out" of the English alphabet by various finger positions on one hand. Figure 6.3 shows the fingerspelling, or manual, alphabet.

Total Communication, the Rochester Method, and Cued Speech

As we mentioned earlier, total communication is now the method of choice for most educators of hearing-impaired students. Depending on the particular child and situa-

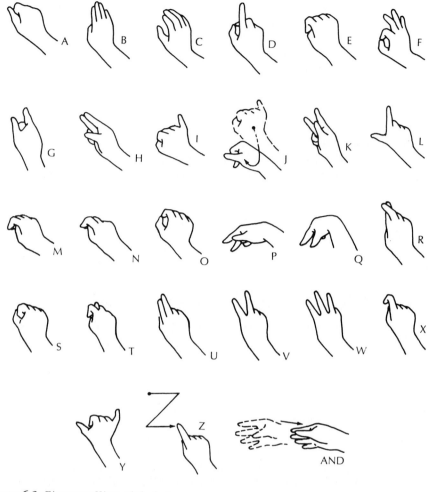

Figure 6.3 *Fingerspelling alphabet.*
SOURCE: L. J. Fant, Jr., *Say it with Hands* (Silver Springs, Md.: National Association for the Deaf, 1971), pp. 1–2.)

tion, the teacher uses a combination of such techniques as auditory training, speechreading, sign language, and fingerspelling.

The **Rochester method** is similar to total communication in that it blends aspects of oralism and manualism by combining fingerspelling and the oral method. It is not widely used, though, because it results in a very slow rate of presentation (Moores and Maetas y Moores, 1981).

Cued speech is a method of augmenting speechreading. In cued speech the individual uses hand shapes to represent specific sounds while the spoken words are produced. Eight hand shapes represent different consonants and four hand positions cue vowels, with diphthongs being represented by gliding from the beginning to the ending vowel. Nicholls and Ling (1982) report the results of a study that showed cued speech to be a viable means of communication for deaf individuals.

Closely related to the principles behind cued speech is the development of the autocuer. The autocuer is a minicomputer that "hears" words spoken to a hearing-impaired person and flashes symbols onto the lenses of a pair of eyeglasses. The symbols, like hand signals in cued speech, are visual cues to help differentiate sounds that look alike to the hearing-impaired speechreader.

Administrative Arrangements

Hearing-impaired students can be found in settings ranging from regular classrooms to residential institutions. With the passage of PL 94-142, more and more hearing-impaired children are being served in regular classrooms. According to the U.S. Department of Education (see Figure 1.2), however, only about 38 percent of hearing-impaired students are educated in regular classrooms. And the figures are undoubtedly drastically lower for hearing-impaired students who also have other handicapping conditions, such as blindness.

One of the major reasons professionals and parents have been hesitant to mainstream large numbers of hearing-impaired students is the great difficulties they have with the English language. Residential facilities have been a major influence in fostering the concept of a "deaf community" or a deaf subculture (Meadow, 1972). One reason for this is that residential facilities are much more likely to hire deaf teachers than are day programs. Another is that many deaf parents place their deaf children in residential facilities.

The practice of mainstreaming for hearing-impaired students is gaining momentum. Educators are becoming aware that hearing-impaired children, particularly the

A total communication approach is a blend of oral and manual methods. (Melissa Grimes-Guy/Photo Researchers)

less severe cases, are best served as close to the mainstream as possible. In the resource room situation, the teacher can work as much as is needed on a one-to-one basis with the child. Once ready, the child can gradually be reintegrated into the regular classroom.

There are, however, a number of adjustments that the regular class teacher will have to make to accommodate the hearing-impaired child. The majority of hearing-impaired children who are currently mainstreamed have mild or moderate hearing losses, but a substantial number have severe or profound losses (Karchmer and Trybus, 1977). In other words, there is a good chance that the regular class teacher will receive a child who has very little hearing. A number of suggestions for handling the hearing-impaired child in the regular classroom are included in the final section of this chapter. A most important thing to keep in mind in educating hearing-impaired children in regular classrooms is that close physical proximity does not guarantee social interaction between hearing-impaired and nonhandicapped peers (Antia, 1985; Soderhan and Whiren, 1985). The teacher must structure situations that facilitate interaction.

Whether an integrated situation will work depends to a certain extent on the degree of hearing loss. In 1975 an Ad Hoc Committee to Define Deaf and Hard of Hearing provided some general guidelines regarding integration of hearing-impaired children with normal-hearing peers (see Table 6-2). These guidelines were endorsed again in 1986 (Brill, MacNeil, and Newman, 1986).

Table 6-2   Guidelines for Integration of Hearing-Impaired and Normal-Hearing Peers

Hearing Threshold Levels (ISO)	Probable Impact on Communication and Language	Present-Day Implications for Educational Settings	
		*Type**	*Probable Need*
Level I** 26–54 dB	Mild	Full integration Partial integration Self-contained	Most frequent Frequent Infrequent
Level II 55–69 dB	Moderate	Full integration Partial integration Self-contained	Frequent Most frequent Infrequent
Level III 70–89 dB	Severe	Full integration Partial integration Self-contained	Infrequent Most frequent Frequent
Level IV 90 dB and above	Profound	Full integration Partial integration Self-contained	Infrequent Frequent Most frequent

SOURCE: Report of the Ad Hoc Committee to Define Deaf and Hard of Hearing, *American Annals of the Deaf 120* (1975), 510. Reprinted with permission.

* *Full integration* means hearing-impaired children are totally integrated into regular classes for hearing students, with special services provided under the direction of specialists in educational programs for the deaf and hard of hearing. *Partial integration* means the children take all classes in a regular school, some on an integrated basis and some on a self-contained basis. *Self-contained* means the children attend classes exclusively with other deaf and/or hard-of-hearing classmates in regular schools, special day schools, or special residential schools.

** It is assumed that these decibel scores were obtained by a qualified audiologist using an average of scores within the frequency range commonly considered necessary to process linguistic information.

Research on the relative benefits of the kind of educational placement is not definitive. Most researchers agree that the specific needs of each child must be considered in any decision about placement. The extent of the child's hearing impairment, the amount of preschool training or treatment he or she may have received, the ability of the parents to understand and implement these educational programs, the child's readiness (or lack of it) to use oral or manual techniques as well as his or her readiness to be integrated into a regular class setting—all will affect the success or failure of the special education framework.

No one can flatly say that a particular type of service is better than another. For example, Meadow (1975), in reviewing the literature, notes that social and intellectual development within any setting is influenced to a large extent by whether or not the parents of the child are deaf. Deaf children of deaf parents appear to do quite well in a residential placement, whereas deaf children of hearing parents do not (Schlesinger and Meadow, 1972). Why this is true we do not know. It could be that hearing parents place a deaf child in an institution out of frustration, while deaf parents do so because they believe it to be the best place. If this is so, it might be true that deaf children have better social interactions with deaf parents. In other words, deaf children of deaf parents may be better adjusted to begin with than deaf children of hearing parents. Another factor might be that deaf parents, because they are much more likely than hearing parents to use signing with their children, are better able to supplement the educational program of a residential facility that stresses manualism.

Technological Advances

A number of technological advances have made it easier for hearing-impaired individuals to communicate with the hearing world, thus opening up previously blocked avenues of communication to them. This explosion of technology has taken place primarily in four areas: computer-assisted instruction, the television, the telephone, and the hearing aid.

Computer-Assisted Instruction

Many professionals are pointing to microcomputers as an excellent means of delivering instruction to hearing-impaired students. Although much research remains to be done, evaluations thus far suggest the benefits of microcomputers for this population of individuals. For example, they have been used for such things as teaching lipreading (Hight, 1982). And Prinz and his colleagues have developed programs for teaching reading, writing, and sign language (Prinz and Nelson, 1985; Prinz, Pemberton, and Nelson, 1985). The Prinz program allows the child to press a sequence of words, or a sentence, which results in the sentence appearing on the screen, along with a picture of the sentence and the appropriate signs. Prinz et al. provide the following rationale for the advantages of their interactive microcomputer system:

> The approach employs a complete novel interactive computer system that allows the child to initiate communication to a skilled teacher about a topic of interest by means of a combination of printed words on the keyboard and any already available language modes (sign, fingerspelling, and/or speech). From the outset of instruction, then, the child has the excitement of using printed words as another way of sharing ideas and feelings with others (1985, p. 446).

The availability of captions, as in this scene from "Little House on the Prairie," now makes television more accessible to hearing-impaired people. (National Captioning Institute, Inc.)

Television Captioning and Teletext

TELEVISION CAPTIONING   There are two types of television captions—open and closed. **Open captions,** used with certain programs in the 1970s, were seen on all television screens. Their use was short-lived, primarily because the general viewing audience complained that they were distracting. In the 1980s **closed captions** became available. These captions are visible only on television sets equipped with a special decoder. Because the general public does not see the captions, closed captioning has become a viable means for hearing-impaired individuals to watch television.

TELETEXT   Some hearing-impaired individuals are also taking advantage of teletext. **Teletext** gives the individual access to information such as news, cultural calendars, and community announcements on his or her television screen. In addition, teletext can be used as a means of presenting captions for television programming (Blatt, 1982).

Telephone Adaptations

Hearing-impaired individuals have traditionally had problems using telephones because of acoustic feedback, noise from the closeness of the telephone receiver to their hearing aids, and the fact that speechreading cues cannot be used. The development of the **teletypewriter (TTY),** which connects with a telephone, has thus been welcomed. The TTY allows the hearing-impaired person to communicate through type with anyone who also has a TTY.

One of the TTY's major drawbacks is that it limits the deaf person's opportunity to communicate with hearing individuals. Even though research has demonstrated that deaf and hearing individuals are capable of communicating with one another by means of TTYs (Geoffrion, 1982), very few people other than those who are deaf have reason to own a TTY. Work is currently under way to enable an individual with a TTY to communicate with those who do not have one. The **Superphone,** for instance, can be used by a deaf person to communicate with anyone who has a pushbutton phone (Stoker, 1982). The Superphone changes the typed message into an electronic voice for the hearing person. The hearing individual can then "type" back a message by pushing the touch-tone buttons. The resulting message shows up on the deaf individual's TTY.

Hearing Aids

A basic feature of any program for hearing-impaired students is the use of hearing aids. Advances in technology have increased the usefulness of these devices to such an extent that teachers of deaf students need to know their advantages and limitations well. A nationwide survey (Karchmer and Kirwin, 1977) found that 79 percent of hearing-impaired students use hearing aids at least some of the time in the classroom. In fact, 67 percent reported that they used a hearing aid all the time in the classroom.

Hearing aids differ in size, cost, and efficiency. The various kinds range from wearable hearing aids to group auditory training units that can be used by a number of children at the same time. The wearable hearing aid—the type most familiar to the general public—comes in a number of models. Some are inserted within the external auditory canal, some are built into glasses, and some are placed behind the ear. The most powerful kind of wearable aid consists of a unit worn on the clothing with an attached earpiece. In general, the more inconspicuous the hearing aid, the less powerful it is. With recent advances in the manufacture of miniature transistors, however, the efficiency of very small units has increased dramatically. This has resulted in a marked increase in the use of in-the-ear and behind-the-ear aids, especially the former. In fact, Sanders (1982) notes that the percentage of in-the-ear aids sold has increased fivefold in the last fifteen years or so. Apparently this increase in the use of ear-level hearing aids has not led to the decline in hearing sensitivity that was feared by some professionals (Meadow, Yannacone, Schlesinger, Yannacone, Lage, and Hynes-Peterson, 1981). With continuing rapid advances in hearing aid technology, most authorities predict that these smaller hearing aids will become even more popular in the years to come.

Group auditory trainers are used in school situations in which it is desirable to provide amplification for a group of children. Group trainers, because they do not need to be small enough to wear, are usually more powerful and give better sound quality than the most advanced individual aids. For a long time a major limitation of the group unit was that it confined the movements of both teacher and children. The teacher's microphone and the children's headphones were plugged into the auditory unit. Although still seen occasionally today, these "hard-wire" systems have rapidly given way to wireless FM systems that allow greater mobility (Niemoeller, 1978).

There are many misconceptions regarding the use of hearing aids. Here are a few of the most common ones:

Hearings aids come in a variety of sizes and shapes, and effective teachers of hearing-impaired students will learn as much as possible about the functioning of different kinds of hearing aids. (Suzanne Szasz/Photo Researchers)

1. There is a widespread belief that a person with sensorineural losses cannot benefit at all from a hearing aid. Although those with sensorineural losses are generally more difficult to help through amplification, they can almost always be helped.

2. Some people believe that hearing aids are never appropriate for mild or severe deficits. With the increase in the power and quality of hearing aids, however, there is no reason not to at least try a hearing aid no matter how mild or great one's hearing loss is.

3. It is often mistakenly assumed that losses in the high-frequency range cannot be corrected. This *was* true when hearing aids could only be worn on the body—the rubbing of the hearing aid on clothing generated low-frequency sound, which was then amplified so that it "drowned out" the high frequencies. Today even aids that are worn on the body are not so subject to this problem because of the development of the *electret microphone*—a microphone that greatly reduces problems associated with clothing friction against the aid as well as distortion due to mechanical feedback.

Hearing aids are an integral part of educational programming for many hearing-impaired individuals. Technological advances that seem certain to occur over the next several years will make it even more necessary for teachers of hearing-impaired children to understand what hearing aids can and cannot do. It is well to keep in mind that there is still much that we do not know about why and how hearing aids are or are not effective for certain individuals. As Sanders notes:

> It is frequently acknowledged . . . that current hearing aid selection for adults and children alike lacks a systematic general theory as to specific requirements for optimal amplification. Nor is there a single well-documented method for selecting an aid. (1982, p. 196)

This lack of a systematic general theory and method for hearing aid selection makes communication among child, parent, and professionals crucial. Only if teachers and parents are willing to try out different systems and accept feedback from the child on their effectiveness will a child be able to profit optimally from amplification.

Holiday Inn Hotel System Unveils New Visual Alert System for Hearing-Impaired Guests

The Holiday Inn hotel system has announced the development of a visual alert system (VAS) especially designed to assist the deaf or hard-of-hearing traveler.

The multiple-function system, the first of its kind in the hotel industry, alerts the hearing-impaired person to a smoke alarm, a door knock, or a telephone ring through use of a sound-activated receiver housed in a small, portable box. A strobe light encased in the electronic unit flashes when any of the functions are initiated.

"The visual alert system, which has been under study at Holiday Inns Inc. for almost a year, answers the special concerns of the deaf or hard-of-hearing traveler," said Alan Kirkpatrick, Washington Region vice president of the Holiday Inn Hotel Group. "Even with the current public interest in disabled citizens and their rights, the hearing-impaired population is often overlooked because theirs is an invisible handicap. The VAS is simple to operate and will provide an unprecedented level of comfort and security for our hearing-impaired guests."

Holiday Inns will place the VAS units in 123 company-owned or -managed hotels by July 1 and also will make it available to the chain's franchise hotels. There will be no charge to the guest for use of the system. Signage in the hotel lobby will inform guests when the VAS is available.

The alert system was tested at various Holiday Inn hotels and at several schools for the deaf over the past year by the company's research and development department. The system was developed by Customized Engineering Services of Laurel, Md.

The VAS is encased in a high-impact plastic and blends in with contemporary hotel room furnishings. The units are sized for a bedside table or credenza. A series of red lights on top of the electronic box indicate which alert function is in progress.

The Holiday Inn hotel system has been an industry leader in providing services for the handicapped traveler. Holiday Inn was the first hotel chain to equip special rooms for the wheelchair traveler and the first chain to make room reservations via Telecommunication Devices for the Deaf (TDD). Some 30,000 TDD users made reservations at Holiday Inn hotels last year.

SOURCE: *Journal of Rehabilitation of the Deaf*, 19(2), (1985) iii.

SPECIAL CONSIDERATIONS IN EDUCATING THE PRESCHOOL CHILD

Starting in the 1970s there has been a sharp increase in public school and state-supported residential school involvement in preschool programming for hearing-impaired children. Before, preschool programs were usually not "educational"; few teachers of deaf students were involved in them, and social, cognitive, and linguistic concerns were largely ignored. Moores (1978) cites three factors that impelled the increase in educational programming for the preschool hearing-impaired child:

1. Many professionals were concerned about the poor academic performance of hearing-impaired children in the elementary grades. It was their hope that earlier intervention would reduce poor school performance.
2. The movement in general education toward compensatory education (e.g., Head Start) also influenced educators of hearing-impaired children to look to preschool education as a way to solve a variety of academic problems.
3. The measles epidemic of 1964–1965 produced more hearing-impaired children, many of whom had additional handicaps. In anticipation of their entrance into elementary school in the early 1970s, educators set up preschool programs to help these children.

To this list can be added the passage of PL 94-142 (see Chapter 1), which mandates that early education programs be made available to, among other categories, hearing-impaired children.

Given that professionals have made a commitment to preschool programming for hearing-impaired children, the question remains concerning what types of programs are the most effective. In her review of early intervention programs for hearing-impaired children, Meadow-Orlans (1987) has reached a number of interesting conclusions. She notes that, in general, the earlier the intervention is begun, the better the chances for its effectiveness. In addition, she lists the following implications of research on early intervention with hearing-impaired children:

1. A strong emphasis on parent counseling, probably both in the form of parent groups and individual sessions. This means that staff people should have some training in counseling and/or should have regular access to an experienced mental health professional. Groups both for mothers and for fathers, singly or together, seem optimal.
2. Staff people with training in audiology who check hearing aids daily to make sure they are working properly. On-site capabilities, either in the home or at the center, to test hearing aids and to provide new ear molds when necessary are essential.
3. Staff training in and strong commitment to encouraging speech and developing oral skills. A natural interactional approach to the development of these skills seems optimal, and the inclusion and encouragement of parental involvement is of prime importance.
4. Inclusion of sign language as a "normal" program component for all parents and children. The view that sign language is a helpful communicative adjunct for all hearing-impaired children and a necessary tool for language acquisition

in severely and profoundly deaf children helps parents avoid the painful choice of oral *or* sign language training and encourages a more rapid adjustment to the child's hearing handicap. A moderate rather than a militant approach to teaching and learning a different communicative mode is a positive indicator.

5. A flexible approach to "matching" family language needs and program capacities. This would mean that staff would have, or attempt to include, varieties of sign language that are used by deaf parents enrolled in the program and that the sign language system taught to hearing parents is one which they can learn most readily—probably a sign language system based on English grammar and syntax with fewer rather than more complex inflectional forms. Sign language training should include help for communicating in a visual mode as well as mere vocabulary and structure. Encouragement of body language, facial expression, and attention-getting strategies is helpful to parents who are accustomed to rely more exclusively on auditory communication.

6. The presence of deaf persons in the program as staff or as resources, either full-time or part-time, is indicative of a positive attitude about the condition of deafness that can be very helpful to parents' envisioning their children as productive, competent, contented hearing-impaired adults. Interaction with deaf adults can help hearing-impaired children begin to develop a positive identity. (Meadow-Orlans, 1987, pp. 356–357)

Although most educators tend to focus on the effects of early intervention on the child's development, parents too can benefit from some intervention programs. Greenberg (1983), for example, reported on a preschool program in Vancouver, British Columbia, in which a program of total communication was delivered to children under 3 years of age, along with counseling for their parents. The parents reported less stress than a control group of parents who did not receive the program.

SPECIAL CONSIDERATIONS IN EDUCATING THE ADOLESCENT AND ADULT

Before the mid-1960s the only institution established specifically for the postsecondary education of hearing-impaired students was Gallaudet College (now Gallaudet University). Except for this one institution, hearing-impaired individuals were left with no choice but to attend traditional colleges and universities. These programs, of course, were generally not equipped to handle the special needs of hearing-impaired students. So it is little wonder that a study by Quigley, Jenne, and Phillips (1968) was able to identify only 224 hearing-impaired graduates of regular colleges and universities in the United States between 1910 and 1965. It is also not surprising that the occupational status of hearing-impaired individuals is not up to par with that of the hearing population (Boatner, Stuckless, and Moores, 1964; Moores, 1969; Schein and Delk, 1974). Although hearing-impaired individuals can make good employees, many are unemployed and a large proportion are overqualified for the jobs they hold. They are overrepresented in the manual trades and underrepresented in professional and managerial positions.

It was findings such as these that led to the expansion of postsecondary programs. The government, through the allocation of federal money, has funded a wide variety of postsecondary programs for hearing-impaired students. Starting in 1965, the National Technical Institute for the Deaf (NTID) (established at the Rochester Institute of Technology) was founded. The NTID program, emphasizing training in technical fields, complements the liberal arts orientation of Gallaudet University. At NTID some of the hearing-impaired students also attend classes with hearing students at the Rochester Institute of Technology. Research has indicated that this mainstreaming is related to better academic achievement and future career adjustment (Saur, Coggiola, Long, and Simonson, 1986).

Following the establishment of NTID, there was an explosion of postsecondary programs. A college and career guide for deaf students published by Gallaudet University and NTID lists 145 postsecondary programs in the United States and Canada for hearing-impaired students (Rawlings, Karchmer, DeCaro, and Egelston-

Show Business

Broadway Has a New Language

The deaf are no longer a silent minority

Read these words aloud and imagine that there is no one in the state of Texas who could ever hear them without difficulty. That will give some idea of the number of Americans who are deaf or hard of hearing. There are approximately 14 million such people in the U.S., and until very recently they have been the true silent minority, unheard as well as unhearing.

Now all that is changing. In March PBS, NBC and ABC began captioning some of their programs, sending out signals that can be converted into subtitles on specially adapted sets. PBS's *Masterpiece Theater* is captioned, and so are such shows as ABC's *Vega$* and NBC's *Real People*. Some advertisers, who realize what a vast market they have been missing, are even captioning their commercials.

One deaf performer, *Sesame Street's* Linda Bove, was so popular with the show's preschool audience that she became a regular member of the cast, playing the part of a deaf actress and spawning entire playgrounds of tots weaving tiny finger patterns in the air. At least one major theater, Los Angeles' Mark Taper Forum, reserves two performances of every production for the deaf, with a translator using sign language at the side of the stage to tell what the actors are saying. A major breakthrough came last month when *Children of a Lesser God*, a play about the romance of a deaf woman and a hearing man, virtually swept the Tonys, Broadway's equivalent of the Oscars. The most surprising award was to Phyllis Frelich, 36, the first deaf person ever to have a lead role on Broadway. She won over such established stars as Maggie Smith and Blythe Danner.

The story was inspired by Frelich's own. Playwright Mark Medoff (*When You Comin' Back, Red Ryder?*) was fas-

cinated by the interplay between Frelich, already an accomplished actress with the National Theater of the Deaf, and her hearing husband, Robert Steinberg, 39, a stage manager and lighting designer. Medoff, who is head of the drama department of New Mexico State University, promised to write her a play. When he finished it, he invited the couple to New Mexico in January 1979 to rehearse it. Says Medoff: "I picked their brains for months in an effort to find out more about what happens when a deaf person and a hearing one fall in love and try to build a life together."

Frelich has none of the anger and bitterness of Sarah, the character she plays, but she does share Sarah's pride and her belief that the world of silence is as rich and worthwhile as the world of sound. Frelich also has Sarah's dependence on her hearing husband, who translates conversation to her through sign language. Medoff learned about a few of the smaller adjustments in such a unique partnership. Steinberg, for instance, initially was uneasy listening to music that his wife could not enjoy; his guilt is transferred to Sarah's stage husband, James, who has pangs of remorse when he listens to Bach.

Having grown up in a world of silence, Frelich actually feels no envy for those who can hear. Her parents were deaf, and genetics made her and her eight brothers and sisters deaf as well. None of them found not being able to hear a great handicap, and she has little patience for do-gooders. "Most people I would meet were extremely patronizing," she says, signing rapidly to her husband, who puts her words into speech for TIME's Elaine Dutka. " 'Look at this wonderful deaf person,' they'd think, and want to use me in some way. Mark Medoff, though, seemed very sincere."

In New Mexico State University's production of *Children*, Steinberg, the only one around who knew how to sign, played the part of James. But when Gordon Davidson took the play to the Mark Taper Forum, John Rubinstein, 33, a more experienced actor, took on the role. His father, Piano Virtuoso Arthur Rubinstein, had trained him as a musician, and he turned out to have a natural talent for the language of hand and fingers. It took him only three weeks to learn to sign the role fluently. "I fell in love with the whole concept of sign," he says, "communicating physically and poetically." What makes the role so difficult is that he must speak for two. Says he: "This is definitely the longest role ever written. For 2½ hours each evening I talk nonstop, with no time to swallow, burp or clear my throat. Not even Hamlet or Lear talks that long."

The play underwent some major revisions. In Los Angeles, Sarah was so proud and isolated that it seemed unlikely that anyone like James would ever love her. In New York she is still proud, but Frelich allows her own radiance to shine through, making Sarah infinitely more attractive. The producers were nervous about how audiences would react to a play in which one of the two leading characters never speaks a word, but their fears obviously were groundless. *Children* is doing so well that a road company is already being planned to set out across the country in November.

Many people still find it difficult to believe that anyone who acts as well as Frelich is really deaf, and backstage visitors are often surprised and stunned to discover that she cannot hear them. "The play will undoubtedly help bridge the gap in the understanding of hearing people," she says, "but there is still a long way to go." And where will Frelich herself go? "Jobs for deaf actresses aren't plentiful," she admits, "but who knows what can happen in the future? I have a lot more dreams."
—*By Gerald Clarke*

Dodd, 1986). By law, Gallaudet and NTID are responsible for serving students from all fifty states and territories. Some of the others serve students from several states, from one state only, or from a specific district only.

Programs at universities that specialize in courses of study for hearing-impaired students frequently provide a variety of special services as well (Rawlings, Trybus, and Biser, 1978). Some of these special provisions are sign language interpreters, training in manual communication for students and instructors, note-taking services, tutoring, and vocational counseling and placement programs. And since the late 1970s and early 1980s, universities that have not traditionally provided programs for hearing-impaired students have begun to provide special services for such students (Flexer, Wray, and Black, 1986).

There is still room for improvement in postsecondary programming for and occupational status of hearing-impaired adults, but available evidence indicates that much progress has been made since the establishment of more programs at the postsecondary level. Some of the conclusions Moores (1978) reached in his review of studies on the effectiveness of postsecondary technical programs are these:

1. The majority of former students perceived their training favorably.
2. There was upward movement in the occupational status of the former students.
3. Former students reported more job satisfaction than had been found prior to the establishment of these programs.
4. Any problems that do arise on the job are more likely due to difficulties in communication than to poor job skills.

Another point about postsecondary education needs to be emphasized. Such training can only be as strong as the training the student receives earlier in elementary and secondary schools. Postsecondary education is not a cure-all. Its success depends on a solid elementary and secondary school foundation.

In addition to the need for formal schooling, some hearing-impaired adults require counseling to help them cope with potential problems related to such things as work and family life. With regard to the latter, for example, counseling may be particularly helpful for those deaf parents who have hearing children. There has been considerable debate among authorities about whether or not the language of hearing children of deaf parents is impaired. Research suggests that such children will not experience oral language delays if their deaf parents use oral language with them and if they are exposed to normal speakers through, for example, preschool programming (Schiff-Myers, 1982). This effect holds even for the hearing children of parents whose speech is not very intelligible and who use signs along with oral expression to communicate with their children. Counseling deaf parents to expose their children to as much oral language as possible is thus important.

MANAGING THE CHILD IN SCHOOL

There are a number of suggestions for handling the special problems of hearing-impaired children in the regular class. Most of these recommendations are based on a commonsense understanding of the special problems of such children.

1. The teacher should pay particular attention to the quality and quantity of social interaction engaged in by the hearing-impaired student. Merely placing

hearing-impaired and nonhandicapped students together does not guarantee appropriate social interaction. For one thing, hearing-impaired students in regular classrooms have a tendency to interact more with the teacher than with their nonhandicapped peers (Antia, 1985). The teacher should discourage the hearing-impaired child from always seeking him or her out for help. Other students in the class can be asked to take turns helping the hearing-impaired student in areas in which he or she is having particular problems.

2. The teacher should allow special seating arrangements for hearing-impaired children so they can take full advantage of as many visual and auditory cues as possible. The best seating will vary according to the particular arrangement of the room and the kind of classroom activity that is going on. For example, when the teacher is standing in front of the class and primarily lecturing, the child should be seated in the front of the class in order to hear better and also see better for speechreading. The optimum distance is about six feet from the teacher; any closer than that may be too near for the child to pick up the range of visual cues he or she uses during speechreading. In a small group discussion it is often best for the hearing-impaired student to be seated in front of the room, but to one side, so that he or she can have a better view of both teacher and classmates (Ross, 1982). Because optimum seating will vary from one situation to another, it is a good idea for the teacher to allow the student the freedom to move his or her chair about the room (Sanders, 1982). This will permit the child to position himself or herself to take advantage of visual and auditory cues.

3. Auditory and visual distractions should be kept to a minimum. Although such distraction may not always be under the control of the teacher, excessive noises from the hall, other rooms, and the outside should be eliminated, especially when the teacher is talking. Environmental noises are also a problem for children with hearing aids, since all noises are amplified for them (Stassen, 1973).

4. Speechreading will be facilitated if the teacher speaks "naturally." People have a tendency to try to sound out words with exaggerated movements of the mouth when talking to hearing-impaired people. But since hearing-impaired children are trained to read lips that form words naturally, any deviation from the normal pattern only confuses them.

5. The teacher should be aware of how important it is that his or her face and body be fully visible to the hearing-impaired student. It is often difficult to break such long-established teaching habits as talking while facing the chalkboard, but every effort should be made to do so. The teacher should also be sure that his or her face is well lighted and, in particular, should avoid situations in which there is backlighting behind his or her head (Sanders, 1982).

6. Because they do not understand what is being said or because they are self-conscious about their speech being imperfect, hearing-impaired students often withdraw from class discussions. It is important for the teacher to determine which of these two factors might be operating. Ross (1982) recommends enticing such children to join class discussions by making them a member of a "team" in a classroom exercise, by at first asking them questions that only require monosyllabic answers, and by at first calling on them to read orally only short passages. If their hesitancy to speak is due to self-consciousness, these techniques should help to draw them out.

Symptoms the Regular Classroom Teacher Should Watch For

It is not unusual for children with mild hearing losses and even, at times, for those with more severe problems to go through a number of years of schooling before their disability is detected. Such children may learn to compensate for their loss in most situations so that the problem is not readily apparent to teachers and parents. Unfortunately, however, such children are usually at a distinct disadvantage compared to their classmates. They often miss out on a lot of what is occurring in the class. Since they don't realize themselves that they have a hearing loss, they are prime candidates for becoming frustrated and anxious learners.

Association of Hearing Loss with Other Problems

Certain children are more likely to have learning difficulties because of medical problems that are often associated with hearing loss:

- The child who misses school frequently because of earaches, sinus congestion, and related disorders should be watched closely. Such illnesses are sometimes a source of temporary or permanent hearing losses.
- The child who suffers from allergies can also be a candidate for hearing loss. Usually seasonally related, allergies can cause a child annually to suffer from head congestion severe enough to bring about reduced hearing acuity for a few days to a number of weeks.

Characteristics

There are a number of behavioral characteristics that the regular teacher should be aware of as possible indicators of hearing problems:

- Any child who exhibits behaviors that would be characteristic of learning disabilities, emotional disturbance, or mental retardation should have his or her hearing checked by an audiologist. It is not uncommon for a child to be misdiagnosed and hence misplaced in a class for learning disabilities, for example, when in fact the real problem is a hearing loss.
- In particular, a child who has problems either in understanding spoken language or in speaking should be suspected as having a hearing loss until it is proven otherwise.
- The child who appears inattentive and lost in daydreams may also have a hearing loss. Such a child may be considered unable to follow directions when in fact he or she has not heard the teacher's instructions.
- The child with a mild hearing loss may appear distracted and confused at times. This disorientation may be more evident when there are extraneous noises inside or outside the classroom.

7. The teacher needs to be aware that some hearing-impaired children have learned certain coping skills that make them look as if they understand what is going on in the classroom when in fact they do not. As Ross (1982) points out, they are good at imitating their peers by raising their hands when they do, laughing when they do, and generally doing what other students are doing in order to blend in with their classmates. It is particularly difficult for hearing-

impaired students to follow group discussions because of the quick interchanges that occur among students and between the teacher and students. One recommendation is that the teacher call by name each child before he or she speaks so that the hearing-impaired student can orient to whoever is about to talk (Ross, 1982).

8. The teacher should encourage the child to ask questions. When it is necessary to repeat something, the teacher should try to rephrase the instructions. Some words and phrases are easier to speechread than others, and rephrasing increases the chances that the child will be exposed to words he or she can understand (McConnell, 1973).

9. The teacher should make every effort to employ visual aids. The use of transparencies on an overhead projector is a good way to do this. Simply writing instructions on the chalkboard is another good method. Providing the hearing-impaired student with a written outline of what is about to be covered and a written summary of what has been covered in class are highly recommended techniques. Another good idea is to have another student in the class help out by taking notes for the hearing-impaired classmate. This student can use carbon paper or paper that produces several copies from one impression (Ross, 1982).

For the teacher who is interested in learning more about the educational problems of the hearing-impaired child, Gildston (1973) presents a list of recommendations, some of which we have already given here.

SUMMARY

In defining hearing impairments, professionals with an educational orientation are concerned primarily with the extent to which the hearing loss affects ability to speak and understand language. The time of onset of the hearing problem is therefore important. Those who are deaf at birth or before language develops are at a greater disadvantage than those who acquire their deafness after the arrival of language. The former are referred to as having *prelingual deafness,* and the latter as having *postlingual deafness.* Professionals favoring a physiological viewpoint define *deaf* children as those who cannot hear sounds at or above a certain intensity level; they call others with hearing impairments *hard of hearing.* The generally accepted definition reflects a more educational orientation: A deaf person is one who is unable to process language through audition, with or without a hearing aid, whereas a hard-of-hearing person *can* do this.

The U.S. Department of Education reports that .17 percent of the school-age population receives services for hearing impairment. Some authorities believe that a lot of hard-of-hearing children are not being served.

The three most commonly used types of tests for hearing acuity are pure-tone audiometry, speech audiometry, and specialized tests for very young or hard to test children. In determining hearing ability, the examiner attempts to find out the intensity of sound (measured in decibels) that a person can hear at different frequency levels (measured in hertz). This is done using prerecorded pure tones or speech. Very young children, as well as those who may for various reasons have difficulty understanding what is expected of them or in voluntarily responding, must often be tested in other ways. In play audiometry, the examiner sets up a play situation in which the child is taught to respond in particular ways on the basis of sounds. Testing is also done by observation and measurement of certain reflexive responses, such as the Moro reflex and orienting response. Evoked-response audiometry is another method used to measure hearing.

Professionals often classify causes of hearing

loss based on the location of the problem within the hearing mechanism. *Conductive* losses are impairments that interfere with the transferral of sound along the conductive pathway of the ear. Such problems take place in the outer ear (the auricle) or the middle ear. *Sensorineural* problems are confined to the complex inner ear, and are thus apt to be much more serious and hard to treat.

Impairments of the outer ear are caused by such things as infections of the external canal, objects put into the ear by children, tumors, buildup of earwax, or perforation of the eardrum. Usually middle-ear troubles occur because of some malfunction of one or more of the three tiny bones, or ossicles, in the middle ear—the malleus, incus, and stapes. Otitis media, allergy problems that cause the eustachian tube to swell, otosclerosis, and tumors are among problems that can occur in the middle ear. Otitis media is considered the most common problem of the middle ear, and is especially prevalent among children with Down syndrome or cleft palate. The most common causes of inner-ear troubles are linked to hereditary factors. Acquired hearing losses of the inner ear include those due to bacterial infections (such as meningitis), viral infections (such as mumps and measles), prenatal infections of the mother (such as maternal rubella, congenital syphilis, and cytomegalovirus), and deprivation of oxygen at birth.

Impairment of hearing ability can have a profound effect on people, largely because of the language and academic orientation of American society. It appears that the earlier the hearing loss occurs, the greater the English language deficit. And there is evidence that early hearing loss begins to exert an effect on language at a very early age: Babies born deaf begin to exhibit less babbling and different patterns of babbling by as early as 8 months of age. But even with serious hearing loss, there are very few people who cannot be taught some use of the English language.

Whether or not one believes that a hearing impairment results in lowered intelligence is largely dependent on how one views the relationship between thought and language. Some theorists hypothesize that thought is dependent on spoken language; they believe hearing-impaired individuals are intellectually subaverage. Those who believe hearing-impaired people are on an intellectual par with hearing people point to theories that thought and language are independent. There is growing awareness that sign language is as true a language as spoken language. Research supports the position that hearing impairment does not necessarily lead to intellectual retardation. Using nonverbal rather than verbal tests of intelligence, investigators have generally found that hearing-impaired students score in the normal range of intelligence. And those who do score in the retarded range frequently have additional handicaps—for example, blindness.

Academic achievement does suffer in hearing-impaired students. Surveys show that only about one-half of hearing-impaired students by age 20 are able to read at the mid-fourth-grade level. Even in arithmetic, one of their better academic areas, they demonstrate severe underachievement. The reason for such pronounced achievement deficits is the strong dependence of academic achievement on English language skills. There is some evidence that intensive and systematic instruction can greatly reduce the amount of academic retardation.

Because communication is vital to social and personality development, people with hearing impairments tend to have a higher incidence of "problems of living"—including social and vocational problems. However, the primary determinant of whether the hearing-impaired individual will develop behavioral problems is the degree to which others accept his or her disability. Communicative isolation from the hearing population sometimes causes those with hearing problems to stay within a societal subgroup of their own—in fact, the deaf community appears to be exceptionally cohesive. Some authorities have recommended social skills training for hearing-impaired students in order to counteract their tendency toward shy and withdrawn behavior.

For many years there were two basic approaches to teaching hearing-impaired youngsters. The oralists believed it was crucial for the deaf child to learn to develop his or her remaining hearing ability and to learn to communicate orally. The manualists held that very few people considered deaf have enough hearing ability to be able to communicate orally, so they emphasized methods such as sign language. Historically, oralism prevailed as the method of choice. Today, however, most deaf educators recognize that a combination of oralism and manualism—called total communication—is the most logical choice for most deaf students.

Auditory training and speechreading are two types of oral methods. Auditory training usually involves the development of awareness of sound, the ability to make gross discriminations among environmental stimuli, and the ability to discriminate among speech sounds. In *speechreading,* sometimes inappropriately referred to as lipreading, the hearing-impaired child is taught to use a number of visual cues, not just those associated with the lips. These may come from the environment; or they may be associated with the message but not part of speech production; or they may be directly related to speech sounds. A variety of manual techniques are used by and for hearing-impaired people. *American Sign Language* (Ameslan) is one. Another is *fingerspelling,* the spelling out of every letter of every word.

Hearing-impaired students can be found in a variety of settings, ranging from regular classrooms to residential settings. Mainstreaming of hearing-impaired pupils is growing in popularity, but is still not used with many hearing-impaired children, especially those classified as deaf. The language problems exhibited by many hearing-impaired children are a major deterrent to integration into regular classrooms. Where a

child is placed depends on the severity of the child's hearing loss, previous learning experiences, and other factors. When a hearing-impaired student is placed in a regular classroom, the teacher will need to make extra efforts to ensure that he or she interacts with other children in the class.

Numerous technological advances are helping hearing-impaired individuals to lead more independent lives. These innovations are occurring primarily in the areas of computer-assisted instruction, television, telephones, and hearing aids.

There are now many programs for hearing-impaired preschoolers. Research indicates that in order for such programs to be successful, they should have a cognitive-academic emphasis. In addition, manual and oral techniques should be integrated from the beginning of programming. Until the mid-1960s there was very little special provision for the postsecondary education of hearing-impaired students. This relative neglect was undoubtedly responsible for their traditional overrepresentation in manual trades. Since the establishment of more and better postsecondary programs, the employment picture has been improving. There are now over 60 postsecondary programs for hearing-impaired students; Gallaudet and the National Technical Institute for the Deaf are two of the major institutions serving the hearing-impaired population. The latter has a successful program of integrating hearing-impaired with hearing students in some classes at the Rochester Institute of Technology.

REFERENCES

Allen, T. E., White, C. S., & Karchmer, M. A. (1983). Issues in the development of a special edition for hearing-impaired students of the seventh edition of the Stanford Achievement Test. *American Annals of the Deaf, 128,* 34–39.

Antia, S. (1985). Social integration of hearing-impaired children: Fact or fiction? *The Volta Review, 87*(6), 297–298.

Baker, C., & Battison, R. (1980). *Sign language and the deaf community: Essays in honor of William C. Stokoe.* National Association of the Deaf.

Bellugi, U., & Klima, E. S. (1978). Structural properties of American Sign Language. In L. S. Liben (Ed.), *Deaf chil-*

dren: Developmental perspectives. New York: Academic Press.

Bender, R. E. (1981). *The conquest of deafness.* Danville, Ill.: The Interstate Printers & Publishers, Inc.

Blatt, J. (1982). Teletext: A new television service for home information and captioning. *The Volta Review, 84,* 209–217.

Bluestone, C. D. (1978). Eustachian tube function and allergy in otitis media. *Pediatrics, 61,* 753–760.

Boatner, E., Stuckless, E., & Moores, D. F. (1964). *Occupational status of the young deaf adults of New England*

and their need and demand for a regional technical vocational training center. West Hartford, Conn.: American School for the Deaf.

Brill, R. G., MacNeil, B., & Newman, L. R. (1986). Framework for appropriate programs for deaf children. *American Annals of the Deaf, 131*(2), 65–77.

Carhart, R. (1970). Development and conservation of speech. In H. Davis & S. R. Silverman (Eds.), *Hearing and deafness* (3rd ed.). New York: Holt, Rinehart and Winston.

Castiglia, P. T., Aquilina, S. S., & Kemsley, M. (1983). Focus: Nonsuppurative otitis media. *Pediatric Nursing, 9,* 427–431.

Davis, H. (1978a). Abnormal hearing and deafness. In H. Davis & S. R. Silverman (Eds.), *Hearing and deafness* (4th ed.). New York: Holt, Rinehart and Winston.

Davis, H. (1978b). Audiometry: Other auditory tests. In H. Davis & S. R. Silverman (Eds.), *Hearing and deafness* (4th ed.). New York: Holt, Rinehart and Winston.

Davis, H. (1978c). Abnormal hearing: Prevention and treatment. In H. Davis and S. R. Silverman (Eds.), *Hearing and deafness* (4th ed.). New York: Holt, Rinehart and Winston.

Fant, L. J. (1971). *Say it with hands.* Silver Springs, Md.: National Association for the Deaf.

Flexer, C., Wray, D., & Black, T. (1986). Support group for moderately hearing-impaired college students: An expanding awareness. *The Volta Review, 88*(4), 223–229.

Fry, D. B. (1966). The development of a phonological system in the normal and the deaf child. In F. Smith & G. A. Miller (Eds.), *The genesis of language: A psycholinguistic approach.* Cambridge, Mass.: M.I.T. Press.

Furth, H. G. (1964). Research with the deaf: implications for language and cognition. *Psychological Bulletin, 62,* 145–164.

Furth, H. G. (1971). Linguistic deficiency and thinking: Research with deaf subjects 1964–1969. *Psychological Bulletin, 76,* 58–72.

Furth, H. G. (1973). *Deafness and learning: A psychosocial approach.* Belmont, Calif.: Wadsworth.

Geoffrion, L. D. (1982). The ability of hearing-impaired students to communicate using a teletype system. *The Volta Review, 84,* 96–108.

Gildston, P. (1973). The hearing impaired child in the classroom: A guide for the classroom teacher. In W. H. Northcott (Ed.), *The hearing impaired child in a regular classroom.* Washington, D.C.: Alexander Graham Bell Association for the Deaf.

Goodhill, V., & Guggenheim, P. (1971). Pathology, diagnosis, and therapy of deafness. In L. E. Travis (Ed.), *Handbook of speech pathology and audiology.* Englewood Cliffs, N.J.: Prentice-Hall.

Greenberg, M. T. (1983). Family stress and child competence: The effects of early intervention for families of deaf infants. *American Annals of the Deaf, 128,* 407–417.

Hanshaw, J. B. (1982). On deafness, cytomegalovirus, and neonatal screening. *American Journal of Diseases of Children, 136,* 886–887.

Hight, R. (1982). Lip-reader trainer. Teaching aid for the hearing impaired. *American Annals of the Deaf, 127*(5), 564–568.

Hoemann, H. W., & Briga, J. S. (1981). Hearing impairments.

In J. M. Kauffman & D. P. Hallahan (Eds.), *Handbook of special education.* Englewood Cliffs, N.J.: Prentice-Hall.

Holiday Inn hotel system unveils new visual alert system for hearing-impaired guests. (1985). *Journal of Rehabilitation of the Deaf, 19*(2), iii.

Jensema, C. J., Karchmer, M. A., & Trybus, R. J. (1978). *The rated speech intelligibility of hearing impaired children: Basic relationships and detailed analysis.* Washington, D.C.: Gallaudet University, Office of Demographic Studies, March.

Karchmer, M. A., & Kirwin, L. A. (1977). *The use of hearing aids by hearing impaired students in the United States.* Washington, D.C.: Office of Demographic Studies, Gallaudet University.

Karchmer, M. A., Milone, M. N., & Wolk, S. (1979). Educational significance of hearing loss at three levels of severity. *American Annals of the Deaf, 124,* 97–109.

Karchmer, M. A., & Trybus, R. J. (1977). *Who are the deaf children in the mainstream programs?* Washington, D.C.: Office of Demographic Studies, Gallaudet University, October.

Klima, E. S., & Bellugi, U. (1979). *The signs of language.* Cambridge, Mass.: Harvard University Press.

Lenneberg, E. H. (1966). The natural history of language. In F. Smith & G. A. Miller (Eds.), *The genesis of language: A psycholinguistic approach.* Cambridge, Mass.: M.I.T. Press.

Lenneberg, E. H. (1967). *Biological foundations of language.* New York: Wiley.

Liben, L. S. (1978). Developmental perspectives on the experiential deficiencies of deaf children. In L. S. Liben (Ed.), *Deaf children: Developmental perspectives,* New York: Academic Press.

Ling, D., & Ling, A. (1978). *Aural habilitation.* Washington, D.C.: Alexander Graham Bell Association for the Deaf.

Loeb, R., & Sarigiani, P. (1986). The impact of hearing impairment on self-perceptions of children. *The Volta Review, 88*(2), 89–100.

McConnell, F. (1973). Children with hearing disabilities. In L. M. Dunn (Ed.), *Exceptional children in the schools: Special education in transition* (2nd ed.). New York: Holt, Rinehart and Winston.

Martin, F. N. (1981). *Introduction to audiology* (2nd ed.). Englewood Cliffs, N.J.: Prentice-Hall.

Meadow, K. P. (1980). *Deafness and child development.* Berkeley, CA: University of California Press.

Meadow, K. P. (1968). Early manual communication in relation to the deaf child's intellectual, social, and communicative functioning. *American Annals of the Deaf, 113,* 29–41.

Meadow, K. P. (1972). Sociolinguistics, sign language and the deaf sub-culture. In T. J. O'Rourke (Ed.), *Psycholinguistics and total communication: The state of the art.* Washington, D.C.: American Annals of the Deaf.

Meadow, K. P. (1975). Development of deaf children. In E. M. Hetherington (Ed.), *Review of child development research* (Vol. 5). Chicago: University of Chicago Press.

Meadow, K. P. (1984). Social adjustment of preschool children: Deaf and hearing, with and without other handicaps. *Topics in Early Childhood Special Education, 3,* 27–40.

Meadow, K. P., Yannacone, C. G., Schlesinger, H. S., Yannacone, C. Y., Lage, R. V., & Hynes-Peterson, J. (1981). Performance of deaf children using ear-level and body-worn hearing aids. *The Journal of Auditory Research, 21,* 181–186.

Meadow-Orlans, K, P. (1987). An analysis of the effectiveness of early intervention programs for hearing-impaired children. In M. J. Guralnick & F. C. Bennett (Eds.), *The effectiveness of early intervention for at-risk and handicapped children* (pp. 325–362). New York: Academic Press.

Moog, J., & Geers, A. (1985). EPIC: A program to accelerate academic progress in profoundly hearing-impaired children. *The Volta Review, 87*(6), 259–277.

Moores, D. F. (1969). The vocational status of young deaf adults in New England. *Journal of Rehabilitation of the Deaf, 2,* 29–41.

Moores, D. F. (1978). *Educating the deaf: Psychology, principles, and practices.* Boston: Houghton-Mifflin.

Moores, D. F. (1982). *Educating the deaf: Psychology, principles, and practices.* (2nd ed.). Boston: Houghton-Mifflin.

Moores, D. F., & Maestas y Moores, J. (1981). Special adaptations necessitated by hearing impairments. In J. M. Kauffman & D. P. Hallahan (Eds.), *Handbook of special education.* Englewood Cliffs, N.J.: Prentice-Hall.

Myklebust, H. R. (1964). *The psychology of deafness* (2nd ed.). New York: Grune & Stratton.

Newby, H. A. (1971). Clinical audiology. In L. E. Travis (Ed.), *Handbook of speech pathology and audiology.* Englewood Cliffs, N.J.: Prentice-Hall.

Nicholls, G. H., & Ling, D. (1982). Cued speech and the reception of spoken language. *Journal of Speech and Hearing Research, 25,* 262–269.

Niemoeller, A. E. (1978). Hearing aids. In H. Davis & S. R. Silverman (Eds.), *Hearing and deafness* (4th ed.). New York: Holt, Rinehart and Winston.

Novelli-Olmstead, T., & Ling, D. (1984). Speech production and speech discrimination by hearing-impaired children. *The Volta Review, 86,* 72–80.

Pelton, S., & Whitley, P. (1983). Otitis media: Current concepts in diagnosis and management. *Pediatric Annals, 12,* 207–218.

Prinz, P. M., & Nelson, K. E. (1985). A child-computer-teacher interactive method for teaching reading to young deaf children. In D. Martin (Ed.), *Cognition, education, and deafness: Directions for research and instruction* (pp. 124–127). Washington, D.C.: Gallaudet University Press.

Prinz, P. M., Pemberton, E., & Nelson, K. (1985). The ALPHA Interactive Microcomputer System for teaching reading, writing, and communication skills to hearing-impaired children. *American Annals of the Deaf, 130*(4), 441–461.

Quigley, S., Jenne, W., & Phillips, S. (1968). *Deaf students in colleges and universities.* Washington, D.C.: Alexander Graham Bell Association for the Deaf.

Rawlings, B. W., Karchmer, M. A., DeCaro, J., & Egelston-Dodd, J. (Eds.) (1986). *College and career programs for the deaf.* (6th Ed.). Washington, D.C.: Gallaudet University.

Rawlings, B. W., Trybus, R. J. & Biser, J. (1978). *A guide to college/career programs for deaf students.* Washington, D.C.: Office of Demographic Studies, Gallaudet University, December.

Report of the Ad Hoc Committee to Define Deaf and Hard of Hearing. (1975). *American Annals of the Deaf, 120,* 509–512.

Ross, B. M., & Hoemann, H. (1975). The attainment of formal operations: A comparison of probability concepts in deaf and hearing adolescents. *Genetic Psychology Monographs, 91,* 61–119.

Ross, M., with Brackett, D., & Maxon, A. (1982). *Hard of hearing children in regular schools.* Englewood Cliffs, N.J.: Prentice-Hall.

Sanders, D. A. (1982). *Aural rehabilitation* (2nd ed.). Englewood Cliffs, N.J.: Prentice-Hall.

Saur, R., Coggiola, D., Long, G., & Simonson, J. (1986). Educational mainstreaming and the career development of hearing-impaired students: A longitudinal analysis. *The Volta Review, 88*(2), 79–88.

Schein, J. D., & Delk, M. T. (1974). *The deaf population of the United States.* Silver Spring, Md.: National Association of the Deaf.

Schiff-Myers, N. B. (1982). Sign and oral language development of preschool hearing children of deaf parents in comparison with their mothers' communication system. *American Annals of the Deaf, 127,* 322–330.

Schildroth, A. (1986). Hearing-impaired children under age 6: 1977 & 1984. *American Annals of the Deaf, 131*(2), 85–90.

Schlesinger, H. S., & Meadow, K. P. (1972). *Sound and sign: Childhood deafness and mental health.* Berkeley: Univ. of California Press.

Schow, R., & Nerbonne, M. (Eds.). (1980). *Introduction to aural rehabilitation.* Baltimore: University Park Press.

Silverman, S. R. (1971). The education of deaf children. In L. E. Davis (Ed.), *Handbook of speech pathology and audiology.* Englewood Cliffs, N.J.: Prentice-Hall.

Smith, M. A., Schloss, P. J., & Schloss, C. N. (1984). An empirical analysis of a social skills training program used with hearing impaired youths. *Journal of Rehabilitation of the Deaf, 18*(2), 7–13.

Soderhan, A. K., & Whiren, A. P. (1985). Mainstreaming the young hearing-impaired child: An intensive study. *Journal of Rehabilitation of the Deaf, 18*(3), 7–14.

Stassen, R. A. (1973). *I have one in my class who's wearing hearing aids.* In W. H. Northcott (Ed.), *The hearing impaired child in a regular classroom.* Washington, D.C.: Alexander Graham Bell Association for the Deaf.

Stoel-Gammon, C., & Otomo, K. (1986). Babbling development of hearing-impaired and normally hearing subjects. *Journal of Speech and Hearing Disorders, 51,* 33–41.

Stoker, R. G. (1982). Telecommunications technology and the hearing impaired: Recent research trends and a look into the future. *The Volta Review, 84,* 147–155.

Stuckless, E. R., & Birch, J. W. (1966). The influence of early manual communication on the linguistic development of deaf children. *American Annals of the Deaf, 111,* 452–460.

Sullivan, P. M. (1982). Administration modifications on the WISC-R Performance Scale with different categories of deaf children. *American Annals of the Deaf, 127,* 780–788.

Thomas, C. L. (1985) (Ed.). *Taber's cyclopedic medical dictionary* (15th Ed.). Philadelphia: F. A. Davis, Co.

Trybus, R. J., & Karchmer, M. A. (1977). School achievement scores of hearing impaired children. National data on achievement status and growth patterns. *American Annals of the Deaf, 122,* 62–69.

Vernon, M., & Koh, S. D. (1971a). Effects of oral preschool

compared to early manual communication on education and communication in deaf children. *American Annals of the Deaf, 116,* 569–574.

Vernon, M., & Koh, S. (1971b). Effects of manual communication on deaf children's educational achievement, linguistic competence and skills, and psychological development. *American Annals of the Deaf, 115,* 527–536.

Vygotsky, L. S. (1962). *Thought and language.* New York: Wiley.

Watson, B., Goldgar, D., Kroese, J., & Lotz, W. (1986). Nonverbal intelligence and academic achievement in the hearing impaired. *The Volta Review, 88*(5), 151–158.

Wilbur, R. B. (1979). *American sign language and sign systems.* Baltimore: University Park Press.

Wiley, J. (1971). A psychology of auditory impairment. In W. M. Cruickshank (Ed.), *Psychology of exceptional children and youth* (3rd ed.). Englewood Cliffs, N.J.: Prentice-Hall.

Williams, B. R. (1985). The education of the deaf: Past, present, future. *Journal of Rehabilitation of the Deaf, 19*(2), 1–3.

Williamson, W. D., Desmond, M. M., LaFevers, N., Taber, L. H., Catlin, F. I., & Weaver, T. G. (1982). *American Journal of Diseases of Children, 136,* 902–905.

Wrightstone, J. W., Aranow, M. S., & Moskowitz, S. (1963). Developing reading test norms for deaf children. *American Annals of the Deaf, 108,* 311–316.

7

Visual Impairment

JILL: God, I can't find anything in my place. The ketchup usually winds up in my stocking drawer and my stockings are in the oven. If you really want to see chaos, come and look at . . . (*She catches herself, self-consciously*), I mean . . . I meant . . .

DON: I know what you mean. Relax. I'm no different from anyone else except that I don't see. The blindness is nothing. The thing I find hard to live with is other people's reactions to my blindness. If they'd only behave naturally. Some people want to assume guilt—which they can't because my mother has that market cornered—or they treat me as though I were living in some Greek tragedy, which I assure you I'm not. Just be yourself.

JILL: I'll try . . . but I've never met a blind person before.

DON: That's because we're a small, very select group—like Eskimos. How many Eskimos do you know?

JILL: I never thought blind people would be like you.

DON: They're not all like me. We're all different.

JILL: I mean . . . I always thought blind people were kind of . . . you know . . . spooky.

DON: (In a mock-sinister voice) But, of course. We sleep all day hanging upside-down from the shower rod. As soon as it's dark, we wake up and fly into people's windows. That's why they say, "Blind as a bat."

(*Leonard Gershe, "Butterflies Are Free"*)

ot unlike anyone with a disability, the blind person wants to be treated like everyone else. Most blind people do not seek pity or even unnecessary help. Although they may need assistance in some situations, in the main they prefer to be independent. They appreciate the sensitivity of others, but they want to be reminded of their similarities rather than their differences.

Visual impairments seem to evoke more awkwardness than any other disability. Why are we so uncomfortably aware of blindness? For one thing, blindness is *visible*. We often do not realize a person has impaired hearing, for example, until we actually talk to that person. The vast majority of mentally retarded individuals are indistinguishable from others on the basis of physical appearance. The visually impaired person has a variety of symbols—white cane, thick or darkened glasses, a guide dog.

Another possible contributor to our awkwardness around blind people is the role that eyes play in social interaction. Poets, playwrights, and songwriters have long recognized how emotionally expressive the eyes can be. We have all experienced how uncomfortable it can be to talk with someone who does not make eye contact with us. Think of how often we have heard someone say, or have ourselves said, that we prefer to talk "face to face" on an important matter rather than over the telephone. It is logical to assume that in social interactions we rely to a great degree on the expressiveness of people's eyes to judge how they are responding to what we are saying, and the lack of such feedback could contribute to our feeling uncomfortable around visually impaired individuals. That such discomfort is due primarily to unfamiliarity with blind people is evidenced by the fact that sighted people who work with visually impaired individuals apparently do not have these feelings.

Too, research has shown that most of us have a special fear of blindness (Conant and Budoff, 1982). One reason may be that our eyes appear so vulnerable. The organs of hearing and thinking, for example, feel safely tucked away; eyes, on the other hand, seem dangerously exposed. So, despite the fact that blindness is by far the least prevalent of all disabilities, we dread it. Another reason we fear loss of vision is that the sense of sight is linked so closely with the traditional concept of beauty. We derive great pleasure from our sight. Our feelings about others are often largely based on physical characteristics that are visually perceived. It is not until we talk with or read about a blind person's appreciation of sounds, smells, and touches that we begin to realize that sight is not the only sense that enables us to enjoy beauty.

One other point made in the introductory dialog should be underscored. As Don says, "We're all different." In this chapter we hope to change the idea that visually impaired children are all alike in some odd way. We start by presenting a fact most people do not know: The majority of blind people can actually see.

DEFINITION AND CLASSIFICATION

The area of visual impairment does not have a great number of definitions. The field does share with most of the other areas of exceptionality, however, considerable disagreement about the best definition. The two most common ways of describing visual impairment are the legal and educational definitions. The former is the one laypeople and those in the medical professions use; the latter is the one educators favor.

The legal definition, which involves assessment of visual acuity and field of vision, is used to determine whether or not an individual qualifies for legal benefits available

MISCONCEPTIONS
ABOUT VISUALLY IMPAIRED PEOPLE

Myth	*Fact*
Legally blind people have no sight at all.	Only a small percentage of those who are legally blind have absolutely no vision. The majority have a useful amount of functional vision.
Most legally blind people use Braille as their primary method of reading.	The majority of legally blind individuals use print (even if it is in large type) as their primary method of reading. In addition, a recent trend shows that more blind people who cannot benefit from the use of print are now using aural methods (listening to tapes or records), rather than Braille.
Blind people have an extra sense that enables them to detect obstacles.	Blind people do *not* have an *extra* sense. They can develop an "obstacle sense" provided they have the ability to hear.
Blind people automatically develop better acuity in their other senses.	Through concentration and attention, blind individuals learn to make very fine discriminations in the sensations they obtain. This is not automatic, but rather represents a better *use* of received sensations.
Blind people have superior musical ability.	The musical ability of blind people isn't necessarily any better than that of sighted people. Apparently many blind individuals pursue musical careers because this is one way in which they can achieve success.
Blind people are helpless and dependent.	With a good attitude and favorable learning experiences, a blind person can be as independent and possess as strong a personality as a sighted person.
If partially sighted people use their eyes too much, their sight will deteriorate.	Only in rare conditions is this true; visual discrimination ability can actually be improved through training and use. Wearing strong lenses, holding books close to the eyes, and using the eyes as much as possible cannot harm vision.
Blind children automatically develop superior powers of concentration that make them good listeners.	Good listening is primarily a learned skill. Although many visually impaired individuals do develop good listening skills, this is the result of work on their part because they are dependent upon these skills for so much of the information they gain from the environment.
Guide dogs take blind people where they want to go.	The guide dog does not "take" the blind person anywhere; the person must first know where he or she is going. The dog is primarily a safeguard against unsafe areas or obstacles.

to blind people. (Some of these benefits include tax advantages and money for special materials.) The American Medical Association proposed this definition in 1934, and it is now accepted by the American Foundation for the Blind. A *legally blind person* is said to be one who has visual acuity of 20/200 or less in the better eye even with correction (e.g., glasses) or whose field of vision is so narrowed that its widest diameter subtends an angular distance no greater than 20 degrees. The fraction 20/200 means that the person sees at 20 feet what a person with normal vision sees at 200 feet. (Normal visual acuity is thus 20/20.) The inclusion of a narrowed field of vision in the legal definition means that a person may have 20/20 vision in the central field of vision but may have severely restricted peripheral vision.

In addition to this medical classification of blindness, there is also a category referred to as partially blind or partially sighted. Partially blind or partially sighted individuals, according to the legal classification system, are those people whose visual acuity falls between 20/70 and 20/200 in the better eye with correction.

Many professionals, particularly educators, have found the legal classification scheme inadequate. They have observed that visual acuity is not a very accurate predictor of how people will function or use whatever remaining sight they have. Although a small percentage of legally blind individuals have absolutely no vision, the vast majority are able to see. Willis (1976), for example, found in an extensive study of 26,433 legally blind students that only 18 percent were totally blind. Her study also dramatically demonstrated that legal blindness does not mean the person does not have a useful amount of functional vision. She found that 52 percent of these students used large- or regular-print books as their primary reading mode; 3 percent used both large-print books and Braille, 21 percent used only Braille, and 24 percent used aural methods (tapes or records). Clearly, being classified legally blind does not mean that an individual will be unable to read print of some kind. Willis also reports a definite trend toward less use of Braille in favor of print and aural materials. (**Braille,** a system in which raised dots are used to allow blind people to "read" with their fingertips, consists of a quadrangular cell containing from one to six dots whose arrangement denotes different letters and symbols.)

Many of those who recognize the limitations of the legal definition of blindness and partial sightedness favor the educational definition. For educational purposes, blind individuals are those who are so severely impaired they must be taught to read by Braille or by the use of aural methods (audiotapes and records); partially sighted individuals can read print, though they need to use magnifying devices or books with large print. Because it stresses the educational variable of method of reading instruction, educators prefer this definition, even though it is not as quantitatively precise as the legal one.

PREVALENCE

As with other areas of special education, prevalence figures for visual impairment vary widely. For example, the Report of the Subcommittee on Rehabilitation of the National Institute of Neurological Diseases and Blindness (1971) estimated that from 0.15 to 0.56 percent of the general population is legally blind. But even the higher of these two figures indicates that blind people are a relatively small part of the population.

Two factors make the percentages even smaller in terms of educational concerns. First, blindness is primarily an adult disability. Most estimates indicate that blindness

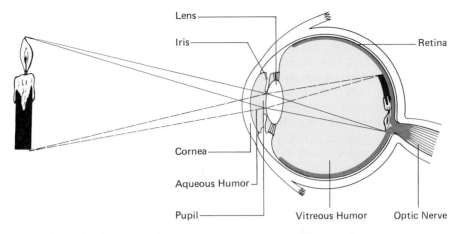

Figure 7.1 *The basic anatomical features of the eye and the visual process.*
SOURCE: Adapted from National Society for the Prevention of Blindness, Pub. V-7, 1964.

is approximately one-tenth as prevalent in school-age children as in adults. Second, these figures are based on the legal definition of blindness. Since many legally blind children can read print, they are not considered blind educationally. As we noted in Chapter 1, the U.S. Department of Education has reported that .07 percent of individuals preschool through grade 12 are being served as visually handicapped.

ANATOMY AND PHYSIOLOGY OF THE EYE

The anatomy of the visual system is extremely complex, so our discussion here will focus just on basic characteristics. Figure 7.1 shows the functioning of the eye. The physical object being seen ends up as an electrical impulse sent through the optic nerve to the visual center of the brain, the occipital lobes. Before reaching the optic nerve, light rays reflecting off the object being seen pass through several structures within the eye. The light rays:

1. Pass through the **cornea** (a transparent cover in front of the iris and pupil), which performs the major part of the bending (refraction) of the light ray so that the image will be focused.
2. Pass through the **aqueous humor** (a watery substance).
3. Pass through the **pupil** (the contractile opening in the middle of the **iris,** the colored portion of the eye that contracts or expands depending on the amount of light striking it).
4. Pass through the **lens,** which refines and changes the focus of the light rays so that they pass through the **vitreous humor** (a transparent gelatinous substance).
5. Come to a focus on the **retina** (the back portion of the eye containing nerve fibers connected to the optic nerve).

MEASUREMENT OF VISUAL ABILITY

Visual acuity is most often measured with the **Snellen chart.** It consists of rows of letters (for individuals who know the alphabet) or *E*s (for the very young and for those who cannot read). In the latter case, the *E*s are arranged in various positions, and the person's task is to indicate in what direction the "legs" of the *E*s are facing. Each row corresponds to the distance at which a person with normal vision can discriminate the direction of the *E*s. (There are eight rows, one corresponding to each of the following distances: 15, 20, 30, 40, 50, 70, 100, and 200 feet.) People are normally tested at the 20-foot distance. If they can distinguish the direction of the letters in the 20-foot row, they are said to have 20/20 central visual acuity for far distances. If they can distinguish only the much larger letters in the 70-foot row, they are said to have 20/70 central visual acuity for far distances.

One of the problems in using the Snellen chart for measuring visual ability is that it is not an accurate predictor of how well the child will be able to read print. Visual acuity is measured for distant, but not for near, objects. That is why it is necessary to report the results of this test in terms of central visual acuity for *far* distances. Many educational activities, particularly reading, require visual ability at close distances. A special Snellen chart, to be used at a distance of 14 inches, has been developed for the assessment of near vision. Another near vision test is the **Jaeger chart,** which is made up of lines of type in different sizes. One useful aspect of the Jaeger chart is that the results can be interpreted in terms of what kinds of reading materials can be used by the visually impaired person—store catalogs, children's books, adult books.

Barraga and her colleagues have developed an assessment instrument—the **Diagnostic Assessment Procedure (DAP)**—to assess visual functioning rather than acuity (Barraga, 1983; Barraga and Collins, 1979; Barraga, Collins, and Hollis, 1977). A 150-lesson curriculum accompanies the DAP; The DAP itself is composed of 40 tasks divided into 8 categories. Here is a listing of the 8 categories, along with task examples:

A. *Awareness of visual stimuli (2).* Item 1: "Learner moves eyes, head and/or body to light source."
B. *Movement control of eyes, discrimination of shape and color (4).* Item 3: "Learner will look from one light to the other."
C. *Exploration, discrimination, use of objects (6).* Item 7: "Learner will see two lines and move between them."
D. *Discrimination and identification of pictures of objects, people, actions (12).* Item 14: "Learner will match solid color geometric shapes in pictures."
E. *Memory for detail, part-whole relationships, figure-ground discrimination (4).* Item 25: "Learner will identify object partially hidden in picture."
F. *Discrimination, identification, reproduction of abstract figures and symbols (4).* Item 29: "Learner will match abstract figures by single inner detail."
G. *Perception of relationships in pictures, abstract figures, symbols (4).* Item 33: "Learner will relate inner detail in figures of different size."
H. *Identification, perception, reproduction of symbols of single and combined symbols (4).* Item 37: "Learner will identify letters in different types." (Berlá, Rankin, and Willis, 1980, p. 298)

Research thus far on the reliability and validity of the DAP indicates the test's technical merits are quite promising (Berlá, Rankin, and Willis, 1980).

Unfortunately, school screening procedures generally include only the Snellen chart. If a child does poorly on this, he or she should be referred for further testing to an ophthalmologist. (**Ophthalmology** is the science dealing with eye disease.)

Symptoms the Regular Classroom Teacher Should Watch For

Behavior

- Rubs eyes excessively
- Shuts or covers one eye, tilts head or thrusts head forward
- Has difficulty in reading or in other work requiring close use of the eyes
- Blinks more than usual or is irritable when doing close work
- Holds books close to eyes
- Is unable to see distant things clearly
- Squints eyelids together or frowns

Appearance

- Crossed eyes
- Red-rimmed, encrusted, or swollen eyelids
- Inflamed or watery eyes
- Recurring styes

Complaints

- Eyes itch, burn, or feel scratchy
- Cannot see well
- Dizziness, headaches, or nausea following close eye work
- Blurred or double vision

Typical school screening procedures, however, will not help in identifying children whose visual problems relate exclusively to field of vision or near vision. These problems are usually detected when the parent or teacher notices a problem. The National Society for the Prevention of Blindness (1972, p. 19) has listed a number of signs of possible eye problems (see the chart "Symptoms the Regular Class Teacher Should Watch For").

CAUSES

The most common visual problems are the result of errors of refraction. **Myopia** (nearsightedness), **hyperopia** (farsightedness), and **astigmatism** (blurred vision) are all examples of refraction errors that affect central visual acuity. Although each can be serious enough to cause significant impairment (Kerby, in his 1958 study, lists myopia and hyperopia as the most common impairments of partially sighted children), usually glasses or contact lenses can give the individual vision within normal limits.

Myopia results when the eyeball is too long. In this case, the light rays from the object in Figure 7.1 would be in focus in front of rather than on the retina. Myopia affects vision for distant objects, but close vision may be unaffected. When the eyeball is too short, *hyperopia* (farsightedness) results. In this case, the light rays from the object in the diagram would be in focus behind rather than on the retina. Hyperopia affects vision for close objects, but far vision may be unaffected. If the cornea or lens of the eye is irregular, the person is said to have *astigmatism.*

In this case, the light rays from the object in the figure would be blurred or distorted.

Among the more serious impairments are those caused by glaucoma, cataracts, and diabetes. They occur primarily in adults, but each of them, particularly the latter two, can occur in children. **Glaucoma** is a condition in which there is excessive pressure in the eyeball. Left undiagnosed, the condition progresses to the point where the blood supply to the optic nerve is cut off and blindness results.

The cause of glaucoma is presently unknown (although glaucoma can be caused secondarily by other eye diseases), and its onset can be sudden or very gradual. Because its incidence increases dramatically after age 35 and because it can be prevented if detected early, it is often strongly recommended that *all* adults have periodic eye examinations after age 35. A common complaint during early stages of glaucoma is that lights appear to have halos around them (Thomas, 1985). **Cataracts** are caused by a clouding of the lens of the eye, which results in blurred vision. In children the condition is called *congenital cataracts.* Distance and color vision are seriously affected. Surgery can usually correct the problems caused by cataracts. Diabetes can result in **diabetic retinopathy,** a condition resulting from interference with the blood supply to the retina.

Several other visual impairments primarily affect children. It has been estimated that 64 percent of the visual impairments of school-age children are due to prenatal causes (United States Department of Health, Education and Welfare, 1970), many of which are hereditary (Livingston, 1986). Congenital (meaning present at birth) cataracts and glaucoma have already been discussed. Another congenital condition is **coloboma,** a degenerative disease in which the central and/or peripheral areas of the retina are not completely formed. This results in impairment of the visual field and/or central visual acuity. Another prenatal condition is **retinitis pigmentosa,** a hereditary disease resulting in degeneration of the retina. Also included in the prenatal category are infectious diseases that affect the unborn child, such as syphilis and rubella.

One of the most dramatic medical breakthroughs in the discovery of causes involved a condition known as **retrolental fibroplasia (RLF),** which results in scar tissue forming behind the lens of the eye. RLF began to appear in the 1940s. In the early 1950s it was determined that it was caused by an excessive concentration of oxygen administered to premature infants. The oxygen was necessary to prevent brain damage, but it was often given at too high a level. Since then, hospitals have been careful to monitor the amount of oxygen administered to premature infants. But after a sharp decrease in the incidence of RLF, increases in the disease as recent as the early 1970s have been reported (Chase, 1974). This is probably because with medical advances many more premature babies are surviving, but very high levels of oxygen are needed to save them.

Two other conditions resulting in visual problems can be grouped together because both are caused by improper muscle functioning. **Strabismus** is a condition in which the eye(s) is (are) directed inward (crossed eyes) or outward. Left untreated, strabismus can result in permanent blindness because the brain will eventually reject signals from a deviating eye. Fortunately, most cases of strabismus are correctable with eye exercises or surgery. **Nystagmus** is a condition in which there are rapid involuntary movements of the eyes. This usually results in dizziness and nausea. Nystagmus is sometimes a sign of brain malfunctioning and/or inner ear problems.

PSYCHOLOGICAL AND BEHAVIORAL CHARACTERISTICS

Language Development

Most authorities believe that lack of vision does not alter ability to understand and use language. They point to the many studies that show that visually handicapped students do not differ from sighted ones on verbal intelligence tests. They also note that studies comparing visually impaired with sighted children have found no differences with regard to major aspects of language (Bateman, 1965; Matsuda, 1984; McGinnis, 1981; Rogow, 1981). Only a few minor aspects of communication, such as gestures, have been found to differ in visually impaired individuals. Because auditory more than visual perception is the sensory modality through which we learn language, it is not surprising that studies have found blind people to be relatively unimpaired in terms of language functioning. The blind child is still able to hear language and may even be more motivated than the sighted child to use it because it is the main channel through which he or she communicates with others.

Another group of professionals, however, believes that the blind child's language development is different. They do not hold that it is necessarily inherently inferior, but rather that it has some features that can affect the blind child's ways of thinking. A blind clinical psychologist, Thomas D. Cutsforth, in his classic, *The Blind in School and Society: A Psychological Study* (1951), provided much of the impetus for this point of view. He (along with others) maintains that blind people exhibit what is termed **verbalism** or verbal unreality. This is defined as the blind individuals' inappropriate reliance on words and phrases that are not consistent with their sensory experiences. Because blind children explore the world primarily through the auditory, tactual, and olfactory senses, it would seem that their language would reflect this fact as well. Cutsforth found, using a word association task, that blind children tend to use language that reflects visual experiences. To the word "Indian," for example, they were likely to respond with "visual" words such as "red" or "brown."

Cutsforth's idea is that verbalism is used by blind individuals as a means of gaining social approval. The result is that they live in an unreal world in the sense that they do not describe their environment in words connected to their own sensations:

> In its larger aspect the underlying purpose of verbalism is that of meeting social approval. It is an attempt to represent things as nearly as possible as they would appear to others in a social situation. Socially and educationally the blind are expected to appreciate things not as they themselves experience them, but as they are taught how others experience them. For example, a lamb, which is a kindly, woolly, bony, wiggling object, possessing none too delightful an odor, whose feet are generally dirty and sharp and whose mouth and nose are damp and slobbery, is not described as such, but as the snow-white, innocent, gamboling lamb. (Cutsforth, 1951, p. 51)

Cutsforth believes verbalism is taught to blind individuals in the educational system. There is too much emphasis, he says, on teaching blind people to become writers of prose and talkers in the same vein as the sighted. He uses Helen Keller as the prime example of a blind individual who was taught to become an excellent prose writer, but whose writing was a denial of her own experiences:

> The implied chicanery in this unfortunate situation does not reflect upon the writer personally, but rather upon her teacher and the aims of the education system in which she

has been confined during her whole life. Literary expression has been the goal of her formal education. Fine writing, regardless of its meaningful content, has been the end toward which both she and her teacher have striven. Her own experience and her own world were neglected whenever possible, or, when this could not be done, they were metamorphosed into auditory and visual respectability. Her own experiential life was rapidly made secondary, and it was regarded as such by the victim. (pp. 52–53)

The major objection of those who criticize verbalism is that it interferes with the child's cognitive development. Reviews by Nolan and Ashcroft (1969) and Suppes (1974), however, cite evidence that verbalism is not a problem in blind individuals. Harley (1963) found no relationship between personal adjustment and verbalism; and Dokecki (1966), after reviewing the psycholinguistic literature, concluded that there is no basis for the position that verbalism inhibits conceptual development. Though all the evidence is not yet in on this matter, what evidence we do have is not very favorable toward Cutsforth's view. His position is certainly not strong enough to justify discouraging blind children from using visually oriented language. In the words of Warren (1981):

> The educational implications of Cutsforth's view seem clear enough: The use of visually related vocabulary by visually impaired children should not be discouraged. Rather, they should be fully exposed to these words and concepts and special attempts should be made to enhance their meanings. *The goal should be to bring visually impaired children to the point of maximal use of the language used by the surrounding culture,* so that language can aid in meaningful and social interaction, in behavioral self-direction, and in progress within the educational system. (p. 207; italics added)

Intellectual Ability

Performance on Standardized Intelligence Tests

Samuel P. Hayes was the pioneer in the area of intelligence testing of blind individuals. In his classic *Contributions to a Psychology of Blindness* (1941), he reported on the IQs of blind individuals whose cases he had followed over a number of years. He concluded that blindness does not automatically result in lower intelligence. Some children who have shown low IQ scores for a number of years in a sheltered environment suddenly make dramatic gains when given adequate educational opportunities (Hayes, 1942). In a 1950 study, Hayes said that he had not found blind students to be at a disadvantage, particularly in verbal intelligence, and that there is no relationship between the age of onset of blindness and IQ.

The particular instrument Hayes used in many of his studies was the Interim Hayes-Binet, a test he adapted for blind people based on the 1937 revision of the Stanford-Binet. One of the limitations of the Hayes-Binet is that its items at the lowest and highest age levels are not very well standardized (Lowenfeld, 1971). Many professionals also use the verbal portion of the Wechsler Intelligence Scale for Children–Revised (WISC–R) to test blind children.

A number of other intelligence measures are less verbal in nature. Of these, the Blind Learning Aptitude Testing (BLAT) (Newland, 1964) and the Ohwaki-Kohs (Ohwaki, Tanno, Ohwaki, Hariu, Hayasaka, and Miyake, 1960) are among the most popular. They allow assessment of the visually impaired child's abilities in the performance domain. Some believe these performance tests to be more educationally valuable, particularly for totally blind children, because they measure ability to use the tactual sense—an ability required for reading Braille.

Most studies indicate that blind people are not markedly lower than sighted people in IQ as measured by standardized verbal intelligence tests. These results should be regarded with a certain degree of caution, however. Intelligence testing of visually handicapped individuals is generally less valid than intelligence testing of sighted people because of the modifications that must be made in the testing procedures.

Conceptual Abilities

A substantial amount of research on other than standardized verbal intelligence tests suggests that the development of conceptual or cognitive abilities in blind children lags behind that of sighted children (Gottesman, 1973, 1976; Stephens and Grube, 1982; Stephens and Simpkins, 1974; Witkin, Birnbaum, Lomonaco, Lehr, and Herman, 1968). In particular, visually impaired children are more likely to do poorly on tasks requiring abstract thinking; they are much more likely to deal with their environment in concrete terms (Higgins, 1973; Nolan and Ashcroft, 1969; Singer and Streiner, 1966; Suppes, 1974; Tillman, 1967a, b; Zweibelson and Barg, 1967).

That these deficiencies are due to lack of appropriate learning experiences rather than inherent inferiority is supported by studies done by Friedman and Pasnak (1973), Stephens and Grube (1982), and Stephens, Grube, and Fitzgerald (1977). Observing that blind children had been found retarded in the comprehension of conceptual tasks developed by the noted Swiss psychologist Jean Piaget (Hatwell, 1966), Friedman and Pasnak gave blind and sighted children training in the ability to classify objects. They found that such training increased the blind children's ability so significantly that their performance equaled that of the sighted children. The studies by Stephens and her colleagues also showed that the conceptual abilities of blind children improved after they were provided with extensive training on Piagetian tasks. Stephens and Grube point out the importance of conceptual abilities such as classification:

> The disadvantages of deficient classification skills are numerous. For example, they hamper the understanding of set theory and number relationships in mathematics, concepts of nation and state in social studies, and the physical relationships or properties of objects confronted in vocational education classes. Moreover, when students do not have the conceptual basis for understanding or classifying material presented in the classroom, their development of conceptual structures will be delayed. (1982, p. 141)

Spatial Concepts

The concept that appears to cause blind children more difficulty than any other is that of space. But although there are studies showing blind people to be inferior on spatial concepts (Hartlage, 1967; Juurmaa, 1967; Swallow and Poulsen, 1973), a number of studies have demonstrated that spatial conceptualization is not impossible for blind individuals (Birns, 1986; Hartlage, 1973).

Blind people apparently learn spatial concepts by the use of senses other than vision. Hartley mentions that blind people sometimes develop an appreciation of space by noting the time it takes to walk various distances. Other authorities believe the tactual sense is usually used to gain spatial conceptualization, and it is because of the limitations of this sense that blind individuals have difficulty. Telford and Sawrey (1977), for example, state:

> Knowledge of the spatial qualities of objects is gained by the blind largely through touch and kinesthesis. Audition provides clues to the direction and distance of objects which

make sounds, but it gives no idea of the objects as such. Tactual and kinesthetic experiences require direct contact with, or movement around, objects. Thus, distant objects, such as the heavenly bodies, clouds, and the horizon, as well as very large objects such as mountains and other geographical units, or microscopic objects such as bacteria, cannot be perceived and must be conceived only by analogy and extrapolation from objects actually experienced. (pp. 378–379)

Tactual versus Visual Experience

As we have noted, tactual sensation is important for the development of the blind child's concept of space. The tactual sense, in fact, is the primary way in which a variety of concepts are acquired by the blind child. At this point it will be helpful to consider the numerous ways sight and touch differ to gain a better understanding of how blind children experience their environment.

Lowenfeld (1971) states that there are two different kinds of tactual perception: synthetic touch and analytic touch. **Synthetic touch** refers to a person's tactual exploration of objects small enough to be enclosed by one or both hands. Most physical objects are too large for synthetic touch to be useful. For these, analytic touch has to be used. **Analytic touch** involves the touching of various parts of an object and then mentally constructing these separate parts. The sighted person is able to perceive different objects or the parts of one object *simultaneously;* the blind person must perceive things *successively.* A good example of the restricted nature of touch is that of a woman trying to find something in the depths of her handbag. She may well have to grope for quite a while, touching objects successively, before she finds what she wants.

As Warren (1981) noted, blind people are at a distinct disadvantage because they are unable to use sight to help them develop integrated concepts:

> Further, vision plays a vital role in the consolidation of various perceptual attributes into a single, integrated concept. The child can hear a dog barking or panting, can feel the texture of the dog's coat or can experience contact with the dog if one of them runs into the other, and can smell the dog's odor. If he or she has sight of the dog as well, then vision informs him or her that all of these perceptual attributes are parts of the same event. Thus vision serves as an effective bridge among the other experiences, and the growth of the integrated concept of dog is facilitated. If vision is impaired, the task of acquiring the integrated concept is much more difficult. (pp. 195–196)

Another critical difference between sight and touch is that touch requires a great deal more conscious effort. As Lowenfeld (1973b) has observed:

> The sense of touch generally functions only if it is actively employed for the purpose of cognition, whereas vision is active as long as the eyes are open and hearing functions continually unless its organ is obstructed. Therefore, blind children must frequently be encouraged to apply touch for the purpose of cognition. In our society where something like a "touch taboo" prevails from infancy on, encouragement to apply touch is often prevented by a need to avoid social disapproval felt by parents and sometimes by educators. (p. 36)

And as Scott (1982) puts it:

> For the sighted child, the world meets him halfway. What he sees encourages him to move further out into his environment and to explore it. He learns literally hundreds of thou-

sands of things from observation, imitation, and identification, without any effort on his part or on the part of his parents or teachers. The visually impaired child is dependent on others to organize, explain, and interpret the strange and confusing world around him. (p. 34)

Little is known about the tactual sense of the blind child and how best to develop it. We do know, however, that good tactual perception, like good visual perception, relies on being able to use a variety of strategies (Berlá, 1981; Berlá, Butterfield, and Murr, 1976; Berlá and Murr, 1974; Griffin and Gerber, 1982). The blind child who compares a pencil and a ruler, for example, by using such strategies as comparing the length of each to body parts and listening to differences in pitch when each is banged against a table, will have an advantage in gaining an understanding of the differences and similarities between these two objects. One general strategy that is especially important for tactual development of blind children is the ability to focus exploration on the most important stimulus features (Davidson, 1972)—those parts of the object that make it what it is. Research has also demonstrated that the earlier the blind child is trained in the use of such strategies, the more beneficial the training will be for tactual development (Berlá, 1981).

Importance of Age at Onset and Degree of Impairment for Concept Development

That many blind children lag behind sighted youngsters in their acquisition of concepts is not in question. It should be kept in mind, however, that this is not true for all visually impaired individuals, especially those who are partially sighted (Brekke, Williams, and Tait, 1974; Tobin, 1972) and those who have become blind after birth. Partially sighted children may still exhibit difficulties in conceptual development, but they will generally be at a distinct advantage over totally blind children. The value of even a small degree of sight can be enormous in helping children tie things together in order to form concepts. Likewise, children who are able to gain some visual experience before losing their sight will be able to rely on these experiences to some degree. Although it is not impossible for children who are blind from birth to acquire some concepts as rapidly as children who become blind after a few years of sight (Birns, 1986), most professionals agree that children blind from birth generally have a more difficult time learning many concepts. Such things as degree of impairment, age at onset, and motivation often determine how much difficulty the visually impaired child will have in conceptual thinking.

Strengths of Visually Impaired Individuals

It should be apparent by now that blind people are not a homogeneous group. And despite their difficulties in cognitive development, they display strengths in some areas. For example, a study by Witkin et al. (1968) indicated that visually impaired people develop an increased ability in attention because their reliance on other senses is necessarily greater, and absorbing information from other sensory modalities requires a great deal of attention. Blind people have been shown to be very good at listening tasks. In addition, they score high on measures of creativity (Halpin, Halpin, and Torrance, 1973; Halpin, Halpin, and Tillman, 1973; Tisdall, Blackhurst, and Marks, 1971).

Visually impaired individuals are able to compensate in many ways for their sensory handicap. Furthermore, Friedman and Pasnak's 1973 study, which we discussed earlier, is encouraging because it indicates that training can make up for the lack of appropriate learning experiences.

Mobility

Probably the most important ability for the successful adjustment of most visually impaired individuals is their mobility—their skill in moving about in their environment. And mobility skills depend to a great extent on spatial ability. Authorities have delineated two ways that the visually impaired person can process spatial information—as a sequential route or as a map depicting the general relation of various points in the environment (Dodds, Howarth, and Carter, 1982; Fletcher, 1981; Herman, Chatman, and Roth, 1983; Rieser, Gurth, and Hill, 1982). The latter method, referred to as **cognitive mapping,** is preferable because it offers more flexibility in navigating an environment. Consider three sequential points—*A, B,* and *C.* A sequential mode of processing spatial information restricts a person's movement so that he or she can move from *A* to *C* only by way of *B.* But a person with a cognitive map of points *A, B,* and *C* can go from *A* to *C* directly without going through *B.*

No matter which conceptualization of space—sequential or map—visually impaired individuals have, there is little doubt that they are at a distinct disadvantage in mobility relative to their sighted peers. For one thing, they are less able, or unable altogether, to rely on visual imagery. As Herman et al. (1983) point out, the "power of the visual-type image may lie in the simultaneously availability of all spatial locations . . ." (p. 165). In addition, visually impaired travelers must rely much more on memory for their representation of space than sighted people do (Hollyfield and Foulke, 1983).

You have no doubt observed blind people who move relatively easily through crowded city streets; you may also have seen others so disoriented that they actually endanger themselves and others merely by walking down a quiet street. Determining what makes one blind person's mobility skills better than another's is not easy. For example, common sense seems to tell us that mobility would be better among those who have more residual vision, but this does not appear to be the case. *Motivation* to become mobile is believed to be the most important factor. Warren and Kocon (1974) cite studies that suggest that partially sighted individuals have greater attitude problems than those who are blind. Possibly partially sighted people are more frustrated than blind individuals because they can see a little—but not enough to be completely at ease in moving about. This frustration may lead them to give up and become dependent on others. Blind individuals, on the other hand, are more likely to be motivated to learn to use as many cues as possible because they know they cannot rely on any visual help.

We might also expect early loss of vision to be more harmful to mobility than later loss, but there is considerable disagreement among authorities on whether this is true. Again, Warren and Kocon (1974) note that those who become visually impaired later in life may have greater adjustment difficulties. With proper motivation, however, these people should be able to profit from a visual frame of reference acquired through previous experiences (Warren, Anooshian, and Boolinger, 1973). They can relate their new reliance on nonvisual modalities to previous visual perceptions. In addition, they have an advantage over those who have been blind from birth since they have been able to develop the rudiments of mobility, such as learning to walk as infants (Scholl, 1973).

"Obstacle Sense"

A large part of a blind person's skill in mobility is the result of ability to detect physical obstructions in the environment. A blind person walking along the street often seems to be able to "sense" an object in his or her path. This ability has come to be known as the "obstacle sense"—an unfortunate term since many laypeople, and some professionals, have taken it to mean that the blind somehow develop an extra sense. This is not true. A number of experiments, most of which were done at Cornell University, have shown that blind people can become very proficient at picking up cues in their surroundings (Ammons, Worchel, and Dallenbach, 1953; Kellogg, 1962; Rice, Feinstein, and Schusterman, 1965; Warren and Kocon, 1974; Worchel and Dallenbach, 1947; Worchel, Mauney, and Andrew, 1950). With practice, they are able to detect subtle changes in the pitch of high-frequency echoes as they move toward objects. Actually, they are taking advantage of the **Doppler effect,** a physical principle that says the pitch of a sound rises as a person moves toward its source. There is nothing special about being blind that allows one to develop this sense.

Although the obstacle sense can be important for the mobility of a blind person, by itself it will not make its user a highly proficient traveler. It is merely an aid. Extraneous noises in the environment (traffic, speech, rain, wind) can make the obstacle sense unusable. Also, it requires a person to walk at a fairly slow speed in order to be able to react in time.

The Myth of Sensory Acuteness

Along with the myth that blind people have an extra sense is a general misconception that with the loss of sight, blind people automatically develop better acuity in their other senses. This is not true. For example, they do not have lowered thresholds for sensation in touch and hearing. What they are able to do is make better use of the sensations they obtain. Through concentration and attention, they learn to make very fine discriminations. Another common belief that has been found to be a misconception (Pitman, 1965) is that blind people are superior in musical ability. Apparently they frequently follow musical careers, and some become accomplished musicians, because music is an avenue through which they can achieve success.

Stevie Wonder at the keyboard. It is a misconception that being blind automatically results in superior musical ability. Blind people frequently follow musical careers because hearing is a sense they can use to achieve success.
(Emerson/NARAS/Sygma)

Academic Achievement

Very few studies have been made of the academic achievement of visually impaired children and sighted children. Many professionals agree that direct comparisons are questionable, primarily because the two groups must be tested under such different conditions. For example, there are Braille and large-type forms of the Stanford Achievement Test for grades 2 through 12 (Morris, 1974). But because reading Braille is an inherently slower process than reading print and because most visually impaired children who do read print read at a slow speed (Nolan and Ashcroft, 1969), the visually impaired child is usually allowed to take a longer time on the tests.

Despite the problems involved in measuring achievement in visually impaired children, some gross generalizations can be made from the research that has been done. There is more than a little evidence to suggest that both partially sighted and blind children are behind their sighted peers when equated on *mental age* (Bateman, 1963; Bateman and Wetherell, 1967; Lowenfeld, 1945; Nolan and Ashcroft, 1969; Oseroff and Birch, 1971; Suppes, 1974). Another generally accepted conclusion is that the academic achievement of visually impaired children is not affected as greatly as that of hearing impaired children. Hearing is evidently more important for school learning than seeing. It may also be that stimuli important for learning can be more easily and effectively presented to a person with no sight than to a person with no hearing. Lowenfeld (1971) thinks, for instance, that an increase in the use of auditory sources in instruction for blind students has resulted in less academic impairment than was once the case.

Social Adjustment

There is a great deal of conflicting evidence on whether visually impaired individuals are less well adjusted than their sighted peers. Since the research does not show visually impaired children to be generally maladjusted, we can conclude that personality problems are not an inherent condition of blindness. Cutsforth (1951) was among the first to stress that if maladjustment does occur in a blind person, it is more than likely due to the way society has treated him or her. In essence, it is society's reaction to the blind person that determines adjustment or lack of it.

When visually impaired individuals are not accepted by those who are nonhandicapped, many professionals believe it is because some of them have difficulty attain-

Very little research data supports the notion that visually impaired individuals have an inordinate amount of personality problems. Most are capable of normal community and social adjustment. (Bodhan Hrynewych/Southern Light)

America's Boswell Drives into the Dark

Dudley Doust on a Remarkable Player

After he had stooped to feel the texture of the grass, and finger the edge of the cup, Charley Boswell paced with his caddie across the green to his ball. He counted as he went . . . 48, 49, 50 feet. "It's mostly downhill," said his caddie, crouching to line up the face of Boswell's putter. "Take off about 10 feet, and putt it like a 40-footer."

Boswell stroked the ball. It sped across the green, climbed and fell, curved, slowed down and dropped with a rattle into the hole. Boswell grinned: "Did you see that one?" Yes, I had seen it. But he hadn't. Charley Boswell is blind. In fact, he is one of the most remarkable blind sportsmen in the world and playing off a handicap as low as 12, he has won the United States Blind Golfers' Association Championship 17 times.

Putting, oddly enough, is one of Boswell's strong departments. Given, of course, the fact that his caddie reads the putt, his execution is immaculate. "A tip that we blind golfers can pass on to the sighted player," he said, "I don't worry about the breaks on a green. Don't try to curb your putt because, as Bobby Jones always said, every putt is a straight putt and let the slopes do the work."

A few weeks ago I met Boswell in California, where he was playing a benefit match for the Braille Institute of America. He had come up from Alabama, where he is the State Commissioner in the Department of Revenue, a remarkable enough job, and now he was walking to the second tee on a course in the lush Coachelle Valley. A wind blew down from the mountains. "Funny thing," he said, "wind is really the only thing that bothers me. It affects my hearing, and that ruins my sense of direction."

On the second tee his caddie, who is his home professional back in Alabama, lined up the face of Boswell's driver and stepped away. Boswell, careful not to lose this alignment, did not waggle his clubhead. He paused, setting up some inner rhythm, and swung with the certainty of a sighted player. He groaned as the ball tailed off into a slice.

"There are two ways I can tell if I hit a good shot," he said, frowning. "I can feel it through the clubhead and, more important, I finish up high on my follow-through. Come on, let's walk. I can't stand golf carts—they bother my judgment of distance."

Boswell has been walking down darkened fairways since shortly after the Second World War. Blinded when a German antitank gun scored a direct hit on his vehicle in the Ruhr, he was sent back to an American hospital for rehabilitation. A former grid-iron footballer and baseball player, Boswell did not take easily to pampered, supervised sport.

"I tried swimming, and it bored me. I tried horseback riding until I rode under a tree and got knocked off. I tried ten-pin bowling, and that wasn't any good either—I fell over the ball-track." He laughed, idly swinging his club as he walked. "Then one day this corporal came in and suggested we play golf. I told him to get the hell out of my room."

Boswell had never swung a golf club in his life but, a few days later, aged 28, he gave it a try: "He handed me a brassie. I took six practice swings, and then he teed one up and I hit it dead centre, right out of the sweet spot. I tell you, I was lucky. If I'd missed the ball that first time I would have quit golf." There are no false heroics about Boswell.

Some holes later he, or rather we, found his ball in a bunker. The bunker shot was clearly the most difficult shot in Boswell's bag. Playing it required him to break two Rules of Golf: he not only needed his usual help from someone to line up his club but, to avoid topping the ball, or missing it altogether, he had to ground his club in the sand. "Also, I can't get fancy and cut across the ball," he said. "I have to swing square to the line of flight. I have to play it like an ordinary pitch."

These handicaps, he later pointed out, were in part counterbalanced by the actual advantages of being blind on a golf course. Boswell, for instance, is never tempted to play a nine-iron when a seven-iron will do the job. "In a match blind players play the course, not their opponents, because we can't see what they're doing anyway," he said, on the way to a score of 91 which, for him, was neat but not gaudy. "You know, I was once playing with Bob Hope, and he said: 'Charley, if you could see all the trouble on this golf course, you wouldn't be playing it.' And I suppose he was right."

SOURCE: Dudley Doust, *The Sunday Times,* London, February 6, 1977. Reprinted by permission.

ing certain social skills, such as exhibiting appropriate facial expressions. And teaching visually impaired students social skills can be a very challenging task, because such skills are traditionally acquired through modeling and feedback using sight (Farkas, Sherick, Matson, and Loebig, 1981; Stewart, Van Hasselt, Simon, and Thompson, 1985; Van Hasselt, 1983). However, a number of investigators have been successful in teaching social skills to visually impaired students using behavioral principles (Van Hasselt, 1983).

In another area related to social adjustment, some authorities have noted that visually impaired individuals often lag behind their sighted peers in obtaining accurate sex information (Welbourne, Lifschitz, Selvin, and Green, 1983). Because the usual way in which we gain information about sex is through the sense of sight, the visually impaired person can be at a distinct disadvantage. The topic of how best to teach human sexuality (whether it should be done in the home or in school) is a hotly debated issue. Suggestions range from the use of raised-line drawings of dolls that can simulate sexual intercourse to the use of live human models.

Stereotypic Behaviors

An impediment to good social adjustment for a few visually impaired individuals is **stereotypic behaviors** or **stereotypies.** These are repetitive, stereotyped movements such as rocking or rubbing the eyes. For many years the term **blindisms** was used to refer to these behaviors, because it was thought that they were manifested only in blind people. But such behaviors are also sometimes characteristic of severely retarded and disturbed children who have normal sight. Stereotypic behaviors and stereotypies are more appropriate terms because they stress the *repetitiveness* of the behaviors, which is the main point.

There are three major competing theories regarding the causes of stereotypic behaviors:

1. *Sensory Deprivation.* Children with low levels of sensory stimulation, such as blind children, attempt to make up for this deprivation by stimulating themselves in other ways. Thurrell and Rice (1970) present a strong case for this position. They found a greater frequency of eye rubbing among children with minimal vision compared to those with a higher degree of vision or no vision at all. They believe that children with minimal vision are able to gain stimulation from neural impulses through pressure applied to the eyes. Totally blind children cannot.

2. *Social Deprivation.* Even with adequate sensory stimulation, social isolation can cause individuals to seek added stimulation through stereotypic behaviors

(Warren, 1977, 1981). Some evidence for this position has been found by Berkson (1973), whose studies with animals suggest that social isolation, even within a relatively rich sensory environment, can lead to stereotypic behaviors.

3. *Retreat to Familiar Patterns of Behavior under Stress.* Arguing that even sighted children sometimes regress to less mature patterns of behavior, a number of researchers (Knight, 1972; Smith, Chethik, and Adelson, 1969; Stone, 1964) hold that stereotypic behaviors may be the child's way of retreating to "safer ground" in order to cope with stressful situations.

We have no conclusive evidence that any one of these three explanations is a single causal theory of stereotypic behaviors. It is safest to assume, therefore, that some combination of the three provides the best explanation for their occurrence.

Behavior modification has frequently been used with disturbed and retarded children (Foxx and Azrin, 1973) to eliminate self-stimulatory behaviors. Caetano and Kauffman (1975) achieved a dramatic reduction in self-stimulatory rocking mannerisms in two third-grade girls who were residents of a state school for the blind. The behavior modification techniques they used were feedback and reminders, coupled with token reinforcement. Every 15 seconds a clicking noise was made with a shopping counter, and then each girl was tapped on the shoulder (if she had been rocking during the previous 15-second interval) or given 5 points (if she had not been rocking) which she could later exchange for toys or trinkets. As the girls became more aware of and able to control their rocking, the length of the intervals was gradually increased and the number of points given was gradually decreased so that eventually praise for not rocking was enough.

EDUCATIONAL CONSIDERATIONS

Lack of sight can severely limit a person's experiences because a primary means for obtaining information from the environment is not available. What makes the situation even more difficult is that educational experiences in the typical classroom are frequently visual. Nevertheless, most experts agree that visually impaired students should be educated in the same general way as sighted children. Some modifications are needed, but the same general educational principles can be applied. The important difference to keep in mind in considering visually impaired children is that they will have to rely on other sensory modalities to acquire information. The extent to which a child can rely upon vision varies according to the degree of useful sight remaining.

Four major areas require special modifications for the child with little or no sight: (1) Braille, (2) use of remaining sight, (3) listening skills, and (4) mobility training. The first three pertain directly to academics, particularly reading; the last refers to skills needed for everyday living. The most classroom adaptations, of course, are needed for reading.

Braille

In nineteenth-century France Louis Braille, himself blind, introduced the basic system of writing for blind people that is used today. Braille actually based his alphabet on a system that had been developed by a French officer, Charles Barbier, for writing messages that could be read at night. The Braille method was offered as a replacement for raised-line letters. It was not adopted by everyone immediately, however,

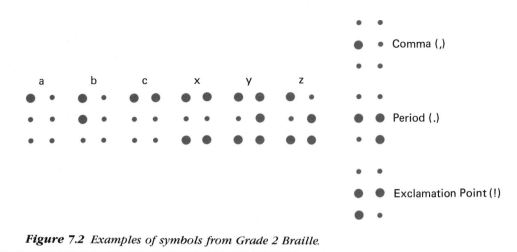

Figure 7.2 *Examples of symbols from Grade 2 Braille.*

and there was considerable debate about whether it or other systems of raised dots developed later were better. But in 1932 Standard English Braille was established as the standard code (Lowenfeld, 1973a). This made it possible for all Braille readers to read material, no matter who had trained them.

The basic unit of Braille is a quadrangular "cell" containing anywhere from one to six dots. The different forms of Braille vary primarily in the number of contractions used. Grade 1 Braille, for example, contains no contractions; Grade 2 Braille, on the other hand, makes considerable use of contractions and the shortened forms of words. In fact, Grade 2 Braille contains 189 contractions and short-form words and 31 punctuation and composition marks. Grade 1 Braille is easier to learn because it is more literal. But Grade 2 Braille is the popular choice because it requires much less space and can be written and read much faster. Figure 7.2 contains some examples of symbols from Grade 2 Braille.

There are primarily two means of writing in Braille—the Perkins Brailler and the slate and stylus. The **Perkins Brailler** (Figure 7.3) has six keys, one for each of the six dots of the cell. The keys, when depressed simultaneously, leave an embossed print on the paper. More portable than the Perkins Brailler, but more difficult to use, is the **slate and stylus** (Figure 7.4). The stylus must be pressed through the openings of the slate, which holds the paper between its two halves. The slate and stylus is also slower because the stylus makes an indentation in the paper, so the Braille cells have to be written in reverse order.

Research has shown that the reading of Braille requires processes very similar to those used when the sighted person learns to read print. The perceptual unit used by visually impaired children, however, is the cell itself rather than words or sentences (Nolan and Kederis, 1969).

Learning to read Braille is much more difficult than learning to read print. As Hanninen (1975) notes, Braille contractions are not logical and do not correspond to phonetic rules. Besides the contractions, other features make Braille reading more complex than print reading. Braille reading relies on memory to a great extent. Because the perceptual unit is the single cell, readers are forced to perceive the material much more sequentially. They cannot perceive a number of words at once,

Figure 7.3 *A Perkins Brailler in use.* (Irene B. Bayer/Monkmeyer)

as can sighted persons reading print. Hanninen also notes that reversal problems (reading or writing letters or words backward) are more likely to occur with Braille. Spelling problems are also more likely because of the use of contractions.

Attesting to the fact that Braille is a more complex process than print reading is research indicating that the speed of reading Braille is much slower. Ashcroft (1963), for example, found that blind high school students average about 90 words

Figure 7.4 *A slate and stylus in use.* (Frink/Monkmeyer)

per minute. Henderson (1973), in reviewing the literature on Braille reading rates, notes that the speed varies greatly according to the kind of material being read, but that the reading of Braille has been shown to be consistently much slower than the reading of print by sighted readers.

Another factor that limits the usefulness of Braille is that the books are very large and take up a great deal of storage space. It is also difficult to obtain some reading material in Braille, even though the American Printing House for the Blind and the Library of Congress provide extensive services.

Use of Remaining Sight

Because of the many problems associated with reading Braille and because the vast majority of visually impaired children have quite a bit of useful vision, many professionals advocate that visually impaired individuals use that vision. They state that teachers should encourage visually impaired children to use their sight as much as possible. Hanninen (1975), for instance, believes that most visually handicapped students should read print. He cites the greater speed of reading print, the ability to portray pictures and diagrams, and the greater accessibility of reading material as reasons.

For many years there was a great deal of resistance to having visually impaired children use their sight in reading and some other activities. There have been many myths about this issue. Among the most common are these: (1) holding books close to the eyes harms the eyes; (2) strong lenses hurt the eyes; and (3) using the eyes too much injures them (Hanninen, 1975). At one time classes for partially sighted students were called "sight conservation" or "sight-saving" classes, reflecting the popular assumption that using the eyes too much causes them to deteriorate. It is now recognized that only in very rare conditions is this true. In fact, studies have shown that visually handicapped individuals can actually be trained to use what visual abilities they do have to better advantage (Barraga, 1964; Barraga and Collins, 1979; Collins and Barraga, 1980).

The two general methods of aiding visually impaired children to read print are large-print books and magnifying devices. Large-print books are simply books printed in larger-size type. This text, printed primarily for sighted readers, is done in 10-point type. Figure 7.5 shows print in 18-point type. Type sizes for visually impaired readers range up to 30-point type; 18-point is one of the most popular.

The major difficulties with large-type books are similar to those associated with Braille books. A great deal of space is required to store them. In addition, they are of limited availability although, along with the American Printing House for the Blind, a number of commercial publishers are now publishing and marketing large-print books (see box). The *New York Times* publishes a large-type edition for visually impaired readers; it comes out once a week, and the type is three times the size of regular newspaper type.

Magnifying devices range from glasses and hand-held lenses to closed-circuit television scanners that present enlarged images on a TV screen. These devices can be used with normal-size type or large-type books.

Figure 7.5

This is an example of 18-point type.

Listening Skills

The importance of listening skills for blind children cannot be overemphasized. The less a child is able to rely upon sight for gaining information from the environment, the more crucial it is that he or she become a good listener. Bischoff (1979) and Hatlen (1976) note that many professionals still assume that good listening skills will develop automatically in blind children. This is unfortunate, for it is now evident that blind children do not spontaneously compensate for poor vision by magically developing superior powers of concentration. In most cases, they must be taught how to listen. Bischoff (1979) lists a number of commercially available curriculum materials designed to teach children listening skills.

Listening skills are becoming more important than ever because of the popularity of recorded material as a method of teaching visually impaired individuals. Visually handicapped children and adults now have access to records and tapes and a variety of recording devices. The American Printing House for the Blind and the Library of Congress are major sources for these materials.

The major advantage of using recordings rather than Braille or large-print books is that the person can cover the same material much more quickly. There are four basic ways of using recordings, and these differ primarily in the speed with which the information is presented. The slowest way is for the material to be both recorded and played at a normal speed. Even this method, which results in a rate of about 150 to 175 words per minute, allows the person to "read" much faster than would be possible with Braille. Another way is for the person making the recording to speak at a faster rate. The listener can also play the tapes at a faster speed. This, however, like playing a 33⅓ rpm record at 45 rpm, results in a distracting "Donald Duck effect." By far the most satisfactory method in terms of efficiency is to use a compressed-speech device. The idea behind this method is to discard very small segments of the speech. This discarding can be done at random, or a computer can be used to ensure that only certain speech sounds (vowels rather than consonants) are eliminated.

The many investigations of the relative reading speed of Braille, large-type print, and compressed speech have consistently shown the last to be the most efficient. The same amount of information can be comprehended, but at a much faster rate. Harley (1973), for example, cites Morris's 1966 study in which accelerated speech was found to be between 155 to 360 percent more efficient than Braille or large type. In addition, Tuttle (1974) found listening to a recording at normal speed to be twice as fast as Braille, and compressed speech three times as fast. Tuttle also reviewed the literature in this area and concluded that the optimum rate for compressed speech is 275 words per minute for average or above-average students, and about 250 words per minute for below-average students.

There are some disadvantages to using recordings. First, there is the danger that the child will come to rely too heavily on them and will not learn to use residual vision. Moreover, recordings are not available for everything. This is especially true of such everyday materials as newspapers and street signs. Hanninen (1975) notes that listening to recordings requires a great deal of concentration. Any momentary lapse in attention will cause the child to miss what is being said.

Mobility Training

How well individuals cope with a visual disability depends to a great extent on how well they are able to move about. Whether a person withdraws from the social environment or becomes independent depends greatly on mobility skills. There are

Large-Print Publishing: The Eyes Have It

You may have noticed in your local bookstore a section devoted to large-print books. Though sales of individual titles remain small—4,000 is a best seller for a large-print book—more and more such titles are appearing every month and there is now a book club for readers of large-print books.

The guru of the large-print book in the United States is a third-generation San Franciscan named Lorraine Marchi, who is founder and head of the National Association for the Visually Handicapped (NAVH). Her interest in the subject began in the early 1950s when she discovered that there was no reading material available for her son who had just entered the first grade. Though not legally blind, he did have serious vision impairment.

"There are 498,000 legally blind people, and they are served by 800 agencies," says Lorraine Marchi. "But there are close to 11 million people who are visually handicapped, which means that even with the best correction, the vision in their better eye is less than normal. Among other things, that means in most states the denial of a driver's license on grounds of vision." It was for this group, and for the 90 percent of legally blind people who had some usable vision, that Mrs. Marchi set up the NAVH.

Among the organization's first aims was to make school-related textbooks available in large print for the visually handicapped. The first four large-print books it published in San Francisco in the 1950s included a fifth-grade speller and three social studies books for the third grade. The NAVH now has a backlist of about 200 books. In the 1960s, an English firm called Ulverscroft began to do large-type editions for adults and a few years later Franklin Watts followed suit here. In the late 1960s, Mrs. Marchi persuaded major publishers including Harper & Row, Simon and Schuster, Prentice-Hall, Scribners and Walker & Co. to give large-print publishing for adults a try, but all later abandoned it because, she says, the small press runs made the books money losers. Walker & Co. has since returned to the large-print market.

The concept of "large print" has different interpretations, but the NAVH has a list of standards that make 16-point type a desideratum. A point equals 1/72 of an inch. Normal book type generally runs from 9 to 11 points, and Book Report is printed in 8.5 point type. "But," says Mrs. Marchi, "point size is only one factor. The amount of white space between lines, the blackness of the type, and the color of the paper are among other important considerations."

Though large-print books are only a small part of its overall business, the biggest name in the field is G. K. Hall, a Boston publisher that is strong in the library market. Probably its best-known division is Twayne, which does critical and biographical works aimed at college students. Hall began to do large-print books in 1970—buying rights from other publishers—and now issues 200 titles a year, primarily fiction. According to Janice Meagher, who has been Hall's executive editor for large-print titles since Jan. 1, the company's best-selling title in the area is probably the *Merriam-Webster Dictionary for Large-Print Users,* first issued in 1975. Hall also does well with *The Fanny Farmer Cookbook* and with a series of original anthologies including *Best-Loved Poems in Large Print.* Reflecting the fact that readers of large-print books tend to be older people, another best-selling book on the Hall list is *Sex After Sixty.*

The other two major publishers in the large-print field are both run by people who once worked for G. K. Hall—Phillips Treleaven, who was president of Hall and now heads the Thorndike Publishing Company, and John Curley, a former marketing man with Hall who is boss of John Curley & Associates.

Thorndike is located in the town of Thorndike, Maine, which has a population of 500—"more cows than people," as Phillips Treleaven describes it. The company publishes 88 titles a year, plus 36 romances imported from the British arm of Harlequin Books, Mills & Boone. Its best-seller so far has been *Lake Wobegon Days* by Garrison

Keillor, but it also has high hopes for its recently published edition of Jean Auel's *The Mammoth Hunters.* Because of the larger type size involved, the book was published in two volumes.

In addition to its large-print line, Thorndike also has done about 30 books of local interest in regular type sizes. *How to Talk Yankee,* a humorous book by schoolteacher Gerald E. Lewis on the language of New England, has sold 90,000 copies for Thorndike.

A lover of Cape Cod, John Curley used to commute into Boston from South Yarmouth, Massachusetts, when he worked for Hall. Now he runs his business from there and can go out for a swim or a game of golf whenever he wants. Curley does nothing but large-print books. The company does about 250 titles a year, including two romances, two mysteries and two westerns every month. Starting next January, the number of westerns will rise to three a month. According to John Curley's daughter, Mary, who works for the company, its best-selling author is probably Zane Grey. Titles on Curley's upcoming fall list include *The Patient Has the Floor* by Alistair Cooke, *Tefuga* by Peter Dickinson, John Hersey's *Hiroshima* and biographies of John Wayne and Ethel Merman.

Walker & Co., a mainstream New York publisher, concentrates on "inspirational classics" in its large-print line including *The Prophet* by Khalil Gibran, *Jonathan Livingston Seagull* by Richard Bach, *Strength to Love* by Martin Luther King and *The Power of Positive Thinking* by Norman Vincent Peale. Walker has 67 large-print books in its backlist.

A new entry in the large-print sweepstakes is Isis, a company based in Oxford, England. Its American marketing is handled out of Brooklyn, N.Y., by Allen Kleiman, a librarian specializing in services for the aging, and his wife Rhonda. Isis has done about 50 books so far, issuing three nonfiction titles and two fiction each month. Its best seller so far has been *Dr. Christiaan Barnard's Arthritis Handbook* and in the fall it will be publishing Barnard's *Your Healthy Heart.*

An important development in the large-print field is the establishment—as part of the Doubleday group of book clubs (which includes the Literary Guild)—of the Doubleday Large Print Home Library. The club gets its selections from books under contract to its fellow clubs in the Doubleday group. Current offerings include *I'll Take Manhattan* by Judith Krantz, *High Jinx* by William F. Buckley Jr., *Break In* by Dick Francis and *Murder at the FBI* by Margaret Truman. For information, write to the club in Garden City, N.Y. 11534-1104. The club also has an 800 number: 800-343-4300, ext. 355.

Another source for users of large-print books is the library maintained by the NAVH, 22 West 21st Street, New York 10010 (telephone 212-889-3141). Up to two large-print books can be checked out of the library at any given time and mailed anywhere in the country. The NAVH also provides vision information, book catalogs and a free newsletter.

The latest development in the large-print field harks back to the beginnings of the NAVH and Mrs. Marchi's frustration at not being able to obtain books for her son. G. K. Hall has begun to publish children's books in large type, including such classics as *Five on a Treasure Island* by Enid Blyton, *Mrs. Frisby and the Rats of NIMH* by Robert C. O'Brien and *Are You There God? It's Me, Margaret* by Judy Blume. And they are excited by their seven-volume edition of C. S. Lewis's *The Chronicles of Narnia,* due in the fall.

And a sign of the times. While marketing people at the large-print companies see their main audience as the growing population of older people, they think there may be a secondary audience in another group: younger people who work in front of computer screens all day and come home with very tired eyes.

SOURCE: Charles Monaghan, *Washington Post Book World,* June 29, 1986, pp. 15, 16. © The Washington Post.

two aspects to mobility: mental and physical orientation (Warren and Kocon, 1974). The ability to form a mental representation of the environment can be developed by the use of embossed maps or small tabletop models of large-scale environments (Herman, Herman, and Chatman, 1983). Besides the obstacle-detection skills mentioned earlier, physical mobility is usually aided in any one of four ways: (1) human guides, (2) guide dogs, (3) the Hoover cane, and (4) electronic devices.

Human Guides

The human guide undoubtedly enables the visually disabled person to have the greatest freedom in moving about safely, but this arrangement is not practical in most cases. Furthermore, too much reliance on another person causes a dependency that can be harmful.

Guide Dogs

Contrary to popular notions, the use of a guide dog is also not recommended very often. Extensive training is required to teach the visually impaired person how to use a guide dog properly. For example, individuals who obtain their guide dogs from The Seeing Eye, Inc., in Morristown, N.J., attend a "boarding school" for 27 days to learn to care for their dogs and to use them effectively (Annual Report, The Seeing Eye, Inc., 1985). This extended training, as well as the fact that guide dogs are large and walk fast, make them particularly inappropriate for children. In addition, like any pet, they must be cared for. Another disadvantage—again, contrary to what most people think—is that a dog does not "take" the blind person anywhere. The blind person must first know where he or she is going; the dog is primarily a safeguard against walking into dangerous areas.

Hoover Cane

The **Hoover cane** (long cane), developed after World War II, is the aid most often recommended. The visually impaired person sweeps the cane in an arc, lightly tapping the ground in front of him or her. The long cane makes it possible to detect obstacles and changes in the terrain.

Electronic Devices

A number of sophisticated electronic devices can be used as sensors of objects in the environment. Some of them are still experimental; most are quite expensive. Representative examples are the Laser cane and the Sonicguide.™ These devices operate on the principle that human beings, like bats, can learn to locate objects by means of echoes.

The **Laser cane** has the advantage of being used in the same way as the Hoover cane or as a sensing device that emits three beams of infrared light (one up, one down, and one straight ahead) that are converted into sound when they strike objects in the path of the blind traveler. Farmer (1975) gives the following interesting description of a Laser cane user's method of "navigating" under the difficult conditions presented by snowy weather. Although it is obvious that the narrator is an accomplished traveler, note the degree of complexity and precision needed to use the device properly.

The following is from a taped interview with a Laser cane user: "The element in travel that requires probably the most understanding by the traveler is when there is a great deal of snow on the ground and you don't have any well-defined shoreline. The ability to utilize the long cane technique will get you from point A to point B, but you're not going to be able to know when to make your right-angle turn into your particular house. Now, in my situation, where there are two rows of townhouses facing each other with roughly 40 to 45 feet in between the two rows of houses, this would normally pose a tremendous problem in picking out the right house—that's assuming that . . . you don't count steps— that's a cop-out! Under these circumstances, you've got the Laser Cane and every other home has a gas lamp set back seven or eight feet from what would be a sidewalk if it weren't covered with snow. So it is admissible to find your way (and I do) from one lamp post to the next with the laser beam and obviously when I get to the third lamp post, that's mine.

"Now the spindle or shaft on the lamp post is very thin, so it's possible under cold conditions to miss feeling the tactile stimulation that those narrow spindles present—and I've done this. When I come to the end of the road, there are ten shallow down stairs to a lower level. I've worked my way through this snow field clear to the end, on occasions, and missed every confounded lamp post and, after I didn't know what post I was process- ing, the sensible thing to do was to go all the way to the end and then work my way back; because when you're at the steps, you're oriented, you know exactly where you are and I have a landmark that I can trust. Now I work my way back using the only clues I have, the three lamp posts, and again the third one is mine.

"What I've learned to do is to find a reference of seven feet on each side, then I know I'm in the middle of the sidewalk. If I've been lucky and it's freshly fallen snow, there is about an inch or two of slope down from the grass to where the sidewalk is because the grass will accumulate snow and hold it that much quicker than the sidewalk. The sidewalk takes about one to one-and-a half inches of snowfall to cool down to the temperature to accumu- late. Then it takes a hell of a lot of fine cane touching the snow to follow that shoreline. But with a combination of that and the Laser Cane reaching out to the lamp post, you're OK!

"Here is a good example of where long cane technique, by shorelining, is employed to maintain a parallel relationship with the landmarks and the Laser Cane is used to 'reach out' across the shoreline to locate and keep track of the landmarks as they are approached. The Laser Cane, having that outreach, is just the additional element needed to reinforce, not your touch but your hearing. Being adventitiously blind, I have had to learn how to hear—and there are gaps in it. This Laser Cane tends to fill in the gaps in my hearing and I think I am just about 70 percent as efficient in traveling with hearing and touch as a congenitally blind person is with his hearing. Now without the Laser Cane, I'm about 30 percent as efficient. Now what I've said no doubt applies to electronic mobility guidance devices in general and that may not seem like very much, but it is a tremendous improve- ment!" (From L. W. Farmer, "Travel in Adverse Weather Using Electronic Mobility Guid- ance Devices," *New Outlook for the Blind,* 1975, *69,* 439–451. American Foundation for the Blind)

A number of researchers have worked on the development of the **Sonicguide**™ and devices closely related to it with visually impaired individuals ranging in age from infancy to adulthood (Bower, 1977; Kay, 1973; Strelow and Boys, 1979). Figure 7.6 shows the device being used with a 7-month-old infant who has been blind from birth. Although still very much in the experimental stages, this ultrasonic aid may eventually help blind infants to gain awareness of their spatial environment and objects within it. The device, worn on the head, emits ultrasound and converts reflections from objects into audible sound. Infants can learn about an object in their environment through three characteristics of the sound echoed back to them: (1) *Pitch* indicates distance of the object—high pitch signifies distant objects, low pitch

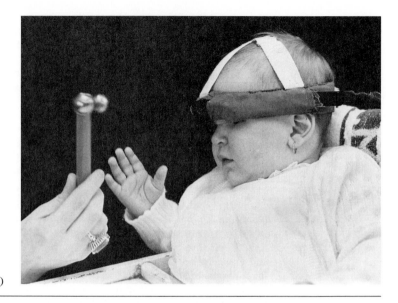

Figure 7.6 *A blind baby, with the help of an ultrasonic device worn on the head, learns to locate an object held by an adult.* (Rick Gemel)

close ones. (2) *Loudness* indicates size—loud means large, soft means small. (3) *Clarity of the sound* indicates texture—a clear sound refers to a hard-surfaced object, a fuzzy sound to a soft object. Also, since the auditory signal is directed to both ears, the infants can learn the direction of the object in the environment.

Because the Sonicguide™ is still experimental, there are a number of unresolved issues relating to its use. There is controversy, for example, over the optimum age at which it should be introduced. Aitken and Bower (1982) present data indicating that benefits of the device diminish substantially if it is introduced after the age of one year. Strelow (1983), on the other hand, suggests that introducing the Sonicguide™ at too early an age may be a waste of time because young infants may not be developmentally ready for its use. Strelow does note, however, that when introducing the device to older children, one needs to be aware that well-established competing behaviors may interfere with learning how to use the cues from the Sonicguide.™ ". . . the children find their own ways of dealing with spatial problems, and, however inadequate these may be, the children cling to them even though they may be detrimental to learning how to use the aid effectively" (1983, p. 437).

One intensive longitudinal study indicates that, if a period of auditory training is provided before introduction of the device, infants as young as 9 months can benefit from the Sonicguide™ (Harris, Humphrey, Muir, and Dodwell, 1985). Harris et al. had the parents of Kathy, a blind infant, begin auditory training with her at 6 months of age by doing such things as calling to her from one side or the other and then rewarding her with words and affection. By the age of 9 months, Kathy showed marked improvement in her use of the sonic aid. Data collected at regular intervals from 9 months until 4 years of age showed that she explored her environment more efficiently when she was wearing the sonic aid than when she was not. Kathy's progress, however, took a considerable amount of training. As Harris et al. state: "In conclusion, we, like other researchers, have found that a blind infant can learn to use a sonar aid for a variety of purposes. However, as the work with Kathy indicated, each milestone must be preceded by a lengthy period of diligent training" (p. 11).

Another issue raised by Strelow (1983) is whether devices like the Sonicguide™

might not actually delay language development. He speculates that intensive exposure to the sound from the aid might interfere with perception of speech sounds. These are all issues that need to be addressed with further research.

In considering electronic mobility devices, a word of caution is in order. Because of their amazing technology, it is easy to become too optimistic about these devices. None of them can just be picked up by the blind person and used without extensive practice. In addition, none of them should be used without more conventional techniques such as the Hoover cane (except in the case of the Laser beam cane, which can substitute for the Hoover cane) (Farmer, 1975). Another problem with these electronic devices mentioned by Strelow and Boys (1979) is that rapid technological advances are quite likely to make a device obsolete before the individual has learned how to use it properly.

All the various mobility methods and aids require visually impaired individuals to rely a great deal on memory. With this in mind, Hollyfield and Foulke (1983) have underscored the importance of practice:

> Because blind pedestrians are less able than sighted pedestrians to acquire the spatial information they need while traveling, they must depend more on their memorial representations of space. Acquiring a memorial representation of space is a skill that can be improved by practice, and blind pedestrians who are learning to travel independently should be given enough practice to establish firmly the habit of remembering to remember space. (p. 209)

How the blind or partially sighted child responds to mobility training depends to a great extent on attitude and previous learning experiences. Simply fitting a blind child with an appropriate mobility aid is not the answer. Training the child to develop orientation and mobility skills requires not only patience and specific teaching techniques, but an insight into the personality of the individual child as well.

Special Instructional Aids

In recent years a minor explosion in technology has resulted in new electronic devices for use in the instruction of visually impaired individuals. Among the first of these was the **Optacon.** This device consists of a camera that converts print into an image of individual letters delivered to the fingers by vibrating pins. The Optacon has not become popular because it does not allow the person to "read" very fast and it is expensive. Tobin and James (1974) found that users of the Optacon were generally able to read only about 5 to 11 words per minute. In addition, their survey indicated that it was not useful for occupational purposes. A major advantage of the Optacon, however, is that it makes many more materials, such as newspapers and magazines, accessible.

Another innovation is the **Kurzweil Reading Machine.** This is a small computer that converts print into speech. By placing the material face down on a scanner, the individual hears the material being "read" by an electronic voice. As with the Optacon, expense limits widespread ownership by individuals. But the Kurzweil Reading Machine is currently in use at a large number of schools, colleges, libraries, and other agencies (Orlansky and Rhyne, 1981). Its major advantage over the Optacon is that it allows the person to read at a level at least as fast as human speech.

Genensky has developed the **Interactive Classroom Television System** for use with partially sighted children (Genensky, Petersen, Clewett, and Yoshimura, 1978). With TV cameras and monitors at both the child's and the teacher's desks, child and

Advances in technology and in teaching visually impaired students enable these children to see enlarged images on the screen. (Rhoda Sidney/Monkmeyer Press)

teacher can keep in constant visual contact. In this way, for example, the child can see an enlarged image of what the teacher is writing on the chalkboard.

For those who still wish to use Braille as a medium for instruction, the **Portable Braille Recorder (PBR)** is proving to be both a time- and space-saver. The blind person records Braille onto tape cassettes and can play them back on the machine's reading board. A big advantage over traditional Braille methods is that the recorded material takes up much less space.

A variety of other special aids is available for use in mathematics instruction. There are now commercially available a number of talking calculators (Melrose and Goodrich, 1984). These devices "talk" to users by "saying" the numbers as they are punched and then "saying" the answer. Less exotic than talking calculators are tactually oriented procedures that have been used for years for sighted people. The **Cranmer abacus,** an adaptation of the Japanese abacus, is a small device consisting of beads that can be manipulated for math computations. Struve, Cheney, and Rudd (1980) advocate **Chisanbop,** a Korean method of using the fingers for calculating.

Administrative Arrangements

There are four major alternative educational placements for the visually impaired child: residential school, special class, resource room, and itinerant teacher. Variations of these arrangements exist, but these are the ones most often used. The order of the list reflects the extent to which the child is integrated with regular classroom children. The residential facility is the most segregated and the itinerant teacher program the most integrated.

Most states operate residential institutions for visually impaired individuals. One advantage of these institutions is that, given the very low prevalence of visually

Impediments to Independent Travel for Visually Impaired People: Rapid Rail Transit as an Example

Most of us who are sighted do not stop to consider how difficult our environment can be for the independent travel of the visually impaired person. Some prime examples of society-made dangers confronting the visually impaired traveler can be found in our subways. Jackson, Peck, and Bentzen (1983) conducted a study of the rapid rail systems of Atlanta, Boston, and Philadelphia. Their findings were based on the experiences of visually impaired individuals as they traversed each of these rapid rail systems, as well as on their own personal observations. The following indicates just a few of the many problems encountered.

Problems Experienced by Visually Impaired Travelers on Rapid Rail Transit Trips

Accessibility within the Station

Requirement: User must perceive and understand information about the correct platform, train, and direction.
Problems:

Some signs were located too high or in inconsistent locations.[a]

Some signs were poorly lit, which hindered attempts to read them.[a]

Some signs were dirty or defaced.[a]

Some signs had low contrast between print and background or had high color saturation.[a]

Some signs were written only in small print.[a]

There were no large print maps.[a]

Requirement: User must approach fare barrier or ticket booth.
Problems:

There was no standard location of the entry gate or turnstile, which made it difficult to locate the appropriate gate.[c]

There was no textured or otherwise tactually discernible path to gate that could be used consistently.[c]

There were narrow turnstiles that were difficult to pass through with dog guides.[c]

There was no standard location for information and change booths.[c]

There was no distinction between entry and exit turnstiles in some places.[c]

The "handicapped gate," which the user was supposed to push when the buzzer sounded, was texturally unmarked, and the traveler pushed on the area adjacent to the gate rather than on the gate itself.[d]

Requirement: User must manipulate currency or show "proof of payment."
Problems:

There were farecard machines in which the farecard had to be inserted in a unique manner.[c]

There were coin or token slots that had no contrast to the rest of the fare-collection device, which made finding the slot a matter of trial and error.[b]

Requirement: The user must travel along the platform to wait for the train.
Problems:

There were station platform edges marked with badly faded painted lines which were not sufficiently distinct from their adjacent area.[a]

There were station platform edges without guard rails.[b]

There were station platform edges with texture strips that were not of sufficient contrast to the adjacent area to serve as tactile warnings.[c]

Requirement: The user must be able to avoid hazards.
Problems:

There were cracks and breaks in the pavement that could cause falls.[c]

There were litter baskets in potential travel paths.[b]

There were newspapers and display racks in potential travel paths.[b]

There were poles and columns in potential travel paths.[b]

There were protruding telephone kiosks which did not project low enough to be detected by a cane.[c]

Requirement: The user must negotiate vertical movement.
Problems:
There were handrails that did not project beyond the top or bottom of stairs.[b]

There were cluttered and littered stairs.[c]

There were no clear visual or textural markings that indicated the top step, which in some cases was the sidewalk.[a]

There were breaks in handrails at landings, which caused confusion when staircases changed direction at landings.[b]

Requirement: The user must identify the correct train.
Problems:
There were no train announcements of destination in the station.[b]

There were trains that sat silently in the station, and they could not be recognized until their doors closed.[d]

Requirement: The user must observe and approach the train door area and enter the vehicle.
Problems:
There were open spaces between cars on trains which were mistaken for doors.[c]

The gap between the platform and train could cause one to stumble.[b]

Access within the Vehicle

Requirement: The user must identify a vacant seat.
Problem:
On some trains no seats were designated for the elderly or handicapped.

Requirement: The user must move along the aisle, possibly during train movement, or must ride standing.

Problems:
There was a lack of standard locations of posts to grasp for maintaining balance.[b]

No auditory warning was given before the train accelerated or decelerated to a halt.[b]

Requirement: The user must identify the desired stop or station.
Problems:
There were no station announcements on some trains.[b]

There were no tactile maps available.[b]

Requirement: The user must identify the desired stop or station.
Problems:
There was no forewarning of the side of the car on which the doors would open.[b]

Accessibility upon Leaving the Station

Requirement: The user must be able to leave the station.
Problems:
Some exit turnstiles were made of floor-to-ceiling horizontal bars, which were dangerous when in motion.[b]

There were "blind" alleys that were unmarked or marked only with visual signs.[b]

General Systemwide Problems

Problems:
Route information available by telephone was incomplete or was not expanded for blind users (e.g., the number of stops between entry and exit stations was not available).[b]

There were no raised or braille signs to identify such places as rest rooms.[b]

There were no auditory cues to beckon travelers to safe exits in an emergency.[b]

[a] Problem for legally blind individuals with some residual vision.

[b] Problem for all types of subjects.

[c] Problem for totally blind and for legally blind individuals with some residual vision.

[d] Problem for totally blind individuals.

SOURCE: Material from "Visually Handicapped Travelers in the Rapid Rail Transit Environment" by R. M. Jackson, A. F. Peck, and B. L. Bentzen, *Journal of Visual Impairment and Blindness,* Vol. 77, no. 10. © 1983 by American Foundation for the Blind Inc. and reproduced by kind permission of American Foundation for the Blind, 15 West 16th Street, New York, NY 10011.

impaired children in the general population, they allow for the concentration of a number of specialized services in one place (Warren, 1981). Today, however, this kind of placement is much less popular than it once was. Whereas virtually all visually impaired children were educated in residential institutions in the early 1900s, now virtually all receive their education in public schools. Much of this shift away from residential placements took place in the 1970s; from 1971 to 1981, the visually impaired residential population dropped 16 percent, while the public school visually impaired population increased 105 percent (McIntire, 1985). Most professionals believe that the residential facility should be used only as a last resort. Since the 1970s the trend has been not to place blind children in institutions unless they have additional limiting handicaps, such as mental retardation or deafness.

Also indicative of the prevailing philosophy of integrating exceptional with non-handicapped children is the fact that many residential facilities have established cooperative arrangements with public schools. One such example is the Community Adjustment Program (CAP), a joint program between the Western Pennsylvania School for Blind Children and the Allegheny Intermediate Unit Vision Program (Stewart, Van Hasselt, Simon, and Thompson, 1985). The staff of the residential facility concentrates on training independent living skills such as mobility, personal grooming, and home management in a five-week summer program, while the public school personnel emphasize academics. The future of residential programs for visually impaired students will no doubt include many more such cooperative arrangements (McIntire, 1985).

The special class plan is still a relatively popular placement. Within this framework the child, who lives at home, spends all instructional time in one class separated from other children in the school. Resource and itinerant teacher arrangements are gaining favor today, especially since the passage of PL 94-142 (see Chapter 1), and more visually impaired children are being kept in the regular classroom for a portion of the day. In keeping with this trend, resource and itinerant teacher strategies are increasing. The resource teacher deals with the child for only a portion of the day or week; the rest of the child's time is spent with sighted peers in the regular classroom. In addition, the resource teacher consults with the child's regular class teacher to provide advice and assistance. The itinerant teacher does not have a classroom; he or she travels from school to school, working with children and consulting with regular teachers. Given the low prevalence of visually handicapped children, this concept is quite popular, particularly in sparsely populated areas.

SPECIAL CONSIDERATIONS IN EDUCATING THE PRESCHOOL CHILD

For many years psychologists and educators considered the normally sighted infant as almost totally lacking in visual abilities during the first half year or so of life. In the 1960s and 1970s, however, there was an explosion of research studies indicating that as early as the first few weeks after birth the sighted infant is capable of making relatively sophisticated visual discriminations (Hetherington and Parke, 1986).

The young sighted infant is able to take in a great deal of information about the environment. This makes it easy to understand why the visually impaired infant, particularly the totally blind child, is at a distinct disadvantage as immediately as the first few weeks after birth. As Warren (1981) has observed, visual impairment impedes blind infants' access to the extended environment. Vision allows young children continuous exposure to the environment; without it, they are slow to learn what kinds of things exist outside their own bodies. This restricted range of interaction with the environment can have serious consequences for cognitive development. It is for this reason that Warren, among others, maintains that the infant with severe visual impairment has a high risk of being seriously delayed in cognitive development by about 18 months of age.

Fraiberg's (1977) observations are also relevant here. She notes that totally blind infants are slow to reach out for sound. While sighted infants are reaching out to grasp things they see by about 6 months of age, totally blind children do not reach out to things they hear until late in the first year. Fraiberg speculates that this delay in reaching for sound is why totally blind infants, although physically ready at the normal age, are late to crawl. Until they learn there is something "out there" that might be worth pursuing, they will not begin to crawl out into the environment. Another handicap facing some blind infants is that their parents are too restrictive about allowing them to explore their environment. It is understandable that parents would be concerned for the safety of their blind child, but it is necessary for them to strive for the proper amount of caution.

It is sometimes difficult for parents to adjust to the birth of a blind infant. There is often an overwhelming sense of grief. Professionals working in early intervention programs for blind infants often recommend that initial efforts focus on helping parents cope with their own reactions to having a blind child (Fraiberg, 1975; Fraiberg, Smith, and Adelson, 1969; Maloney, 1981). As Fraiberg et al. have stated:

> When we first encounter these parents they are nearly always immobilized by grief and they are without hope. If this was a first pregnancy we can see ruins of parental daydreams all about us. There may be a "baby book" in which nothing is written. Usually there are no pictures of the baby. The gift toys for the new baby, the rattles, cuddle toys, the cradle gym

Opportunities for exploration of the environment are crucial for the preschool blind child. (Karen Rosenthal/Stock, Boston)

are put away. "What can he do with them?" Grandparents, relatives, friends, all participate in a conspiracy of silence. . . .

So to our amazement, we were usually the first visitors to these mourning households who could say such things as, "He's a fine baby," "He's a beautiful baby," or "He is such an active baby!" and apart from anything else we did for our families, we were often the first people in the lives of these young couples who cared about the baby, who talked to the baby, asked to hold him, admired his accomplishments, found him a person. (Fraiberg, Smith, and Adelson, 1969, p. 123)

Fraiberg's (1975) program stresses the need for strong emotional attachment to the infant. Without strong affectional ties, she believes, the infant will not progress cognitively. Once these bonds are established, work can begin on language, cognitive, and mobility training.

One area of particular importance in preschool programming for visually impaired children is that of motor development (Dubose, 1976; Palazesi, 1986). Unfortunately, for many years professionals did not begin training motor development and mobility until visually impaired children were in the early elementary grades. Today, most authorities agree that mobility training should begin in preschool. Palazesi (1986) recommends that about 20 minutes be set aside every day for structured movement training: "The sequence of activities should follow a similar pattern: sessions should begin with stretching and bending activities and small movements; as the session progresses, movement builds and activities climax with large muscle movements across space." (p. 576)

SPECIAL CONSIDERATIONS IN EDUCATING THE ADOLESCENT AND ADULT

Two closely related major areas are difficult for some visually impaired adolescents and adults—independence and employment. Most authorities agree that some of the blind person's major impediments to securing an appropriate job lie in the area of independent living.

Independent Living

Perhaps the single most important thing to keep in mind when working with visually impaired adolescents or adults is that it is often a constant struggle for them to develop and maintain a sense of independence. A common mistake is to assume that such an individual is helpless. This feeling may be rooted in our own experiences. When we enter a dark room for the first time, we feel defenseless, fearful. Visually impaired people, however, have had many opportunities to become accustomed to seeing little. They are not at the same disadvantage as sighted people who suddenly find themselves in a situation in which there is little or no visibility.

Many people think of blindness in terms of street beggars selling pencils, and they feel pity for someone in this position (Lowenfeld, 1973b), although there are those who claim that blind beggars are in reality very independent and have exceptionally strong personalities (Cutsforth, 1951; Scott, 1969). In *The Making of Blind Men,* Scott lays the blame for the dependency of blind people on the numerous organizations, agencies, and programs created to serve them. He claims that blind people become dependent on the agencies for services and employment because they are *taught* to play a dependent role by these agencies. Of course, organizations for the

Sex education is an important component of independent living preparation for blind students. (Edith G. Haun/Stock, Boston)

blind vary in the degree to which they foster dependency. Scott's criticism should be kept in mind, however, for there is a real danger that some of these agencies may unwittingly be working against the very goals they espouse for handicapped people.

Both sighted and visually impaired individuals have been cited as possible contributors to the dependency some visually impaired people exhibit. Rickelman and Blaylock (1983) conducted a survey of blind persons in which, among other things, they asked them to indicate how sighted individuals might respond to blind people so as to decrease their dependent behavior. Following are their main suggestions:

1. *Respecting and encouraging the blind person's individuality, capabilities, and independence:* Do not assume that because you can do something more conveniently or quickly you should automatically do it for the blind person.

   Blind people often do not need help. Ask, "Can I be of assistance?" instead of initiating help. Do not feel embarrassed or rejected if a blind person declines your offer of assistance.

   Avoid being oversolicitous or overly protective. Blind people have the right to make mistakes, too.

The qualities and characteristics of the blind are as individual as the sighted. Respect this individuality.

2. *Talking with the blind:* Feel free to approach and talk to a blind person. You have the right to ask any questions you wish. The blind person has the right to respond as he wishes.

   Identify yourself before beginning a conversation or offering assistance.

   Approach a blind person without embarrassment, fear, or pity.

   If you are uncomfortable being around or associating with a blind person, admit it openly to the person. Neither the sighted nor the blind profit from avoiding each other.

   When you leave the presence of a blind person, always let him or her know that you are leaving.

   Talk in a normal tone of voice. Do not assume deafness or other disability.

   If your business is with a blind person, speak directly to the person rather than to sighted companions or relatives to get information.

3. *Becoming knowledgeable about guide techniques:* Let the blind person take your arm and walk slightly behind you. Never take his or her arm and push the blind person ahead of you. Walk at a normal pace.

   Always go through a door ahead of a blind person, telling him or her which way the door opens.

4. *Miscellaneous:* If you work in security at an airport, realize that the canes many blind people use are made of fiberglass and will not set off the metal detector.

   If you work with blind people in a dentist's or physician's office, always orient them to the waiting, examining, or treatment room. Explain what is expected of them and the steps of any procedures to be done.*

Some visually impaired individuals accuse themselves of contributing to their own dependency. Jernigan (1982) provides an illustrative incident from his own experiences:

> Early in my freshman year I went to one of my professors and said to him, "I want to do everything that's needed. I don't want any special favors or privileges. I want to compete on terms of equality with the other students here. I really want to be able to perform, and I believe I can. As I have said, I don't want you to give me special favors or privileges. Once in a while there may be a few things that I will need to do a little differently, but I hope there won't be many such things and that they won't be sufficient to make a difference in my overall performance.
>
> "Specifically," I said, "since fitting footnotes onto a sheet of typing constitutes some problem, I would hope that I would be able to omit footnotes from term papers and themes. I shall certainly do all the research involved, and will type the papers myself."
>
> That is what I told my professor. It sounds pretty good. Don't you think? It's a fairly plausible argument. I put [sic] all of the right words: "no special favors, no special treat-

---

* B. L. Rickelman and J. N. Blaylock, "Behaviors of Sighted Individuals Perceived by Blind Persons as Hindrances to Self-reliance in Blind Persons," *Journal of Visual Impairment and Blindness,* Vol. 77, No. 1. © 1983 by the American Foundations for the Blind, Inc. and reproduced by the kind permission of the American Foundation for the Blind, 15 West 16th Street, New York, NY 10011.

ment, no unreasonable privileges." Then, I asked the professor: "Is it all right if I proceed in that manner?"

His answer was blunt and to the point.

"Hell no," he barked. "It's not all right. Look, you have come here telling me that you can compete on terms of equality, and you have made all of this speech about how you want to do it on equal terms with everybody else. You also say you are capable of doing competitive work in college. Now, you either can or you can't.

"I could let you get by without the footnotes, and probably nobody would criticize me for it. But when you are through with my classes and are graduating, you are going to want a recommendation. At that time you'll get your feelings hurt if I say, 'He's not capable of competing on terms of real equality with others, but he can do a good job considering that he's blind.' You won't like it if I say that. Therefore, you are either going to pass my courses in such a way that I can honestly give you good recommendations, or I'll flunk you. Take it either way you want it."

That was one of the finest things that ever happened to me, because I had gone there with a good line prepared to snow the man, and I am not sure that I even knew that I was trying to do it. I typed his papers, by the way, and put the footnotes on them. There was no problem at all in doing it. I am afraid that if he had permitted it I might have taken the easy way out and paid a terrible price for it.

Not all blind persons are as lucky as I was. Too many are faced with people who say to them, "You don't need to do this." Unfortunately too many blind people accept the proffered assistance and (more often than not) never realize the high price they pay for the success they achieve in avoiding whatever it is they get out of or are talked into not doing.

When you are blind how do you manage to do the different things you need to do? Very often we begin by assuming that we need a lot more so-called "accommodation" than we do. Remember: There is no such thing as a free lunch. You pay for everything.*

Although there may be disagreement among professionals about who exactly is to blame for the dependency of some visually impaired people, there is little disagreement that they present special problems for the teaching of daily living skills. It is extremely important that the visually impaired individual, especially by adolescence, develop the independent living skills taken for granted by sighted people. Visually impaired adolescents need to be taught such skills as how to work household appliances (lighting a pilot light on a gas stove can be a particular problem), eat at the table, and prepare food for cooking.

Employment

Only about one-third of working-age blind adults are employed, and those who are working are often overqualified for the jobs they hold (Pfouts and Nixon, 1982). Most authorities agree that school personnel need to take an active role in helping visually impaired students develop appropriate career aspirations and job performance skills (Graves and Lyon, 1985). And many professionals also believe that, although the emphasis on such preparation should be strongest in secondary school, it should begin in elementary school. Unfortunately, research indicates that service

---

* K. Jernigan, "Competing on Terms of Equality," *The Braille Monitor,* January 1982, pp. 5–6. Reprinted with permission.

providers for visually handicapped students do not always believe that they are able to meet the students' career development needs. One survey of rehabilitation counselors and teachers, for example, led to the conclusion that visually impaired individuals need more exposure to career development tasks, experiences, and resources (Bagley, 1985).

Authorities now also recognize that job training is more likely to succeed if it takes place in regular work settings rather than in simulated settings in the classroom (Storey, Sacks, and Olmstead, 1985; Winkley, 1985). (As we noted in Chapter 2, community-based work instruction has also proved advantageous for retarded people.) The advantages of community-based instruction are described by Storey et al. (1985):

> The transfer of skills from a simulated environment (classroom) to an actual work environment (assembly line, clerical, or technical), for visually impaired students, might create . . . difficulties. For example, conditions such as industrial lighting and sound, physical obstacles, and social interactions with normally sighted adult co-workers cannot be simulated in a classroom environment. The community classroom model allows students to participate in real work settings with the supervision of a special education instructor. The purpose of the training is not only to teach specific job tasks but to give students a variety of real work experiences. In doing so, the students will be better prepared to make career decisions as adults. In addition, such an approach gives students the opportunity to develop generic work behaviors (i.e., punctuality, grooming, following directions, social skills) which will carry over to other work or community environments. (p. 481)

Storey et al. report data for a 17-year-old visually impaired student enrolled in a community-based training program, the Technological Employment Project (Gaylord-Ross, Forte, Gaylord-Ross, in press). This student, having received training in a branch office of AT&T, successfully learned the job skills of a long-distance operator, a position that has become highly technical in recent years.

MANAGING THE CHILD IN SCHOOL

With the increased attendance of visually disabled children in regular classrooms, teachers are having to learn to handle the special problems relating to their needs. Hanninen (1975) has made a number of suggestions, which we have summarized in the following six points:

1. Visually handicapped children should be required to care for their own materials as part of the effort to foster a sense of independence.
2. A sighted child in the class can at times act as a guide, as long as the visually disabled children do not become too dependent on him or her.
3. Blind children should be treated like sighted peers; the same general expectations should be maintained for all the children.
4. Interpersonal interaction between blind children and sighted peers should be encouraged.
5. Blind children should be encouraged to participate in as many activities as possible. Alternative activities should be arranged if it is not possible for them to join in with the rest of the class.
6. Visually impaired children should be given the same kinds of special tasks (such as watering plants) given to other children.

ONE PROFESSIONAL'S PERSPECTIVE

Rebecca (Ricki) G. Curry

B. A., Experimental Psychology and English, Brown University

M. Ed., Special Education for the Visually Impaired and Early Childhood Education, University of Virginia

Current Position: Itinerant teacher of visually impaired students, Piedmont Regional Education Program, serving five counties in central Virginia

Ms. Curry has been a teacher of visually impaired children since 1976. Her current caseload includes 12 students, ranging in age from 3 to 17 years. Because Ms. Curry operates as an itinerant teacher, she travels among 10 different schools in 4 counties to see these 12 students. Her current caseload contains children ranging in intelligence from gifted to severely retarded and ranging in visual acuity from 20/70 to totally blind (the majority are legally blind). In addition to visual impairment, many of them have other disabilities as well.

As an itinerant teacher, Ms. Curry's schedule is extremely variable. Only about 25 percent of her time is involved in actual instruction, about 50 percent is spent in case management (consultation with teachers, evaluations, visits to ophthalmologists with students), and about 25 percent is spent in travel to and from schools.

We asked Ms. Curry the following series of questions:

What influenced your decision to be a teacher of visually im-

paired youngsters? When I was in sixth grade I became very interested in handicapped children, probably because books about such children were popular in our class. I waded through Helen Keller's autobiography, read *Karen* by Marie Killilea several times and also read a book called *Follow My Leader* which is about a boy who loses his sight through an accident and has a special teacher who comes to teach him. I found the idea of adapting to blindness just fascinating, especially reading with a code. I spent some time getting involved in all different kinds of codes—Braille, fingerspelling, even Morse code. As I went through school I focused more on physically handicapped children, especially those with cerebral palsy. I spent a summer during high school as a volunteer in a camp for CP children and decided that what I wanted to become was a physical therapist. I went to a liberal arts college and planned to go into physical therapy in graduate school, not realizing that the area is so specialized that it's extremely difficult to transfer into a program or begin a program after finishing college. Luckily, while I was discovering that I had probably lost my chance at physical therapy by attending a school which didn't offer the prerequisite courses, I

also started to realize that I was more interested in influencing the minds of children than their bodies. Somehow I discovered that there was a whole field of education that I had never heard of before, and that was special education. I remembered my early fascination with Braille and the adaptations to blindness and realized that special education for blind children offered everything I was looking for: a profession that involved working with handicapped children; interesting problems of reading and mobility to which to adapt; the chance to have a tremendous influence on the intellectual and personal development of individual children; a close and continued relationship with children and their families over a period of years.

If you could change one thing about your job, what would it be? The most frustrating thing about my job is that I spend comparatively little of my time actually teaching visually impaired children. Although I enjoy the variety of responsibilities that being an itinerant teacher entails, those responsibilities too often limit teaching time. I'm also often operating in areas where I'm not trained, simply because there is no one else available to become involved with the student or the family.

What major changes have occurred in your field since you began teaching? Because of better child-find activities since PL 94-142, more children with other severe handicaps are being looked at more closely and found to have visual deficits secondary to their handicapping conditions. Therefore, our population has changed to include many children for whom visual impairment is a secondary problem and relatively few children who are only visually impaired. At the same time, fewer children are being placed in residential schools for the blind because of new legislation. The residential schools now serve very few "normal" blind children and are serving a population of mostly multiply impaired blind children. These changes have placed a great strain on the public school systems that are now required to deal with visually impaired children in their regular classrooms or by providing special classes. It has been difficult to convince many people in regular education that visually impaired children can function in their schools and deserve to be there.

Another major change since I began teaching is the proliferation of new technology aimed at serving visually impaired people. Paper Braille is no longer the only reading medium—now Optacons and electronic Braille machines like the Versabraille are available. Talking calculators and voice outputs for computers have also expanded the information and learning mediums available for my students.

Pick the one student in your career with whom you've had the most success and describe your involvement with him or her. In my second year of teaching in a residential school, a child moved up into my class who was something of a case study in the effects of deprivation. She came to the school at age 6 with the skills of an infant—no language other than screams, not toilet-trained, no ability to chew solid foods. Apparently, she had been left in a crib and treated like a baby for six years. In two years of school her teacher had taught her the basic skills of living. When she came to me she was eight years old and had the skills of a 3-year-old. While it didn't seem that she was retarded, her delays were still so great that we all wondered whether trying to teach her academic skills would be a long and ultimately losing proposition. I had her for four years,

and it took every bit of four years to bring her from a level of primitive language, rote counting, and simple matching to the point where she could recognize the entire Braille alphabet, use a brailler to write her name and simple sentences, and read simple sentences with comprehension. Her progress was so slow that I was never sure I wasn't wasting her time and mine by trying to teach her to read. At age 12, after four years of intense teaching, she had a Braille sight vocabulary of about 50 words, and she understood what reading was all about. I felt magnificent. Here was a child that *I* taught to read. Because she was a Braille reader, there was no incidental learning. Her only reading materials were the ones I produced for her. I had the pleasure of knowing that this child was able to read because I had made the decision to invest great amounts of her time and mine in teaching her.

Describe the most interesting student you've ever had and what made him or her so interesting. Robert is now 3½ years old and I've been working with him since he was about 9 months old. When he was first identified as visually impaired (he is totally blind), it was thought by everyone involved—his doctors, parents, teachers and myself—that blindness would be his only handicap. His blindness is caused by a genetic condition that is also associated with hearing loss and retardation, but at his evaluation by a genetic ophthalmologist his parents were told that since he had come along so far without any apparent complications it was likely that he would develop normally. He was a little over a year old at that time. His parents and I proceeded to deal with him as a "normal" blind child—giving him concrete experiences, language stimulation, gross motor experiences, and so on. But by

the time he was 2 years old I, at least, had serious questions about Robert's overall development. He had no language that I could understand and very poor fine motor skills. He spent a lot of time "tuned out" and seemed detached from other people. Over the past year and a half it has been very difficult for his parents and myself to view Robert as a "normal" blind child. He has developed language, but it is stilted and comprised mostly of learned phrases. In other areas Robert has made even less progress. He still lacks social responsiveness. He shows no desire to act upon his environment— when pleasant stimulation stops, Robert makes no move to get it started again. For example, if he is being tickled, Robert will laugh and obviously enjoy the tickling but when the tickling stops he will not use what language he has to ask for more tickling nor will he use physical prompts to get it to start again. It is most frustrating because we so badly want Robert to somehow become the child we thought he could be as an infant. After several intensive psychological consultations, all of us working with Robert changed our structured approach and have worked as a team to create an open-ended teaching environment in the hope that this would bring out his spontaneity. The result has been that he has found ways to respond in a rote manner to an open-ended problem! We are now facing the fact that he may be incapable of spontaneous response and rote learning may be his only avenue of success. Just as his parents do, I feel responsible somehow for Robert's limitations and I've done a lot of searching back for what part of my teaching was lacking. Even though I know that Robert's condition put him at high risk for problems beside blindness, as a teacher I still have the feeling that it's my responsibility to find the key to this boy.

Hanninen also has a number of suggestions relating to the physical environment of the partially sighted child. Adequate illumination is a must. Seating placement is also very important. The child should be seated so that he or she can best see the chalkboard and other materials. Glossy pictures should be avoided. Visual materials should be free from distracting background. The teacher should be sure to write on the chalkboard in large, clear letters. In addition, because of the great amount of visual attention the child must maintain, frequent rest periods may be necessary.

A number of other suggestions have been made by Orlansky and Rhyne (1981):

1. Sighted peers can help visually impaired children by taking notes for them or making carbon copies of notes they take for themselves.
2. It is beneficial for teachers to say aloud what they are writing on the chalkboard.
3. It is often appropriate for teachers to allow visually impaired children extra time to complete assignments.
4. There are obvious problems associated with teaching math and reading to the visually impaired. Science and geography are also problem areas because they are so visually oriented. Hadary has published a number of exciting ideas for a science curriculum with the visually impaired (Hadary, Cohen, and Weiss, 1979). For geography, embossed maps are available from the American Printing House for the Blind.

Scott (1982) also provides a number of helpful recommendations for teachers.

1. Choose a seat for the blind student that facilitates unobtrusive observation of how that pupil is coping with assigned work.
2. Make available a small table or set of shelves, easily accessible to the visually impaired student, for any special equipment he or she uses.
3. Encourage the blind student to share unique program needs with the teacher. These discussions should be private and confidential, held during recess or after school.
4. Be alert to reward problem-solving and other independent behaviors.
5. Facilitate social interaction by verbalizing the names of those nearby the child and by choosing the blind child occasionally for leadership roles in games and activities.
6. Be alert to make sure that the student understands communication or information presented, and encourage the student to ask for clarification when he or she does not understand.
7. Emphasize how important it is that he or she listens attentively.

The teacher should also make an effort to ensure that the visually handicapped child is familiar with the physical layout of the school. An **IPO relief drawing set** (Melotte and Engle, 1980) may be used to draw a raised-line map of the school for the child. This special type of pen can also be used in a variety of other ways. In interactions with the child, the teacher must be careful to remember that the nonverbal cues used with sighted children are inappropriate for visually impaired students. It is important to verbalize intentions.

Other recommendations relating to teaching everyday living skills have been mentioned by Telford and Sawrey:

Suggestions for the sighted who wish to aid the blind include the following: (a) Teach children to use the Continental technique of eating (holding the fork in the left hand and the knife in the right at all times) rather than the American "cross-over" convention. The former makes the act of eating neater and simpler for the blind. (b) Maintain a routine in table arrangements, tell the location of things "by the clock," and use salt and pepper shakers of different sizes or shapes. Teach children to shake salt and pepper into their hand before putting them on food, so as to estimate the amount. Name and indicate the location of food as it is served. (c) To assist in walking, ask the blind person if he would like to take your elbow. A gentle but firm grip just above your elbow is best. The blind person can then walk about half a step behind you. Start and stop gradually rather than abruptly, and walk in as straight a line as possible. (d) Let the blind person enter a car by himself after you have placed his hand on the car door. . . . (e) In a restaurant, place the blind person's hand either on the chair back or on the seat, and read the menu unless he already knows it. Let him give his order to the waiter. Either touch his hand or tell him the location of such things as ash trays, sugar bowls, salt and pepper shakers. Tell him what his bill is and let him pay the waiter or cashier. (f) When you meet a blind person, shake his hand if he makes a gesture in your direction. Speak directly to him; do not use his sighted companion as an "interpreter." Do not raise your voice. (1977, pp. 390–391)

The most important point to remember in teaching visually impaired children is to help them learn the maximum amount possible, while at the same time encouraging their sense of independence and accomplishment. Part of the purpose of assimilating these children into the regular classroom is to help them learn to function as efficiently as possible in the world.

SUMMARY

The legal definition of blindness and partial sightedness depends on the measurement of visual acuity and field of vision. A legally blind person has visual acuity of 20/200 or less in the better eye even with correction, or has a very narrow (less than 20 degrees) field of vision. Using a visual acuity criterion, partially sighted individuals have visual acuity between 20/70 and 20/200 in the better eye with correction. Educators, however, prefer to define blindness according to how well the visually disabled person functions. For the educator, blind individuals are those who need to be taught to read by Braille or aural methods, whereas partially sighted individuals can read print even though they need to use magnifying devices or books with large print.

The majority of those who are legally blind have some vision. It is important to know that many legally blind children are not educationally blind because they can read print (whether large print or magnified regular print).

Blindness is one of the least prevalent handicapping conditions in childhood. However, blindness is much more prevalent in adults than in children.

The Snellen chart, consisting of rows of letters or of *E*s arranged in different positions, is used to measure visual acuity. A special Snellen chart and the Jaeger chart permit one to determine what kinds of reading material the visually impaired student can use. Barraga's Diagnostic Assessment Procedure measures visual functioning rather than acuity and includes a curriculum. It assesses such things as awareness of visual stimuli, movement control of the eyes, and discrimination and identification of pictures of objects, people, and actions. Despite the existence of these tests, many vision problems are discovered by an alert parent or teacher. Teachers should be aware of a number of symptoms of visual impairment.

Most visual problems are the result of errors of refraction; because of faulty structure and/or malfunction in the eye, the light rays are not focused on the retina. The most common visual impairments are myopia (nearsightedness), hyperopia (farsightedness), and astigmatism (blurred vision). Eyeglasses or contact lenses can usually correct these problems. More serious impairments include glaucoma, cataracts, diabetic retinopathy, coloboma, retinitis pigmentosa, retrolental fibroplasia, strabismus, and nystagmus. Research indicates that about 64 percent of visual handicaps in school-age students are due to prenatal causes, many of which are hereditary.

Most authorities believe that visual handicaps do not influence language development. Performance on standardized intelligence tests indicates that blind students are not markedly lower in verbal intelligence than are sighted students, although modifications must be made for testing visually impaired children. The Ohwaki-Kohs and the Blind Learning Aptitude Test measure ability to use the tactual sense, and some believe these are more meaningful tests for totally blind children.

Blind children do tend to have difficulties forming certain types of concepts. In particular, they have problems with spatial concepts. These conceptual problems are not inherent in blindness, but are the result of lack of appropriate learning experiences. Through extensive training, blind students can improve their ability to form concepts.

Many of the differences between the conceptual abilities of sighted and blind children are due to the fact that the latter must rely primarily on touch to learn about their world. Sight more easily allows one to perceive different objects or parts of an object simultaneously; touch, on the other hand, results in successive perception of most objects. Sight permits easier integration of various perceptions. And touch requires more conscious effort on the part of the individual. Although many questions remain on how best to develop the sense of touch in visually impaired youngsters, research has shown that early training in the use of strategies helps.

Many believe that the most important ability for successful adjustment of visually impaired people is mobility. Mobility is greatly affected by motivation, attitude, and learning experiences. Totally blind persons seem to have fewer attitude difficulties than partially sighted individuals. This has been cited as a reason why they do not appear to be more at a disadvantage than the latter when it comes to mobility. There is much disagreement about whether those who experience early loss of vision are more or less mobile than those who lose their sight later. In any case, researchers have demonstrated that the mobility of visually impaired people is largely dependent on their spatial ability. Those who conceptualize their environment as a cognitive map possess better mobility skills than those who process their environment in a sequential way.

Blind people do not, as is commonly thought, have an inherent obstacle sense. They can develop it, however, provided they possess the vital mode of hearing. Another myth about blind people is that they automatically develop better acuity in other senses. What they actually do is become adept at picking up other sensory cues in their surroundings, thus making better use of their intact senses.

Methods of testing academic achievement of visually impaired students differ substantially from those used in testing sighted youngsters. Evidence suggests that partially sighted and blind children are behind their sighted peers in achievement.

Personality problems are not an inherent condition of visual impairment. Any social adjustment problems a blind individual may have are primarily the result of society's reaction to blindness. Some social skills that come easily to sighted people, such as exhibiting appropriate facial expressions, are difficult but not impossible to teach to visually impaired individuals. The stereotypic behaviors exhibited by a few blind individuals are also an impediment to social acceptance. Behavioral techniques have been used to diminish the frequency of stereotypies.

Educational experiences in regular classrooms are frequently visual. But with some modification in methods, the same general principles of instruction can be applied to both sighted and visually handicapped students. The Braille system of reading may be necessary for those whose vision is so impaired that they cannot read even larger type. There has been a dramatic increase in the number of special electronic devices for use in instruction of visually impaired students; examples are the Optacon, the Kurzweil Reading Machine, and talking calculators.

Currently, authorities believe that children

who have remaining vision should be encouraged to use it as much as possible. In fact, researchers have shown that visual discrimination ability can be improved through systematic training. Audiorecorded materials are being used more and more as educational tools for visually handicapped students. The compressed-speech method, in particular, permits fast and efficient presentation of material.

Mobility is critical to visually impaired people, especially for their ability to lead independent lives. Mobility training can involve the use of human guides, guide dogs, the Hoover cane, and electronic devices such as the Sonicguide™ and Laser cane. Most mobility instructors recommend the Hoover cane for the majority of blind people.

The four basic educational placements for visually impaired children are: the residential school, the special class, the resource room, and the itinerant teacher. The latter two placements, wherein the child spends a great deal of the day in the regular classroom, are now the most frequently used. Residential placement, at one time the most popular alternative, is now recommended only as a last resort. In addition, residential institutions for the blind now have greater percentages than before of individuals who have other handicapping conditions in ad-

dition to visual impairment. One trend is for integrated programming between residential and community-based facilities.

Without special attention, the visually impaired infant may lag behind the sighted infant cognitively. Impaired vision may restrict the infant's interaction with the environment. Early intervention frequently focuses on parental reaction to the child's disability and stresses the need for parent and infant to establish strong emotional ties. Once these bonds are established, work can begin on language, cognitive, and mobility training.

Education for the adolescent and adult stresses independent living and employment skills. Independence is particularly difficult to achieve for some visually impaired individuals, but it is extremely important, especially for work adjustment, that they be able to function independently. A contributing factor to visually impaired people's dependency problems is society, which often mistakenly treats them as helpless. Only about one-third of working-age blind adults are employed, and they are frequently overqualified for their jobs. Authorities are attempting to change this bleak employment picture. One trend is for job training to take place in regular work settings rather than simulated settings in classrooms.

REFERENCES

Aitken, S., & Bower, T. G. R. (1982). The use of the Sonicguide in infancy. *Journal of Visual Impairment and Blindness, 76,* 91–100.

Ammons, C. H., Worchel, P., & Dallenbach, K. M. (1953). Facial vision: The perception of obstacles out of doors by blindfolded and deafened subjects. *American Journal of Psychology, 66,* 519–553.

Annual Report (1985). The Seeing Eye, Inc., Morristown, N.J.

Ashcroft, S. C. (1963). Blind and partially sighted children. In L. M. Dunn (Ed.), *Exceptional children in the schools.* New York: Holt, Rinehart and Winston.

Bagley, M. (1985). Service providers assessment of the career development needs of blind and visually impaired students and rehabilitation clients and the resources available to meet those needs. *Journal of Visual Impairment and Blindness, 79,* 434–443.

Barraga, N. C. (1964). *Increased visual behavior in low vision children.* New York: American Foundation for the Blind.

Barraga, N. C. (1983). *Visual handicaps and learning* (Rev. ed.). Austin, TX: Exceptional Resources.

Barraga, N. C., & Collins, M. E. (1979). Development of efficiency in visual functioning: Rationale for a compre-

hensive program. *Journal of Visual Impairment and Blindness, 73,* 121–126.

Barraga, N. C., Collins, M., & Hollis, J. (1977). Development of efficiency in visual functioning: A literature analysis. *Journal of Visual Impairment and Blindness, 71,* 387–391.

Bateman, B. D. (1963). Reading and psycholinguistic processes of partially seeing children. *Council for Exceptional Children Research Monograph,* Council for Exceptional Children, No. 5.

Bateman, B. D. (1964). The modifiability of sighted adults' perceptions of blind children's abilities. *New Outlook for the Blind, 58,* 133–135.

Bateman, B. D. (1965). Reading and psycholinguistic processes of partially seeing children. *Research Bulletin: American Foundation for the Blind,* No. 8.

Bateman, B. D., & Wetherell, J. L. (1967). Some educational characteristics of partially seeing children. *International Journal for the Education of the Blind, 17,* 33–40.

Berkson, J. (1981). *Animal studies of treatment of impaired young by parents and the social group.* Paper presented at the Conference on the Blind Child in Social Interaction. *Journal of Visual Impairment and Blindness, 75,* 210–214.

Berlá, E. P. (1981). Tactile scanning and memory for a spatial display by blind students. *Journal of Special Education, 15,* 341–350.

Berlá, E. P., Butterfield, L. H., & Murr, M. J. (1976). Tactual reading of maps by blind students: A videomatic behavioral analysis. *Journal of Special Education, 10,* 265–276.

Berlá, E. P., & Murr, M. J. (1974). Psychophysical functions for active tactual discrimination of line width of blind children. *Perception and Psychophysics, 17,* 607–612.

Berlá, E. P., Rankin, E. F., & Willis, D. H. (1980). Psychometric evaluation of the low vision diagnostic assessment procedure. *Journal of Visual Impairment and Blindness, 1980, 75,* 297–301.

Birns, S. L. Age at onset of blindness and development of space concepts: From topological to projective space. *Journal of Visual Impairment and Blindness, 80,* 577–582.

Bischoff, R. W. (1979). Listening: A teachable skill for visually impaired persons. *Journal of Visual Impairment and Blindness, 73,* 59–67.

Bower, T. J. R. (1977). Blind babies see with their ears. *New Scientist, 73,* 255–257.

Brekke, B., Williams, J. D., & Tait, P. (1974). The acquisition of conservation of weight by visually impaired children. *Journal of Genetic Psychology, 125,* 89–97.

Caetano, A., & Kauffman, J. M. (1975). Reduction of rocking mannerisms in two blind children. *Education of the Visually Handicapped, 7,* 101–105.

Chase, J. B. (1974). A retrospective study of retrolental fibroplasia. *New Outlook for the Blind, 68,* 61–71.

Collins, M. E., & Barraga, N. C. (1980). Development of efficiency in visual functioning: An evaluation process. *Journal of Visual Impairment and Blindness, 74,* 93–96.

Conant, S., & Budoff, M. (1982). The development of sighted people's understanding of blindness. *Journal of Visual Impairment and Blindness, 76,* 86–90.

Cowen, E. L., Underberg, R., Verillo, R. T., & Benham, F. G. (1961). *Adjustment to visual disability in adolescence.* New York: American Foundation for the Blind.

Cutsforth, T. D. (1951). *The blind in school and society: A psychological study.* New York: American Foundation for the Blind.

Davidson, P. W. (1972). The role of exploratory activity in haptic perception: Some issues, data, and hypotheses. *Research Bulletin: American Foundation for the Blind,* No. 24, 21–27.

Dodds, A. G., Howarth, C. I., & Carter, D. C. (1982). The mental maps of the blind: The role of previous visual experience. *Journal of Visual Impairment and Blindness, 76,* 5–12.

Dokecki, P. R. (1966). Verbalism and the blind: A critical review of the concept and the literature. *Exceptional Children, 32,* 525–530.

Dubose, R. F. (1976). Developmental needs in blind infants. *New Outlook for the Blind, 70,* 49–52.

Farkas, G. M., Sherick, R. B., Matson, J. L., & Loebig, M. (1981). Social skills training of a blind child through differential reinforcement. *The Behavior Therapist, 4,* 24–26.

Farmer, L. W. (1975). Travel in adverse weather using electronic mobility guidance devices. *New Outlook for the Blind, 69,* 433–451.

Fletcher, J. F. (1981). Spatial representation in blind children. 3: Effects of individual differences. *Journal of Visual Impairment and Blindness, 75,* 46–49.

Foxx, R. M., & Azrin, H. H. (1973). The elimination of autistic self-stimulatory behavior by overcorrection. *Journal of Applied Behavior Analysis, 6,* 1–14.

Fraiberg, S. (1975). The development of human attachments in infants blind from birth. *Merrill-Palmer Quarterly, 21,* 315–334.

Fraiberg, S. (1975). *Insights from the blind.* New York: Basic Books.

Fraiberg, S., Smith, M., & Adelson, E. (1969). An educational program for blind infants. *Journal of Special Education, 3,* 121–139.

Friedman, J., & Pasnak, R. (1973). Accelerated acquisition of classification skills by blind children. *Developmental Psychology, 9,* 333–337.

Gaylord-Ross, C., Forte, J., Gaylord-Ross, R. (in press). The community classroom: Technological vocational training for students with serious handicaps. *Journal of Vocational Special Needs.*

Genensky, S. M., Petersen, H. E., Clewett, R. W., & Yoshimura, R. J. (1978). A second-generation interactive classroom television system for the partially sighted. *Journal of Visual Impairment and Blindness, 72,* 41–45.

Gottesman, M. (1973). Conservation development in blind children. *Child Development, 44,* 824–827.

Gottesman, M. (1976). Stage development of blind children: A Piagetian view. *New Outlook for the Blind, 70,* 94–100.

Graves, W. H., & Lyon, S. (1985). Career development: Linking education and careers of blind and visually impaired ninth graders. *Journal of Visual Impairment and Blindness, 79,* 444–449.

Griffin, H. C., & Gerber, P. J. (1982). Tactual development and its implications for the education of blind children. *Education of the Visually Handicapped, 13,* 116–123.

Hadary, D. W., Cohen, S. H., & Weiss, M. E. (1979). *Laboratory science and art for blind, deaf, and emotionally disturbed children: A mainstream approach.* Baltimore: University Park Press.

Halpin, G., Halpin, G., & Tillman, M. H. (1973). Relationships between creative thinking, intelligence, and teacher-rated characteristics of blind children. *Education of the Visually Handicapped, 5,* 33–38.

Halpin, G., Halpin, G., & Torrance, E. P. (1973). Effects of blindness on creative thinking abilities of children. *Developmental Psychology, 9,* 268–274.

Hanninen, K. A. (1975). *Teaching the visually handicapped.* Columbus: Charles E. Merrill.

Harley, R. K. (1963). *Verbalism among blind children.* New York: American Foundation for the Blind, Series No. 10.

Harley, R. K. (1973). Children with visual disabilities. In L. M. Dunn (Ed.), *Exceptional children in the schools* (2nd ed.). New York: Holt, Rinehart and Winston.

Harris, L., Humphrey, G. K., Muir, D. M., Dodwell, P. C. (1985). Use of the Canterbury Child's Aid in infancy and early childhood: A case study. *Journal of Visual Impairment and Blindness, 79,* 4–11.

Hartlage, L. C. (1967). *The role of vision in the development of spatial ability.* Doctoral dissertation: University of Louisville.

Hatlen, P. (1976). Priorities in educational programs for

visually handicapped children and youth. *Division for the Visually Handicapped Newsletter, 20,* 8–11.

Hatwell, Y. (1966). *Privation sensorielle et intelligence.* Paris: Presses Universitaires de France.

Hayes, S. P. (1941). *Contributions to a psychology of blindness,* New York: American Foundation for the Blind.

Hayes, S. P. (1942). Alternative scales for the mental measurement of the visually handicapped. *Outlook for the Blind and the Teachers Forum, 36,* 225–230.

Hayes, S. P. (1950). Measuring the intelligence of the blind. In P. A. Zahl (Ed.), *Blindness.* Princeton, N.J.: Princeton University Press.

Henderson, F. (1973). Communication skills. In B. Lowenfeld (Ed.), *The visually handicapped child in school.* New York: John Day.

Herman, J. F., Chatman, S. P., & Roth, S. F. (1983). Cognitive mapping in blind people: Acquisition of spatial relationships in a large-scale environment. *Journal of Visual Impairment and Blindness, 77,* 161–166.

Herman, J. F., Herman, T. G., & Chatman, S. P. (1983). Constructing cognitive maps from partial information: A demonstration study with congenitally blind subjects. *Journal of Visual Impairment and Blindness, 77,* 195–198.

Hetherington, E. M., & Parke, R. D. (1986). *Child psychology: A contemporary viewpoint* (3rd ed.). New York: McGraw-Hill.

Higgins, L. (1973). *Classification in congenitally blind children.* New York: American Foundation for the Blind.

Hollyfield, R. L., & Foulke, E. (1983). The spatial cognition of blind pedestrians. *Journal of Visual Impairment and Blindness, 77,* 204–210.

Jackson, R. M., Peck, A. F., & Bentzen, B. L. (1983). Visually handicapped travelers in the rapid rail transit environment. *Journal of Visual Impairment and Blindness, 77,* 469–475.

Jernigan, K. (1982). Competing on terms of equality. *The Braille Monitor,* January 4–14.

Jones, R., Gottfried, N., & Owens, A. (1966). The social distance of the exceptional: A study at the high school level. *Exceptional Children, 32,* 551–556.

Juurmaa, J. (1967). Ability structure and loss of vision. *American Foundation for the Blind Research Series,* No. 18.

Kay, L. (1973). Sonic glasses for the blind: A progress report. *Research Bulletin: American Foundation for the Blind,* No. 25, 25–58.

Kellogg, W. N. (1962). Sonar system of the blind, *Science, 137,* 399–404.

Kerby, C. E. (1958). Causes of blindness in children of school age. *Sight Saving Review, 28,* 10–21.

Knight, J. J. (1972). Mannerisms in the congenitally blind child. *New Outlook for the Blind, 66,* 297–302.

Lewis, M. (1975). The development of attention and perception in the infant and young child. In W. M. Cruickshank and D. P. Hallahan (Eds.), *Perceptual and learning disabilities in children.* Vol. 2, *Research and Theory.* Syracuse: Syracuse University Press.

Lowenfeld, B. (1945). *Braille and talking book reading: A comparative study.* New York: American Foundation for the Blind.

Lowenfeld, B. (1971). Psychological problems of children with impaired vision. In W. M. Cruickshank (Ed.), *Psychology of exceptional children and youth* (3rd ed.). Englewood Cliffs, N.J.: Prentice-Hall.

Lowenfeld, B. (1973a). History of the education of visually handicapped children. In B. Lowenfeld (Ed.), *The visually handicapped child in school.* New York: John Day.

Lowenfeld, B. (1973b). Psychological considerations. In B. Lowenfeld (Ed.), *The visually handicapped child in school.* New York: John Day.

Maloney, P. L. (1981). *Practical guidance for parents of the visually handicapped preschooler.* Springfield, IL: Charles C Thomas.

Matsuda, M. M. (1984). A comparative analysis of blind and sighted children's communication skills. *Journal of Visual Impairment and Blindness, 78,* 1–5.

McGinnis, A. R. (1981). Functional linguistic strategies of blind children. *Journal of Visual Impairment and Blindness, 75,* 210–214.

McIntire, J. C. (1985). The future role of residential schools for visually impaired students. *Journal of Visual Impairment and Blindness, 79,* 161–164.

Melotte, H. E. M., & Engel, F. L. (1980). Reading, writing, and drawing in relief: The IPO Relief Drawing Set. *Journal of Visual Impairment and Blindness, 74,* 155–157.

Melrose, S., & Goodrich, G. L. (1984). Evaluation of voice-output calculators for visually handicapped users. *Journal of Visual Impairment and Blindness, 78,* 17–19.

Morris, J. E. (1966). Relative efficiency of reading and listening for braille and large type readers. 48th American Biennial Conference of the American Association of Instructors of the Blind, Washington, D.C.

Morris, J. E. (1974). The 1973 Stanford Achievement Test series adopted for use by the visually handicapped. *Education of the Visually Handicapped, 6,* 33–40.

National Society for the Prevention of Blindness (1964). Pub. V-7.

National Society for the Prevention of Blindness (1972). *Teaching about vision.*

Newland, T. E. (1964). Prediction and evaluation of academic learning by blind children. II: Problems and procedures in evaluation. *International Journal for the Education of the Blind, 14,* 42–51.

Nolan, C. Y., & Ashcroft, S. C. (1969). The visually handicapped. *Review of Educational Research, 39,* 52–70.

Nolan, C. Y., & Kederis, C. J. (1969). Perceptual factors in Braille word recognition. *American Foundation for the Blind, Research Series,* No. 20.

Ohwaki, Y., Tanno, Y., Ohwaki, M., Hariu, T., Hayasaka, K., & Miyake, K. (1960). Construction of an intelligence test for the blind. *Tohuku Psychologia Fobia, 18,* 45–63.

Oriansky, M. D., & Rhyne, J. R. (1981). Special adaptations necessitated by visual impairments. In J. M. Kauffman & D. P. Hallahan (Eds.), *Handbook of special education.* Englewood Cliffs, N.J.: Prentice-Hall.

Oseroff, A., & Birch, J. W. (1971). Relationships of socioeconomic background and school performance of partially seeing children. *Exceptional Children, 38,* 158–159.

Palazesi, M. A. (1986). The need for motor development programs for visually impaired preschoolers. *Journal of Visual Impairment and Blindness, 80,* 573–576.

Pfouts, J. H., & Nixon, D. G. (1982). The reality of the dream: Present status of a sample of 98 totally blind adults. *Journal of Visual Impairment and Blindness, 76,* 41–48.

Pitman, D. J. (1965). The musical ability of blind children. *Research Bulletin: American Foundation for the Blind,* No. 11, 63–79.

Report of the Subcommittee on Rehabilitation (1971). National Institute of Neurological Diseases and Blindness, Organization for Social and Technical Innovation, Inc.

Rice, C. E., Feinstein, D. H., & Schusterman, R. J. (1965). Echo detection ability of the blind: Size and distance factors. *Journal of Experimental Psychology, 70,* 246–251.

Rickelman, B. L., & Blaylock, J. N. (1983). Behaviors of sighted individuals perceived by blind persons as hindrances to self-reliance in blind persons. *Journal of Visual Impairment and Blindness, 77,* 8–11.

Rieser, J. J., Gurth, D. A., & Hill, E. W. (1982). Mental processes mediating independent travel: Implications for orientation and mobility. *Journal of Visual Impairment and Blindness, 76,* 213–218.

Rogow, S. M. (1981). The appreciation of riddles by blind and visually handicapped children. *Education of the Visually Handicapped, 13,* 4–10.

Schindele, R. (1974). The social adjustment of visually handicapped children in different educational settings. *Research Bulletin: American Foundation for the Blind,* No. 28, 125–144.

Scholl, G. T. (1973). Understanding and meeting developmental needs. In B. Lowenfeld (Ed.), *The visually handicapped child in school.* New York: John Day.

Scott, E. P. (1982). *Your visually impaired student: A guide for teachers.* Baltimore, Md.: University Park Press.

Scott, R. A. (1969). *The making of blind men.* New York: Russell Sage Foundation.

Singer, J. L., & Streiner, B. F. (1966). Imaginative content in the dreams and fantasy play of blind and sighted children. *Perceptual and Motor Skills, 22,* 475–482.

Smith, M. A., Chethik, M., & Adelson, E. (1969). Differential assessments of "blindisms." *American Journal of Orthopsychiatry, 39,* 807–817.

Stephens, B., & Grube, C. (1982). Development of Piagetian reasoning in congenitally blind children. *Journal of Visual Impairment and Blindness, 76,* 133–143.

Stephens, B., Grube, C., & Fitzgerald, J. (1977). *Cognitive remediation of blind students. Final Report, Grant No. G00-74-07445, Office of Education, Bureau for Education of the Handicapped.*

Stephens, B., & Simpkins, K. (1974). *The reasoning, moral judgment, and moral conduct of the congenitally blind.* Final Project Report, H23-3197, Office of Education, Bureau of Education for the Handicapped.

Stewart, I. A., Van Hasselt, V. B., Simon, J., & Thompson, W. B. (1985). The Community Adjustment Program (CAP) for Visually Impaired Adolescents. *Journal of Visual Impairment and Blindness, 79,* 49–54.

Stone, A. A. (1964). Consciousness: Altered levels in blind retarded children. *Psychosomatic Medicine, 26,* 14–19.

Storey, K., Sacks, S. Z., & Olmstead, J. (1985). Community-referenced instruction in a technological work setting: A vocational education option for visually handicapped students. *Journal of Visual Impairment and Blindness, 79,* 481–486.

Strelow, E. R. (1983). Use of the Binaural Sensory Aid by young children. *Journal of Visual Impairment and Blindness, 77,* 429–438.

Strelow, E. R., & Boys, J. T. (1983). The Canterbury Child's Aid: A binaural spatial sensor for research with blind children. *Journal of Visual Impairment and Blindness, 73,* 179–184.

Struve, N. L., Cheney, K. M., & Rudd, C. (1980). Chisanbop for blind math students. *Education of the Visually Handicapped, 11,* 108–112.

Suppes, P. (1974). A survey of cognition in handicapped children. *Review of Educational Research, 44,* 145–175.

Swallow, R. M., & Poulsen, M. K. (1973). An exploratory study of Piagetian space concepts in secondary, low-vision girls. *Research Bulletin: American Foundation for the Blind,* No. 26, 139–149.

Telford, C. W., & Sawrey, J. M. (1977). *The exceptional individual.* 4th Ed., Englewood Cliffs, N.J.: Prentice-Hall.

Thomas, C. L. (Ed.) (1985). *Taber's cyclopedic medical dictionary* (15th ed.), Philadelphia: F. A. Davis Co.

Thurrell, R. J., & Rice, D. G. (1970). Eye rubbing in blind children: Application of a sensory deprivation model. *Exceptional Children, 36,* 325–330.

Tillman, M. H. (1967). The performance of blind and sighted children on the Wechsler Intelligence Scale for Children: Study I. *International Journal for the Education of the Blind, 16,* 65–74 (a).

Tillman, M. H. (1967). The performance of blind and sighted children on the Wechsler Intelligence Scale for Children: Study II. *International Journal for the Education of the Blind, 16,* 106–112 (b).

Tisdall, W. J., Blackhurst, A. E., & Marks, C. H. (1971). Divergent thinking in blind children. *Journal of Educational Psychology, 62,* 468–473.

Tobin, M. J. (1972). Conservation of substance in the blind and partially sighted. *British Journal of Educational Psychology, 42,* 192–197.

Tobin, M. J., & James, R. K. (1974). Evaluating the Optacon: General reflections on reading machines for the blind. *Research Bulletin: American Foundation for the Blind,* No. 28, 145–157.

Tuttle, D. (1974). A comparison of three reading media for the blind: Braille, normal recording, and compressed speech. *Research Bulletin: American Foundation for the Blind,* No. 27, 217–230.

United States Department of Health, Education and Welfare (1970). *Statistics for 1966 on blindness in the model reporting area.* Washington, D.C.: U.S. Government Printing Office.

Van Hasselt, V. B. (1983). Social adaptation in the blind. *Clinical Psychology Review,* 87–102.

Warren, D. H. (1977). *Blindness and early childhood development.* New York: American Foundation for the Blind.

Warren, D. H. (1981). Visual impairments. In J. M. Kauffman & D. P. Hallahan (Eds.), *Handbook of special education.* Englewood Cliffs, N.J.: Prentice-Hall.

Warren, D. H., Anooshian, L. J., & Bollinger, J. G. (1973). Early vs. late blindness: The role of early vision in spatial behavior. *Research Bulletin: American Foundation for the Blind,* No. 26, 151–170.

Warren, D. H., & Kocon, J. A. (1974). Factors in the successful mobility of the blind: A review. *Research Bulletin: American Foundation for the Blind,* No. 28, 191–218.

Webb, N. C. (1974). The use of myoelectric feedback in teaching facial expression to the blind. *Research Bulletin: American Foundation for the Blind,* No. 27, 231–262.

Wellbourne, A., Lifschitz, S., Selvin, H., & Green, R. (1983). A comparison of the sexual learning experiences of visually impaired and sighted women. *Journal of Visual Impairment and Blindness, 77,* 256–259.

Willis, D. H. (1976). *A study of the relationship between*

visual acuity, reading mode, and school systems for blind students—1976. Louisville, Ky.: American Printing House for the Blind.

Winkley, W. M. (1985). World without workshops. *Journal of Visual Impairment and Blindness, 79,* 462–465.

Witkin, H. A., Birnbaum, J., Lomonaco, S., Lehr, S., & Herman, J. L. (1968). Cognitive patterning in congenitally totally blind children. *Child Development, 39,* 767–786.

Worchel, P., & Dallenbach, K. M. (1947). Facial vision: Perception of obstacles by the deaf-blind. *American Journal of Psychology, 60,* 502–553.

Worchel, P., Mauney, J., & Andrew, J. G. (1950). The perception of obstacles by the blind. *Journal of Experimental Psychology, 40,* 170–176.

Zunich, M., & Ledwith, B. E. (1965). Self-concepts of visually handicapped and sighted children. *Perceptual and Motor Skills, 21,* 771–774.

Zweibelson, S., & Barg, C. F. (1967). Concept development of blind children. *New Outlook for the Blind, 61,* 218–222.

8

Physical Disabilities

We thank you Lord, 'cause Freddie's walkin'
We thank you Lord, 'cause Freddie's walkin'
Freddie's wearin' a smile, and rightly so,
'cause now his feet know how to go
We thank you Lord, 'cause Freddie's walkin'

We thank you Lord, 'cause Freddie's walkin'
We thank you Lord, 'cause Freddie's walkin'
Freddie's steppin' out, holdin' his head up high,
with his pretty blue eyes lookin' toward the sky
Oh, thank the Lord, 'cause Freddie's walkin'.

(Chuck Mangione, "Freddie's Walkin'")

I n Western culture people are almost obsessed with their bodies. They don't just want to be healthy and strong, they want to be beautiful—well formed and attractive to others. In fact, some people seem to be more concerned about the impression their bodies make than they are about their own well-being. They may even endanger their health in an effort to become more physically alluring. It is not really surprising, then, that those with physical disabilities must fight two battles—the battle to overcome the limitations imposed by their physical condition and the battle to be accepted by others.

Consider the experiences of the children described in the box on p. 361. Their stories reveal the insensitivity and nonacceptance many children and adults show toward those whose bodies are distorted by disease or accident. Even children whose disease or disability is not readily visible may be shunned by classmates and adults, as in the case of a child with AIDS (Acquired Immune Deficiency Syndrome; see pp. 378–379).

Children with physical disabilities often face more than the problem of acceptance, however. For many, accomplishing the seemingly simple tasks of everyday living is a minor—or major—miracle. Learning to walk, for example, may call for special celebration, as Chuck Mangione's song indicates.

DEFINITION AND CLASSIFICATION

In this chapter we consider children whose primary distinguishing characteristics are nonsensory health or physical problems. For the purposes of this book, children with physical disabilities are defined as those whose nonsensory physical limitations or health problems interfere with school attendance or learning to such an extent that special services, training, equipment, materials, or facilities are required. Our definition excludes children whose *primary* characteristics are visual or auditory impairments, although some physically disabled children have these deficiencies as *secondary* problems. Children who have physical disabilities may also have mental retardation, learning disabilities, emotional disturbance, speech and language disorders, or special gifts or talents. Thus we consider in this chapter those children whose physical condition is the first and foremost concern, but whose additional characteristics may be extremely varied. The child's physical condition is, of course, the proper concern of the medical profession—but when physical problems have obvious implications for education, teaching specialists must enter the scene.

The fact that the primary distinguishing characteristics of children with physical disabilities are medical conditions, health problems, or physical limitations highlights the necessity of interdisciplinary cooperation. There simply *must* be communication between physicians and special educators to maintain the child's health and at the same time develop whatever capabilities the youngster has (see Verhaaren and Connor, 1981a).

There is a tremendous range and variety of physical disabilities. Children may have **congenital anomalies** (defects they are born with), or they may acquire disabilities through accident or disease after birth. Some physical disabilities are comparatively mild and transitory; others are profound and progressive, ending in total incapacitation and early death. So it is difficult to discuss physically disabled children in general. Most of the remainder of the chapter will be organized around specific conditions and diseases falling under one of several categories: neurological impairments; musculoskeletal conditions; congenital malformations; accidents and other conditions; and child abuse and neglect. (For concise descriptions of many

MISCONCEPTIONS ABOUT PHYSICALLY DISABLED PEOPLE

Myth	*Fact*
Cerebral palsy is a contagious disease.	Cerebral palsy is not a disease in the usual sense; it is not contagious or progressive, and there are no remissions; it is a result of brain injury before, during, or soon after birth.
Physical disabilities of all kinds are decreasing because of medical advances.	The number of children with severe disabilities is increasing because modern medical treatment keeps more children alive.
The greatest educational problem involving children with physical disabilities is highly specialized instruction.	The greatest educational problem is teaching the nondisabled about what it is like to have a disability and how disabilities can be accommodated.
The more severely people are crippled, the less intelligence they have.	A person may be severely crippled by cerebral palsy or another condition but have a brilliant mind.
People with epilepsy are mentally ill.	People with epilepsy are not any more or less disposed to mental illness than those who do not have epilepsy.
Arthritis is found only in adults, particularly the elderly.	Arthritic conditions are found in people of any age, including young children.
Physically disabled persons have no need for sexual expression.	Physically disabled persons have sexual urges and need outlets for sexual expression.

physical disabilities and their implications for education, see Blackman, 1984; Bleck and Nagel, 1975.)

PREVALENCE AND NEED

The federal Department of Education for many years estimated that, for special education purposes, approximately 0.5 percent of school-age children have physical disabilities. About half of the physically disabled population was assumed to have cerebral palsy or another crippling condition; the other half were assumed to have chronic health problems or diseases of one sort or another that interfered with schooling. If the 0.5 percent prevalence estimate is correct, then one would expect to find about 200,000 physically disabled children needing special education in the United States.

Figures from the U.S. Department of Education (1986) indicate that about 200,000 students are being served under three special education categories related to physical disabilities: orthopedically handicapped (about 59,000), other health impaired (about 69,000), and multiply handicapped (about 72,000). But the needs of many students with physical disabilities appear to be unmet for many reasons, including the fact that the population of physically disabled children and youth is growing.

An increase in certain physical disabilities during the past two decades has been reported (Batshaw and Perret, 1986; Harkey, 1983; Wilson, 1973). Part of this increase may be due to improvements in the identification of and medical services to health-impaired and crippled children. Ironically, however, medical advances have not only improved the chances of preventing or curing certain diseases and disorders. They have also assured the survival of more children with severe medical problems. Many severely and profoundly handicapped children and those with severe, chronic illnesses who in the past would not have survived long today can have a normal life span (see Batshaw and Perret, 1986; Harkey, 1983; Hobbs, Perrin, and Ireys, 1985; Hobbs, Perrin, Ireys, Moynahan, and Shayne, 1984). So declining mortality rates do not necessarily mean there will be fewer disabled individuals. And improvements in medical care may not lower the number of disabled individuals unless there is also a lowering of risk factors in the environment—factors such as accidents, toxic substances, malnutrition, disease, and interpersonal violence.

The needs of American children with chronic illnesses were highlighted in reports by Hobbs and his colleagues (Hobbs et al., 1985, 1984). Their work, and that of Harkey (1983), indicates that 1 to 2 percent of the child population—that is, at least one million American children—suffer from *severe* chronic illnesses and "live out their lives in a twilight zone of public understanding" (Hobbs et al., 1984, p. 206).

NEUROLOGICAL IMPAIRMENTS

One of the most common causes of physical disability in children is damage to or deterioration of the central nervous system—the brain or spinal cord. Damage to the brain may be so mild as to be undetectable as far as the child's functioning is concerned, or so profound as to reduce the child to a very low level of functioning. There may be focal brain damage (involving a very specific and delimited area, often with specific effects on the child's behavior), or diffuse brain damage (involving a large or poorly defined area, often with generalized behavioral effects).

A brain-damaged child may show a wide variety of behavioral symptoms, including mental retardation, learning problems, perceptual problems, lack of coordination, distractibility, emotional disturbance, and speech and language disorders. (Of course, a child may show any of these behavioral manifestations and not have a damaged brain—see the discussion of brain damage and learning disabilities in Chapter 3.) Other symptoms that indicate brain damage or malfunction are impaired motor function, paralysis, and certain types of seizures.

Even though a person's brain may be intact and functioning properly, he or she may be neurologically impaired because of damage to the spinal cord. Since nerve impulses are sent to and from the extremities by way of the spinal cord, damage to the cord may mean that the child will lose sensation, be unable to control movement, or be incapable of feeling or moving certain parts of the body.

Neurological impairments have many causes, including infectious diseases, hypoxia (oxygen depletion), poisoning, congenital malformations, and physical trauma due to accidents or abuse. Poliomyelitis (polio or infantile paralysis) is an example of an infectious disease that attacks the nerves in the spinal cord or brain and often causes paralysis. Spina bifida is an example of a congenital malformation of the spine usually resulting in paralysis. In many cases of brain damage it is impossible to identify the exact cause of the impairment. The important point is that *when chil-*

Cancer-Stricken Children Find Confidence At Camp

DAUPHIN, Pa. (AP) — A year ago, David Brumbaugh gave himself up for dead after learning he had bone cancer at age 15.

Depressed, he headed for a camp for young cancer patients, where he thought the campers would sit around pitying each other.

He figured wrong.

This year, David is back for a week at Camp Can-Do, in the central Pennsylvania woods. His cancer is responding to treatment and he's counting the days until October, when his chemotherapy is scheduled to end.

"Nobody could tell me I wasn't going to die," he said Thursday. "I just had to go along with the treatment and trust the doctors."

They told him his hair, which fell out during the early stages of treatment, would grow back, and it did. They told him his strength would gradually return, and it did.

The doctors took care of everything but removing David's doubts. Camp took care of that this year by helping him decide to try out for the soccer team when he starts his junior

year in high school in suburban Phiadelphia next month.

"I found out I wasn't as out-of-shape as I thought I was," he said. "I found out there are people who have less of a chance than I do."

David is one of about 70 campers attending Camp Can-Do's fourth summer session. For a week, they ride horses and canoe, play board games, build models, swim and talk with other kids who share their problems and concerns.

"They offer each other hope. They offer each other support," said volunteer camp counselor Dale Perkel, a social service worker at St. Christopher's Hospital for Children in Philadelphia. "They really keep each other going."

David said he feels an obligation to help other campers, especially younger ones, deal with their illnesses and treatment because he can speak from experience about the side effects of drugs.

"Everybody else says they understand, they understand," he said. "But they really can't."

Dr. James F. Balsley, a pediatric oncologist at the Milton S. Hershey Medical

Center, said a child has a 1-in-600 chance of developing cancer. Because of the odds, healthy children aren't accustomed to seeing peers without hair or with disfiguring surgery scars or amputations. So they, and many adults, stare. Others shun young cancer patients.

Even when a medical cure is attained, as it is in about 60 percent of the cases, social acceptance is slow, Balsley said.

Nicole Todd, an 8-year-old camper from Enola whose leukemia is in remission, said some children still keep their distance at school.

"They treat me like they never knew me," the third-grader said. "They just treat me like I'm new there. I just ignore them and I play with the people who do know me and they treat me nice."

Twelve-year-old Jennifer Clites, whose hair is thin and wispy because of her treatments for Hodgkins disease, said the taunts of other children taught her about the way she treats people.

"I don't make fun of anybody anymore," she said.

dren's nervous systems are damaged, no matter what the cause, muscular weakness or paralysis is almost always one of the symptoms. And because these disabled children cannot move about like most youngsters, they typically require special equipment and facilities for their education. We turn now to some specific types of neurological impairments.

Cerebral Palsy

Cerebral palsy is not a disease in the usual sense of the word. It is not contagious, it is not progressive (except that improper treatment may lead to complications), and there are no remissions. Although it is often thought of as a motor problem associated with brain damage at birth, it is actually more complicated. Cerebral palsy can, for practical purposes, be considered part of a syndrome that includes motor dysfunction, psychological dysfunction, convulsions, or behavior disorders due to brain damage. Some individuals show only one indication of brain damage, such as motor impairment; others may show combinations of symptoms. The usual definition of

Neurological impairments such as cerebral palsy or epilepsy, in which there is sometimes the danger of hard falls, may require special protective equipment, like the helmets these children are wearing. (J.W. Myers/Uniphoto Picture Agency)

cerebral palsy refers to a condition characterized by paralysis, weakness, incoordination, and/or other motor dysfunction due to damage to the child's brain before it has matured (Batshaw and Perret, 1986; Crocker, 1983; Healy, 1984). Symptoms may be so mild that they are detected only with difficulty, or so profound that the individual is almost completely incapacitated.

Causes

Anything that can cause brain damage during the brain's development can cause cerebral palsy. Before birth, maternal infections, chronic diseases, physical trauma, or maternal exposure to toxic substances or X rays, for example, may damage the brain of the fetus. During the birth process the brain may be injured, especially if labor or birth is difficult or complicated. Premature birth, hypoxia, high fever, infections, poisoning, hemorrhaging, and related factors may cause harm following birth. In short, anything that results in oxygen deprivation, poisoning, cerebral bleeding, or direct trauma to the brain can be a possible cause of cerebral palsy. Although cerebral palsy occurs at every societal level, it is more often seen in children born to mothers in poor socioeconomic circumstances. Children of the poor have a greater risk of incurring brain damage due to such factors as malnutrition of the mother, poor prenatal and postnatal care, and environmental hazards during infancy (Denhoff, 1976; Thompson, Rubin, and Bilenker, 1983).

Cases in which genetic (chromosomal) factors cause cerebral palsy are rare. In some cases of genetically determined biochemical disorders associated with mental retardation, the child may show evidence of brain damage or cerebral palsy (Denhoff, 1976; Reed, 1975). Although there are many possible causes of cerebral palsy, the actual causes are often unknown. The cause can be identified in only about 60 percent of cases (Batshaw and Perret, 1986).

Types of Cerebral Palsy

It may seem reasonable to classify cerebral palsy according to the time period during which brain damage occurred (prenatal, natal, or postnatal), but ordinarily it is impossible to pinpoint the exact time of the damage. Classification according to degree of involvement (severity) or according to the extent and nature of the damage to the brain has not been successful either, because severity involves subjective judgments. Brain damage cannot be assessed precisely except by autopsy and recently developed technologies (Banker and Bruce-Gregorios, 1983; Werry, 1979a). The two means of classification that have been most widely accepted specify the limbs involved and the type of motor disability.

Classification according to the extremities involved applies not just to cerebral palsy, but to all types of motor disability or paralysis. The most common classifications and the approximate percentage of cerebral-palsied individuals falling into each class (according to Denhoff, 1976) may be summarized as follows:

- **Hemiplegia.** One half (right or left side) of the body is involved (35 to 40 percent).
- **Diplegia.** Legs are involved to a greater extent than arms (10 to 20 percent).
- **Quadriplegia.** All four limbs are involved (15 to 20 percent).
- **Paraplegia.** Only the legs are involved (10 to 20 percent).

Classification according to type of brain damage and consequent type of motor disability includes *pyramidal, extrapyramidal,* and *mixed* types. These may be described as follows, according to Batshaw and Perret (1986):

- **Pyramidal (Spastic).** Individuals with this type have suffered damage to the motor cortex or to the pyramidal tract of the brain. This results in problems with voluntary movements and in spasticity—stiffness or tenseness of muscles and inaccurate voluntary movement. About 50 percent of cases show spasticity.
- **Extrapyramidal (Choreoathetoid, Rigid, and Atonic).** Damage is outside the pyramidal tracts and results in abrupt, involuntary movements and difficulty maintaining posture (choreoathetoid), malleable rigidity or "lead pipe stiffness" (rigid), or floppy muscle tone (atonic). About 25 percent of cases show symptoms associated primarily with extrapyramidal damage.
- **Mixed.** Damage is to both pyramidal and extrapyramidal regions of the brain, and the child shows a mixture of effects (e.g., spasticity in the legs, rigidity in the arms). About 25 percent of cases are classified as mixed.

The regions of the brain that are damaged and the resulting paralysis for several types of cerebral palsy are depicted in Figure 8.1. Emotional state and general activity level may affect a child's movements, with the disorder becoming more apparent when the child is under stress and/or moving about than when he or she is at ease.

Prevalence

The prevalence of cerebral palsy is difficult to determine accurately. In the past a great deal of stigma was attached to the condition, and many parents hesitated to report their children's problems. Many cases occur among the poor and disadvantaged segment of the population and so may not be identified or receive medical treatment. In addition, prevalence estimates are confused by the many handicaps, such as mental retardation and emotional disorders, that can accompany cerebral palsy. There are data indicating that cerebral palsy occurs at a rate of approximately 1.5 per 1000 live births—about 0.15 percent of the child population (Batshaw and

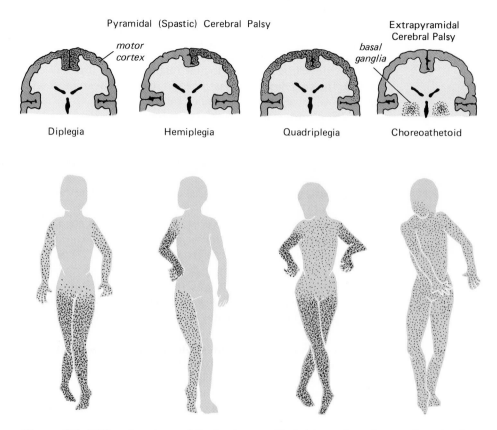

Figure 8.1 *Different regions of the brain are affected in various forms of cerebral palsy. The darker the shading, the more severe is the involvement.*
SOURCE: M. L. Batshaw and Y. M. Perret, *Children with Handicaps: A Medical Primer,* 2nd ed. (Baltimore: Paul H. Brookes, 1986), p. 302.

Perret, 1986; Healy, 1984). More male than female and more white than black children are affected (see Cruickshank, 1976b; Nelson and Ellenberg, 1978; Thompson et al., 1983).

Associated Handicaps and Educational Problems

Research during the past few decades has made it clear that cerebral palsy is a developmental disability—a multihandicapping condition far more complex than a motor disability alone (Cruickshank, 1976a; Batshaw and Perret, 1986). When the brain is damaged, sensory abilities, cognitive functions, and emotional responsiveness as well as motor performance are usually affected. A very high proportion of children with cerebral palsy are found to have hearing impairments, visual impairments, perceptual disorders, speech defects, behavior disorders, mental retardation, or some combination of several of these handicapping conditions in addition to motor disability. They may also exhibit characteristics such as drooling or facial contortions.

Some individuals with cerebral palsy have normal or above-average intellectual capacity, and a few test within the gifted range. The *average* tested intelligence of

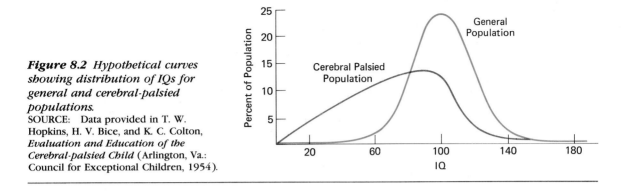

Figure 8.2 *Hypothetical curves showing distribution of IQs for general and cerebral-palsied populations.*
SOURCE: Data provided in T. W. Hopkins, H. V. Bice, and K. C. Colton, *Evaluation and Education of the Cerebral-palsied Child* (Arlington, Va.: Council for Exceptional Children, 1954).

children who are victims of cerebral palsy, however, is clearly lower than the norm (Batshaw and Perret, 1986; Cruickshank, Hallahan, and Bice, 1976; Nelson and Ellenberg, 1978; Thompson et al., 1983). A comparison between the normal distribution of IQs and that for children with cerebral palsy is shown in Figure 8.2. As Cruickshank et al. point out, proper testing of these children requires a great deal of clinical sophistication, since many intelligence tests or specific test items are inappropriate for children with multiple handicaps. Consequently, one must be cautious in interpreting test results for such children.

The educational problems of children who have cerebral palsy are as multifaceted as their handicaps. Not only must special equipment and facilities be provided because the children are physically disabled, but the same special educational procedures and equipment required to teach vision-impaired or hearing-impaired, speech-handicapped, learning-disabled, behavior-disordered, or mentally retarded children are often needed. Careful and continuous educational assessment of the individual child's capabilities is particularly important. Teaching the child who has cerebral palsy demands competence in many aspects of special education and experience in working with a variety of handicapping conditions in a multidisciplinary setting (Best, 1978; Calhoun and Hawisher, 1979; Verhaaren and Connor, 1981a,b; Zadig, 1983).

Epilepsy (Seizure Disorder)

A person has a **seizure** when there is an abnormal discharge of electrical energy in certain brain cells. The discharge spreads to nearby cells, and the effect may be loss of consciousness, involuntary movements, or abnormal sensory phenomena. The effects of the seizure will depend on the location of the cells in which the discharge starts and how far the discharge spreads.

People with epilepsy have recurrent seizures. About 6 percent of the population will have a seizure at some time during life, but most of them will not be diagnosed as having epilepsy because they do not have repeated seizures (Batshaw and Perret, 1986).

Most seizures first occur before the individual is 6 years old or when he or she has reached old age; seizures are primarily a phenomenon of early childhood and old age (Hauser and Kurland, 1975). Seizures beginning before the age of 2 years are usually associated with developmental defects (Cavazzuti, Ferrari, and Lalla, 1984); those with onset after age 25 are usually a sign of organic brain disease. Seizures reflect abnormal brain activity, so it is not surprising that they occur more often in children with developmental disabilities (e.g., mental retardation or cerebral palsy) than in children without handicapping conditions (Batshaw and Perret, 1986; Jacobs, 1983).

Causes

Seizures apparently can be caused by almost any kind of damage to the brain. The most common causes include lack of sufficient oxygen (hypoxia), low blood sugar (hypoglycemia), infections, and physical trauma. Certain conditions, like those named, tend to increase the chances that neurochemical reactions will be set off in brain cells (Batshaw and Perret, 1986). In many cases, the cause is unknown (Wolraich, 1984).

Types of Seizures

The International League Against Epilepsy suggests two major types of seizures: *generalized* and *partial*. A **generalized seizure** involves discharge of cells in a large part of the brain; a **partial seizure** begins in a localized area, and only a small part of the brain is involved. Several subtypes of both generalized and partial seizures have been classified. The important point here is that seizures may take many forms. They may differ along at least the following dimensions:

- *Duration:* They may last only a few seconds or for several minutes.
- *Frequency:* They may occur as frequently as every few minutes or only about once a year.
- *Onset:* They may be set off by certain identifiable stimuli or be unrelated to the environment, and they may be totally unexpected or be preceded by certain internal sensations.
- *Movements:* They may cause major convulsive movements or only minor motor symptoms (e.g., eye blinks).
- *Causes:* They may be caused by a variety of conditions including high fever, poisoning, trauma, and other conditions mentioned previously; but in many cases the cause is unknown.
- *Associated disabilities:* They may be associated with other handicapping conditions or be unrelated to any other medical problem or disability.
- *Control:* They may be controlled completely by drugs so that the individual has no more seizures, or only partially controlled.

Prevalence

Epilepsy (including seizure disorders of all types, but not isolated seizures) occurs in about 0.5 percent of the general population (Wolraich, 1984).

Educational Implications

About half of all children with epilepsy have normal or higher than average intelligence. Among these nonretarded children with epilepsy, however, one may expect to find a higher than usual incidence of learning disabilities (Batshaw and Perret, 1986). Although many children who have epilepsy have other disabilities, some do not. Consequently, both general and special education teachers may be expected to encounter children who have seizures. Besides obtaining medical advice regarding

First Aid for Epileptic Seizures

A major epileptic seizure is often dramatic and frightening. It lasts only a few minutes, however, and does not require expert care. These simple procedures should be followed:

- REMAIN CALM. You cannot stop a seizure once it has started. Let the seizure run its course. Do not try to revive the child.
- If the child is upright, ease him to the floor and loosen his clothing.
- Try to prevent the child from striking his head or body against any hard, sharp, or hot objects; but do not otherwise interfere with his movement.
- Turn the child's face to the side so that saliva can flow out of his mouth.
- DO NOT INSERT ANYTHING BETWEEN THE CHILD'S TEETH.
- Do not be alarmed if the child seems to stop breathing momentarily.
- After the movements stop and the child is relaxed, allow him to sleep or rest if he wishes.
- It isn't generally necessary to call a doctor unless the attack is followed almost immediately by another seizure or the seizure lasts more than ten minutes.
- Notify the child's parents or guardians that a seizure has occurred.
- After a seizure, many people can carry on as before. If, after resting, the child seems groggy, confused, or weak, it may be a good idea to accompany him home.

Courtesy of Epilepsy Foundation of America.

management of the child's particular seizure disorder, teachers should know first aid for epileptic seizures (see box above).

Epilepsy is primarily a medical problem and requires primarily medical attention. Educators are called upon to deal with the problem in the following ways: (1) General and special teachers need to help dispel ignorance, superstition, and prejudice toward people who have epilepsy and provide calm management for the occasional seizure the child may have at school. (2) Special education teachers who work with mentally retarded students or teach children with other developmental disabilities (especially institutionalized or severely and profoundly handicapped youngsters) need to be prepared to manage children's seizures as well as to handle learning problems.

Some nonretarded children who have epilepsy exhibit learning and behavior problems. Stores (1978) reported that learning and behavior problems associated with epilepsy occur more often in boys than in girls and are most often seen in children who have persistent abnormal electrical discharges in the left temporal lobe of the brain. Learning and behavior problems may result from damage to the brain that causes other disabilities in addition to seizures. The problems may also be the side effects of anticonvulsant medication or the result of mismanagement by parents and teachers. Teachers must be aware that seizures of any type may interfere with the child's attention or the continuity of education. Brief seizures may require that the teacher repeat instructions or allow the child extra time to respond. Frequent major convulsions may prevent even a bright child from achieving at the usual rate (Holdsworth and Whitmore, 1974a).

Research has shown that children with epilepsy do have emotional and behavioral problems more often than children without epilepsy (Freeman, Jacobs, Vining, and Rabin, 1984; Hoare, 1984). One must not, however, conclude that epilepsy causes emotional and behavioral problems directly. The stress of having to deal with seizures, medications, and stigma, as well as adverse environmental conditions, is more likely to cause these problems. Moreover, Freeman and his research group have shown that the school adjustment of students with epilepsy can be improved dramatically if they are properly assessed, placed, counseled, taught about epilepsy, and given appropriate work assignments (Freeman et al., 1984).

Spina Bifida

During early fetal development the two halves of the embryo grow together or fuse at the midline. When the closure is incomplete, a congenital "midline defect" is the result. Cleft lip and cleft palate are examples of such midline defects (see Chapter 5). **Spina bifida** is a congenital midline defect resulting from failure of the bony spinal column to close completely during fetal development. The defect may occur anywhere from the head to the lower end of the spine. Because the spinal column is not closed, the spinal cord (nerve fibers) may protrude, resulting in damage to the nerves and paralysis and/or lack of function or sensation below the site of the defect.

The cause of spina bifida is not known, though many factors are suspected (Batshaw and Perret, 1986; Hearey, Harris, Usatin, Epstein, Ury, and Neutra, 1984). Prevalence is estimated at 0.1 percent, making it one of the most common birth defects causing physical disability. There are several different forms of the condition. **Spina bifida occulta** does not result in any neurological disability because the spinal cord does not protrude. Nor is there any outward sign of a defect except occasionally a clump of hair growing from the area of the spine involved, usually in the lower back (see Figure 8.3). The **meningocele** form of spina bifida is distinguished by a tumorlike sac somewhere along the backbone. The sac contains cerebrospinal fluid but no nerve tissue, and there is no sign of neurological disability. In the **myelomeningocele** (or **meningomyelocele**) form, the sac contains the spinal cord or parts of it, and because the nerve fibers are involved, there is neurological damage. A myelomeningocele is often accompanied by paralysis of the legs and of the anal and bladder sphincters because nerve impulses are not able to travel past the defect.

Spina bifida is often accompanied by hydrocephalus, an enlargement of the head caused by excessive pressure of the cerebrospinal fluid (this is a syndrome associated with mental retardation—see Chapter 2); meningitis, a bacterial infection of the linings of the brain or spinal cord; and other congenital abnormalities. Although hydrocephalus and other defects associated with spina bifida may result in mental retardation, spina bifida alone does not result in lowered intelligence.

Surgery to correct the defect is performed in early infancy, and the mortality rate for children with spina bifida is being lowered (meaning, too, that more severely impaired children are surviving and attending school; Korabek and Cuvo, 1986). With proper orthopedic care, the child with spina bifida can learn to get around rather well with braces or crutches or in a wheelchair. Many children can attend regular public school classes. Lack of bowel and bladder control often are the greatest obstacles if the child with spina bifida is to go to regular school.

Poliomyelitis

It is tempting to believe that medical advances alone will wipe out diseases that cripple. But unless people practice preventive health care, the threat of crippling disease continues even though the means to conquer it are available.

Before the mid-1950s, when the Salk vaccine was perfected, **poliomyelitis** (also

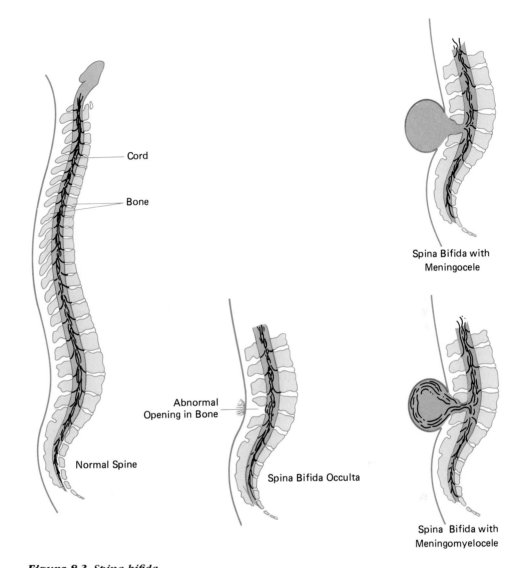

Cord

Bone

Normal Spine

Abnormal
Opening in Bone

Spina Bifida Occulta

Spina Bifida with
Meningocele

Spina Bifida with
Meningomyelocele

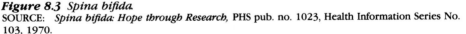

Figure 8.3 *Spina bifida.*
SOURCE: ***Spina bifida: Hope through Research,*** PHS pub. no. 1023, Health Information Series No.
103, 1970.

called polio or infantile paralysis) was a much-feared infectious disease. The polio
virus, which attacks the nerve tissue in the spinal cord and/or brain, left many
thousands of children and young adults crippled. The postpolio individual could be
unaffected neurologically, or left with severe muscular weakness, spasticity, complete paralysis, or skeletal deformities.

Widespread immunization against the disease has virtually eliminated it in the
United States, and most postpolio cases are now past school age (Batshaw and
Perret, 1986). In fact, the March of Dimes organization, which used to raise money
to fight polio, now collects funds to fight birth defects. Nevertheless, there have been

periodic outbreaks of the disease among unvaccinated children, especially in poor areas of the world (*World Health Statistics Report,* 1976). And cases of polio in American children are still being reported (Schonberger, Sullivan-Bolyai, and Bryan, 1978).

Because polio does not affect intelligence directly, children who have had the disease can usually attend regular public school classes if they receive proper ortho- pedic and other medical care.

Multiple Sclerosis

Multiple sclerosis (MS) is primarily a disease of older adolescents and adults. It is a chronic, slowly progressive disease of the central nervous system in which there is a hardening or scarring of the protective myelin sheath of certain nerves. The symp- toms include a variety of sensory problems (especially visual disturbances), tremors, muscle weakness, spasticity, speech difficulties, dizziness, mild emotional distur- bances, and difficulty in walking. Typically, the onset of the disease is slow and hard to recognize. The cause is unknown, and the prognosis is difficult to determine in the individual case (Frankel, 1984). The disease often seems to get better or worse unpredictably. There is no known cure. It is usually recommended that the person with MS lead as normal a life as possible. As a rule, a young person with MS should remain in regular public school classes and receive home instruction when school attendance is impossible.

Other Neurological Impairments

In addition to these conditions, a variety of other rare diseases, disorders, hereditary syndromes, and accidents can result in neurological impairment. The effects of these impairments vary widely and include sensory, motor, and intellectual deficits. The educational needs of students with neurological impairments must be considered on a case-by-case basis.

MUSCULOSKELETAL CONDITIONS

Some children are physically disabled because of defects or diseases of the muscles or bones. Even though they are not neurologically impaired, their ability to move about is affected. Most of the time muscular and skeletal problems involve the legs, arms, joints, or spine, making it difficult or impossible for the child to walk, stand, sit, or use his or her hands. The problems may be congenital or acquired after birth, and the causes include genetic defects, infectious diseases, accidents, or developmental disorders. We will describe two of the most common musculoskeletal conditions: muscular dystrophy and arthritis.

Muscular Dystrophy

Some children are handicapped by a weakening and wasting away of muscular tissue. If there is neurological damage or the muscles are weak because of nerve degenera- tion, the condition is called **atrophy.** When there is no evidence of neurological disease or impairment, the condition is called **myopathy.** The term **dystrophy** is applied to cases in which the myopathy is progressive and hereditary. Although there are many varieties of muscular atrophy and myopathy, some of the most

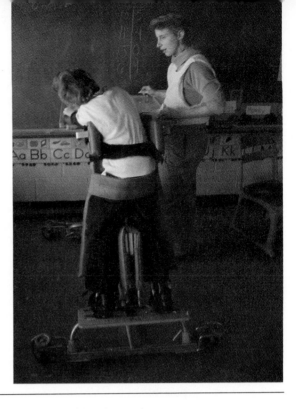

Neurological or musculosketetal conditions that impair ability to sit or stand may require special equipment for working at a table or participating in class. (Alan Carey/The Image Bank)

common serious conditions of this type fall under the general heading of **muscular dystrophy,** a hereditary disease characterized by progressive weakness caused by degeneration of muscle fibers. The exact biological mechanisms responsible for muscular dystrophy are not known, nor is there at present any cure (Batshaw and Perret, 1986; Harkey, 1983).

Two major types of muscular dystrophy are the pseudohypertrophic (Duchenne) form and the facioscapulohumeral (Landouzy-Dejerine) form. The pseudohypertrophic form is found only in boys. It is usually first noticed when the child is learning to walk, and it progresses throughout childhood. By early adolescence the child is often confined to a wheelchair. Pseudohypertrophy (literally false growth) of the muscles of the pelvic girdle, shoulder girdle, legs, and arms gives the child the outward appearance of health and strength, but the muscles are actually being replaced by fatty tissue. The individual seldom lives beyond young adulthood (Harkey, 1983). Facioscapulohumeral muscular dystrophy is found in both boys and girls. The onset is usually in adolescence. Weakness of the shoulders and arms is more prominent than weakness of the legs, and the facial muscles are affected. The progression is slower than in the Duchenne form. Some individuals become totally disabled, though others live a normal life span and are hardly aware of the symptoms.

Problems associated with muscular dystrophy are impairment of physical mobility and the prospect of early total disability or death. In advanced cases complications involving the bones and other body systems are common. One of the primary considerations is maintaining as normal a pattern of activity as possible so that the deterioration or degeneration of muscle tissue is minimized. Although muscular dystrophy itself does not affect intellectual functioning, research indicates that children with the Duchenne form tend to have lower than average verbal IQs (Batshaw and Perret, 1986; Karagan and Zellweger, 1978). Furthermore, when a child with muscular dystrophy has low intelligence, he or she tends to lose ambulation ability sooner, possibly because of lower motivation to continue exercise programs and use braces properly (Ziter and Allsop, 1976).

Arthritis

Pain in and around the joints can be caused by many factors, including a large number of debilitating diseases and conditions known as **arthritis.** Many people think of arthritis as a condition found exclusively in adults, especially the elderly. But arthritic conditions may be found in people of any age, including young children. **Rheumatoid arthritis,** the most common form, is a systemic disease with major symptoms involving the muscles and joints. The cause and cure are unknown, although in juvenile rheumatoid arthritis there are complete remissions in 75 to 80 percent of the cases. According to the U.S. Department of Health, Education and Welfare (1974), approximately 0.08 percent of children under the age of 17 have juvenile rheumatoid arthritis. More girls than boys are affected. Arthritis may vary greatly in severity, from relatively mild inflammation, swelling, and stiffness in the joints and connective tissues to extremely debilitating symptoms accompanied by atrophy and joint deformity. Sometimes there are complications such as fever, respiratory problems, heart problems, and eye infections. Educational considerations for children with arthritis consist of making the school experience as normal as possible.

Among handicapped children, **osteoarthritis** is the most common form. The cartilage around the joint is damaged, the space between the bones becomes smaller and loses its lubrication, and movement becomes painful or impossible. Osteoarthritis is especially likely to occur when the child has a condition in which a joint has been dislocated. Children with cerebral palsy, for example, may have recurring dislocations and suffer from painful arthritis. Surgery to correct the dislocation may also involve repair of the joint to reduce the risk of arthritis (Batshaw and Perret, 1986).

Other Conditions

A wide variety of other congenital conditions, acquired defects, and diseases can affect the musculoskeletal system (see Batshaw and Perret, 1986; Blackman, 1984). Some of these are listed in Table 8-1. In all these conditions, as well as in cases of muscular dystrophy and arthritis, intelligence is unaffected unless there are addi-

Table 8-1 Additional Musculoskeletal Conditions

Condition	Description
Clubfoot	One or both feet are turned at the wrong angle at the ankle.
Scoliosis	Abnormal curvature of the spine.
Legg-Calve-Perthes disease	Flattening of the head of the femur or hipbone.
Osteomyelitis	Bacterial infection of the bone.
Arthrogryposis	Muscles of the limbs are missing or smaller and weaker than normal.
Osteogenesis imperfecta	Bones are formed improperly and break very easily.

tional associated handicaps. Insofar as the musculoskeletal problem itself is concerned, special education is necessary only to overcome the child's mobility deficit, to see that proper posture and positioning are maintained, to provide for education during periods of confinement to hospital or home, and otherwise to make the educational experience as normal as possible.

CONGENITAL MALFORMATIONS

Several of the conditions we have described are always congenital (spina bifida); others are sometimes congenital and sometimes acquired after birth (cerebral palsy). Babies can be born with a defect or malformation of any body part or organ system; here we will give examples of only some of the more common or obvious ones.

Congenital defects occur in about 3 percent of live births (Batshaw and Perret, 1986). Counting birth anomalies that are not noticed at birth but discovered during the first year, congenital defects affect about 6 percent of the population (Bigge and O'Donnell, 1977). Not all these defects are debilitating.

Common Malformations

Congenital malformations of the heart and/or blood vessels leading to or from the heart are particularly serious. More children with congenital heart defects are surviving as advances are being made in heart surgery (Harkey, 1983). Today defects that once would have required an extremely sheltered or restricted life are being repaired so successfully that many children with congenital heart defects can look forward to a life of normal activity.

Congenital dislocation of the hip is a fairly common problem, occurring in about 1.5 of every 1000 live births; eight times more females than males are affected. The defect appears to be genetically determined and tends to run in families. It can usually be corrected with the use of casts or braces until the hip socket grows properly (Bigge and O'Donnell, 1977).

Congenital malformations of the extremities may range from relatively minor abnormalities of the foot or hand (webbing of the fingers or an extra toe) to profound malformations of the legs and arms. Some babies are born with arms or legs completely or partly missing. Minor malformations of the extremities can ordinarily be corrected by plastic or reconstructive surgery; major malformations require the fitting of prosthetic (artificial) devices, perhaps in addition to corrective or reconstructive surgery, and instruction in how to make the best use of the existing extremities.

Congenital malformations of the head and face (craniofacial abnormalities) are serious not only because they are cosmetic defects but also because the brain, eyes, ears, mouth, and nose may be involved. In addition to bizarre appearance, the child may suffer brain damage, visual impairment, auditory impairment, have no sense of smell or taste, or be unable to eat or talk normally. Advances in medicine, especially in plastic and reconstructive surgery, have had two obvious consequences: first, more children with major craniofacial anomalies are surviving than previously; second, children who formerly had to go through life markedly deformed can now often be made quite normal in appearance and be given the ability to see, smell, taste, or eat more normally. The extent to which craniofacial deformities can be corrected is illustrated in the before and after pictures in Figure 8.4.

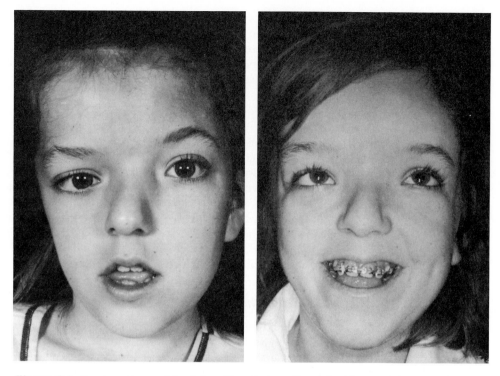

Figure 8.4 *Preoperative and postoperative photos of a girl with craniofacial defects. The preoperative photo (left) shows ocular hypertelorism (eyes abnormally far apart) with orbital dystopia (displacement of the eyes) and malalignment of the nose and facial bones due to a condition known as craniostenosis, in which the growth of the head and/or face is distorted. Notice that the right side of the face is smaller than the left. The postoperative photo (right) shows a much better alignment of the eyes and nose and improvement in facial symmetry.*
SOURCE: Courtesy of Dr. Milton T. Edgerton, Chairman, Department of Plastic Surgery, University of Virginia School of Medicine.

Congenital Malformations and Teratogens

Some children are born with malformed bodies because of a genetic defect—that is, they are destined to be malformed from conception because of the chromosomes contributed by the mother and/or father. Others are damaged at some time during fetal development. In some cases viruses, bacteria, radiation, or chemical substances—**teratogens**—damage the chromosomes of the parent(s) or interfere with normal fetal development. An almost endless list of diseases, drugs taken by the mother, and poisonous substances to which the mother may have been exposed during the course of pregnancy can cause a deformed fetus. Although in the vast majority of cases a specific teratogenic agent cannot be identified, the list of drugs, chemicals, and bacteria known to be capable of producing deformed fetuses is constantly growing.

A particular factor may be teratogenic *only* if the mother (and, indirectly, of course, the fetus) is exposed to it at a certain critical interval. In general, the first trimester is the crucial stage of fetal development. By the end of this first three months of pregnancy all the body parts have developed, though they have not completed their growth in size. For example, if a woman contracts **German mea-**

sles (rubella) during the first trimester, her baby may be born with a deformity. After this period maternal rubella ordinarily presents no danger to the fetus.

Perhaps the most dramatic, and infamous, teratogenic drug is thalidomide. This apparently "safe" sedative or antinausea drug, taken by many pregnant woman in the late 1950s and early 1960s (especially in Europe), was responsible for the birth of thousands of babies with extremely deformed or missing limbs and other peculiar anomalies (Batshaw and Perret, 1986). "Thalidomide babies" typically showed a deformity that is called **phocomelia,** in which the limbs are extremely short or are missing completely, and the hands and feet are attached directly to the torso.

Not as dramatic and infamous, but probably the most frequently used teratogenic drug in contemporary life, is alcohol. Ethanol, the type of alcohol found in beer, wine, and liquor, is known to be capable of causing cancer, mutations, and birth defects (Wilsnack, Klassen, and Wilsnack, 1984). A pregnant woman who drinks alcohol excessively runs the risk of having a baby with **fetal alcohol syndrome** (or **alcohol embryopathy**). Fetal alcohol syndrome is now the most frequent teratogenic damage seen in humans (Obe and Hansjurgen, 1979). The syndrome can range from mild to severe and includes effects such as fetal and postnatal growth retardation, brain damage, mental retardation, hyperactivity, anomalies of the face, and heart failure (Wisniewski and Lupin, 1979) (see also Chapter 2).

ACCIDENTS AND OTHER PHYSICAL CONDITIONS

Falling, burning, poisoning, and mishaps involving bicycles, motorcycles, and automobiles are some of the ways children and youths acquire disabilities. Neurological impairments as well as disfigurement or amputation may result from such accidents; and the physical, psychological, and educational problems range from insignificant to profound. The problem of childhood accidents can hardly be overrated: More children die in accidents each year than are killed by all childhood diseases combined. In 1975 alone more than 28 million children under the age of 16 were injured in accidents (Harmon, Furrow, Gruendel, and Zigler, 1980). Spinal cord injury occurs at a particularly high rate in young persons 15 to 24 years of age because of vehicular accidents (Rutledge and Dick, 1983). Sports injuries also contribute to temporary and permanent disabling conditions of children and youth (Vinger and Hoerner, 1986).

A variety of other physical conditions that may affect children's development and education are summarized in Table 8-2. This is not an exhaustive list; children are susceptible to many more disorders and diseases than those given here. The important thing to remember is that these conditions affect normal bodily functions— breathing, eating, digestion, growth, elimination, healing, or movement. And because these bodily functions are adversely affected, the child may lack vitality, require special medical treatment or therapy, or be unable to participate in some ordinary school activities.

Perhaps the most feared and controversial disease currently known is **Acquired Immune Deficiency Syndrome (AIDS).** The virus that causes the disease— HTLV-III—interferes with the body's immune system, leaving the individual vulnerable to chronic and ultimately fatal infections from a variety of microbes. As of 1987, there is no known cure for the disease, and no vaccine has yet been developed.

First described as a disease of homosexual men (Gottlieb, Schroff, Schanker, Weisman, Fan, Wolf, and Saxon, 1981), AIDS was soon detected among Haitians, intravenous drug users, persons with hemophilia (see Table 8-2), others who had received

Table 8-2   Additional Physical Conditions

Condition	Description
Asthma	Chronic respiratory condition characterized by repeated episodes of difficulty in breathing, especially exhalation.
Cystic fibrosis	Inherited disease characterized by chronic respiratory and digestive problems, including thick, sticky mucus and glandular secretions.
Diabetes	A hereditary or developmental problem of sugar metabolism caused by failure of the pancreas to produce enough insulin.
Nephrosis and nephritis	Disorders or diseases of the kidneys due to infection, poisoning, burns, crushing injuries, or other diseases.
Sickle cell anemia	Severe, chronic hereditary blood disease (occurring primarily among blacks) in which red blood cells are distorted in shape and do not circulate properly.
Hemophilia	A rare, sex-linked disorder in which the blood does not have a sufficient clotting component and excessive bleeding occurs.
Rheumatic fever	Painful swelling and inflammation of the joints (typically following strep throat or scarlet fever) that can spread to include the brain or heart.
Tuberculosis	Infection by the tuberculosis bacterium of an organ system, such as lungs, larynx, bones and joints, skin, gastrointestinal tract, genitourinary tract, or heart.
Cancer	Abnormal growth of cells that can affect any organ system.

blood transfusions, heterosexual prostitutes, and young children (Shannon and Ammann, 1985). Today it is known that the disease can be transmitted through intimate sexual contact with an AIDS patient or a carrier of the virus, through transfusions of blood from patients or carriers, and from contaminated hypodermic needles. There is apparently no way in which a pregnant woman who has AIDS can avoid giving the disease to her baby (Church, Allen, and Stiehm, 1986).

The seriousness of AIDS and the medical concern regarding its control can hardly be overemphasized. Church et al. (1986) describe AIDS as a "devastating epidemic disorder of extraordinary morbidity and mortality. As many as 1 million individuals in the United States may be infected with the virus, and 1% of these have the full-blown disease" (p. 423). About 1.5 percent of the total cases reported are children. By March 1987, 586 AIDS patients under the age of 20 had been reported to the Centers for Disease Control (CDC); more than 30,000 cases in all were reported to the CDC. Some children and youth with AIDS have minimal symptoms. Nevertheless, "[T]hey are, despite the recommendations of the U.S. Centers for Disease Control (CDC), being excluded from school and society, with all of the psychologic implications that befell Hester Prynne, Nathaniel Hawthorne's adulteress" (Church et al., 1986, p. 423).

Right now, prevention of AIDS through antiviral therapy is only a hope; education is the single feasible means of stopping the spread of the disease. Both the U.S. Surgeon General and the National Academy of Sciences have called for massive education programs to prevent a worsening of the epidemic. However, AIDS education and the matter of education for students with AIDS are controversial for two reasons: (1) The disease is usually sexually transmitted, and therefore sex education is involved; (2) fear of the disease creates pressure to exclude infected children and adults from classrooms. The news stories in the box on pp. 378–379 illustrate the highly emotional nature of the issues raised by AIDS. In the case involving 5-year-old Ryan Thomas, the school board had admitted him to school on the condition that he use a separate bathroom that was locked at all other times. The biting incident resulted in his suspension although, according to the news story, the bite did not break the skin and Ryan did not appear, in the opinion of a school psychologist, to be prone to impulsivity or physical acting out. And the board decided not to take any chances that Ryan might bite again, even though there is no evidence that AIDS can be transmitted through a bite.

At this time, it appears that public officials and physicians are likely to maintain a cautious approach toward AIDS, and take few risks of exposing children to the virus. Church et al. (1986) have noted that whether or not a child should be excluded from school depends on the individual case. If the child is extraordinarily sensitive to infection, then school placement may be inappropriate; if the child shows only positive antibody tests, the child should not be excluded. In the opinion of Church et al. (1986), adult AIDS patients who have symptoms of the disease probably will be excluded from the classroom. However, a recent U.S. Supreme Court decision (*School Board of Nassau County, Fla.* v *Arline*) barring discrimination against individuals simply because they are handicapped by an infectious disease suggests that exclusion of teachers and pupils who test positive for AIDS might be prohibited (Migra, 1987).

Church et al. (1986) summarize the recommendations of the Centers for Disease Control with respect to educational placement of children who have the disease:

> As the recommendations from the CDC state, horizontal spread of AIDS to family members, other household contacts, or classmates has not been documented. The presence of virus in saliva and tears, as well as blood, makes such transmission theoretically possible by kissing, sharing toys, and handling secretions (vomitus, respiratory mucus, stools, etc.). However, transmission via this route will be as rare as contracting syphilis from the proverbial toilet seat. Thus, the CDC recommends that children with HTLV-III infections can attend elementary school (and beyond) if they are neurologically and behaviorally normal, without risk to other children or their teachers. Nevertheless, precautions should be taken in the case of accidents (incontinence, nose bleeds, cuts, etc.), thus necessitating the nurse, teacher, and principal knowing the identity of such children. In preschool settings (prior to age 5 years), the predictable need to deal with children's secretions, their shared food and toys, and their uncontrolled behavior led to the recommendation that such children be excluded from this setting (p. 426).

Adolescent Pregnancy

Adolescent pregnancy cannot of course be considered a physical handicap, but to the extent that it interferes with a young person's schooling, special educational provisions are necessary. Furthermore, teenage mothers are ten times more likely than women over 20 to give birth to premature babies (Batshaw and Perret, 1986), to have babies with handicapping conditions (Baldwin and Cain, 1981; Broman, 1981), and to be abusive to their children (Broadhurst, 1986). The problem is not just one of maternal health; it also involves prevention of handicapping conditions (Anastasiow, 1983).

AIDS in School: Walking a Tightrope

Area's Jurisdictions Differ in Their Policies on Instruction

Candis L. Ramelli's high school students have asked the same questions about AIDS so many times that she lists them in shorthand: "Swimming pools," "tears" and "insects."

Those are ways that her students believe acquired immune deficiency syndrome can be transmitted. Ramelli sets them straight. No case of the deadly disease has been traced to casual contact, crying or insect bites.

"The only thing [students] know when they arrive is that it's fatal," said Ramelli, 38, who has taught sex education classes at T.C. Williams High School for four years.

Alexandria, which begins instruction about AIDS in the fourth grade, is among several local public school systems already doing what U.S. Surgeon General C. Everett Koop recently asked all educators to do: To teach children about the disease early and often.

Prince George's County and the District also begin teaching general information about AIDS in elementary schools. Arlington, Howard, Montgomery and Prince William counties wait until the middle grades. Many programs in the area began only in the past year or two, when public concern about AIDS rose dramatically.

At the far end of the scale from Alexandria is Fairfax County, which effectively prohibits early instruction about AIDS by means of a School Board policy that forbids the mention of homosexuality in a classroom until the upper grades. Most cases in this country have been among homosexuals, but AIDS is increasingly becoming a heterosexual concern. Fairfax has no AIDS education now but is expected to approve a lesson on AIDS for inclusion in 10th grade biology classes this year.

"We have had a very conservative sex education program because of community desires," explained Mary Anne Lecos, the county's assistant superintendent for instruction.

But other educators argue that students must be taught about AIDS, even if it is a highly charged subject. "You just cannot afford not to tell kids," said Jean Hunter, a family life curriculum specialist in Alexandria. "That's why you teach driver's ed. It's not so they can drive a car. It's so they drive it more responsibly."

Most area school systems say their AIDS education programs provoke little controversy because they were installed with approval of parent advisory groups. But one suburban teacher said she thinks very carefully before she discusses AIDS in class: "You're walking a tightrope. You don't want to be sued." She requested that her name not be used because in the past she has received harassing phone calls and visits from critics of sex education. . . .

Biting Incident Shatters Plan for 5-Year-Old to Attend Class

ATASCADERO, Calif.—Last month, when 5-year-old Ryan Thomas, clutching his oldest brother's hand, marched bravely past a crowd of reporters and into kindergarten for the first time, Robin and Judy Thomas thought the worst was over. Enduring icy stares at the Safeway and answering probing personal questions at a dozen school board meetings had finally paid off: Their youngest son, who has AIDS, was enrolled in public school.

School officials in this coastal town, relieved by the absence of pickets, thought they had taken every possible precaution. Parents had signed waivers permitting their children to be in Ryan's class. Teacher Lori Parker knew what to do if he cut himself or got sick. A bathroom stall had even been set aside exclusively for Ryan's use.

Four days later all hope for an uneventful year at Santa Rosa Road Elementary School was shattered. On Sept. 8, as Parker gathered the class in a semicircle to read a story, Justin Smyers, jealous of the attention Ryan was paying another classmate, elbowed him in the head and yanked his hair, pulling Ryan's face into his lap.

Ryan bit him.

"That was the worst possible thing we could conceive of happening," said principal Chuck Wilbur. Ryan was suspended from school until at least 1987.

"The Bite" as it is known here, has reignited a bitter debate in this community of 19,000 and has made Ryan Thomas, a sweet-faced boy with enormous aqua eyes, an unlikely protagonist in a much bigger drama, a federal court suit filed by his parents seeking his readmission. What happens in his case could have implications for school systems around the country as they grapple with the question of whether, or under what circumstances, to admit approximately 1,000 school-age children who have been exposed to the AIDS virus. . . .

Before Ryan Thomas, the most famous AIDS-related public school case involved 14-year-old Ryan White, who was readmitted to a Kokomo, Ind., junior high school last April after a court ruled that he presented no danger to classmates and that barring him constituted illegal discrimination against a handicapped person. Judges in New York City, New Jersey and Orange County, Calif., have issued similar rulings. . . .

Ryan was born six weeks prematurely, weighing less than four pounds. When he was two weeks old he was flown to Children's Hospital Medical Center of Oakland for emergency treatment that included multiple transfusions. For the next three years he suffered asthma, constant respiratory infections and raging fevers. Until last year the Thomases were baffled by Ryan's incessant illnesses. Then one morning Judy Thomas received a phone call that solved the mystery and forever changed their lives.

The caller was an official of Children's Hospital. A blood donor in Oakland, he said, had recently informed the blood bank that he was dying of AIDS. The hospital was notified and found that the man's blood had been transfused into Ryan's veins. Ryan, the official said, had received AIDS-contaminated blood. . . .

Ryan, the Thomases say, has been "crushed" by the suspension. "He told me he thinks he can't go to school because he's dumb," said his mother. "He loved school, and he cries in the morning because he can't go with his brothers." He spends his days playing with his two dogs and two cats, watching television, especially his favorite video "The Karate Kid," and waiting eagerly for his brothers to come home.

For one hour every afternoon he goes to Santa Rosa school for tutoring after the other children have gone home. . . .

SOURCE: Staff writers D'Vera Cohn and Sandra G. Boodman, *The Washington Post,* November 2, 1986, pp. A1, A33, A34, A35.

Each year over a million American girls between the ages of 15 and 19 become pregnant (about 10 percent of this age group). A large percentage of these pregnancies end in miscarriage or abortion. About 800,000 babies are born to teenage mothers annually (Delatte, Orgeron, and Preis, 1985). Clearly, massive efforts to educate teenagers about pregnancy and child care and to provide for the continued schooling of teenagers who are pregnant or mothers or fathers are needed. Federal law now disallows federal funds to any school system that does not include pregnant girls in its education programs.

CHILD ABUSE AND NEGLECT

Since the early 1960s there has been national interest among child health specialists in the **battered child syndrome** (Kempe, Silverman, Steele, Droegemueller, and Silver, 1962). Klein and Stern define the syndrome as "frank unexplained skeletal trauma or severe bruising or both, or such neglect as to lead to severe medical illness or immediate threat to life" (1971, p. 15). Public Law 93-247, passed in 1974, defines child abuse and neglect as "physical or mental injury, sexual abuse, negligent treatment, or maltreatment of a child under the age of 18 by a person who is responsible for the child's welfare under circumstances which indicate that the child's health or welfare is harmed or threatened." Although the definition of child abuse is not simple and current prevalence estimates are not reliable, it is known that many thousands of children ranging in age from newborns to adolescents are battered or abused each year in the United States. They are beaten, burned, sexually molested, starved, or otherwise neglected or brutalized by their parents or other older persons.

The consequences of child abuse may be permanent neurological damage, other internal injuries, skeletal deformity, facial disfigurement, sensory impairment, or death. Psychological problems are an inevitable outcome of abuse. Evidence indicates that the abuse of children is increasing. Abuse and neglect by adults is now a leading cause of injury—both physical and psychological—and death among children. Unfortunately, congressional action to prevent abuse and provide services to abusive families has been weak (Blumberg, 1984; Chase-Lansdale, 1984; Fontana, 1984; Gerbner, Ross, and Zigler, 1980; Helfer, 1984).

Child abuse and neglect constitute one of the most complex problems confronting our society today. There is a need for better understanding of the nature and extent of the problem among both the general public and professionals. Education for parenting and child management, including family life education in the public schools, is an obvious need in our society (Broadhurst, 1986). Without concerted effort on the part of all professionals, as well as a strong coalition of political constituencies, the problem will not be satisfactorily addressed. Since abuse and injury vary so greatly from case to case, the special educational provisions appropriate for abused and neglected children range from special attention by regular classroom teachers to residential or hospital teaching.

Teachers can play an extremely important role in detecting, reporting, and preventing child abuse and neglect because, next to parents, they are the people who spend the most time with children. It is therefore vital that teachers be aware of the indicators that a child is being abused or neglected at home. (Types of neglect and indications of abuse are listed in Table 8-3.) Teachers must also be aware of the reporting procedures that should be followed when they suspect abuse or neglect. These vary from one area and state to another, but ordinarily the teacher is required to report suspected cases of child abuse or neglect to a school administrator or public health official (Broadhurst, 1986). A professional who fails to report child abuse or neglect may be held legally liable.

Children who are already disabled physically, mentally, or emotionally are more at risk for abuse than are nonhandicapped children (Watson, 1984; Zirpoli, 1986). Because the disabled children are more vulnerable and dependent, abusive adults find them easy targets. The poor social judgment and limited experience of many handicapped children make them even more vulnerable to sexual abuse. Moreover, some of the characteristics of handicapped children are sources of additional stress for their caretakers and may be contributing factors in physical abuse—they often require more time, energy, money, and patience than nonhandicapped children. Parenting any child is stressful; parenting a handicapped child can demand more than some parents are prepared to give. It is not surprising that handicapped children are disproportionately represented among abused children and that the need for training is particularly great for parents of handicapped children.

Table 8-3 Types of Child Neglect and Indications of Abuse

Types of Neglect

Abandonment: Totally or for long periods of time.

Lack of Supervision: Young children left unattended at home or in the care of others too young to protect them.

Lack of Adequate Clothing and Poor Personal Hygiene: Severe diaper rash, children who are dirty, unbathed, or lice ridden.

Lack of Medical or Dental Care: Unmet health needs, lack of immunizations and dental care.

Lack of Adequate Nutrition: Insufficient quantity and/or quality of food resulting in severe developmental lags or "failure-to-thrive."

Lack of Adequate Shelter: Dangerous and unsanitary housing.

Lack of Emotional Stimulation: Physical and mental retardation syndromes and/or "failure-to-thrive."

Lack of Education: Chronic absenteeism.

Indications of Abuse

A child may be abused if he or she:

1. is unduly afraid of others, especially of parents.
2. is kept confined (e.g., in a crib, playpen, or cage) for long periods of time.
3. shows evidence of repeated skin injury or other injuries.
4. has injuries that are inappropriately treated in terms of bandages and medications.
5. appears undernourished.
6. is given inappropriate food, drink, or medicine.
7. is dressed inappropriately for weather conditions.
8. is passive and avoids parental confrontation.
9. is aggressive, demanding, hyperactive.
10. shows evidence of overall poor care.
11. is constantly irritable and cries often.
12. takes over the role of parent and tries to be protective or otherwise take care of parent's needs—"role reversal."

SOURCE: Vincent J. Fontana, "Introduction—The Maltreatment Syndrome of Children," *Pediatric Annals*, 1984, *13*, p. 739. Reprinted with permission.

PSYCHOLOGICAL AND BEHAVIORAL CHARACTERISTICS

Academic Achievement

It is impossible to make many valid generalizations about the academic achievement of physically disabled children because they vary so widely in the nature and severity of their conditions. Many youngsters with physical disabilities have erratic school attendance because of hospitalization, visits to physicians, the requirement of bed rest at home, and so on. Some learn well with ordinary teaching methods; others require special methods because they are mentally retarded or sensorily impaired in addition to being physically disabled. Because of the frequent interruptions in their schooling, some fall considerably behind their agemates in academic achievement, even though they have normal intelligence and motivation. Some children with mild or transitory physical problems experience no academic deficiencies at all; others experience severe difficulties. Some students who have serious and chronic health problems still manage to achieve at a high level. Usually these high-achieving physically disabled children have high intellectual capacity, high motivation, and teachers and parents who make every possible special provision for their education. The children who are neurologically impaired are, as a group, most likely to have intellectual and perceptual deficits and therefore to be behind their agemates in academic achievement (see Batshaw and Perret, 1986; Hobbs et al., 1985; Verhaaren and Connor, 1981a,b).

Personality Characteristics

Research does not support the notion that there is a "personality type" associated with any physical disability (DeLoach and Greer, 1981; Lewandowski and Cruickshank, 1980; Newman, 1980). Physically disabled children are as varied in their psychological characteristics as nondisabled children, and they are apparently responsive to the same factors that influence the psychological development of the average youngster. How they adapt to their physical limitations and how they respond to social-interpersonal situations greatly depends on how parents, siblings, teachers, peers, and the public react to them (Bigge and O'Donnell, 1977; Miezio, 1983).

Public Relations

Public attitudes can have a profound influence on how physically disabled children see themselves and on their opportunities for psychological adjustment, education, and employment. If the reaction is one of fear, rejection, or discrimination, physically disabled people may spend a great deal of energy trying to hide their stigmatizing differences (Goffman, 1963). If the reaction is one of pity and an expectation of helplessness, people with disabilities will tend to behave in a dependent manner. To the extent that other people can see children with physical handicaps as persons who have certain limitations but are otherwise just like everyone else, disabled children and youth will be encouraged to become independent and productive members of society.

Several factors seem to be causing greater public acceptance of people with physical handicaps. Professional and civic groups encourage support and decrease fear of handicapped people through information and public education. Government insistence on the elimination of architectural barriers that prevent handicapped citizens from using public facilities serves to decrease discrimination. Programs to encourage hiring of handicapped workers help the public to see those with physical disabilities as constructive, capable people. Laws that protect *every* child's right to public education are bringing more individuals into contact with severely and profoundly handicapped children. Public agencies are including physically disabled youth in their programs. For example, the National Park Service has begun a program in which young people with a variety of physical disabilities—including severe arthritis, cerebral palsy, multiple sclerosis, and spinal cord injuries—work as staff members during the summer (Satz, 1986). This program has not only benefitted the disabled participants, but made the public and the Park Service more sensitive to the needs of disabled persons. All these changes are encouraging more positive attitudes toward handicapped children and adults (DeLoach and Greer, 1981). But there is no doubt that many children with physical disabilities are still rejected, feared, pitied, or discriminated against. The more obvious the physical flaw, the more likely it is that the person will be perceived in negative terms by the public.

Public policy regarding children's physical disabilities has not met the needs of most such children and their families (Hobbs et al., 1984, 1985). Particularly as successful medical treatment prolongs the lives of more and more children with severe chronic illnesses and other disabilities, issues of who should pay the costs of treatment and maintenance (which are often enormous) and which children and families should receive the limited available resources are becoming critical (Lyon, 1985).

Family Reactions

The reactions of a child's family to a physical handicap can worsen or offset the negative influence of public reaction. The psychological effect of having a handicapped child is dramatic, regardless of the nature or cause of the condition It is inevitable that the family of a seriously handicapped child will experience shock, disappointment, depression, and a feeling that somehow fate has been unfair to them (Lyon, 1985; Roos, 1975). Parents often feel shame and guilt, and are frequently frustrated by well-meaning but incompetent professionals or "experts" who do not understand their problems.

In his novel *Something Happened,* Joseph Heller (1974) poignantly expresses the feelings of the central character and his wife about their brain-damaged son.

> "If only we hadn't had him," my wife used to lament. "He'd be so much better off if he'd never been born."
>
> "Let's kill the kid," I used to joke jauntily when I thought he was just innately fractious (I used to carry color snapshots of all three of my children in my wallet. Now I carry none), before I began to guess there might be something drastically wrong.
>
> I don't say that anymore.
>
> (Poor damaged little tyke. No one's on your side.)
>
> He is a product of my imagination. I swear to Christ I imagined him into existence.
>
> We do feel guilty. We do blame ourselves. We're sorry we have him. We're sorry people know we do. We feel we have plenty to be ashamed of. We have him. (pp. 532–533)

The potential for psychological havoc in the family because of a physically disabled child is great. Such a child almost invariably demands a disproportionate amount of the family's financial resources, energy, and time. The parents may blame one another, neglect each other or their children, or try to deny that their child is disabled. Siblings may resent the child and the extra care and attention he or she must have. The child may be overprotected and infantilized, or neglected and denied normal experiences, or even tormented and abused by the family. The family can also be a source of strength and contribute immeasurably to the child's own healthy adjustment (see Turnbull and Turnbull, 1985, for examples of family reactions, and Miezio, 1983, for suggestions for families of the disabled).

Many people are unaware of the enormous financial burdens borne by the families of chronically ill children. It is not unusual for such families to spend 25 percent or more of their total spendable income on the disabled child's care (Hobbs et al., 1984). Naturally this financial burden adds to their psychological stress.

Children's Reactions

As we suggested earlier, children's reactions to their own physical disabilities are largely a reflection of the way they have been treated by others. Shame and guilt are learned responses; children will have such negative feelings only if others respond to them by shaming or blaming them (and those like them) for their physical differences. Children will be independent and self-sufficient (within the limits of their physical disability) rather than dependent and demanding only to the extent that they learn how to take care of their own needs. And they will have realistic self-perceptions and set realistic goals for themselves only to the extent that others are honest and clear in their appraisal of their condition.

However, certain psychological reactions are inevitable for the physically disabled child, no matter how he or she is treated. The wish to be nondisabled and participate in the same activities as most youngsters, and the fantasy that the disability will disappear, are to be expected. With proper management and help, the child can be expected eventually to accept the disability and live a happy life, even though he or she knows the true nature of the condition (Bigge and O'Donnell, 1977; DeLoach and Greer, 1981; Wright, 1960). Fear and anxiety, too, can be expected. It is natural for children to be afraid when they are separated from their parents, hospitalized, and subjected to medical examinations and procedures that may be painful. In these situations, too, proper management can minimize emotional stress. Psychological trauma is not a necessary effect of hospitalization. The hospital environment may in fact be better than the child's home in the case of abused and neglected children (see Verhaaren and Connor, 1981a; Werry, 1979b).

Other important considerations regarding the psychological effects of a physical handicap include the age of the child and the nature of the disability (e.g., whether it is congenital or acquired, progressive or not). But even these factors are not uniform in their effects. A child with a relatively minor and short-term physical disability may become more maladjusted, anxious, debilitated, and disruptive than another child with a terminal illness because of the way the child's behavior and feelings are managed. Certainly understanding the child's and the family's feelings about the disability are important. But it is also true that managing the consequences of the child's behavior is a crucial aspect of education and rehabilitation (Bigge and O'Donnell, 1977).

It may seem reasonable to expect more frequent psychological depression and suicide attempts among physically disabled adolescents and young adults than among their nonhandicapped peers, since disability does impose psychological stress. However, Bryan and Herjanic (1980) concluded that "the association between handicaps and depression, suicide attempts, and suicide has not been clearly established" (p. 64). It is true that a disabled youth must go through a difficult period of learning to accept a disability, its permanence, and its personal and social implications. It is equally true that adolescents without physical disabilities find the task of establishing an identity difficult.

PROSTHETICS, ORTHOTICS, AND ADAPTIVE DEVICES FOR DAILY LIVING

A **prosthesis** is an artificial replacement for a missing body part (an artificial hand or leg); an **orthosis** is a device that replaces a function no longer present in a part of a person's body (a brace or a device that allows a person to do something; see Figures 8.5 to 8.8). Adaptive devices for daily living include a variety of adaptations of

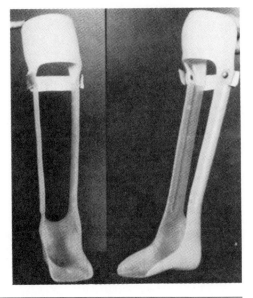

Figure 8.5 *Examples of thermoform leg braces. The braces are molded to fit the contour of the wearer's leg and hold the knee, ankle, and/or foot in a more correct or acceptable position. The orthoses are lighter in weight, more functional, and cosmetically more acceptable than older-style braces and can be worn with a variety of footwear.*
SOURCE: J. C. Drennan and J. R. Gage, "Orthotics in Cerebral Palsy," in G. H. Thompson, I. L. Rubin, and R. M. Bilenker (Eds.), *Comprehensive Management of Cerebral Palsy* (Orlando, Fla.: Grune & Stratton, 1983), pp. 206, 208. Reprinted by permission of Grune & Stratton, Inc.

ordinary items found in the home, office, or school that make performing the tasks required for self-care and employment easier for the person who has a physical disability, such as a device to aid bathing or handwashing or walking.

The most important principles to keep in mind are use of residual function, simplicity, and reliability. For example, an artificial hand is operated by the muscles of the arm, shoulder, or back. A person without legs must be taught to use his arms to move himself about in a wheelchair, or to use torso and arms to get about on artificial legs (perhaps using crutches or a cane in addition).

Two points regarding prosthetics, orthotics, and residual function must be kept in mind. First, residual function is often important even when a prosthesis, orthosis, or adaptive device is not used. For example, it may be crucial for the child with

Figure 8.6 *A drinking cup equipped with a special handle can be used by someone who has little or no ability to grasp.*
SOURCE: Photos 8.6 through 8.8 courtesy of Laura Vogtle, Children's Rehabilitation Center, University of Virginia.

Figure 8.7 *Devices to assist a physically disabled person in eating. Notice that the plate is attached to the table with suction cups to keep it from moving. The metal rim around the plate (a "plate guard") keeps food from being accidentally pushed off the plate and provides help in getting food onto the utensil. The eating utensil shown is a "spork," a combination spoon and fork. With a spork, the person can both spear and scoop food without changing utensils. The band around the hand, with the fitting holding the spork, is a "universal cuff," a very simple, practical orthotic device. The cuff allows a person who has no grasp to hold and use common objects, such as eating utensils, pencils, paint brushes, and pointers.*

cerebral palsy or muscular dystrophy to learn to use the affected limbs as well as possible without the aid of any special equipment because using residual function alone will make the child more independent and may help to prevent or retard physical deterioration. Too, it is often more efficient for a person to learn not to rely completely on a prosthesis or orthosis as long as he or she can accomplish a task without it.

Second, spectacular technological developments often have very limited meaning for the immediate needs of the majority of physically disabled individuals. It may be years before expensive experimental equipment is tested adequately and marketed at a cost most people can afford, and a given device may be applicable only to a small group of individuals with an extremely rare condition (Moore, 1985). For a long time to come, common "standby" prostheses, orthoses, and other equipment adapted to the needs of the individual will be the most practical devices. A few common devices that are helpful to persons with various physical disabilities are shown in Figures 8.6 to 8.10. (See Bigge and O'Donnell, 1977; DuBose and Deni,

Figure 8.8 *A ball-bearing feeder in use. This orthotic device is counterbalanced so that a person who has use of his hand, but not his arm and shoulder, can perform tasks such as feeding. The arm and shoulder can be moved into position with almost no effort using the feeder, allowing the person to grasp or manipulate objects with the fingers. This orthosis is often needed by individuals with muscular dystrophy or high spinal-cord injury.*

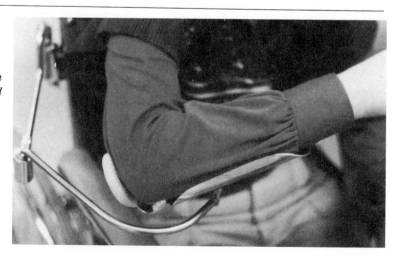

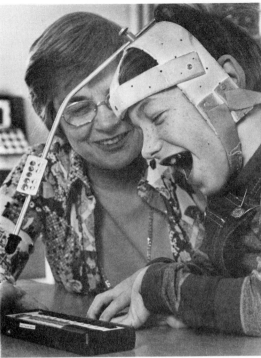

Figure 8.9 *The head stick is a very useful device for individuals who cannot use their hands. It can be used for pointing, writing, dialing a phone, operating switches, etc., in addition to typing. The wand can be adjusted for angle and length and can be replaced with a pencil, paint brush, or other tool.* (George Bellerose, Stock, Boston.)

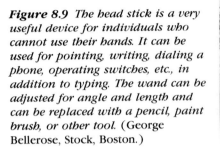

Figure 8.10 *Rehabilitation engineers are redesigning wheelchairs for use in off-the-street recreational and work environments. These all-terrain chairs allow disabled persons to engage in work and play that formerly were difficult or impossible for them.* (Rehabilitation Medical Center, Information Services, University of Virginia.)

387

1980; Fraser and Hensinger, 1983; Verhaaren and Connor, 1981b, for many additional illustrations of such devices.)

We do not mean to downplay the importance of technological advances for physically disabled people. Our point here is that the greatest significance of a technological advance often lies in how it changes seemingly "ordinary" items or problems. For example, technological advances in metallurgy and plastics have led to the design of much more functional braces and wheelchairs. The heavy metal-and-leather leg braces—which were cumbersome, difficult to apply, and not very helpful in preventing deformity or improving function—formerly used by many children with cerebral palsy or other neurological disorders have been largely supplanted by braces constructed of thermoform plastic (see Figure 8.5). Wheelchairs are being built of lightweight metals and plastics and redesigned to allow users to go places inaccessible to the typical wheelchair (see Figure 8.10). And an increasing number of computerized devices are improving the movement and communication abilities of people with disabilities.

EDUCATIONAL CONSIDERATIONS

Too often we think of people who have physical disabilities as being helpless or unable to learn. It is easy to lower our expectations for them because we know that they are indeed unable to do some things. We forget that many people with physical disabilities can learn to do most or all of the things most nondisabled persons do, though sometimes they must perform these tasks in a different way (for example, a person who does not have the use of her hands may have to use her feet or mouth). Accepting the limitations imposed by physical disabilities without trying to see how much disabled people can learn or how the environment can be changed to allow them to respond more effectively is an insulting and dehumanizing way of responding to physical differences.

Educating physically disabled students is not so much a matter of special instruction for the disabled youngsters as it is of educating the nondisabled population. Physically disabled people solve many of their own problems, but their lives are often needlessly complicated because the nondisabled give no thought to what life is like for someone with specific physical limitations. Simple design adaptations in buildings, furniture, household appliances, and clothing can make it possible for someone with a physical disability to function as efficiently as a nondisabled person in a given environment, be it home, school, or community (see box, pp. 389-390).

Behavior Modification Procedures

Some of the most effective teaching techniques that can be used with disabled children are derived from the principles of behavior modification. Basically, they are the same strategies used with other children: a sequence of steps is determined—beginning with what the child can already do and leading to an ultimate goal—and the child's performance of each successive step is rewarded. Such techniques are especially effective because they focus on specific behavioral responses and on maximizing motivation to perform (Hanson and Harris, 1986).

Individualized Education Programs (IEPs)

Students with complex physical disabilities typically require a wide array of related services as well as special education. The IEPs for such students tend to be particularly specific and detailed. The instructional goals and objectives often include

"Uncomplicated" Fashions Designed for Handicapped

Some days Teresa White's joints are so stiff that she cannot stand to pull on pants. She must lean against a wall. A social worker who worked in rehabilitation of the disabled and elderly, Mrs. White now knows—and lives—the daily frustrations of her former patients. She suffers from rheumatoid arthritis.

"Buttons can be so frustrating," she said recently at her home in the northeast part of town. "It seems very simple, but sometimes buttoning can take so long. I get very frustrated."

Some 30 million disabled Americans share Mrs. White's frustrations. For the vast majority, fashionable clothing is out of the question. They search clothing racks for loose-fitting garments with large zippers and buttons or elasticized waists. If they are able to find easy-access clothing, it is often dowdy. But along came M. Dolores Quinn, a fashion design professor at Drexel University here, who has begun a quiet revolution.

"There is no reason why the physically disabled cannot have elegant, beautiful, un-complicated and fashionable clothing—garments that are easy to put on and keep on," she said in a recent interview.

Four summers ago, Miss Quinn was planning a course for her students when she concluded that they should learn to work within limits. "Students hadn't been directing their thinking toward boundaries, that discipline we all apply on a daily basis," she recalled. So she assigned them a project of designing clothing for the physically handi-capped.

Her able-bodied students taped their fingers together to experience the difficulty of dressing with limited hand motion, tried dressing with only one arm and confined themselves in other ways to understand the dressing limitations of a disabled person. They talked with handicapped people, nurses, and therapists. By the end of the summer the students had turned out garments that were not only comfortable and easily donned and doffed, but where stylish in design.

That summer course was the seed that grew into Miss Quinn's "Design Within Limits" project. With funds from Drexel, the National Endowment for the Arts, several foundations and private contributors, she opened a design laboratory from which have come attractive functional prototype clothes for men and women with physical limita-tions, including the following:

- Slacks that convert to shorts with horizontal zippers that make prosthesis fitting easier for an amputee.
- A wrap skirt, for easy access, with several pleats at the side. Its matching pleat-front vest has no buttons.
- A tissue-like navy nylon raincoat designed for wheelchair-bound women. Gathered across the bodice and trimmed in narrow blue and green piping, it features a hood that drops to become a cowl collar. People in wheelchairs told Miss Quinn that they do not like to sit on a lot of bulky fabric, so she designed the raincoat with a slit from the midback to the hem.
- Slacks with two diagonal zippers from the waist to the side seams, allowing the front panel to drop easily, useful for people who wear a catheter.
- Stretch denim jeans designed with horizontal pleats over a Lycra backing at the knee. This accordion-like design gives more stretch room at the knee and keeps pant legs from riding up for people in wheelchairs.
- Slacks with vertical zippers in each side seam from waist to ankle, which are use-ful for those who wear braces and need extra width in getting a foot into a pant leg.
- Pockets are handy for people in wheelchairs but the conventional placement of pockets, in side seams, is inconvenient and bulky. Miss Quinn designed pockets that can be attached to a waistband in front.

> In designing clothing for the physically disabled, Miss Quinn and her students have learned from the handicapped themselves what is comfortable and how important style is to the disabled person's self-concept. Last year, Miss Quinn conducted a study with 30 disabled clients, including Mrs. White, who selected and rated custom-made garments.
>
> Once the competition is held and winning designs are selected in various categories, Miss Quinn hopes to interest manufacturers in making and marketing the "Design Within Limits" line. She knows the market is out there and she already has a simple gray-on-white "Design Within Limits" label with its trademark registered.
>
> SOURCE: Martha Jablow, New York Times News Service. Copyright © 1981 by The New York Times Company. Reprinted with permission.

seemingly minute steps, especially for young children with severe handicaps. Hanson and Harris (1986) provide an example of an IEP for Dan, a child who was born prematurely. Dan, now 26 months of age, has been diagnosed as having cerebral palsy and retrolental fibroplasia (RLF; see Chapter 7). Excerpts from his IEP are shown in Table 8.4. Note that the IEP includes multiple objectives in each of five areas: gross motor, communication, preacademic, fine motor and cognitive, and self-help. Only the initial objectives for the first goal in each area are shown in Table 8-4.

Educational Placement

Physically disabled children may be provided an education in any one of several different settings, depending on the type and severity of the condition, the services available in the community, and the medical prognosis for the condition. If such children ordinarily attend regular public school classes but must be hospitalized for more than a few days, they may be included in a class in the hospital itself. If they must be confined to their homes for a time, a visiting or homebound teacher may provide tutoring until they can return to regular classes. In these cases, which usually involve accident victims or conditions that are not permanently and severely crippling, relatively minor, commonsense adjustments are required to continue the children's education and keep them from falling behind their classmates. At the other extreme, usually involving serious or permanent disabilities, the child may be taught in an institutional school, a special day school, a hospital school, or a special public school class designed specifically for physically disabled children.

In the past many physically disabled children were taught at home, in institutions, or in hospitals. Today most are being integrated into the public schools because of advances in medical treatment: new developments in bioengineering allowing them greater mobility and functional movement; decreases in or removal of architectural barriers and transportation problems; and the movement toward public education for *all* children (Bleck, 1979; Fraser and Hensinger, 1983).

Educational Goals and Curricula

It is not possible to prescribe educational goals and curricula for physically disabled children as a group because their limitations vary so greatly from child to child. Even among children with the same condition, goals and curricula must be determined after assessing the individual child's intellectual, physical, sensory, and emotional characteristics.

Table 8-4 Excerpts From Dan's IEP

Gross Motor

Goals	Objectives	Anticipated Date of Completion
1. Dan will move on hands and knees up at least two stairs.	1.1 Dan will move to a hands-and-knees position, support his weight in this position, and rock backward and forward for 1 minute on 80% of the trials for two of three consecutive days.	November
	1.2 Dan will independently move forward for 2 feet in an alternating pattern on hands and knees (creeping—one hand and opposite knee forward, then other hand and opposite knee forward, and so on) on 80% of the trials for two of three consecutive days.	January
	1.3 Dan will reach forward with one arm to obtain a toy placed 1 foot in front of him while supported on one hand and both knees on 80% of the trials for two of three consecutive days.	February
	1.4 Dan will creep on hands and knees up two stairs on 80% of the trials for two of three consecutive days.	June

Communication

Goals	Objectives	Anticipated Date of Completion
1. Dan will turn toward a familiar voice and to an unfamiliar sound.	1.1 Dan will make eye contact within a few seconds after parent says, "Look at me" on 80% of the occasions for two of three consecutive days.	October
	1.2 Dan will turn his head to the side toward a sound within 10 seconds after the sound is presented on 80% of the trials for two of three consecutive days.	November
	1.3 Dan will look toward the sound source and vocalize when his name is called on 50% of the occasions for two of three consecutive days.	December

Pre-Academic

Goals	Objectives	Anticipated Date of Completion
1. Dan will identify people and objects in his environment.	1.1 Dan will point to family members and at least two other persons when asked on 80% of the occasions for two of three consecutive days.	December
	1.2 Dan will point to an object placed within a group of objects within 30 seconds after he is asked on 80% of the occasions for two of three consecutive days.	March
	1.3 Dan will differentially demonstrate the use of five different objects within 1 minute after he is asked (for example: "What do you do with a cup?") on 80% of the occasions for two of three consecutive days.	June

(table continues)

Fine Motor and Cognitive

Goals	Objectives	Anticipated Date of Completion
1. Dan will visually track objects.	1.1 Dan will visually follow an object continuously from side to side on 80% of the trials for two of three consecutive days.	December
	1.2 Dan will visually follow an object being moved in a circular motion on 80% of the trials for two of three consecutive days.	March
	1.3 Dan will visually follow an object being moved vertically (up and down) on 80% of the trials for two of three consecutive days.	March

Self-Help

Goals	Objectives	Anticipated Date of Completion
1. Dan will drink from a cup and use a spoon.	1.1 Dan will lick food off upper lip independently on at least 80% of the occasions for two of three consecutive days.	October
	1.2 Dan will hold a small cup with one hand and drink from it with little spillage on 80% of the occasions for two of three consecutive days.	January
	1.3 Dan will use a napkin to wipe his mouth after drooling or eating on at least 50% of the occasions for two of three consecutive days.	January

SOURCE: M. J. Hanson and S. R. Harris, *Teaching the Young Child with Motor Delays: A Guide for Parents and Professionals* (Austin, Tex.: PRO-ED, 1986), pp. 30–33.

In terms of education, a physical disability, especially a severe and chronic one that limits mobility, may have two effects. The child may be deprived of educationally relevant experiences that nondisabled children have, and the child may find it impossible to manipulate educational materials and respond to educational tasks the way most children do. For example, a severely crippled cerebral-palsied child cannot take part in most outdoor play activities and travel experiences and may not be able to hold and turn pages in books, write, explore objects manually, or use a typewriter without special equipment.

For children with an impairment that is only physical, curriculum and educational goals should ordinarily be the same as for nondisabled children: reading, writing, arithmetic, and experiences designed to familiarize them with the world about them. In addition, special instruction may be needed in mobility skills, daily living skills, and occupational skills. That is, because of their physical impairments, these children may need special, individualized instruction in the use of mechanical devices that will help them perform tasks that are much simpler for the nondisabled. For children with other handicaps in addition to physical limitations, curricula will need to be further adapted (see Bigge and O'Donnell, 1977; Calhoun and Hawisher, 1979; Hanson and Harris, 1986).

Educational goals for students with severe or profound disabilities must be related to their functioning in everyday community environments. Only recently have educators begun to address the problems of analyzing community tasks (e.g., crossing streets, using money, riding public transportation, greeting neighbors) and planning efficient instruction for severely handicapped individuals (Snell and Browder, 1986). Efficient instruction in such skills requires that teaching occur in the community environment itself.

Links with Other Disciplines

In the opening pages of this chapter we made two points: Physically disabled children have medical problems, and interdisciplinary cooperation is necessary in their education. It is important for the teacher to know what other disciplines are involved in the child's care and treatment, and to be able to communicate with professionals in these areas about the physical, emotional, and educational development of each youngster.

It goes almost without saying that knowing the child's medical status is crucial. Many physically disabled children will need the services of a physical therapist and/ or occupational therapist. The physical therapist and occupational therapist can give valuable suggestions about helping the child use his or her physical abilities to the greatest possible extent, continuing therapeutic management in the classroom, and encouraging independence and good work habits. Teachers should be particularly concerned about how to handle and position the child so that the risk of further

Hospitalization, frightening and painful medical procedures, separation from parents, and demands for learning new and difficult skills often present educational and emotional problems for children with serious physical impairments or diseases.
(Tom McCarthy/The Image Bank)

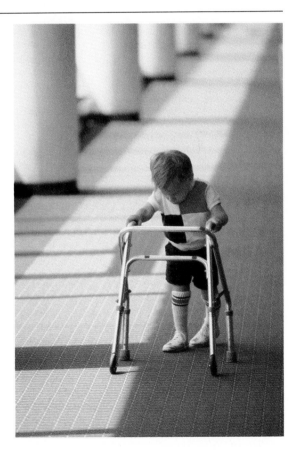

ONE PROFESSIONAL'S PERSPECTIVE

Beverly Metzger

B.S., Special Education (EMR, LD, BD), Ohio University
M.Ed., Special Education-Supervision (Moderately, Severely, Profoundly Handicapped), Kent State University
Current Position: Teacher of a multiply and severely handicapped preschool housed in a regular elementary school and included in the Cleveland Heights-University Heights Public Schools, Ohio

Prior to assuming her current position in 1984, Ms. Beverly Metzger taught mildly retarded students for three years and for one year was a graduate assistant and teacher in an experimental preschool for handicapped and nonhandicapped children, the Early Intervention Program at Kent State University. She now teaches 16 students—7 in the morning and 9 in the afternoon program. Her students range in age from 3 to 6 years: five are girls and 11 are boys. The average mental age of the morning group is about 15 months (ranging from 8 months to 2 years), and the average for the afternoon group is about 3 years (ranging from 9 months to 4 years). Three of the children have cerebral palsy and are nonambulatory; two are visually impaired, seeing only colored objects within one to three feet. Other disabilities of the children include Down syndrome, severe language delays, and emotional and behavioral disorders (including autistic-like behavior) in addition to mental retardation and motor disabilities. Due to the nature of their disabilities and young age,

the IQs of many of the children have not been determined.

Ms. Metzger finds that evenings are essential to complete her many job-related responsibilities which include holding a monthly parent group meeting, contacting speakers, and arranging visits to other programs that serve or might serve her pupils. She spends at least 3 to 5 hours in preparation and planning on weekends. Besides instructional planning, she also must shop for snacks and wash the accumulated laundry (e.g., art smocks and towels).

We asked Ms. Metzger the following questions:

What influenced your decision to be a teacher of children with physical disabilities? I grew up in a community that included a state facility for handicapped people. In my childhood, it was known as a "mental institution." As a volunteer (through church and school), I made several visits to the facility prior to entering college. I engaged in a variety of activities with the residents— singing, crafts, walking, and just talking. I always felt that we volunteered out of pity for those people who were incapable of caring for themselves. Later, as an undergraduate, I chose elementary education as a major, but I continued to do volunteer

work with handicapped people. I also became very good friends with a family who had a severely retarded child with cerebral palsy. The mother was a classmate of mine and convinced me to take a class with her in special education. This class corrected many of the myths that I had harbored about handicapped persons since childhood. I could see that special education was a challenging field, one whose purpose is to educate people with special needs. The class enlightened me regarding the potential of handicapped persons and their right to be educated, not merely segregated from the larger society. After consulting my college advisor, I was convinced that changing my major to special education would gratify my career goals in a helping profession. Teaching developmentally handicapped children (called "educable" at the time) for three years and seeing the increasing integration of handicapped children in public schools made me realize that my skills would soon be lacking, so I returned to school for my masters degree. Working with the Early Intervention Program led me to my current interest in young physically disabled children and to my current position.

If you could change one thing about your job, what would it be? I would provide time for regularly scheduled monthly or bimonthly team meetings involving all related services staff. My students are served by a speech therapist, an occupational therapist, and a physical therapist in addition to my two aides and myself. Regular communication as a team is necessary to promote consistency in programming across disciplines. Time seems to be the one commodity in teaching that always suffers a shortage, so it is difficult to meet with others as a group. Satisfying one need usually results in the sacrifice of another unless professionals have time to communicate. The staff organized one such interdisciplinary meeting, and the benefits were immeasurable. We agreed that we had a lot to learn from one another and became much more sensitive to the "whole" child when discussing our students. It is very easy to view a child from the perspective of your discipline alone, which can be extremely limiting.

What major changes have occurred in your field since you began teaching? Deinstitutionalization has opened a new arena for handicapped individuals. "Mental institutions" have shrunk to small developmental disabilities centers. Handicapped people are taking their places in society—gaining access to life's experiences, as evidenced by increasing numbers of programs in public schools and increasing community group homes. I see this change as positive and equitable. Problems occur, though, when society doesn't change as quickly or willingly as necessary to receive and accommodate handicapped persons. Computers and various adaptive devices are providing for many physically handicapped persons, once imprisoned within their own bodies, an avenue for manifesting their cognitive abilities. However, economic factors are a big issue, and equipment isn't available to all who could benefit. "Least restrictive environment" is being interpreted more precisely to insure more integration, and more families are caring for their handicapped child(ren) at home. This has resulted in numerous services to assist the family. College and university curriculums are becoming broader, yet more specific, in their course offerings. Experimental programs for early intervention are becoming more numerous, and advocacy groups are becoming more vocal about the need for programs for high

risk infants and young children. Accessibility laws have helped insure that physically disabled individuals can enter facilities.

How would you describe your involvement with the student with whom you have had the most successful experience of your career? I had my greatest success with Brenda, who was 5 years old and moderately retarded when I taught her. Because she was motorically delayed, she had a tendency to hyperextend her limbs and head when performing many gross motor tasks. She also had severe behavior problems. At first, she'd sit in a chair for 30 to 60 seconds before sliding onto the floor and becoming rigid. She wouldn't do what I told her to do. If I gave her a physical prompt, she became aggressive toward me, usually ending up in a struggle and self-abusive head banging. I devised a strategy for increasing her in-seat behavior and decreasing her aggression. I praised her for staying in her seat. When she slid out of her chair onto the floor, I knelt beside her, held her hand firmly, and turned my back. When she received no eye contact or other attention, she stopped banging her head; and when I was on the floor with her, she would immediately stand up. When she stood up, I physically assisted her to the chair, then praised her for sitting. Another part of the strategy was using a nylotex "seat belt." The first time she was out of seat during an activity, I put a nylotex strap around her hips, not to restrain her but to cue her that she should be sitting. She quickly learned that the seat belt followed her out-of-seat behavior. It took about four weeks for her to learn, but she will now sit for the duration of a 15-minute activity. A verbal cue is all that's necessary now if she begins to leave her chair. And now that she stays in her seat

the aggression and self-abusive behavior seldom occur.

Describe the most difficult student you've had. I am now serving the most challenging student I've had in my career, a 6-year-old boy who is severely retarded and physically disabled due to extreme hypotonia in his arms and legs. He is severely visually impaired, with function only in his right eye (which has had a detached retina and now has a cataract). He is nonambulatory. He also has a history of respiratory problems and has an overexpanded chest secondary to prolonged use of a respirator. He is nonverbal but appears to have normal hearing. He has frequently been hospitalized during the school year due to various illnesses and eye difficulties. Frequent absences make it difficult to program consistently and evaluate his progress. The visual problems also are interfering with many tasks we attempt. We've noted some progress during the 5 months, however. He was sitting only 15 to 20 minutes per day at the beginning of the school year; now he sits for at least two hours. He has graduated from two adaptive chairs into a regular chair with only one nylotex strap for his hips and a foot rest because the chair itself is too high for him. He also cried quite frequently at the beginning of the program, but he rarely cries now unless he's physically uncomfortable. He has adjusted beautifully to the classroom environment. He also is partially participating in his feeding. He can grasp a spoon and bring it to his mouth. The deteriorating vision has somewhat affected his ability to assist in feeding. He is also standing by using a walker independently for one minute per day. Although he's very challenging, he remains a joy to the staff, and his successes breed optimism in all who work with him.

physical disability is minimized and independent movement and manipulation of educational materials are most efficiently learned.

Specialists in prosthetics and orthotics design and build artificial limbs, braces, and other devices that help physically disabled individuals function more conventionally. By conferring with such specialists, the teacher will get a better grasp of the function and operation of a child's prosthesis or orthosis and understand what the child can and cannot be expected to do.

Social workers and psychologists are the professionals with whom most teachers are quite familiar. Cooperation with them may be particularly important in the case of a physically disabled child. Work with the child's family and community agencies is often necessary to prevent lapses in treatment. The child may also be particularly susceptible to psychological stress, so the school psychologist may need to be consulted to obtain an accurate assessment of intellectual potential.

Speech/language therapists are often called upon to work with physically disabled children, especially those with cerebral palsy. The teacher will want advice from the speech/language therapist on how to maximize learning of speech and language.

SPECIAL CONSIDERATIONS IN EDUCATING THE PRESCHOOL CHILD

Two concerns of all who work with young physically disabled children are (1) early identification and intervention and (2) development of communication. Identifying signs of developmental delay so that intervention can begin as early as possible is important in preventing disabilities and maximizing the outcome of therapy. Communication skills are often difficult for the physically disabled child to learn, and they are one of the critical objectives of any preschool program (see Chapter 5).

Probably the first and most pervasive concerns of teachers of young physically disabled children should be handling and positioning. *Handling* refers to how the child is picked up, carried, held, and assisted; *positioning* refers to providing support for the child's body and arranging instructional or play materials in certain ways. Proper handling makes the child more comfortable and receptive to education. Proper positioning maximizes physical efficiency and ability to manipulate materials. It also inhibits undesirable motor responses while promoting desired growth and motor patterns (Fraser and Hensinger, 1983).

What constitutes proper positioning for one child may not be appropriate for another. It is important that the teacher of physically disabled children be aware of some general principles of positioning and handling; in addition, he or she must work closely with physical therapists and physicians so that each child's particular needs are met.

The physical problems that most often require special handling and positioning involve muscle tone. Some children have **spastic** muscles—chronic increased muscle tone. As a result, their limbs are either flexed or extended all the time. If nothing is done to counteract the effects of the chronic imbalance of muscle tone, the child develops **contractures**—permanent shortening of muscles and connective tissues that results in deformity and further disability. Other children have athetosis or fluctuating muscle tone that results in almost constant uncontrolled movement. If these movements are not somehow restrained, the child cannot accomplish many motor tasks successfully. Still other children have muscles that are **hypotonic.**

These children appear floppy—their muscles are flaccid and weak. The hypotonia may prevent them from learning to hold up their heads, sit, or stand. All these muscle tone problems can occur together in the same child; they can occur with varying degrees of severity; and they can affect various parts of the body differently.

Another major problem that involves handling and positioning is the presence of abnormal reflexes. These are reflexes that most children exhibit during certain developmental periods but do not show after a given age. An example is the **asymmetrical tonic neck reflex (ATNR),** which babies normally show from birth to about 4 months but which is definitely abnormal or pathological if exhibited by a child who is a year old. The stimulus that elicits ATNR is turning the head to either side while lying on the back. The reflex is characterized by extension of the arm and leg on the side toward which the head is turned and flexion of the other arm and leg (see Figure 8.11). Utley, Holvoet, and Barnes (1977) have noted the problems caused by a pathological ATNR: First, rolling over is difficult or impossible; second, the child who is on all fours will collapse if the face is turned to either side; third, the child may not be able to get both hands to the midline for manual activities; fourth, self-feeding and walking are difficult.

Figure 8.11 *Asymmetrical tonic neck reflex. As shown in this illustration, the ATNR causes a student to assume a "fencing" position every time his head is turned.*
SOURCE: B. A. Fraser and R. N. Hensinger, *Managing Physical Handicaps: A Practical Guide for Parents, Care Providers, and Educators* (Baltimore: Paul H. Brooks Publishing Company), p. 167. Copyright © 1983. Used with permission.

The teacher of young physically disabled children concentrates first on gross-motor responses such as head control, rolling over, sitting, standing, and walking. The head control program (see box on pp. 401-402) is an example of the teaching objectives and procedures a teacher might employ. Fine-motor skills such as reaching, grasping, and releasing, and self-help skills such as feeding, toileting, and dressing, are priorities. The severely handicapped child who is far beyond preschool age may still be functioning at a very early developmental level. Consequently, the muscle tone, posture, and movement problems we discuss here, as well as the teaching objectives we have just mentioned, apply to some older physically disabled children as well.

Handling and positioning the physically disabled child demand attention to support of the child's body at various points and how various postures influence muscle tone and ability to move. There are several key points—neck and spine, shoulder girdle, and pelvic area—where support should be given because pressure on these points controls muscle tone in the extremities and influences voluntary movement. Picking up, carrying, or handling children without attention to support at these key points may only make the child's voluntary movement more difficult (Hanson and Harris, 1986; Utley et al., 1977). Simple adaptive equipment is frequently required to keep the physically disabled child positioned properly for movement and learning. Often such equipment can easily be made (DuBose and Deni, 1980; Fraser and Hensinger, 1983; Hanson and Harris, 1986; Verhaaren and Connor, 1981a,b). Three examples of such positioning equipment are shown in Figures 8.12, 8.13, and 8.14. Some adaptive equipment for positioning can be purchased, but it often needs to be tailored to the needs of the individual child.

But teaching young children with physical disabilities does not stop with handling, positioning, and gross motor skills. The teacher will also work on social, cognitive, and communication skills as the child acquires motor abilities. Learning to be responsive to people, learning how to make social initiations, learning to play with others, and learning problem-solving skills, for example, are important goals for which the teacher must develop instructional strategies.

SPECIAL CONSIDERATIONS IN EDUCATING THE ADOLESCENT AND ADULT

Two areas of concern stand out clearly for physically disabled adolescents and young adults: careers and sociosexuality. Adolescents begin contemplating and experimenting with jobs, social relations, and sexuality in a direct and serious way. For the adolescent with a physical disability, these questions and trial behaviors are often especially perplexing, not just to themselves but to their families as well. "Can I get and hold a satisfying job?" "Can I become independent?" "Will I have close and lasting friendships?" "Will anyone find me physically attractive?" "How can I gratify my sexual needs?" Ordinary adolescents have a hard time coming to grips with these questions and the developmental tasks they imply; adolescents with physical disabilities often have an even harder time.

As we pointed out in our discussion of psychological characteristics, there is no formula for predicting the emotional or behavioral problems a person with a given physical disability will have. Much depends on the management and training the person has received. So it is particularly important to provide both career education and sociosexual education for physically disabled students.

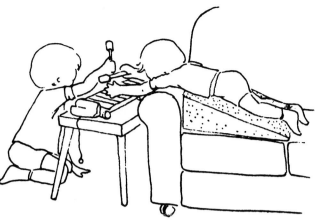

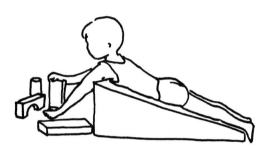

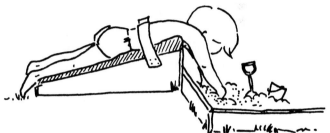

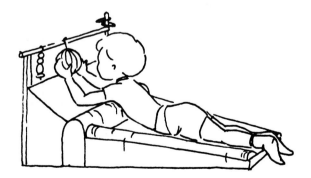

Figure 8.12 *Children positioned on wedges so they are free to use their arms and hands to reach and grasp. A wedge can be made of foam rubber, padded boards, or rolled blankets or towels to achieve proper support and positioning.*
SOURCE: N. R. Finnie, *Handling the Young Cerebral Palsied Child at Home.* 2nd ed. Copyright © 1974 by Nancie R. Finnie, F.C.S.P. Additions for U.S. edition copyright © 1975 by E. P. Dutton. Reprinted by permission of the publisher, E. P. Dutton and Wm. Heinemann Medical Books, London.

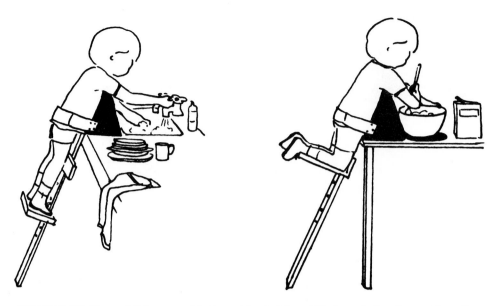

Figure 8.13 *Some children need to be supported in a tilted semi-standing or kneeling position by a board so they can work at a table or counter. Special features of a prone board are its adjustability and devices to keep the child securely in place and properly positioned.*
SOURCE: N. R. Finnie, *Handling the Young Cerebral Palsied Child at Home* (New York: Dutton, 1975).

Figure 8.14 *Various adaptive equipment can be devised for maintaining a child in a side-lying position. Boards forming a right angle can be used, as shown here, but sandbags or even the right angle formed by a wall and the floor can be used.*
SOURCE: R. F. DuBose, and K. Deni, "Easily Constructed Adaptive and Assistive Equipment," *Teaching Exceptional Children,* 1980, *12,* 116–123. Copyright 1980 by The Council for Exceptional Children. Reprinted with permission.

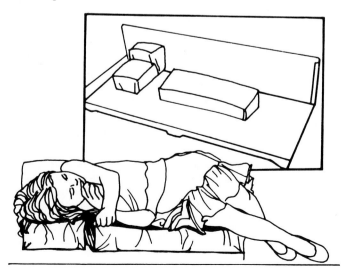

Head Control

Teaching gross motor activities to physically disabled young children requires careful attention to the developmental sequence in which motor skills are acquired, to proper positioning during training, and to specific teaching activities and consequences. The goal of helping a child acquire head control may be achieved only if a sequence of objectives and teaching procedures is carefully developed. Here are the initial objectives in a head control program:

Objective 1.1: Child Lifts Head to Clear Chin

Position: Lying on stomach (prone)
Materials needed: Favorite toy or object
Teaching activities:

1. Place child on his stomach on a blanket or a wedge.
2. Present a sound stimulus, such as a bell or rattle, or a visual stimulus, such as a brightly colored toy, to encourage the child to lift his head. Say "Head up."
3. Practice this activity to both sides so that the child can lift his head and turn to either side.

Consequences:

(+) 1. Praise the child and stroke his back if he successfully lifts his head to clear his chin.
(−) 2. If the child does not lift his head, present the sound or visual stimulus again and physically lift the child's head to look at the object. Praise him for the assisted head-lifting.

Objective 1.2: Child Turns Head from Side to Midline

Position: Lying on back (supine)
Materials needed: Favorite toy or object, wedge
Teaching activities:

1. Place child on her back on a blanket or a wedge. *Note:* If the child tends to "push back" with her head while lying flat on her back, you may want to position her in back-lying on a wedge to help to prevent this.
2. Present a visual stimulus, such as a brightly colored toy, in the child's line of vision. (For children with visual impairment, you may use a sound stimulus, such as a bell or rattle.)
3. Hold the stimulus about 12 inches from the child's eyes and move it toward the midline. Say, "Watch the toy."
4. It is important to encourage the child to bring the head into midline because this position will help to decrease the influence of abnormal primitive reflexes that may serve to prevent normal movement.

Consequences:

(+) 1. Praise the child if she turns her head to follow the visual stimulus from one side toward the midline.
(−) 2. If the child does not turn her head, gently turn it for her with your fingertips on her chin. Praise her as you assist her through the motion.

Additional Objectives

Objective 1.3: Child Maintains Head in Midline, Lying on Back
Objective 1.4: Child Lifts Head 45°, Lying on Stomach

Objective 1.5: Child Maintains Head up in Supported Sitting
Objective 1.6: Child Lifts Head 90°, Lying on Stomach
Objective 1.7: Child Maintains Head in Line with Body, Tipping from Side to Side
Objective 1.8: Child Maintains Head in Line with Body During Pull-to-Sit
Objective 1.9: Child Lifts and Maintains Head Up During Assisted Rolling
Objective 1.10: Child Maintains Head Vertical, Tipping Side to Side
Objective 1.11: Child Maintains Chin Tuck During Pull-to-Sit

SOURCE: M. J. Hanson and S. R. Harris, *Teaching the Young Child with Motor Delays: A Guide for Parents and Professionals* (Austin, Tex.: PRO-ED, 1986), pp. 94–95.

Choice of Career

For the physically disabled adolescent or young adult, career considerations are extremely important (Fonosch, Arany, Lee, and Loving, 1982). In working out an occupational goal, it is vital to realistically appraise the individual's specific abilities and disabilities and to assess motivation carefully. Some disabilities clearly rule out certain occupational choices. With other disabilities, high motivation and full use of residual function may make it possible to achieve unusual professional status. For instance, Tom Dempsey, one of football's best field-goal kickers, had a congenitally deformed arm, hand, and foot.

One of the greatest problems in dealing with physically disabled adolescents is helping them attain a truly realistic employment outlook. Intelligence, emotional characteristics, and work habits must be assessed as carefully as physical limitations. Furthermore, the availability of jobs, the demands of certain occupations, and possible discrimination in certain fields must all be taken into account. The child who is mentally retarded and has severe spastic quadriplegia is obviously not going to have a career as a lawyer, a laboratory technician, or a clerk-typist. But what of one who has severe spastic quadriplegia and a bright mind? Such a person may be able to overcome both the physical limitation and the associated social stigma and be successful in a profession, such as law, in which the work is more mental than physical.

There are no simple conclusions regarding the occupational outlook for physically handicapped students. Those with mild or transitory handicapping conditions may not be affected at all in their occupational choices. Some with relatively mild physical disabilities may be unemployed, or even unemployable, because of inappropriate social and emotional behavior or poor work habits; they may need vocational rehabilitation training in order to function even in a sheltered workshop. Some people with severe physical disabilities are able to use their intelligence, social skills, and residual physical abilities to the fullest and become competitive employees (or employers) in demanding occupations.

Ryan (1979) describes one model career development program for severely disabled youth that served individuals ranging from 14 to 25 years of age. Their educational levels ranged from high school freshman to college senior, and they had a variety of disabilities including spinal cord injuries, spina bifida, cerebral palsy, multiple sclerosis, and neuromuscular disorders. A summer work program was set up in which the students went through several phases: interview, evaluation, and assessment prior to acceptance in the program; applications and interviews similar

Participation in social life and sociosexual activities are often special concerns of youth with physical disabilities. (© Bohdan Hrynewych/Southern Light)

to standard hiring practices; placement and training in a paying job for the summer; and counseling sessions, career seminars, and job-seeking skills seminars. The jobs for which the participants were hired included clerical, secretarial, educational, technical, engineering, computer, and social service positions. Most of the participants obtained full-time jobs or went on to more extensive preparation for careers.

Sociosexuality

Until fairly recently handicaps of most kinds, but particularly physical disabilities, were assumed to cancel human sexuality. People who were not whole physically, especially if they had limited mobility, were thought of as having no sex appeal for anyone and as having little or no ability or right to function sexually. These ideas are reflected in the words of William L. Rush, a physically disabled young man whose romantic feelings were rejected by the first young women he felt he loved:

> Only two roads are open for the severely physically handicapped in dealing with their feelings of love: the road of expecting and accepting only platonic love or the road of fantasizing. Neither is very satisfactory. (Rush, 1977, p. 6)

Fortunately attitudes and experiences are changing. It is now recognized that handicapped people have a right to family life education, including sex education, and to a full range of human relationships, including appropriate sexual expression (Duncan and Canty-Lemke, 1986; Edmonson, 1980). Sociosexual education for physically disabled students, like such education for nonhandicapped children and youths, should begin early, continue through adulthood, and include information about the structure and functions of bodies, human relationships and responsibilities, and alternative modes of sexual gratification.

Physically disabled youths need to experience close friendships and warm physical contact that is not sexually intimate. But it is neither realistic nor fair to expect physically disabled people to keep all their relationships platonic or to limit themselves to fantasy. Most physical disability, even if severe, does not in itself kill sexual desire or prevent sexual gratification; nor does it preclude marriage and children. The purpose of special education and rehabilitation is to make exceptional individuals' lives as full and complete as possible. In the case of youths with physical disabilities, this may involve teaching or providing alternative means of sexual stimulation and accepting sexual practices and relationships that are different from the norm, as discussed by Lewandowski and Cruickshank (1980). With sensitive education and rehabilitation, satisfying sociosexual expression can be achieved by all but a small minority of physically disabled persons (DeLoach and Greer, 1981).

MANAGING THE CHILD IN SCHOOL

For the regular classroom teacher with a student who is physically disabled, it is important to know that several immediate courses of action may be necessary:

1. Medical information must be obtained regarding the child's condition and the ways it will limit his or her participation in school.
2. The child must be given every opportunity to continue school work to the extent possible. If the youngster must be hospitalized during the school year, it may be necessary to inquire about the hospital's school program (if it has one) and to cooperate with the hospital's teachers or send work for the child to complete.
3. If the child must be confined to the home, an itinerant, homebound, or visiting teacher may be a possibility, or work can sometimes be sent from the school.
4. Good communication must be maintained with the child's family; the cooperation and encouragement of parents and other family members is vital in assuring every handicapped child the maximum opportunity for success in life. In general, the goal should be to continue and support the youngster's contact with school and to keep him or her from falling behind in school work, while at the same time not pressing the child beyond the limits imposed by the existing medical condition.
5. When disabled children return to school after having been hospitalized or confined to the home, it is important to make them feel welcome, to explain the disabling condition to their classmates, and to treat them as much like nondisabled youngsters as possible.
6. It may be necessary to consult other professionals regarding what can and cannot be expected of such children. Remember that the students will take their cues from the teacher about how to treat the physically disabled members of the class.

SUMMARY

Physically disabled children are considered to be those whose nonsensory physical limitations or health problems interfere with school attendance or learning to such an extent that special services, training, equipment, materials, or facilities are required. These children may have other disabilities such as mental retardation and emotional disturbance. The medical nature of the problem highlights the need for interdisciplinary cooperation in special education procedures.

Because of improvements in identification of and medical services to health-impaired and crippled children, mortality rates have been declining. But is does not follow that the number of children with disabilities is also declining. In fact, more people are surviving with disabilities that must be treated and dealt with socially and educationally.

The most common conditions and diseases are neurological impairments, musculoskeletal conditions, and congenital malformations.

Children with neurological impairments have suffered damage to or deterioration of the central nervous system. Their behavioral symptoms include mental retardation, learning problems, perceptual-motor dysfunction, paralysis, seizures, and emotional disturbance. The causes of neurological impairments include infectious diseases, hypoxia, poisoning, congenital malformations, accidents, and child abuse.

Cerebral palsy, a condition characterized by paralysis, weakness, incoordination, and/or other motor dysfunction, accounts for about half of the physically impaired children in the United States. Classification of cerebral palsy is generally made according to the limbs involved and the type of motor disability. The educational problems of cerebral-palsied children are varied because of the multiplicity of the behavioral symptoms; a careful clinical appraisal must be made of each individual in order to determine the type of special education needed.

Seizures are caused by an abnormal discharge of electrical energy in the brain. They may be generalized or partial. Recurrent seizures are referred to as epilepsy. Most people with epilepsy are able to function normally, except when having a seizure. Intelligence is not affected by epilepsy, so educational procedures consist chiefly of attaining a knowledge of the disorder and how to manage seizures and a commitment to help dispel the ignorance and fear connected with seizures.

Spina bifida is a congenital midline defect resulting from failure of the bony spinal column to close completely during fetal development. The resulting damage to the nerves generally causes paralysis and/or lack of function below the site of the defect. This disability affects approximately 0.02 percent of the population; its causes are as yet unknown. Hydrocephalus and meningitis often accompany spina bifida. With proper orthopedic care and corrective surgery, many children affected by this condition can attend regular classes. Other neurological impairments include poliomyelitis and multiple sclerosis.

A number of physical disabilities derive from musculoskeletal conditions in which there are defects or diseases of the muscles or bones. Children with such disabilities have a range of difficulties in walking, standing, sitting, or using their hands. Muscular dystrophy is a degenerative disease causing a progressive weakening and wasting away of the muscle tissues. Progressing physical immobility and the prospect of total disability or death make this condition especially difficult on victims. But intellectual capacity is not affected, and with proper motivation and educational procedures, most of these children can benefit from special educational programs. Arthritis is a disease that causes acute inflammation around the joints; its symptoms vary from mild to profound, and it can affect children as well as adults. These and other musculoskeletal conditions do not cause lowered intelligence, so educational considerations include overcoming the child's deficit in mobility so that he or she can continue learning in as normal a way as possible.

Congenital malformations, treated here as a separate category of physical disabilities, can be acquired through neurological impairment or musculoskeletal difficulties. Spina bifida is always congenital; cerebral palsy may or may not be congenital. There can also be inherited malformations of the heart and/or blood vessels;

dislocations of the hip, abnormalities of the extremities (webbed or extra fingers or toes) or of the head and face. Some malformations are caused by faulty chromosomes contributed by the mother and/or father. Teratogens, deformity-producing factors that interfere with normal fetal development, can cause damage during the gestation period, with fetal alcohol syndrome now the most common.

Accidents that bring about neurological impairment, disfigurement, or amputation are an important cause of physical disability among children. AIDS, a fatal viral infection discovered only a few years ago, is forcing controversial decisions regarding sex education and exclusion of sufferers from school. No evidence suggests that the AIDS virus is transmitted by casual contact, and at this time in most cases little justification for excluding students with AIDS from school can be found. Abused and neglected children represent an alarming and large category of physically impaired children. Many thousands of children each year are damaged—emotionally and physically—by adults who neglect, burn, beat, sexually molest, starve, and otherwise brutalize them. Children with disabilities are more likely to be abused. Those who teach must be especially alert to signs of possible child abuse and neglect.

As a group, physically disabled children represent the total range of impairment, and their behavioral and psychological characteristics thus vary greatly. The necessity for hospitalization, bed rest, prosthetic devices, and so on means that their academic achievement is dependent upon individual circumstances, motivation, and the caliber of care received both at home and at school. The two major effects of a physical disability, especially if it is severe or prolonged, are that a child may be deprived of educationally relevant experiences, and that he or she may not be able to learn to manipulate educational materials and respond to educational tasks the way most children do.

There does not appear to be a distinct personality type associated with particular physical disabilities. The reactions of the public, family, peers, and educational personnel—as well as the child's own reactions to the disability—are all closely interwoven in the determination of any particular child's personality and in that child's degree of motivation, progress, and attitude. Given ample opportunity to develop educationally, socially, and emotionally in as normal a fashion as possible, many physically disabled children are able to make a healthy adjustment to their impairments.

Behavior modification techniques have been valuable in helping physically disabled children to achieve and perform at a maximum level. In any decisions involving the type of special education the physically disabled child should receive, individual characteristics (intellectual, sensory, physical, and emotional) must be considered. Along with scholastic education, the child may also need special assistance in daily living, mobility, and occupational skills. Consequently, many other disciplines may become involved. The major considerations are to help each physically impaired child become as independent and self-sufficient in daily activities as possible; to provide basic academic skills; and to prepare the child for the acquisition of advanced educational and/or occupational skills that will allow him or her the basic human right of being a fulfilled, contributing, functioning member of human society. Special considerations for the preschool child include handling and positioning. For adolescents and young adults, careers and sociosexuality are particularly important.

REFERENCES

Anastasiow, N. J. (1983). Adolescent pregnancy and special education. *Exceptional Children, 49,* 396–401.

Baldwin, W., & Cain, V. S. (1981). The children of teenage parents. In F. Frustenberg, R. Lincoln, & J. Menken (Eds.), *Teenage sexuality, pregnancy and childbearing* (pp. 265–279). Philadelphia: University of Pennsylvania Press.

Banker, B. Q., & Bruce-Gregorios, J. (1983). Neuropathology. In G. H. Thompson, I. L. Rubin, & R. M. Bilenker (Eds.), *Comprehensive management of cerebral palsy.* New York: Grune & Stratton.

Batshaw, M. L., & Perret, Y. M. (1986). *Children with handicaps: A medical primer.* Baltimore: Paul H. Brookes.

Best, G. A. (1978). *Individuals with physical disabilities: An introduction for educators.* St. Louis: C. V. Mosby.

Bigge, J., & O'Donnell, P. (1977). *Teaching individuals with physical and multiple disabilities.* Columbus: Charles E. Merrill.

Blackman, J. A. (Ed.). (1984). *Medical aspects of developmental disabilities in children birth to three* (rev. 1st ed.). Rockville, Md.: Aspen.

Bleck, E. E. (1979). Integrating the physically handicapped child. *The Journal of School Health, 49,* 141–146.

Bleck, E. E., & Nagel, D. A. (Eds.). (1975). *Physically handicapped children: A medical atlas for teachers.* New York: Grune & Stratton.

Blumberg, M. L. (1984). Sexual abuse of children—causes, diagnosis, and management. *Pediatric Annals, 13,* 753–758.

Broadhurst, D. D. (1986). *Educators, schools, and child abuse.* Chicago: National Committee for Prevention of Child Abuse.

Broman, S. H. (1981). Long-term development of children born to teenagers. In K. G. Scott, T. Field, & E. G. Robertson (Eds.), *Teenage parents and their offspring* (pp. 195–224). New York: Grune & Stratton.

Bryan, D. P., & Herjanic, B. (1980). Depression and suicide among adolescents and young adults with selective handicapping conditions. *Exceptional Education Quarterly, 1*(2), 57–66.

Calhoun, M. L., & Hawisher, M. (1979). *Teaching and learning strategies for physically handicapped students.* Baltimore: University Park Press.

Campbell, P. H., Green, K. M., & Carlson, L. M. (1977). Approximating the norm through environmental and child-centered prosthetics and adaptive equipment. In E. Sontag, J. Smith, & N. Certo (Eds.), *Educational programming for the severely and profoundly handicapped.* Reston, Va.: Council for Exceptional Children.

Cavazzuti, G. B., Ferrari, P., & Lalla, M. (1984). Follow-up study of 482 cases with convulsive disorders in the first year. *Developmental Medicine and Child Neurology, 26,* 425–437.

Chase-Lansdale, L. (1984). The Child Abuse Prevention and Treatment Act of 1983. *Washington Report, 1*(1), 1–6.

Church, J. A., Allen, J. R., & Stiehm, E. R. (1986). New scarlet letter(s), pediatric AIDS. *Pediatrics, 77,* 423–427.

Cruickshank, W. M. (Ed.). (1976a). *Cerebral palsy: A developmental disability* (3rd rev. ed.). Syracuse, N.Y.: Syracuse University Press.

Cruickshank, W. M. (1976b). The problem and its scope. In W. M. Cruickshank (Ed.), *Cerebral palsy: A developmental disability* (3rd rev. ed.). Syracuse, N.Y.: Syracuse University Press.

Cruickshank, W. M., Hallahan, D. P., & Bice, H. V. (1976). The evaluation of intelligence. In W. M. Cruickshank (Ed.), *Cerebral palsy: A developmental disability* (3rd rev. ed.). Syracuse, N.Y.: Syracuse University Press.

Delatte, J. G., Orgeron, K., & Preis, J. (1985). Project SCAN: Counseling teen-age parents in a school setting. *Journal of School Health, 55*(1), 24–26.

DeLoach, C., & Greer, B. G. (1981). *Adjustment to severe physical disability: A metamorphosis.* New York: McGraw-Hill.

Denhoff, E. (1976). Medical aspects. In W. M. Cruickshank (Ed.), *Cerebral palsy: A developmental disability* (3rd rev. ed.). Syracuse, N.Y.: Syracuse University Press.

Dikmen, S., Matthews, C. G., & Harley, J. P. (1975). The effect of early versus late onset of major motor epilepsy upon cognitive-intellectual performance. *Epilepsia, 16,* 73–81.

DuBose, R. F., & Deni, K. (1980). Easily constructed adaptive and assistive equipment. *Teaching Exceptional Children, 12,* 116–123.

Duncan, D., & Canty-Lemke, J. (1986). Learning appropriate social and sexual behavior: The role of society. *The Exceptional Parent, 16*(5), 24–26.

Edmonson, B. (1980). Sociosexual education for the handicapped. *Exceptional Education Quarterly, 1*(2), 67–76.

Eiben, R. M., & Crocker, A. C. (1983). Cerebral palsy within the spectrum of developmental disabilities. In G. H. Thompson, I. L. Rubin, & R. M. Bilenker (Eds.), *Comprehensive management of cerebral palsy.* New York: Grune & Stratton.

Finnie, N. R. (1975). *Handling the young cerebral palsied child at home.* New York: Dutton.

Fonosch, G. G., Arany, J., Lee, A., & Loving, S. (1982). Providing career planning and placement services for college students with disabilities. *Exceptional Education Quarterly, 3*(3), 67–74.

Fontana, V. J. (1984). Introduction—The maltreatment syndrome of children. *Pediatric Annals, 13,* 736–744.

Frankel, D. (1984). Long-term care issues in multiple sclerosis. *Rehabilitation Literature, 45,* 282–285.

Fraser, B. A., & Hensinger, R. N. (1983). *Managing physical handicaps: A practical guide for parents, care providers, and educators.* Baltimore: Paul H. Brooks.

Freeman, J. M., Jacobs, H., Vining, E., & Rabin, C. E. (1984). Epilepsy and the inner city schools: A school-based program that makes a difference. *Epilepsia, 25,* 438–442.

Gerbner, G., Ross, C. J., & Zigler, E. (Eds.). (1980). *Child abuse: An agenda for action.* New York: Oxford University Press.

Goffman, E. (1963). *Stigma: Notes on the management of spoiled identity.* Englewood Cliffs, N.J.: Prentice-Hall.

Gottlieb, M. S., Schroff, R., Schanker, H. M., Weisman, J. D., Fan, P. T., Wolf, R. A., & Saxon, A. (1981). *Pneumocystis carinii* pneumonia and mucosal candidiasis in previously healthy homosexual men: Evidence of a new acquired cellular immunodeficiency. *New England Journal of Medicine, 305,* 1425–1431.

Hanson, M. J., & Harris, S. R. (1986). *Teaching the young child with motor delays.* Austin, Tex.: Pro-Ed.

Harkey, J. (1983). The epidemiology of selected chronic childhood health conditions. *Children's Health Care, 12,* 62–71.

Harmon, C., Furrow, D., Gruendel, J., & Zigler, E. (1980). Childhood accidents: An overview of the problem and a call for action. *Newsletter of the Society for Research in Child Development,* Spring.

Hauser, W. A., & Kurland, L. T. (1975). The epidemiology of epilepsy in Rochester, Minnesota, 1935 through 1967. *Epilepsia, 16,* 1–66.

Healy, A. (1984). Cerebral palsy. In J. A. Blackman (Ed.), *Medical aspects of developmental disabilities in children birth to three,* rev. 1st ed. (pp. 31–37). Rockville, Md.: Aspen.

Hearey, C. D., Harris, J. A., Usatin, M. S., Epstein, D. M., Ury, H. K., & Neutra, R. R. (1984). Investigation of a cluster of anencephaly and spina bifida. *American Journal of Epidemiology, 120,* 559–564.

Helfer, R. E. (1984). The epidemiology of child abuse and neglect. *Pediatric Annals, 13,* 745–751.

Heller, J. (1974). *Something happened.* New York: Knopf.

Hoare, P. (1984). The development of psychiatric disorder among schoolchildren with epilepsy. *Developmental Medicine and Child Neurology, 26,* 3–13.

Hobbs, N., Perrin, J. M., & Ireys, H. T. (1985). *Chronically ill children and their families.* San Francisco: Jossey-Bass.

Hobbs, N., Perrin, J. M., Ireys, H. T., Moynahan, L. C., & Shayne, M. W. (1984). Chronically ill children in America. *Rehabilitation Literature, 45,* 206–213.

Holdsworth, L., & Whitmore, K. (1974a). A study of children with epilepsy attending ordinary schools. Part I: Their seizure patterns, progress, and behavior in school. *Developmental Medicine and Child Neurology, 16,* 746–758.

Holdsworth, L., & Whitmore, K. (1974b). A study of children with epilepsy attending ordinary schools. Part II: Information and attitudes held by their teachers. *Developmental Medicine and Child Neurology, 16,* 759–765.

Hopkins, T. W., Bice, H. V., & Colton, K. C. (1954). *Evaluation and education of the cerebral palsied child.* Arlington, Va.: Council for Exceptional Children.

Jacobs, I. B. (1983). Epilepsy. In G. H. Thompson, I. L. Rubin, & R. M. Bilenker (Eds.), *Comprehensive management of cerebral palsy.* New York: Grune & Stratton.

Karagan, N., & Zellweger, H. (1978). Early verbal disability in children with Duchenne muscular dystrophy. *Developmental Medicine and Child Neurology, 20,* 435–441.

Kempe, C. H., Silverman, F. N., Steele, B. B., Droegemueller, W., & Silver, H. K. (1962). The battered child syndrome. *Journal of the American Medical Association, 181,* 17–24.

Klein, M., & Stern, L. (1971). Low birth weight and the battered child syndrome. *American Journal of Diseases of Children, 122,* 15–18.

Korabek, C. A., & Cuvo, A. J. (1986). Children with spina bifida: Educational implications of their medical characteristics. *Education and Treatment of Children, 9,* 142–152.

Lewandowski, L. J., & Cruickshank, W. M. (1980). Psychological development of crippled children and youth. In W. M. Cruickshank (Ed.), *Psychology of exceptional children and youth* (4th ed.). Englewood Cliffs, N.J.: Prentice-Hall.

Lyon, J. (1985). *Playing god in the nursery.* New York: Norton.

Miezio, P. M. (1983). *Parenting children with disabilities: A professional source for physicians and guide for parents.* New York: Marcel Dekker.

Migra, T. (1987). Impairment due to infectious disease ruled a handicap. *Education Week, 6*(24), 1, 21.

Moore, J. (1985). Technology is not magic. *The Exceptional Parent, 15*(7), 41–42.

Nelson, K. B., & Ellenberg, J. H. (1978). Epidemiology of cerebral palsy. *Advances in Neurology, 19,* 421–435.

Newman, J. (1980). Psychological problems of children and youth with chronic medical disorders. In W. M. Cruickshank (Ed.), *Psychology of exceptional children and youth* (4th ed.). Englewood Cliffs, N.J.: Prentice-Hall.

Obe, G., & Hansjurgen, R. (1979). Mutagenic, cancerogenic, and teratogenic effects of alcohol. *Mutation Research, 65,* 229–259.

Reed, E. W. (1975). Genetic abnormalities in development.

In F. D. Horowitz (Ed.), *Review of child development research* (Vol. 4). Chicago: University of Chicago Press.

Robinson, N. M., & Robinson, H. B. (1976). *The mentally retarded child: A psychological approach* (2nd ed.). New York: McGraw-Hill.

Roos, P. (1975). Parents and families of the mentally retarded. In J. M. Kauffman & J. S. Payne (Eds.), *Mental retardation: Introduction and personal perspectives.* Columbus: Charles E. Merrill.

Rush, W. L. (1977). Feelings of love. *The Exceptional Parent, 7*(6), 2–6.

Rutledge, D. N., & Dick, G. (1983). Spinal cord injury in adolescence. *Rehabilitation Nursing, 8*(6), 18–21.

Ryan, P. A. (1979). Widening their horizons: A model career development program for severely physically disabled youth. *Rehabilitation Literature, 40,* 72–74.

Satz, J. (1986). Another first: The National Park Service opens summer work programs to students with disabilities. *The Exceptional Parent, 16*(2), 19–22.

Shannon, K. M., & Ammann, A. J. (1985). Acquired immune deficiency syndrome in childhood. *Journal of Pediatrics, 106,* 332–342.

Schonberger, L. B., Sullivan-Bolyai, J. Z., & Bryan, J. A. (1978). Poliomyelitis in the United States. *Advances in Neurology, 19,* 217–227.

Scott, D. (1973). *About epilepsy* (rev. ed.). New York: International Universities Press.

Snell, M. E., & Browder, D. M. (1986). Community-referenced instruction: Research and issues. *Journal of the Association for Severely Handicapped, 11,* 1–11.

Stores, G. (1978). School-children with epilepsy at risk for learning and behavior problems. *Developmental Medicine and Child Neurology, 20,* 502–508.

Thompson, G. H., Rubin, I. L., & Bilenker, R. M. (Eds.). (1983). *Comprehensive management of cerebral palsy.* New York: Grune & Stratton.

Torres, F. (1969). Convulsive disorders: A working classification and guidelines for diagnosis and treatment. *Medical Times, 97,* 152–156.

Turnbull, A. P., & Turnbull, H. R. (Eds.). (1985). *Parents speak out: Then and now* (2nd ed.). Columbus: Charles E. Merrill.

U.S. Department of Education. (1984). *Sixth annual report to Congress on the implementation of Public Law 94-142, The Education for All Handicapped Children Act.* Washington, D.C.: U.S. Government Printing Office.

U.S. Department of Education. (1986). *Eighth annual report to Congress on the implementation of the Education of the Handicapped Act,* Vol. 1. Washington, D.C.: author.

U.S. Department of Health, Education and Welfare. (1974). *Prevalence of chronic skin and musculoskeletal conditions—United States 1969.* Vital and Health Statistics, Series 10, No. 92.

Utley, B. L., Holvoet, J. F., & Barnes, K. (1977). Handling, positioning, and feeding the physically handicapped. In E. Sontag, J. Smith, & N. Certo (Eds.), *Educational programming for the severely and profoundly handicapped.* Reston, Va.: Council for Exceptional Children.

Verhaaren, P., & Connor, F. (1981a). Physical disabilities. In J. M. Kauffman & D. P. Hallahan (Eds.), *Handbook of special education.* Englewood Cliffs, N.J.: Prentice-Hall.

Verhaaren, P., & Connor, F. (1981b). Special adaptations

necessitated by physical disabilities. In J. M. Kauffman & D. P. Hallahan (Eds.), *Handbook of special education.* Englewood Cliffs, N.J.: Prentice-Hall.

Vinger, P. F., & Hoerner, E. F. (Eds.). (1986). *Sports injuries: The unthwarted epidemic* (2nd ed.). Littleton, Mass.: PSG Publishing Company.

Watson, J. D. (1984). Talking about the best kept secret: Sexual abuse and children with disabilities. *The Exceptional Parent, 14*(6), 15–20.

Werry, J. S. (1979a). Organic factors. In H. C. Quay & J. S. Werry (Eds.), *Psychopathological disorders of childhood* (2nd ed.). New York: Wiley.

Werry, J. S. (1979b). Psychosomatic disorders, psychogenic symptoms, and hospitalization. In H. C. Quay & J. S. Werry (Eds.), *Psychopathological disorders of childhood* (2nd ed.). New York: Wiley.

Wilsnack, S. C., Klassen, A. D., & Wilsnack, R. W. (1984). Drinking and reproductive dysfunction among women in a 1981 national survey. *Alcoholism: Clinical and Experimental Research, 8,* 451–458.

Wilson, M. I. (1973). Children with crippling and health disabilities. In L. M. Dunn (Ed.), *Exceptional children in the schools* (2nd ed.). New York: Holt, Rinehart & Winston.

Wisniewski, K., & Lupin, R. (1979). Fetal alcohol syndrome and related CNS problems. *Neurology, 29,* 1429–1430.

Wolraich, M. L. (1984). Seizure disorders. In J. A. Blackman (Ed.), *Medical aspects of developmental disabilities in children birth to three,* rev. 1st ed. (pp. 215–221). Rockville, Md.: Aspen.

World Health Statistics Report. (1976). Geneva: World Health Organization, Vol. 29, No. 2.

Wright, B. A. (1960). *Physical disability: A psychological approach.* New York: Harper & Row.

Zadig, J. M. (1983). The education of the child with cerebral palsy. In G. H. Thompson, I. L. Rubin, & R. M. Bilenker (Eds.), *Comprehensive management of cerebral palsy.* New York: Grune & Stratton.

Zirpoli, T. J. (1986). Child abuse and children with handicaps. *Remedial and Special Education, 7*(2), 39–48.

Ziter, F. A., & Allsop, K. G. (1976). The diagnosis and management of childhood muscular dystrophy. "Clinicians must provide the best care and support possible." *Clinical Pediatrics, 15,* 540–548.

9

Giftedness

I think Jim Gillis was a much more remarkable person than his family and his intimates ever suspected. He had a bright and smart imagination and it was of the kind that turns out impromptu work and does it well, does it with easy facility and without previous preparation, just builds a story as it goes along, careless of whether it is proceeding, enjoying each fresh fancy as it flashes from the brain and caring not at all whether the story shall ever end brilliantly and satisfactorily or shan't end at all. Jim was born a humorist and a very competent one. When I remember how felicitous were his untrained efforts, I feel a conviction that he would have been a star performer if he had been discovered and had been subjected to a few years of training with a pen. A genius is not very likely to ever discover himself; neither is he very likely to be discovered by his intimates; they are so close to him that he is out of focus to them and they can't get at his proportions; they cannot perceive that there is any considerable difference between his bulk and their own. They can't get a perspective on him and it is only by a perspective that the difference between him and the rest of their limited circle can be perceived.

(The Autobiography of Mark Twain)

P eople who are gifted, or at least have the potential for giftedness, can go through life unrecognized. As Mark Twain pointed out (see page 411), they may seem unremarkable to their closest associates. Sometimes gifted children and youth go undiscovered because their families and intimates simply place no particular value on their special abilities. Sometimes they are not recognized because they are not given the necessary opportunities or training. Especially in the case of those who are poor or members of minority groups, gifted children may be deprived of chances to demonstrate and develop their potential. How many more outstanding artists and scientists would we have if every talented child had the opportunity and the training necessary to develop his or her talents to the fullest possible extent? There is no way of knowing, but it is safe to say we would have more.

Unlike mental retardation and other handicapping conditions, giftedness is something to be fostered, not eliminated. Yet giftedness is not something a child can show without risk of stigma and rejection (Perry, 1986; Tannenbaum, 1986). Many people have a low level of tolerance for those who are intellectually superior or who eclipse the ordinary individual in some area of achievement. A child who achieves far beyond the level of his or her average peers may be subject to criticism or social isolation by other children or their parents. Had Jim Gillis been discovered, given a few years of training with a pen, and become a gifted writer, it is possible that some of his intimates would have found his giftedness hard to accept.

Some of the problems presented by giftedness parallel those presented by the handicapping conditions we have discussed in the other chapters of this book. For instance, the definition and identification of gifted children involve the same sort of difficulties that exist in the case of retarded and disturbed children. But there is an underlying philosophical question regarding giftedness that makes us think differently about this exceptionality. Most of us feel a moral obligation to help those who are at some disadvantage compared to the average person, who have a deficiency that prevents them from achieving an ordinary level of competence unless they are given special help. In the case of gifted students, though, we may wonder about our moral obligation to help those who are already advantaged to become even better, to distinguish themselves further by fulfilling the highest promise of their extraordinary resources. It is on this issue—the desirability or necessity of helping our most capable children become even better—that special education for gifted students is likely to founder.

DEFINITION

Gifted children are in some way superior to a comparison group of other children of the same age. Beyond this almost meaningless statement, you will find little agreement about how gifted children should be defined (Cassidy and Johnson, 1986; Cornell, 1984; Gallagher, 1985; Kontos, Carter, Ormrod, and Cooney, 1983a,b; Maker, 1986; Renzulli and Owen, 1983). The disagreements are due primarily to differences of opinion regarding the following questions:

1. *In what way are gifted children superior?* Are they superior in general intelligence, insight, creativity, special talents, achievements in academic subjects or in a valued line of work, moral judgment, or some combination of such factors?

The authors are indebted to Dr. Carolyn M. Callahan of the University of Virginia for her invaluable assistance in the preparation of this chapter.

MISCONCEPTIONS ABOUT GIFTEDNESS

Myth	*Fact*
Gifted people are physically weak, socially inept, narrow in interests, and prone to emotional instability and early decline.	Although there are wide individual variations, gifted individuals as a group tend to be exceptionally healthy, well adjusted, socially attractive, and morally responsible.
Gifted individuals are in a sense "superhuman."	Gifted people are not "superhuman"; rather, they are human beings with extraordinary gifts in particular areas.
Gifted children are usually bored with school and antagonistic toward those who are responsible for their education.	Gifted children usually like school and adjust well to their peers and teachers.
Gifted people tend to be mentally unstable.	Those who are gifted are likely to be well-adjusted, emotionally healthy people.
We know that 3 to 5 percent of the population is gifted.	The percentage of the population that is gifted depends on the definition of giftedness that one uses. Some definitions include only 1 or 2 percent of the population, others over 20 percent.
Giftedness is a stable trait, always consistently evident in all periods of a person's life.	Some gifted people's remarkable talents and productivity develop early and continue throughout life; in other cases, a person's gifts or talents are not noticed until adulthood, and occasionally a youngster who shows outstanding ability becomes a nondescript adult.
Gifted people do everything well.	Some people known as gifted have superior abilities of many kinds; others are clearly superior in only one area.
A person is gifted if he or she scores above a certain level on intelligence tests.	IQ is only one indication of giftedness. Creativity and high motivation are as important indications as general intelligence.
Gifted students will excel without special education. Students who are truly gifted need only the incentives and instruction that are appropriate for all students.	Some gifted children will perform at a remarkably high level without special education of any kind. Some will make outstanding contributions even in the face of great obstacles to their achievement. But most will not come close to achieving at a level commensurate with their potential unless their talents are deliberately fostered by incentives and instruction that are appropriate for their advanced abilities.

Perhaps nearly everyone is gifted in some way or other. What kind of giftedness is most important? What kind of giftedness should we try to encourage?

2. *How is superiority measured?* Is it by standardized tests of aptitude, teacher judgments, past performance in school or in everyday life, or by some other means? If it is measured in one particular way, then some individuals will be overlooked. If past performance is the test, then we are defining giftedness after the fact. What measurement techniques can we have confidence in? What measurements will tell us which children have the potential to become gifted?

3. *To what degree must a child be superior in order to be considered gifted?* Must the child do better than 50 percent, 80 percent, 90 percent, or 99 percent of the comparison group? The number of gifted individuals will vary depending on the criterion (or criteria) for giftedness. What percent of the population do we want to be gifted?

4. *Who should comprise the comparison group?* Should it be every child of the same chronological age, the other children in the child's school, all children of the same ethnic or racial origin, or some other grouping? Almost everyone is the brightest or most capable in some group. What group should set the standard?

You may have concluded already that giftedness is whatever we choose to make it, just as mental retardation is whatever we choose to say it is. Someone can be considered gifted (or retarded) one day and not the next simply because we have changed an arbitrary definition. There is no inherent rightness or wrongness in the definitions professionals use. Some definitions may be more logical, more precise, or more useful than others, but we are still unable to say they are more "correct" in some absolute sense. We have to struggle with the concept of giftedness and the reasons for identifying gifted individuals before we can make any decisions about definition. Our definition of giftedness will be shaped to a large extent by what our culture believes is most useful or necessary for its survival.

Even the terminology of giftedness can become rather confusing. Besides the word "gifted," a variety of other terms have been used to describe individuals who are superior in some way: "talented," "creative," "insightful," "genius," and "precocious," for example. **Precocity** refers to remarkably early development. Many highly gifted children show precocity in particular areas of development, such as language, music, or mathematical ability, and the rate of intellectual development of all gifted children exceeds the rate for nongifted children. **Insight** may be defined as separating relevant from irrelevant information, finding novel and useful ways of combining relevant bits of information, or relating new and old information in a novel and productive way. **Genius** has sometimes been used to indicate a particular aptitude or capacity in any area. More often, it has been used to indicate extremely rare intellectual powers (extremely high IQ or creativity). **Creativity** refers to the ability to express novel and useful ideas, to sense and elucidate novel and important relationships, and to ask previously unthought of, but crucial, questions. The word **talent** ordinarily has been used to indicate a special ability, aptitude, or accomplishment. **Giftedness,** as we use the term in this chapter, refers to cognitive (intellectual) superiority (not necessarily of genius caliber), creativity, and motivation in combination and of sufficient magnitude to set the child apart from the vast majority of agemates and make it possible for him or her to contribute something of particular value to society (Renzulli, Reis, and Smith, 1981).

Changes in the Definition of Giftedness

The traditional definition of giftedness is based on general intelligence as measured by an individually administered intelligence test, usually the Stanford-Binet or the Wechsler Intelligence Scale for Children—Revised. That is, children have traditionally been considered gifted if they scored above a particular level on the Binet or the WISC—R. A definition of giftedness based solely on IQ was used in the classic studies of gifted children by Lewis Terman and his associates (published under the general title *Genetic Studies of Genius*). This definition (high IQ) has been used in many other studies and programs for the gifted. In recent years, however, there has been great dissatisfaction with the use of IQ as the single (or even most important) criterion for defining giftedness. The reasons for this include recognition of the limitations of IQ tests, reconceptualization of the nature of intelligence, and additional research and thinking on the nature of giftedness (Humphreys, 1985; Renzulli and Delcourt, 1986; Sternberg and Davidson, 1983, 1985).

Limitations of Intelligence Tests

A relatively restricted range of performances is sampled by an intelligence test. Even though the performances or abilities are important ones and remarkably predictive of achievement on a statistical basis, an individual may possess capacities that cannot be tapped by an intelligence test but that are important enough to be used in defining giftedness. It has also been argued that intelligence tests (especially the standard individual tests) are biased in favor of white middle-class children and against groups of minority racial or ethnic origin. The argument is that because of differences in language and cultural values, gifted children who are not Caucasian and middle class often are unable to score as high as white middle-class children of comparable intelligence. In short, it has been recognized that intelligence and giftedness are more complex than the relatively narrow band of performances required to score exceptionally high on an intelligence test.* Furthermore, giftedness seems to be characterized by qualitative differences in thinking and insightfulness, which may not be clearly reflected by performance on intelligence tests (see Rosenbloom, 1986; Sternberg and Davidson, 1983). The box on p. 416 illustrates the type of insight that might be shown by a student who is gifted in mathematics.

Reconceptualization of Intelligence

The first widely used test of general intelligence, the Binet, was designed to predict whether or not children would fail in school (Tyler, 1976). The tests developed after the Binet were designed for basically the same purpose and have been compared, for validation, to the Binet. The majority of the items on these tests sample verbal ability (general information, comprehension, vocabulary). In the 1950s Guilford (1959, 1967, 1975) began to extend and elaborate on the various abilities that make up intelligence. His descriptions of more than 100 different facets of intelligence led to interest in devising new tests. In particular, Guilford's work stimulated interest in creativity, one aspect of which he called **divergent thinking**

---

* Recall that the limitations of IQ have become obvious also in the definition of mental retardation. An exceptionally low IQ by itself is no longer sufficient to define mental retardation, but must be accompanied by deficits in adaptive behavior (see Chapter 2 and Zigler and Farber, 1985).

Insight: A Qualitative Difference in Thinking

The thinking of gifted children is qualitatively different from that of ordinary people. Many times I have, in classes of gifted children, written on the blackboard:

$$1 + 2 + 4 + 8 + \text{ and so on } + 1024 = ?$$

and asked the children to find the sum. Very often, I have hardly stated the problem before someone shouts out "2047!" If I ask, "How did you get it so fast?," a typical answer might be "1 + 2 is 3, and 4 more is 7, and the sum is always one less than the next number."

When I teach the same topic to average college students, I must explain the concept of a geometrical progression, how to recognize this problem as such, how to derive a formula for the sum, and then show how to apply it to this special case. The gifted children have a capacity for insights which cannot be taught at any level. If this ability exists, it can be developed and stimulated.

SOURCE: P. C. Rosenbloom, "Programs for the Gifted in Mathematics," *Roeper Review,* 1986, *8,* 243.

(as contrasted with **convergent thinking**). Whereas the usual tests of intelligence assess the ability to think deductively and arrive at a single answer that could be scored "right" or "wrong," Guilford's work inspired interest in tests of creativity, especially assessment of the ability to think inductively and suggest many different potential answers. His delineation of the many facets of human intelligence led to dissatisfaction with previous conceptualizations of "general" intelligence or "primary mental abilities" (Maker, 1986). Nevertheless, today researchers are again searching for the cognitive characteristics that define *general* intelligence (Grinder, 1985). For example, Sternberg and Davidson (1983) describe *insight* skills, which they believe may be the primary characteristics that define intellectual giftedness. Although giftedness may be manifested by performance in specific domains (e.g., mathematics, writing, visual arts, interpersonal skills, music), the factor that makes such performance possible may be general intelligence (Horowitz and O'Brien, 1985).

New Ideas about Giftedness

A variety of definitions of giftedness have been proposed during the past two decades, including the following:

- Exceptional academic achievement
- Exceptional creativity
- Existence of special talents
- Superior achievement beyond peers in any valued line of activity
- Inclusion in the top X percent of children according to any criterion of giftedness

The problem is that each of these definitions, taken alone, may include some children who are not gifted (who do not eventually contribute something of extraordinary value to society) and exclude some children who are. For example, a

Giftedness and talent of many different kinds are recognized. Margaret Mead is recognized as an eminent scholar in the social sciences; Ralph Sampson, a UPI and AP college basketball player of the year and pro basketball star, is recognized for his athletic prowess; Itzhak Perlman is recognized for his musical genius. (David Austen/Stock, Boston; Jerry Wachter/Focus on Sports, Inc.; Children's Television Workshop)

child may be extremely high in IQ but not high in creativity and may fail to produce anything particularly worthwhile or beneficial to society. A high-achieving child may be simply an extremely hard worker who has little imagination or capacity to create anything of value. The highly creative child may not have the ability or motivation to channel inventiveness into productive activity. A child with a special talent, perhaps an extraordinary drummer or basketball player, may not have the resources of intelligence and creativity necessary to become recognized as a person of outstanding ability. Children may achieve well beyond the level of their agemates in a single valued line of activity but show no other signs of giftedness, or they may be in the top 5 percent of their class in their particular school but barely in the top third of students nationally.

Perhaps giftedness is not a fixed or absolute human characteristic. A person may be gifted if the conditions are right for gifted performance—if, besides possessing above-average ability and creativity, the person is given opportunities and incentives to perform at an extraordinarily high level. Perhaps we should speak of people who exhibit *gifted behavior* rather than of *gifted people,* because people typically act gifted only under particular circumstances. These are relatively new ideas about giftedness that have been suggested by Keating (1980) and Renzulli et al. (1981).

More recently, Horowitz and O'Brien (1985) have conceptualized giftedness, retardation, and all levels of performance between these extremes in terms of a developmental model. Giftedness may be thought of as a superior to extraordinary developmental outcome resulting from the joint function of a relatively unimpaired and invulnerable organism and a facilitative environment. That is, a child can attain a gifted level of performance only when he or she is (a) relatively free of biological impairments, (b) mostly invulnerable to environmental stresses that tend to limit performance, and (c) reared in an environment that supports performance.

An important assumption of Horowitz and O'Brien's model is that children may function as gifted or nongifted in specific domains. For example, a cerebral palsied child could not perform at a gifted level in a motor performance impaired by his or her brain injury. This child might, however, function at the gifted level with respect to cognitive development or in motor skills unimpaired by his or her brain injury. A child whose legs alone are seriously affected by cerebral palsy might become an eminent scientist or violinist, but this child could not become a gifted dancer. Furthermore, with the right technology, this child's motor performance could be improved.

The interactions among environment and organism hypothesized by Horowitz and O'Brien are depicted in Figure 9.1. The figure shows a cube shaped so that the curved surface represents the performance of children under various combinations of vulnerability, impairment, and environmental facilitation. The far upper corner (A) represents gifted performance, which would be produced by an unimpaired, invulnerable organism in a highly facilitative environment. The near lower corner (B) represents profound retardation or developmental failure, which would be the product of severe impairment and vulnerability in a nonfacilitative environment. The right upper corner (C) represents the optimal developmental outcome that can be expected in a facilitative environment, given an impaired and vulnerable organism. The left upper corner (D) represents the optimal outcome given an unimpaired and invulnerable child in a nonfacilitative environment. Note that the right and left corners represent the best outcomes that can be expected under the poorest circumstances—outcomes that, while optimal for the individual child, do not represent giftedness. Outcomes do not reach the gifted level at the left corner of the

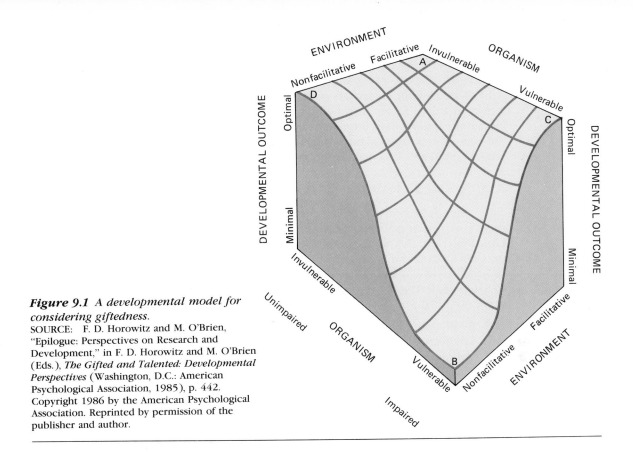

Figure 9.1 *A developmental model for considering giftedness.*
SOURCE: F. D. Horowitz and M. O'Brien, "Epilogue: Perspectives on Research and Development," in F. D. Horowitz and M. O'Brien (Eds.), *The Gifted and Talented: Developmental Perspectives* (Washington, D.C.: American Psychological Association, 1985), p. 442. Copyright 1986 by the American Psychological Association. Reprinted by permission of the publisher and author.

Gifted children have superior cognitive abilities that allow them to compete with older individuals of average intellect. (Timothy Eagan/Woodfin Camp & Associates)

model because the child's environment does not facilitate performance; at the right corner, giftedness is not achieved because the organism is damaged.

In short, giftedness today is seen as a much more complex phenomenon than it was even a decade ago. It is being redefined in terms of new concepts in developmental psychology and intelligence. The field is moving toward an appreciation of the neurophysiological factors involved in gifted performance and the ways in which general intelligence is manifested in various domains of human endeavor.

A Suggested Definition

As we mentioned earlier, an adequate definition of giftedness includes the requirement that a person show at least the *potential* for making a remarkable and valued contribution to the human condition. The problem, then, is one of predicting future performance. Given what is known about people whose achievements have been remarkable, we believe that gifted children should be defined (as suggested by Renzulli et al., 1981) for purposes of education as those who have demonstrated or show potential for:

1. High ability (including high intelligence)
2. High creativity (the ability to formulate new ideas and apply them to the solution of problems)
3. High task commitment (a high level of motivation and the ability to see a project through to its conclusion)

The reason for using the multiple-criterion definition is that all three characteristics—high ability, high creativity, and high task commitment—seem to be necessary for truly gifted performance in any field (Renzulli, 1978).

Figure 9.2 illustrates the notion that giftedness is defined as a combination of these three characteristics (the shaded area shared by the three circles), but only when an individual applies them to performance in a specific endeavor. In an operational definition of giftedness, general ability is less important than specific performance; as Renzulli et al. (1981) state, "We do not offer courses or college majors in IQ, nor do people pursue careers or avocational activities in ideational fluency or semantic transformations . . . these are general abilities within the clusters that are *brought to bear* on specific areas of human expression" (p. 27).

PREVALENCE

Federal financial assistance for special education for gifted and talented students ended in 1981 (Stronge, 1986). Consequently, the U.S. Department of Education does not publish an official prevalence estimate of giftedness. However, it has been assumed in federal reports and legislation that 3 to 5 percent of the school population could be considered gifted or talented (Mitchell and Erickson, 1978; Sisk, 1981).

Obviously the prevalence of giftedness is a function of the definition chosen. If giftedness is defined as the top X percent on a given criterion, the question of prevalence has been answered. Of course, if X percent refers to a percentage of a national sample, the prevalence of gifted pupils in a given school or cultural group may vary from the comparison group. When IQ is used as the sole or primary criterion for giftedness, more gifted children will come from homes of higher socioeconomic status, have fewer siblings, and have better-educated parents (Barbe, 1956; Fisch, Bilek, Horrobin, and Chang, 1976). Although giftedness by nearly any

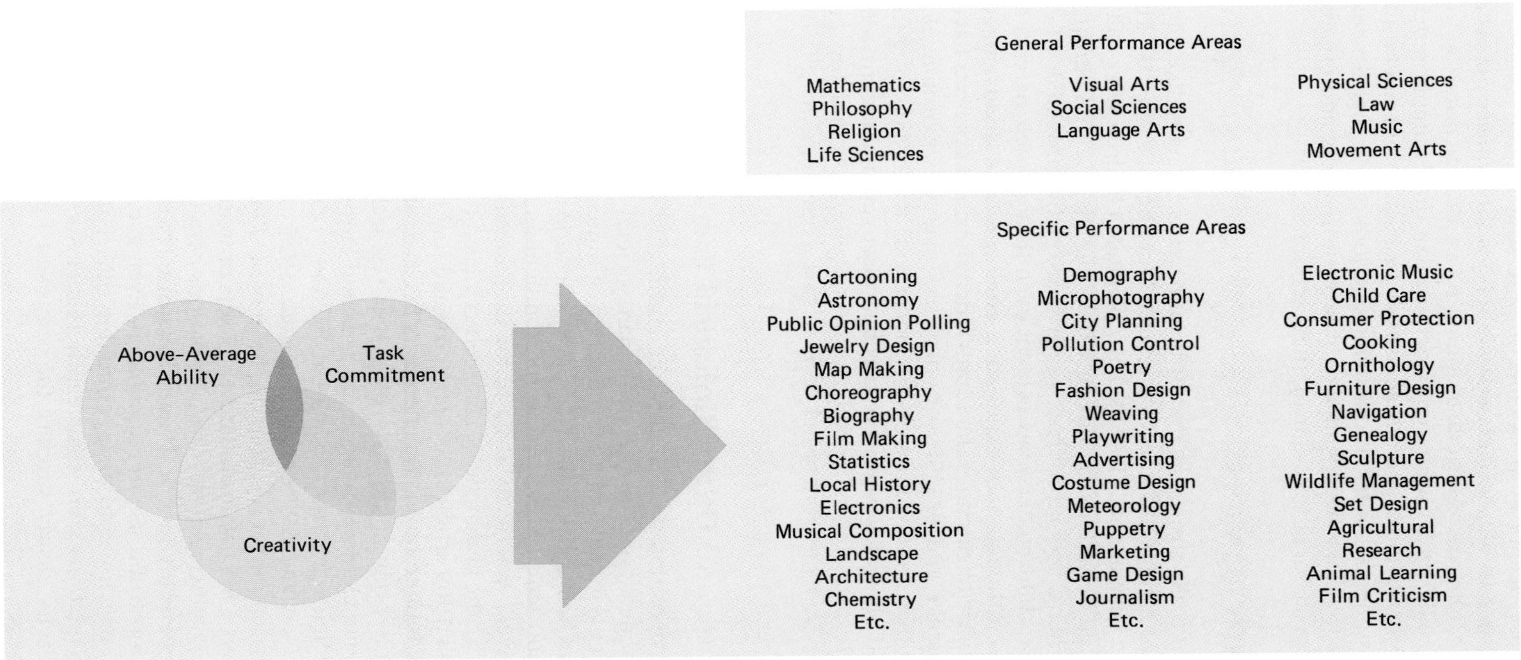

General Performance Areas

Mathematics	Visual Arts	Physical Sciences
Philosophy	Social Sciences	Law
Religion	Language Arts	Music
Life Sciences		Movement Arts

Specific Performance Areas

Cartooning	Demography	Electronic Music
Astronomy	Microphotography	Child Care
Public Opinion Polling	City Planning	Consumer Protection
Jewelry Design	Pollution Control	Cooking
Map Making	Poetry	Ornithology
Choreography	Fashion Design	Furniture Design
Biography	Weaving	Navigation
Film Making	Playwriting	Genealogy
Statistics	Advertising	Sculpture
Local History	Costume Design	Wildlife Management
Electronics	Meteorology	Set Design
Musical Composition	Puppetry	Agricultural Research
Landscape Architecture	Marketing	Animal Learning
Chemistry	Game Design	Film Criticism
Etc.	Journalism	Etc.
	Etc.	

Above-Average Ability

Task Commitment

Creativity

Figure 9.2 *Graphic representation of the definition of giftedness.*
SOURCE: J. S. Renzulli, S. M. Reis, and L. H. Smith, *The Revolving Door Identification Model* (Mansfield, Conn.: Creative Learning Press, 1981), p. 28. Reprinted with permission.

definition occurs in all socioeconomic strata, gifted children are not distributed equally across all social classes when IQ is the primary means of identification. This is one of the reasons for abandoning IQ as the sole criterion for defining giftedness.

Renzulli (1982) argues convincingly that the assumption that only 3 to 5 percent of the population is gifted is needlessly restrictive and may result in many potentially gifted students' contributions being overlooked. He suggests that 15 to 25 percent of all children may have sufficient ability, motivation, and creativity to exhibit gifted behavior at some time during their school career.

ORIGINS OF GIFTEDNESS

It is not really surprising that brilliant parents are more likely to have gifted children than are parents of average or retarded intelligence. We also know that an impoverished environment is less likely to produce children who will fulfill their potential for gifted behavior than one in which models of gifted performance, opportunities for learning, and appropriate rewards are richly provided. Of course, the giftedness of some children becomes evident even though their parents are intellectually dull and even though they experience environmental disadvantages. But the statistical probability of giftedness increases when the child's parents have higher than average intelligence and provide a better than average environment for the child. Some things that are not fully understood about the origins of giftedness and will take particularly well-designed research to discover, include the *relative* contribution of **genetic** and environmental factors to giftedness and the *precise nature* of the genetic and environmental factors that contribute to giftedness (see Gallagher, 1985).

Genetic and Other Biological Factors

The proposition that intelligence and highly valued abilities are inherited is not a very popular one in our egalitarian society. It can be used as a springboard for arguments for selective reproduction of humans (with intelligence or other characteristics being the primary factors in selection of mates) and as a reason to downplay the importance of improving environmental conditions for citizens already born or conceived. Americans' distaste for the notion that intelligence is inherited is illustrated by the avalanche of outraged criticism that followed the publication of Arthur Jensen's 1969 article in which he argued that black children do not score as high as white children on intelligence tests because of genetic factors. Nevertheless, a considerable body of child development research supports the assertion that among Caucasian children living in America and Europe, 50 to 75 percent of the *variation* in intelligence is due to genetic factors (Bouchard and McGue, 1981; Freeman, 1981; Newland, 1976; Scarr-Salapatek, 1975).

One example of research on the genetic contribution to giftedness is provided by Nichols (1965), who studied 1507 sets of twins who took the National Merit Scholarship Qualifying Tests. The correlations between the scores of **monozygotic** (one-egg, genetically identical) and **dizygotic** (two-egg, not genetically identical) twins on various subtests were compared. Even accounting for periods of separation and illness, which would have resulted in different environmental conditions for twins, the correlations were significantly higher for identical than for nonidentical twins. The results clearly support the argument for a genetic factor in intelligence or giftedness.

Biological factors that are not genetic may also contribute to the determination of intelligence. Nutritional and neurological factors, for example, may partially determine how intellectually competent a child becomes. In previous chapters we pointed out that severe malnutrition in infancy or childhood, as well as neurological damage at any age, can result in mental retardation. But does it follow that superior nutrition and neurological status early in life contribute to superior intelligence?

Fisch et al. (1976) provide data that show no relationship between neurological status and superior intelligence at 7 years of age. Over a period of years they followed the development of 2023 children born at the University of Minnesota hospitals. The incidence of neurological or physical abnormality, infection, anoxia, and trauma in the newborn period was the same for children who at the age of 7 years had low (79 or less), average (80–119), or superior (120 or higher) IQs. In addition, it was found that definite neurological abnormality at age 1 and at age 7 and inadequate speech, language, or hearing at age 5 were not significantly less common among the children with superior IQs than among those with average intelligence (although these abnormalities were significantly more common among children with low IQs). From the time they were a year old, the children of superior intelligence were found to have a significantly larger head circumference than children of average IQs, and the superior children were significantly taller and heavier than those of average intelligence from the time they were 4 years old.

Fisch and associates found head circumferences to be the earliest biological indicator of superior intelligence. Motor performance measures and neurological data obtained in infancy did not distinguish intellectually superior children (see also Willerman and Fiedler, 1974). These findings "would suggest that studies that are concerned with intellectual superiority must be formulated differently from those dealing with intellectual impairment" (Fisch et al., 1976, p. 485). It is not known whether the earliest superior physical characteristics (head circumference, height, and weight) of intellectually superior children represent the effects of a superior physical and social environment, a genetic effect that becomes obvious only after the child has attained the age of a year or more, or a combination of environmental and genetic effects. Studies of the gifted, such as Terman's classic studies, typically have shown them to be physically superior to others of lesser intelligence in characteristics such as height, weight, attractiveness, and health in adulthood as well as in childhood. However, it is not clear whether these physical characteristics are a result of the generally superior environments of the gifted or of another factor that accounts for superior intellect (see also Cornell, 1984; Gallagher, 1966).

More males than females are considered gifted and creative. By an overwhelming margin, men achieve outstanding status and recognition more frequently than women of the same age. However, there is no conclusive evidence that these performance differences are the result of biological differences. The available research points far more clearly to social and cultural expectations as an explanation for the disproportionate number of males who are recognized as gifted (Callahan, 1979, 1981; Eccles, 1985).

In summary, genetic factors clearly are involved in the determination of giftedness. Environmental influences alone cannot account for the fact that some individuals perform so far above the average. We emphasize, however, that an individual does not inherit an IQ. What is inherited is a collection of genes that, along with experiences, determine the limits of intelligence and other abilities (Zigler and Farber, 1985).

Environmental Factors

Since the beginning of systematic, longitudinal studies of gifted children by Terman (1926), the finding that gifted children are more likely to come from homes in which the parents are above average in income and education than from less privileged homes has been confirmed and reconfirmed many times. Predictably, Fisch and his colleagues (1976), for example, found that superior parental social and educational background was the best correlate of superior intelligence in their sample of 7-year-olds (see also Willerman and Fiedler, 1974). Certainly it is true that gifted children are found in all social strata, including poor homes where the parents may have little or no education and lower than average intelligence. This has been recognized since Terman's early studies. But there are some who have persistently denied any correlation between giftedness (at least as it is defined here) and the socioeconomic and educational levels of the parents. Marland, for example, in his 1972 report to Congress, said, "The assumption that the gifted and talented come from privileged environments is erroneous" (p. 17). Had Marland's statement been *"only* from privileged environments," it would have been accurate. The idea that there is no correlation appears to be supported only by wishful thinking.

Beyond the obvious general advantages often found in homes of higher socioeconomic and educational level (more intellectual stimulation from adults, fewer children, greater encouragement for achievement, more reading material, increased opportunities for travel, and other enriching experiences), we do not know precisely *how* superior home environments are related to higher intelligence.

Research has shown that parents differ greatly in their attitudes toward and management of their gifted children. Some parents view having a gifted child as positive, some as negative; fathers appear to see their children as gifted less often than mothers (Cornell, 1983, 1984). A study of individuals who have been successful in a variety of fields has shown that the home and family, especially in the child's younger years, are extremely important (Bloom, 1982; Bloom and Sosniak, 1981). The following were found to occur in the families of highly successful persons:

- Someone in the family (usually one or both parents) had a personal interest in the child's talent and provided great support and encouragement for its development.
- Most of the parents were role models (at least at the start of their child's development of talent), especially in terms of life style.
- There was specific parental encouragement of the child to explore, to participate in home activities related to the area of developing talent, and to join the family in related activities. Small signs of interest and capability by the child were rewarded.
- Parents took it for granted that their children would learn in the area of talent, just as they would learn language.
- Expected behaviors and values related to the talent were present in the family. Clear schedules and standards for performance appropriate for the child's stage of development were held.
- Teaching was informal and occurred in a variety of settings. Early learning was exploratory and much like play.
- The family interacted with a tutor/mentor and received information to guide the child's practice (interaction included specific tasks to be accomplished, information or specific points to be emphasized or problems to be solved, a set time by which the child could be expected to achieve specific goals and objectives, and the amount of time to be devoted to practice).

- Parents observed practice, insisted that the child put in the required amount of practice time, provided instruction where necessary, and rewarded the child whenever something was done especially well or when a standard was met.
- Parents sought special instruction and special teachers for the child.
- Parents encouraged participation in events (recitals, concerts, contests, etc.) in which the child's capabilities were displayed in public.

One may conclude that children who realize their potential for accomplishment most fully have families that are stimulating, directive, supportive, and rewarding of their abilities (see Besemer and Besemer, 1986). Research does not, however, indicate much else about how families encourage gifted performance. Moreover, little is known regarding the appropriate and helpful involvement of parents in their gifted children's schooling (Callahan and Kauffman, 1982; Colangelo and Dettmann, 1983; Page, 1983).

Several studies, including Terman's early work, have found that some cultural or ethnic groups (especially Jews) produce a higher than average number of gifted children even when differences in socioeconomic level are taken into account (Gallagher, 1966; Mistry and Rogoff, 1985). Lesser, Fifer, and Clark (1965) found mental ability higher in middle-class than in lower-class children. They also found that some ethnic groups scored higher in some areas. It may be that striving for upward social mobility and the high value attached to achievement in specific areas among certain cultural and ethnic groups contribute to giftedness. (Remember that motivation to achieve is an important feature of our definition.) However, in all studies of social and cultural factors related to giftedness it has been difficult or impossible to separate these factors from genetic influences.

Cultural factors that work against the development and recognition of gifted females were reviewed by Callahan (1979, 1981) and Eccles (1985). Females simply

Environmental conditions that contribute to the development of giftedness include opportunities to learn advanced skills, guidance and support from parents or other adults, appropriate role models, encouragement to explore interests and talents, availability of special teachers, clear expectations for achievement, and recognition for performance.
(*left*: Larry Mulvehill/Photo Researchers; *right*: Michal Heron/Woodfin Camp & Associates)

have not been provided with the motivation to enter into many academic disciplines or careers that have by tradition been dominated by males, such as chemistry, physics, medicine, and dentistry. When females do enter these fields, they are often rewarded inappropriately (according to irrelevant criteria or with affection rather than promotion) for their performance. English literature has tended to portray females as wives, mothers, or "weaker" sisters who are either dependent on males or sacrifice themselves for the sake of males who are dominant. These barriers to giftedness in females have only recently been brought forcefully to public attention, and it is too early to tell what benefits will result from their removal.

In summary, environmental influences have much to do with how a child's genetic endowment is expressed in performance. But neither environment nor genetics can be entirely responsible for the performance of gifted or retarded individuals. Genetic factors apparently determine the range within which a person will function, and environmental factors determine whether the individual will function in the lower or upper reaches of that range. One's collection of genes constitutes a **genotype:** the expression of that genotype in performance, which is referred to as a **phenotype,** is determined by environmental factors. That is, genetic factors (genotype) set the upper and lower limits; environmental factors determine the actual level of functioning (phenotype) within those limits. How much, then, can performance be improved by environmental enrichment? Zigler and Farber (1985) comment as follows:

> We . . . assert that it would be just as difficult for environmental intervention to raise a genotype for an IQ of 60 to a phenotypic expression of 100 as it would be to change a 100 IQ genotype to 140. This viewpoint reflects the growing disillusionment with the "naive environmentalism of the 60's" (see Scarr, 1981). Put more succinctly, retarded children cannot be made normal. Producing genius, which has become something of a cottage industry in recent years, is likewise destined to be a futile effort. (p. 400)

SCREENING AND IDENTIFICATION

Measurement of giftedness is a complicated matter. Some components cannot be assessed by traditional means. In addition, the particular definition of giftedness will determine how test scores are interpreted. But if it is indeed important to identify gifted children early so that they will be aided in the development of their special potential to make a unique and valuable contribution to society, then it is important that good screening and measurement methods be used.

Effectiveness and Efficiency of Screening Techniques

Renzulli and Smith (1977) suggest some definitions of effectiveness and efficiency. They define *effectiveness* in terms of the appropriateness of children's placement in special programs for gifted students, appropriateness being determined by ratings of regular classroom teachers and special program teachers. *Efficiency* is defined as "(a) the amount of time (in terms of professional and clerical staff/hours) that was devoted to identification activity and (b) the cost in dollars for carrying out these activities" (p. 513). According to Renzulli et al. (1981), a case study approach, in which aptitude and achievement test scores, teacher ratings, past academic performance, parent ratings, and self-ratings are taken into account, has advantages over the more traditional procedures based only on test scores. The advantages are greater efficiency and effectiveness, using Renzulli and Smith's (1977) definition, and greater effectiveness in identifying minority group students (Renzulli, 1973). Note that part of the case study approach is obtaining aptitude (intelligence) and achievement test scores. This approach uses *additional* information; it does not substitute other sources of data for test scores.

Devices are now available to help structure and objectify teachers' judgments. Renzulli, Hartman, and Callahan (1975) have presented a Scale for Rating Behavioral Characteristics of Superior Students. The teacher is asked to rate each pupil on a series of four-point scales related to four different classes of characteristics: learning, motivation, creativity, and leadership. The items on which the teacher rates students were derived from research studies of the characteristics of gifted individuals. Rating scales also serve another purpose: they provide guidance for the classroom teacher who must deal with gifted children. A good rating scale will help the teacher define giftedness more clearly and thus know what characteristics to watch for and foster in children.

Renzulli and Delcourt (1986) note that four criteria have been used in identifying gifted students: (1) test scores, (2) academic mastery in specific domains (e.g., mathematics), (3) creative productivity in specific domains or interdisciplinary areas, with products being assessed by teacher judgment and student interest and willingness to pursue advanced follow-up activities, and (4) long-range creative productivity (the ultimate criterion, which can be used to identify gifted persons only after the fact of their performance). Test scores have been the most widely used criteria, although selection on the basis of testing alone is now widely viewed as inappropriate:

> The test-score-as-criterion design has undoubtedly been popular because of its convenience and tidiness of arbitrarily equating giftedness with certain levels of IQ scores. But the performance-based designs help us to raise important issues about how one uses . . . intelligence *and other* potentials in situations that require the display and development of gifted behaviors. As one person put it, "I know IQ is important, but you just can't major in IQ." (Renzulli and Delcourt, 1986, p. 23)

Measuring Creativity

Nearly every definition of giftedness that is taken seriously today includes an explicit statement that the gifted person is highly creative (see Torrance, 1986). But how can creativity be measured? As Petrosko (1978) notes, measuring creativity presents a challenging paradox—devising a standardized way of capturing a nonstandard behavioral product. Because of the convenience of test scores, to which Renzulli and Delcourt (1986) referred, researchers and publishers are often pressured to devise creativity tests. But as Treffinger (1986) has commented:

> We must recognize that creativity is one of the most complex of human functions; it is unrealistic to expect that there ever will be (or that there should be) a single, easily administered, simply scored test booklet that educators can use to decide who is at least one standard deviation above other students in creativity. (p. 16)

Tests have been criticized as inadequate measures of creativity on much the same grounds that tests have been criticized as measures of intelligence. That is, scores on the tests are affected by many factors that have nothing to do with the actual ability one wishes to measure. Instead of defining creativity in terms of test scores, Wallach

(1985) notes that "creativity may be best understood as what characterizes the work done at the cutting edge of a given field by those who have mastered it" (p. 117). Wallach suggests that research should focus on the identification of discipline-specific approaches to improving instruction and the study of creative people's accomplishments as they develop across their entire life spans.

What does creative performance entail? How can it be fostered? Answers to these questions demand analysis of the structure of the particular discipline. The box on p. 429 is an example of a gifted mathematician's approach to fostering creativity in mathematics. Many of us find the notion of creativity in mathematics foreign, although we may readily understand what is involved in creativity in other disciplines.

PHYSICAL, PSYCHOLOGICAL, AND BEHAVIORAL CHARACTERISTICS

Although intellectual precocity has been recognized throughout recorded history (see Benbow and Stanley, 1983; Hollingworth, 1942, Stanley, 1975), there has been a persistent stereotype of the gifted individual as one who is physically weak, socially inept, narrow in interests, and prone to emotional instability and early decline. Terman's early studies, and many others, shattered the myth that giftedness carries with it a set of undesirable characteristics. In fact, it now appears that gifted children tend to be superior in every way—in intelligence, in physique, in social attractiveness, in achievement, in emotional stability, even in moral character. The danger now is a developing stereotype of the gifted child as "superhuman," as someone immune to ordinary frailties and defects.

This new stereotype probably has its roots in a misunderstanding of (or simply insufficient attention to) two statistical phenomena: dispersion of scores around a mean and intercorrelation among characteristics. Although it is true that *as a group* gifted people are superior in almost every characteristic, individuals deviate from the mean for the group. There are indeed gifted children who are weak, small, sickly, socially obtuse, underachieving, unattractive, or otherwise below par compared to agemates of normal intelligence. Gifted children who are handicapped have been neglected, partly because it is hard for us to entertain the thought that handicapped people can be superior in any way (Maker, 1977; Whitmore and Maker, 1985) or that gifted people may have disabilities (Fox, Brady, and Tobin, 1983). Gifted children as a group have specific characteristics that show about as much variation around the mean as the variation shown by any other group around its mean.

Furthermore, the intercorrelation among the characteristics of gifted children can be misleading. For example, could it be that physical superiority actually is a characteristic of children of higher socioeconomic status, many of whom happen to be gifted? It is not really clear which attributes of children who are superior in ability, creativity, and motivation are just coincidental with giftedness. Here, of course, we will be making generalizations about a group, not individuals.

Physical Characteristics

As we have mentioned, study after study, beginning with Terman's work, has shown that gifted children as a group are taller, heavier, stronger, more energetic, and healthier than other children their age who have average intelligence (Martinson,

Creative Work in Mathematics

Most school people have no conception of creative work in mathematics. When I teach gifted students, I start them on "baby research," at whatever level they are ready for. Since even in special classes for the gifted, there are usually wide variations in ability, I like to give problems where it is easy to get some interesting results, but where one can go as far as one's ability permits.

Thus with very young children (6–7 years old), I may tell about Lower Slobbovia, where there are only pennies and 2-cent pieces. How many ways can a Slob make 5 cents into change? The children may give the answers:

Number of pennies	Number of 2-cent pieces
1	2
3	1
5	0

Thus 3 ways in all. We then set up a table for recording our data:

Number of cents	Number of ways to make change
1	
2	
3	
4	
5	3
6	
7	
8	
9	

Now the children work out the rest of the table. They soon see a pattern. Can we predict the next entry in the table? Can we predict further ahead, say the number of ways a Slob can make 15 or 20 cents? Is there a reason for the pattern? They are encouraged to make conjectures and test them. Then we investigate what happens in Upper Slobbovia, where they have only pennies and 3-cent pieces. For homework they examine the situation if these countries unite, so that now there are pennies, 2-cent and 3-cent pieces.

Then, I tell the pupils to invent their own countries, each with its own coinage. Each is to investigate the change problem in his/her own country, look for patterns, test predictions, search for reasons. When they report their results, we compare them. Are there relations between the patterns for different countries?

This is an example of a problem that can be studied at every level from first grade to post-doctoral. Each student can do something interesting, but how far he can go depends only on his ability. When he knows algebra or geometry or calculus he can dig deeper.

Another example is: imagine that you are living on the surface of a cone. Assume that you can measure, calculate, and reason, but you cannot fly off your world to see it from the outside. What can you find out about your world? What are the shortest paths, the "straight lines"? Where are all the points 5 inches from a given point? Make parallel columns on the blackboard. In one column write what you know about the geometry on a plane, a flat world. In the other column, write the corresponding facts about your conical world. Thus each fact that the students know about geometry suggests a natural problem about the cone. At the elementary and junior high school levels the pupils will work largely empirically. At the high school level they will search for proofs. They may investigate similarly a spherical or a cylindrical world, or some other surface of their own choice.

I have given these examples to show concretely what sort of thing can be done in mathematics for the gifted. Many educators are unaware of the fascinating possibilities for creative work in mathematics, and the alternatives to feeding the students the same stale old dish of beans at a faster pace.

SOURCE: P. C. Rosenbloom, "Programs for the Gifted in Mathematics," *Roeper Review*, 1986, *8*, 245.

Brightest Girls Find Their Place At Mary Baldwin

STAUNTON (AP) — When Katie Burkhardt was 4, her parents thought she might have a learning disability. They told a neurologist of Katie's trouble with spelling, how she would sometimes reverse the order of the letters.

The doctor didn't seem worried. He gently reminded Michael and Rita Burkhardt that their daughter was learning to spell two or three years earlier than most children do.

Katie, of Virginia Beach, never lost that head start. This week she will start classes at Mary Baldwin College in Staunton as a rangy, tanned 14-year-old with brown eyes and a great white smile.

She expects to have her high school diploma and a bachelor's degree by the time she is 18. She hasn't made up her mind about a career, but she could be a lawyer before she is old enough to buy a bottle of champagne to celebrate. She could be a doctor at 22.

Katie and 26 other girls from 13 to 15 years of age attend Mary Baldwin's Program for the Exceptionally Gifted, or PEG, where they can earn a college degree at about the same time their friends back home finish high school.

The program, in its second year, is the only place in the country where extremely talented girls can combine high school and college study at a women's college.

The PEG students are among the brightest in the country. Their IQs range from 130 to nearly 170; 100 represents normal intelligence for adults. When they took the Scholastic Aptitude Test in seventh and eighth grades, they scored from 950 to 1,400. A perfect SAT score is 1,600, and 1,400 is high enough for even the most selective colleges.

Christine Garrison, director of the program, calls her students "light-year kids" because they are intellectually so far ahead of others their own age. "Even in a group of gifted kids they stand out ahead," she said.

"How about making sure we come across as real people, and not just little brains going to college?" said Katie Sharrar, 15, of Greeneville, Tenn., who has always resented the idea that being gifted meant being some kind of freak.

"It's a gift, but it's also a label," said Betsy Carson, 14, of Winston-Salem, N.C.

All of them came through public school systems. Some hated the prospect of high school, where they would be unchallenged, where it is often hard for a girl to be a good student and well-liked at the same time. Others, such as Katie Burk-

SOURCE: *The Charlottesville Daily Progress,* September 1, 1986, pp. B1, B16.

1961, 1973). Terman and Oden (1959) followed gifted children identified in Terman's earlier work (1926) into middle age and found that they maintained their superior physical characteristics. Many gifted children are outstanding in athletic ability and are superior competitors in a variety of sports.

Two cautions are in order. First, although gifted children clearly tend to outstrip their average agemates in both mental and physical characteristics by the time they are several years old, their superiority does not appear to be detectable at birth or even during the first year in most cases. Willerman and Fiedler (1974) and Fisch et al. (1976) found no reliable evidence from tests of motor or mental ability during the first year of life that would predict later precocity. Second, since there is a sizable correlation between IQ and socioeconomic status, the apparent physical superiority of gifted children may be a result of nonintellectual factors. Laycock and Caylor (1964), for example, found that the physical superiority of gifted children was less marked when they were compared to their less gifted siblings (who, of course, were of nearly identical socioeconomic background).

hardt, who would have gone to the 10th grade in Green Run High School this year, found it hard to sacrifice friends, activities and traditions of high school.

Lest anyone think the girls are simply cloistered for five years, by their second year they are usually taking several courses at Mary Baldwin with regular college students. They are required to volunteer with a community organization, such as a library or a nursing home, and Garrison sets up academic and social events with gifted students from nearby schools.

The program costs $11,145 a year. All but four students receive financial aid from the college and the state, although they cannot get grants and loans because they are too young.

What produces exceptionally gifted children?

"Academically talented kids tend to come from families that value knowledge," said Barbara A. Kerr, an expert on gifted education who teaches at the University of Iowa. "There does seem to be an inherited component having to do with memory and reasoning, but what's critical is an environment where a kid gets exposure to challenge and a love for learning."

Katie Burkhardt was born in Japan and raised in a variety of small towns in the Midwest and East before her family moved to Virginia Beach three years ago. Her father is sales director for PMI Inc. in Chesapeake, which makes concrete products, and her mother is a homemaker.

"The intelligence is there — we didn't really do anything to get that," Michael Burkhardt said. "That's a gift from God. The plan was that the intellect would almost take care of itself. We really tried to develop her personality, her decision-making processes."

Katie's parents encouraged her to try a lot of different things, to play the cello, to ride horses, to join dance classes. And especially to make friends.

When they first moved to Virginia Beach, Katie was in sixth grade, having her toughest year ever. "Kids would continually torment her and laugh at her on the bus because she was so smart," her father said. "She would come home and cry."

Gradually, with a lot of effort, she made friends and kept her grades up, managing straight A's last year as a ninth-grader.

While advocates of the handicapped have been fighting for years for mainstreaming, moving handicapped children into classes with regular students, research on highly gifted children suggests that they profit most by being with others of the same abilities.

"These kids need other bright people," said Garrison, who directed gifted programs in the Albemarle County schools and taught at the University of Virginia before coming to Mary Baldwin.

Kerr said research shows, generally, "bright kids do not benefit from constant exposure to the same-age peers who are intellectually average. If they're always right, if they're always the best 100 percent of the time, they learn contemptuousness."

By contrast, gifted children who have been able to compete with others of the same ability "learn what it's like to fail, learn what it's like to not be the best, learn what it's like to compete, learn compassion," said Kerr, author of the book "Smart Girls, Gifted Women."

"Our society still does such a good job of socializing for mediocrity," she said.

Nicole Angresano, 15, of Lynchburg admitted that she intentionally kept her grades down so she would fit in better with the pupils around her.

Some of the PEG girls said they immediately felt a sense of relief when they got to meet others their own age with the same ability to think.

Educational and Occupational Characteristics

Gifted children tend to be far ahead of average children in academic achievement. They learn to read easily; many of them are taught to read by their parents or teach themselves before they enter school. They have been shown to be more advanced in reading than in areas that require manual dexterity, such as writing and art, and more advanced in reading than math, which depends more on sequential development of concepts and skills (Gallagher, 1966). Contrary to popular opinion, which pictures gifted students as constantly bored with and antagonistic toward school, it has been found that most gifted children like school and love to learn (Gallagher, 1966). Many gifted students are younger than their classmates, because of their superior academic performance. The box above describes a program in Staunton, Virginia, for highly gifted girls. In this program, girls may complete a four-year college degree by the age at which most students finish high school. While only the most highly gifted are so far advanced beyond their agemates, some gifted stu-

Gifted children typically have high motivation to achieve and pursue their creative interests. (Susan McCartney/Photo Researchers)

dents start school earlier or advance through the grades more quickly than their age peers.

Not surprisingly, gifted people tend to enter occupations demanding greater than average intellectual ability, creativity, and motivation. Most find their way into the ranks of professionals and managers, and a high proportion distinguish themselves among their peers in adulthood. Occupationally, as educationally, they are winners (Feldman, 1984; Gallagher, 1985; Terman, 1926; Terman and Oden, 1959).

But again, it is important to remember that this description does not hold true for *every* gifted person. It is not unusual for a gifted child to go unrecognized by school personnel, to become unpopular with teachers because of such characteristics as inquisitiveness, unusual knowledge and wit, or boredom with unchallenging school work. It is an unfortunate fact that much talent goes to waste because school personnel are oblivious of the needs of gifted children or refuse to alter the lockstep plan of education for the sake of superior students.

Social and Emotional Characteristics

Gifted children tend to be happy and well liked by their peers. Many are social leaders at school. Most are emotionally stable and self-sufficient and are less prone to neurotic and psychotic disorders than average children. They have wide and varied interests and perceive themselves in positive terms (Coleman and Fultz, 1985; Janos and Robinson, 1985; Reynolds and Bradley, 1983; VanTassel-Baska, 1983).

When gifted students complain, what are their gripes? Galbraith (1985) studied the complaints of over 400 gifted students in six states. Approximately equal numbers of boys' and girls' responses to surveys and interviews were obtained. The

---

The Eight Great Gripes of Gifted Kids

1. No one explains what being gifted is all about—it's kept a big secret.
2. The stuff we do in school is too easy and it's boring.
3. Parents, teachers and friends expect us to be perfect, to "do our best" all the time.
4. Kids often tease us about being smart.
5. Friends who *really* understand us are few and far between.
6. We feel too different and wish people would accept us for what we are.
7. We feel overwhelmed by the number of things we can do in life.
8. We worry a lot about world problems and feel helpless to do anything about them.

SOURCE: J. Galbraith, "The Eight Great Gripes of Gifted Kids: Responding to Special Needs," *Roeper Review,* 1985, 7, 16.

---

students ranged in age from 7 to 18 years. The eight most frequent complaints are listed in the box above. Notice that most of these gripes are not peculiar to students identified as gifted. However, Galbraith's findings do suggest that gifted students need more than intellectual challenge in order to feel good about themselves and use their special abilities to the fullest.

One common and persistent, but erroneous, notion regarding gifted people, especially those who excel in the arts, is that they are prone to mental disease. The idea that there must be something of the lunatic in the creative genius has not been an easy one to get rid of (see Leo, 1984; Lombroso, 1905; Madden, 1833; and Sanborn, 1885, for fascinating comments on genius and insanity*). Even Freud theorized that artists turn away from the real world and toward creative endeavors because of unconscious conflicts. Such ideas have made it especially difficult to destroy the myth that creative excellence is linked to mental illness rather than to mental health. It is true that some great artists, musicians, and scientists have gone through periods of mental instability or psychosis, but their achievements were probably made in spite of, not because of, their emotional distress.

McNiff has pointed out that creative productions by psychotic individuals can be more logically explained as indications of emotional health than of emotional illness. In describing the art of a chronic schizophrenic woman, he states:

> Instead of attributing Priscilla's artistic production to psychopathological factors, one could argue that her intensely expressive art is a manifestation of personality strength. In communicating her thoughts and feelings through the visual arts, she is clearly functioning on a highly motivated and highly integrated behavioral level by consciously resolving many artistic problems that confront her in the course of her work—a level involving well developed ego controls that have not yet manifested themselves in her more general functioning. (1974, p. 12)

The misconception that gifted people tend to be social misfits and emotional cripples was abetted by a classic study by Leta Hollingworth of children who tested

---

*Lombroso wrote, "Just as giants pay a heavy ransom for their stature in sterility and relative muscular and mental weakness, so the giants of thought expiate their intellectual force in degeneration and psychoses. It is thus that the signs of degeneration are found more frequently in men of genius than even in the insane" (p. vi).

Gifted students often participate in technical or scientific activities that are characteristically pursued by adults.
(Ellis Herwig/Taurus Photos)

at 180 or higher IQ on the Stanford-Binet. She reported that these children were quite isolated from their peers and not very well adjusted as adults. But we should check into the representativeness of her sample of gifted children:

> In twenty-three years' seeking in New York City and the local metropolitan area, the densest center of population in this country and at the same time a great intellectual center attracting able persons, I have found only twelve children who test at or above 180 IQ (S-B). This number represents the winnowing from thousands of children tested, hundreds of them brought for the testing because of their mental gifts. (Hollingworth, 1942, p. xiii)

To categorize gifted people as those with IQs of 180 or higher is roughly like categorizing retarded individuals as only those with IQs of 20 or less (Zigler and Farber, 1985). Certainly it is reasonable to expect that children with such very high IQs might have more social problems and emotional difficulties than the more typical gifted child with an IQ in the 130 to 150 range, although follow-up research does not indicate that this is the case (Feldman, 1984). Most societies have a great deal of trouble dealing with extreme deviance of any kind, and someone with an IQ of 180 is certainly unusual. However, to characterize all extremely gifted people as maladjusted and eccentric plainly contradicts the facts (Gross, 1986; Reynolds and Bradley, 1983).

Again, it is well to consider *individual* children. The young genius may have unique problems in socialization, although the extraordinary resources that go with genius may equip such a child to handle unusual social situations (see Gross, 1986). If the child is fortunate enough to have intelligent and caring parents in addition to superior mental powers, it is reasonable to expect that social adjustment will be quite good. Mike Grost, a child with an extremely high (over 180) IQ, was described by his mother as a happy and gregarious boy who could easily adapt to play with his peers or to social relationships with adults, as the situation demanded. His wit and charm helped him achieve acceptance among classmates at Michigan State University even at the tender age of 10. Here is one example of how things went in his college classes:

> "Now today our topic is 'Changing Sexual Mores' in the societies and cultures under study . . . let there be light! . . . nobody wants to open the discussion, eh? Maybe we should all go home and I'll take your reticence into consideration the next . . . well, our 10-year-old is going to volunteer some insightful remarks—go ahead . . ."
>
> "Well, not that I speak from experience, but . . ."
>
> Pandemonium.
>
> "Quiet! Quiet! Class! Ahem! Perhaps, Mike, you had better qualify your position."
>
> "Yes sir, I apologize for unwittingly disrupting the class. And may I say that I didn't mean to imply that anyone else in this class *could* speak from experience . . ."
>
> Chaos. (Grost, 1970, p. 133)

All this is not to say that gifted students are immune to social and emotional problems. They may be particularly susceptible to difficulties if they have extremely high IQs or if they are subject to social conditions, such as peer pressure toward mediocrity, that mitigate against mental health (Janos and Robinson, 1985). It should come as no surprise to find that gifted students become upset and maladjusted when they are discriminated against and prevented from realizing their full potential (see box on p. 436). But that reaction is not peculiar to any group of children, exceptional or average along any dimension. Finally, it should be noted that, as in the case of physical superiority, socioeconomic status may partially account for the apparent social superiority of gifted children and youth. Higher socioeconomic status is a correlate of social acceptance and emotional health, and its relative influence compared to the influence of cognitive superiority is unknown.

Moral and Ethical Characteristics

There is a tendency among most of us to hope that those who are the brightest are also the best—that moral attributes such as fairness, honesty, compassion, and justice go along with intelligence. Gifted individuals should be able to do the right as they see it, and they should be able to see the right more quickly or more profoundly than the average person. However, the corruptibility of major figures in every profession in every society raises questions about the moral and ethical superiority of gifted persons. The atrocities of the Nazis in Germany, some of whom were able, creative, motivated individuals, testify to the fact that gifted and talented people *can* make criminal use of their potential. But are the moral and ethical shortcomings of these figures characteristic of gifted people as a group?

Here again, we must qualify the discussion by stating that there are individual differences among gifted people and that not every gifted person will be characterized by the description that fits the group. Most studies show gifted people to be superior to average individuals in concern for moral and ethical issues and in moral behavior (Gallagher, 1985). At an earlier age than most, gifted children tend to be concerned with abstract concepts of good and evil, right and wrong, justice and injustice (Galbraith, 1985; Hollingworth, 1942, Martinson, 1961; Terman, 1926). They tend to be particularly concerned with social problems and the ways they can be resolved. The immoral, unethical gifted individual seems to be the exception

Being Gifted: Some Unhappy Feelings

On Being Gifted, written by twenty gifted and talented high school students, contains a few brief comments by fourth-, fifth-, and sixth-graders from Norwich, Connecticut that illustrate the negative self-perceptions and social stigma that gifted and talented students sometimes experience.

Peer Pressure

To many with exceptional talents a problem arises concerning their peers and contacts with other people. Of course the gifted student is proud of his powers but his peer group makes it very difficult for him.

People with special gifts get a great deal of attention from the society around them. For me it is not as great a problem as for others simply because I am in my own age group. However, prodding, teasing, and resentment do present themselves as foolish obstacles.

Students in my peer group are jealous about my ability. I do my best to share with them my knowledge and I try to help them whenever possible but all this is to no avail. (Jealousy stirs teasing—which gets to be a drag.)

Caught in the Middle

As I sit in a classroom of a smalltown high school, I am listening to the teacher begin a lecture for the day. He asks a question regarding the assigned homework, chapter 25 in our book. I raise my hand and respond correctly to his query. He continues to ask questions and I continue to answer them. After a couple of rounds I begin to look around sheepishly to see if anyone else has his hand raised. No one does so I answer again. I hear annoyed mutterings from my classmates. I just know they're thinking, "She thinks she knows everything." So in a futile effort to conform and satisfy them, I sink down in my seat just a little and let the rest of the questions slide by. The teacher becomes angry that no one has read the assignment and feels he must repeat the chapter. And another day is wasted.

So goes it, and unfortunately, too often. As a result, I do not feel challenged nor do I attempt to be when I find myself in such a class. One alternative, which in my school is extremely limited, is to sign up for those courses which are designed for people planning to major in that specific area. But alas, not enough teachers, nor enough money in the budget for books or supplies. So suffer, kid!

Pressures from Teachers

Often our peers get their cues when our teachers begin to reject us. This often happens when an instructor feels threatened by the exceptional student. In my school this takes the form of neglect. The teacher does not fill my needs because he will not devote extra time to me and often totally ignores my suggestions.

Often, instructors, though not actually threatened, feel that the gifted student has had enough recognition and therefore bypass him. Many times one of my teachers has preferred to work extremely hard with his favorite remedial workshop student than to talk to me. This sort of behavior has caused me to doubt my priorities concerning education.

Who's on Our Side?

Occasionally teachers seem to be foes rather than allies. Unfortunately, many times teachers are on an ego trip, preferring to help slower students so that they might appear to be all-powerful and all-knowing.

If a student happens to learn rapidly or already has a knowledge of the subject from prior exposure, the teacher develops a deep resentment for the child.

In my case, I had a teacher of algebra who developed this type of resentment. I understood the material because of previous contact with the subject. I seldom missed problems on tests, homework or on the board; when I did, I caught his wrath.

I don't know the psychological reasons; I only know this situation shouldn't exist.

SOURCE: *On Being Gifted* (New York: American Association for Gifted Children, 1978), pp. 21–29.
© 1978 by the American Association for Gifted Children. Used by permission of Walker & Co.

rather than the rule. It may be that gifted people are the ones who have the greatest potential for helping individuals and societies resolve their moral and ethical dilemmas. It is worth remembering that almost any definition of giftedness will include people who are recognized as moral giants (Gruber, 1985).

ATTITUDES TOWARD GIFTED CHILDREN AND THEIR EDUCATION

It is relatively easy to find sympathy for handicapped children, but more than a little difficult to turn that sympathy into public support for effective educational programs. It is difficult to elicit sympathy for gifted children, and next to impossible to arrange sustained public support for education that meets their needs (Tannenbaum, 1979, 1986). When the Russians launched the world's first artificial satellite in the late 1950s, American pride and competitiveness and the obsession with "national security" aroused special interest in gifted children who could keep us in the space race. But when America pulled far ahead, society's attitudes toward the most capable of our children reverted to the traditional indifference or even resentment.

As many writers have pointed out, support for education of gifted and talented students runs in cycles. When national security is a major concern, programs for the gifted flourish because excellence is seen as a means of defense; when the nation feels secure from outside threats, programs are allowed to wither in favor of emphasis on educational equity. Gallagher (1986) and Gold (1986) note that the relative emphasis on equity and excellence is an international as well as a national phenomenon.

At present, federal legislation and funding for gifted students in elementary and secondary schools is nonexistent. However, state funds allocated for education of gifted students have increased significantly during the past few years (Mitchell, 1986). Nevertheless, monies spent on education of gifted and talented students are minuscule in comparison to funds allocated for handicapped students. Clearly, a rationale is needed to argue the case for special education for our most able students.

We can state two rational arguments for providing special education for gifted children:

1. Every child is entitled to public education that meets his or her needs. Because of their exceptional abilities, gifted children need special education if they are to realize their potential for personal fulfillment and social contribution. To deny gifted children special education suited to their needs is to deny them equal opportunity, their birthright as American citizens.
2. Society will be best served if the talents of its most capable problem solvers are cultivated. Gifted children are the most precious natural resource for solving the future problems of society, and that resource can be ignored only at great peril. As Terman remarked, "It should go without saying that a nation's resources of intellectual talent are among the most precious it will ever have. The origin of genius, the natural laws of its development, and the environmental influences by which it may be affected for good or ill, are scientific problems of almost unequaled importance for human welfare" (1926, p. v).

These two arguments for providing special education for gifted students—do it for the sake of the children and do it for the sake of us all—obviously have not been enough to bring about either a wave of sentiment or a flurry of action on their behalf. In fact, the attitude we often encounter is that if gifted children are really so capable, they will find ways to help themselves.

Very recently, however, national interest in the education of gifted students has increased, sparked by President Reagan's National Commission on Excellence in Education—the "A Nation at Risk" report published in 1983 (see Council for Exceptional Children, 1984). Federal legislation supporting education of gifted children has been proposed, and many states have increased their budgets for educating their gifted children (Association for the Gifted, 1984; Mitchell, 1986). Nevertheless, gifted children and youths remain the most underserved population in our nation's schools. Programs for gifted students are not yet safe from antagonistic attitudes and attacks on their evaluation (see Baer, 1980; Callahan, 1983; Council for Exceptional Children, 1984; Gallagher, 1985; Karnes, 1983; Keating, 1980; Myers and Ridl, 1981; Renzulli, 1980; Sapon-Shevin, 1984).

Gallagher (1986) describes American society's attitude toward gifted and talented students as a love-hate relationship. Our society loves the good things that gifted people produce, but it hates to acknowledge superior intellectual performance. Opponents of special education for gifted students argue that it is inhumane and un-American to segregate gifted students for instruction, to allocate special resources for the education of those already advantaged, and that there is a danger of leaving some children out when only the ablest are selected for special programs (Baer, 1980; Myers and Ridl, 1981; Sapon-Shevin, 1984). Yet segregation in special programs, allocation of additional resources, and stringent selectivity are practices enthusiastically endorsed by the American public when the talent being fostered is athletic. The opposition develops only when the talent is academic or artistic.

Let us take a closer look at the arguments against special education for gifted and talented students that have been advanced by Baer (1980), Myers and Ridl (1981), and Sapon-Shevin (1984). Note that the same arguments can be used against special education for handicapped children.

1. The children cannot be identified with great reliability (compare the difficulties in identifying ED, LD, and EMR students).
2. More children are identified in some social classes or ethnic groups than in others.
3. Identified children receive special educational resources that others do not, although many nonidentified students could profit from those same resources.
4. Students may have special needs in one area but not in another, or at one time but not at another.
5. Identified students are set apart from their peers in a way that may stigmatize them.

In our opinion, one cannot argue against special education for gifted and talented students without arguing against special education in general, for all special education involves the recognition of individual differences and the accommodation of those differences in schooling.

The lack of research evidence supporting the effectiveness of educational programs for gifted students is also a factor underlying the fickle support of education for such children. There is simply not enough scientific research clearly indicating that gifted children become gifted adults who contribute to the social welfare or are personally fulfilled because of the influence of special education programs (Weiss and Gallagher, 1982). Although it can be argued on the basis of sound logic, common sense, and anecdotal reports that special education should be provided for gifted children, it is impossible to point to controlled research studies showing the effects of such education. Given this failure to prove the effectiveness of special education, it is perhaps understandable that taxpayers are not clamoring for programs and politicians are not allocating funds for the education of gifted students (Callahan, 1983). Callahan (1986) suggests that the wrong questions are often asked in evaluating programs. When the primary objective of a program is the provision of education that is appropriate for the capabilities of the students, then the major evaluation questions should involve the appropriateness of the education provided, not the outcome of producing more productive citizens.

Legal arguments for education of gifted students are quite different from those for education of handicapped students. Much of the litigation for educating handicapped children was based on the fact that handicapped children were being excluded from school or from regular classes, leading to the argument that they were being denied equal protection of law. Gifted students are seldom denied an education or access to regular classes, so the legal basis for special provisions to meet their needs is less clear (Stronge, 1986).

NEGLECTED GROUPS OF GIFTED STUDENTS

There has been recent concern for neglected groups—gifted children and youth who are disadvantaged by economic needs, racial discrimination, handicaps, or sex bias—and it is not misplaced. We must face two facts: (1) Gifted children from higher socioeconomic levels already have many of the advantages, such as more appropriate education, opportunities to pursue their interests in depth, and intellectual stimulation, that special educators recommend for those who are gifted. (2) There are far too many disadvantaged and handicapped gifted individuals who have been overlooked and discriminated against, resulting in a tremendous waste of human potential.

The Problem of Underachievement

Students may fail to achieve at a level consistent with their abilities for a variety of reasons. Many females achieve far less than they might because of social or cultural barriers to their selection of or progress in certain careers. Students who are members of racial or ethnic minorities are often underachievers because of bias in identification or programming for their abilities. Students with obvious handicaps are frequently overlooked or denied opportunities to achieve. Still, underachievement cannot be explained simply by sex, race, or handicap discrimination; many males, nonminority, and nonhandicapped students also are underachievers. Underachievement of gifted and talented children can result from any of the factors that lead to underachievement in any group, such as emotional conflicts or a poor home environment. A very frequent cause is an inappropriate school program—school work that is unchallenging and boring because the gifted student has already mastered most of the material. And gifted underachievers often develop negative self-images and negative attitudes toward school (Delisle, 1982; Whitmore, 1980). When a student shows negative attitudes toward school and self, any special abilities he or she may have are likely to be overlooked.

Whitmore (1986) suggests that lack of motivation to excel is usually a result of a mismatch between the student's motivational characteristics and opportunities provided in the classroom. Students are typically highly motivated when (1) the social climate of the classroom is nurturant, (2) the curriculum content is relevant to the students' personal interests and is challenging, and (3) the instructional process is appropriate to the students' natural learning style. Whitmore suggests an approach to the problem of underachievement that is consistent with gifted students' advanced reasoning abilities. First, the teacher should study the problem systematically by observing the student's performance and behavior in various settings. Second, the teacher should share those observations with the student, indicating the hypothesized causes of the problem. Third, the teacher should attempt to develop a sense of partnership between the student and the parent or teacher(s) involved in the problem.

This sense of partnership is most likely to evolve when the teacher works with the student to define the problem precisely in terms of specific behavior and its probable consequences, generate alternative ways in which the student and adults could respond to the problem, select an alternative, and evaluate the outcome (or select another alternative if the prior attempt failed). This approach is consistent with the suggestion of Belcastro (1985) that behavior modification techniques may enhance certain desirable attributes of gifted students—their ability to analyze situations and devise means of coping with hostile or boring environments.

Underachievement must not be confused with nonproductivity (Delisle, 1981). A lapse in productivity does not necessarily indicate that the student is underachieving. Gifted students should not be expected to be constantly producing something remarkable. But this points up our difficulty in defining giftedness: How much time must elapse between episodes of creative productivity before we say that someone is no longer gifted or has become an underachiever? We noted earlier that giftedness is in the performance, not in the person. Yet we know that the unrelenting demand for gifted performance is unrealistic and can be inhumane.

Gifted Minority Students

Three characteristics may be used to define gifted students with unique needs because of their minority status: cultural diversity, socioeconomic deprivation, and geographic isolation (Baldwin, 1985). These characteristics may occur singly or in combination. They create unique needs for different reasons. Children from minority cultural groups may be viewed negatively, or the strengths and special abilities valued in their culture may conflict with those of the majority (see box, p. 441). Children reared in poverty may not have toys, reading materials, opportunities for travel and exploration, good nutrition and medical care, and many other advantages typically provided by more affluent families. Lack of basic necessities and opportunities for learning may mask intelligence and creativity. Children living in remote areas may not have access to many of the educational resources that are typically found in more populated regions.

Adjustments must be made in identification procedures and programming to include minorities in education of gifted and talented students. Different cultural and ethnic groups place different values on academic achievement and areas of performance. Stereotypes can easily lead us to overlook intellectual giftedness or to over- or under-rate children on any characteristic because they do not conform to our expectations based on their ethnic identity or socioeconomic status (Baldwin, 1985; Callahan, 1981; Sisk, 1981).

A Minority within a Minority: The Culturally Different Gifted and Talented

In 1975, a special conference was held to which twenty gifted and talented high school juniors and seniors were invited. One outcome of the conference was publication of a book, *On Being Gifted,* which was written entirely by the young participants. The reflections of these young people on their experiences and feelings and their recommendations for other gifted and talented youths make fascinating reading. One of the topics dealt with by several of the contributors is the problems of cultural minorities. A young native American wrote:

Are You a Minority within Our Gifted and Talented Minority?

Our Indian culture views gifted and talented youth in a type of religious manner. For our part, it takes quite a bit of intelligence to understand what goes on around us—such as the religious ceremonies. The elderly people believe you are nothing unless as an Indian you know you *are* an Indian and are fully aware of your culture.

But, in retrospect, we have the same interpretations of various aspects in life, whether it be of old legends or of religious beliefs.

Sometimes I am quite confused over certain things because of my two different cultures. I feel you have to adjust yourself to completely understand society *now.*

Educational opportunities for gifted and talented native Americans are a lot stronger now. There are more chances for higher education at more institutions, but we definitely need an even greater force to educate the rural gifted and talented native American.

Living in a rural area is undoubtedly different from living in an urbanized residence. I don't have much of an opportunity to increase my learning ability. Libraries and various other learning centers are situated in distant places requiring transportation and time for further studying. Yet, living in a rural area does have a basic learning value also, such as studying in secluded places where "city noise" is non-existent or sometimes just studying life itself. We have time and a place to do that without distraction.

Although I feel I have matured quite fast in the last several months since early admission to the local university, my life has not changed much because of my so-called "unique learning needs." Other than that, our school requires the usual classes to be taken in order to graduate with a certain amount of credit hours. This is where kids become bored. We all need a change of environment which goes along with selecting a wider variety of chosen fields. I myself became very depressed when higher educational opportunities were non-existent for students with unique learning needs. In addition, our community also fails to cooperate. *I mean, there are all these organizations helping the underachieving students, when I feel I need help, too!*

SOURCE: *On Being Gifted* (New York: American Association for Gifted Children, 1978). © 1978 by the American Association for Gifted Children. Used by permission of Walker & Co.

Handicapped Gifted Students

The education of gifted handicapped students is a field that is just emerging (Whitmore and Maker, 1985). The major goals of the field today are identification of gifted students with specific disabilities, research and development, preparation of professionals to work with gifted handicapped children and youth, improvement of interdisciplinary cooperation for the benefit of such children and youth, and preparation of students for adult living.

A substantial percentage of eminent persons have been handicapped (Porter, 1982). Nevertheless, the special abilities of handicapped people are often overlooked. Whitmore and Maker (1985) note that our stereotypic expectations for disabled people frequently keep us from recognizing their abilities. For example, if a child lacks the ability to speak or to be physically active, or presents the image associated with intellectual dullness (e.g., drooling, slumping, dull eyes staring), we tend to assume that the child is mentally retarded. The following is an example of how the gifted handicapped child is typically overlooked:

> Kim was classified at birth as "profoundly handicapped," owing to cerebral palsy of severe degree. Early treatment began with a physical therapist and a language development specialist, but at 7 years of age, Kim still had extremely limited motor control and no expressive language. Confined to a wheelchair, she slumped considerably and had difficulty holding her head erect. Her droopy posture, continual drooling, and lack of language skills led professionals to design educational experiences for her that were identical to those provided for mentally retarded children. She was placed in a public school for the profoundly and multiply handicapped, in which development of basic self-help skills comprised the principal educational goals.

> Kim's parents, who were teachers, had observed through the years her increased effort to communicate with her eyes and began to believe there was more intellect within that severely limited body than they had assumed. They stimulated her with questions and problems to solve while providing her with a relatively simple means of indicating responses. When a group of students from the school for multiply handicapped were scheduled to be mainstreamed into an open-space elementary school, they insisted that Kim be included. After two months of stimulation in a normal classroom setting, the provision of an adapted communicator she could manage, and participation in a more normal instructional program, Kim evidenced remarkable development. She exhibited a capacity to learn quickly and to remember exceptionally well; superior problem-solving and reasoning skills; and a keen interest in learning. Within four months she was reading on grade level (second) despite missing two years of appropriate reading instruction in school. An adapted form of the Stanford-Binet was administered, and her performance qualified her as mentally gifted. (Whitmore and Maker, 1985, p. 16)

We do not want to foster the myth that giftedness is found as often among handicapped students as among those who are not handicapped. But clearly gifted handicapped students have been a neglected population. Whitmore and Maker (1985) estimate that at least 2 percent of handicapped children may be gifted (recall that 3 to 5 percent is the typical estimate for the general population).

EDUCATIONAL CONSIDERATIONS

Today, the consensus of leaders in the field is that special education for gifted and talented students should have three characteristics: (1) a curriculum designed to accommodate the students' advanced cognitive skills, (2) instructional strategies consistent with the learning styles of gifted students in the particular content areas of the curriculum, and (3) administrative arrangements facilitating appropriate grouping of students for instruction. Fox and Washington (1985) note that these characteristics are consistent with the recommendations of a 1972 report to Congress by Sidney Marland, who was then the U.S. commissioner of education. Although special education for gifted and talented students is not mandated by federal law or regulation, the Marland report has influenced state plans.

States and localities have devised a wide variety of plans for educating gifted students. Generally, the plans can be described as providing **enrichment** (additional experiences provided to students without placing them in a higher grade) or **acceleration** (placing the students ahead of their age peers). Seven plans for grouping students and modifying the curriculum for gifted and talented students are described by Weiss and Gallagher (1982) as follows:

1. *Enrichment in the classroom:* Provision of a differentiated program of study for gifted pupils by the classroom teacher within the regular classroom, without assistance from an outside resource or consultant teacher.
2. *Consultant teacher program:* Differentiated instruction provided within the regular classroom by the classroom teacher with the assistance of a specially trained consultant teacher.
3. *Resource room/pullout program:* Gifted students leave the classroom on a regular basis for differentiated instruction provided by a specially trained teacher.
4. *Community mentor program:* Gifted students interact on an individual basis with selected members of the community for an extended time period on a topic of special interest to the child.
5. *Independent study program:* Differentiated instruction consists of independent study projects supervised by a qualified adult.
6. *Special class:* Gifted students are grouped together and receive instruction from a specially trained teacher.
7. *Special school:* Gifted students receive differentiated instruction in a specialized school established for that purpose.

Not every community offers all the options listed here. In fact, there is great variation in the types of services offered within the school systems of a given state and from state to state. As one might expect, large metropolitan areas typically offer more program options than small towns or rural areas. New York City, for example, has a long history of special high schools for gifted and talented students.

The future holds particularly exciting possibilities for the education of gifted and talented students. Fox and Washington (1985) note that advances in telecommunications, the presence of microcomputers in the home and classroom, and the call for excellence in American education are three developments with implications for educating our most able students. Telecommunications, including instructional television, telephone conferencing, and electronic mail, are technological means of facilitating the interaction of gifted students and their teachers over wide geographical areas. These communication systems are important for extending appropriate education to gifted students in rural and remote areas. The possible uses of microcomputers for enhancing the education of gifted students are enormous. Using software tutorials, accessing data banks, playing or inventing computer games that are intellectually demanding, writing and editing in English and foreign languages, learning computer languages, and solving advanced problems in mathematics are only a few of the possibilities. The concern for excellence, especially in science and math education, spurred by the report of the National Commission on Excellence in Education in the early 1980s, is an important impetus for educating gifted students. If efforts to reform American education are continued and if they include attention to upgrading instruction for students at all levels of ability, then special programs for gifted and talented students may become more common.

ONE PROFESSIONAL'S PERSPECTIVE

Paul W. Dugger

B.A., Earth Sciences, Pacific Lutheran University
M.A., Public School Administration, Pacific Lutheran University
Current Position: District Coordinator of programs for the highly capable (QUEST) in Puyallup School District, Washington

Mr. Paul Dugger began his career as a regular elementary teacher in 1972. He has been in his current position for over six years. As program coordinator, Mr. Dugger is assisted by two half-time teachers and a secretary aide. The QUEST program currently serves 144 elementary students from 15 public and 3 private schools in the Puyallup area. The resource center for the program includes 4 classrooms centrally located in the district. Students are selected for QUEST on the basis of ability and achievement measures, coupled with parent and teacher evaluations of creativity, performance, and task commitment. The students range in IQ from about 130 to 160 (average about 140), and their academic achievement is between 2 and 8 grade levels ahead of their age-mates'. About half of the students in the program are boys and half girls; about 8 percent are Asian and 3 percent are black or Native American, reflecting the composition of the school community. QUEST programming substitutes for one day each week in the students' neighborhood schools. Students are transported to the resource center, in which they are grouped with other students having like needs. Methods, materials, and organizational procedures are clearly different from the regular class in content, process, and product.

We asked Mr. Dugger the following series of questions:

What influenced your decision to become a teacher-administrator of high ability students? I chose education because I enjoy learning and sharing. Science especially attracted me because of my own quest for knowledge. I could not function in a static environment. Change revitalizes me. I began my career in teaching at the intermediate level and taught fifth grade for four years, the last three in an open-concept school in which I was free to be innovative and work especially with the more highly capable students. I transferred to the primary grades to gain expertise at that level. While there, I focused on developing science curricula and worked again with the most capable students. I decided to obtain a masters degree in administration and a principal's credential. During my administrative internship I was asked to develop and implement the district's newly envisioned gifted education program. I accepted and completed my internship in that capacity.

If you could change one thing about your job, what would it be? The most frustrating aspect of my present position is my inability to perform at my highest level due to conflicting demands on my time. I am constantly being torn between teaching and administrative tasks. Taking care of all the administrative paperwork inherent in developing, maintaining, and accounting for the program impinges on the time I could be spending on curriculum development and lesson preparation. Due to the nature of the curriculum, a greater amount of time is required for lesson preparation and correction of students' work. I feel I could have greater impact on the students I teach through increased communication with their teachers and neighborhood schools. I'd like to be a greater advocate for the needs of highly capable students when the district is making decisions about testing, textbook selection, or programming. And I'd like to have time to identify and link highly capable students with educational experiences that aren't available in the local district.

What major changes have occurred in the field since you began teaching? The most important change is increased awareness of the need for differentiated programming for the gifted and talented. Entire issues of many professional journals, as well as many popular magazines, have been devoted to this topic in recent years. Programs are spreading. A flood of teaching materials aimed at gifted and talented students has permeated teaching resource catalogs. Many of these materials are of questionable quality, although I am encouraged by the increasing focus on appropriate curriculum. Finally, there has been an increase in inservice opportunities for teachers and in graduate and undergraduate coursework in gifted education.

Describe for us the one student in your career with whom you

have had the most success.
Most of my "success stories" involve maintenance of skills and attitudes rather than dramatic turnarounds. The great majority of academically gifted and talented students are very well adjusted and exhibit high performance in school. For these students, the role of the educator is to recognize, cultivate, and encourage their abilities and provide an optimal match of instruction and individual needs. Many times the strongest students lose interest because they are not consistently challenged to exceed their present level of knowledge and understanding. Scott was a student who required special handling, however.

From a very early age, Scott had an exceptional curiosity, especially about reading, mathematics, and science. He began reading when he was 2 and was reading books on his own by age 3, at which age he also understood basic concepts of addition, subtraction, and multiplication. I met Scott when he was a first grader. His mother was worried because Scott told her "some of the things we are doing at school are not fun because I already know how to do them." Although testing indicated that his IQ was 147 and that he was reading at the 4.2 grade level and performing math at the 2.7 grade level, he was substantially below his age peers in physical development, especially fine motor skills. His first grade teacher was reluctant to have him attend the QUEST program, but his mother persisted and Scott was placed in the resource center one day per week. He continued in the gifted program during second and third grade. His mother related that "Scott began to tune out school in second grade, but QUEST kept him interested and enthusiastic in school." He is now in sixth grade—still small for his age (under 60 pounds), still having difficulty with written work due to poor motor skills, but maintaining an excitement for learning and a feeling of self-worth. He has developed lasting friendships with his intellectual peers which carries over into his home life. Scott says, "I have not only learned vast amounts of knowledge, but enjoyed it. I feel that QUEST has helped me and many others in that here we are not held back by people who are not as willing or able to learn."

How would you describe your work with the most difficult student with whom you've worked? Mike was referred to QUEST following testing by a school psychologist. He'd been referred for testing by his first grade teacher, who wrote "This is Mike's second year in first grade. Mike has been performing much below his abilities in reading, arithmetic, and penmanship. He makes many demands on the teacher and has occasionally disrupted the class in reading because of his behavior. Mike does not relate well to his peer group."

Mike's father indicated that he showed many signs of exceptional brightness as a preschooler. His lack of success in school was, therefore, unexpected. Daydreaming, uncooperative behavior, and limited ability to socialize with peers all seemed to contribute to his difficulties in school since kindergarten.

The psychologist reported that Mike seemed to enjoy the testing and wanted to please; however, his progress was frequently interrupted by a seeming compulsion to share ideas on how test items could be restructured or the instructions altered, demands to know why certain items were included, and information regarding the exact number of children of different ages who had passed various items. Mike also spent a great deal of time discussing his proposed inventions. The psychologist noted, "Failure to pay sufficient attention to directions often caused him not to get credit for very simple initial items on both verbal and nonverbal tasks. In general, he quickly grew impatient with work he perceived as easy and would do it incorrectly. On the other hand, he would show almost instant insight and total delight when performing teenage level tasks." His full-scale IQ was 127, but the psychologist felt that Mike's impatience and failure to attend to work he characterized as easy, in addition to his need to restructure tasks to his own liking, probably lowered his score.

The psychologist's findings did not qualify Mike for a learning disability program. So he was retained in a regular first grade classroom, provided with weekly counseling sessions, and enrolled in the QUEST program one day per week. He is now in sixth grade and continues to exhibit most of the problem behaviors described in first grade. He is a year and a half older than the other students in his class. His social skills are very poor, and he is a chronic underachiever. His report cards contain many D and F grades because he does not complete assignments. Mike has been in and out of counseling and has experienced deep depression. He dislikes school but shows enthusiasm for the gifted program. Although he experiences the same underachievement and inability to relate to peers in QUEST, he values the stimulation.

Mike will attend junior high school next year. He lacks the motivation, organization, and social skills to succeed. He was in the school system for over two years and had been labeled a failure before anyone recognized his high ability. Earlier identification and appropriate programming may have transformed Mike into a well-adjusted productive student.

Acceleration

Acceleration has not been a very popular plan, except with extremely gifted students. Nevertheless, the evidence in favor of acceleration is quite positive (Benbow and Stanley, 1983; Gross, 1986; Stanley, 1977, 1978, 1979: Stanley and McGill, 1986). Feldhusen, Proctor, and Black (1986) summarize the research on advanced placement of precocious students as follows:

> Examination of the research literature reveals that acceleration contributes to academic achievement. No negative effects on social or emotional development have been identified. If adjustment problems occur, they tend to be minor and temporary in nature. Conversely, failure to advance a precocious child may result in poor study habits, apathy, lack of motivation, and maladjustment. (p. 27)

Opponents of acceleration fear that gifted children who are grouped with older students will suffer negative social and emotional consequences, or that they will become contemptuous of their age peers. Proponents of acceleration argue that appropriate curriculums and instructional methods are available only in special schools or in regular classes for students who are older than the gifted child. Furthermore, proponents argue that by being grouped with other students who are their intellectual peers in classes in which they are not always first or correct, gifted students acquire a more realistic self-concept and learn tolerance for others whose abilities are not so great as their own. So far, the evidence seems clearly to support acceleration, especially in the case of the most gifted students.

Models of Enrichment

Renzulli (1977) has noted that many of the activities provided for children under the guise of "special education for the gifted and talented" cannot be justified. If gifted or average children spend their time playing games designed to foster creativity or problem-solving strategies, they are not being served well. If the traditional content-oriented curriculum (which emphasizes pouring facts into children's heads) is replaced by an equally inane process-oriented curriculum (which emphasizes pouring cognitive processes into children's heads), no real progress has been made. A defensible program for gifted pupils must state how education for them will be the same as and how it will be different from education for all children.

One model of enrichment that has received widespread attention is that described by Renzulli and his colleagues as the "Revolving Door Model" (Delisle and Renzulli, 1982; Renzulli, 1983; Renzulli et al., 1981). This model is based on the notion that children exhibit gifted behavior in relation to particular projects or activities on which they bring to bear their above-average ability, creativity, and task commitment (see Figure 9.3). Students selected into a "talent pool" through case study identification methods are engaged in enrichment activities that involve individual or small-group investigation of real-life problems; they become practicing pollsters, politicians, geologists, editors, and so on. The teacher (1) helps students translate and focus a general concern into a solvable problem, (2) provides students with the tools and methods necessary to solve the problem, and (3) assists students in communicating their findings to authentic audiences (i.e., consumers of information). Students may stay in the enrichment program as long as they have the ability, creativity, and motivation to pursue productive activities that go beyond the usual curriculum for students their age. Table 9-1 lists additional enrichment activities in which students identified for the talent pool may participate.

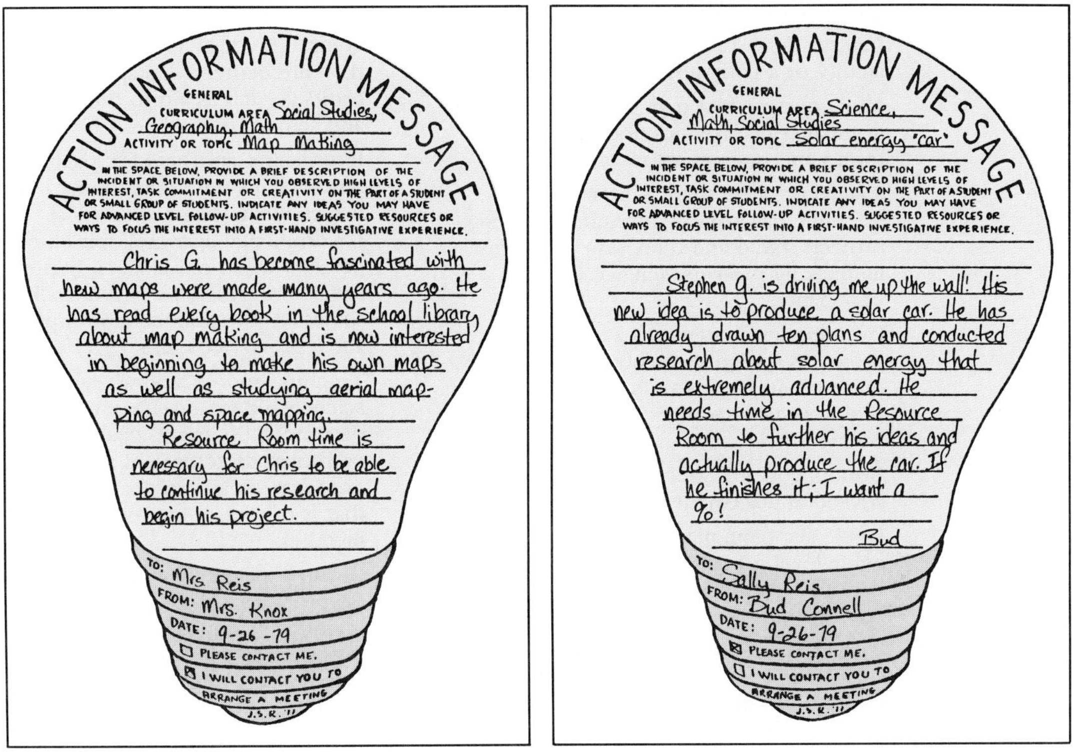

Figure 9.3 *Action information messages.*
SOURCE: J. S. Renzulli, S. M. Reis, and L. H. Smith, *The Revolving Door Identification Model* (Mansfield, Conn.: Creative Learning Press, 1981), pp. 86–87. Reprinted with permission.

Renzulli's enrichment model is designed to be operative during the regular academic year in elementary and secondary schools. The focus is on harnessing gifted students' ability, creativity, and commitment to a task to produce useful information and products. Examples of how gifted elementary and secondary school students can produce valuable information and products are provided by the cases of Monty Tew and Tom Churchill. Monty, a 10-year-old elementary school student in Texas, invented a device that converts the energy of sound waves into useful electrical energy (*Bulletin of the National/State Leadership Training Institute on the Gifted and Talented,* August, 1980). According to a United Press International story dated October 10, 1976, at the age of 15 Tom learned to forecast the weather with greater than 90 percent accuracy, a level better than that achieved by the National Weather Service. He began by forecasting the weather as a hobby and included his forecasts in the school newspaper he started in the third grade. Before he was old enough to get a driver's license, he had won $16,000 on a TV quiz show, done spots on local radio stations, and become a meteorologist for a cable TV station. He had appeared on network talk shows and had been considered as a once-a-week forecaster for ABC-TV's *AM America.* These boys' information and products were not a result of Renzulli's enrichment program, although they might have been. Renzulli and his colleagues describe projects in which gifted students design and complete studies

Table 9-1   Additional Services for Talent Poor Members

Independent study with a member of the faculty or a community resource person.

Mini-courses, field trips, and special seminars organized around particular topics and interest areas.

Special projects such as literary and scientific magazines, community action projects, radio and television programs, filmmaking projects, science fairs, newspapers.

Participation in new or existing club programs within the school and through other organizations such as 4-H Clubs, Junior Achievement, Scouting, Outward Bound.

Honors courses, special seminars, and advanced placement courses.

Grade skipping, placement in advanced grade-level groups, summer courses, adult education and community college courses, correspondence courses.

Participation in community programs such as amateur theatrical groups, symphonies, artists' workshops, community festivals, restoration projects, day-care centers, and special service projects such as aid to the handicapped, and senior citizens.

Internships, apprenticeships, and mentorships with community professionals, businesses, local governmental agencies, museums, and persons who hold leadership positions in special interest groups such as historical societies, environmental groups, animal shelters, service clubs.

Teaching and/or laboratory assistance to science and art teachers, media center personnel, librarians, coaching staff, band or chorus director, and any other faculty or staff person who deals with an area that is of special interest to a Talent Pool member.

Group and individual counseling, special experiences in career exploration, visits to college campuses, and career-day experiences with persons who work in areas of potential interest.

SOURCE: J. S. Renzulli, S. M. Reis, and L. H. Smith, *The Revolving Door Identification Model* (Mansfield, Conn.: Creative Learning Press, 1981), p. 80. Reprinted with permission.

that are useful to the community—surveying community attitudes toward environmental and economic issues, for example. At the University of Virginia a summer enrichment program for gifted elementary and secondary school students makes use of the university environment and personnel, which are not typically available to youngsters.

TEACHERS OF GIFTED STUDENTS

Teaching gifted students may at first thought seem easy. Who would not like to teach students who are particularly bright, creative, and motivated? In reality, teachers of gifted students, just like other special and general education teachers, are vulnerable to burnout (Dettmer, 1982). Gifted and talented students often challenge the "system" of school, and they can be verbally caustic. Their superior abilities and unusual or advanced interests demand teachers who themselves are highly intelligent, creative, and motivated (see Callahan, 1981; Lindsey, 1980).

The teacher must be adept at assessing students' abilities, interests, and commitment to tasks and skilled at helping other teachers recognize the characteristics that indicate a student could profit from special education. Frequent communication with regular teachers, observation, interpretation of test scores, and interviews with students, parents, and other professionals are required to identify gifted students. Figure 9.3 contains examples of "action information messages" devised by Renzulli et al. (1981) to help teachers communicate about students who may profit from an

Special Schools Open Worlds for Gifted Kids

Susan Wong didn't want to attend a "regular" high school; she suspected that the courses would be boring. Today, as a 14-year-old freshman at Stuyvesant High School in Manhattan, Wong is working on an independent project in a chemistry lab—and loving it.

"If I hadn't gotten in here," she says, "I don't know what I would have done."

Stuyvesant High looks like any other high school—with smooching couples and flying books—but its bulletin boards are layered with Shakespearean puns in Latin, applications for archaeological digs and posters that tease, "So you want to win a Nobel Prize . . ."

Stuyvesant is the oldest (1904) of the USA's 14 public high schools catering to 2.3 million gifted and talented kids. And New York has the most schools with four—Stuyvesant, Bronx High School of Science, Brooklyn Tech and the twin-campus La Guardia High School of Music and the Arts.

Most of these special schools—which many students must travel an hour or more to reach—stress science and math, but students also must complete English, social studies and other typical courses.

Optional classes, however, far exceed the usual high school fare with law, calculus, anatomy, Chinese and other advanced offerings. At Brooklyn Tech, for example, it's not unusual for students to complete eight or 10 years' worth of science before graduation.

SOURCE: Carol Atwater, *USA Today,* April 13, 1983, p. 3D. Copyright 1983 *USA Today*. Excerpted with permission.

enrichment program. When these messages are received by the special teacher, they must be followed up by observations and interviews with the teachers and students involved. If the follow-up indicates that the student could profit from enrichment activities, then the special teacher must devise a management plan specifying the method of study, resources to be used, activities to be pursued, intended products of the study, and intended audiences for the information. Only a teacher with broad interests, extensive information, and abundant creative energy will be able to accomplish the identification, instruction, and guidance of gifted students.

Lindsey (1980) suggests many personal, professional, and instructional characteristics that are important for teachers of gifted students, including the following:

- Understands, accepts, respects, trusts, and likes self
- Is sensitive to, supports, respects, and trusts others
- Has high intellectual, cultural, and literary interests
- Is flexible, open to new ideas
- Desires to learn; has high achievement needs and enthusiasm
- Is intuitive, perceptive
- Is committed to excellence
- Is democratic rather than autocratic
- Is innovative and experimental rather than conforming
- Uses problem-solving; doesn't jump to unfounded conclusions
- Seeks involvement of others in discovery
- Develops flexible, individualized programs
- Provides feedback; stimulates higher mental processes
- Respects creativity and imagination

Renzulli (1980) has said that these traits are pure "American Pie" and one would hope that *all* teachers would show them. One is probably safe in assuming, however, that teachers must exceed most of their pupils in creativity, intelligence, energy, and task commitment. Consequently, a teacher of gifted students must be above the average for all teachers on many of these traits (see Gallagher, 1985; Karnes, 1983).

SPECIAL CONSIDERATIONS IN EDUCATING THE PRESCHOOL CHILD

Early identification of exceptional abilities is important. Tests have particular limitations in identifying young gifted children. Intelligence test scores of young children are not very stable; they tend to change a lot over a period of time, so that without other information they are not very good indicators of even potential giftedness. Robinson, Roedell, and Jackson (1979) believe that tests of academic achievement are useful in early identification if they are used as part of a carefully chosen and competently administered test battery. The battery must sample a wide range of abilities and must allow the child to demonstrate his or her *best* performance. Some tests designed for young children simply do not contain items difficult enough to tap skills at the top of the gifted child's ability. Furthermore, many young children are not easy to test. They are anxious or shy or so inquisitive about the testing materials that a particularly experienced and skillful examiner is required for accurate assessment of their abilities.

Robinson et al. (1979) note that young gifted children can be identified by the fact that they exhibit skills like those of ordinary children who are older. For example, an 18-month-old child may use language like that of most children who are 30 months; a 3-year-old may do multiplication and division problems like those done by average third-graders; or a 4-year-old may be able to read and draw maps as well as most adults (see examples of Chris and Jonathan in box). Robinson (1977) argues that gifted youngsters are not qualitatively different in cognitive characteristics, only quantitatively different. That is, their minds do not work in an essentially different way from the minds of most children; they only work faster and at a more advanced level. Gifted children, according to Robinson, are not cognitively different; they are developmentally advanced.*

Any program for meeting the educational needs of young gifted children must take into account the fact that they can perform like older children in particular skill areas. The conclusion of some researchers (Robinson, 1977; Robinson et al., 1979) is that since gifted children are only quantitatively different in their abilities, they do not need special programs. Instead, what young gifted children need is the freedom to make full and appropriate use of the school system as it now exists. They need the freedom to study with older children in specific areas where their abilities are challenged. Gifted children need to be able to get around the usual eligibility rules so they can go through the ordinary curriculum at an accelerated rate. Unfortunately, relatively few gifted preschoolers receive the kind of educational programming that is appropriate for their abilities. This is especially the case for young gifted children who are also handicapped, poor, or from minority families (Karnes, 1983; Karnes, Shwedel, and Lewis, 1983).

---

* Recall that in Chapter 2 we discussed the theory that mentally retarded children are not cognitively different from most children, but rather show a developmental delay or lag in learning. These theories suggest that the cognitive characteristics of retarded individuals are the mirror image of those of gifted ones.

The Gifted Preschooler: Chris and Jonathan

Chris came running into the house, bubbling over with excitement, "Mommy, mommy. I did it! I put the bird back together. Its bones were scattered all around. Look, I have a skeleton of a bird! I guess I am a paleontologist for real! Let's go to the library and find out what species it is."

Chris, only 4, resembles Stephen Gould, world renowned paleontologist whose interest also began at an early age. A visit to the dinosaur exhibit at the American Museum of Natural History inspired both to the world of paleontological inquiry. Will Chris eventually become a paleontologist? Chris has both advanced knowledge and an all-consuming interest in paleontology.

From this scenario we can attest readily to his superior levels in vocabulary development and comprehension skills. Intense interest, in-depth knowledge, and accelerated development in language provide positive evidence of giftedness. But more important, these characteristics strongly imply that Chris has educational needs different from most 4-year-olds.

Will these special needs be met within the school setting? Unfortunately there are a limited number of educational programs adequately equipped to address the unique requirements of children like Chris. Chris' parents, like most parents of bright preschoolers, voice their concern since many of these youngsters are already reading, composing original stories, and computing simple addition and subtraction problems on their own.

One would only have to listen and watch children like Chris to confirm the need for such services. These children frequently demonstrate advanced vocabularies and often an early ability to read. In addition, they seem to learn easily and spontaneously. Logic appears early in some bright youngsters, often to the embarrassment of adults.

For instance, Jonathan, at 3, requested a grilled cheese sandwich at a restaurant. The waitress explained that grilled cheese was not on the menu. Jonathan, determined to have his way, queried, "Do you have cheese and bread?" The waitress nodded, "We do . . ." "Then," Jon blurted, "do you have a pan?" Jon got his sandwich. When the sandwich arrived, the waitress took beverage orders. Jonathan ordered a milkshake, but this time the waitress was one step ahead. "Jonathan, we have milk and ice cream, but I'm sorry we don't have any syrup." To which Jon asked, "Do you have a car?"

Other youngsters may show advanced abilities in number concepts, maps, telling time, and block building. Their skills in such activities far exceed that of their age-mates. Not only do these characteristics define gifted preschoolers but also provide a rationale and structure for intervention.

SOURCE: S. Baum, "The Gifted Preschooler: An Awesome Delight," *Gifted Child Today,* 1986, *9*(4), 42–43.

Gifted preschoolers may be intellectually superior and have above-average adaptive behavior and leadership skills as well (Childs, 1982; Perez, Chassin, Ellington, and Smith, 1982). Their advanced abilities in many areas, however, do not mean that their development will be above average across the board. Emotionally, they may develop at an average pace for their chronological age. Sometimes their uneven development creates special problems of social isolation, and adults may have unrealistic expectations for their social and emotional skills because their cognitive and language skills are so advanced (see Gross, 1986). They may require special guidance by sensitive adults who not only provide appropriate educational environments for them, but also discipline them appropriately and teach them the skills

Gifted preschool children demonstrate an ability to do things that older children of average ability do. (Daemmrich/Stock, Boston)

required for social competence (Baum, 1986; Roedell, 1985). They may need help, for example, in acquiring self-understanding, independence, assertiveness, sensitivity to others, friend-making skills, and social problem-solving skills.

SPECIAL CONSIDERATIONS IN EDUCATING THE ADOLESCENT AND ADULT

If there is a central issue in the education of gifted adolescents, it is that of acceleration versus enrichment. Proponents of enrichment feel that gifted students need continued social contact with their age peers. They argue that gifted students should follow the curriculum of their agemates and study topics in greater depth. Proponents of acceleration feel that the only way to provide challenging and appropriate education for those with special gifts and talents is to let them compete with older students. They argue that since the cognitive abilities of gifted students are advanced beyond their years, they should proceed through the curriculum at an accelerated pace (see box on pp. 430–431 describing program at Mary Baldwin College).

One of the most articulate proponents of acceleration is Julian Stanley, who directs a special program of accelerated study in mathematics at Johns Hopkins University in Baltimore. His project, the Study of Mathematically Precocious Youth (SMPY), is a longitudinal research program that began in 1971 (Benbow and Stanley,

1983; George, 1979; Stanley, 1977, 1978, 1979; Stanley and George, 1978; Stanley and McGill, 1986). Each year a mathematics talent search is conducted in the seventh, eighth, and ninth grades of the Baltimore metropolitan area. Students who have already scored in the top 5 percent on an achievement test are given two tests designed primarily for above-average eleventh- and twelfth-graders: the College Board's Scholastic Aptitude Test, mathematical part (SAT-M), and the Mathematics Achievement Test, Level I. Individual students are then given counseling about educational options.

Depending on how precocious they are in mathematics, their motivation to do advanced study, and personal considerations, the students may pursue a variety of acceleration programs such as skipping a grade, doing early part-time college study, earning college credit by examination or correspondence courses, entering college early, or attending special fast-paced classes. The students will be followed over a period of more than two decades to observe their achievements and personal adjustment.

The outcomes of the SMPY program are reported to be very positive and include increased zest for learning and for life, enhanced feelings of self-worth and accomplishment, and reduction of egotism and arrogance (Stanley, 1977). Furthermore, these positive results have apparently been obtained also in the Minnesota Talented Youth Mathematics Program (Keating, 1979). Acceleration may be the better choice for students who are precocious in areas of study requiring reasoning that is not dependent on social experience. For students whose precocity is in areas requiring verbal skills and social reasoning, such as literature, it is more feasible to devise enrichment that is an adequate substitute for grade acceleration.

MANAGING THE CHILD IN SCHOOL

A particularly heavy responsibility for the welfare of gifted children falls on the regular classroom teacher because, although no reliable figures are available to indicate what percentage of gifted students are being served by special education, it is abundantly clear that the great majority are being educated in regular classrooms with average classmates. There are four basic things the regular classroom teacher should do to help prevent needless waste of talent:

1. The teacher should periodically review the characteristics of all the pupils in the class to guard against overlooking any child who may be gifted. Which students show particular ability, creativity, and task commitment? Are there pupils in the class, especially those who are economically disadvantaged or members of a minority group, whose abilities may be less obvious according to white middle-class standards or who may be masking their abilities because of peer pressure for conformity?

2. The teacher must analyze and adjust his or her educational requirements for gifted pupils. Is the gifted child turned off to education because the work is not challenging or is not suitable for his or her superior intellectual powers? Is the gifted child underachieving simply because he or she is not being given appropriate work? Especially with the underachieving child it is important to present specific educational tasks in a structured environment with the firm and consistent expectation that they will be completed. For a helpful annotated listing of teaching resources and references, see Karnes and Collins (1980).

3. The teacher must seek out the resources of the school and community that can be used to the advantage of gifted children. Are there other teachers or older students with knowledge of the problems and methods of inquiry in a field of special interest who can help the child in independent study or small-group activities? Are there community residents with special expertise who are willing to tutor the child or use him or her as an assistant?

4. The teacher should support whatever movement there may be in the school system toward establishing special programs for gifted pupils. Are there parents of gifted children whose pleas for special programs can be encouraged? Are there workshops for teachers? Does the school system employ resource teachers or specialists who will help regular classroom teachers find methods, materials, and community resources?

SUMMARY

Disagreements about definitions of giftedness center around the questions of exactly *how* gifted children are superior; how this superiority is measured; the degree to which the individual must be superior in order to be considered gifted; and who should make up the comparison group. Even the terms used can be confusing: *Precocity* indicates remarkable early development; *insight* involves separating relevant from irrelevant information and combining information in novel and productive ways; *genius* refers to rare intellectual powers; *creativity* has to do with the ability to express novel and useful ideas, to see novel relationships, to ask original and crucial questions; *talent* indicates a special ability within a particular area. In this chapter *giftedness* is considered to be cognitive superiority, creativity, and motivation in combination and of sufficient magnitude to set the individual apart from the majority of agemates and make it possible for him or her to contribute something of unique value to the society.

In recent years the use of the individually administered intelligence test as the only basis for defining giftedness has met with increasing dissatisfaction for several reasons. First, traditional intelligence tests are limited. Second, intelligence is being reconceptualized by leading researchers, who are searching for cognitive characteristics that define *general* intelligence. The thinking of gifted people appears to be *qualitatively* different from that of average individuals, perhaps along such dimensions as insightfulness. Third, new ideas about giftedness include the hypothesis that gifted performance is attainable only when a child is relatively free of biological impairments, mostly invulnerable to environmental stresses that limit performance, and reared in an environment that is supportive of performance. However, children exhibit gifted performance in specific domains; it would be possible, for example, for a physically disabled child to attain giftedness in any area not impaired by that child's specific physical disability.

It is suggested that giftedness be defined as demonstration of high ability, high creativity, and high task commitment. Therefore, a given child may be gifted at one time or in one situation and not in another. Giftedness is not an absolute, fixed human characteristic. Consequently the prevalence of giftedness is not known precisely. Perhaps 15 to 25 percent of the population has the potential for exhibiting gifted behavior at some time during their schooling.

The relative contribution of genetic and environmental factors to giftedness is not known, nor is the precise nature of these factors. But the evidence strongly suggests that the statistical probability of giftedness increases when a child's parents are higher than average in intelligence and provide a better than average environment. Although the correlation between superior intelligence and an above-average social and educational family background is positive, many socioeconomically disadvantaged children are also gifted. Current research suggests that one's collection of genes (genotype) set the upper and lower limits of performance; the actual performance (phenotype) within those limits is determined by environmental factors.

Early identification of gifted children is important, partly because such children have the potential to make valuable contributions to society. The most effective and efficient means of screening for giftedness is a case study approach, which includes aptitude and achievement test scores, teacher ratings, past academic performance, parent ratings, and self-ratings. Test scores alone are now seen as an inadequate basis for identification of gifted students. Creativity is an important aspect of giftedness, although measuring creativity is very difficult. Creativity is best understood as a characteristic of the behavior of people who have mastered a given field and are working at the cutting edge of their discipline.

The stereotype of brilliant people as physically weak, socially inept, and prone to emotional instability still exists. But considered as a group, gifted individuals tend to be superior not only in intelligence but also in physique, social attractiveness, achievement, emotional stability, and even moral character. They are not, however, "superhuman." Gifted people tend to excel in academic and occupational pursuits, although there are still many underachieving gifted children. Socially and emotionally, intellectually superior individuals tend, as a group, to be happy, well liked, stable, and less apt to have psychotic and neurotic disorders than average people. Despite historical and psychoanalytic theories to the contrary, genius and insanity are not inextricably linked. Like most of us, brilliant people can be corrupt and unscrupulous, but the majority appear to have a great concern for moral and ethical issues and behavior.

Current attitudes toward special education for gifted students leaves much to be desired. Those who argue against special education for gifted students may in reality be arguing against special education for any type of exceptional child. In recent years interest in education of gifted children has increased, but most gifted students in American public schools still receive no special services appropriate to their abilities.

Neglected groups of gifted students include underachievers—those who fail to achieve at a level consistent with their abilities, whatever the reason. Underachievement is often a problem of minority and handicapped students, whose special abilities tend to be overlooked due to biased expectations and/or the values of the majority.

Education of gifted and talented students should have three characteristics: curriculum designed to accommodate advanced cognitive skills, instructional strategies consistent with learning styles in particular curriculum areas, and administrative facilitation of grouping for instruction. Programs and practices in the education of gifted students are extremely varied and include special schools, acceleration, special classes, tutoring, and enrichment during the school year or summer. Administrative plans for modifying the curriculum include enrichment in the classroom, use of consultant teachers, resource rooms, community mentors, independent study, special classes, and special schools. Teachers of gifted students should exhibit characteristics that are desirable for all teachers, but probably must be particularly intelligent, creative, energetic, enthusiastic, and committed to excellence. Future developments in the education of gifted students will likely be influenced by telecommunications, the use of microcomputers in home and classroom, and the pressure for excellence in American schools.

Special considerations for the preschool child include providing stimulation to foster giftedness, early identification of special abilities, and special provisions, such as acceleration, to make education appropriate for the child's advanced skills. Acceleration versus enrichment is a central issue in the education of gifted adolescents and young adults. Programs of acceleration (especially in mathematics, in which students skip grades or complete college-level work early) have been evaluated very positively.

The regular classroom teacher has a large responsibility because the majority of gifted children receive their education alongside their average classmates. It is important, therefore, that teachers periodically review the characteristics of all pupils to ascertain which ones are intellectually exceptional. Teachers should also be prepared to analyze and adjust the educational requirements for gifted pupils. Perhaps the most important thing regular teachers can do is to support and encourage movements toward establishing special programs, for gifted children are a precious natural resource.

REFERENCES

Association for the Gifted. (1984). H.R. 5596: Answering your questions. *TAG Update, 8*(1), 1–2.

Baer, N. A. (1980). Programs for the gifted: A present or paradox? *Phi Delta Kappan, 61,* 621–623.

Baldwin, A. Y. (1985). Programs for the gifted and talented: Issues concerning minority populations. In F. D. Horowitz & M. O'Brien (Eds.), *The gifted and talented: Developmental perspectives* (pp. 251–295). Washington, D.C.: American Psychological Association.

Barbe, W. B. (1956). A study of the family background of the gifted. *Journal of Educational Psychology, 47,* 302–309.

Baum, S. (1986). The gifted preschooler: An awesome delight. *Gifted Child Today, 9*(4), 42–45.

Belcastro, F. P. (1985). Gifted students and behavior modification. *Behavior Modification, 9,* 155–164.

Benbow, C. P., & Stanley, J. C. (Eds.), (1983). *Academic precocity: Aspects of its development.* Baltimore: Johns Hopkins University Press.

Besemer, S., & Besemer, J. (1986). Raising a creative kid. *Gifted Child Today, 9*(3), 6–9.

Bloom, B. S. (1982). The role of gifts and markers in the development of talent. *Exceptional Children, 48,* 510–522.

Bloom, B. S., & Sosniak, L. A. (1981). Talent development vs. schooling. *Educational Leadership, 39,* 86–94.

Bouchard, T. J., & McGue, M. (1981). Familial studies of intelligence: A review. *Science, 212,* 1055–1059.

Callahan, C. M. (1979). Gifted women. In A. H. Passow (Ed.), *The 78th yearbook of the National Society for the Study of Education, Part I. The gifted and talented: Their education and development.* Chicago: University of Chicago Press.

Callahan, C. M. (1981). Superior abilities. In J. M. Kauffman & D. P. Hallahan (Eds.), *Handbook of special education.* Englewood Cliffs, N.J.: Prentice-Hall.

Callahan, C. M. (1983). Issues in evaluating programs for the gifted. *Gifted Child Quarterly, 27*(1), 3–7.

Callahan, C. M. (1986). Asking the right questions: The central issue in evaluating programs for the gifted and talented. *Gifted Child Quarterly, 30,* 38–42.

Callahan, C. M., & Kauffman, J. M. (1982). Involving gifted children's parents: Federal law is silent, but its assumptions apply. *Exceptional Education Quarterly, 3*(2), 50–55.

Cassidy, J., & Johnson, N. (1986). Federal and state definitions of giftedness: Then and now. *Gifted Child Today, 9*(6), 15–21.

Childs, R. E. (1982). A comparison of the adaptive behavior of normal and gifted five and six year old children. *Roeper Review, 4*(2), 41–43.

Clark, B. (1979). *Growing up gifted.* Columbus: Charles E. Merrill.

Colangelo, N., & Dettmann, D. F. (1983). A review of research on parents and families of gifted children. *Exceptional Children, 50,* 20–27.

Coleman, J. M., & Fultz, B. A. (1983). Special class placement, level of intelligence, and the self-concepts of gifted children: A social comparison perspective. *Remedial and Special Education, 6*(1), 7–12.

Cornell, D. G. (1983). Gifted children: The impact of positive labeling on the family system. *American Journal of Orthopsychiatry, 53,* 322–335.

Cornell, D. G. (1984). *Families of gifted children.* Ann Arbor, Mich.: UMI Research Press.

Council for Exceptional Children. (1984). Reply to "A Nation at Risk": Report of the CEC Ad Hoc Committee to Study and Respond to the 1983 Report of the National Commission on Excellence in Education. *Exceptional Children, 50,* 484–494.

Delisle, J. (1981). The non-productive gifted child: A contradiction of terms? *Roeper Review, 3,* 20–22.

Delisle, J. (1982). The gifted underachiever: Learning to underachieve. *Roeper Review, 4,* 16–18.

Delisle, J. R., & Renzulli, J. S. (1982). The revolving door identification and programming model: Correlates of creative production. *Gifted Child Quarterly, 26*(2), 89–95.

Dettmer, P. (1982). Preventing burnout in teachers of the gifted. *Gifted/Creative/Talented,* January–February, 37–41.

Eccles, J. S. (1985). Why doesn't Jane run? Sex differences in educational and occupational patterns. In F. D. Horowitz & M. O'Brien (Eds.), *The gifted and talented: Developmental perspectives* (pp. 251–295). Washington, D.C.: American Psychological Association.

Feldhusen, J. F., Proctor, T. B., & Black, K. N. (1986). Guidelines for grade advancement of precocious children. *Roeper Review, 9,* 25–27.

Feldman, D. H. (1984). A follow-up of subjects scoring above 180 IQ in Terman's "Genetic Studies of Genius," *Exceptional Children, 50,* 518–523.

Fisch, R. O., Bilek, M. K., Horrobin, J. M., & Chang, P. (1976). Children with superior intelligence at 7 years of age. *American Journal of Disease of Children, 130,* 481–487.

Fox, L. H., Brady, L., & Tobin, D. (Eds.), (1983). *Learning-disabled/gifted children.* Baltimore: University Park Press.

Fox, L. H., & Washington, J. (1985). Programs for the gifted and talented: Past, present, and future. In F. D. Horowitz & M. O'Brien (Eds.), *The gifted and talented: Developmental perspectives* (pp. 197–221). Washington, D.C.: American Psychological Association.

Freeman, J. (1981). The intellectually gifted. In K. I. Abroms & J. W. Bennett (Eds.), *Genetics and exceptional children.* San Francisco: Jossey-Bass.

Galbraith, J. (1985). The eight great gripes of gifted kids: Responding to special needs. *Roeper Review, 7,* 15–18.

Gallagher, J. J. (1966). *Research summary on gifted child education.* Springfield: Illinois State Department of Education.

Gallagher, J. J. (1985). *Teaching the gifted child* (3rd ed.). Boston: Allyn & Bacon.

Gallagher, J. J. (1986). Our love-hate affair with gifted children. *Gifted Child Today, 9*(3), 47–49.

Gallagher, J. J., & Weiss, P. (1979). *The education of gifted and talented students: A history and prospectus.* Washington, D.C.: Council for Basic Education.

George, W. C. (1979). The talent search concept: An identification strategy for the intellectually gifted. *Journal of Special Education, 13,* 221–237.

Gold, M. J. (1986). Gifted: Not "The same the whole world over." *Roeper Review, 8*(4), 252–256.

Grinder, R. E. (1985). The gifted in our midst: By their divine deeds, neuroses, and mental test scores we have known them. In F. D. Horowitz & M. O'Brien (Eds.), *The gifted and talented: Developmental perspectives* (pp. 5–35). Washington, D.C.: American Psychological Association.

Gross, M. (1986). Radical acceleration in Australia: Terence Tao. *Gifted Child Today, 9*(4), 2–11.

Grost, A. (1970). *Genius in residence.* Englewood Cliffs, N.J.: Prentice-Hall.

Gruber, H. E. (1985). Giftedness and moral responsibility: Creative thinking and human survival. In F. D. Horowitz & M. O'Brien (Eds.), *The gifted and talented: Developmental perspectives* (pp. 301–330). Washington, D.C.: American Psychological Association.

Guilford, J. P. (1959). Three faces of intellect. *American Psychologist, 14,* 469–479.

Guilford, J. P. (1967). *The nature of human intelligence.* New York: McGraw-Hill.

Guilford, J. P. (1975). Varieties of creative giftedness, their measurement and development. *Gifted Child Quarterly, 19,* 107–121.

Hollingworth, L. S. (1942). *Children above 180 IQ, Stanford-Binet: Origin and development.* Yonkers-on-Hudson, N.Y.: World Book Company.

Horowitz, F. D., & O'Brien, M. (1985). Epilogue: Perspectives on research and development. In F. D. Horowitz & M. O'Brien (Eds.), *The gifted and talented: Developmental perspectives* (pp. 437–454). Washington, D.C.: American Psychological Association.

Humphreys, L. G. (1985). A conceptualization of intellectual giftedness. In F. D. Horowitz & M. O'Brien (Eds.), *The gifted and talented: Developmental perspectives* (pp. 331–360). Washington, D.C.: American Psychological Association.

Janos, P. M., & Robinson, N. M. (1985). Psychosocial development in intellectually gifted children. In F. D. Horowitz & M. O'Brien (Eds.), *The gifted and talented: Developmental perspectives* (pp. 149–195). Washington, D.C.: American Psychological Association.

Jensen, A. (1969). How much can we boost IQ and scholastic achievement? *Harvard Educational Review, 39,* 1–123.

Karnes, F. A., & Collins, E. C. (1980). *Handbook of instructional resources and references for teaching the gifted.* Boston: Allyn & Bacon.

Karnes, M. B. (Ed.). (1983). *The underserved: Our young gifted children.* Reston, Va.: Council for Exceptional Children.

Karnes, M. B., Shwedel, A. M., & Lewis, G. F. (1983). Short-term effects of early programming for the young gifted handicapped child. *Exceptional Children, 50,* 103–109.

Kauffman, J. M. (1981). Historical trends and contemporary issues in special education in the United States. In J. M. Kauffman & D. P. Hallahan (Eds.), *Handbook of special education.* Englewood Cliffs, N.J.: Prentice-Hall.

Keating, D. P. (1979). Secondary school programs. In A. H. Passow (Ed.), *The 78th yearbook of the National Society for the Study of Education, Part I. The gifted and talented.* Chicago: University of Chicago Press.

Keating, D. P. (1980). Four faces of creativity: The continuing plight of the intellectually underserved. *Gifted Child Quarterly, 24*(2), 56–61.

Khatena, J. (1982). *Educational psychology of the gifted.* New York: Wiley.

Kontos, S., Carter, K. R., Ormrod, J. E., & Cooney, J. B. (1983a). Reversing the revolving door: A strict interpretation of Renzulli's definition of giftedness. *Roeper Review, 6*(1), 35–39.

Kontos, S., Carter, K. R., Ormrod, J. E., & Cooney, J. B. (1983b). Another look at the revolving door: A reply to Renzulli. *Roeper Review, 6*(1), 41–42.

Laycock, F., & Caylor, J. S. (1964). Physiques of gifted children and their less gifted siblings. *Child Development, 35,* 63–74.

Leo, J. (1984). The ups and downs of creativity. *Time,* October, 8, 76.

Lesser, G., Fifer, G., & Clark, D. H. (1965). Mental abilities of children from different social-class and cultural groups. *Monographs of the Society for Research in Child Development, 30,* Serial No. 102.

Lindsey, M. (1980). *Training teachers of the gifted and talented.* New York: Teachers College Press.

Lombroso, C. (1905). *The man of genius* (2nd ed.). New York: Walter Scott.

Madden, R. R. (1833). *The infirmities of genius* (Vol. II). Philadelphia: Carey, Lea, & Blanchard.

Maker, C. J. (1977). *Providing programs for the gifted handicapped.* Reston, Va.: Council for Exceptional Children.

Maker, C. J. (1986). Education of the gifted: Significant trends. In R. J. Morris & B. Blatt (Eds.), *Special education: Research and trends* (pp. 190–221). New York: Pergamon.

Marland, S. P. (Submittor). (1972). *Education of the gifted and talented: Report to the Congress of the United States by the U.S. Commissioner of Education.* Washington, D.C.: U.S. Government Printing Office.

Martinson, R. A. (1961). *Educational programs for gifted pupils.* Sacramento: California Department of Education.

Martinson, R. A. (1973). Children with superior cognitive abilities. In L. M. Dunn (Ed.), *Exceptional children in the schools* (2nd ed.). New York: Holt, Rinehart and Winston.

McNiff, S. A. (1974). The myth of schizophrenic art. *Schizophrenia Bulletin,* Issue No. 9, Summer 12–13.

Mistry, J., & Rogoff, B. (1985). A cultural perspective on the development of talent. In F. D. Horowitz & M. O'Brien (Eds.), *The gifted and talented: Developmental perspectives* (pp. 125–144). Washington, D.C.: American Psychological Association.

Mitchell, B. (1986). Current state efforts in gifted/talented education in the United States. *Roeper Review, 8,* 272–274.

Mitchell, P., & Erickson, D. K. (1978). The education of gifted and talented children: A status report. *Exceptional Children, 45,* 12–16.

Myers, D. G., & Ridl, J. (1981). Aren't all children gifted? *Today's Education, 70,* 15–20.

Newland, T. E. (1976). *The gifted in socio-cultural perspective.* Englewood Cliffs, N.J.: Prentice-Hall.

Nichols, R. C. (1965). *The inheritance of general and specific ability.* Research Report No. 1, Evanston, Ill.: National Merit Scholarship Corporation.

Page, B. A. (1983). A parent's guide to understanding the behavior of gifted children. *Roeper Review, 5*(4), 39–42.

Perez, G. S., Chassin, D., Ellington, C., & Smith, J. A. (1982). Leadership giftedness in preschool children. *Roeper Review, 4*(3), 26–28.

Perry, S. M. (1986). I'm gifted . . . and I'm not supposed to know it. *Gifted Child Today, 9*(3), 52–54.

Petrosko, J. M. (1978). Measuring creativity in elementary school: The current state of the art. *Journal of Creative Behavior, 12*(2), 109–119.

Porter, R. M. (1982). The gifted handicapped: A status report. *Roeper Review, 4,* 24–25.

Renzulli, J. S. (1973). Talent potential in minority group students. *Exceptional Children, 39,* 437–444.

Renzulli, J. S. (1977). *The enrichment triad model: A guide for developing defensible programs for the gifted and talented.* Wethersfield, Conn.: Creative Learning Press.

Renzulli, J. S. (1978). What makes giftedness? Re-examining a definition. *Phi Delta Kappan, 60*(3), 180–184, 261.

Renzulli, J. S. (1980). Will the gifted child movement be alive and well in 1990? *Gifted Child Quarterly, 24*(3), 3–9.

Renzulli, J. S. (1982). Dear Mr. and Mrs. Copernicus: We regret to inform you . . . *Gifted Child Quarterly, 26*(1), 11–14.

Renzulli, J. S. (1983). Guiding the gifted in the pursuit of real problems: The transformed role of the teacher. *Journal of Creative Behavior, 17*(1), 49–59.

Renzulli, J. S., & Delcourt, M. A. B. (1986). The legacy and logic of research on identification of gifted persons. *Gifted Child Quarterly, 30,* 20–23.

Renzulli, J. S., Hartman, R. K., & Callahan, C. M. (1975). Scale for rating the behavioral characteristics of superior students. In W. B. Barbe & J. S. Renzulli (Eds.), *Psychology and education of the gifted* (2nd ed.). New York: Irvington.

Renzulli, J. S., & Owen, S. V. (1983). The revolving door identification model: If it ain't busted don't fix it: if you don't understand it don't nix it. *Roeper Review, 6*(91), 39–41.

Renzulli, J. S., Reis, S. M., & Smith, L. H. (1981). *The revolving door identification model.* Mansfield Center, Conn.: Creative Learning Press.

Renzulli, J. S., & Smith, L. H. (1977). Two approaches to identification of gifted students. *Exceptional Children, 43,* 512–518.

Reynolds, C. R., & Bradley, M. (1983). Emotional stability of intellectually superior children versus nongifted peers as estimated by chronic anxiety levels. *School Psychology Review, 12,* 190–194.

Robinson, H. B. (1977). Current myths concerning gifted children. In *Gifts, talents, and the very young.* Ventura,

Calif.: National/State Leadership Training Institute on the Gifted and Talented.

Robinson, H. B., Roedell, W. C., & Jackson, N. E. (1979). Early identification and intervention. In A. H. Passow (Ed.), *The 78th yearbook of the National Society for the Study of Education, Part I. The gifted and talented.* Chicago: University of Chicago Press.

Roedell, W. C. (1985). Developing social competence in gifted preschool children. *Remedial and Special Education, 6*(4), in press.

Rosenbloom, P. C. (1986). Programs for the gifted in mathematics. *Roeper Review, 8,* 243–246.

Sanborn, K. (1885). *The vanity and insanity of genius.* New York: George J. Coombes.

Sapon-Shevin, M. (1984). The tug-of-war nobody wins: Allocation of educational resources for handicapped, gifted, and "typical" students. *Curriculum Inquiry, 14,* 57–81.

Scarr, S. (1981). *Race, social class and individual differences in IQ.* Hillsdale, N.J.: Erlbaum.

Scarr-Salapatek, S. (1975). Genetics and the development of intelligence. In F. D. Horowitz (Ed.), *Review of child development research* (Vol. 4). Chicago: University of Chicago Press.

Sisk, D. (1981). Educational planning for the gifted and talented. In J. M. Kauffman & D. P. Hallahan (Eds.), *Handbook of special education.* Englewood Cliffs, N.J.: Prentice-Hall.

Stanley, J. C. (1975). Intellectual precocity. *Journal of Special Education, 9,* 29–44.

Stanley, J. C. (1977). Rationale of the study of mathematically precocious youth (SMPY) during its first five years of promoting educational acceleration. In J. C. Stanley, W. C. George, & C. H. Solano (Eds.), *The gifted and the creative: A fifty-year perspective.* Baltimore: Johns Hopkins Press.

Stanley, J. C. (1978). Educational non-acceleration: An international tragedy. *G/C/T, 1*(3), 2–5, 53–57, 60–63.

Stanley, J. C. (1979). The study and facilitation of talent for mathematics. In A. H. Passow (Ed.), *The 78th yearbook of the National Society for the Study of Education, Part I. The gifted and talented.* Chicago: University of Chicago Press.

Stanley, J. C., & George, W. C. (1978). Now we are six: the ever expanding SMPY. *G/C/T, 1*(1), 9–11, 43–44, 50–51.

Stanley, J. C., & McGill, A. M. (1986). More about "Young entrants to college: How did they fare?" *Gifted Child Quarterly, 30,* 70–73.

Sternberg, R. J., & Davidson, J. E. (1983). Insight in the gifted. *Educational Psychologist, 18,* 51–57.

Sternberg, R. J., & Davidson, J. E. (1985). Cognitive development in the gifted and talented. In F. D. Horowitz & M. O'Brien (Eds.), *The gifted and talented: Developmental perspectives* (pp. 37–74). Washington, D.C.: American Psychological Association.

Stronge, J. H. (1986). Gifted education: Right or privilege? *Gifted Child Today, 9*(3), 52–54.

Tannenbaum, A. J. (1979). Pre-Sputnik to Post-Watergate concern about the gifted. In A. H. Passow (Ed.), *The 78th yearbook of the National Society for the Study of Education, Part I. The gifted and talented.* Chicago: University of Chicago Press.

Tannenbaum, A. J. (1986). Reflection and refraction of light on the gifted. *Roeper Review, 8,* 212–218.

Terman, L. M. (1926). *Genetic studies of genius. Vol. I: Mental and physical traits of a thousand gifted children* (2nd ed.). Palo Alto, Calif.: Stanford University Press.

Terman, L. M., & Oden, M. H. (1959). *Genetic studies of genius, Vol. V: The gifted group at midlife.* Palo Alto, Calif.: Stanford University Press.

Torrance, E. P. (1986). Glimpses of the "Promised Land." *Roeper Review, 8,* 246–251.

Treffinger, D. J. (1986). Research on creativity. *Gifted Child Quarterly, 30,* 15–19.

Treffinger, D. J., Renzulli, J. S., & Feldhausen, J. F. (1975). Problems in the assessment of creative thinking. In W. B. Barbe & J. S. Renzulli (Eds.), *Psychology and education of the gifted* (2nd ed.). New York: Irvington.

Tyler, L. E. (1976). The intelligence we test—An evolving concept. In L. B. Resnick (Ed.), *The nature of intelligence.* Hillsdale, N.J.: Lawrence Erlbaum Associates.

VanTassel-Baska, J. (1983). Profiles of precocity: The 1982 midwest talent search finalists. *Gifted Child Quarterly, 27,* 139–144.

Wallach, M. A. (1985). Creativity testing and giftedness. In F. D. Horowitz & M. O'Brien (Eds.), *The gifted and talented: Developmental perspectives* (pp. 99–123). Washington, D.C.: American Psychological Association.

Weiss, P., & Gallagher, J. J. (1982). *Report on education of gifted* (Vol II). Chapel Hill, N.C.: Frank Porter Graham Child Development Center.

Whitmore, J. R. (1980). *Giftedness, conflict, and underachievement.* Boston: Allyn & Bacon.

Whitmore, J. R. (1986). Understanding a lack of motivation to excel. *Gifted Child Quarterly, 30,* 66–69.

Whitmore, J. R., & Maker, C. J. (1985). *Intellectual giftedness in disabled persons.* Rockville, Md.: Aspen.

Willerman, L., & Fiedler, M. F. (1974). Infant performance and intellectual precocity. *Child Development, 45,* 483–486.

Zigler, E., & Farber, E. A. (1985). Commonalities between the intellectual extremes: Giftedness and mental retardation. In F. D. Horowitz & M. O'Brien (Eds.), *The gifted and talented: Developmental perspectives* (pp. 387–408). Washington, D.C.: American Psychological Association.

10

Normalization and Attitudes toward Disabled People

Come writers and critics
Who prophesies with your pen
And keep your eyes wide
The chance won't come again.
And don't speak too soon
For the wheel's still in spin
And there's no tellin' who
That it's namin'
For the loser now
Will be later to win
For the times they are a-changin'.

(Bob Dylan, "The Times They Are A-Changin'")

he lyrics of Bob Dylan's song, "The Times They Are A-Changin'" (see p. 461), could have been written for the field of special education. The last several years have seen especially dramatic changes in the education of exceptional individuals. And current thinking of special education authorities, as reflected in the professional literature, indicates the field is poised for still more changes.

In this chapter we explore the major changes taking place in the field. The chapter is divided into three main sections: Normalization, Deinstitutionalization, and Mainstreaming. Although we believe in the logic of this division, it should also become evident that many of the issues separated under these three headings are interrelated. For example, much of what we discuss in this chapter is derived from the topic to which we now turn—normalization.

NORMALIZATION

Normalization, first espoused in Scandinavia (Bank-Mikkelsen, 1968, 1976) and later popularized in the United States by Wolfensberger (1972), is the philosophical belief that every disabled person should have an education and living environment as close to normal as possible. No matter what the type or level of the individual's disability, normalization dictates that he or she should be integrated as much as possible into the larger society. PL 94-142's insistence on the *least restrictive environment* was a direct result of lobbying by advocates for handicapped people to get the principle of normalization legally mandated.

In this section, we explore some of the major themes in special education that derive their impetus from the normalization principle. These are included under the headings The Antilabeling Movement, The Disability Rights Movement, Society's Attitudes Toward Handicapped Newborns, Technology and the Goal of Normalization, and The Media's Treatment of Disabilities.

The Antilabeling Movement

Some people fear that attaching a "special education" label to a child can cause that child to suffer feelings of unworthiness, or to be viewed by the rest of society as a deviant and hence grow to feel unworthy.

There are at least three different sources of the antilabeling movement:

1. Many more ethnic-minority children are labeled as handicapped, particularly "mentally retarded."
2. There has been a growing appreciation of the ecological approach to deviance.
3. There is a trend toward viewing exceptional children as quantitatively rather than qualitatively different from normal children.

We will discuss each of these closely related factors, and then take a look at some of the research data on the effects of labeling.

Overrepresentation of Minority-Group Members Among the Retarded Population

It is an indisputable fact that a disproportionate number of those labeled retarded are minority children. The U.S. Office of Civil Rights, for example, reported that 38 percent of students in classes for the mildly retarded in the United States were black,

MISCONCEPTIONS
ABOUT EXCEPTIONAL INDIVIDUALS

Myth	*Fact*
Labeling a child "retarded," "disturbed," or "blind" is totally inappropriate.	Although there are dangers in using labels, there are advantages as well. Labels are an efficient way of describing a general set of characteristics and are useful in making appeals for services for specific groups of exceptional children. Labels of some kind are necessary for efficient communication about any group of children.
Mainstreaming has been embraced wholeheartedly by general educators.	General educators are often reluctant to accept exceptional children into their classrooms. A good deal of pre- and in-service training is required to prepare regular educators to work with exceptional students.
Technology can only have a positive influence on the education of handicapped individuals.	Technology undoubtedly has led to, among other things, greater independence for disabled people. However, one should guard against the potential for dependency on technology. In other words, some handicapped people might come to rely too much on technology rather than working at developing their own skills.
Physicians are always in a position to advise parents about what kind of "quality of life" their handicapped newborn child will have.	In many cases no one is able to predict the future development of handicapped infants. And some have questioned whether it is possible to define "quality of life."
Deinstitutionalization is easily achieved.	Communities need to be educated before group homes can be established without resistance.
Group homes can only be established in marginal neighborhoods; if set up in other kinds of neighborhoods, property values will decline.	If handled appropriately, group homes can be set up in almost any kind of neighborhood without causing declines in property values.
Research has established beyond a doubt that special classes are ineffective and that mainstreaming is effective.	Research comparing special versus mainstream placement has been inconclusive. In fact, many are now saying that these "efficacy studies" are not very helpful in deciding the issue of what the best placement is for exceptional children. Instead, researchers are focusing on finding ways of making mainstreaming work more effectively.

but that only 16 percent of the nation's schoolchildren were black (Messick, 1984). Whether this discrepancy occurs because of mislabeling has been debated in the literature, with reputable authorities on both sides of the issue. More important for our discussion here is that a prevailing philosophy for those who believe the over-representation is inappropriate is that the label of retardation is damaging to the individual.

One of the first professionals to champion the position that labeling minority children as retarded is harmful was Jane Mercer. Mercer believes that one of the evils of labeling is that the label comes to be viewed as an *inherent attribute* of the person. Mental retardation, for example, is seen as a disease within the *individual* instead of being viewed within the *social environment* in which it occurs. Put simply, behavior that constitutes retardation or emotional disturbance in one society or social milieu may not be so considered in another society or social situation. As Mercer states:

> In this context, mental retardation is not a characteristic of the individual, but rather, a description of an individual's location in a social system, the role he is expected to play in the system, and the expectations which others in the system will have for his behavior. Mental retardation is an achieved status. (1970, pp. 383–384)

An Ecological Approach to Deviant Behavior

Mercer's views are shared by psychologists and sociologists who favor an **ecological approach** (Braginsky and Braginsky, 1974; Goffman, 1963; Hobbs, 1975; Rhodes, 1967; Szasz, 1974). This position stresses the interaction between the individual and the social environment. To a large extent, handicaps are viewed as being caused by social forces. For example, retardation, as we know it, would not exist in a society that did not value intelligent, adaptive behavior. Ecological theorists maintain that labels are metaphors that "have laid the groundwork for thinking about so-called handicaps as social constructions rather than as objective conditions" (Bogdan, 1986, p. 344).

Those espousing an ecological position also embrace what has been termed **symbolic interaction theory** (Blumer, 1969). As Bogdan (1986) states:

> The cliché beauty is in the eye of the beholder embodies the emphasis of the symbolic interactionist approach. We all know, but seldom take seriously when conducting research, that objects, people, situations, life, and the world do not carry their own meaning, rather meaning is conferred upon them. To put it another way, meaning does not lie in things; the interpretation or definition that the viewer imputes is paramount. For symbolic interactionists, the subjects of investigation are how people define the world and the process by which that understanding is constructed. Human beings are foremost interpreting, defining, symbolic creatures, whose behavior can only be understood by entering the defining process.
>
> Conferring meaning is not an autonomous act; human beings are social and meaning develops through interaction with others. (p. 345)

What this means for special education, Bogdan argues, is that disability is a socially created construct. Its existence is dependent upon social interaction (see cartoon, box, p. 465.) Only in a very narrow sense, according to Bogdan, does a person *have* a disability. For example, the fact that a person cannot see only sets the stage for his or her being labeled as "blind." Once we designate a person as blind, there are a variety

Cutter John Cuts through Prejudicial Barriers

Most special education professionals and handicapped people themselves would agree that there are many ways to break down attitudinal barriers toward disabled people. And humor may be one of the most effective weapons against such prejudices. If that is the case, then the well-aimed salvos of Cutter John, the creation of Pulitzer Prize-winner Berke Breathed, may be doing their fair share of winning the war against stereotypical and negative attitudes toward handicapped people.

Appearing in the comic strip "Bloom County," syndicated by the *Washington Post*, Cutter John takes a no-nonsense approach to his disability. He has his tenderhearted moments with his girlfriend, Bobbi, and he loves to joyride with his penguin companion, Opus, whose friendship he won when Opus realized they were "birds of a feather" because they both had "a couple of useless limbs." He is at his best, however, when he directly, but gently and humorously, forces others to confront their own feelings about his having a disability. The strip below demonstrates in the blink of an eye what theorists often take several paragraphs to explain when positing that disability is a socially created construct whose existence is dependent upon social interaction.

©1983 Washington Post Writers Group. Reprinted with permission.

of undesirable consequences, according to symbolic interactionists. Our interactions with the blind person are different because of the label. We view the person primarily in terms of the blindness. We tend to interpret everything the blind person can or cannot do in terms of the blindness, and the label of blindness takes precedence over other things we may know about the individual. This labeling opens the door for viewing the blind person in a stereotypical and prejudicial manner because, once labeled, we tend to think of all blind people as being similar to one another but different from the rest of society:

> The way we think about people with alleged disabilities is filled with judgments about good or bad, normal and abnormal (Bogdan & Biklen, 1977). The meaning of disability in special education goes far beyond the alleged physical, behavioral, and psychological differences. Disability has symbolic meaning that must be looked at in terms of what society honors and what it degrades. Society's thoughts about intelligence, confidence, beauty, and winning must be understood in order to understand what we mean when we mockingly call someone *retarded* or *blind as a bat*. Our society has traditionally been structured to bring shame to people with alleged disabilities. Symbolic interactionists understand that only a small part of problems of discrimination are technical—providing

physical access to wheelchairs, building communication systems for nonverbal people. The problems of disability are much more social; they are located much deeper in the seams of our society than professionals in the field of special education acknowledge. (Bogdan, 1986, p. 351)

Quantitative versus Qualitative Conception of Deviance

Some authorities have noted that exceptional individuals can be viewed as qualitatively or quantitatively different from nonhandicapped people (Telford and Sawrey, 1977; Zigler and Balla, 1982). Proponents of the *qualitative approach* believe that exceptional children are qualitatively different in behavior from other children and that each type of exceptionality has its own specific personality and behavioral characteristics. The qualitative conception often leads to using the label to "explain" the behavior of the child. When a handicapped child performs inappropriately or gets into trouble, it is all too often attributed solely to the child's exceptionality. This results in such statements as "He does poorly in school *because* he is learning disabled," or "She gets into trouble with the police *because* she is a juvenile delinquent." This kind of thinking unfortunately perpetuates stereotypes and does not really explain the behavior. Labels such as "learning disabled" and "emotionally disturbed" refer to individuals with a wide range of behaviors and characteristics. In reality, the individuals with a given label differ from one another about as much as they differ from their nonhandicapped peers.

According to the *quantitative approach* to exceptionality, exceptional individuals differ from nonhandicapped people in some behaviors in degree but not in kind. Most authorities today favor the quantitative approach. In our chapter on mental retardation, for example, we discussed research evidence which suggests that children classified as mentally retarded do not learn in a qualitatively different way from nonretarded individuals of the same mental age. It is the contention of Zigler and Balla (1982), for example, that the retarded individual does not go through different developmental learning stages; instead, he or she progresses *more slowly* through the same stages as the nonretarded individual.

Research on the Effects of Labeling

A frequently cited study purporting to show the potential harmful effects of labeling exceptional children is that of Rosenthal and Jacobsen (1968). It has been so well publicized, in fact, that we often hear and see references to the "Rosenthal effect" (sometimes called the "self-fulfilling prophecy"). In this study the experimenters administered a group intelligence test to elementary school children. The test was explained as a method of determining a child's potential for a growth spurt in intelligence. After the test the investigators provided each teacher with a list of children who were said to be likely to show large gains during the year. Actually about 20 percent were randomly assigned the status of "potential bloomers." Later in the school year, the same test was administered again. This time Rosenthal and Jacobsen found the children who had been labeled as potential bloomers after the first test achieved significantly higher scores than the rest of the children. They believe that such changes were due to expectancy cues conveyed by the teachers. It has since been pointed out, however, that the Rosenthal and Jacobsen study contained many methodological flaws (Barber and Silver, 1968a, 1968b; Snow, 1969;

Thorndike, 1968), and attempts to replicate the results have not been successful (Fleming and Anttonen, 1971).

Most authoritative reviews of the literature on labeling have concluded that evidence for a relationship as dramatic as that claimed by Rosenthal and Jacobsen is limited at best (Gottlieb and Leyser, 1981; Keogh and Levitt, 1976; MacMillan and Becker, 1977; MacMillan, Jones, and Aloia, 1974). MacMillan, Jones, and Aloia, for example, made the following statement regarding labeling and its relationship to self-concept and peer acceptance:

> . . . no evidence has been found of a direct relationship between self-concept and labeling. . . . Some investigators found lower self-concepts in labeled and/or special-class students (Borg, 1966; Jones, 1973; Mann, 1960; Meyerowitz, 1962); others found the opposite (Drews, 1962; Goldberg, Passow, and Justman, 1961); and one researcher reported no difference (Bacher, 1965). And the methodological problems inherent in the vast majority of these studies render their findings difficult to interpret. (p. 246)

> To summarize, the evidence of the effect of labeling and/or placement on peer acceptance is open to several conflicting interpretations. Clearly, the results of these studies are inconclusive. (p. 247)

There is research evidence, however, that most people tend to view a labeled person differently from a nonlabeled one (Foster, Ysseldyke, and Reese, 1975; Herson, 1974; Langer and Abelson, 1974; Salvia, Clark, and Ysseldyke, 1973). People are more likely both to expect deviant behavior from labeled individuals and to rate nonhandicapped individuals as possessing abnormal traits if they are provided with the misinformation that the individuals are deviant.

In summary, then, research on labeling indicates that expectations and views of the handicapped can be biased by labels. However, there is as yet no clear-cut evidence showing that this influences the behavior or personality traits of handicapped individuals themselves. It is difficult to imagine that being labeled handicapped would not affect a person's feelings about himself or herself; however, research to support this view conclusively has yet to be done (see Burbach, 1981, for further discussion).

We must be careful not to let labels for handicapping conditions lead to inappropriate restrictions on children's exploration of their environment and participation in activities. (Glyn Cloyd/Taurus Photos)

Some Possible Advantages of Labeling

Given the logical likelihood that labeling *might* result in negative consequences, are there any reasons for doing it? Five reasons are usually given for the continued use of labeling:

1. It is often noted that federal and local funding of special education programs is based on labeling. This reasoning, however, says nothing regarding the value of labeling in and of itself. Because funding guidelines use labels does not mean that these labels are appropriate.

2. It is maintained by some that labeling a population helps professionals communicate with one another about children. For example, in assessing a research study it is helpful to know that the investigation was carried out with visually impaired, hearing-impaired, or mentally retarded children. Unfortunately such labels are not always clear.

3. One can make a relatively strong case that with the abolition of the present labels a new set of labels and/or descriptive phrases would evolve to take their place. In other words, children with special problems will probably always be perceived as being different. People do not necessarily need a label to recognize individual differences in behaviors related to school learning.

4. Whether it is right or wrong, labeling helps spotlight the problem for the general public. Gallagher notes: "Like it or not, it is a fine mixture of compassion, guilt, and social conscience that has been established over these many years as a conditioned response to the label 'mental retardation' that brings forth . . . resources [monies for specialized services]" (1972, p. 531). The taxpayer is more likely to react sympathetically to something that can be labeled. Gallagher maintains that the crux of the labeling problem is that it does not always guarantee appropriate services.

5. Labeling may, to a certain extent, actually make the nonhandicapped majority more tolerant of the handicapped minority (Fiedler and Simpson, 1987). Gottlieb and Leyser (1981) speculate that the label may influence people to view the handicapped more favorably by justifying some of the latter's inappropriate behavior. For example, it is probably fairly common for the nonhandicapped adult to tolerate the socially immature play behavior of the child next door who is mentally retarded while finding the same behavior unacceptable in his or her own child.

The Disability Rights Movement

In their quest for normalization, more and more handicapped people have become disability activists. They are a part of a disability rights movement that in the late 1970s began to confront various societal institutions which proponents believe discriminate against handicapped people.

In many ways, the seeds of the movement were sown in the civil rights movement of the 1960s. Disability activists claimed that they, like blacks and other ethnic groups, were an oppressed minority. They even coined the term *handicapism* (a parallel of racism) (Bogdan and Biklen, 1977). **Handicapism** is "a set of assumptions and practices that promote the differential and unequal treatment of people because of apparent or assumed physical, mental, or behavioral differences" (Bogdan and Biklen, 1977, p. 14).

More and more disabled people are forming their own organizations to work toward greater community acceptance. (Alan Carey/The Image Works)

Indeed, on social and economic grounds a strong case can be made that handicapped people qualify as a minority in the same sense as many ethnic groups:

> The minority status of a group can be determined by comparing their position with dominant portions of the population on crucial social and economic indicators. According to this standard, despite the flaws in available statistics, there seems to be little doubt disabled people deserve to be considered a minority group. Persons with disabilities experience the highest unemployment rate and the most prevalent levels of welfare dependency in the country. They have been disproportionately exposed to persistent poverty and inadequate schools, housing, transportation, and other services. Even the exclusion of disabled individuals from voting booths, juries, and political meetings seems to parallel the barriers impeding other groups which have struggled to gain equal rights. (Hahn, 1986)

Goals of the Disability Rights Movement

To combat what they perceive as handicapism, activists have goals for the disability rights movement that are very similar to those for the civil rights movement:

> The first question that we must address (and the key to understanding the disability rights movement) is: "What is the goal of disability rights?" For individual disabled people, it is accessible public transportation, community-based independent living support services, sign language interpreters, mobility skills training, adequate housing, appropriate medical care, communications access and aids, appropriate and adequate employment, and mobility aids.

> For all disabled persons, however, the ultimate goal is the freedom to choose, to belong, to participate, to have dignity and the opportunity to achieve. It is the end of the caste of the handicapped and the stereotypes and prejudices that persons with disabilities lack essential human attributes necessary to be considered a part of organized society (Funk, 1986)

Barriers to the Disability Rights Movement

Although more and more disabled people—and professionals too—are supporting the disability rights movement, there are several impediments to its achieving the same degree of impact as the civil rights movement. We will discuss four. First, some believe that the political climate in the United States has not been conducive to fostering yet another rights movement. Whereas the civil rights movement of the 1960s was spawned in an era of liberal ideology, the disability rights movement has coincided with a more conservative climate (Gartner and Joe, 1986).

Second, some of the activists themselves have been unable to agree on the best ways to meet the movement's general goals. For example, some believe that disabled individuals should receive special treatment in such things as tax exemptions or reduced public transportation fares. Others maintain that such preferential treatment fosters the image of handicapped people being dependent on the nonhandicapped for charity (Gartner and Joe, 1986).

Third, we have pointed out repeatedly in this book, handicapped people are an incredibly heterogeneous population. While general goals can be the same for all handicapped people, specific needs vary greatly, depending to a large extent on the particular type and severity of handicap the person has. The *particular* problems a blind, severely retarded adolescent faces are considerably different from those of a Vietnam veteran who has lost the use of his legs. Although activists admit it would not be good for the public to believe that all handicapped people are alike any more than they already do (Gartner and Joe, 1986), the heterogeneity does make it more difficult for disabled people to join forces on specific issues.

But perhaps what has been most missing and what is hardest to achieve is a sense of pride. The civil rights movement for blacks and the women's movement fostered a sense of pride in those groups. For example, there has been no equivalent of the "Black is beautiful" slogan within the disability rights movement. Although to some it may seem odd to be proud of one's disability, Carol Gill, a psychologist and disability activist, believes strongly that that is what is needed to ignite the movement. Here is a summary of a speech she gave to the West Los Angeles chapter of the California Association of the Physically Handicapped, as reported in *The Disability Rag.* (The *Rag*, as it is sometimes called, has become the leading publication outlet for disability activists; see box, pp. 472–473.)

> "We're separated by time and place; we're isolated. We don't see each other for a long time sometimes; we're tired from our disabilities. Sometimes our disabilities decrease our tolerance to be up and doing things. These things can be overcome, but it takes a lot of emotional effort."
>
> But after Gill lists all these problems, she is quick to stress that, "There are strong psychological reasons for developing a disability culture.
>
> "A disability culture movement can foster disability pride. It promotes pride in us; it allows us to project a positive image to the public." It also provides what Gill calls "fortification." "We renew each other and our strength through shared experiences and rituals.
>
> "If we express our culture in some unified way, we're signalling; we're communicating what our values, goals, and identity are." This, says Gill, is one of the strongest values of a culture. "Through our culture, we can recruit people. When we present a strong image, it motivates people to want to belong. They want to be part of something that powerful. . . .
>
> "We don't need to be foster children of the 'able-bodied culture,' " says Gill. "We can have our own family!
>
> "That doesn't mean we don't still want our majority culture family we were born into; but we also want one that responds more to our experience."
>
> While we're groping for that, says Gill, "We may go through a very frightening period in which we feel we're rejecting our birth roots; we're rejecting the security we had; the only sense of belonging we've felt we had"—similar, says Gill, to what adolescents go through.

"In order to really form their own identity, people give up for awhile the identity they were born with. They need to separate from their parents and think about who they are. . . .

"I think that's what we as disabled people go through," says Gill. "I think it's what other minority groups go through when they develop a pride movement. . . .

"But if we had some rituals to identify with—as part of who we are—they could renew our faith in each other and ourselves and make us aware we do have common experiences. . . .

We need our songs; songs about the disability struggle, the political struggle, about our hopes for what will happen some day. We don't have those things—things that other minority groups have.

"Maybe we need more slogans. We need to wear symbols of what we believe in or what we've experienced—on t-shirts, on buttons—when we're out in the streets. It could be something as small as a button with a slogan on it—but if it's one that all disabled people come to know as meaningful, then when we go out in public and wear it, we signal to each other what we're about.

"I think of the black culture movement and the black civil rights movement and black pride. Some people went all out. They wore dashikis, they did their hair in cornrows, they wore beads from Africa. But others just maybe let their hair go natural instead of straightening it. People participated at different levels. But the message they were all saying was, 'We're proud of who we are. We're a people that is not inferior—but different.'" . . .

What Gill encourages people to do, "—sensitively, I hope—and carefully—is to say, 'Yes, I'm a part of my family of origin, but I'm also something else—and it isn't a betrayal to my family that gave birth to me to explore this 'something else' that I am. In fact it may be necessary in order for me to be whole. It may really be necessary for me to say, 'I also belong to another family.'"

"And when I talk about it in terms of 'family,' that's when I get the most tears; that's when it hits home.

"Once we get people to realize they have this need, once we conquer our fear of facing the fact that we do need another family—a disability family—then I think it will really begin." (Johnson, 1987, pp. 4, 6, 9, 10)

Society's Attitudes toward Handicapped Newborns

The recent revolution in neonatal technology has made it possible to keep alive many newborn children who previously would have died because of various illnesses. Unfortunately, many of these infants who now survive are seriously disabled. The disabilities are sometimes so severe that some physicians and parents have serious reservations about whether these newborns should be kept alive. And, in fact, medical treatment has often been withheld from such children, resulting in their death, even though it was impossible to predict with complete accuracy how severe the disabilities would eventually have been. Hentoff (1985), for example, provides the following illustrations of how difficult it is to predict the future physical and mental status of some newborns:

Some physicians' prophecies about imperfect babies are shown to be startlingly wrong when the child has a chance to live long enough to confound the prediction. A particularly vivid illustration of auguries turned upside down appeared as part of *Death in the Nursery*,

Puncturing The Pathos for The Disabled

Instead, the Gadfly 'Rag' Seeks the Removal of Barriers

By David Streitfeld
Washington Post Staff Writer

The advertisement by the National Society to Prevent Blindness seems inoffensive. Designed to produce a catch in the throat and induce a little checkbook action, it no doubt does both.

"Save the Stars," reads the text, which is illustrated by a photo of the night sky. "When you lose your vision, you lose the stars. You lose the sunsets. The rainbows. The snowflakes and moonlight. This year, 50,000 Americans will lose all that and more. Forever. Yet in many cases, blindness can be prevented . . . Help us save the stars. Give to Prevent Blindness."

Simple, touching and effective, no? Not according to readers of The Disability Rag, a spirited magazine out of Louisville, Ky. Their reactions were a tad harsher.

"They're worrying about me seeing stars," said one. "I wish they'd worry about why we never see paychecks." Another commented: "It reinforces the myth that blind people's lives are unbearably sad, and that's simply not true."

The advertisement may be well-meaning, but it "goes for the negative, and plays on the fears of everyone who can see," says Rag editor Mary Johnson. "A sighted person reads that and says, 'How awful it would be to be blind!' Of all the ways they could have got people to contribute money, they chose the one that made blindness look tragic and pathetic."

The 4,200-circulation Rag, which claims to be the only periodical that covers disability as a civil rights issue, takes aim at anyone or anything that, in the magazine's opinion, patronizes, stereotypes or takes advantage of the disabled. As with the Prevent Blindness ad, which ran in the magazine's "We wish we wouldn't see . . . " section, it's not reluctant to tackle groups devoted to improving conditions for the disabled. Some other recent targets:

■ Telethons for the handicapped. ("Why isn't the space program—or Star Wars defense research—paid for by a national telethon? . . . [Why is it that] vital services for disabled people—and research for cure, research this country pays such lip service to—must await the nickel-and-dime generosity of people who give money out of 'thankfulness' that they're not like the poor unfortunates they believe their money is going to 'save.' ")

■ The National Handicapped Sports and Recreation Association slogan "If I can do this, I can do anything." ("What do the people who are learning to live by that slogan do when they come up against an attitude in society they can't conquer? Or a real barrier like a flight of stairs?")

■ Ads for cosmetic surgery—including breast enlargement, hip reductions through suctioning, nose jobs—that promise easy payment plans and "hotel-like" accommodations. ("A decade ago, many of us in disability rights longed for the day when hospital visits, surgery, prostheses—all the things that society shunned but we were forced to endure—would seem a normal part of everyday life. Why couldn't a stay in a hospital be treated like a stay in a hotel, we wondered? . . . Now that the day of hotel-like hospital accommodations has come . . . we discover that packaging medical services hasn't done what we hoped at all: it hasn't made it more acceptable to be 'imperfect.' It's done just the opposite.")

■ And then there's exercise guru Richard Simmons, whose *Reach for Fitness: A Special Book of Exercises for the Physically Challenged* has provoked special ire.

"His whole approach tends to sanctify the concept that disabled people have to 'overcome' and they're very 'special,' " says Johnson. "It's real sappy, and also misguided and superficial. He's gotten on this bandwagon—help the gimps and be trendy at the same time."

It reminds her, she adds, of the "dress for success" philosophy that asserted that the solution to a woman's pay inequities was to buy a nice navy blue suit. "It's trivializing the very real problems that are caused by society . . . All this junk about 'challenging,' where you become good by exercising and making your body perfect—I never can figure out what those people are supposed to do when they need to ride a city bus and they can't get on it."

The Rag doesn't spend all its time firing broadsides. Features in the November-December issue include a book review, an article on the abuse of the handicapped by attendants and family, and several personal testimonies. Yet every piece displays an underlying conviction that the problems of the disabled aren't just medical, but can arise out of prejudice, denial of access and discrimination.

"We wanted disabled people to realize that getting about is not totally up to them," says Cass Irvin, the Rag's publisher and a contributing editor. "Society needs to take some responsibility for people getting around easier. That's why we have roads and mass transit, and that's why we should have accessible buses." Buses are a frequent topic in the Rag: The editors estimate that fewer than 10 cities in the country have satisfactory public transport systems.

Some of those who work with the disabled have mixed views of the Rag, seeing it as well-intentioned but abrasive. Says John Kemp, general counsel for the National Easter Seal Society and the director of its telethon:

"They cover a perspective that no one else does, and they provide a valuable service by rounding out readers' perspectives." He adds, however, that "I resent the strident, shoot-from-the-hip approach. Much of what the Rag offers is good, but the accusatory tone they use can diminish the impact of their message."

As for their criticism of telethons, "It would be wonderful if we could get the federal government to accept its responsibility to provide all disabled people with minimal but essential services. But until then, money will have to come from elsewhere, like telethons."

Bob Ruffner, the director of public affairs for the President's Committee on Employment of the Handicapped, also sees the Rag as a "strong voice for those who may not be associated with a lot of well-organized groups. It's very forceful in arguing that disabled people should get their heads out of the clouds and confront society with their needs."

The Rag, some critics feel, often places more importance on being disabled and staying that way than on taking risks with technology that might remove the barriers.

"There can be dignity in disability, but this is a world of hearing, sight and ambulation, and if you could accomplish these things, life would certainly be easier," says Kemp. "I'm a quadruple amputee, and if I could miraculously grow arms and legs, I would take them in a second."

———

Ask the 38-year-old Johnson if she is disabled, and she'll reply: "Not yet."

Most people are handicapped at some point in their lives, she notes. Pregnancy, breaking your leg while skiing, back problems or a heart attack—all make it harder to get around. "The chances of me remaining undisabled through the rest of my life are small. If we create a society that doesn't erect barriers when people go through a disability phase, I'll be a lot better off personally."

The Rag's only full-time staffer, Johnson was an activist in the civil rights and women's movements. She got involved with a local disability group in her home town of Louisville, and that experience led to the 1980 launching of the magazine.

"We kept feeling frustrated because there was much that needed to be said that wasn't," says the 41-year-old Irvin, who has been severely disabled since she was a child and uses a wheelchair. "Part of the problem is geography and part is physical access—how are you going to get the disabled to work together if they can't even get together? There needed to be some way for people to connect."

The Rag's budget has always been minimal. With no money to do any fancy artwork, the magazine once illustrated an article about McDonald's by photocopying a mess of french fries. ("We're a rag. What can I say?" laughs the editor. "Maybe some day we'll look as beautiful as Arizona Highways, but not soon.")

The magazine's goals, on the other hand, are enormous. They include the removal of enough barriers so any handicapped person in any community can get to work and the design of all new housing so everyone can use it, no matter what their physical condition.

"All their lives the disabled have been told they can't do things on their own. It's a huge psychological internalization of dependency," says Johnson. "If we can retool society, a generation will grow up that won't have to live in a special world if they become paralyzed."

Isn't this all a little far-fetched? Does The Disability Rag really believe that in this era of lowered expectations, monstrous budget deficits and 7 percent unemployment, society can afford to redo itself?

"Massive new government expenditures don't seem likely," agrees Ruffner. "But utopian ideas—ideas that can be translated into social action—start in places like the Rag. How else can you build a movement among people who have been left out? Its purpose is to build a fire."

"I suppose people would have once said that racism was a fact of life," Johnson says. "If you talked to a southerner in the '40s, the fact that a black person should be allowed to use the same restroom as a white person may have been fine and good, but they weren't going to do it.

"Social change is a very long process, but we hope to keep at it until people understand."

The Disability Rag, P.O. Box 145, Louisville, Ky. 40201, is available in regular type, large print or cassette. Subscription is $9 a year ($6 if you're on a tight budget, $12 if you're generous, $15 if you want it sent first class).

a 1983 series on the Boston television station WNEV-TV. The segment focused on two classmates in a West Haven, Connecticut, elementary school, Jimmy Arria and Kimberly Mekdeci. The boy, born prematurely, had weighed only four and half pounds at birth, contracted pneumonia a day later, and suffered seizures. The girl was born with spina bifida.

A pediatrician suggested to the parents of both infants that they choose death as the preferred management option. Kimberly Mekdeci's father remembers that doctor saying that his daughter would probably grow up to be a vegetable. The quality of Jimmy Arria's life, the doctor predicted, would be very poor.

Jimmy Arria is [now] a good student; Kim is also bright. (p. 58)

Nevertheless, the practice of withholding treatment from handicapped newborns has been relatively common. Duff and Campbell (1973) report, for example, that in one special-care nursery forty-three infants died in a two and one half year period because treatment was withheld from them.

In the 1980s, however, some have denounced the withholding of treatment from any handicapped newborn. Some have argued that this denouncement indicates a more positive attitude toward exceptional individuals. They make the case that an index of a society's attitudes toward handicapped people is how that society resolves the moral dilemma of caring for handicapped infants. They believe a society that allows doctors and parents to decide not to treat handicapped infants is one that does not place much value on the lives of handicapped individuals.

The Baby Doe Case

Much of the controversy surrounding the treatment of handicapped newborns arose out of the Baby Doe case in Indiana. In April 1982 a baby was born with Down syndrome. He also had an abdominal obstruction requiring surgery, a relatively common physical problem accompanying Down syndrome. The parents of Baby Doe, in consultation with their physician and knowing that without the surgery the baby would die, decided not to have the surgery performed. The baby died on April 15, 1982.

The case gained widespread media attention and also spurred the federal government to institute rules and regulations requiring the treatment of all infants, no matter how severe their defects. The U.S. Health and Human Services Department's first rules were struck down in a U.S. District Court on May 23, 1984. However, in the summer of 1984 the U.S. Senate passed a compromise bill that, while redefining child abuse to include the withholding of medical treatment from disabled infants, states that doctors are not required to provide extraordinary treatment to all severely and profoundly handicapped infants. If death or lifelong coma are likely to result or where treatment would otherwise be futile, heroic efforts are not required. Interestingly, this measure had the endorsement of a number of diverse groups, including the National Association for Retarded Citizens of the United States, the Spina Bifida Association, civil rights advocates, and anti-abortion groups. In fact, the only major group to oppose it was the American Medical Association (AMA).

Quality of Life Issues

The AMA has opposed federal regulations because it insists that decisions regarding the treatment of handicapped newborns must be left to the discretion of parents in consultation with their physician. In addition, the AMA maintains that in advising parents, a most important consideration should be the quality of life to be expected for the child. Unfortunately, defining "quality of life" is not an easy task. Experts in situational ethics differ not only on the definition of the term, but even on whether it is possible to define it at all.

Fletcher (1979) maintains that before one attempts to define quality of life, it is necessary to define "humanness." He proposes that the criteria for humanness include: minimum intelligence, self-awareness, self-control, a sense of time, a sense of futurity, a sense of past, the capacity to relate to others, concern for others, communication, control of existence, curiosity, change and changeability, balance of rationality and feeling, idiosyncrasy, and neocortical functioning. Under Fletcher's criteria, many mentally retarded individuals would not be considered human.

Disagreeing with Fletcher are Childress (1981) and the Association for Persons with Severe Handicaps. Childress is highly critical of attempts such as Fletcher's to define quality of life:

> Attempts to formulate satisfactory criteria of "quality of life" or "meaningful life" have been notoriously vague and inconclusive. . . .
>
> . . . Joseph Fletcher's criteria of "humanhood" are . . . suspect because they are framed in terms of standard of utility or social worth, i.e., the individual's potential contribution to society. . . .
>
> The difficulties and dangers are evident. Perhaps the language of "quality of life" or "meaningful life" is too loose and vague, too susceptible to corruption by judgments of social worth, and too easily directed against the senile and mentally retarded. At the very least, such slogans should be replaced by "the patient's best interest." Such a shift will not resolve all difficulties or avoid all risks, for the criteria of "the patient's best interest" are by no means evident. (pp. 45–46)

The Association for Persons with Severe Handicaps published a monograph titled *Legal, Economic, Psychological and Moral Considerations on the Practice of Withholding Medical Treatment from Infants with Congenital Defects* (Guess, Dussault, Brown, Mulligan, Orelove, Comegys, and Rues, 1984) that explores a wide range of issues surrounding the withholding of treatment from handicapped newborns. The association is very much opposed to withholding treatment on the basis of a diagnosis of, or prognosis for, mental retardation or related handicapping conditions. Regarding the issue of defining quality of life, the monograph's authors state:

Some may argue that "quality of life" is not quantifiable, but most of us can recognize happiness when we see it. (David H. Grossman/Photo Researchers, Inc.)

In the final analysis, it may be that quality of life and attempts to define it are just as illusive as efforts to devise criteria or inventories for bestowing humanness, and that attempts to predicate life sustaining medical decisions on some presumed happiness scale are doomed to the same problem where a few make choices for those who cannot speak for themselves (i.e., the newborn with a handicap). It may further be that the quality of life and the reverence for the sanctity of life are essentially nonexclusive, and are not to be perceived as one *versus* the other. . . .

In sum, the quality of life issue is, in many respects, an indictment of society's own attitudes towards persons with handicapping conditions, and the opportunity to participate in society might well be the problem of the nonhandicapped population. In this case, the decision to withhold treatment to infants who are severely handicapped is justified primarily on the perception of them as a commodity. And, as noted by Smith (1974):

> The error we want to avoid is the notion that we should solve our limited resource problem simply by assessing the "quality" of the output. Such an approach leads one to think that the ideal result is either a "perfect" baby or a "dead" baby (p. 46).

There is little doubt that the survival of handicapped newborns is a complex issue. Whether considered from the perspective of a professional or a parent, resolution of the problem is no easy matter. No matter where one stands on the issue, one should agree that the recent open discussion is a healthy sign for special education as a profession and for handicapped people themselves. Whereas in the past decisions regarding the treatment of handicapped newborns were sometimes made on the almost automatic assumption that defective babies were destined to lead meaningless lives, the difference that special educators and other professionals can make in the lives of many of these handicapped infants is now being recognized.

Technology and the Goal of Normalization

Technology is rapidly changing the way special educators and other professionals work with exceptional individuals. In addition, it is changing how handicapped people themselves participate in various aspects of society, from leisure to job activities. Throughout this book we have provided numerous examples of how technology has bettered the lives of handicapped people. In particular, some technologies have helped handicapped individuals lead more independent lives (see box on pp. 478–480). By allowing for greater independence, technology is making it possible for more and more handicapped people to take part in activities that previously were inaccessible to them. Thus technology serves in many instances as a means for achieving normalization.

Some people have expressed the opinion that technology can, in some cases, actually work against the goal of normalization. Professionals have mentioned two ways in which this might happen. First, there is the danger that some handicapped individuals might be too quick to rely on technology for assistance instead of working to improve their own abilities. Reliance on artificial means of interacting with the environment when more natural means are possible could jeopardize a person's quest for normalization. A controversy reported in the March 1984 issue of *The Braille Monitor* highlights how sensitive some handicapped individuals are to the issue of technology and independence. The National Federation of the Blind of New Mexico was upset about an electronic guidance system for blind people being used at the University of New Mexico. In this system wires under the floor transmit a signal to an electronic cane used by the blind person. The cane acts as a receiver, beeping whenever it is near a wire. Fred Schroeder, president of the National Federation of the Blind of New Mexico, wrote a letter to the developer of the electronic system in which he listed his complaints:

> The guidance system which you have had installed . . . poses a limitation to independent travel rather than an opening of new freedom of movement for the blind.

> The fundamental problem with an electronic guidance system is the philosophical premise upon which it is based. The underlying attitude behind its creation stems from an image of the hopeless, helpless blind groping their way timidly through the world fraught with danger and uncertainty.

> By installing an electronic guidance system the public is reinforced in its belief that the blind are unable to travel without elaborate accommodation. . . . Our success in improving social and economic conditions for the blind has come from our ability to adapt ourselves to the world rather than relying on the benevolence of the world to adapt to us.

Some professionals fear that an emphasis on technology may be dehumanizing (Cavalier and Mineo, 1986; McMurray, 1986). They argue there is a danger that a heavy stress on technology leads to viewing disabled people as "broken persons," like broken machines whose parts need fixing (Cavalier and Mineo, 1986). An indication of this dehumanization, they claim, is the tendency for technologists to concentrate on trying to fit handicapped people into existing technology, rather than developing technology to fit the needs of disabled individuals.

Although most technology does not usurp the independence of exceptional individuals and technology need not lead to dehumanization, a couple of points are worth keeping in mind. First, those who develop technology for handicapped people need to consult with them at every stage of research and development. The consumer needs to be considered.

As technology becomes even more sophisticated, the issue of independence will become ever more important. One general guideline might be that if the technology allows handicapped people to do something they could not do without it, then the technology is in their best interest. If, however, it allows them to do something new or better but at the same time imposes new limitations, then one might need to weigh the technology's benefits.

The Media's Treatment of Disabilities

A few investigations of how the media portray handicaps were conducted a number of years ago (e.g., Altheide, 1977; Byrd, Byrd, and Allen, 1977; Nunnally, 1957; Steadman and Cocazza, 1977). It was not until the mid-1980s that disability activists began to take strong stands, and to claim that the media have been often guilty of representing handicapped people in stereotypic and inaccurate ways.

Electronic Media

We discuss films and TV together here, since the findings regarding each have been highly similar—probably because a large part of TV's treatment of disability has occurred in films or made-for-TV movies although prime-time and daytime serials also offer up a disproportionate number of handicapped people, especially those who qualify as mentally ill (Cassata, Skill, and Boadu, 1979; Fruth and Padderud, 1985; Wahl and Roth, 1982). Two of the most influential critics on the topic of TV's

Personal Computers Increase Independence of Handicapped Users

To begin his workday, Thomas Shworles maneuvers his electric wheelchair over to his computer, braces his right hand on a special metal keyboard overlay and begins working.

Mr. Shworles suffers from a muscle disorder that has incapacitated his left arm and both legs and left him with only partial control of his right hand and forearm. He operates his wheelchair with a breath-control switch. And he runs his computer's word-processing program with the aid of the special keyboard overlay, a cover with holes above each key that helps prevent accidental key depression . . .

That accessory to a home computer means that the 52-year-old Mr. Shworles, who retired four years ago as a medical sociologist and counselor, can work at home (in a converted sewing room) as the head of a Chicago-based consumer group focused on computers and the disabled. "It's purely thrilling to know that I can turn on this machine and have access to scores of files," he says. "I couldn't walk over to a file cabinet and handle that many folders." . . .

For Tom Shworles and a growing number of people with disabilities, the computer offers a kind of personal revolution. It can mean employment and a greater degree of independence and equality. . . .

'Equalizer Gun'

"Putting the right computerized information tools in the hands of the disabled is like giving them an equalizer gun," Mr. Shworles says. "This technology is like the six-gun in the old West. It puts the weak and the strong, the meek and the aggressive on a par."

That unlikely six-shooter is being used by the blind in the form of talking computers, Braille keyboards and Braille word-processing programs. It can become a super "telephone" that quickly sends messages for the deaf or computerized synthetic voice for those who can't speak. . . .

But in order for the disabled to become truly part of the new computerized society, most experts agree that such research must be speeded up. A hungry general consumer market is constantly pushing the technology toward new frontiers, thus ever challenging disabled users of computers to adapt to the changes. . . .

Expanded Opportunities

Access to computers is crucial for the disabled primarily because the machines can greatly expand their job opportunities. That access would make many offices and some factory jobs possible as well as let some disabled people join the growing number of people who work by "telecommuting," or transferring their work product electronically from their homes to an office across town or across the country.

For John Boyer, who is both deaf and blind, computers have meant a 10-year career as a programmer and, recently, the beginning of his own company, Computers to Help People Inc. The Madison, Wis., company's purpose is to train disabled people to use computers in their work and to do research and develop software for that purpose.

Mr. Boyer settled on his programming career during college partly because it was one of the few in which the experts welcomed him. "To be respected in this society, you have to have a job, and that's as it should be," he says, speaking confidently after an assistant repeats an interviewer's questions by quickly using a kind of sign language to "finger-spell" each word into the palm of his hand. . . .

The first person hired by Mr. Boyer is Michael Reece, a 30-year-old computer programmer who has cerebral palsy and who uses a mouth stick to type on a terminal keyboard.

Because of their disabilities, Mr. Boyer and Mr. Reece use a computer to talk with each other. After Mr. Reece types a message on the computer screen, Mr. Boyer uses an Optacon, a device made by Telesensory Systems of Mountain View, Calif., that can "read" words on a video monitor and then translate them into a tactile display. . . .

"It bugs me when people ask how I can use a computer since I can't see," says Roger Petersen, a consultant. "A computer responds to arbitrary streams and pulses, and it doesn't care if they are coming to it through a joy stick or a sip-and-puff switch, or if the output is in Braille or on a screen. . . .

That adaptability contracts [sic] with what Mr. Shworles calls "the old broken-person model" or the approach that assumes an individual's life will be controlled by his disabilities. The construction of wheelchair ramps and graded curbstones began when the disabled focused on the need to change their environment rather than letting that environment control their lives.

A comparable goal for computer use is to adapt the various kinds of machines and operating systems to make them readily accessible to disabled people. Gregg Vanderheiden, director of the University of Wisconsin's Trace Center, says that will often require the use of special devices designed for those who can't manipulate standard computer keyboards, even with pointing sticks. Those devices are called "keyboard emulators" and were developed for commercial use at the university. . . .

The keyboard emulator is a critical development because it means the disabled can use the software developed for the general market. It would be nearly impossible to duplicate the already-huge library of programs in the ways that might be needed to fit particular disabilities.

Mr. Vanderheiden likens the keyboard emulator to the ramps that now are commonly built into sidewalk curbs. "If we'd thought of putting in those curb cuts in the first place, we wouldn't have had to go back and do it," he says. "So as we're building our information highways, we have to make sure we don't forget the technical 'curb cuts' that are necessary for some people to have access to them." . . .

Inevitable Move

"Computer companies are seeing their technology driven toward rapid innovation as a way of capturing a large market share," says Craig Heckathorne, a rehabilitation engineer at Northwestern University. "Engineers can't match that level of resources. While we can technically emulate computers, I wonder if we'll have the resources to keep pace."

He says one solution is for disabled consumers to begin pressuring computer companies to make their new machines accessible from the start. And the industry's slow but inevitable move toward standardizing computer-operating systems and languages would be even more important to the disabled.

The general consumer is likely to benefit, however, from research being done specifically for the disabled. At Michigan State University, John Eulenberg, director of the artificial-language laboratory, has fitted about 20 severely disabled people who also can't speak with custom-made personal computers that include synthetic voices. The effort involves advanced research that Prof. Eulenberg, a linguist and computer scientist, hopes will eventually result in computers that can pick up impulses directly from the central nervous system.

One of the short-term goals already has been achieved. Computers with synthetic voices are being built for people with severe physical handicaps at rehabilitation centers around the country, even though research on some of the customized systems costs hundreds of thousands of dollars. Prof. Eulenberg says that if there can be "talking" microwave ovens, there should be a way for voice-disabled people to talk. "The essence of being human is being able to communicate," he adds.

Special-Interest Groups

. . . "Disabled consumers will have to keep pounding on the doors of the rehabilitation network with computer companies and telling them to look at things the way we do," Mr. Schworles says. "It's imperative that people with disabilities become their own priests. No one can tell them what's the best computer system for them."

SOURCE: Jeanne Saddler, *The Wall Street Journal,* February 7, 1984, pp. 1, 18. Reprinted by permission of *The Wall Street Journal.* © Dow Jones & Company, Inc. (1984). All rights reserved.

and movies' treatment of disability are Lauri Klobas and Paul Longmore. Klobas writes for *The Disability Rag* (see box, pp. 472–473) and is preparing a book in which she reviews over 400 TV episodes that involve a handicapped character. The "report card" she has kept on TV for several years contains virtually all failing grades (see *TV Guide* article by Kalter pp. 483–484). Longmore (1985), approaching the topic from a sociological perspective, also cites numerous instances of misrepresentation of disability in electronic media.

Jane Fonda and Jon Voight in the movie "Coming Home." Critics of disabilities in the media point to "Coming Home" as one of the few movies that portrays disabilities accurately. (© 1987 United Artists Pictures. All rights reserved.)

Both Klobas (1985) and Longmore (1985) fault TV and films for stereotyping handicapped individuals. Between them, Klobas and Longmore assert that TV and films use five common disability images. They portray the handicapped person as one or more of the following: criminal, monster, suicidal, maladjusted, or sexually deviant. The most prevalent characterization, Longmore claims, is that of the maladjusted disabled person:

> The plots follow a consistent pattern: the disabled central characters are bitter and self-pitying because, however long they have been disabled, they have never adjusted to their handicaps, and have never accepted themselves as they are. Consequently, they treat nondisabled family and friends angrily and manipulatively. At first, the nondisabled characters, feeling sorry for them, coddle them, but eventually they realize that in order to help the disabled individuals adjust and cope they must "get tough." The stories climax in a confrontation scene in which a nondisabled character gives the disabled individual an emotional "slap in the face" and tells him or her to stop feeling sorry for themselves. Accepting the rebuke, the disabled characters quit complaining and become well-adjusted adults. (Longmore, 1985, p. 34)

Longmore maintains that these characterizations reinforce common prejudices and stereotypes—for instance, images of handicapped people as criminals (Dr. Strangelove is used as an example) foster three common prejudices. Disabled individuals:

1. have been punished for doing evil,
2. are embittered by their fate, and
3. resent nonhandicapped people and seek to destroy them.

These prejudices offer the viewer absolution for any difficulties faced by handicapped people and allow nonhandicapped people to "blame the victims" for their own problems. Rarely do movie themes acknowledge society's role in creating attitudinal barriers for handicapped people.

When TV does attempt to portray handicapped people in a positive light, it often ends up highlighting phenomenal accomplishments—a one-legged skier, a wheelchair marathoner, and so forth. This superhero image, according to some disability activists, is a mixed blessing. It does promote the notion that being disabled does not automatically stop one from achieving. Activists claim, however, that such human interest stories:

> suggest that disabled people can best prove their social acceptability, their worthiness of social integration, by displaying some physical capability. Finally, these features also reiterate, with the active complicity of the disabled participants themselves, the view that disability is a problem of individual emotional coping and physical overcoming, rather than an issue of social discrimination against a stigmatized minority. (Longmore, 1985, p. 35).

Although disability activists, for the most part, have been extremely displeased with TV's handling of disabilities, they have been more complimentary of TV advertising that uses disabled characters (Longmore, 1985). Beginning in the mid-1980s, a few TV commercials have used handicapped people. Those who watched the 1984 Summer Olympics, for example, were treated to a Levi jeans commercial showing a group of young people going down the street in time to music. One of the characters was in a wheelchair. Ads such as this one, and others using handicapped actors, have been applauded by activists because they present handicapped people in a casual or

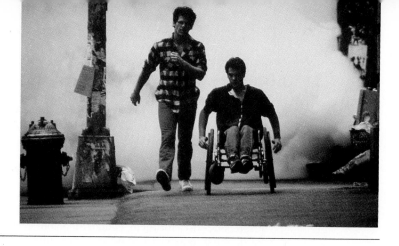

This commercial for Levi Strauss 501 Jeans has been applauded by disabled people and special education professionals. It shows a disabled person in a natural and nonstereotypical way. (Levi Strauss)

"normalized" manner. They promote what activists call "disability cool," an approach that neither denies nor overdoes the handicap (see *TV Guide* article by Kalter in the box on pp. 483–484).

Written Media

LITERATURE   Several professionals have pointed out that literature often reinforces negative stereotypes about disabled people (Kent, 1986; Kriegel, 1986). Considering physical disabilities, for example, Kriegel states that Melville's Ahab is an example of a physically handicapped person being portrayed as evil. Even more important, he is depicted as demonic *because* of his disability. His obsession over the loss of his leg drives him to seek revenge on the great white whale. In addition to the depiction of physically handicapped people as evil, Kriegel notes that another literary image is that of the charity case, like Dickens' Tiny Tim.

Kent's (1986) analysis focused on 24 twentieth-century novels and plays, which contained a total of 27 disabled women characters. She states that the predominant characterization of these women is one of passivity, helplessness, and victimization. Almost one-third of them, in fact, owe their disability to an act of violence or an accident, with the accident often being due to someone else's carelessness. According to Kent, relationships with men are rarely normal. The man is either perversely attracted to the woman because of her disability, or he is repulsed by it. In either case, the man's feelings toward the woman center on the disability: The disability defines the relationship.

JOURNALISM   Few writers have focused on journalism's treatment of disability. What analyses have been done, however, have not been favorable. For example, two separate critiques (Baer, 1984; Biklen, 1986) of how the press covered a particular situation germane to special education (the Baby Jane Doe case, which is similar in some respects to the Baby Doe case we discussed on p. 474) pointed out that a number of inaccuracies and misleading comments were published. Perhaps more important from a disability rights perspective, the press focused almost exclusively on the dramatic, although admittedly important, question of whether the infant should live or die and who should decide, while largely ignoring the issue of society's obligation to provide services for disabled people (Biklen, 1986).

Simmons and Kameenui (1986) systematically investigated the treatment of one specific category of special education, learning disabilities, in popular magazines such as *Time, Reader's Digest, Better Homes and Gardens,* and *McCall's.* They found

Good News: The Disabled Get More Play on TV
Bad News: There Is Still Too Much Stereotyping

He wears fashionable black-leather pants. He suavely kisses a reporter's hand. He dispenses buttons with his name on them. And, as he slips a cassette of his TV appearances into the VCR—bit spots from *T.J. Hooker, AfterMASH* and *Hill Street Blues*—he says, as if stunned by his own brilliance, "This will blow you away." Like so many Hollywood hopefuls, Henry Holden is a tireless self-promoter, determined to reach the top: "It's gonna happen," he says. "I will emerge." But unlike others, if he does, he'll be getting there on crutches.

Holden—who contracted polio at age 4—is one of an emerging generation of performers who see their roles on a larger stage; they are not only actors but activists—leading players in a fight against stereotypes and discrimination. . . .

Lauri Klobas, who keeps tabs on what she calls "phys diz show biz" for a feisty rights magazine named The Disability Rag, tracks at least three such stories a week. Ace's old girl friend shows up in a wheelchair on ABC's *The Love Boat;* an accident paralyzes a high-school boy on NBC's *Highway to Heaven.* And that's not counting the regulars—such as Victoria Ann-Lewis, who, post-polio, plays a secretary on CBS's *Knots Landing,* or Hugh Farrington, a paraplegic, who's a police lieutenant on ABC's *T.J. Hooker.* . . .

The good news about this Disability Chic, say the activists, is that characters with disabilities are more often portrayed by performers with disabilities. They filled about 150 roles last year, mostly on TV, compared with some 20 only five years ago, says Tari Susan Hartman, executive director of California's Media Access Office. Even better news, they say, is that TV makes more use of disabled actors in "nonspecific" roles—where their disability is not central to the part. Only a few years ago, you never saw a disabled person in a TV ad. Today, they rush for Big Macs, tout Plymouth Voyagers, pop wheelies in Levi Strauss jeans. But there's bad news, too: TV may have increased the quantity of these roles, but it's done little to improve their quality. And how do the disabled rate their present TV image? Says Holden, "It's garbage."

Your basic "crip show," say those in the know, is drawn from the charity model—the telethon. Disabled characters are often just larger versions of "Jerry's kids"—poor, afflicted creatures who need us open-minded able-bodied folk to buck them up. Darn it, such stories imply, if only they would quit being bitter and learn to accept themselves!

. . .

As every TV scriptwriter knows, deformity of the body is a sure sign of deformity of the soul. That theme carries from one of the all-time most popular shows, ABC's *The Fugitive,* in which a "one-armed man" was the *real* killer of David Janssen's hapless TV-wife, to one of the most acclaimed, PBS's *The Jewel in the Crown,* in which that vile racist, Ronald Merrick, lost an arm in battle. It's probably all that pent-up, self-pitying bitterness, Klobas jokes, that makes the disabled such villains. And never mind the projected fears of the nondisabled.

The flip side of TV's "bitter crip" is its "supercrip." Here, say the activists, disabled people are portrayed as courageous, inspirational, superhuman. Blind people, for instance, are commonly endowed with miraculous powers. In a 1983 episode of CBS's *Simon & Simon,* a blind woman witnesses a crime. Later, riding between A.J. and Rick, she spots the getaway car. How? She recognizes the sound of its engine and the smell of its exhaust. Of course! "Smellovision," Klobas calls this. "Watch enough TV and you'll think that blind people walk around sniffing you." Which is not to say that overcoming the obstacles of life is not the stuff of basic human drama. Only to note that TV's disabled people must go to such extraordinary lengths to do so. In HBO's "The Terry Fox Story," based on real life, a young amputee hops across country on one leg. "Sure, it raised money for cancer research and sure, it showed the human capacity for achievement," says Alan Toy, who walks with a brace and who's appeared in shows ranging from *Airwolf* to *Trauma Center.* "But a lot of ordinary disabled people are made to feel like failures if they haven't done something extraordinary. They may be bankers or factory workers—proof enough of their usefulness to society. Do we have to be 'supercrips' in order to be valid? And if we're not so super, are we 'invalid'?"

Some people with disabilities *are* extraordinary, of course, and many wage a difficult struggle for self-worth. But the problem with both the "supercrip" and "bitter crip" stories, say disability-rights activists, is that they treat disability exclusively as a drama of personal adjustment—with no social context. The issue is reduced to one of individual character and courage—rather than of societal stigma and discrimination. And the real concerns of disabled people are rarely explored—access to buildings, unemployment, prejudice. "Viewers would rather think of disability as a problem of emotional coping," says Dr. Paul Longmore, a cultural historian at the University of Southern California. "That way they can let themselves off the hook. 'It's not *our* problem,' they can think. 'It's someone else's'." . . .

There *are* signs of progress, however, particularly where this new generation of disabled people has some input into production. Take the 1983 episode of NBC's *Hill Street Blues,* based on a story by Darrell Ray and Alan Toy. Detective Belker parks in a handicapped space, only to find that a militant young man in a wheelchair, assertive about his civil rights, has painted the car in protest. When Belker hauls him into the precinct house, he gets a funky lesson in just how inaccessible bathrooms are to wheelchairs. . . .

Most often these days, TV's "crip shows" are a mixture of old stereotypes and new consciousness. "Producers and writers have picked up that something's going on out there, but they're not quite sure what it is," says Longmore. "So you see a lot of contradictions." Ray and Toy's *Hill Street Blues* episode, considered a milestone by many, still starred an able-bodied actor. And against their wishes, the militant character he played gets killed in the end, implying, perhaps, that the price of his defiance was death. . . .

What these actors and activists would like to see is what they call "disability cool"—an approach that neither denies their disability nor overdoes it. Most everyone, they say, feels physically imperfect, and almost everyone struggles to overcome difficulties from indebtedness to divorce. Disabilities *are* different—but, says Templeton, "They don't have to be such a big deal."

Will TV ever make that leap? "Perhaps not soon enough to get my star on Hollywood Boulevard," muses Ann-Lewis. Henry Holden replies with characteristic chutzpah: "Two years from now I'll be on the cover of TV GUIDE, crutches and all." He walks past framed cover portraits on his way to the elevator and, as the doors close behind him, shouts out one last thought. "Wish me luck," he says—and can't resist adding, "Break a leg."

SOURCE: Joanmarie Kalter, *TV Guide,* May 31, 1986, pp. 40–44. Reprinted with permission from *TV Guide*® Magazine. Copyright © 1986 by Triangle Publications, Inc., Radnor, Pennsylvania.

that these magazines generally attribute neurological causes for learning disabilities, but they foster the idea that education holds the key to treatment. Regarding the specifics of causes and treatments, however, a great variety of opinion was expressed. Simmons and Kameenui concluded that this diversity is a general reflection of how learning disabilities professionals view their field.

Conclusions: The Media

Those who criticize the media's treatment of issues relating to disability have made a strong case by pointing to the many instances in which disabled individuals were portrayed in an inappropriate manner. More systematic research on this topic, however, might help to document even more convincingly the failure of the media to educate rather than merely entertain (Crowley, 1986). In addition to providing information on how often and in what manner handicapped people appear in the media, further research could help to clarify some interesting issues. For example, how much of the media's depiction of disabled people is a reflection of society's views toward disabilities, and how much does it actually shape society's attitudes? Another important question is whether different characterizations have different effects on attitudes. For instance, does the superhero result in better or worse public perceptions than the maladjusted characterization? Are any of these portrayals better than no exposure at all? Finally, an important issue is how much disabled people, in general, agree with activists' harsh criticism of the media. It would be interesting to know which portrayals draw the strongest criticisms from disabled people themselves, and why.

DEINSTITUTIONALIZATION

The first part of the twentieth century witnessed a growth in the numbers of large residential facilities. Starting in the late 1960s, however, the trend has been to place exceptional individuals in closer contact with the community. More and more exceptional children are being raised by their families. In addition, smaller facilities, constructed within local neighborhoods, are now common. Halfway houses are being used as a placement for disturbed individuals who no longer need the more isolated environment of a large institution. For the retarded population, group homes are being used to house small numbers of individuals whose retardation may range from mild to severe.

One of the reasons large residential institutions are less popular today is that both the general public and the special education profession have become aware of the grossly inadequate care provided by many of them. Blatt and Kaplan's now-classic *Christmas in Purgatory* (1966), a pictorial essay on the squalid conditions of institutional life, did much to raise sentiment against institutions. This book and others like it have shown how bad residential living for exceptional individuals *can* be. But a caution is in order here. Not all institutions are dehumanizing and grossly mismanaged. Actually, there is great variety in the quality of institutional programs.

In addition, a number of cautions regarding the reality of deinstitutionalization should be noted. Like mainstreaming, deinstitutionalization is doomed to fail unless careful steps are taken to ensure its success. Merely placing retarded individuals in group homes is not enough. Such variables as caretaker experience, accessibility to support services, and the degree of acceptance by the surrounding community are important to the success of a group home (Eyman, Demaine, and Lei, 1979; Sutter, 1980).

It is difficult to overemphasize the importance of community acceptance. Homeowners often hesitate to accept group homes for retarded people in their neighborhoods. Kastner, Reppucci, and Pezzoli (1979) devised a study that demonstrated this hesitancy. They had surveyors interview homeowners about their attitudes toward mentally retarded people. In one condition, the surveyors implied that a nearby house that was for sale was being considered as a group home for retarded people; in another condition, no such "threat" was implied. They found that people in the "threat" condition were more likely to respond negatively on items relating to the effects of integrating retarded individuals into neighborhoods. The difficulties surrounding placement of group homes in suburban neighborhoods was the topic of a segment on CBS's *60 Minutes* ("Not My Street," November 2, 1980, produced by

Steve Glauber). The neighbors interviewed on this show were extremely upset about the placement of five retarded men in a typical suburban home on a typical suburban block. The resentment of the neighbors, in fact, was mentioned as a prime reason why two of the men were eventually moved back into a larger institution. The depth of feeling such homes can cause in a neighborhood is evident from the fact that shortly after this show was aired, another nearby house targeted as a group home was set afire.

But setting up group homes does not always spell disaster for either the residents or their neighbors. David and Sheila Rothman (1984) present a case history of the deinstitutionalization of the 5,400-bed Willowbrook State School in New York that can be used as a model of how to go about preparing communities for group homes. The Rothmans note that throughout the history of this massive court-ordered deinstitutionalization in the 1970s, *"Once a group home opened, it was never the object of vandalism or even picketing"* (p. 196). In addition, neighborhood property values did not decline. And the former Willowbrook residents were not placed in marginal neighborhoods. The Rothmans cite a number of factors that led to this relatively smooth establishment of group homes:

> Behind this achievement was MPU's [Metropolitan Placement Unit] readiness to back off a site when a well-organized community was incensed. . . . The location of group homes thus represented something of a compromise between the state and the citizenry. So, too, MPU was not averse to adjusting its placement plans to locate a home in the least desirable section of a highly desirable neighborhood and thus mute opposition. Brooklyn's Community Board 15, where a Save Our Community organization kept its lively vigil on would-be intruders, approved a group home for 3730 Shore Parkway, in part because the owner lived in California and could not be influenced by its opposition, but in part, too, because the block itself, although quite pleasant, was cut off from the rest of the area by a parkway. . . .
>
> The formal procedures that MPU followed contributed, too, to this successful outcome. Opponents exhausted a number of administrative and judicial remedies, and in so doing, exhausted themselves. With ample opportunity to argue their case, they were far more resigned to the home at the end of the hearings than at the beginning. To be sure, had the situation later proved disastrous, had the retarded gone about begging for food, the administrative process would have become irrelevant. But by the same token, were these procedures absent, the community might have remained so hostile as to be incapable of noticing that the lawns were mowed, the retarded cared for, and the real estate values holding firm. . . .
>
> So community placement was accomplished without putting Willowbrook's residents into the wastelands of the city, without altering property values, and without ruining neighborhoods. Sometimes a community's fear of change far exceeds the impact of change, at least on it. For the retarded children and adults lucky enough to move into the community, the change was momentous, in terms of both the quality of the care they received and the life chances they enjoyed (pp. 196–199).

Research on the Effects of Placement in Large Residential Institutions

Many investigators have attempted to determine the effects of living in large facilities on an individual's psychological development. Most of this work has been done on mental retardation institutions. (In Great Britain a great deal of the research has been done by Tizard, 1970, and his colleagues. In the United States Zigler and his colleagues—Butterfield and Zigler, 1965; McCormick, Balla, and Zigler, 1975; Zigler, Balla, and Butterfield, 1968; Zigler, Butterfield, and Capobianco, 1970; Zigler and Williams, 1963—have been heavily involved in this work.) The following conclusions are based on the reviews of Balla (1976), Butterfield (1967), and Zigler (1973):

1. Institutionalization can result in a lowering of cognitive abilities. The most likely areas to be affected are those involving verbal and abstract abilities.
2. Whether cognitive deficiencies are due to decreased intelligence per se or are the result of motivational changes is a debatable issue. There is evidence showing that institutionalization can deprive retarded individuals of social reinforcement.
3. Not all retarded individuals are affected in the same way by institutionalization. For example, those who have come from a socially deprived home environment to an institution are less likely to be harmed by being placed in an institution.
4. Most important, not all institutions are alike. Some can produce positive changes in an individual. Those that make an effort to provide a noninstitutional atmosphere are more likely to produce positive behavioral changes in the residents. In other words, a restrictive regimen can be harmful; a program offering residents an opportunity to live as normally as possible can be beneficial. Wolfensberger's concept of "normalization" is important here (see Soeffing, 1974; Wolfensberger, 1972). He believes that every attempt should be made to make retarded individuals' living, working, and playing arrangements like those of the rest of society.

Research on the Effects of Placement in Community Residential Facilities

Because the trend to place individuals in community residential facilities (CRFs) only started in the 1970s, not a great deal of research has been conducted on the effects of such placement. Most authorities agree, however, that at the very least the potential for better treatment is higher in smaller CRFs than in larger residential facilities. Researchers have demonstrated that the fewer the number of residents served in a residential setting, the more likely it is that the treatment environment will be characterized as positive and homelike (Rotegard, Hill, and Bruininks, 1983). In addition, the limited research done thus far suggests that residents of CRFs achieve better adjustment than do residents of larger facilities. The following conclusions are drawn from studies of CRFs:

1. Movement from larger facilities to CRFs results in better adaptive behavior (Conroy, Efthimiou, and Lemanowicz, 1982; Kleinberg and Galligan, 1983).
2. CRFs provide more social and occupational opportunities for their residents than do larger institutions (Jacobson and Schwartz, 1983).
3. Successful adjustment of CRF residents is related to personal variables such as good vocational skills and mild behavior problems, as well as to environmental factors such as appropriate social supports and clinical services (Jacobson and Schwartz, 1983). With regard to the latter, it is important that residents in the CRF be provided with genuine access to the various community service agencies.

Is Life in a CRF Really Normal?

The reason for moving individuals out of large institutions and into smaller community residential facilities is to provide them with a more normal existence. It is fair to ask, then, how close these small group living arrangements come to achieving the goal of normalization, especially with severely and profoundly handicapped persons. In other words, do individual residents actually participate in the small-group living experience? The answer to this question undeniably varies according to which group home one visits, but Rothman and Rothman, in their investigation of group homes in New York, were able to find CRFs in which residents participated actively and meaningfully in the group life of the home.

The first impression of group-home life at the Lincoln Apartments may be of an elaborate puppet show. Normalization seems a script for the staff-puppeteers to follow as they manipulated the resident-puppets. One puppet is very bright, another very funny, another very affectionate, but all these characteristics appear to be imposed by the staff on residents who are too handicapped physically and mentally to be capable of scripting their own parts. So when one resident wears a Mets cap and has a schedule of the team's game on his wall, the staff is assigning him an interest that he does not possess. Similarly, when the residents sit in front of the TV set with their legs up, the staff is arranging a scene. When two boys of the same age are said to have exchanged gifts, once again there is the suspicion that the staff has set the stage and written the lines. The group home takes on the quality of a performance—an amiable one, to be sure. The atmosphere is relaxed and the residents well cared for; there is no bad puppet. The staff relates to everyone without making anyone into a scapegoat. So even if group homes were nothing more than elaborate puppet shows, that would justify them.

Sustained observation of the daily routine alters this initial impression. Perhaps the enterprise had begun as a puppet show, but in *Pinocchio* fashion, life had been breathed into the puppets. The residents, too, were involved in making some of the decisions. They were not simply plopped in front of the TV, but often "asked" for programs by giving the staff signals that a casual observer might miss. Albert and Ted, both nonverbal, had word boards (one with thirty words, the other with eighty). When they wanted to watch television, they would move a spastic arm until it more or less hit the character for TV. The staff would respond by positioning them in front of the set. There is no way of knowing how much they understood of the program. But they made the request, and that required effort and forethought.

The residents' imprecise gestures meant that the staff, like parents of an infant, had to listen and watch for clues. What was surprising was how many signals the residents transmitted. Sounds or flailing gestures that at first appeared random were deliberate attempts to gain assistance. . . .

There was an unspoken contract between staff and residents, which both honored. The staff had taught that it would respond to signals by residents that expressed their own will. The residents, in turn, made the effort, knowing it would be rewarded.

Rothman and Rothman also address the question of whether group homes are ever really integrated into the social fabric of the community. According to the Rothmans, it is really a matter of what you mean by integration:

It may also be time to bury the question of whether group homes are or are not in the community. If critics go on at length about the difficulty of getting normals to be friends with the retarded—as though community living is the equivalent of intimate ties—supporters get rhapsodic about the visit to the museum or the zoo—as if living in a community involves a checklist of events attended. Are group homes in the community? No, if one means choosing acquaintances by preference (not by the accident of a shared residence), or attending different functions with different social circles (basketball games with one, weddings with another). Yes, if by community one is talking about visibility (so that residents are better protected from abuse) or convenient location (so that staff would prefer to work there). And finally, yes, if one means the opportunity to exercise some degree of choice and enjoy a variety of life's ordinary experiences.

A month after a number of blind and deaf clients from Willowbrook moved into their group home, they and their staff went out for a walk. A few minutes later, it started to rain and the clients, to the staff's bewilderment and horror, started to take off their clothes. As the counselors frantically tried to keep them covered, it dawned on them that the clients assumed it was shower-time at the facility. They had never before felt the rain.

SOURCE: David J. Rothman and Sheila M. Rothman, *The Willowbrook Wars*, pp. 228–229 and 252–253. Copyright © 1984 by David J. Rothman and Sheila M. Rothman. Reprinted by permission of Harper & Row, Publishers, Inc.

4. Evidence suggests that better resident care is generally associated with staff job satisfaction, and studies indicate that there is better job satisfaction in CRFs with decentralized, community-oriented service delivery systems (Jacobson and Schwartz, 1983).

MAINSTREAMING

Many professionals have viewed **mainstreaming**—the integration of handicapped students into general education classes—as the primary method by which schools can help exceptional children achieve normalization. Even though the concept of mainstreaming has been around for several years, there have been changes in how special educators have approached the topic. For this reason, we have organized our discussion according to two different time periods—the efficacy studies era (ca. 1950–1980) and the post-efficacy studies era (ca. 1980–present). The dates for these phases are estimates; no single event marked the end of one era and the beginning of the next.

The Efficacy Studies Era (ca. 1950–1980)

For several years it was the preoccupation of special educators to conduct studies comparing handicapped children's placement in various types of service delivery configurations, e.g., special classes versus general education classrooms, special classes versus resource rooms, and so forth. From 1950 to 1980, at least 50 such studies were conducted (Carlberg and Kavale, 1980). Commonly referred to as "the efficacy studies" by special educators, the studies were the source of considerable debate. Results were sometimes mixed, and further complicating the picture was the fact that the results tended to be different for academic versus social outcomes. In general, the studies suggested that special class placement was of little benefit in terms of academic achievement, but there was some evidence suggesting that regular class placement tended to result in a lower acceptance of handicapped students by their nonhandicapped peers (Gottlieb, Alter, and Gottlieb, 1983; Strain and Kerr, 1981).

Although results were sometimes contradictory, many believed the efficacy studies were cause for indictment of special classes for exceptional children. In the absence of strong evidence that special classes were effective, especially with regard to achievement, many special educators called their existence into question. The most famous indictment came in an article by Lloyd Dunn (1968) entitled "Special Education for the Mildly Retarded—Is Much of It Justifiable?" in which he concluded there was no evidence to justify the existence of special classes for this population. In essence, what authorities like Dunn were saying was that, since special classes required segregrating handicapped children from their peers, the burden of proof was on those who set up special classes to prove their effectiveness.

The End of the Efficacy Studies Era

Around 1980, special educators began to lose their enthusiasm for both conducting and reviewing standard efficacy studies. Although efficacy studies (e.g., Wang and Birch, 1984a) and reviews of efficacy studies (e.g., Carlberg and Kavale, 1980; Leinhardt and Pallay, 1982; Madden and Slavin, 1983) did not come to a complete stop at this time, their frequency did begin to wane substantially, for at least four reasons:

1. After so many studies, there were still no clear-cut answers. The mixed results were a source of frustration.
2. Numerous authorities pointed out that with a few rare exceptions (e.g., Budoff and Gottlieb, 1976; Goldstein, Moss, and Jordan, 1965) efficacy studies, on the whole, were methodologically inadequate (Gottlieb, Alter, and Gottlieb, 1983; Keogh and Levitt, 1976; MacMillan and Becker, 1977; Robinson and Robinson, 1976; Tindal, 1985). One of the major flaws was that the students were not randomly assigned to special versus general education classes. Those selected to go into special classes could very likely have been much more difficult to teach than those left in the regular classes. This was not always a case of researchers not having an adequate grasp of research methodology. Investigators were understandably hesitant for ethical reasons in many cases to assign students randomly. If they or school personnel believed one setting to be more beneficial, they often believed they would have a hard time defending placement of a child in the one they believed to be less appropriate. The fact that randomization in most cases is not possible has caused some to question the results of earlier efficacy studies and to lose interest in conducting any more.
3. The majority of efficacy studies were conducted so long ago (many date back to the 1950s) that they are in many ways an unfair test of the effectiveness of different service delivery options (Hallahan and Keller, 1986). One can probably assume that both mainstreaming practices as well as special class instructional procedures have improved since many of the studies were conducted.
4. One of the primary reasons why research comparing the effectiveness of various service delivery options has been so contradictory is that, by focusing on *physical placements* to the exclusion of what goes on in those settings, researchers have overestimated the role settings per se play in affecting children's learning or social development (Bickel and Bickel, 1986; Hallahan and Keller, 1986; Lakin, 1983). In other words, researchers have tended to view

One of the problems with the efficacy studies was that they focused on physical placement and did not address what kind of instruction goes on in those settings. (Jeff Lowenthal/Woodfin Camp & Associates)

the setting as the critical variable and have often neglected to delve more deeply into what goes on in that setting in terms of instruction.

These factors figured heavily in ending the emphasis on efficacy studies as a way of approaching the issue of mainstreaming. Essentially, they were neutral with regard to the question of whether special classes were effective or not—those arguing in favor of special classes said that efficacy studies were inconclusive and mainstreaming advocates said that their very inconclusiveness was reason to abolish special classes. In any case, the concerns about efficacy research set the stage for what we have called the post-efficacy studies era.

The Post-Efficacy Studies Era (ca. 1980–present)

Since about 1980, those advocating mainstreaming have used two general arguments:

1. Some, who have written on the topic from the perspective of advocates, have emphasized ethical issues: Mainstreaming is the *right* thing to do because, unlike special class and resource class programming, it does not require segregating handicapped students from their peers.
2. Some, in general agreement with the arguments concerning overemphasis on physical setting in most efficacy studies, have begun to look at the educational process with the goal of finding ways of facilitating the principle of mainstreaming. They have investigated different ways of structuring what goes on in the classroom, as well as different ways in which educational personnel can be used to enhance the chances of successful mainstreaming.

Ethical Arguments for Mainstreaming

Cruickshank (1977) was among the first to point out that for some professionals, the question of appropriate placements for exceptional children is less of a research issue than an ethical one. Although they may refer to research when appropriate, their emphasis is more on the philosophical conviction that mainstreaming is right because it is more ethical and moral than are placements, such as special classes and resource rooms, that segregate handicapped students from nonhandicapped peers. These advocates are often aligned with the disability rights movement and believe that labeling children as handicapped is detrimental. The best of their arguments are viewed by many as eloquent and compelling. For example, one mainstreaming advocate, who is also a disability rights activist, has written:

> There is much to be done to honor the commitment to ourselves and to those with handicapping conditions. The guarantee of access must be met. We will have failed the students and the virtue which propelled P.L. 94-142, however, if we use it to shove into special education students who do not need to be there, if we allow misguided benevolence to be the motivating force rather than the struggle to improve education for all students, or if we permanently handicap those we place in special education. Sadly, too much of what goes on under the label of benefit to children takes the form of "disabling help." (Gartner, 1986, p. 76)

Implementing the Principle of Mainstreaming

There are a variety of recommendations about how to better the chances that mainstreaming will work. We will briefly discuss six of the most common strategies.

1. To encourage general education teachers to use teaching practices with handicapped students that have been found to be effective with nonhandicapped students.
2. To use special educators as teacher consultants to help general education teachers cope with the special problems presented by handicapped youngsters.
3. To establish prereferral teams to ensure that only those who truly need special education services are identified for them.
4. To structure classroom activities to encourage cooperative learning among students of different ability levels.

As more and more handicapped students are being mainstreamed, better ways of meeting their needs are being implemented. (Will McIntyre/Photo Researchers, Inc.)

5. To structure classroom activities so that nonhandicapped students act as tutors for their handicapped peers.
6. To use commercially available curriculum materials designed to change nonhandicapped students' attitudes toward their handicapped peers.

ENCOURAGING GENERAL EDUCATION TEACHERS TO USE EFFECTIVE TEACHING PRACTICES   In the late 1970s, educational researchers began experimentally to address the question of which teaching behaviors in general education classrooms lead to student achievement. This body of literature has been referred to as the **effective teaching research.** Those conducting effective teaching studies have arrived at a relatively consistent set of findings (Rosenshine, 1983; Walberg, 1984). Although very few of these investigators have included handicapped students in their samples, they have often included low-achieving pupils. A review of experiments that included students who were younger, slower, and/or had little prior knowledge concluded that teachers were most effective with these students when they:

> structure the learning; proceed in small steps at a brisk pace; give detailed and redundant instructions and explanations; provide many examples; ask a large number of questions and corrections, particularly in the initial stages of learning new material; have a student success rate of 80% or higher in initial learning; divide seatwork assignments into smaller assignments; and provide for continued student practice so that students have a success rate of 90%–100% and become rapid, confident, and firm. (Rosenshine, 1983, pp. 336–337)

And in one of the few studies to include handicapped mainstreamed students, a similar set of teaching behaviors were identified as related to handicapped children's success: providing positive feedback, giving sustaining feedback, responding supportively to students in general, responding supportively to low-ability students, responding supportively to learning problem behaviors, asking questions that receive correct student responses, ensuring high success rate, using time efficiently, manifesting a low rate of intervention for misbehavior, using punitive interventions infrequently, using few punitive responses, criticizing responses infrequently, disciplining students infrequently, using little time for student transitions, and having a low rate of off-task time (Larrivee, 1985).

Some special and general educators have stated that results of the teaching effectiveness literature should be used as a way of fostering successful mainstreaming. They maintain that, if general education teachers would engage in more of these successful teaching behaviors, they could teach many of the handicapped children who usually go to special or resource classes (Reynolds and Lakin, 1987; Wang, Reynolds, and Walberg, 1986).

One program that has been designed to implement effective teaching principles is the Adaptive Learning Environments Model (ALEM) developed by Margaret Wang and her colleagues (Wang and Birch, 1984a, b; Wang, Peverly, and Randolph, 1984; Wang and Walberg, 1983). ALEM classrooms have served many different types of exceptional children, as well as gifted students integrated with nonhandicapped peers. ALEM has two major components—a prescriptive learning element and a self-responsibility element. The prescriptive learning component, based on the teaching effectiveness literature, is highly structured, has built-in diagnostic procedures, and stresses having the student progress through the curriculum at his or her own pace. The self-responsibility segment of ALEM is less structured, and it involves such activities as having students plan and manage their own learning activities.

Mainstreaming in Reverse

Traditionally, most people think of mainstreaming in terms of placing a few handicapped children in classes primarily composed of nonhandicapped students. Some professionals, however, have advocated what has come to be called **reverse mainstreaming**—that is, the placement of a few nonhandicapped children in classes primarily composed of handicapped children. McCann, Semmel, and Nevin (1985) have presented the following arguments for the potential benefits of reverse mainstreaming versus traditional mainstreaming:

> Many of the conditions which characterize reverse mainstreaming appear more conducive to prosocial peer interaction than do those typical of traditional mainstreaming:

> Handicapped students are clearly not minority group members identified as "different" in special education classrooms. They do not lose their group affiliation, and they are not placed in the position of entering extant social groups when nonhandicapped peers are brought into the special class. The burden of achieving social acceptance is shifted to the nonhandicapped student, and teachers have discretion in selecting socially appropriate students to send to special classes. The ratio of handicapped to nonhandicapped students favors intergroup social interaction, since the majority of available peers are handicapped. Special education teachers are more likely to be aware of the need for and methods of providing special programming to facilitate positive social interaction, e.g., cooperative learning activities. Visits to special classes may reduce nonhandicapped students' fears and ignorance of these classes, with concomitant reductions in stigma associated with them. Further, reverse mainstreaming may provide opportunities for handicapped students to establish friendships with nonhandicapped students which may become critical sources of social acceptance when the handicapped student is mainstreamed in regular classes.

Although the rationale for reverse mainstreaming is well articulated, further research is needed to answer certain questions. So far there are few data available on its effectiveness. We do not even know how widespread reverse mainstreaming is. In addition, research is lacking on such things as the optimum length of time for integration and the optimum blend of pupil (handicapped and nonhandicapped alike) characteristics such as age, sex, and types of disabilities.

One fear raised is that nonhandicapped children will be harmed by reverse mainstreaming because it might expose them to inappropriate models. Although more research is needed on this topic, one study found no negative influence of reverse mainstreaming on nonhandicapped preschoolers (Odom, Deklyen, and Jenkins, 1984). The nonhandicapped preschoolers were integrated with mildly and moderately handicapped preschoolers at a ratio of 1 to 2. The researchers found no differences between an integrated group and a nonintegrated group on measures of intelligence, communication, and social development. Noting the small-scale nature of their study, however, they did caution that to "understand further the developmental effect of integrated special education on nonhandicapped children, replications in different settings, possibly with different proportions of handicapped children and different curriculum models, are recommended" (Odom et al., p. 47).

Research on the effectiveness of ALEM for handicapped students has been promising but inconclusive. Researchers have not always been consistent in reporting the specific effects of the program on the handicapped children involved. Some (e.g., Gallagher, 1986) have criticized the authors of ALEM studies for lack of precision in reporting procedures and sample characteristics. Critics of the program have been few thus far, and it is fair to say that ALEM has a large group of supporters, with one report (Wang and Birch, 1984b) stating that as of 1984 ALEM was being used in over 150 school districts in over 28 states.

USING TEACHER CONSULTANTS   Although only a handful of states offer certification in **teacher consultation,** there has been since the early 1980s an ardent group of professionals from around the country who are advocates of teacher consultation (Idol-Maestas, 1983; Idol-Maestas, 1986; Knight, Meyers, Paolucci-Whitcomb, Hasazi, and Nevin, 1981; Lew, Mesch, and Lates, 1982; Nelson and Stevens, 1981). A variety of personnel can provide consultation to the general education teacher, but resource teachers or school psychologists most often deliver such services. Teacher consultation is defined as:

> supportive services provided to classroom teachers to assist with academic and social behavior problems of mildly and moderately handicapped students. As defined and discussed by Idol-Maestas (1983) this support can be provided for academic and behavioral assessment, appropriate academic placement, child management systems, and utilization of data-based instruction to ensure academic and behavioral growth of all students. (Idol-Maestas, 1986, p. 8)

Authorities have cited a number of advantages of teacher consultation. Some of these are: (1) It is cost-efficient because the consultant can have an impact on many students; (2) general educators learn strategies for working with a variety of students, some of whom may be identified as handicapped and some of whom may not; (3) it allows for flexibility with regard to when and in what quantity services are provided; and (4) it keeps handicapped youngsters in the mainstream (Idol-Maestas, 1986).

There has been relatively little research on the effectiveness of teacher consultation, but the few studies done have been encouraging (Idol-Maestas, 1981; Knight et al., 1981; Lew et al., 1982; Marotz-Sprague and Nelson, 1979; Miller and Sabatino, 1978; Nelson and Stevens, 1981; Nevin, Paolucci-Whitcomb, Duncan, and Thibodeau, 1982; Paolucci-Whitcomb and Nevin, 1985). Some have noted that the greatest impediment to successful implementation of teacher consultation is that most states do not have separate certification requirements for this type of professional (Haight, 1984; Nelson and Stevens, 1981). Without this, they point out, it is difficult to define the role of teacher consultants.

ESTABLISHING PREREFERRAL TEAMS   Closely aligned with the notion of teacher consultation is the practice of using **prereferral teams (PRTs).** Both involve professionals helping general education teachers deal with students who have problems in their classrooms. There are three essential ways in which they differ, however. First, teacher consultants are individuals, and PRTs consist of groups. Second, as indicated by their title, PRTs' emphasis is on keeping students from being formally referred for special education services. Although teacher consultants can and do often serve the same purpose, they put less stress on the notion of limiting referrals and usually do work with students identified as handicapped. Third, teacher consultants are invariably other than general education teachers, whereas some believe that general educators are the essential members of PRTs.

The role of the PRT is to work with classroom teachers to recommend different strategies for working with youngsters exhibiting academic and/or behavioral problems. One of the primary goals is to establish "ownership" of these types of children with general and not special educators. In other words, PRTs try to keep referrals to special education down by stressing that general educators need to try as many alternative strategies as possible before deciding that difficult-to-teach students need to become the primary responsibility of special educators.

Because of this emphasis on general education's ownership, some have maintained that general educators are the most important team members (Chalfant, Psych, and Moultrie, 1979; Gerber and Semmel, 1984, 1985). A major justification for using classroom teachers to make decisions regarding referral to special education is that they may have information on individual children that is even more important than the usual standardized test data:

> Teachers observe tens of thousands of discrete behavioral events during each school day. Formal tests of ability and achievement are based on analysis of only small samples of student behavior. Clearly teachers have available to them, if they choose to use it, a far richer and varied sample of student behavior than the typical "test." (Gerber and Semmel, 1984, p. 141)

There is very little research on the effectiveness of PRTs. The few evaluations that have been done indicate two things: (1) They do cut down on the number of referrals to special education, and (2) team members and administrators report that they are effective (Schram et al., 1984).

ENCOURAGING COOPERATIVE LEARNING   Much emphasis is placed on competition in the traditional regular class. This focus, some believe, is detrimental to the success of all students, especially those who are handicapped or of lower ability (D. Johnson and R. Johnson, 1984, 1986; Slavin, 1983). D. and R. Johnson have found that **cooperative learning**—involving handicapped and nonhandicapped peers in situations in which they must cooperate with one another—leads to better attitudes on the part of the nonhandicapped toward their handicapped peers as well as better attitudes of handicapped students toward themselves.

The Johnsons believe that cooperative situations foster differentiated, dynamic, and realistic views of group members, including the handicapped students taking part in the cooperative venture. By *differentiated,* they mean that a child is viewed as possessing more attributes than just the stereotypic ones that accompany his or her label. And by *dynamic,* they mean that a child's attributes may not be viewed by other group members as relevant to all aspects of the task at hand. They state:

> New information on the handicapped peer is admitted into one's impression as it becomes relevant. Thus, if a peer is visually impaired, this category may be noted when the group is trying to read what the teacher has written on the blackboard, but it is forgotten when the group discusses the material they are studying. The conceptualization of the handicapped peer stays in a dynamic state of change, open to modification with new information, and takes into account situational factors.

> When nonhandicapped students work closely with a handicapped peer, the boundaries of the handicap [become] . . . more and more clear. Although handicapped students may be able to hide the extent of their disabilities when they are isolated, [cooperation] . . . promotes a realistic as well as differentiated view of the handicapped students. If a handicapped member of a learning group cannot read or speak clearly, the other members of the learning group become highly aware of the fact. With the realistic perception, however, there also comes a decrease in the primary potency of the handicap and a decrease in the stigmatization connected to the handicapped student. (Johnson and Johnson, 1984, pp. 126–127)

Table 10-1   Cooperation versus Competition

Compared with competitive and individualistic learning situations, working cooperatively with peers:

1. Will create a pattern of promotive interaction, in which there is
   a. more direct face-to-face interaction among students;
   b. an expectation that one's peers will facilitate one's learning;
   c. more peer pressure toward achievement and appropriate classroom behavior;
   d. more reciprocal communication and fewer difficulties in communicating with each other;
   e. more actual helping, tutoring, assisting, and general facilitation of each other's learning;
   f. more open-mindedness to peers and willingness to be influenced by their ideas and information;
   g. more positive feedback to and reinforcement of each other;
   h. less hostility, both verbal and physical, expressed towards peers.

2. Will create perceptions and feelings of
   a. higher trust in other students;
   b. more mutual concern and friendliness for other students, more attentiveness to peers, more feelings of obligation to and responsibility for classmates, and desire to win the respect of other students;
   c. stronger beliefs that one is liked, supported, and accepted by other students, and that other students care about how much one learns and want to help one learn;
   d. lower fear of failure and higher psychological safety;
   e. higher valuing of classmates;
   f. greater feelings of success.

SOURCE: D. Johnson and R. Johnson, "Classroom Learning Structure and Attitudes toward Handicapped Students in Mainstream Settings: A Theoretical Model and Research Evidence", in R. L. Jones (Ed.), *Attitudes and Attitude Change in Special Education: Theory and Practice* (Reston, Va.: The Council for Exceptional Children, 1984). Reprinted with permission.

And once the teacher places handicapped and nonhandicapped students in small, heterogeneous groups for the purpose of working toward a common goal, Johnson and Johnson state that a number of positive things will happen (see Table 10-1).

Although the Johnsons' use of cooperative learning has led to positive changes in attitudes, they have been less successful in affecting achievement. They have looked at achievement in only a few of their studies (Armstrong, D. Johnson, and Balow, 1981; D. Johnson, and R. Johnson, 1982; Nevin, D. Johnson, and R. Johnson, 1982; D. Johnson and R. Johnson, 1982), and the results have been mixed. An investigator who has designed cooperative learning situations which have led to achievement gains, however, is Robert Slavin.

Although only a few of Slavin's studies have included formally identified handicapped students, he has used cooperative learning with low-ability students. He concludes that, in order for there to be positive effects on achievement, cooperative learning must involve two elements: (1) There must be group incentives, and (2) there must be individual accountability. What should be avoided are situations in which the group's solution to a problem can be found by just one or two members. One way of doing this is to base rewards on the group's average so that each individual's score contributes to the total score of the group (Slavin, 1983).

USING PEER TUTORS   Yet another recommended method of integrating handicapped students into the mainstream is peer tutoring. **Peer tutoring** is defined as one student tutoring another. Professionals have advocated using handicapped children as tutors as well as tutees. When a handicapped child assumes the role of tutor, the tutee is usually a younger peer.

Research results on the effectiveness of peer tutoring are mixed (Gerber and Kauffman, 1981; Osguthorpe and Scruggs, 1986; Scruggs and Richter, 1986). There is evidence suggesting that mildly handicapped students can benefit academically when serving as tutor or tutee. There is little empirical data, however, to show that it improves self-concept.

An important caution to keep in mind is that, contrary to what some educators believe, peer tutoring is not a time-saver (Gerber and Kauffman, 1981). A good peer tutoring situation requires continuous organization and monitoring by the teacher.

USING CURRICULUM MATERIALS TO CHANGE ATTITUDES   Curriculum materials have been developed to enlighten regular education students about exceptional children. These materials often involve activities constructed to teach children about different aspects of disabilities, such as causes and characteristics, as well as to let students explore their feelings about handicapped children. Sapon-Shevin (1983) has reviewed a number of these materials, ranging from full-blown curricula such as *Accepting Individual Differences* (Cohen, 1977) and *What If You Couldn't?: An Elementary School Program about Handicaps* (Children's Museum of Boston, 1978) to individual books such as *Don't Feel Sorry for Paul* (Wolf, 1974). Many of these approaches involve a variety of media, as well as a variety of activities. One especially creative approach is *Kids on the Block. Kids* is a puppet show, with

Kids on the Block, Inc. produces handicapped puppets who perform in scripts designed to entertain young elementary school children as well as inform them about different kinds of handicaps.
(The Kids on the Block, Inc., Alexandria, Virginia)

Hal's Pals™, a collection of handicapped dolls, is available from For Challenged Kids, a not-for-profit corporation. (Mattel, Inc., 5150 Rosecrans Ave., Hawthorne, CA 90250)

Muppet-like puppets that have different kinds of handicaps (e.g., mental retardation, cerebral palsy, emotional disturbance, and visual impairment). It comes with scripts designed to get across basic concepts about exceptional children and a variety of curriculum suggestions.

Although more and more schools are using materials that purportedly teach children in regular education about exceptional students, very few efforts have been made to evaluate these curricular modifications systematically. One encouraging study (Hazzard and Baker, 1982) was an evaluation of *Feeling Free* (Barnes, Berrigan, and Biklen, 1978; Brightman, Storey, and Richman, 1978; Sullivan, Brightman, and Blatt, 1979). *Feeling Free* is a multimedia program consisting of films, activities, discussion topics, and books. Hazzard and Baker assessed the effects of the program on children in grades three through six. Although *Feeling Free* did not produce benefits in all areas measured, it did increase students' knowledge of disabilities. In addition, children who received the program exhibited more positive perceptions of handicapped people and a better understanding of how to handle situations involving disabled peers.

The Regular Education Initiative

Beginning in the mid-1980s, some began to argue that special education, especially for mildly handicapped students, is too separate from general education. They have advocated what has been termed the **regular education initiative.** In essence, the goal of the initiative is to make general education be more responsible for the education of handicapped children. (In addition, some have recommended that the initiative should also have general education serve economically disadvantaged children, who have traditionally been educated under compensatory education, and bilingual children.)

This movement has drawn much of its impetus from the beliefs that pulling out students for specialized instruction is unethical and that mainstreaming can be effectively implemented with the use of such techniques as "effective teaching" practices, teacher consultants, prereferral teams, cooperative learning, peer tutoring, and special curriculum materials. Advocates of the initiative have ranged from professionals to the Assistant Secretary for the Office of Special Education and Rehabilitative Services, U.S. Department of Education, Madeleine C. Will (Biklen and Zollers, 1986; Reynolds and Lakin, 1987; Reynolds, Wang, and Walberg, 1987; Wang and Reynolds, 1985; Wang, Reynolds, and Walberg, 1986; Will, 1986).

Although initiative advocates have been extremely critical of special education, most have not called for an end to special education. But they have recommended a radical departure from what they perceive to be a sharp distinction between special and general education:

> If we are to correct the flawed vision, to refine the vision, not obliterate what is good in present vision, not destroy what we have worked so hard to achieve, then an atmosphere of trust will have to be created. Success will mean constant input from parents, administrators, teachers, and state and local governments. It will mean acceptance of the general applicability of special education techniques beyond the confines of the special education class. Success will mean the creation of a more powerful, more responsive education system, one with enhanced component parts. It will not mean that the role of special education teachers and other special assistance providers will be eliminated or diminished. It does not mean the consolidation of special education into regular education. Nor will it mean placing an overwhelming and unfair financial burden on *one* part of the system.
>
> It does mean that special programs must be allowed to use their knowledge base and services to prevent students with learning problems from reaching the point of failure in the educational system.
>
> It does mean that programs must be allowed to establish a partnership with regular education to cooperatively assess the educational needs of students with learning problems and to cooperatively develop effective educational strategies for meeting those needs.
>
> In the delivery of educational services to meet individualized needs, it does mean that administrators and teachers must be allowed to collectively contribute skills and resources to carry out appropriate educational plans.
>
> It does mean the nurturing of a shared commitment to the future of all children with special learning needs. (Will, 1986, pp. 414–415)

Some supporters have forwarded a two-part plan for implementation of their ideas:

> The first part of the initiative involves the joining of demonstrably effective practices from special, compensatory, and general education to establish a general education system that is more inclusive and that better serves all students, particularly those who require greater-than-usual educational support. The second part of the initiative calls for the federal government to collaborate with a number of states and local school districts in encouraging and supporting experimental trials of integrated forms of education for students who are currently segregated for service in separate special, remedial, and compensatory education programs. (Reynolds, Wang, and Walberg, 1987, p. 394)

Why Is Special Education Missing from the National Excellence Reports on Education?

The mid-1980s witnessed a burgeoning concern over the quality of our schools. A number of reports and publications drew widespread attention from both professionals and the general public because of their alarmingly negative portrayal of schools in the United States (e.g., Boyer, 1983; Goodlad, 1984; National Commission on Excellence in Education, 1983; Sizer, 1984). Many professionals viewed these assessments as generally accurate and long overdue. They have also welcomed the attention to education in the hope that the nation will turn its attention to reforming many aspects of education, such as teacher preparation and teacher salaries. And there have followed reports recommending changes in teacher education (Carnegie Forum on Education and the Economy: Task Force as a Teaching Profession, 1986; The Holmes Group, 1986).

From special education's perspective, it is interesting that the reports had very little to say about special education's place in the "reform movement." There are at least four interpretations for this minimal reference to special education. First, it may be that the authors did not find anything to criticize in special education. Second, it may be that the authors equated achieving excellence in schools with meeting the needs of the most able students and neglected the less able, handicapped population (Sapon-Shevin, 1987). Third, it may be that general educators view special education as a separate enterprise (Pugach, 1987), something they do not have the expertise on which to pass judgment. A fourth explanation, one that is embraced by a few of the more radical regular education initiative proponents, is that the reports tended to exclude special education because they were describing an ideal situation; and in an ideal educational system special education would not exist in its current form:

> Thus, I applaud the fact that special education is not a major focus of the Sizer, Boyer, and Goodlad reports. I celebrate the vision of these authors in focusing on descriptions of responsive, effective systems of general education. And to special educators, I say that "the ball is in our court," and until we are willing to examine our flawed assumptions about children and teachers and become integral members of the general education community, we cannot expect either to be featured in reform reports or to be involved in construction of the next era of public education in the United States. (Lilly, 1987, p. 326)

No matter which of the above explanations, or combinations of explanations, is the correct one, the relative absence of special education in these reports should give special educators pause. Even if one does not accept the position that special education as it presently operates does not deserve to be included in an ideal system, the neglect of special education does suggest a lack of communication between general and special educators.

There are indications that, although the original reform reports neglected special education, steps will be taken to remedy this situation. It is anticipated that the American Association of Colleges for Teacher Education and the Council for Exceptional Children, as well as some of the teacher education reform groups, will begin to address this issue (Viadero, 1987).

OPPOSITION TO THE REGULAR EDUCATION INITIATIVE   Many special educators have concerns about the initiative. For example, the Teacher Education Division of the Council for Exceptional Children (the major professional organization in special education) issued a position paper questioning some of the basic assumptions of the initiative (Teacher Education Division, CEC, 1986a). Among other things, the paper states that the initiative is too critical of existing special education services and that some types of special education classes are needed for some students:

The manner in which proponents assert their positions may serve to defeat the initiative. These negative statements will surely lead to resistance among many who could work as change agents in achieving constructive outcomes. To set up an either/or impression is neither a good plan for marketing an innovation, nor an effective strategy of planned change. Our argument is substantiated by the fact that there is a better rationale for the "regular education initiative" than assumptions about the quality of special education (and other special programs). The best rationale for the initiative is, of course (from special education's viewpoint), that two-thirds of the nation's students with handicaps are in fact enrolled in general education classes for all or part of the school day. To improve the instruction they are receiving, both in general education and in special services, should be the focus. . . .

Assumptions adopted by proponents of the "regular education initiative" imply that special education services for students with mild to moderate handicaps should be minimized or perhaps eventually terminated. While the improvement of instruction for special-needs learners in general education classrooms is a goal that we genuinely endorse, the TED Executive Committee cannot support an initiative that might ultimately interfere with the provision of more intensive services for children whose mild to moderate handicaps might require such services. Hopefully, large numbers of special needs learners will indeed receive the most excellent instruction and related services within general education. This would not, however, preclude the need for other alternatives for some students. The real issue at the outset should not be simply WHERE (in what setting) to provide instruction, but HOW to improve instruction in various modes. A variety of options should be available for special needs learners. Many of these should be possible in general education; others will more appropriately be offered in different situations. Form *follows* function. (pp. 11–12)

TED also formed a 76-member task force that formulated over 250 questions regarding the initiative. The questions ranged widely in scope, from such things as legal rights of parents and students to certification requirements for general educators to definition of who the initiative's mildly and moderately handicapped are to whether general education wants to assume a more responsible role for special education's students. It is this latter point that, perhaps more than any other, has caused widespread concern among special educators. How willing is general education to take over the function of serving these difficult-to-teach youngsters? As the task force stated:

In the proposals being advanced for restructuring the service delivery system, it appears that special education is assuming the responsibility for change in general education. While this is admirable, it may impede progress because it may not stimulate the ownership of others who are depicted as becoming responsible for implementing this change. This initiative cannot be expected to succeed without the support and active involvement of the general education community. (Teacher Education Division, CEC, 1986b, p. 19)

ARE GENERAL EDUCATORS READY FOR MAINSTREAMING?   Actually, special educators were addressing the question of general education's willingness to accept mainstreaming long before the regular education initiative. A number of surveys conducted in the 1970s led to the conclusion that general educators were far from ready to embrace mainstreaming. The usual finding was that general educators did not believe they were prepared to cope with the special problems of exceptional children (Hudson, Graham, and Warner, 1979; McGinity and Keogh, 1975; Middleton, Morsink, and Cohen, 1979; Payne and Murray, 1974).

It could be argued that, since these surveys were conducted some time ago, they may not reflect current attitudes. Few states, for example, required that teachers take any coursework concerning handicapped students, let alone courses on teaching techniques for exceptional children, until the mid-1970s.

There is little evidence available on how well prepared today's general education teachers are to work with mildly or moderately handicapped students. One study did find that the most effective teachers were the least willing to accept handicapped students into their classes (Gersten, Walker, and Darch, in press). And some have argued that general education teachers should not necessarily be blamed for their reluctance to work with handicapped students:

> It should be recalled that until very recent years the history of education in this country was that mentally retarded children were educated in self-contained classes by teachers who were specially trained to deal with their problems. Until the mid-1960s many school systems paid teachers a salary differential for being willing and certified to teach retarded children. Many special and regular education teachers euphemistically referred to the salary differential as "battle pay." Special education classes were more often than not located in an isolated section of the school building so that the special and regular education children would not interact very much. Special education teachers were often socially isolated from the remainder of the school faculty. When regular education teachers were taught about mentally retarded children, differences rather than similarities were stressed. Given the historical fact that mentally retarded children were always considered to be "different" it is little wonder that teachers today feel as they do, i.e., incompetent to teach mentally retarded children. (Gottlieb and Leyser, 1981, p. 61)

> The message [of the regular education initiative] to teachers is clear: "Instruct every student effectively, even the most difficult to teach; manage all behavior problems, no exceptions; *we* know that if you are not lazy or incompetent or uncaring you can do this, but it is *your* job." The good teacher never complains, never gives up, always succeeds, no matter the adversity. . . .

> We need to ask ourselves some hard questions. How reasonable are our expectations for teachers? Do we approach the analysis of problem situations with a bias toward finding incompetence in teachers? And does our expectation that general education alternatives will be totally exhausted before a student is identified as behaviorally disordered contribute to our underservice to such students? . . . I have a strong suspicion that many of us in university life would change our perceptions of what is possible, what is reasonable, and what is desirable were we to assume classroom teachers' responsibilities—assume them indefinitely, not just for a month or a semester, but as a career. Perhaps we should not drive the argument for exhausting general education alternatives to the point of exhausting teachers. (Kauffman, 1986, pp. 16–17)

The Future of Mainstreaming

As we head toward and into the last decade of the twentieth century, some of the most intriguing questions facing the field of special education involve the concept of mainstreaming. Few doubt that mainstreaming is desirable, that it has since the passage of PL 94-142 resulted in better conditions for many exceptional students, and that it can yet be improved upon. Many questions do remain, however, regarding how it is to be implemented, especially in relation to the role and responsibility of general education. Whether and in what ways general and special educators can create a partnership that results in better educational opportunities for *all* children will be a formidable challenge for the future.

SUMMARY

There are numerous changes taking place in the field of special education. Many of them are captured in the interrelated concepts of *normalization, deinstitutionalization,* and *mainstreaming*.

Normalization—the philosophical belief that every exceptional individual should be provided with an education and living environment as close to normal as possible—has been the focus of special education professionals for a number of years. It served, for example, as an underpinning to the concept of the *least restrictive environment* of PL 94-142. The principle has been used by special educators to examine a number of ideas and practices, such as the antilabeling movement, the disability rights movement, society's attitudes toward handicapped newborns, and media treatments of disabilities.

The antilabeling movement has arisen out of the fear that labeling children for placement in special classes will have a stigmatizing effect. The number of minority children specified as mildly retarded raises the question of discriminatory labeling to segregate such children. *Ecological theorists* maintain that the interaction between social environment and individual is crucial in determining handicaps. Ecological theorists also espouse *symbolic interaction theory,* which posits that people and things, by themselves, have no meaning; meaning is *given* to people and things by other people. Therefore, for the symbolic interactionist, disability is a socially created construct—one is disabled only insofar as other people perceive him or her to be disabled. Another theme that has contributed to the antilabeling movement is that some believe exceptional individuals are quantitatively rather than qualitatively different from nonhandicapped people in their behavior.

Research on the effects of labeling indicates that it does have a biasing effect on perceptions of handicapped people. However, although it is logical that labels would have an effect on handicapped individuals themselves, there is no solid evidence that this is the case.

There are several reasons why labeling is still practiced. First, federal and local funding of special education programs is based on labeling. Second, some people maintain that labeling helps professionals communicate about what kinds of children are being referred to. Third, it is believed by some that if the current labels were abolished, another set would take their place. Fourth, right or wrong, labeling helps to spotlight problems for the general public. Finally, labeling may help in some cases to make the nonhandicapped majority more tolerant of the handicapped minority.

Since the late 1970s, there has been a strong disability rights movement. Basing many of their arguments on the premise that society promotes *handicapism* (analogous to racism), disability activists have argued that the disability rights movement can be considered similar to the civil rights movement and that handicapped people are another oppressed minority. Although the disability rights movement has gained momentum, it has not had the same kind of impact as the civil rights movement. First, the political climate has not been especially conducive. Second, movement members have not always been able to agree on goals. Third, because of the heterogeneity of the handicapped population, the problems individuals face are sometimes quite specific, making it difficult for individuals to join forces on issues. Finally, and perhaps most important, handicapped people have a difficult time achieving a sense of pride.

Another theme closely related to concern for normalization is the issue of how society treats handicapped newborns. Although the withholding of treatment from defective newborns has been a relatively common practice for years, the ethical problems surrounding this issue did not gain the spotlight until the 1980s. The fact that the common practice is being questioned indicates that society now has a more positive attitude toward handicapped people, as well as a more optimistic view of the value of special education and related disciplines for this population.

It is interesting to consider technology vis-à-vis normalization. Technology has undoubtedly contributed to normalization by allowing greater independence and making it possible for more handicapped people to take part in activities that were previously inaccessible. Some have cautioned, however, that disabled people might in certain instances come to rely on technology to help them do things they could do on their own. Those who are engaged in developing equipment for handicapped people need to consult closely with disabled people, themselves, so that technology can be used most appropriately.

Some researchers and activists have raised questions about how the media portray disabilities. Critics have stated, for example, that TV and movies often portray disabled people in stereotypical ways—for example, as criminals, monsters, suicide-prone, maladjusted, sexually deviant, and/or superheros. The latter category—superhero—is an effort to characterize exceptional individuals in a positive light, but many critics maintain that it actually does the opposite. All these characterizations, claim critics, serve to reinforce prejudicial and stereotypical views of handicapped people. Written media, both literature and journalism, have also been analyzed and found guilty of inaccurate and stereotypical characterizations. Those attacking the media have pointed to instances of inappropriate depictions of handicapped people. Although they have made a strong case that the media are guilty of negative portrayals, more systematic research might strengthen their arguments.

Deinstitutionalization is part of the trend to move exceptional individuals into closer contact with community and home so that they can enjoy as normal a life as possible. Group homes, or community residential facilities (CRFs), are increasingly being used as placements for more severely handicapped individuals. Many who were formerly maintained in full-time large institutional settings are now taking part in community and family living. It is evident that community education and cooperation are needed before CRFs can be successful. Where professionals have taken care to prepare the community for the placement of group homes, however, there has been little trouble.

Research has revealed that placement in large residential facilities can result in a lowering of cognitive abilities, possibly because social reinforcement is missing and motivation is lowered. Research on the effects of placement in CRFs is just beginning. However, studies indicate that movement from larger institutions to CRFs results in better adaptive behavior and that CRFs provide more social and occupational opportunities than larger institutions. Successful adjustment of CRF residents is related to personal variables such as good vocational skills and mild, as opposed to severe, behavior problems, as well as environmental factors such as appropriate social support and clinical services. Better resident care is also related to job satisfaction of the group home staff.

Mainstreaming—the integration of exceptional students with nonhandicapped students—is viewed by many as the primary way in which the schools can foster normalization. Concerns for mainstreaming can be roughly divided into an efficacy studies era (ca. 1950–1980) and a post-efficacy studies era (ca. 1980–present). In the efficacy studies era, researchers conducted numerous studies comparing students in special education classes with those in general education classes. Many authorities have become disenchanted with the value of these studies. First, the studies often came up with contradictory results. Second, the vast majority contained methodological flaws. Third, they were conducted so long ago that they might not be representative of what goes on in either mainstream or special classes today. And finally, the focus of the studies was on physical settings, instead of what goes on in those settings.

The post-efficacy studies era has consisted of professionals writing about mainstreaming from two general orientations. Some have approached the topic primarily from an advocacy point of view. Others have been interested primarily in determining the most effective ways of enhancing the success of mainstreaming. Those taking an advocacy stance have argued that mainstreaming is more ethical than separate special programs because the latter are a form of segregation.

Several strategies have been presented for bettering the chances of mainstreaming's success. Six of the most common are: (1) encouraging general education teachers to use "effective teaching" practices, (2) using teacher consultants, (3) establishing prereferral teams, (4) setting up cooperative learning situations, (5) using peer tutors, and (6) using commercially available curriculum materials designed to change attitudes.

"Effective teaching research" refers to studies conducted in general education classrooms that look at which teaching behaviors lead to student achievement. Teaching behaviors that have been found to be related to student achievement for low-achieving pupils are: structuring the learning; proceeding in small steps at a brisk pace; giving detailed and redundant instructions and explanations; providing many examples; asking a large number of questions and corrections, particularly in the early stages of learning new material; having a student success rate of 80 percent or higher in initial learning; dividing seatwork assignments into smaller segments; and providing for continued practice so that students have a success rate of 90 to 100 percent. Some have suggested that these behaviors should also lead to higher achievement on the part of exceptional children. Research on the application of effective teaching principles to handicapped students is just beginning.

Teacher consultants have been recommended in order to assist general education teachers in working with exceptional students in the classroom. There has been relatively little research on the effectiveness of these consultants. Some have stated that the greatest impediment to successful implementation is that many states lack separate certification requirements for consultant teachers.

Prereferral teams (PRTs) are also used to help classroom teachers. They are designed to ensure that the teacher uses alternative strategies for teaching hard-to-teach children before they are referred to special education. Very little research has been done on PRTs. Evaluation efforts have found that school personnel believe they are beneficial and that they do cut down on the number of referrals to special education.

Some are recommending the use of cooperative learning—having students work together on problems—to facilitate mainstreaming. Those who have used cooperative learning with a mixture of handicapped and nonhandicapped students have found that it has resulted in positive changes in attitudes of the nonhandicapped youngsters toward their handicapped peers. Effects on achievement have been mixed. Some who have used cooperative learning with low-ability students who were not formally identified as handicapped have found achievement gains when they have structured the situations to include group incentives and individual accountability.

Peer tutoring can involve nonhandicapped students tutoring handicapped students or vice versa. Research suggests that it does benefit exceptional children academically, but there are little data to show that it affects self-concept.

Curriculum materials designed to teach general education students about disabled students and how to get along with them better are available. There have been few systematic attempts to evaluate these materials, although one study has provided encouraging results.

Beginning in the mid-1980s, some professionals started what has been called the "regular education initiative." Advocates state that general education should be primarily, or entirely, responsible for the education of mildly handicapped students (and some have also included moderately handicapped students), as well as economically disadvantaged and bilingual students. They have requested that schools try such programs on an experimental basis. Some have questioned some of the basic assumptions of the initiative. One of the major concerns is that the initiative does not take into account that general education does not want to take over more responsibility for educating exceptional students. One of the major issues concerning the education of handicapped children in the future is whether and in what ways general and special educators will be able to work together.

REFERENCES

Altheide, D. L. (1977). Mental illness and the news: The Eagleton story. *Sociology and Social Research, 61*(2), 138–155.

Armstrong, B., Johnson, D. W., & Balow, B. (1981). Effects of cooperative vs. individualistic learning experiences on interpersonal attraction between learning-disabled and normal progress elementary school students. *Contemporary Educational Psychology, 6,* 102–109.

Bacher, J. H. (1965). The effect of special class placement on the self-concept of the adolescent mentally retarded in relation to certain groups of adolescents. *Dissertation Abstracts, 25,* 2846–2847.

Baer, S. (1984). The half-told story of Baby Jane Doe. *Columbia Journalism Review,* November–December, 35–38.

Balla, D. (1976). Relationship of institution size to quality of care: A review of the literature. *American Journal of Mental Deficiency, 81,* 117–124.

Bank-Mikkelsen, N. E. (1968). Service for mentally retarded children in Denmark. *Children, 15,* 198–200.

Bank-Mikkelsen, N. E. (1976). Administrative normalisering. *S.A.-Nyt, 14*(9), 3–6.

Barber, T. X., & Silver, M. J. (1968). Fact, fiction, and the experimenter bias effect. *Psychological Bulletin, 70,* 1–29.

Barnes, E., Berrigan, C., & Biklen, D. (1978). *What's the difference?* Syracuse, N.Y.: Human Policy Press.

Bickel, W. E., & Bickel, D. D. (1986). Effective schools, classrooms, and instruction: Implications for special education. *Exceptional Children, 52*(6), 489–500.

Biklen, D. (1986). Framed: Journalism's treatment of disability. *Social Policy,* Winter, 45–51.

Biklen, D., & Zollers, N. (1986). The focus of advocacy in the LD field. *Journal of Learning Disabilities, 19*(10), 579–586.

Blatt, B., & Kaplan, F. (1966). *Christmas in Purgatory: A photographic essay on mental retardation.* Boston: Allyn & Bacon.

Blumer, H. (1969). *Symbolic interactionism.* Englewood Cliffs, N.J.: Prentice-Hall.

Bogdan, R. (1986). The sociology of special education. In R. J. Morris & B. Blatt (Eds.), *Special education: Research and trends* (pp. 344–359). New York: Pergamon.

Bogdan, R., & Biklen, D. (1977). Handicapism. *Social Policy, 7*(5), 14–19.

Borg, W. R. (1966). *Ability grouping in the public schools.* Madison, Wis.: Dembar Educational Research Services, Inc.

Boyer, E. L. (1983). *High school: A report on secondary education in America.* New York: Harper and Row.

Braginsky, B. M., & Braginsky, D. D. (1974). The mentally retarded: Society's Hansels and Gretels. *Psychology Today, 7*(10), 18–30.

Brightman, A., Storey, K., & Richman, L. (1978). *Feeling free: An invitation to teachers.* Cambridge, Mass.: American Institutes for Research.

Budoff, M., & Gottlieb, J. (1976). Special-class EMR children mainstreamed: A study of an aptitude (learning potential) × treatment interaction. *American Journal of Mental Deficiency, 81,* 1–11.

Burbach, H. J. (1981). The labeling process: A sociological analysis. In J. M. Kauffman & D. P. Hallahan (Eds.), *Handbook of special education.* Englewood Cliffs, N.J.: Prentice-Hall.

Butterfield, E. C. (1967). The role of environmental factors in the treatment of institutionalized mental retardates. In A. A. Baumeister (Ed.), *Mental retardation: Appraisal, education, and rehabilitation.* Chicago: Aldine.

Butterfield, E. C., & Zigler, E. (1965). The influence of differing institutional social climates on the effectiveness of social reinforcement in the mentally retarded. *American Journal of Mental Deficiency, 70,* 48–56.

Byrd, E. K., Byrd, P. D., & Allen, C. M. (1977). Television programming and disability. *Journal of Applied Rehabilitation Counseling, 8*(1), 28–32.

Carlberg, C., & Kavale, K. (1980). The efficacy of special versus regular class placement for exceptional children: A meta-analysis. *Journal of Special Education, 14,* 295–309.

Carnegie Forum on Education and the Economy: Task Force on Teaching as a Profession (1986). *A nation prepared: Teachers for the 21st century.* New York.

Cassatta, M. B., Skill, T. D., & Boadu, S. O. (1979). In sickness and health. *Journal of Communications,* Autumn, 73–78.

Cavalier, A., & Mineo, B. A. (1986). The application of technology in the home, classroom, and work place: Unvoiced premises and ethical issues. In A. Gartner & T. Joe (Eds.), *Images of the disabled/disabling images.* New York: Praeger.

Chalfant, J. C., Psych, M. V., & Moultrie, R. (1979). Teacher assistance teams: A model for within-building problem solving. *Learning Disability Quarterly, 2,* 85–96.

Children's Museum of Boston with WGBH Boston. (1978). *What if you couldn't? An elementary school program about handicaps.* Weston, Mass.: Burt Harrison & Co.

Childress, J. F. (1981). *Priorities in biomedical ethics.* Philadelphia: Westminster Press.

Cohen, S. (1977). *Accepting individual differences.* Allen, Tex.: Developmental Learning Materials.

Conroy, J., Efthimiou, J., & Lemanowicz, J. (1982). A matched comparison of the developmental growth of institutionalized and deinstitutionalized mentally retarded clients. *American Journal of Mental Deficiency, 86,* 581–587.

Crowley, E. P. (1986). *Television and disability: A literature review.* Unpublished manuscript, University of Virginia, Charlottesville, Virginia.

Cruickshank, W. M. (1977). Guest editorial. *Journal of Learning Disabilities, 10,* 193–194.

Drews, E. M. (1962). *The effectiveness of homogeneous and heterogeneous ability grouping in ninth grade English classes with slow, average, and superior students.* Unpublished manuscript, Michigan State University, East Lansing.

Duff, R. S., & Campbell, A. G. M. (1973). Moral and ethical dilemmas in the special care nursery. *New England Journal of Medicine, 289,* 890–894.

Dunn, L. M. (1968). Special education for the mildly retarded—Is much of it justifiable? *Exceptional Children, 35,* 5–22.

Eyman, R. K., Demaine, G. C., & Lei, T. (1979). Relationship between community environments and resident changes in adaptive behavior: A path model. *American Journal of Mental Deficiency, 83,* 330–338.

Fielder, C. R., & Simpson, R. L. (1987). Modifying the attitudes of nonhandicapped high school students toward handicapped peers. *Exceptional Children, 53*(5), 342–349.

Fleming, E. S., & Anttonen, R. G. (1971). Teacher expectancy as related to the academic and personal growth of primary-age children. *Monographs of the Society for Research in Child Development, 36,* Ser. No. 145.

Fletcher, J. (1979). *Humanhood: Essays in biomedical ethics.* Buffalo, N.Y.: Prometheus Books.

Foster, G. G., Ysseldyke, J. E., & Reese, J. H. (1975). "I wouldn't have seen it if I hadn't believed it." *Exceptional Children, 41,* 469–473.

Fruth, L., & Padderud, A. (1985). Portrayals of mental illness in daytime television serials. *Journalism Quarterly, 62*(2), 384–387.

Funk, R. (1986). Disability rights: From caste to class in the context of civil rights. In A. Gartner and T. Joe (Eds.), *Images of the disabled/disabling images.* New York: Praeger.

Gallagher, J. J. (1986). Learning disabilities and special education: A critique. *Journal of Learning Disabilities, 19*(10), 595–601.

Gallagher, J. J. (1972). The special education contract for mildly handicapped children. *Exceptional Children, 38,* 527–535.

Gartner, A. (1986). Disabling help: Special education at the crossroads. *Exceptional Children, 53*(1), 72–76.

Gartner, A., & Joe, T. (1986). Introduction. In A. Gartner and T. Joe (Eds.), *Images of the disabled/disabling images.* New York: Praeger.

Gerber, M. M., & Kauffman, J. M. (1981). Peer tutoring in academic settings. In P. S. Strain (Ed.), *The utilization of classroom peers as behavior change agents* (pp. 155–187). New York: Plenum.

Gerber, M. M., & Semmel, M. I. (1984). Teacher as imperfect test: Reconceptualizing the referral process. *Educational Psychologist, 19,* 137–148.

Gerber, M. M., & Semmel, M. I. (1985). Microeconomics of referral and reintegration: A paradigm for evaluation of special education. *Studies in Educational Evaluation, 11*(1), 13–29.

Gersten, R., Walker, H., & Darch, C. (in press). Relationships between teachers' effectiveness and their tolerance for handicapped students: An exploratory study. *Exceptional Children.*

Goffman, E. (1963). *Stigma: Notes on the management of a spoiled identity.* Englewood Cliffs, N.J.: Prentice-Hall.

Goldberg, M. L., Passow, A. H., & Justman, J. (1961). *The effects of ability grouping.* Unpublished manuscript, Teacher's College, Columbia University, New York.

Goldstein, H., Moss, J., & Jordan, L. J. (1965). *The efficacy of special class training on the development of mentally retarded children.* Urbana: University of Illinois Press.

Goodlad, J. I. (1984). *A place called school.* New York: McGraw-Hill.

Gottlieb, J. (1980). Improving attitudes toward retarded children by using group discussion. *Exceptional Children, 47,* 106–111.

Gottlieb, J., Alter, M., & Gottlieb, B. W. (1983). Mainstreaming mentally retarded children. In J. L. Matson & J. A.

Mulich (Eds.), *Handbook of mental retardation* (pp. 67–77). New York: Pergamon Press.

Gottlieb, J., & Leyser, Y. (1981). Facilitating the social mainstreaming of retarded children. *Exceptional Education Quarterly, 1*(4), 57–69.

Guess, D., Dussault, B., Brown, F., Mulligan, M., Orelove, F., Comegys, A., & Rues, J. (1984). *Legal, economic, psychological and moral considerations on the practice of withholding medical treatment from infants with congenital defects* (Monograph No. 1). Seattle, Wash.: The Association for Persons with Severe Handicaps.

Gunzburg, H. E. (1981). Editorial. *The British Journal of Mental Subnormality, XXVII,* 45–46.

Hahn, H. (1986). Civil rights for disabled Americans: The foundation of a political agenda. In A. Gartner & T. Joe (Eds.), *Images of the disabled/disabling images.* New York: Praeger.

Haight, S. L. (1984). Special education teacher consultant: Idealism versus realism. *Exceptional Children, 50,* 507–515.

Hallahan, D. P., & Keller, C. E. (1986). *Learning disabilities: A study of studies.* Charleston: West Virginia State Department of Education.

Hazzard, A. P., & Baker, B. L. (1982). Enhancing children's attitudes toward disabled peers using a multi-media intervention. *Journal of Applied Developmental Psychology, 3,* 247–262.

Hentoff, N. (1985). The awful privacy of Baby Doe. *The Atlantic Monthly,* January, pp. 54–62.

Herson, P. F. (1974). Biasing effects of diagnostic labels and sex of pupils on teachers' view of pupils' mental health. *Journal of Educational Psychology, 66,* 117–122.

Hobbs, N. (1975). *The futures of children.* San Francisco: Jossey-Bass.

Hudson, F., Graham, S., & Warner, M. (1979). Mainstreaming: An examination of the attitudes and needs of regular classroom teachers. *Learning Disability Quarterly, 2,* 58–62.

Idol-Maestas, L. (1981). A teacher training model: The resource/consulting teacher. *Behavioral Disorders, 6,* 108–121.

Idol-Maestas, L. (1983). *Special educator's consultation handbook.* Rockville, Md.: Aspen Systems.

Idol-Maestas, L. (1986). *Draft of teacher consultation task force.* Unpublished manuscript.

Jacobson, J. W., & Schwartz, A. A. (1983). The evaluation of community living alternatives for developmentally disabled persons. In J. L. Matson & J. A. Mulich (Eds.), *Handbook of mental retardation* (pp. 39–66). New York: Pergamon Press.

Johnson, D. W., & Johnson, R. (1984). Classroom learning structure and attitudes toward handicapped students in mainstream settings: A theoretical model and research evidence. In R. L. Jones (Ed.), *Attitudes and attitude change in special education: Theory and practice* (pp. 118–142). Reston, Va.: The Council for Exceptional Children.

Johnson, D. W., & Johnson, R. (1982). Effects of cooperative and individualistic instruction on handicapped and nonhandicapped students. *Journal of Social Psychology, 118,* 257–268.

Johnson, D. W., & Johnson, R. (1986). Mainstreaming and cooperative learning strategies. *Exceptional Children, 52*(6), 553–561.

Johnson, M. (1987). Emotion and pride. *The Disability Rag,* January–February, pp. 1, 4–7, 9–10.

Jones, R. L. (1973). *Educational alienation, fatalism, school achievement motivation, and self-concepts in mental retardates.* Unpublished manuscript, University of California-Riverside.

Kalter, J. (1986). Disability chic, *TV Guide,* May 31, pp. 40–42, 44.

Kauffman, J. M. (1986). *Strategies for the nonrecognition of social deviance.* Paper presented at the 10th Annual Conference on Severe Behavior Disorders of Children and Youth, November, Tempe, Arizona.

Kastner, L. S., Reppucci, N. D., & Pezzoli, J. J. (1979). Assessing community attitudes toward mentally retarded persons. *American Journal of Mental Deficiency, 84,* 137–144.

Keogh, B. K., & Levitt, M. L. (1976). Special education in the mainstream: A confrontation of limitations? *Focus on Exceptional Children, 8,* 1–11.

Kent, D. (1986). Disabled women, portraits in fiction and drama. In A. Gartner & T. Joe (Eds.), *Images of the disabled/disabling images.* New York: Praeger.

Kleinberg, J., & Galligan, B. (1983). Effects of deinstitutionalization on adaptive behavior of mentally retarded adults. *American Journal of Mental Deficiency, 88*(1), 21–27.

Klobas, L. (1985). TV's concept of people with disabilities: Here's lookin' at you. *The Disability Rag,* January–February, pp. 2–6.

Knight, M. F., Meyers, H. W., Paolucci-Whitcomb, R., Hasazi, S., & Nevin, A. (1981). A four-year evaluation of consulting teacher service. *Behavioral Disorders, 6,* 92–100.

Kriegel, L. (1986). The cripple in literature. In A. Gartner & T. Joe (Eds.), *Images of the disabled/Disabling images.* New York: Praeger.

Lakin, K. C. (1983). A response to Gene V. Glass. *Policy Studies Review, 2*(1), 233–240.

Langer, E. J., & Abelson, R. P. (1974). A patient by any other name . . . : Clinician group differences in labeling bias. *Journal of Consulting and Clinical Psychology, 42,* 4–9.

Larrivee, B. (1985). *Effective teaching for successful mainstreaming.* New York: Longman.

Leinhardt, G., & Pallay, A. (1982). Restrictive educational settings: Exile or haven? *Review of Educational Research, 52,* 557–578.

Lew, M., Mesch, D., & Lates, B. J. (1982). The Simmons College Generic Consulting Teacher Program. *Teacher Education and Special Education, 5*(2), 11–16.

Lilly, M. S. (1987). Lack of focus on special education in literature on educational reform. *Exceptional Children, 53*(4), 325–326.

Longmore, P. K. (1985). Screening stereotypes: Images of disabled people. *Social Policy, 16*(1), 31–37.

MacMillan, D. L., & Becker, L. D. (1977). Mainstreaming the mildly handicapped learner. In R. D. Kneedler & S. G. Tarver (Eds.), *Changing perspectives in special education.* Columbus, Ohio: Charles E. Merrill.

MacMillan, D. L., Jones, R. J., & Aloia, G. F. (1974). The mentally retarded label: A theoretical analysis and review of research. *American Journal of Mental Deficiency, 79,* 241–261.

Madden, N. A., & Slavin, R. E. (1983). Mainstreaming students with mild handicaps: Academic and social outcomes. *Review of Educational Research, 53,* 519–569.

Mann, M. (1960). What does ability grouping do to the self-concept? *Childhood Education, 26,* 357–360.

Marotz-Sprague, B., & Nelson, C. M. (1979). The in-service consultant: A role for teacher trainers working with behavior disorders in the schools. *Monograph in Behavioral Disorders,* 24–37.

McCann, S. K., Semmel, M. I., & Nevin, A. (1985). Reverse mainstreaming: Nonhandicapped students in special education classrooms. *Remedial and Special Education.*

McCormick, M., Balla, D., & Zigler, E. (1975). Resident-care practices in institutions for retarded persons: A cross-institutional, cross-cultural study. *American Journal of Mental Deficiency, 80,* 1–17.

McGinity, A. M., & Keogh, B. K. (1975). *Needs assessment for inservice training: A first step for mainstreaming exceptional children into regular education.* Technical Report, University of California, Los Angeles.

McMurray, G. L. (1986). Easing everyday living: Technology for the physically disabled. In A. Gartner & T. Joe (Eds.), *Images of the disabled/disabling images.* New York: Praeger.

Mercer, J. (1970). Sociological perspectives on mild mental retardation. In H. C. Haywood (Ed.), *Social-cultural aspects of mental retardation.* Englewood Cliffs, N.J.: Prentice-Hall.

Messick, S. (1984). Assessment in context: Appraising student performance in relation to instructional quality. *Educational Researcher, 13*(3), 3–8.

Meyerowitz, J. H. (1962). Self derogations in young retardates and special class placement. *Child Development, 33,* 443–451.

Middleton, E. J., Morsink, C., & Cohen, S. (1979). Program graduates' perception of need for training in mainstreaming. *Exceptional Children, 45,* 256–261.

Miller, T. L., & Sabatino, D. A. (1978). An evaluation of the teacher consultation model as an approach to mainstreaming. *Exceptional Children, 45*(2), 86–91.

National Commission on Excellence in Education (1983). *A nation at risk: The imperative for educational reform.* Washington, D.C.: U.S. Department of Education.

Nelson, C. M., & Stevens, K. B. (1981). An accountable model for mainstreaming behaviorally disordered children. *Behavioral Disorders, 6*(2), 82–91.

Nevin, A., Johnson, D. W., & Johnson, R. (1982). Effects of group and individual contingencies on academic performance and social relations of special needs students. *Journal of Social Psychology, 116,* 41–59.

Nevin, A., Paolucci-Whitcomb, P., Duncan, D., Thibodeau, L. A. (1982). The consulting teacher as a clinical researcher. *Teacher Education and Special Education, 5*(4), 19–29.

Nunnally, J. C. (1957). The communication of mental health information: A comparison of opinions of experts and the public with mass media presentations. *Behavioral Science,* July, 222–230.

Odom, S. L., Deklyen, M., & Jenkins, J. R. (1984). Integrating handicapped and nonhandicapped preschoolers: Developmental impact on nonhandicapped children. *Exceptional Children, 51,* 41–48.

Osguthorpe, R. T., & Scruggs, T. E. (1986). Special education students as tutors: A review and analysis. *Remedial and Special Education, 7*(4), 15–25.

Paolucci-Whitcomb, P., & Nevin, A. (1985). Preparing consulting teachers through a collaborative approach between university faculty and field-based consulting teachers. *Teacher Education and Special Education, 8*(3), 132–143.

Payne, R., & Murray, C. (1974). Principals' attitudes toward integration of the handicapped. *Exceptional Children, 41,* 123–125.

Powell, T. H., Aiken, J. M., & Smylie, M. A. (1982). Treatment or involuntary euthanasia for severely handicapped newborns: Issues of philosophy and public policy. *The Journal of the Association for the Severely Handicapped, 6*(4), 3–10.

Pugach, M. (1987). The national education reports and special education: Implications for teacher preparation. *Exceptional Children, 53*(4), 308–314.

Reynolds, M. C., & Lakin, K. C. (1987). Noncategorical special education: Models for research and practice. In M. C. Wang, M. C. Reynolds, & H. J. Walberg (Eds.), *Handbook of special education: Research and practice.* New York: Pergamon.

Reynolds, M. C., Wang, M. C., & Walberg, H. J. (1987). The necessary restructuring of special and regular education. *Exceptional Children, 53*(5), 391–398.

Rhodes, W. C. (1967). *The disturbing child: A problem of ecological management, 33,* 449–455.

Robinson, N. M., & Robinson, H. B. (1976). *The mentally retarded child* (2nd ed.). New York: McGraw-Hill.

Rosenshine, B. (1983). Teaching functions in instructional programs. *The Elementary School Journal, 83*(4), 335–354.

Rosenthal, R., & Jacobsen, L. (1968). *Pygmalion in the classroom.* New York: Holt, Rinehart & Winston.

Rotegard, L. L., Hill, B. K., & Bruininks, R. H. (1983). Environmental characteristics of residential facilities for mentally retarded persons in the United States. *American Journal of Mental Deficiency, 88*(1), 49–56.

Rothman, D. J., & Rothman, S. M. (1984). *The Willowbrook wars.* New York: Harper & Row.

Saddler, J. (1984). Home work: Personal computers increase independence of handicapped users. *The Wall Street Journal,* February 7, pp. 1, 18.

Salvia, J., Clark, G. M., & Ysseldyke, J. E. (1973). Teacher retention of stereotypes of exceptionality. *Exceptional Children, 39,* 651–652.

Sapon-Shevin, M. (1987). The national education reports and special education: Implications for students. *Exceptional Children, 53*(4), 300–306.

Sapon-Shevin, M. (1983). Teaching children about differences: Resources for teaching. *Young Children, 38*(2), 24–32.

Schram, L., Semmel, M. I., Gerber, M. M., Bruce, M. M., Lopez-Reyna, N., & Allen, D. (1984). *Problem solving teams in California.* University of California at Santa Barbara.

Scruggs, T. E., & Richter, L. (1986). Tutoring learning disabled students: A critical review. *Learning Disability Quarterly, 9,* 2–14.

Simmons, D. C., & Kameenui, E. J. (1986). Articulating learning disabilities for the public: A case of professional riddles. *Learning Disability Quarterly, 9*(4), 304–314.

Sizer, T. R. (1984). *Horace's compromise: The dilemma of the American High School.* Boston: Houghton Mifflin.

Slavin, R. E. (1983). When does cooperative learning increase student achievement? *Psychological Bulletin, 94,* 429–445.

Smith, K., Johnson, D. W., & Johnson, R. (1982). Effects of cooperative and individualistic instruction on the achievement of handicapped, regular, and gifted students. *Journal of Social Psychology, 116,* 277–283.

Smith, O. H. (1974). On letting some babies die. *Hastings Center Studies, 2,* 37–46.

Snow, R. E. (1969). Unfinished Pygmalion. *Contemporary Psychology, 14,* 197–199.

Soeffing, M. Y. (1974). The way to know: Normalization of services for the mentally retarded—A conversation with Dr. Wolf Wolfensberger. *Education and Training of the Mentally Retarded, 9,* 202–208.

Steadman, H. J., & Cocozza, J. J. (1977). Selective reporting and the public's misconceptions of the criminally insane. *Public Opinion Quarterly, 41*(4), 523–533.

Strain, P. S., & Kerr, M. M. (1981). *Mainstreaming of children in schools: Research and programmatic issues.* New York: Academic Press.

Sullivan, M., Brightman, A., & Blatt, J. (1979). *Feeling free.* Reading, Mass.: Addison-Wesley.

Sutter, P. (1980). Environmental variables related to community placement failure in mentally retarded adults. *Mental Retardation, 18,* 189–191.

Szasz, T. S. (1974). Our despotic laws destroy the right to self-control. *Psychology Today, 8*(7), 19–24, 29, 127.

Teacher Education Division, CEC. (1986a). *A message to all TED members concerning the National Inquiry into the Future of Education for Students with Special Needs.* Washington, D.C.

Teacher Education Division, CEC. (1986b). *Formulation of questions: The National Inquiry into the Future of Education for Students with Special Needs.* Washington, D.C.

Telford, C. W., & Sawrey, J. M. (1977). *The exceptional individual* (3rd ed.). Englewood Cliffs, N.J.: Prentice-Hall.

The Holmes Group (1986). *Tomorrow's teachers: A report of the Holmes Group.* East Lansing, Mich.: The Holmes Group, Inc.

Thorndike, R. L. (1968). Review of Pygmalion in the classroom. *American Educational Research Journal, 5,* 708–711.

Tindal, G. (1985). Investigating the effectiveness of special education: An analysis of methodology. *Journal of Learning Disabilities, 18,* 101–112.

Tizard, J. (1970). The role of social institutions in the causation, prevention and alleviation of mental retardation. In H. C. Haywood (Ed.), *Social-cultural aspects of mental retardation.* New York: Appleton-Century-Crofts.

Tymchuk, A. J. (1976). A perspective on ethics in mental retardation. *Mental Retardation, 14,* 44–47.

Viadero, D. (1987). Long overlooked, special education may soon get reformer's attention. *Education Week,* January 14, pp. 1, 21.

Wahl, O. F., & Roth, R. (1982). Television images of mental illness: Results of a metropolitan media watch. *Journal of Broadcasting, 26,* 599–605.

Walberg, H. J. (1984). Improving the productivity of America's schools. *Educational Leadership, 41*(8), 19–30.

Walker, H. M., McConnell, S., Holmes, O., Todis, B., Walker, J., & Golden, N. (1983). *ACCEPTS: A children's curriculum for effective peer and teaching skills.* Austin, Tex.: Pro-Ed Publishers.

Wang, M. C., & Birch, J. W. (1984a). Comparison of a full-time mainstreaming program and a resource room approach. *Exceptional Children, 51,* 33–40.

Wang, M. C., & Birch, J. W. (1984b). Effective special education in regular classes. *Exceptional Children, 50,* 391–398.

Wang, M. C., Peverly, S., & Randolph, R. (1984). An investigation of the implementation and effects of a full-time mainstreaming program. *Remedial and Special Education, 5*(6), 21–32.

Wang, M. C., & Reynolds, M. C. (1985). Avoiding the "Catch 22" in special education reform. *Exceptional Children, 51*(6), 499–502.

Wang, M. C., Reynolds, M. C., & Walberg, H. J. (1986). Rethinking special education. *Educational Leadership, 44*(1), 26–31.

Wang, M. C., & Walberg, H. J. (1983). Adaptive instruction and classroom time. *American Educational Research Journal, 20,* 601–626.

Will, M. C. (1986). Educating children with learning problems: A shared responsibility. *Exceptional Children, 52*(5), 411–415.

Wolf, B. (1974). *Don't feel sorry for Paul.* Philadelphia: Lippincott.

Wolfensberger, W. (1972). *The principle of normalization in human services.* Toronto: National Institute on Mental Retardation.

Zigler, E. (1973). The retarded child as a whole person. In D. K. Routh (Ed.), *The experimental psychology of mental retardation.* Chicago: Aldine.

Zigler, E., & Balla, D. (1982). Introduction: The developmental approach to mental retardation. In E. Zigler & D. Balla (Eds.), *Mental retardation: The developmental difference controversy* (pp. 3–8). Hillsdale, N.J.: Lawrence Erlbaum Associates.

Zigler, E., Balla, D., & Butterfield, E. C. (1968). A longitudinal investigation of the relationship between preinstitutional social deprivation and social motivation in institutionalized retardates. *Journal of Personality and Social Psychology, 10,* 437–445.

Zigler, E., Butterfield, E. C., & Capobianco, F. (1970). Institutionalization and the effectiveness of social reinforcement: A five- and eight-year follow-up study. *Developmental Psychology, 3,* 253–263.

Zigler, E., & Williams, J. (1963). Institutionalization and the effectiveness of social reinforcement: A three-year follow-up study. *Journal of Abnormal and Social Psychology, 66,* 197–205.

Glossary

Acceleration. Educating gifted students by placing them in grade levels ahead of their peers in one or more academic subjects.

Acquired aphasia. Loss or impairment of the ability to understand or formulate language due to accident or illness.

Acquired Immune Deficiency Syndrome (AIDS). A fatal virus illness resulting in a breakdown of the immune system. Currently, no known cure exists.

Adventitious deafness. Deafness occurring through illness or accident in an individual who was born with normal hearing.

Air conduction test. Administration of a pure-tone hearing test using earphones; results are compared to those of *bone conduction* test.

Alcohol embryopathy. Fetal alcohol syndrome.

American Sign Language (Ameslan). A signing system for the hearing-impaired that has its own grammatical rules and is considered by many to be a true language.

Amniocentesis. A medical procedure that allows examination of the amniotic fluid around the fetus; sometimes recommended to determine the presence of abnormality.

Analytic touch. Involves the touching of various parts of an object and then mentally constructing these separate parts.

Anoxia. Reduced supply of oxygen for a long enough time to cause brain injury.

Apert's syndrome. A condition characterized by a narrowing of the skull such that proper development of the brain is inhibited; results in mental retardation if not surgically corrected.

Aphasia (dysphasia). Loss or impairment of the ability to understand or formulate language; caused by neurological damage.

Apraxia. The inability to move the muscles involved in speech or other voluntary acts.

Aqueous humor. A watery substance between the cornea and the lens of the eye.

Arthritis. A disease involving inflammation of the joints.

Arthrogryposis. A congenital condition in which muscles of the limbs are missing or smaller and weaker than normal, resulting in stiffness or deformity of the limbs and trunk.

Articulation. Refers to the movements the vocal tract makes during production of speech sounds; enunciation of words and vocal sounds.

Asthma. A chronic respiratory condition in which the individual experiences repeated episodes of difficulty in breathing (dyspnea).

Astigmatism. Blurred vision caused by an irregular cornea or lens.

Asymmetrical Tonic Neck Reflex (ATNR). A normal reflex in babies up to about four months of age in which turning the head to one side results in extension of the arm and leg on the side toward which the head is turned and flexion of the opposite arm and leg. It is an abnormal reflex indicative of brain injury in infants older than about four months.

Ataxia. A condition characterized by awkwardness of fine and gross motor movements, especially those involved with balance, posture, and orientation in space; a type of *cerebral palsy*.

Athetosis. A condition in which there are sudden involuntary, jerky, writhing movements, especially of the fingers and wrists; a type of *cerebral palsy*.

Atresia. A condition in which the external auditory canal isn't formed completely.

Attributions. Explanations given by people for their successes and failures. Attributions may be internal or external.

Atrophy. Degeneration of tissue, such as muscles or nerves.

Audiogram. A graphic representation of the weakest sound a person can hear at several frequency levels.

Audiology. A science dealing with hearing impairments, their detection, and remediation.

Audiometric zero (zero decibel level). Lowest level at which normal people can hear.

Auditory training. The procedure of teaching deaf or hard-of-hearing children to make full use of their residual hearing ability.

Augmentative communication. Alternative forms of communication that do not use the oral sounds of speech.

Aura. A sensation, such as the perception of certain odors, sounds, images, etc., sometimes experienced just before a seizure.

Auricle. The visible part of the ear, composed of cartilage; collects the sounds and funnels them via the external auditory canal to the eardrum.

Autism. A childhood disorder characterized by extreme withdrawal, self-stimulation, cognitive deficits, language disorders, and onset before the age of 30 months.

Battered Child Syndrome. Evidence of physical, psychological, and/or sexual abuse or neglect of a child that is threatening to the child's health or life.

Behavioral assessment (direct daily measurement). A method of observing and recording particular behaviors continually over a specific length of time.

Blindisms. Repetitive, stereotyped movements such as rocking or eye rubbing; also characteristic of some severely retarded and disturbed children.

Bone conduction test. Refers to administration of tones to the forehead using a vibrator, to categorize a hearing problem; results are compared to those of *air conduction* test.

Braille. A system in which raised dots are used to allow blind people to "read" with their fingertips; consists of a quadrangular cell containing from one to six dots whose arrangement denotes different letters and symbols.

Brain dysfunction. A term applied to those in whom there is suspected malfunctioning of the brain; used instead of the term "brain damage" or "brain injury" because it does not specify tissue damage. Many professionals, especially educators, have avoided use of this term because of its ambiguity.

Cancer. Abnormal growth of cells in any of the body's organ systems.

Canterbury Child's Aid. An electronic device used by the visually impaired to help them in mobility. It operates on the principle that the individual can learn to locate objects by means of echoes.

Cataracts. A condition caused by a clouding of the lens of the eye; affects color vision, and distance vision.

Cerebral palsy (Little's disease, congenital spastic paralysis). A condition characterized by paralysis, weakness, incoordination, and/or other motor dysfunction due to brain damage.

Cerumen (earwax). A bitter substance in the ear; can repel insects and discourage their entry into deeper parts of the ear.

Chisanbop. A Korean method of using the fingers for math calculations; recommended by some for use with the visually impaired.

Chromosome. A rod-shaped entity in the nucleus of the cell; contains *genes,* which convey hereditary characteristics.

Chronological age. Refers to how old a person is; used in comparison with *mental age* (see glossary) to determine the IQ score of an individual:

$$IQ = \frac{MA}{CA} \times 100.$$

Cleft palate, cleft lip. Condition in which there is a rift or split in the upper part of the oral cavity or the upper lip.

Closed caption. TV program captions visible only on sets equipped with a decoder.

Clubfoot. A congenital condition in which one or both feet are turned at the wrong angle at the ankle.

Cluttering. Excessive speed of speaking plus disorganized sentence structure and articulation problems as well as repetition.

Cochlea. A snail-shaped organ that lies below the vestibular mechanism; its parts convert the sound coming from the middle ear into an electrical signal in the inner ear, which is transmitted to the brain.

Cognitive behavior modification. A training approach that emphasizes teaching individuals to control their own thought processes; often used with learning-disabled children who are in need of an educational approach that stresses self-initiative and the use of learning strategies.

Cognitive mapping. A nonsequential way of conceptualizing the spatial environment that allows a visually impaired person to know where several points in the environment are simultaneously; allows for better mobility than does a strictly sequential conceptualization of the environment.

Cognitive training. Training procedures designed to change thoughts or thought patterns.

Coloboma. A degenerative disease in which the central and/or peripheral areas of the retina are incompletely formed, resulting in impairment of the visual field and/or central visual acuity.

Community residential facility (CRF). A place, usually a group home, in an urban or residential neighborhood where from about three to ten retarded adults live under supervision.

Comprehension monitoring. The ability to keep track of one's own comprehension of reading material and to make adjustments in order to comprehend better while one is reading; often deficient in learning-disabled students.

Congenital. Existing at birth.

Congenital anaphthalmos. Lack of development of the eye and parts of the brain; usually characterized by mental retardation.

Congenitally deaf. Deafness that is present at birth; can be caused by genetic factors, by injuries during fetal development, or by injury incurred at birth.

Contractures. Permanent shortening of muscles and connective tissues and consequent distortion of bones and/or posture due to neurological damage.

Convergent thinking. The tendency to think deductively and arrive at a single answer that could be scored "right" or "wrong."

Cornea. A transparent cover in front of the iris and pupil in the eye; responsible for most of the refraction of the light rays in the focusing of an object.

Cranium bifidum (encephalocele). A midline defect in which part of the brain protrudes through the back of the skull or into the nose and throat.

Cranmer abacus. An adaptation of the Japanese abacus for the visually impaired that consists of beads that can be manipulated through touch for math computations.

Creativity. Ability to express novel and useful ideas, to sense and elucidate new and important relationships, and to ask previously unthought of, but crucial, questions.

Criterion-referenced test. A procedure used to determine a child's level of achievement; when this level is established, a criterion, or goal, is set to fix a level at which the child *should* be achieving.

Cued speech. A variation of the total communication approach in which hand shapes represent specific sounds at the same time that spoken words are produced.

Cultural-familial retardation. Mild retardation with no evidence of brain pathology in someone from an economically disadvantaged background.

Curriculum-based assessment. This approach to assessment is a formative evaluation method designed to evaluate performance in the particular curriculum to which students are exposed. It usually involves giving students a small sample of items from the curriculum in use in their schools. Proponents of this assessment techniques argue that it is preferable to comparing students with national norms or using tests that do not reflect the curriculum content learned by students.

Cystic fibrosis. An inherited disease characterized by chronic respiratory and digestive problems.

Decibel. A unit of relative intensity of a sound; zero decibels designates the point at which people with normal hearing can just detect sound.

Defective syntax. Inability to put words together in order to express ideas in grammatically complete sentences.

Deviance. Behavior that is at variance with the socially accepted norm.

Diabetes. A hereditary or developmental problem of sugar metabolism caused by a failure of the pancreas to produce enough insulin; *diabetes mellitus* is the common type.

Diabetic retinopathy. A condition resulting from interference of the blood supply to the retina; the fastest-growing cause of blindness.

Diagnostic-prescriptive center. Facilities provided for exceptional children; usually such children are placed there for a short time so their needs can be assessed and a plan of action established for their education.

Dimensional classification. Classification of behavior disorders according to several types or dimensions comprised of behaviors that statistical analyses indicate tend to occur together.

Diplegia. A condition in which the legs are paralyzed to a greater extent than the arms.

Direct instruction. A method of teaching academics, especially reading and math, that is similar to behavior analysis. It places emphasis on structure among solution strategies and the selection of examples.

Divergent thinking. The ability to think inductively and suggest many different potential answers.

Dizygotic. Refers to twins who are not genetically identical because they came from two separate eggs.

Doppler effect. Term used to describe the phenomenon of the pitch of a sound rising as the listener moves toward the source of that sound.

Double hemiplegia. A condition in which both halves of the body are paralyzed but, unlike in *quadriplegia,* the two sides are affected differently.

Down syndrome. A condition resulting from a chromosomal abnormality; characterized by mental retardation and such physical signs as slanted-appearing eyes, flattened features, shortness, tendency toward obesity. The three major types of Down syndrome are the *trisomy* 21, *mosaicism,* and *translocation* types.

Dysacusis. An inner-ear condition that causes difficulties in understanding speech.

Dysarthria. A condition in which brain damage causes impaired control of the muscles used in articulation.

Dyslexia. An impairment of the ability to read.

Dystrophy. Hereditary, progressive weakening and wasting away of muscle tissue in which there is no evidence of neurological disease.

Echolalia. The meaningless repetition (echoing) of words that have been heard.

Echolocation device. Invented by Kay and developed by Bower, a device that emits high-frequency sound waves, which bounce off objects; loudness of signal warns the sightless person of the size of an object, and pitch indicates distance.

Ecological approach. A position that stresses the interaction between the individual and his environment; proponents of this position believe that labeling a child's exceptionality is harmful.

Educable mentally retarded (EMR). The traditionally used educators' classification label for an individual whose IQ is between 50 and 75; are considered to be capable of learning basic academic subjects; loosely corresponds to the AAMD category of *mild retardation.*

Electrodermal audiometry (EDA). Used in testing young and/or hard-to-test children; based on measurement of skin resistance in response to sounds.

Electroencephalogram (EEG). A graphic recording of the brain's electrical impulses.

Emotional lability. Frequent changes of mood.

Encephalitis. An inflammation of the brain; can affect the child's mental development adversely.

Endogenous. A term used to refer to mental retardation caused by social or genetic factors; infrequently used today.

Enrichment. Provision of additional learning experiences for gifted students while they remain in the grade level appropriate for their chronological age.

Epilepsy. A recurrent convulsive disorder.

Eustachian tube. The tube connecting the middle ear and the throat.

Evoked-response audiometry. A technique involving electroencephalograph measurement of changes in brain-wave activity in response to sounds.

Executive control processes. Strategies an individual can use to do better on a variety of tasks involving concept learning, memory, attention, and language; an example would be rehearsal of to-be-learned items on a memory task; often deficient in learning-disabled and mentally retarded children.

Exogenous. A term used to refer to mental retardation caused by brain damage; infrequently used now.

Expressive language disabilities. Problems associated with the inability to express oneself verbally.

External locus of control. A personality characteristic in which individuals believe chance factors or people other than themselves are responsible for personal successes and failures; analogous to *outer-directedness.*

External otitis (swimmer's ear). An infection of the skin of the external auditory canal.

Fetal alcohol syndrome. Associated with excessive drinking of alcohol during pregnancy. Defects range from mild to severe, including growth retardation, brain damage, mental retardation, hyperactivity, anomalies of the face, and heart failure.

Fingerspelling. A spelling-out of the English alphabet by various finger positions on one hand.

Fluency. The flow with which oral language is produced.

Focal seizure. A partial seizure involving a discharge in a fairly circumscribed part of the brain, thus causing only a limited motor or sensory effect.

Functional. Nonorganic; without apparent structural or organic cause.

Functional academics. Practical skills rather than academic learning.

Galactosemia. A disease involving the body's inability to metabolize galactose; a metabolic genetic disorder that can result in mental retardation.

Gene. Responsible for hereditary characteristics; arranged at specific locations in the chromosomes within each cell.

Generalized seizure. A seizure involving a large part of the brain.

Genetics. The biological study of heredity.

Genius. A word sometimes used to indicate a particular aptitude or capacity in any area; rare intellectual powers.

Genotype. An individual's particular genetic constitution which determines his or her range of potential functioning.

German measles. (See rubella.)

Giftedness. Refers to cognitive (intellectual) superiority, creativity, and motivation of sufficient magnitude to set the child apart from the vast majority of agemates and make it possible for him/her to contribute something of particular value to society.

Glaucoma. A condition in which there is excessive pressure in the eyeball; the cause is unknown, but if untreated, blindness results.

Group auditory trainers. Devices that amplify sound for a group of hearing-impaired individuals. Wireless FM systems allow freedom of movement for teacher and students.

Handicapism. A term used by activists who fault the unequal treatment of handicapped individuals. This term is parallel to the term *racism,* coined by those who fault unequal treatment based on race.

Hemiplegia. A condition in which one half (right or left side) of the body is paralyzed.

Hemophilia. A rare, sex-linked disorder of the blood; occurs almost exclusively in males and is transmitted through a recessive gene carried by the mother.

Herpes simplex. A type of venereal disease that can cause cold sores or fever blisters; if it affects the genitals and is contracted by the mother-to-be in the later stages of fetal development, it can cause mental subnormality in the child.

Hertz (Hz) unit. A measurement of the frequency of sound; refers to highness or lowness of a sound.

Homophenes. Sounds that are identical in terms of revealing movements (visible articulatory patterns).

Hoover cane. A long cane that is swept in an arc in front of the person to detect obstacles and changes in the terrain. Most often recommended for the blind as a mobility aid.

Hospital and homebound instruction. A service to provide for the educational needs of exceptional children who are unable to attend the regular school because of their handicapping problem.

Hydrocephalus. A condition characterized by enlargement of the head due to excessive pressure of the cerebrospinal fluid.

Hyperactivity. A higher degree of inappropriate motor activity than is considered typical for a particular age group.

Hyperopia. Farsightedness; usually results when the eyeball is too short.

Hypertonic. Muscle tone that is too high; muscles that are too tense.

Hypoglycemia. A condition characterized by abnormally low blood sugar.

Hyporesponsive. Slow to respond; opposite of *hyperactive* or distractible; characteristic of some learning-disabled children.

Hypotonic. Muscle tone that is too low; flabby muscles.

Hypoxia. Deficiency in the amount of oxygen reaching the tissues of the body.

Impulsivity. The tendency to respond quickly without carefully considering the alternatives; responding without adequate reflection.

Incus. Anvil-shaped bone in the ossicular chain of the middle ear.

Individualized education program (IEP). P.L. 94-142 requires that an IEP be drawn up by the educational team for each exceptional child; the IEP must include a statement of present educational performance, instructional goals, educational services to be provided, and criteria and procedures for determining that the instructional objectives are being met.

Informal reading inventory (IRI). A procedure used to appraise a child's level of reading competence in a particular area; consists of sequentially graded reading paragraphs.

Inner-directedness. A personality characteristic in which individuals rely on their own resources to solve problems; analogous to *internal locus of control.*

Insight. Ability to separate and/or combine various pieces of information in new, creative, or useful ways.

Interactive Classroom Television System. A system that allows the teacher to present material at the chalkboard that is then transmitted as an enlarged image to a TV monitor on a student's desk. It is designed to permit the teacher and the visually-impaired student to keep in visual contact with one another.

Internal locus of control. A personality characteristic in which individuals believe they are responsible for their own successes and failures; analogous to *inner-directedness.*

IPO relief drawing set. Special type of drawing materials that allow one to draw raised lines; used to draw maps for the visually impaired.

IQ (Intelligence Quotient). A measure of intellectual functioning; determined by dividing *mental age* (the age level at which the person is functioning) by *chronological age* and multiplying by 100.

IQ-achievement discrepancy. Academic performance markedly lower than what would be appropriate for a student's intellectual capability.

Iris. The colored portion of the eye; contracts or expands depending on the amount of light striking it.

ISO standard. The International Standard Organization's determination of the average hearing levels, in which slight hearing loss is considered to be from 27 to 40 dB loss; mild 41 to 55 dB loss; marked 56 to 70 dB loss; severe 71 to 90 dB loss; and extreme 91 dB or more loss.

Itinerant teacher. Goes from school to school on a regular schedule to perform special instructional services for exceptional children; also consults with regular teacher about special problems or techniques.

Jaeger chart. Used in determining visual competence; composed of lines of type in different sizes; makes possible interpretation of results in terms of what kinds of reading materials can be used for the person with the visual disability.

Kinesthesis. The sensation of bodily movements as perceived through the muscles, tendons, and joints; the feeling of movement.

Kurzweil Reading Machine. A computerized device that converts print into speech for the visually impaired. The user places the printed material over a scanner that then "reads" the material aloud by means of an electronic voice.

Language. An arbitrary code or system of symbols to communicate meaning.

Language disorder. A lag in the ability to understand and express ideas that puts linguistic skill behind an individual's development in other areas, such as motor, cognitive, or social development.

Larynx. The structure in the throat containing the vocal apparatus (vocal cords); *laryngitis* is a temporary loss of voice due to inflammation of the larynx.

Laser cane. Operates on the principle that the individual can learn to locate objects by means of echoes. Can be used by the visually impaired like a Hoover cane (see glossary), or can be used as an electronic device for aid in mobility.

Learned helplessness. A motivational term referring to a condition wherein a person believes that no matter how hard he or she tries, failure will result.

Least restrictive environment (LRE). A legal term referring to the fact that exceptional children must be educated in as "normal" an environment as possible.

Legg-Calve-Perthes disease. A condition involving a flattening of the head of the femur or hip bone, and including destruction of bone tissue, pain, muscular spasm, or limping. Usually occurs in children age 3 to 11.

Lens. A structure that refines and changes the focus of the light rays passing through the eye.

Locus of control. A motivational term referring to how people attribute their successes or failures; people with an *internal* locus of control believe that they themselves are the reason for success or failure, whereas people with an *external* locus of control believe outside forces (e.g., other people) influence how well they perform.

Malleus. Hammer-shaped bone in the ossicular chain of the middle ear.

Mediation. A strategy of attaching a verbal label to something so that it can be more easily remembered.

Meningitis. A bacterial or viral infection of the linings of the brain or spinal cord.

Meningocele. A tumorlike sac containing cerebrospinal fluid; a type of *spina bifida*.

Mental age. Refers to the IQ test score that specifies the age level at which an individual is functioning.

Mental retardation. A condition in which the individual has below-average intellectual functioning abilities; both IQ and adaptive skills are considered today as measures of the level of retardation; those who are retarded were traditionally divided by IQ test scores as *educable, trainable,* and *custodial;* today the more commonly used AAMD division includes *mild, moderate, severe,* and *profound* categories.

Metacognitive skills. Those abilities that people use to know their own cognitive processes. Metacognition refers to one's understanding of what strategies are available for learning and what strategies are best used in which situations.

Metacognitive strategy instruction. Providing alternative thinking strategies to students in order to facilitate the learning process.

Microcephalus. A condition causing development of a small head with a sloping forehead; proper development of the brain is prevented, resulting in mental retardation.

Mild retardation. A classification used by the AAMD to specify an individual whose IQ test score is between 55 and 68 or 69; corresponds to educators' label of *educable retarded;* individual is capable of learning basic academic subjects.

Minimal brain dysfunction (MBD). A term used to describe a child who shows behavioral but not neurological signs of brain injury; the term is not as popular as it once was, primarily because of its lack of diagnostic utility—i.e., some children who learn normal show signs indicative of MBD.

Mixed cerebral palsy. A type of cerebral palsy in which several types, such as *athetosis* and *spasticity,* occur together.

Mixed dominance. A term describing a person whose preferred anatomical sides are mixed—e.g., right-eyed, left-footed, and right-handed. Occurs slightly more frequently in learning-disabled compared to normal children, but not enough to be diagnostically useful; for example, many individuals who learn normally are mixed dominant.

Modeling. Showing or demonstrating to others how to perform particular behaviors.

Moderate retardation. A classification used by the AAMD to specify an individual whose IQ test score is between 40 and 55; corresponds to educators' label of *trainable retarded;* individual can usually learn functional academics and vocational skills.

Monoplegia. A condition in which only one limb is paralyzed.

Monozygotic. Refers to twins who are genetically identical because they came from the same egg.

Morphology. The study within psycholinguistics of word formation; of how adding or deleting parts of words changes their meaning. Learning-disabled students often make morphological errors in their language.

Mosaicism. A type of Down syndrome in which some of the cells, owing to faulty development, have an extra chromosome, and some do not.

Multiple sclerosis. A chronic, slowly progressive disease of the central nervous system in which there is a hardening or scarring of the protective myelin sheath of certain nerves.

Muscular dystrophy. A hereditary disease characterized by progressive weakness caused by degeneration of muscle fibers; the two major types are *facioscapulohumeral* and *pseudohypertrophic.*

Mutation. A change in one or more of the genes, the arrangement of genes, or the quantity of chromosomal material.

Myelomeningocele (meningomyelocele). A tumorlike sac containing part of the spinal cord itself; a type of *spina bifida.*

Myopathy. A weakening and wasting away of muscular tissue in which there is no evidence of neurological disease or impairment.

Myopia. Nearsightedness; usually results from a too-long eyeball.

Nephritis. A chronic disease of the kidneys characterized by swelling of the body tissues.

Nephrosis. A degenerative kidney disease.

Neurosis (psychoneurosis). A condition marked by anxiety, inability to cope with inner conflicts; doesn't interfere as seriously with everyday activity as does *psychosis.*

Noise. A term used to describe features of the environment or the speaker—poor acoustics in a room or poor syntax in a speaker—that contribute to a person's difficulty in hearing sounds.

Nonsheltered work environments. Work environments in which handicapped persons are engaged in competitive employment side by side with nonhandicapped coworkers.

Nonsupperative otitis. Inflammation of the middle ear that occurs without an infection; often preceded by infectious otitis media. (See *serous otitis media.*)

Normalization. A philosophical belief in special education that every individual, even the most handicapped, should have an educational and living environment as close to normal as possible.

Nystagmus. A condition in which there are rapid involuntary movements of the eyes; sometimes indicates a brain malfunction and/or inner ear problems.

Obturator. An artificial device used to close an opening; sometimes employed to close a cleft palate.

Open caption. TV captions that can be seen on all sets; used with selected programs since the 1970s.

Ophthalmology. The science of dealing with eye diseases.

Optacon. A device used to enable the blind to "read." Consists of a camera that converts print into an image of letters, which are then produced via vibration onto the finger.

Organic. Inherent, inborn; involving known neurological or structural abnormality.

Orthosis. A device designed to restore, partially or completely, a lost function of the body (e.g., a brace or crutch).

Orthotics. A professional specialty concerned with restoration of lost function of body parts with braces, adaptive devices, etc.

Ossicles. Three tiny bones (*malleus, incus,* and *stapes*) that together make possible an efficient transfer of sound waves from the eardrum to the *oval window,* which connects the middle ear to the inner ear.

Osteogenesis imperfecta. A hereditary condition in which the bones are formed improperly and break very easily.

Osteomyelitis. A bacterial infection of the bone.

Otitis media. Inflammation of the middle ear.

Otology. The medical specialty dealing with the ear and its diseases.

Otosclerosis. A hereditary disease of the bone in which the *stapes* bone is abnormally attached to the *oval window* of the ear.

Outer-directedness. A personality characteristic in which individuals rely on people other than themselves for cues to solve problems; analogous to *external locus of control.*

Oval window. Connects the middle and inner ear.

Palate. The roof of the mouth.

Paraplegia. A condition in which both legs are paralyzed.

Partial seizure. A seizure beginning in a localized area and involving only a small part of the brain.

Pathsounder. A device worn around a blind person's neck that emits a noise when an object is approached.

Peer tutoring. A method that can be used to integrate handicapped students in regular classrooms, based on the notion that students can effectively tutor one another. The role of learner or teacher may be assigned to either the handicapped or the nonhandicapped student.

Perception. An individual's ability to process stimuli meaningfully; the ability to organize and interpret sensory information.

Perceptual-motor match. A concept forwarded by Newell Kephart that motor development precedes sensory (especially visual) development; most child development research evidence does not substantiate this theory.

Perkins Brailler. A system making it possible to write in *Braille;* has six keys, one for each of the six dots of the cell, which leave an embossed print on paper.

Perseveration. Persistent repetition of an activity or behavior.

Pharynx. The back of the throat leading from the nasal and mouth passages to the *larynx.*

Phenotype. An individual's actual level of functioning within limits set by genetic constitution and its interaction with environmental influences.

Phenylketonuria (PKU). A metabolic genetic disorder caused by the inability of the body to convert phenylalanine to tyrosine; an accumulation of this phenylalanine results in abnormal brain development.

Phocomelia. A deformity in which the limbs of the baby are very short or missing completely, with the hands and feet attached directly to the torso-like flippers; a syndrome commonly resulting from maternal use of the drug thalidomide during pregnancy.

Phonation. The processes involved in control of the breath stream to produce speech sounds.

Phonology. The study of how individual sounds make up words.

Physically disabled. Not able to perform significant physical activities required in everyday living that most persons

of the same age and sex are able to perform without special assistance.

Physically handicapped. Individuals whose nonsensory physical limitations or health problems interfere with school or learning to such an extent that they require special education.

Pitch. The tonal frequency (high or low tone) of one's voice.

P.L. 94-142. The Education for All Handicapped Children Act, which contains a mandatory provision stating that beginning in September 1978, in order to receive funds under the Act, every school system in the nation must make provision for a free, appropriate public education for every child between the ages of 3 and 18 (extended to ages 3 to 21 by 1980) regardless of how, or how seriously, he may be handicapped.

Play audiometry. A method of testing hearing in which young children are taught to respond to an auditory signal within a game situation.

Poliomyelitis (polio, infantile paralysis). An infectious disease that attacks the nerve tissue in the spinal cord and/or brain.

Portable Braille Recorder. A tape cassette system for recording Braille that takes up less space than the larger Perkins-Brailler. (See *Perkins Brailler* in glossary.)

Postlingual deafness. Deafness occurring after the development of speech and language.

Pragmatics. The study within psycolinguistics of how one uses language in social situations; emphasis is on functional use of language rather than its mechanics. Learning-disabled students often have problems in the pragmatics of language.

Preacademic skills. Behaviors that are needed *before* formal academic instruction can begin (e.g., ability to identify letters, numbers, shapes, and colors).

Precocity. Remarkable early development.

Prelingual deafness. Deafness that occurs before the development of spoken language, usually at birth.

Prepalate. The upper lip and upper gum ridge, including the alveolar process.

Process test. A procedure to determine the effectiveness of psychological (usually perceptual or linguistic) processes.

Profound retardation. A classification used by the AAMD to specify an individual whose IQ test score is below 25; corresponds to educators' label of *custodial retarded.*

Prosody. The patterns of stress and rate given to spoken words; rhythm.

Prosthesis. A device designed to replace, partially or completely, a part of the body (e.g., artificial teeth or limbs).

Prosthetics. A professional specialty concerned with replacing missing body parts with artificial substitutes (*prostheses*).

Psychoanalysis. A system developed by Sigmund Freud to treat mental/emotional disorders; unconscious motivations are considered to be at the root of such problems.

Psychoneurosis (neurosis). A condition marked by anxiety, inability to cope with inner conflicts; doesn't interfere as seriously with everyday activity as does *psychosis.*

Psychosis. A major mental disorder exhibited in seriously disturbed behavior and lack of contact with reality; childhood *schizophrenia* and *autism* are forms of psychosis.

Pupil. The contractile opening in the middle of the iris of the eye.

Pure-tone audiometry. A system whereby tones of various intensities and frequencies are presented to determine a person's hearing loss.

Quadriplegia. A condition in which all four limbs are paralyzed.

Readiness skills. Skills deemed necessary before academics can be learned (e.g., attending skills, the ability to follow directions, knowledge of letter names).

Reauditorization. A defect in the ability to understand and recognize words so that they can be remembered and retrieved for later use.

Receptive language disabilities. Difficulties that derive from the inability to understand spoken language.

Reciprocal teaching. A teaching method in which students and teacher are involved in dialogue to facilitate reading comprehension.

Reflex audiometry. The testing of responses to sounds by observation of such reflex actions as the orienting response and the Moro reflex.

Regression-based discrepancy formula. A formula used to determine the extent of a person's failure to perform academic tasks in accordance with intellectual capability that takes into account the statistical correlation between achievement and IQ scores.

Regular Education Initiative. A philosophy that maintains that general education, rather than special education, should be primarily responsible for the education of mildly (and some moderately) handicapped students.

Residential school. A facility in which the exceptional child receives twenty-four-hour care, usually away from his or her home community.

Resonance. Refers to the quality of the sound imparted by the size, shape, and texture of the organs in the vocal tract.

Resource teacher. Typically provides services for exceptional children and their teachers within one school; assesses the particular needs of such children and sometimes teaches them individually or in small groups, using any special materials or methods that are needed; consults with regular teachers, advising on the instruction and management of the child in the classroom and demonstrating instructional techniques.

Retina. The back portion of the eye, containing nerve fibers connected to the optic nerve.

Retinitis pigmentosa. A hereditary disease resulting in degeneration of the retina.

Retinoblastoma. A hereditary disease characterized by a malignant tumor of the eye; associated with above-average intelligence.

Retrolental fibroplasis (RLF). A condition resulting from administration of an excessive concentration of oxygen at birth; causes scar tissue behind the lens of the eye.

Reverse mainstreaming. The practice of placing nonhandicapped students in classes that are predominantly composed of handicapped students.

Rheumatic fever. A condition sometimes following a strep throat or scarlet fever; noted by painful swelling and inflammation of the joints.

Rheumatoid arthritis (Still's disease). A systemic disease with major symptoms involving the muscles and joints.

Rigidity cerebral palsy. A rare type of cerebral palsy that is characterized by diffuse, continuous muscle tension and consequent "lead-pipe" stiffness.

Rochester Method. A "total" method of teaching communication to hearing-impaired people that utilizes both manual and oral techniques and principles.

Rubella (German measles). A serious viral disease, which, if it occurs during the first trimester of pregnancy, is likely to cause a deformity in the fetus.

Schizophrenia. Psychotic behavior manifested by loss of contact with reality, bizarre thought processes, and inappropriate actions.

Scoliosis. Curvature of the spine, either congenital or acquired from poor posture, disease, or muscular weakness due to certain conditions such as *cerebral palsy* or *muscular dystrophy.*

Seizure (fit, convulsion). A sudden alteration of consciousness, usually accompanied by motor activity and/or sensory phenomena; caused by an abnormal discharge of electrical energy in the brain.

Self-instructional training. A type of cognitive behavior modification (see glossary) technique that requires individuals to talk aloud and then to themselves as they solve problems.

Self-monitoring. A type of cognitive behavior modification (see glossary) technique that requires individuals to keep track of their own behavior.

Semantic. Pertaining to meaning in language.

Serous otitis media. Inflammation of the middle ear that occurs without an infection; often preceded by infectious otitis media. (See *nonsupperative otitis media.*)

Severe retardation. A classification used by the AAMD to specify an individual whose IQ test score is between 25 and 40; educational efforts usually concentrate on basic communication and self-help skills.

Severely and profoundly handicapped (SPH). A term applied to mentally retarded individuals whose IQs fall below 25; these are the most seriously impaired of the mentally retarded, and they are often characterized by physical and sensory impairment as well as mental retardation.

Sheltered workshop. A facility that provides a structured environment for handicapped persons in which they can learn skills; can be either a transitional placement or a permanent arrangement.

Sickle cell anemia. A severe, chronic blood disease that occurs only in those who inherit the abnormal sickle gene from both parents; the gene produces an abnormal form of hemoglobin; occurs almost exclusively among blacks.

Sign language. A manual system in which there is sometimes similarity between the configuration of each gesture and the meaning it represents.

Slate and stylus. A method of writing in *Braille* in which the paper is held in a slate while the stylus is pressed through openings to make indentations in the paper. With this method the *Braille* cells are written in reverse order, and thus it is more difficult to use than the *Perkins Brailler.*

Snellen chart. Used in determining visual competence; consists of rows of letters or Es arranged in different positions; each row corresponds to the distance at which a normally sighted person can discriminate the letters; does not predict how accurately a child will be able to read print.

Sociopath. A person whose behavior is aggressively antisocial and who shows no remorse or guilt for misdeeds.

Sociopathic. Behavior characteristics of a *sociopath;* someone who exhibits behavior characteristics of a *sociopath.*

Sonic glasses. Developed by Kay (1973); operates on the principle that humans, like bats, can learn to locate objects by means of echoes.

Spastic. Sudden, involuntary contraction of muscles that makes accurate, voluntary movement difficult; a type of *cerebral palsy*.

Spasticity. A condition in which there are sudden, involuntary contractions of the muscles, causing voluntary movements to be difficult and inaccurate; a type of *cerebral palsy*.

Special day schools. Provide all-day, segregated educational experience for exceptional children.

Special self-contained class. Enrolls exceptional children with a particular diagnostic label; usually children in such a class need full-time instruction in this placement, and are only integrated with their normal classmates for a few activities, if any.

Speech. Forming and sequencing oral language sounds during communication.

Speech audiometry. A technique that tests a person's detection and understanding of speech rather than using pure tones to detect hearing loss.

Speech disorder. Oral communication that exhibits poor or abnormal use of the vocal apparatus; is unintelligible or so inferior that it draws attention to itself and causes anxiety, feelings of inadequacy, or inappropriate behavior in the speaker.

Speech flow. The sequence of rhythm with which speech sounds are produced.

Speech-Plus Talking Calculator. An electronic calculator designed especially for use with the visually impaired. The device "says" the numbers aloud as they are punched and "says" the answers aloud.

Speechreading. A method that involves teaching children to use visual information from a number of sources to understand what is being said to them; more than just *lipreading*, which uses only visual clues arising from the movement of the mouth in speaking.

Speech Reception Threshold (SRT). The decibel level at which a person can understand speech.

Spina bifida. A congenital midline defect resulting from failure of the bony spinal column to close completely during fetal development.

Spina Bifida Occulta. A nonhandicapping form of spina bifida in which the spinal cord is not injured and the only outward sign of the defect may be a clump of hair growing from the affected region of the back.

Standard deviation. A measure of the amount by which an individual test score differs from the *mean* (average) score; a statistical construct that divides normal distribution into areas, making it possible to predict the percentage that falls above or below a score.

Standardized achievement test. A procedure to determine a child's relative achievement level; administered to a large group of children so that any one child's score can be compared to the norm.

Stapes. Stirrup-shaped bone in the ossicular chain of the middle ear.

Status epilepticus. A condition in which an individual has continuous seizures.

Stereotypic behaviors. Any of a variety of repetitive behaviors (e.g., eye rubbing) that are sometimes found in the blind or seriously retarded. Sometimes referred to as stereotypies or blindisms.

Stereotypies. (See *stereotypic behaviors*)

Stimulus reduction. A concept largely forwarded by Cruickshank; an approach to teaching distractible and hyperactive children that emphasizes reducing extraneous (nonrelevant to learning) material.

Strabismus. A condition in which the eyes are directed inward (crossed eyes) or outward.

Structured program. A concept largely forwarded by Cruickshank; emphasizes a teacher-directed approach in which activities and environment are structured for distractible and hyperactive children.

Stuttering. Speech characterized by abnormal hesitations, prolongations, and repetitions; may be accompanied by grimaces, gestures, or other bodily movements indicative of a struggle to speak, anxiety, blocking of speech, avoidance of speech.

Superphone. A device that enables a deaf person to communicate with someone who has a pushbutton phone; it changes keyboard message typed by the deaf person into an electronic voice; the hearing person can then type a response on the phone keys that will appear on the deaf person's typewriter.

Sweep test. An audiometric test designed to rapidly screen people to determine whether or not they have hearing impairment.

Symbolic interaction theory. A theory that suggests interaction between individuals gives meaning to things. It posits that constructs such as "disability" are socially created; a person has a disability because others believe that he/she has a disability.

Syntax. The way words are joined together to structure meaningful sentences.

Synthetic touch. Refers to a person's tactual exploration of objects that are small enough to be enveloped by one or both hands.

Syphilis. A venereal disease that can cause mental subnormality in a child, especially if it is contracted by the mother-to-be during the latter stages of fetal development.

Tactual vocoder. A device that transforms sound into vibrations.

Talent. A special ability, aptitude, or accomplishment.

Tay-Sachs disease. An inherited condition that can appear when both mother and father are carriers; results in brain damage and eventual death; it can be detected before birth through amniocentesis (see *amniocentesis*).

Teletext. System for presenting information on a standard television screen which the viewer can see whenever he or she wishes; requires a decoder and keypad for retrieving information.

Teletypewriter (TTY). A device connected to a telephone by a special adapter; allows communication between the hearing and hearing impaired over the telephone.

Temperament. Inborn behavioral style, including general level of activity, regularity or predictability, approach or withdrawal, adaptability, intensity of reaction, responsiveness, mood, distractibility, and persistence. The temperament is present at birth but may be modified by parental management.

Teratogens. Deformity-producing factors that interfere with normal fetal development.

Tinnitis. Roaring or ringing noises in the ear.

Total communication approach. An approach for testing the hearing impaired that blends oral and manual techniques.

Trainable mentally retarded (TMR). The traditionally used educators' classification label for an individual whose IQ is between 25 and 50; corresponds to AAMD categorization of *moderate retardation;* the educational emphasis is on self-help and vocational skills.

Transition programming. A program to provide mentally retarded individuals with educational support during the transition from school to workplace. The degree of support provided will vary according to the individual's handicapping condition.

Translocation. A type of Down syndrome in which the extra chromosome (the result of faulty development) in the twenty-first set breaks off and attaches itself to another of the chromosome pairs.

Tremor cerebral palsy. A rare type of cerebral palsy that is characterized by rhythmic, involuntary movement of certain muscles.

Triplegia. A condition in which three limbs are paralyzed; a type of cerebral palsy.

Trisomy 21. A type of Down syndrome in which the twenty-first chromosome is a triplet, making forty-seven, rather than the normal forty-six, chromosomes in all.

Tuberculosis. An infectious disease potentially causing tissue destruction in many organ systems, particularly the lungs.

Tuberous sclerosis. A rare type of brain disease; a biochemical disorder caused by an abnormal dominant gene; can result in mental retardation ranging from mild to severe.

Tympanic membrane (eardrum). The anatomical boundary between the outer and middle ear; the sound gathered in the outer ear vibrates here.

Uvula. The rear part or "tail" of the soft palate that can be seen hanging down in the back of the throat.

Velopharyngeal incompetence. The inability to build up sufficient air pressure in the oral cavity and prevent the escape of air from the nasal cavity while articulating sounds.

Velum. The soft palate.

Verbalism (verbal unreality). A blind person's supposed inappropriate reliance on words and phrases that are not consistent with his or her sensory experiences.

Vestibular mechanism. Located in the upper portion of the inner ear; consists of three soft, semicircular canals filled with a fluid that is sensitive to head movement, acceleration, and other movements related to balance.

Vibrotactile pulser. A device used by Azrin, Jones, and Flye (1968) to deliver a rhythmic pulse to the palm of the hand; used in a behavior modification technique aimed at helping children learn to read faster.

Visual Efficiency Scale. Developed by Barraga (1970); assesses visual functioning rather than acuity; measures such things as discrimination for light-dark intensity, size, position in space, and spatial perspective.

Vitreous humor. A transparent gelatinous substance that fills the eyeball between the retina and the lens of the eye.

Work-Study program. A program designed to introduce students to a variety of vocational opportunities while still in school. On-the-job training is provided, and the student's performance is evaluated.

Index

AUTHOR INDEX

SUBJECT INDEX